KT-521-488

Isle of Lewis
106/107
Stornoway

WESTERN ISLES OR HEBRIDES

Durness
Bettyhill
Thurso
108/109
110/111
Wick

Helmsdale

Ullapool
Dornoch
102/103

Gairloch
100/101
Inverness
104/105
Elgin
Banff
Fraserburgh
Peterhead

N. Uist
98/99

Kyle of Lochalsh
92/93
Grantown-on-Spey

S. Uist
Skye
90/91

Kingussie
94/95
Aberdeen
96/97
Stonehaven

Mallaig
Fort William

Pitlochry
Montrose
Forfar

84/85
Mull
86/87
Oban
Crieff
Dundee
88/89
St Andrews

Inveraray
Perth

Jura
Stirling

Islay
76/77
Edinburgh
80/81
Dunbar
82/83
Berwick-upon-Tweed

78/79
Largs Glasgow
Lanark
Peebles

Ayr

Campbeltown
Moffat
72/73
Jedburgh
74/75
Alnwick

70/71 Girvan
Dumfries

Stranraer
68/69
Hexham
Carlisle
Newcastle upon Tyne
Durham

62/63
Penrith
64/65
66/67
Whitby
Workington
Keswick
Darlington
Whitehaven

Isle of Man
Ramsey
Kendal
Northallerton
Ripon
Scarborough
Douglas
Barrow-in-Furness
56/57
Lancaster
58/59
York
60/61
Bridlington

Blackpool
Blackburn
Bradford
Leeds
Kingston upon Hull

Southport
Manchester
Doncaster
Grimsby
Anglesey
Liverpool
50/51
52/53
Sheffield
54/55

Holyhead
Llandudno
Chester
Lincoln
Skegness

Caernarfon
48/49

Crewe
Stoke-on-Trent
Nottingham
Boston
Cromer
Pwllheli
Bala
Derby
46/47
38/39
40/41
42/43
44/45
Norwich
Dolgellau
Stafford
Leicester
Peterborough
Lowestoft
Shrewsbury
Montgomery

Birmingham
Aberystwyth
Kidderminster
Warwick
Northampton
Cambridge
Ipswich
28/29
Presteigne
Worcester
34/35
36/37
Cardigan
Lampeter Hereford
30/31
32/33
Banbury
Colchester
Fishguard
Cheltenham
Luton
26/27
Pembroke
Carmarthen
Monmouth
Gloucester
Oxford
Aylesbury
Hertford
Chelmsford
Swansea
18/19
Swindon
LONDON
24/25
Cardiff
20/21
Reading
Chatham
Margate
Bristol
Newbury
Bath
Guildford
Dover
Ilfracombe
Minehead
Wells
Salisbury
Winchester
T. Wells
8/9
Taunton
10/11
Southampton
14/15
16/17
Bude
Portsmouth
Brighton
Hastings
Exeter
Dorchester
12/13
Bournemouth
Eastbourne
Launceston
Lyme Regis

Newquay
Weymouth 6/7
Isle of Wight
2/3
Plymouth Torbay
4/5
Penzance

Isles of Scilly

116/117
Lerwick
114/115
SHETLAND ISLANDS

Fair Isle

112/113
Kirkwall
ORKNEY ISLANDS

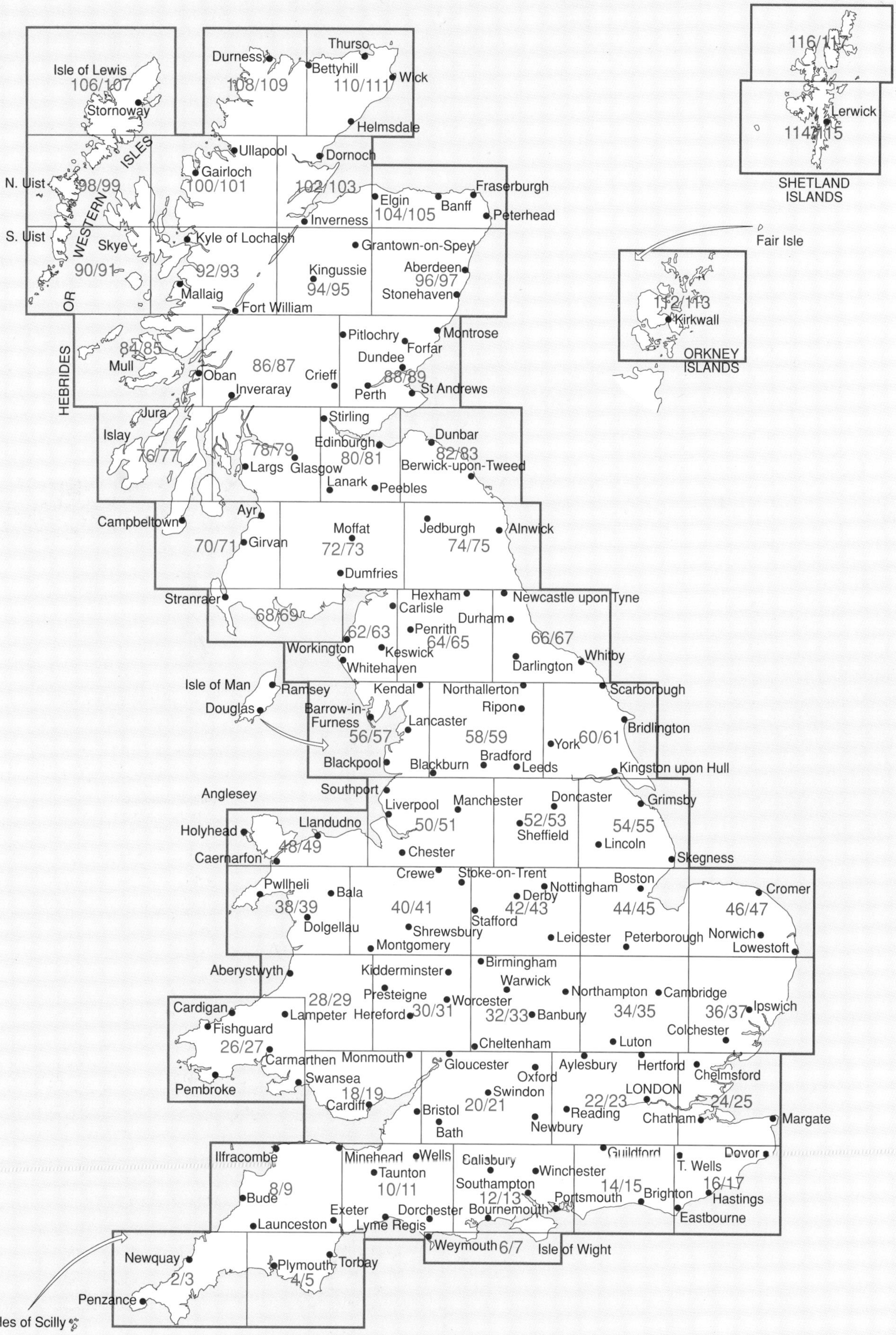

ORDNANCE SURVEY

ROAD ATLAS

of Great Britain

BCA

LONDON · NEW YORK · SYDNEY · TORONTO

This edition published 1992
by BCA by arrangement with

Ordnance Survey and Hamlyn
Romsey Road   an imprint of
Maybush   Reed International Books Ltd
Southampton   Michelin House, 81 Fulham Road
SO9 4DH   London SW3 6RB

CN 5306

First published 1983

Fifth edition 1992
First impression 1992

The representation in this atlas of a road is no evidence
of the existence of a right of way.

Made, printed and published in Great Britain

CONTENTS

Front Endpaper: Legend, Key to Map Pages

IV Route Planning

X Restricted Motorway Junctions

XI Motorways and Major Routes

XII Road Signs

XIV Radio Information and Distances

XVI National Parks, Forest Parks and Long Distance Paths

1 Legend to 1:250 000 Scale Maps

2 Ordnance Survey 1:250 000 Scale Maps

118 London Area

122 Central London

129 Street Index to Central London Maps

134 Town Plans

134 Aberdeen, Bath, Birmingham
135 Blackpool, Bournemouth, Bradford, Brighton
136 Bristol, Cambridge, Canterbury
137 Cardiff, Cheltenham, Chester
138 Coventry, Croydon, Derby, Dundee
139 Durham, Edinburgh, Exeter
140 Glasgow, Gloucester, Hull
141 Leeds, Liverpool
142 Leicester, Manchester, Middlesbrough
143 Milton Keynes, Newcastle, Oxford
144 Norwich, Nottingham
145 Peterborough, Plymouth, Portsmouth, Reading
146 Salisbury, Sheffield, Shrewsbury
147 Southampton, Stratford, Swansea, York

148 Ferry Ports

148 Dover, Fishguard, Folkestone, Harwich and Felixstowe
149 Holyhead, Plymouth, Newhaven, Poole
150 Portsmouth, Ramsgate, Stranraer, Sheerness

151 Channel Tunnel Information

152 Airports

152 Aberdeen, Birmingham International, East Midlands, Edinburgh,
    Glasgow, Stansted
153 Gatwick, Luton, Manchester, Prestwick, Leeds and Bradford
154 Heathrow

155 Index to 1:250 000 Scale Maps

*Back Endpaper: M25 and Routes into London
            Routes into Liverpool and Manchester*

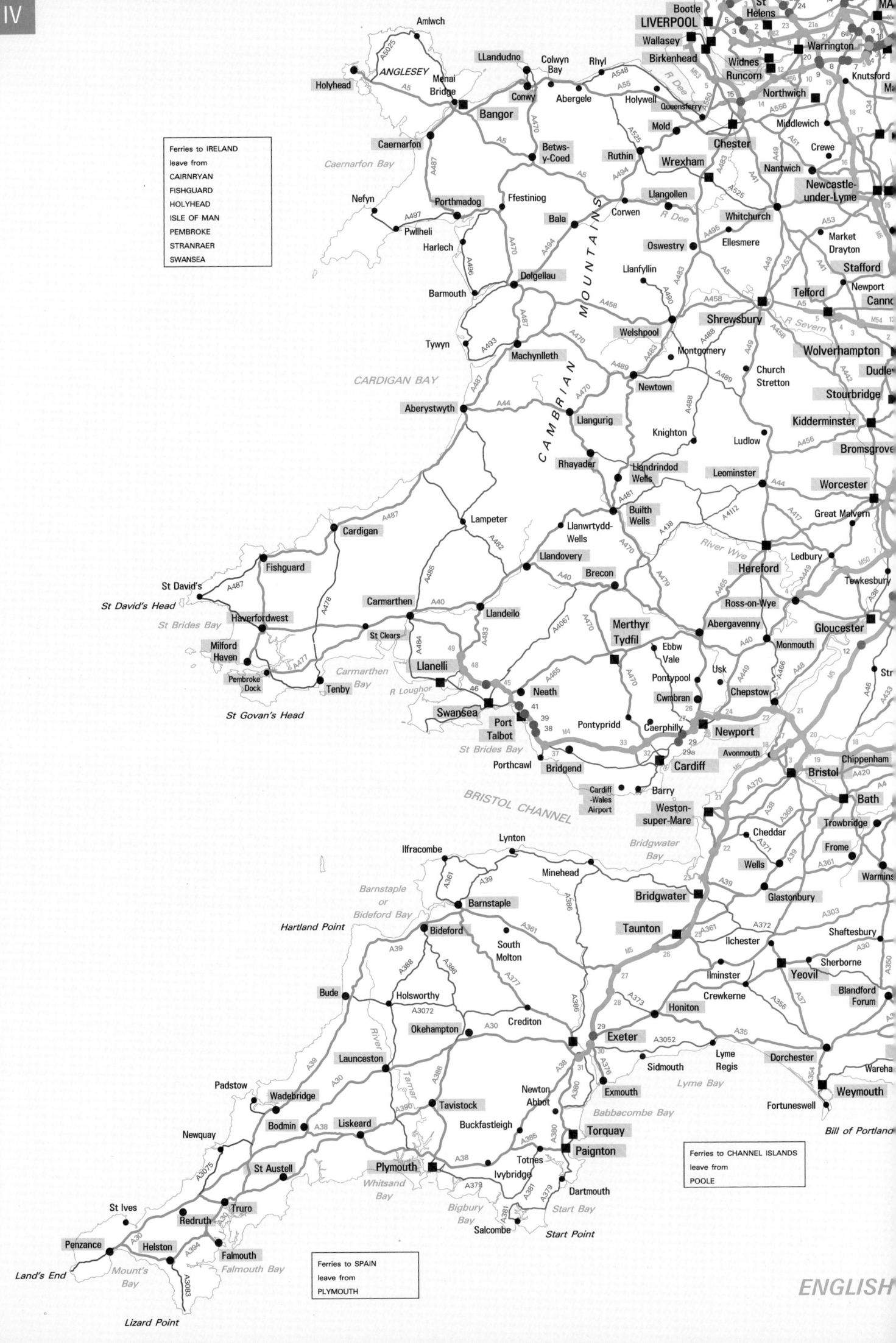

V

ROUTE PLANNING

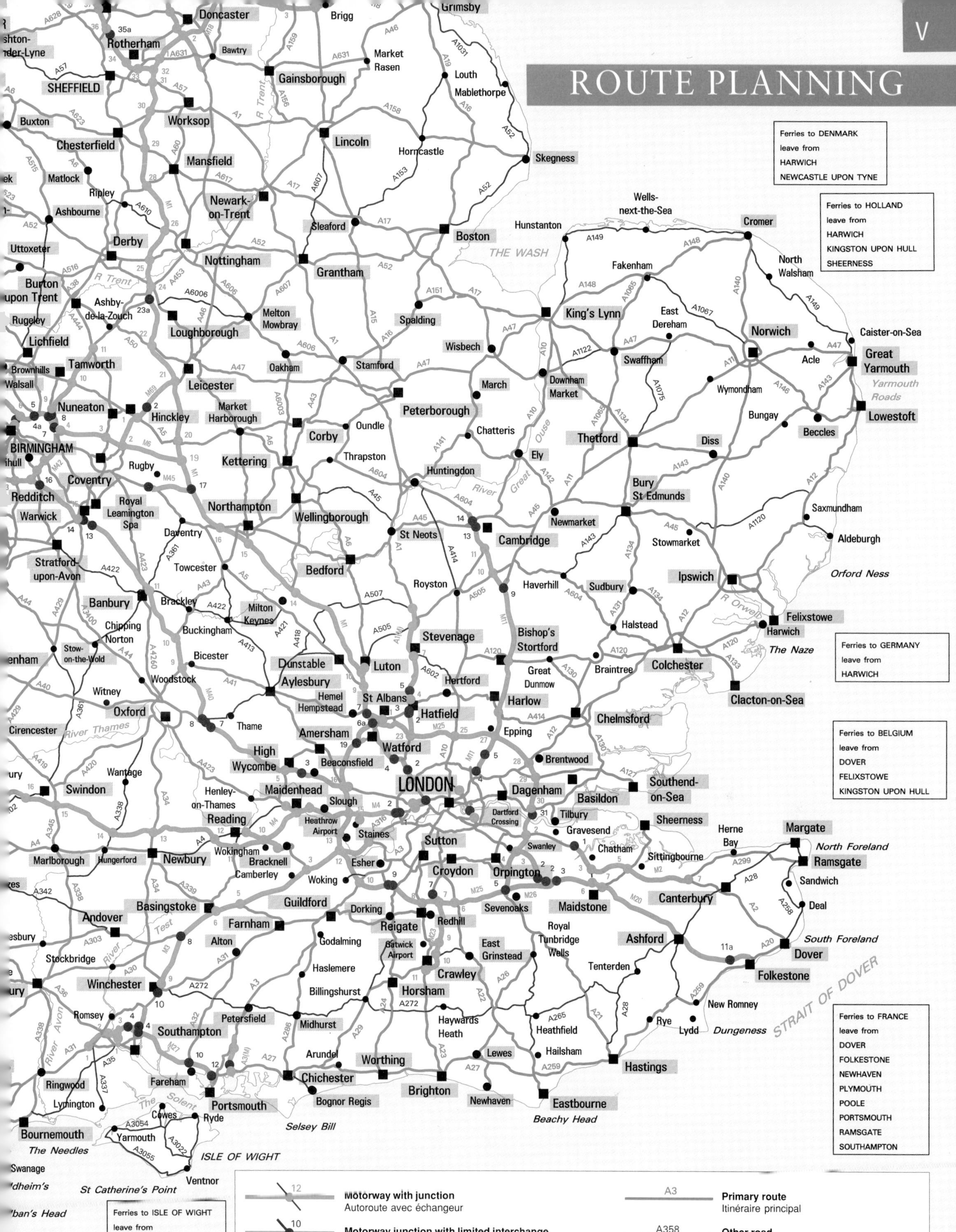

Ferries to DENMARK
leave from
HARWICH
NEWCASTLE UPON TYNE

Ferries to HOLLAND
leave from
HARWICH
KINGSTON UPON HULL
SHEERNESS

Ferries to GERMANY
leave from
HARWICH

Ferries to BELGIUM
leave from
DOVER
FELIXSTOWE
KINGSTON UPON HULL

Ferries to FRANCE
leave from
DOVER
FOLKESTONE
NEWHAVEN
PLYMOUTH
POOLE
PORTSMOUTH
RAMSGATE
SOUTHAMPTON

Ferries to ISLE OF WIGHT
leave from
LYMINGTON
PORTSMOUTH
SOUTHAMPTON

Legend:

12 — Motorway with junction / Autoroute avec échangeur

10 — Motorway junction with limited interchange / Echangeur partiel

— — Motorway under construction / Autoroute en construction

A3 — Primary route / Itinéraire principal

A358 — Other road / Autre route

Exeter — Primary route destination / Localité signalisée sur un itinéraire principal

Scale 1:1 375 000 or about one inch to 22 miles
Echelle 1/1 375 000

0   20   40   60 miles
0 20 40 60 80 100 kilometres

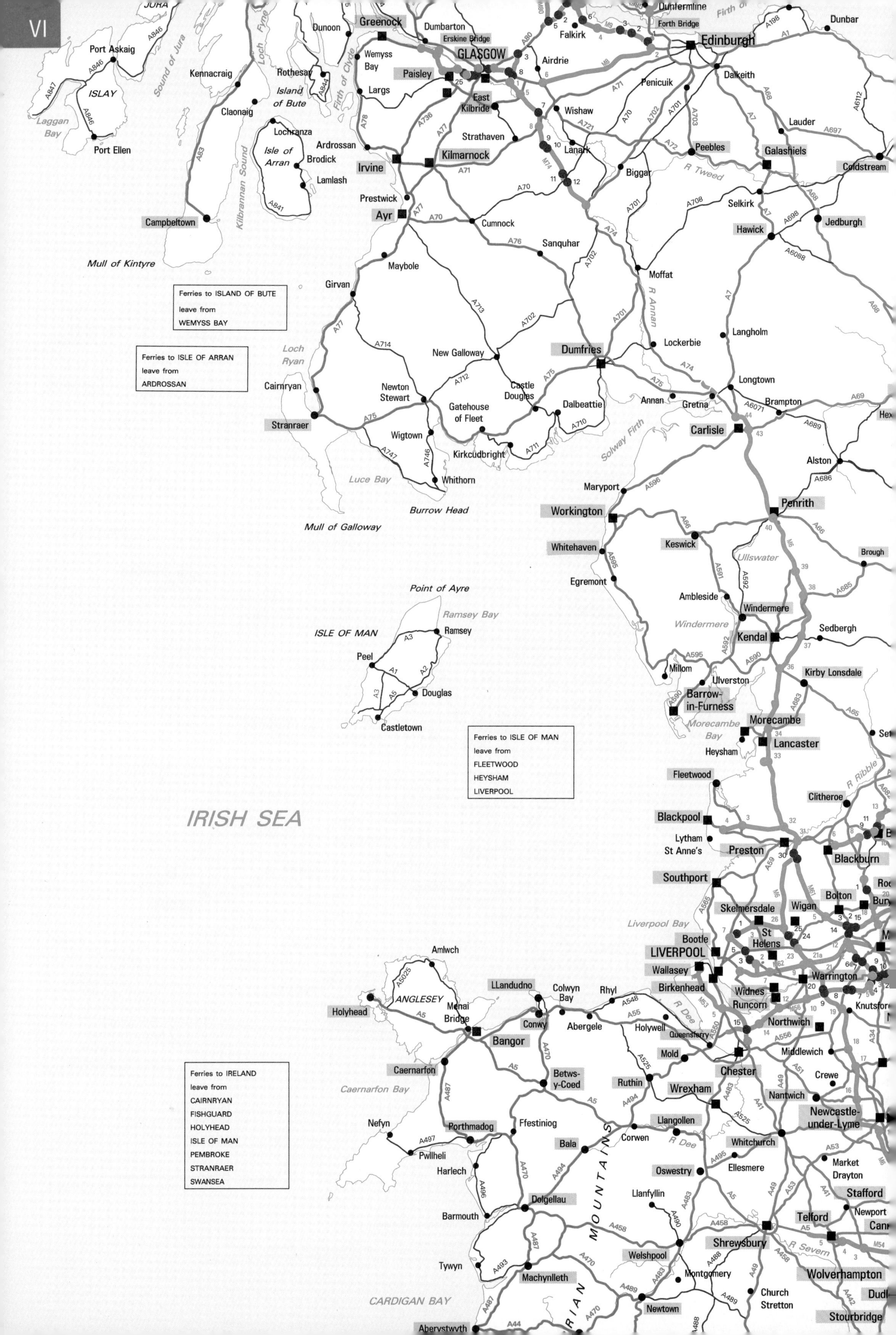

JURA

Port Askaig
A846
Kennacraig
Dunoon
Greenock
Dumbarton
Erskine Bridge
Dunfermline
Forth Bridge
Firth of
Falkirk
M9
Edinburgh
Dunbar
A198
A1
Rothesay
ISLAY
Claonaig
Island of Bute
Wemyss Bay
Paisley
GLASGOW
Airdrie
Penicuik
Dalkeith
Lauder
A697
Laggan Bay
Port Ellen
Largs
East Kilbride
Wishaw
A71
A702
A701
A703
A7
Galashiels
Coldstream
Lochranza
Ardrossan
Brodick
Isle of Arran
Strathaven
Lanark
Biggar
Peebles
A72
R Tweed
Hawick
Jedburgh
A6088
Lamlash
Irvine
A71
Kilmarnock
A721
Selkirk
A698
Campbeltown
Prestwick
Ayr
A77
Cumnock
Sanquhar
A76
Moffat
A7
Langholm
Mull of Kintyre
Maybole
A70
A74
Lockerbie
Longtown
Brampton
A69
Hex

Girvan
Ferries to ISLAND OF BUTE leave from WEMYSS BAY

Loch Ryan
A714
New Galloway
Dumfries
A75
Annan
Gretna
Carlisle
43
A689
Alston
A686

Ferries to ISLE OF ARRAN leave from ARDROSSAN

Cairnryan
Newton Stewart
A712
Castle Douglas
Dalbeattie
A710
Solway Firth
44
A6071

Stranraer
A747
A746
Wigtown
Gatehouse of Fleet
A711
Kirkcudbright
Maryport
A596
Penrith
Brough
A686

Luce Bay
Whithorn
Workington
Keswick
Ullswater
40
39
A66
A685

Burrow Head
Mull of Galloway
Whitehaven
A595
Egremont
Ambleside
Windermere
Sedbergh
38
A684

Point of Ayre
Ramsey Bay
Ramsey
ISLE OF MAN
A3
Peel
A1
A2
Douglas
Castletown
Millom
Ulverston
Barrow-in-Furness
Kendal
A590
A591
A592
Windermere
A595
A682
A690
36
37
Kirby Lonsdale
A65

Ferries to ISLE OF MAN leave from FLEETWOOD HEYSHAM LIVERPOOL

IRISH SEA

Heysham
Morecambe
Morecambe Bay
Lancaster
34
33
Set

Fleetwood
Clitheroe
13
11
A59

Blackpool
32
B

Lytham St Anne's
Preston
Blackburn
Amlwch
A5025
ANGLESEY
Menai Bridge
A5
Holyhead
LLandudno
Colwyn Bay
Rhyl
A548
Southport
Skelmersdale
26
Wigan
Bolton
Bury
Roc
A580
A570

Bootle
St Helens
25
24
14
15
LIVERPOOL
Wallasey
Birkenhead
Widnes
Runcorn
Warrington
Knutsford
M
A34

Caernarfon
Bangor
Conwy
Abergele
Holywell
Queensferry
Northwich
Middlewich
A556

Caernarfon Bay
A487
A470
Betws-y-Coed
Mold
A525
Chester
Crewe
A51
A49
Nantwich
Newcastle-under-Lyme
A53
A41

Nefyn
Porthmadog
Ffestiniog
Ruthin
A494
Wrexham
A483
Whitchurch
Market Drayton
A525

Pwllheli
A497
Bala
Llangollen
Corwen
R Dee
Ellesmere
Oswestry
A495
A5
Stafford
M6

Harlech
A496
Dolgellau
A494
A458
Llanfyllin
Shrewsbury
Telford
Newport
Can
M54

Barmouth
A493
Tywyn
A487
Machynlleth
A489
Welshpool
Montgomery
A488
A483
Church Stretton
A49
Wolverhampton
Dudl

CARDIGAN BAY
A470
Newtown
A489
A44
Stourbridge

Aberystwyth

Ferries to IRELAND leave from CAIRNRYAN FISHGUARD HOLYHEAD ISLE OF MAN PEMBROKE STRANRAER SWANSEA

MOUNTAINS
R Severn
R Dee
R Ribble
R Annan
Liverpool Bay

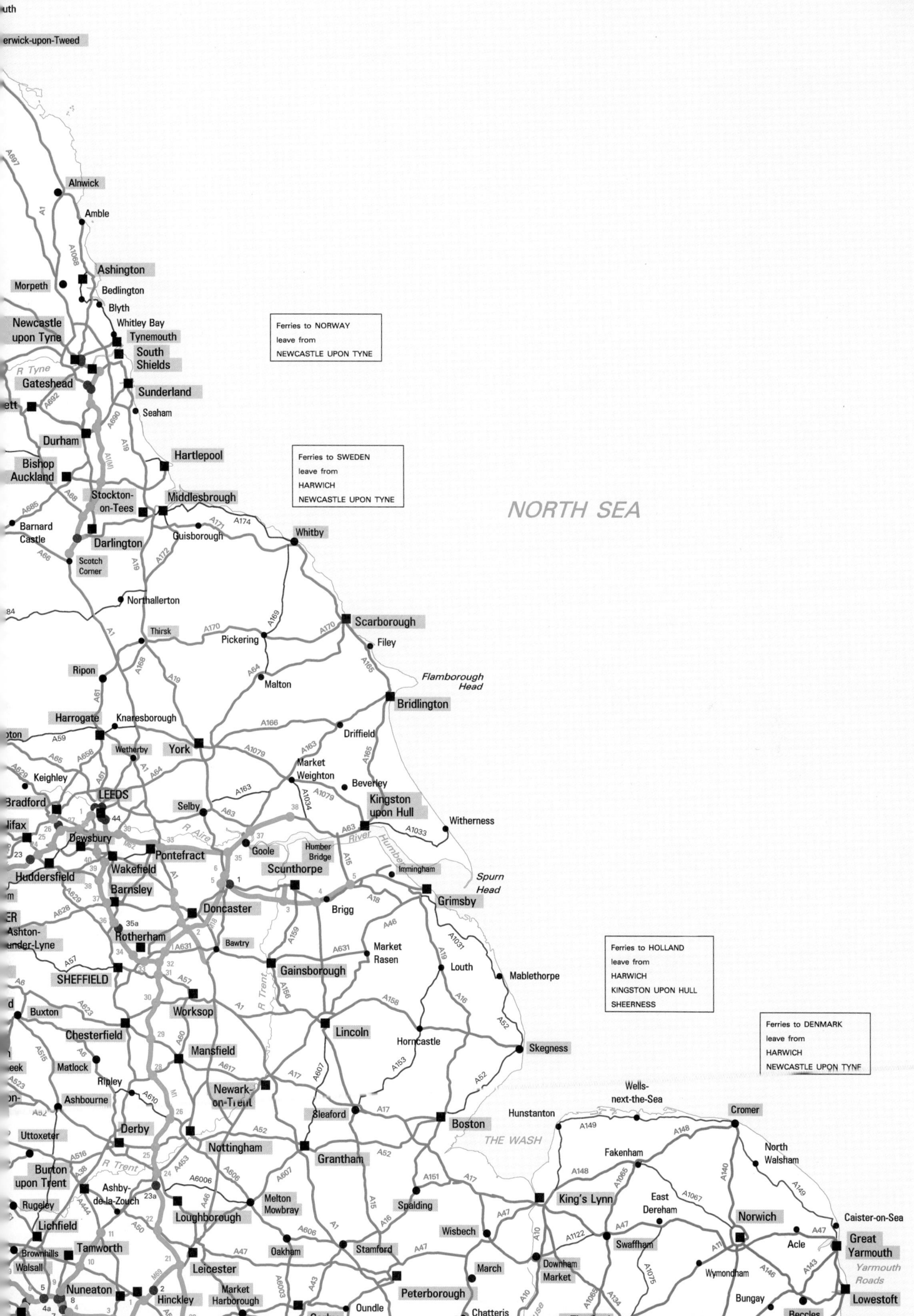

's Head
uth

erwick-upon-Tweed

A697

Alnwick

A1

Amble

A1068

Morpeth

Ashington
Bedlington
Blyth
Whitley Bay
Newcastle
upon Tyne
Tynemouth
South
Shields
R Tyne
A692
Gateshead
ett
Sunderland
A690
Seaham
Durham
A19
Bishop
Auckland
A68
A1(M)
A685
Stockton-
on-Tees
Middlesbrough
Barnard
Castle
A66
Darlington
Scotch
Corner
A19
A172
Guisborough
A171

A174

Whitby

Ferries to NORWAY
leave from
NEWCASTLE UPON TYNE

Ferries to SWEDEN
leave from
HARWICH
NEWCASTLE UPON TYNE

NORTH SEA

84
A1
Northallerton
A168
A19
A170
A163
Scarborough
Thirsk
Pickering
Filey
Ripon
A61
A64
Malton
A65
Flamborough
Head
Harrogate
Knaresborough
A166
Bridlington
ton
A59
Wetherby
York
A1079
Driffield
A165
A829
Keighley
A65
A658
A61
A1
A64
Market
Weighton
A163
Beverley
Bradford
Selby
A163
A1034
A1079
Kingston
upon Hull
lifax
Leeds
1
A63
Witherness
23
Dewsbury
M62
R Aire
38
A1033
Pontefract
Goole
Humber
Bridge
River Humber
Huddersfield
Wakefield
Scunthorpe
Immingham
Spurn
Head
Barnsley
A18
A629
A628
35a
Doncaster
Brigg
Grimsby
Ashton-
under-Lyne
Rotherham
A631
Bawtry
A631
A46
A57
A623
SHEFFIELD
Gainsborough
Market
Rasen
A6
A158
Louth
A16
Buxton
A623
A60
Worksop
A1
A156
Mablethorpe
Chesterfield
A52
A516
Mansfield
Lincoln
Horncastle
Skegness
eek
Matlock
A617
A607
A153
A623
Ripley
Newark-on-Trent
A17
Ashbourne
A610
A6
R Trent
A52
Sleaford
A17
Boston
Hunstanton
Wells-
next-the-Sea
Cromer
Uttoxeter
A516
Derby
A52
Grantham
A52
THE WASH
A149
A148
North
Walsham
Burton
upon Trent
A38
Nottingham
A606
A607
A151
Spalding
King's Lynn
Fakenham
A148
A1065
A140
Rugeley
Ashby-
de-la-Zouch
A453
A6006
Melton
Mowbray
A15
A606
A1
Wisbech
A47
East
Dereham
A1067
Norwich
Caister-on-Sea
Lichfield
A50
Loughborough
A47
Oakham
Stamford
A47
March
A1122
Swaffham
A47
A11
Acle
A47
Brownhills
Walsall
Tamworth
A47
Leicester
A6003
A43
Peterborough
Downham
Market
A1075
Wymondham
A146
Great
Yarmouth
Nuneaton
Hinckley
Market
Harborough
A6
Corby
Oundle
A141
Chatteris
Thetford
Bungay
Diss
Beccles
Lowestoft

Ferries to HOLLAND
leave from
HARWICH
KINGSTON UPON HULL
SHEERNESS

Ferries to DENMARK
leave from
HARWICH
NEWCASTLE UPON TYNE

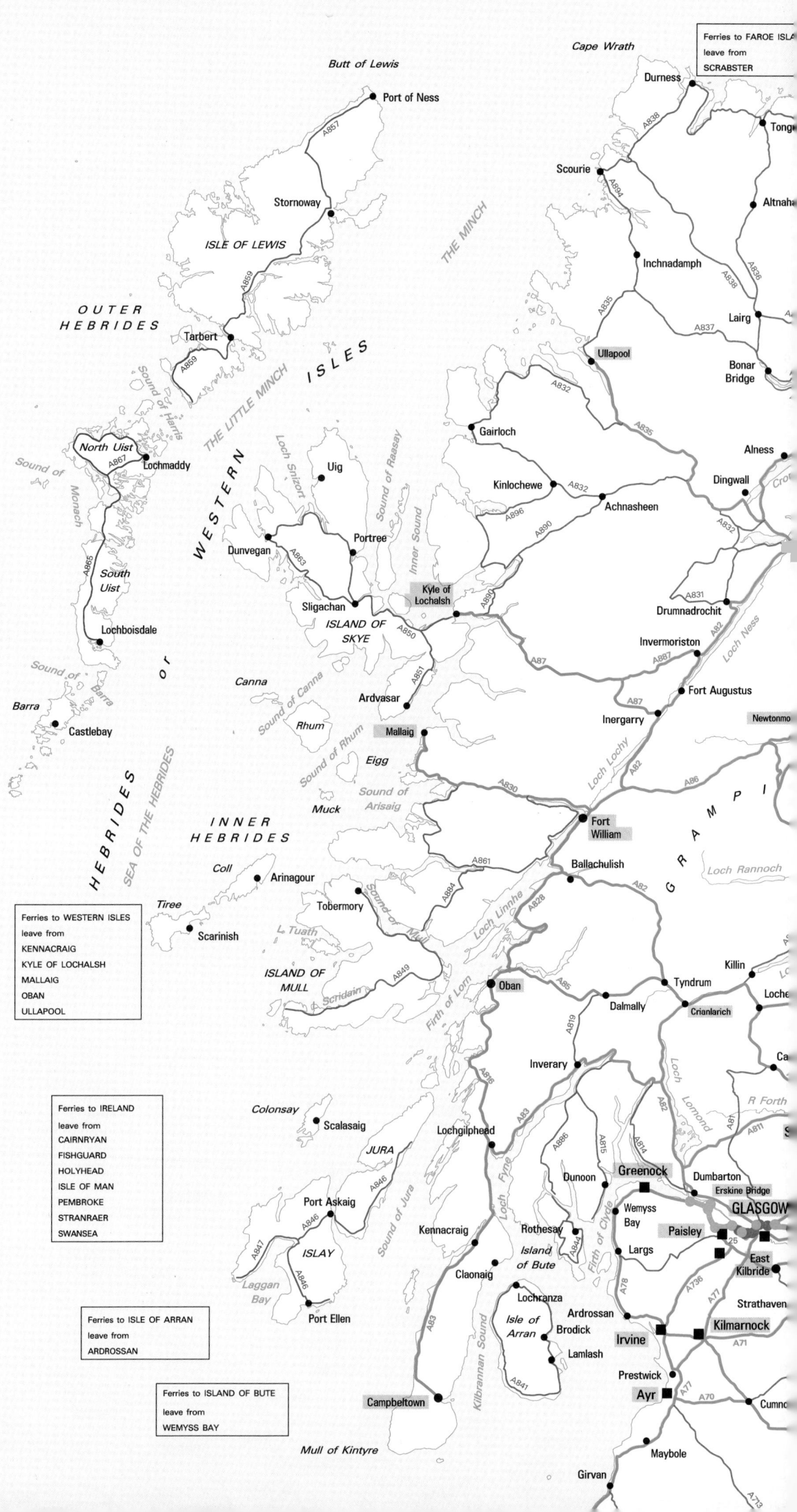

Cape Wrath

Butt of Lewis

Port of Ness

Durness

Ferries to FAROE ISLA
leave from
SCRABSTER

Tong

A957

Scourie

Altnaha

A838

A894

A836

Stornoway

Inchnadamph

ISLE OF LEWIS

A835

Lairg

A837

A859

THE MINCH

Ullapool

Bonar
Bridge

OUTER
HEBRIDES

Tarbert

A832

Alness

A859

Gairloch

A835

Dingwall

Sound of Harris

THE LITTLE MINCH

North Uist

A867

Lochmaddy

Uig

A896

Kinlochewe

A832

Crc

Achnasheen

A890

A832

Loch Snizort

Sound of Raasay

WESTERN

Portree

Dunvegan

A863

Drumnadrochit

A831

A865

South
Uist

Inner Sound

Sligachan

Kyle of
Lochalsh

Invermoriston

A82

A887

Loch Ness

Lochboisdale

ISLAND OF
SKYE

A850

Fort Augustus

A87

Sound of Monach

ISLES

Canna

A851

Ardvasar

Inergarry

Newtonmo

Barra

Sound of Canna

Rhum

Mallaig

Loch Lochy

A92

A86

Castlebay

Eigg

Sound of Rhum

A930

Sea of the Hebrides

Muck

Sound of
Arisaig

Fort
William

GRAMPI

Loch Rannoch

INNER
HEBRIDES

Coll

Arinagour

A861

Ballachulish

A82

Scridain

Loch Linnhe

Tobermory

Tiree

Scarinish

L. Tuath

Killin

Ferries to WESTERN ISLES
leave from
KENNACRAIG
KYLE OF LOCHALSH
MALLAIG
OBAN
ULLAPOOL

ISLAND OF
MULL

A849

A894

Oban

A85

Tyndrum

Loch

Dalmally

Crianlarich

Ca

A819

Sound of Mull

Firth of Lorn

Inverary

R Forth

Colonsay

Scalasaig

A83

Loch Lomond

A82

A84

A811

S

JURA

Lochgilphead

Greenock

Dumbarton

A886

A815

A814

Erskine Bridge

Ferries to IRELAND
leave from
CAIRNRYAN
FISHGUARD
HOLYHEAD
ISLE OF MAN
PEMBROKE
STRANRAER
SWANSEA

Dunoon

GLASGOW

A846

Port Askaig

Wemyss
Bay

Paisley

Firth of Clyde

A846

Rothesay

A844

Largs

East
Kilbride

ISLAY

Kennacraig

Island
of Bute

A78

A847

A846

Claonaig

A736

A77

Strathaven

Ferries to ISLE OF ARRAN
leave from
ARDROSSAN

Lochranza

Kilmarnock

A71

Port Ellen

Ardrossan

Loch Fyne

Isle of
Arran

Brodick

Irvine

Kilbrannan Sound

A83

Lamlash

Ferries to ISLAND OF BUTE
leave from
WEMYSS BAY

Prestwick

A77

Ayr

A841

Campbeltown

A70

Cumno

Maybole

Mull of Kintyre

Girvan

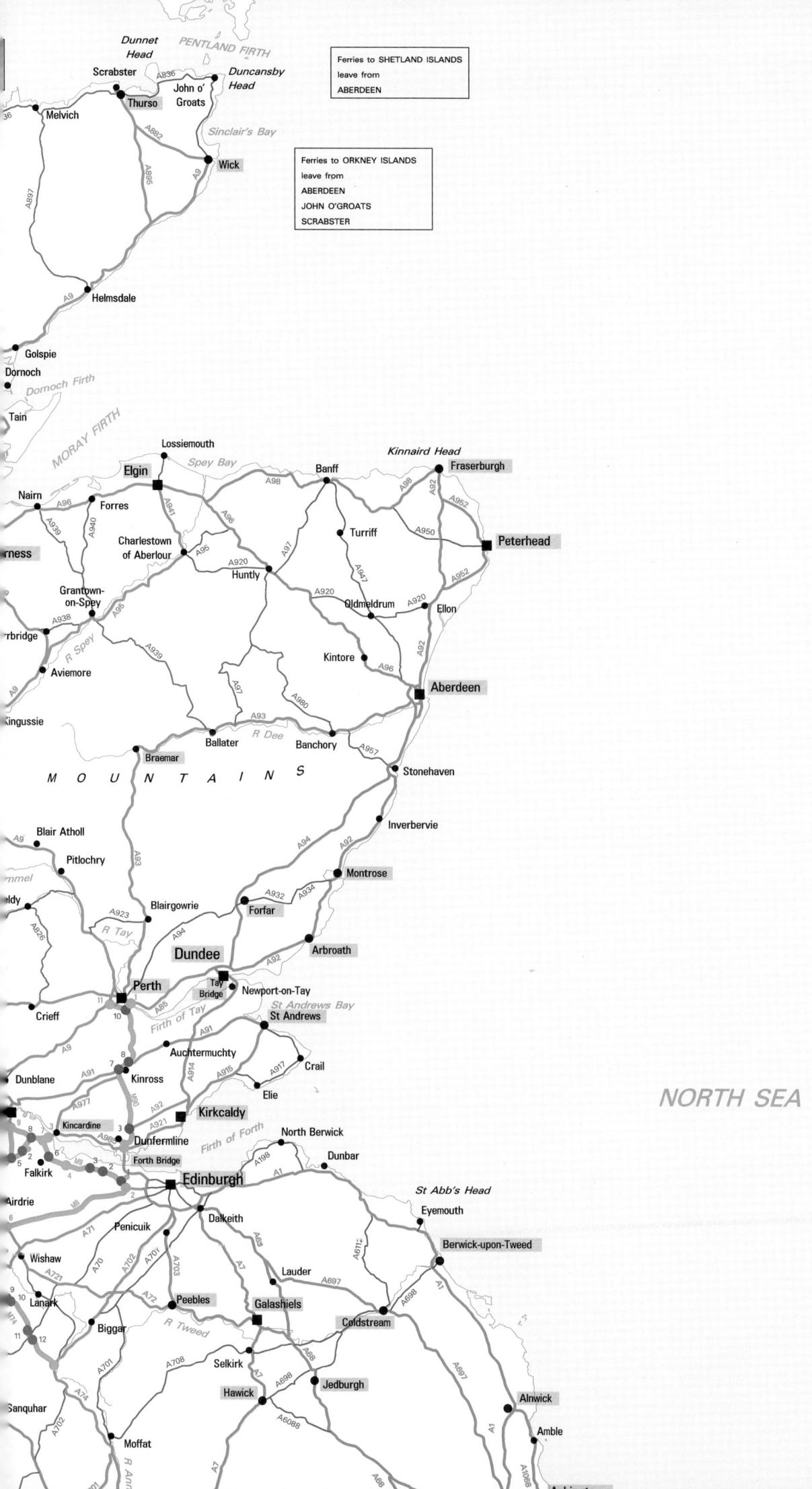

RESTRICTED MOTORWAY JUNCTIONS

M1

	Southbound	Northbound
46	No access	
45	No exit	No access
44	No access	No exit
35A	No exit	
23A	No exit to A453	No access from A453
17	No exit	No access
7	No access	No exit
6A	No access from M25	No exit to M25
4	No access	No exit
2	No access	No exit

M2

	Eastbound	Westbound
1	No access from A2 westbound	No exit to A2 eastbound

M3

	Eastbound	Westbound
8	No exit; access from A303 only	Exit to A303 only; no access
10	No access	No exit
14	No exit	No access

M4

	Eastbound	Westbound
46	No exit	No access
41	No access	No exit
39	No access; no exit	No exit
38		No access
29	No exit	No access from A48(M)
2	No exit or access from A4 westbound	No exit or access from A4 eastbound
1	No exit to A4 westbound	No access from A4 eastbound

M5

	Southbound	Northbound
10	No access	No exit
12	No exit	No access
29	No exit	No access

M6

	Southbound	Northbound
30	No access	No exit
25	No exit	No access
24	No access	No exit
20	No direct access from M56 eastbound	No direct exit to M56 eastbound
10A	No exit	No access
5	No exit	No access
4A	No access; exit to M42 only	No exit; access from M42 southbound only

M11

	Southbound	Northbound
14	No access from A1307 or A45 eastbound	No exit to A1307 or A45 westbound
13	No exit	No access
9	No exit	No access
5	No exit	No access
4	No access; no exit to A406 eastbound	No exit; no access from A406 westbound

M20

	Eastbound	Westbound
2	No access	No exit
3	No exit	
11A	No access	No exit

M23

	Southbound	Northbound
7	No access from A23 northbound	No exit to A23 southbound

M25

	Eastbound	Westbound
5	No access to M26 from A21	No exit to A21 from M26
9 (Central)	No access; no exit	
9 (North)		No access; no exit
19	No access	No exit
21	No exit to M1 southbound; no access from M1 northbound	No exit to M1 southbound; no access from M1 northbound

M27

	Eastbound	Westbound
4 (West)	No access	No exit
4 (East)	No exit	No access
10	No exit	No access
12	No access	No exit

M40

	Eastbound	Westbound
16	No access	No exit
14	No access	No exit
13	No exit	No access
8	No access	No exit
L	No exit	No access
7	No exit	No access
3	No exit	No access

M42

	Southbound	Northbound
1	No access	No exit
7	Access from M6 only; no exit	Exit to M6 West only; no access
7A	No access; no exit	Exit to M6 East only; no access
8	Exit to M6 only; no access	Access to M6 only; no exit

M45

	Eastbound	Westbound
L	No access	No exit

M53

	Southbound	Northbound
11	No access	No access

M56

	Eastbound	Westbound
15	No exit	No access
9	No direct access	No direct exit to M6 southbound
8	No access; no exit	No exit
7		No access
4	No exit	No access
2	No exit	No access
1	No exit to A34 southbound or M63 westbound	No access from A34 southbound or M63 westbound; no exit to M63

M57

	Southbound	Northbound
3	No access	No exit
5	No access	No exit

M58

	Eastbound	Westbound
1	No exit	No access

M61

	Southbound	Northbound
9	No exit	No access
3		No access
2		No access from A580 eastbound

M62

	Eastbound	Westbound
14	No exit to A580; no access from A580 westbound	No exit to A580 eastbound; no access from A580
15	No exit	No access
23	No access	No exit

M63

	Southbound	Northbound
7	No exit	
9	No exit to B5103 northbound; no access from A5103 northbound	
10	No exit to M56 or to A34 northbound	No exit to A34 northbound; no access from M56
11	No access	No exit
13	No exit	No access
14	No exit	No exit; no access
15	No access	

M65

	Eastbound	Westbound
9	No access	No exit
11	No access	No access

M66

	Southbound	Northbound
1	No exit	No access
12	No access	

M67

	Eastbound	Westbound
1	No access	No exit
2	No exit	No access

M69

	Southbound	Northbound
2	No access	No exit

M180

	Eastbound	Westbound
1	No access	No exit

A3(M)

	Southbound	Northbound
L	Junction with unclassified road, no exit	Junction with unclassified road, no access

M8

	Eastbound	Westbound
25	No access from A739 northbound	No access from A739 northbound
23	No exit	No access
22	No exit	No access
21	No access	No exit
20	No exit	No access
18		No access
16	No exit	No access
14	No access	No exit
9	No access	No exit
8		No access from A8 eastbound, A89 eastbound or M73 southbound

M9

	Eastbound	Westbound
8	No exit	No access from M876 northbound
6	No access	No exit
3	No exit	No access
2	No access	No exit
1	No exit	No access

M73

	Southbound	Northbound
3	No access from A80 northbound	No exit to A80 southbound
2	No access from A89; no exit to M8 (Junction 8) or A89	No exit to A89; no access from M8 (Junction 8) or A89

M74

	Southbound	Northbound
7	No access	No exit
9	No access	No exit; no access
10	No exit	
11	No access	No exit
12	Exit to A74 only, end of motorway	Access from A74 only

M80

	Southbound	Northbound
5	No exit	No access

M90

	Southbound	Northbound
10	No exit to A912	No access from A912
8	No exit	No access
7	No access	No exit

M876

	Eastbound	Westbound
2	No access	No exit

A1(M)

	Southbound	Northbound
L	Junction with A69, no exit	Junction with A69, no access
L	Junction with A66(M), no exit	Junction with A66(M), no access
5	No exit; no access	No exit
3	No access	
2	No exit	

MOTORWAYS AND MAJOR ROUTES

ROAD SIGNS

SIGNS GIVING ORDERS

These signs are mostly circular and those with red circles are mostly prohibitive

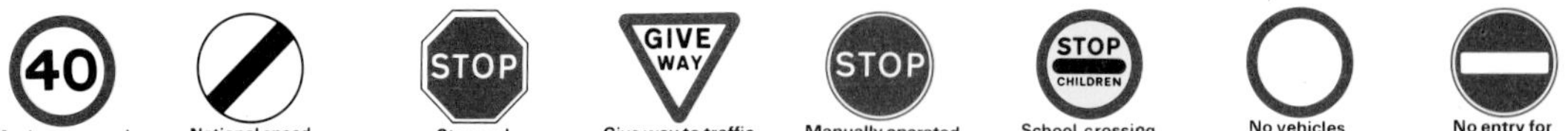
40
STOP
GIVE WAY
STOP
STOP
CHILDREN

Maximum speed · National speed limit applies · Stop and Give Way · Give way to traffic on major road · Manually operated temporary 'STOP' sign · School crossing patrol · No vehicles · No entry for vehicular traffic

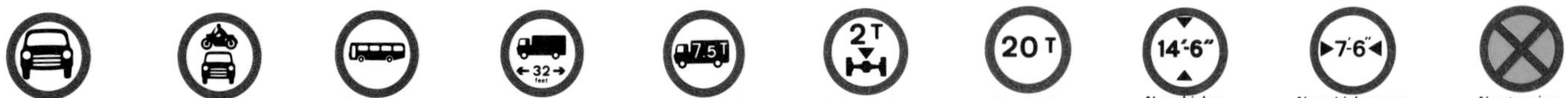
32
7.5T
2T
20T
14'6"
7'6"

No motor vehicles except solo motorcycles, scooters or mopeds · No motor vehicles · No vehicles with over 12 seats except regular scheduled, school and works buses · No vehicle or combination of vehicles over length shown · No goods vehicles over maximum gross weight shown (in tonnes) · Axle weight limit in tonnes · No vehicles including load over weight shown (in tonnes) · No vehicles over height shown · No vehicles over width shown · No stopping (Clearway)

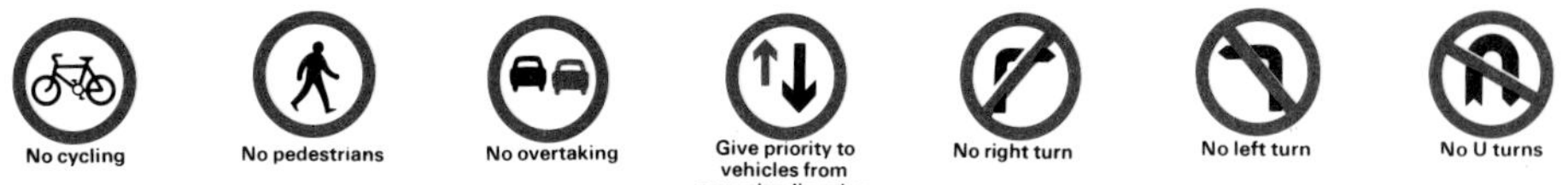

No cycling · No pedestrians · No overtaking · Give priority to vehicles from opposite direction · No right turn · No left turn · No U turns

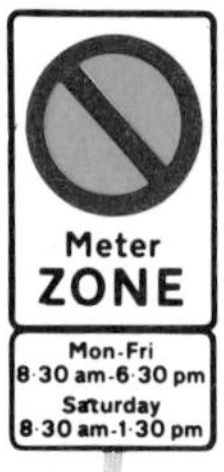
Meter
ZONE
Mon-Fri
8·30 am-6·30 pm
Saturday
8·30 am-1·30 pm

Entrance to controlled parking zone

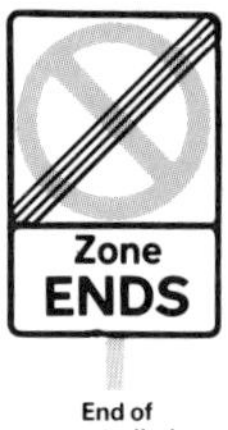
Zone
ENDS

End of controlled parking zone

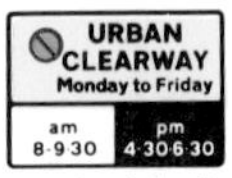
URBAN
CLEARWAY
Monday to Friday
am
8·9·30
pm
4·30·6·30

No stopping during times shown except for as long as necessary to set down or pick up passengers

Plates below some signs qualify their message

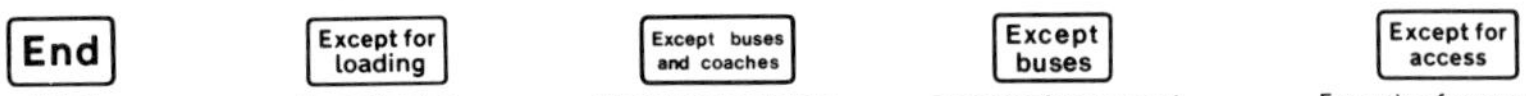
End
Except for loading
Except buses and coaches
Except buses
Except for access

End of restriction · Exception for loading/unloading goods · Exception for vehicles with over 12 seats · Exception for stage and scheduled express carriages, school and works buses · Exception for access to premises and land adjacent to the road where there is no alternative route

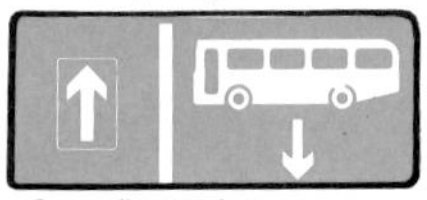

Contra-flow bus lane

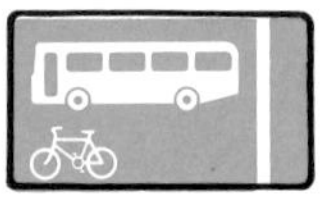

With-flow bus and cycle lane

Signs with blue circles but no red border mostly give positive instruction

30
30

Ahead only · Turn left ahead (right if symbol reversed) · Turn left (right if symbol reversed) · Keep left (right if symbol reversed) · Vehicles may pass either side to reach same destination · Route to be used by pedal cycles only · Minimum speed · End of minimum speed · Mini-roundabout (roundabout circulation – give way to vehicles from the immediate right) · One-way traffic (Note: compare circular "Ahead only" sign) · **Shared pedal cycle and pedestrian route**

WARNING SIGNS

Mostly triangular

Roundabout · Cross roads · T junction · Staggered junction · Dual carriageway ends · Road narrows on both sides · Road narrows on right (left if symbol reversed)

Humps for ½ mile

Distance over which road humps extend

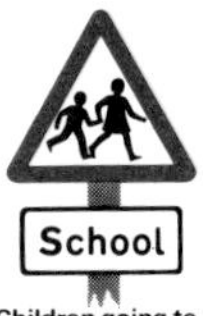
School

Children going to or from school

Change to opposite carriageway (may be reversed) · Slippery road · Two-way traffic straight ahead · Two-way traffic crosses one-way road · **Traffic merges from left/right with equal priority** · Double bend first to left (may be reversed) · Bend to right (or left if symbol reversed)

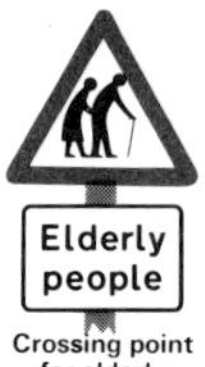
Elderly people

Crossing point for elderly people (blind or disabled if shown)

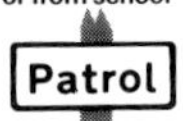
Patrol

School crossing patrol ahead (Some signs have amber lights which flash when patrol is operating)

10%
20%

Steep hill downwards · Steep hill upwards · **Hump bridge** · **Uneven road** · Traffic signals · Failure of light signals · Pedestrian crossing

Gradients may be shown as a ratio i.e. 20% = 1:5

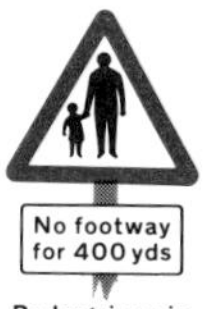
No footway for 400 yds

Pedestrians in road ahead

Safe height 16'-6"

Overhead electric cable; plate indicates maximum height of vehicles which can pass safely

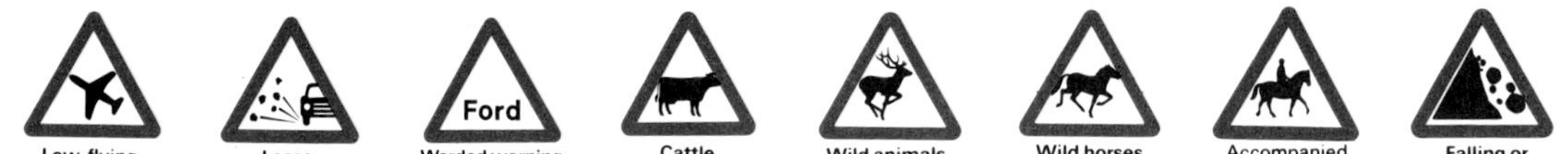
Ford

Low-flying aircraft or sudden aircraft noise · Loose chippings · Worded warning sign · Cattle · Wild animals · Wild horses or ponies · Accompanied horses or ponies crossing the road ahead · Falling or fallen rocks

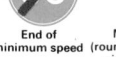

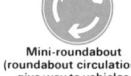

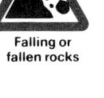

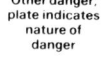

Fallen tree

Other danger; plate indicates nature of danger

14'6"

Height limit (e.g. low bridge)

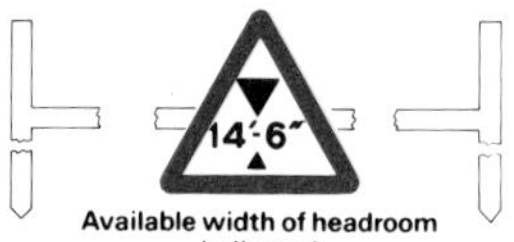
14'6"

Available width of headroom indicated

Opening or swing bridge ahead · Quayside or river bank · **Cycle route ahead** · Road works

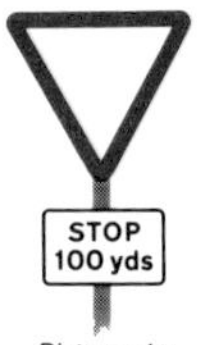
STOP 100 yds

Distance to "STOP" line ahead

1 mile

Distance to tunnel

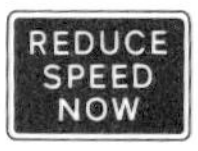
REDUCE SPEED NOW

Plate below some signs

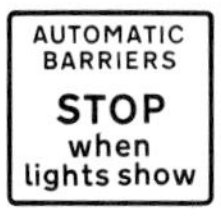
AUTOMATIC BARRIERS
STOP
when
lights show

Plate to indicate a level crossing equipped with automatic barriers and flashing lights

Level crossing with barrier or gate ahead · Level crossing without barrier or gate ahead · Level crossing without barrier (the additional lower half of the cross is used when there is more than one railway line)

Risk of Grounding

Risk of grounding of long low vehicles at level crossing

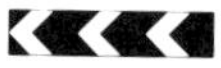

Sharp deviation of route to left (or right if chevrons reversed)

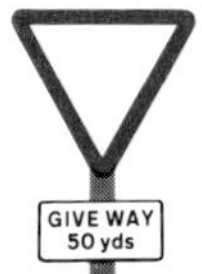
GIVE WAY 50 yds

Distance to "Give Way" line ahead

DIRECTION SIGNS
Signs on motorways
Mostly rectangular
Blue backgrounds

Start of motorway and point
from which motorway
regulations apply

"Count-down" markers at exit from motorway
(each bar represents 100 yards to the exit).
Green-backed markers may be used on primary
routes and white-backed markers with red bars
on the approaches to concealed level crossings

Distance to service area with fuel,
parking and cafeteria facilities
(The current petrol price may be shown
in pence per gallon or litre,
or may be omitted)

On approaches to junctions
(junction number on black background)

Downward pointing arrows mean
"Get in lane"

The panel with the sloping arrow
indicates the destinations which can be
reached by leaving the motorway
at the next junction

At a junction leading directly into a motorway

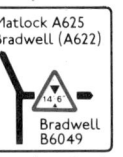

Route confirmatory sign
after junction

End of motorway

Signs on primary routes
Green backgrounds

At the junction

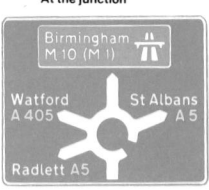

On approaches to junctions (The blue panel
indicates that the motorway commences from
the junction ahead. The motorway shown in
brackets can also be reached by proceeding in
that direction)

Ring road

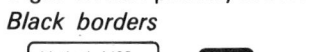

On approaches to junctions

Route
confirmatory
sign
after junction

Route confirmatory sign after junction

Primary Routes

These form a national network of recommended through routes which complement the motorway
system.
Selected places of major traffic importance are known as Primary Route Destinations
and are shown on this map thus **EXETER** Distances and directions to such destinations are
repeated on traffic signs which, on primary routes, have a green background or, on motorways,
have a blue background.
To continue on a primary route through or past a place which has appeared as a destination on
previous signs, follow the directions to the next primary destination shown on the green-backed signs.

Signs on non-primary routes
Black borders

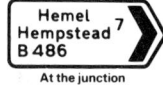

On approaches to junctions
(a symbol may sometimes be
shown to indicate a warning
of a hazard or prohibition on a
road leading from a junction)

Ring road

At the junction

Local direction signs
Blue borders

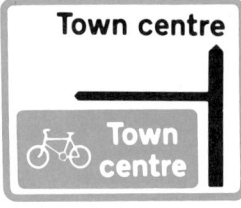

On approaches to junctions
(where there is a different route
for pedal cycles this may be
shown in a blue panel)

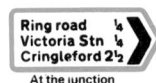

On approaches to junctions

Direction to toilets
with access for the disabled

At the junction

Airport

Direction to camping
and caravan site

Picnic site

INFORMATION SIGNS
All rectangular

Parking place for
towed caravans

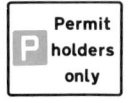

Parking restricted to use
by people named on sign

One-way street

Bus lane on road
at junction ahead

Appropriate traffic lanes
at junction ahead

No through
road

With-flow pedal cycle lane

Recommended route
for pedal cycles

Tourist
information
point

Permanent
reduction in
available lanes.
e.g. two-lane
carriageway
reducing to one

Temporary lane closure

The number and position of arrows and
bars may be varied according to lanes
and ahead

Hospital
ahead

Advance warning of
restriction or prohibition
ahead

Priority over vehicles
from opposite
direction

Other direction signs

Advisory route for lorries

Holiday route

Railway Museum 3
follow
Tourist attraction

Diversion route

Wrest Park
Ancient monument in the care of
English Heritage

Council Offices
Public Library
Route for pedestrians

Marton 3
Recommended route for pedal
cycles to place shown

Lane control signals

White arrow — lane available to traffic facing the sign. Red crosses — lane closed to traffic facing the sign.

RADIO INFORMATION AND DISTANCES

Distances are shown in miles and in *italics* kilometres

National Radio Information

BBC National Radio gives frequent road and weather information

The frequencies used are:

	kHz/metres	VHF(MHz)
Radio 1	1053/285	**97.7 - 99.6**
	1089/275	
Bournemouth	1485/202	
Merseyside	1107/271	
National FM coverage due in 1994		
Radio 2		**88.1 - 90.2**

Radio 4	198/1515	**92.5 - 95.8**
		103.5-105.0
Aberystwyth	198/1515	
Aberdeen	1449/207	
Carlisle	1485/202	
London	720/417	
Plymouth	774/388	
Redruth	756/397	
Tyneside	603/498	
Radio 5	693/433	
	909/330	
Mid Wales	990/303	
Radio Scotland	810/370	**92.5 - 94.7**
W Scotland		**97.7 - 99.4**
Radio Aberdeen	990/303	**92.7 - 94.5**
Radio Highland		**92.5 - 94.6**
		104.9
Radio Orkney		**92.7 - 93.7**
Radio Shetland		**92.7**
Radio Solway	585/513	**93.1 - 94.7**
Radio Tweed		**92.8 - 93.9**
		103.6
Radio Wales	882/340	**95.1-95.9**
Mid Wales	1125/267	
Radio Clwyd	657/457	
Radio Cymru		**92.5-94.5**
Blaenavon		**104.0**
Wenvoe		**96.8**

Distance Chart

(miles / kilometres in italics. Each row is labelled by its city at the right.)

```
London
503/810  Aberdeen
211 445 /340 716  Aberystwyth
394 177 317 /634 285 510  Ayr
338 182 311 134 /544 293 501 216  Berwick-upon-Tweed
105 420 114 289 264 /169 676 183 465 425  Birmingham
226 308 153 180 193 123 /364 496 246 290 311 198  Blackpool
100 564 207 436 412 147 270 /161 908 333 702 663 237 435  Bournemouth
482 59 405 143 148 377 268 524 /776 95 652 230 238 607 431 843  Braemar
52 556 235 446 390 163 286 92 534 /84 895 378 718 628 262 460 148 859  Brighton
122 493 125 370 352 81 204 82 458 137 /196 793 201 595 566 130 328 132 737 220  Bristol
54 458 214 357 294 100 208 154 426 106 144 /87 737 344 575 473 161 335 248 686 171 232  Cambridge
157 490 105 382 368 103 209 117 470 182 45 179 /253 789 169 615 592 166 336 188 756 293 72 288  Cardiff
301 221 224 93 87 196 87 343 181 353 277 264 289 /484 356 360 150 140 315 140 552 291 568 446 425 465  Carlisle
159 344 176 235 198 94 94 235 310 211 175 116 197 142 /256 554 283 378 319 151 151 378 499 340 282 187 317 229  Doncaster
71 576 282 465 409 176 297 174 553 82 186 125 238 372 231 /114 927 454 748 658 283 478 280 890 132 299 201 383 599 372  Dover
434 67 376 117 113 349 239 495 52 486 430 391 441 152 275 505 /698 108 605 188 182 562 385 797 84 782 692 629 710 245 443 813  Dundee
378 125 320 73 57 292 183 439 91 430 373 335 385 96 219 449 56 /608 201 515 117 92 470 295 707 146 692 600 539 620 154 352 723 90  Edinburgh
172 569 201 456 428 157 282 82 534 146 76 220 121 353 251 248 506 450 /277 916 323 734 689 253 454 132 859 267 122 354 195 568 404 399 814 724  Exeter
260 491 56 373 393 170 209 234 461 291 154 270 112 280 233 331 432 376 230 /418 790 90 600 632 274 336 377 742 468 248 435 180 451 375 533 695 605 370  Fishguard
497 165 430 133 190 392 283 539 125 549 473 460 485 196 338 568 127 144 549 486 /800 266 692 214 306 631 455 867 201 884 761 740 781 315 544 914 204 232 884 782  Fort William
397 145 320 33 101 292 183 439 110 449 373 360 385 96 238 468 83 44 449 376 101 /639 233 515 53 163 470 295 707 177 723 600 580 620 154 383 753 134 71 723 605 163  Glasgow
109 468 102 330 318 56 174 99 419 133 35 123 56 237 150 180 390 334 111 153 433 333 /175 753 164 531 512 90 280 159 674 214 56 198 90 381 241 290 628 538 179 246 697 536  Gloucester
128 495 294 402 345 180 252 228 477 180 241 82 261 309 167 185 442 390 205 505 405 205 /206 797 473 647 555 290 406 367 768 290 388 132 420 497 269 298 711 621 478 563 813 652 330  Great Yarmouth
76 505 281 439 372 167 275 176 504 128 191 67 246 336 194 125 469 413 248 337 532 432 178 82 /122 813 452 707 599 269 443 283 811 206 307 108 396 541 312 201 755 665 399 542 856 695 286 132  Harwich
253 439 111 305 311 148 141 288 311 206 248 216 212 167 339 364 308 282 167 179 /407 707 179 491 501 238 227 463 632 501 332 399 348 341 269 546 586 496 454 269 657 496 290 504 507  Holyhead
536 105 486 199 215 458 348 597 75 588 539 493 549 262 351 607 132 158 618 542 66 166 504 518 545 474 /863 169 782 320 346 737 560 961 121 946 867 793 884 422 565 977 212 254 995 872 106 267 811 834 877 763  Inverness
663 232 615 328 342 587 478 724 202 715 668 620 680 391 478 734 259 285 744 671 195 295 628 645 672 603 129 /1067 373 990 528 550 945 769 1165 325 1151 1075 998 1094 629 769 1181 417 459 1197 1080 314 475 1011 1038 1081 970 208  John O'Groats
206 364 223 251 185 152 127 282 307 258 233 163 244 158 47 277 272 216 309 280 354 254 198 169 232 214 374 501 /332 586 359 404 298 245 204 454 494 415 375 262 393 254 76 446 438 348 497 451 570 409 272 333 373 344 602 806  Kingston-upon-Hull
576 189 499 212 243 471 362 618 159 628 552 539 564 275 417 647 216 226 555 79 179 512 584 611 487 84 189 433 /927 304 803 341 391 758 583 995 256 1011 888 867 908 443 671 1041 299 348 1011 893 127 288 824 940 983 784 135 304 697  Kyle of Lochalsh
297 692 325 570 552 281 405 205 665 289 200 334 245 477 374 346 630 574 123 353 673 573 255 640 571 405 741 868 421 752 /478 1114 523 917 888 452 652 330 1070 465 322 538 394 768 602 589 1014 924 198 568 1081 922 378 676 597 652 1193 1397 678 1210  Land's End
189 327 181 212 156 113 72 255 293 241 194 145 220 119 29 260 258 202 270 237 315 215 159 196 223 164 360 487 55 394 394 /304 526 291 341 251 182 116 410 472 388 312 233 354 192 47 418 415 325 435 381 507 346 256 315 359 264 579 784 89 634 634  Leeds
97 414 153 299 252 39 140 158 378 149 68 142 206 74 188 283 196 202 85 140 402 302 85 140 135 163 461 588 121 481 320 95 /156 666 246 481 406 63 225 254 608 240 193 109 229 332 119 270 562 455 315 336 647 486 137 225 217 262 742 947 195 774 515 153  Leicester
131 383 199 274 224 90 128 209 343 183 171 85 193 181 39 202 314 258 247 255 377 277 136 128 155 200 427 554 44 456 371 68 51 /211 616 320 441 360 145 206 336 552 295 275 137 311 291 63 325 505 415 398 410 607 446 219 206 249 322 687 892 71 734 597 109 82  Lincoln
202 341 104 213 219 39 49 234 307 256 161 201 165 120 86 273 272 216 237 160 316 216 126 240 235 196 382 511 130 395 361 75 100 118 /325 549 167 343 352 150 79 377 494 412 259 324 272 193 138 439 438 348 381 257 509 348 203 386 378 148 615 822 209 636 581 121 161 190  Liverpool
185 340 141 212 196 80 48 227 306 237 161 151 172 119 51 256 271 216 197 126 315 215 126 205 239 124 373 500 95 394 361 40 92 84 /298 547 227 341 315 129 77 365 492 381 259 243 277 192 82 412 436 348 317 203 507 346 203 330 385 200 600 805 153 634 581 64 148 135  Manchester
274 235 273 149 64 207 129 347 201 326 288 230 304 57 114 345 110 110 364 329 253 148 253 281 308 247 268 395 121 318 636 92 187 159 /441 378 439 240 103 333 208 558 323 525 463 370 489 92 183 555 267 177 586 529 407 238 407 452 496 398 431 636 195 512 785 148 301 256  Newcastle-upon-Tyne
114 475 276 382 328 166 234 214 457 163 221 62 241 289 147 174 422 366 282 237 280 366 385 186 20 73 293 498 625 149 564 421 176 119 105 /183 764 444 615 528 267 373 344 735 262 356 100 388 465 237 280 679 589 454 531 781 620 299 32 117 293 498 625 149 564 421 176 119 105  Norwich
122 379 164 274 221 50 111 183 353 174 145 83 153 181 43 193 318 262 221 220 377 277 110 142 150 171 430 557 69 456 345 70 25 35 /196 610 264 441 356 80 179 295 568 280 233 134 246 291 69 311 512 422 356 354 607 446 177 229 241 275 692 896 145 734 555 113 40 56  Nottingham
489 178 412 125 180 384 275 530 141 545 465 452 477 188 350 560 117 123 468 482 92 42 424 497 524 460 134 244 346 65 307 393 368 /787 286 663 201 290 618 443 853 227 871 748 727 768 303 531 901 188 108 858 753 79 148 682 800 843 644 185 393 557 206 494 632 592  Oban
57 483 154 353 324 64 187 90 448 99 74 83 108 260 145 128 413 357 142 205 456 356 52 156 126 209 515 642 192 535 274 168 73 124 /92 777 248 568 521 103 301 145 721 159 119 134 174 418 233 206 665 574 229 330 734 573 84 251 203 336 829 1033 309 861 441 270 117 200  Oxford
218 615 247 492 474 203 328 128 587 212 122 263 167 399 297 276 595 495 157 343 719 619 301 420 360 664 790 355 157 343 293 316 242 293 /351 990 398 792 763 327 528 206 945 341 196 423 269 642 478 444 958 797 253 552 473 528 1069 1271 571 1085 143 509 389 472  Plymouth
70 560 222 430 401 141 264 52 526 48 97 124 142 337 222 130 491 435 120 251 533 433 108 198 146 288 592 719 269 612 241 244 150 201 /113 901 357 692 645 227 425 84 847 77 156 200 229 542 357 209 790 700 193 404 858 697 174 319 235 463 953 1157 433 985 388 393 241 323  Portsmouth
159 360 159 245 190 76 86 216 320 211 161 120 179 152 18 230 291 235 237 173 348 248 126 166 187 149 393 520 65 427 361 33 62 46 /256 579 256 394 306 122 138 348 515 340 259 193 288 245 29 370 468 378 381 346 560 399 203 267 301 240 632 837 105 687 581 53 100 74  Sheffield
150 399 77 269 265 95 98 185 357 208 133 155 111 176 97 133 274 247 80 330 274 179 133 372 272 77 225 282 103 438 567 146 451 303 109 84 117 /241 642 124 433 426 72 158 298 575 335 166 233 179 283 159 356 531 441 288 214 599 438 124 362 354 167 912 235 726 488 175 135 188  Shrewsbury
77 547 201 417 388 128 251 31 512 61 76 131 121 324 209 143 477 421 105 215 520 420 205 153 273 579 706 256 599 228 232 137 188 /124 880 323 671 624 206 404 50 824 98 122 211 195 521 336 230 768 678 169 346 837 676 130 246 439 932 1136 412 964 367 373 220 303  Southampton
402 228 325 51 138 297 188 444 194 454 378 365 390 101 253 477 167 124 454 381 164 87 384 410 435 313 250 379 259 263 578 220 307 282 /647 367 523 82 254 478 303 715 312 731 608 587 628 163 391 761 269 200 731 613 296 135 552 660 700 504 402 610 417 423 930 354 494 454  Stranraer
194 494 73 366 383 119 216 167 483 222 85 217 41 273 217 207 448 392 161 67 469 369 89 294 267 184 535 664 264 548 285 227 158 209 /312 795 117 589 616 192 348 269 777 357 137 349 66 439 349 441 721 631 259 108 755 594 143 473 430 296 861 1069 425 882 459 365 254 336  Swansea
193 319 205 214 148 130 96 269 285 245 211 150 244 121 34 264 250 194 287 261 317 217 176 201 228 188 352 479 37 396 411 24 108 75 /311 513 330 344 238 209 154 433 459 394 340 241 393 195 55 425 402 312 462 420 510 349 283 323 367 303 566 771 60 637 661 39 174 121  York
```

Local Radio

Local radio stations giving road and weather reports. BBC stations are listed in red, Independent Local Radio stations in blue.

	MW (kHz/metres)	VHF (MHz)

1 BBC CWR
94.8
103.7
104.0
Mercia Sound
1359/220 97.0
102.9

2 BBC Essex
729/412 95.3
765/392 103.5
1530/196
Essex Radio
1359/220 96.3
1431/210 102.6

3 BBC Hereford & Worcester
738/406 94.7
104.0
104.6
Radio Wyvern
954/314 97.6
1530/196 102.8

4 BBC Wiltshire Sound
1332/225 103.5
1368/219 103.6
104.3

5 Greater London Radio
1458/206 94.9
Capital Radio
1548/194 95.8
LBC London Broadcasting Company
1152/261 97.3

6 Greater Manchester Radio
1458/206 95.1
Piccadilly Radio
1152/261 103.0

7 Radio Bedfordshire
630/476 95.5
1161/258 103.8
104.5
Chiltern Radio
792/378 96.9
828/362 97.6
Horizon Radio
103.3

8 Radio Bristol
1323/227 94.9
1548/194 95.5
104.6
GWR
936/321 96.3
1161/258 96.5
1260/238 97.2
102.2
103.0

9 Radio Cambridgeshire & Peterborough
1026/292 95.7
1449/207 96.0
CN FM
103.0

10 Radio Cleveland
95.0
95.8
TFM Radio
1170/257 96.6

11 Radio Cornwall
630/476 95.2
657/457 96.0
103.9

12 Radio Cumbria
756/397 95.6
1458/206

13 Radio Derby
1116/269 94.2
95.3
104.5

14 Radio Devon
801/376 94.8
855/351 95.8
990/303 96.0
1458/206 103.4

15 Radio Furness
837/358 95.2
96.1
104.2

16 Radio Gloucestershire
95.0
104.7
Severn Sound
774/388 102.4
103.0

17 Radio Humberside
1485/202 95.9
Viking Radio
1161/258 96.9

18 Radio Kent
774/388 96.7
1035/290 97.6
1602/187 104.2

19 Radio Lancashire
855/351 95.5
1557/193 103.9
104.5

20 Radio Leeds
774/388 92.4
95.3
103.9
Radio Aire
828/362 96.3

21 Radio Leicester
837/358 104.9
Leicester Sound
1260/238 103.2

22 Radio Lincolnshire
1368/219 94.9

23 Radio Merseyside
1485/202 95.8
Radio City
1548/194 96.7

24 Radio Newcastle
1458/206 95.4
96.0
104.4
Metro Radio
1152/261 97.1
103.0

25 Radio Norfolk
855/351 95.1
873/344 104.4
Radio Broadland
1152/261 102.4

26 Radio Northampton
103.6
104.2
Northants 96
1557/193 96.6

27 Radio Nottingham
1584/189 95.5
103.8
Radio Trent
945/317 96.2
999/301 102.8

28 Radio Oxford
95.2

29 Radio Sheffield
1035/290 88.6
94.7
104.1
Radio Hallam
990/303 96.1
1305/230 97.4
1548/194 102.9
103.4

30 Radio Shropshire
1584/189 95.0
96.0

31 Radio Solent
999/300 96.1
1359/221

32 Radio Stoke
1503/200 94.6
Signal Radio
1170/257 102.6

33 Radio Suffolk
95.5
103.9
104.6

34 Radio Sussex
1161/258 95.1
1485/202 95.3
1368/219 104.0
104.5
Southern Sound
1323/227 96.9
97.5
102.4
103.5

35 Radio WM
828/362 95.6
1458/206
Beacon Radio/ WABC
990/303 97.2
1017/295 103.1

36 Radio York
666/450 95.5
1260/238 103.7
104.3

37 BRMB Radio
1152/261 96.4

38 Premier Radio
96.4

39 Devonair Radio
666/450 96.4
954/314 97.0

40 Fox FM
97.4
102.6

41 Hereward Radio
1332/225 102.7

42 Invicta Radio
603/497 95.9
1242/242 96.1
97.0
102.8
103.1

43 Manx Radio
1368/219 89.0
97.2
103.7

44 Marcher Sound
1260/238 97.1
103.4

45 Moray Firth Radio
1107/271 97.4

46 North Sound Radio
1035/290 96.6

47 Ocean Sound
96.7
97.5
Power FM
103.2
South Coast Radio
1170/257
1557/193
1323/227

48 Orchard
102.6

49 Plymouth Sound
1152/261 96.6
97.0

50 Radio Borders
96.8
97.5
103.1
103.4

51 Radio Clyde
1152/261 102.5

52 Radio Forth
1548/194 97.3
97.6

53 Radio Mercury
1521/197 97.5
102.7

54 Radio Tay
1161/258 96.4
1584/189 102.8

55 Radio 210
1431/210 97.0
102.9

56 Red Dragon Radio
1305/230 97.4
1359/221 103.2

57 Red Rose Radio
999/301 97.4

58 SGR
1170/257 97.1
1251/240 102.4

59 Swansea Sound
1170/257 96.4

60 Two Counties Radio
828/362 102.3

61 West Sound
1035/290 96.7

62 Isle of Wight Radio
1242/242

63 Buzz FM
102.4

64 Lincs FM
102.2

65 Minster FM
To be announced

66 Great Yorkshire Radio
990/303
1161/258
1278/235
1305/230
1530/196
1548/194

Liverpool

35								*Manchester*
56								
155	132							*Newcastle-upon-Tyne*
249	212							
220	185	264						*Norwich*
354	298	425						
98	63	157	122					*Nottingham*
158	101	253	196					
308	307	233	477	369				*Oban*
496	494	375	768	594				
157	144	260	145	98	448			*Oxford*
253	232	418	233	158	721			
283	283	410	343	267	587	185		*Plymouth*
455	455	660	552	430	945	298		
234	221	337	186	175	525	77	164	*Portsmouth*
377	356	542	299	282	845	124	264	
72	38	125	146	37	339	135	283	212	*Sheffield*
116	61	201	235	60	546	217	455	341	
58	69	205	82	364	106	225	185	82	*Shrewsbury*
93	111	323	330	132	586	171	362	298	132	
221	208	324	193	162	512	64	151	21	199	170	*Southampton*
356	335	521	311	261	824	103	243	34	320	274	
221	220	158	390	290	176	362	500	277	425		*Stranraer*
356	354	254	628	467	283	583	805	705	423	446	684	
153	187	319	274	169	461	141	206	182	200	118	161	374	*Swansea*
246	301	513	441	272	742	227	332	293	322	190	259	602	
99	64	84	181	77	309	181	333	258	52	133	245	222	251	*York*
159	103	135	291	124	497	291	536	415	84	214	394	357	404	

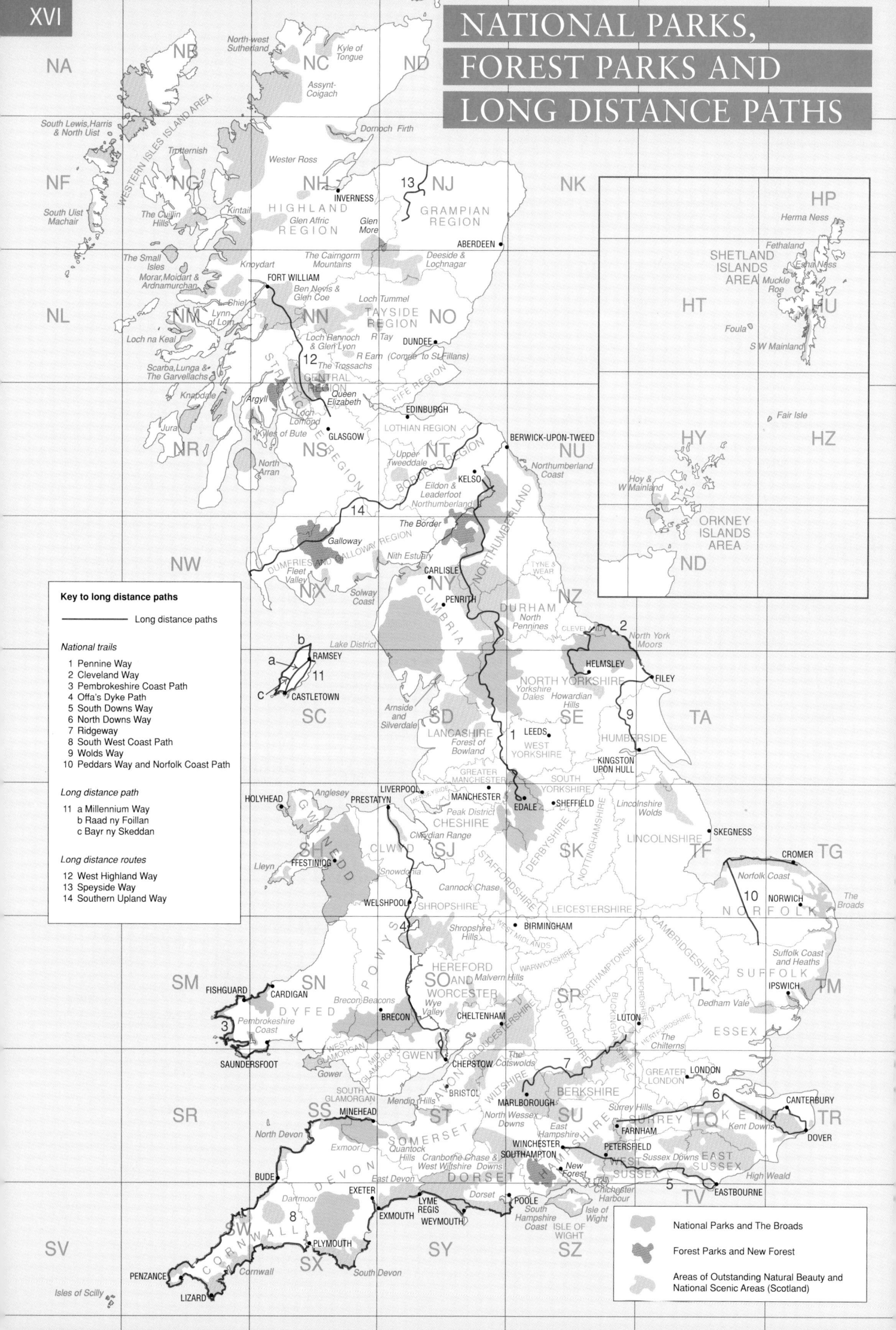

LEGEND TO 4-MILE MAPPING

Strassen

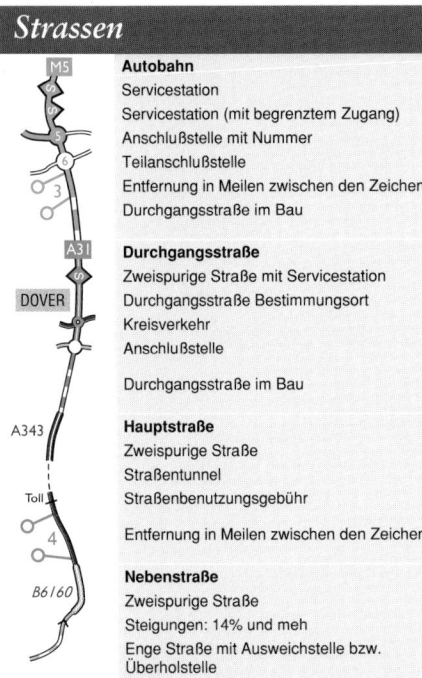

Autobahn
Servicestation
Servicestation (mit begrenztem Zugang)
Anschlußstelle mit Nummer
Teilanschlußstelle
Entfernung in Meilen zwischen den Zeichen
Durchgangsstraße im Bau

Durchgangsstraße
Zweispurige Straße mit Servicestation
Durchgangsstraße Bestimmungsort
Kreisverkehr
Anschlußstelle

Durchgangsstraße im Bau

Hauptstraße
Zweispurige Straße
Straßentunnel
Straßenbenutzungsgebühr

Entfernung in Meilen zwischen den Zeichen

Nebenstraße
Zweispurige Straße
Steigungen: 14% und meh
Enge Straße mit Ausweichstelle bzw.
Überholstelle

Sonstige Straßen

Routes

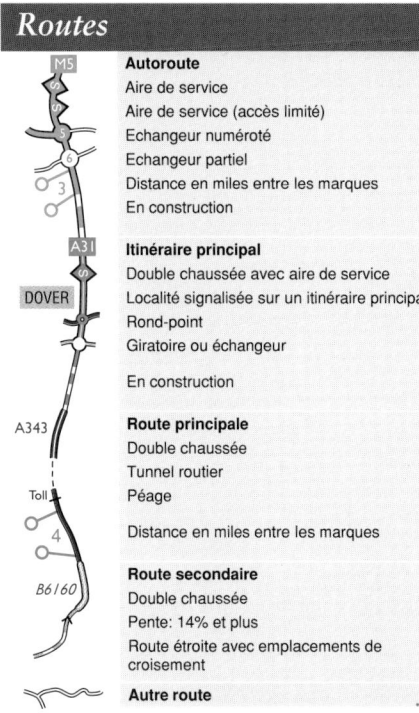

Autoroute
Aire de service
Aire de service (accès limité)
Echangeur numéroté
Echangeur partiel
Distance en miles entre les marques
En construction

Itinéraire principal
Double chaussée avec aire de service
Localité signalisée sur un itinéraire principal
Rond-point
Giratoire ou échangeur

En construction

Route principale
Double chaussée
Tunnel routier
Péage

Distance en miles entre les marques

Route secondaire
Double chaussée
Pente: 14% et plus
Route étroite avec emplacements de croisement

Autre route

Roads

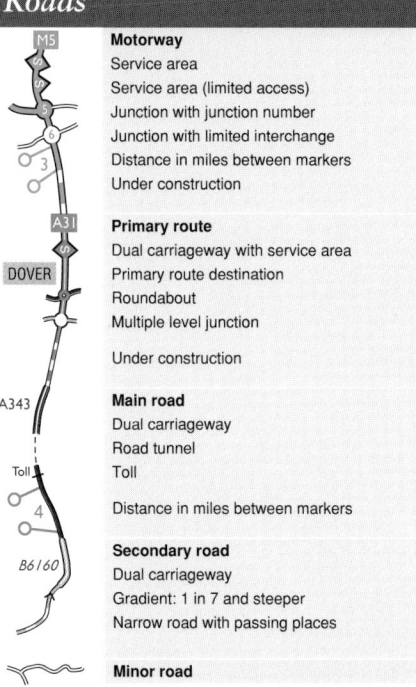

Motorway
Service area
Service area (limited access)
Junction with junction number
Junction with limited interchange
Distance in miles between markers
Under construction

Primary route
Dual carriageway with service area
Primary route destination
Roundabout
Multiple level junction

Under construction

Main road
Dual carriageway
Road tunnel
Toll

Distance in miles between markers

Secondary road
Dual carriageway
Gradient: 1 in 7 and steeper
Narrow road with passing places

Minor road

Tourist Information   Antiquités Sehenswürdigkeit

✝ **Abbey, Cathedral, Priory**
Abbaye, Cathédrale, Prieuré
Abtei, Kathedrale, Priorei

Aquarium
Aquarium
Aquarium

Camp site
Terrain de camping
Campingplatz

Caravan site
Terrain pour caravanes
Wohnwagenplatz

Castle
Château
Schloss

Cave
Caverne
Höhle

Country park
Parc naturel
Landschaftspark

Craft centre
Centre artisanal
Zentrum für Kunsthandwerk

Garden
Jardin
Garten

Golf course or links
Terrain de golf
Golfplatz

Historic house
Manoir, Palais
Historisches Gebäude

Information centre
Bureau de renseignements
Informationsbüro

Motor racing
Courses automobiles
Autorennen

Museum
Musée
Museum

Nature reserve
Sentier de grande randonnée
Naturschutzgebiet

Other tourist features
Autre site intéressant
Sonstige Sehenswürdigkeit

Picnic site
Pique-nique
Picknickplatz

Preserved railway
Chemin de fer touristique
Museumseisenbahn

Racecourse
Hippodrome
Pferderennbahn

Skiing
Piste de ski
Skilaufen

Viewpoint
Belvédère
Aussichtspunkt

Wildlife park
Parc animalier
Wildpark

Zoo
Zoo
Tiergarten

Wolds Way **National trail Long Distance Route**
Sentier de grande randonnee
Fernwanderweg

General Features   Signes Divers   Allgemeine Angaben

⊕ + **Airfield with / without customs facilities**
Aérodrome avec / sans poste de douane
Flugplatz mit / ohne Zolabfergunsstelle

Buildings
Bâtiments
Gebäude

Ⓗ **Heliport**
Héliport
HubschrauberLandeplatz

Lighthouse in use / disused
Phare en usage / désaffecté
Leuchtturm in Gebrauch / außerGebrauch

𝒞 **Motoring organisation telephone**
Téléphone d'associations automobiles
(Automobilen Organisation) Fernsprecher

𝒞 **Public telephone**
Téléphone public
Fernsprechzelle

Radio or TV mast
Pylône de radio / TV
Antennenmast Radio und Fernsehen

Windmill
Moulin à vent
Windmühle

Wood
Bois
Wald

▲ **Youth hostel**
Auberge de jeunesse
Jugendherberge

Antiquities   Antiquités   Historisch Sehenswürdigkeiten

ᚾ **Ancient monument open to the public**
Monument ancien ouvert au public
Altertümliches Denkmal offen für
Öffentlichkeit

Native fortress
Forteresse pré-romaine
Landesfestung

Castle **Other antiquities**
Autres antiquités
Schloß / andere historische
Sehenswürdigkeiten

ROMAN CAMP ▪ **Roman antiquity**
Antiquité romaine
Altertum römisch

Roman road (course of)
Route romaine (course de)
Römische Strasse (Weg)

1066 **Site of battle (with date)**
Champ de bataille historique (avec date)
Kampfplatz (mit Datum)

Boundaries   Limites Grenzen

National
National
National

County, Region or Island Area
Comté, Région ou île
Grafschaft, Region
oder Inselzone

Railways   Chemins de Fer   Bahnlinien

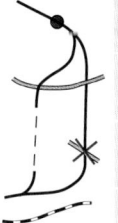

Standard gauge track and station
Voie normale et gare
Normalspurweite Trasse und Bahnhof

Road under, road over
Passage de la route: inférieur / supérieur
Unterführung, Überführung

Tunnel, level crossing
Tunnel, passage à niveau
Tunnel, Bahnübergänge

Narrow gauge track
Voie à écartement étroit
Schmalspur Trasse

Water features   Hydrographie Wassermerkmal

Ferry routes for vehicles (Boat/Hovercraft)
liaisons maritimes (par bateau / par aéroglisseur)
Fähre für Fahrzeuge (Schiff/Luftkissenfahrzeug)

Canal
canal
Kanal

Bridge
pont
Brücke

Lake
lac
See

Foreshore
plage
Vorland

Light-vessel
bateau-feu
Feuerschiff

Ferry route for vehicles
bac pour véhicules
Kurzer Fährweg für Fahrzeuge

Sand
sable
Sand

Relief   Topographie

2000 610	**Heights in feet above mean sea level**
1400 427	Altitude en
1000 305	pieds Erhebung über mittlerem
600 183	Meeresspiegel
0 feet 0 metres	pieds fuß /mètres /meter

Scale

1:250 000 or about 4 miles to 1 inch

| 0 Kilometres | 5 | 10 | 15 |
| 0 Miles | 5 | | 10 |

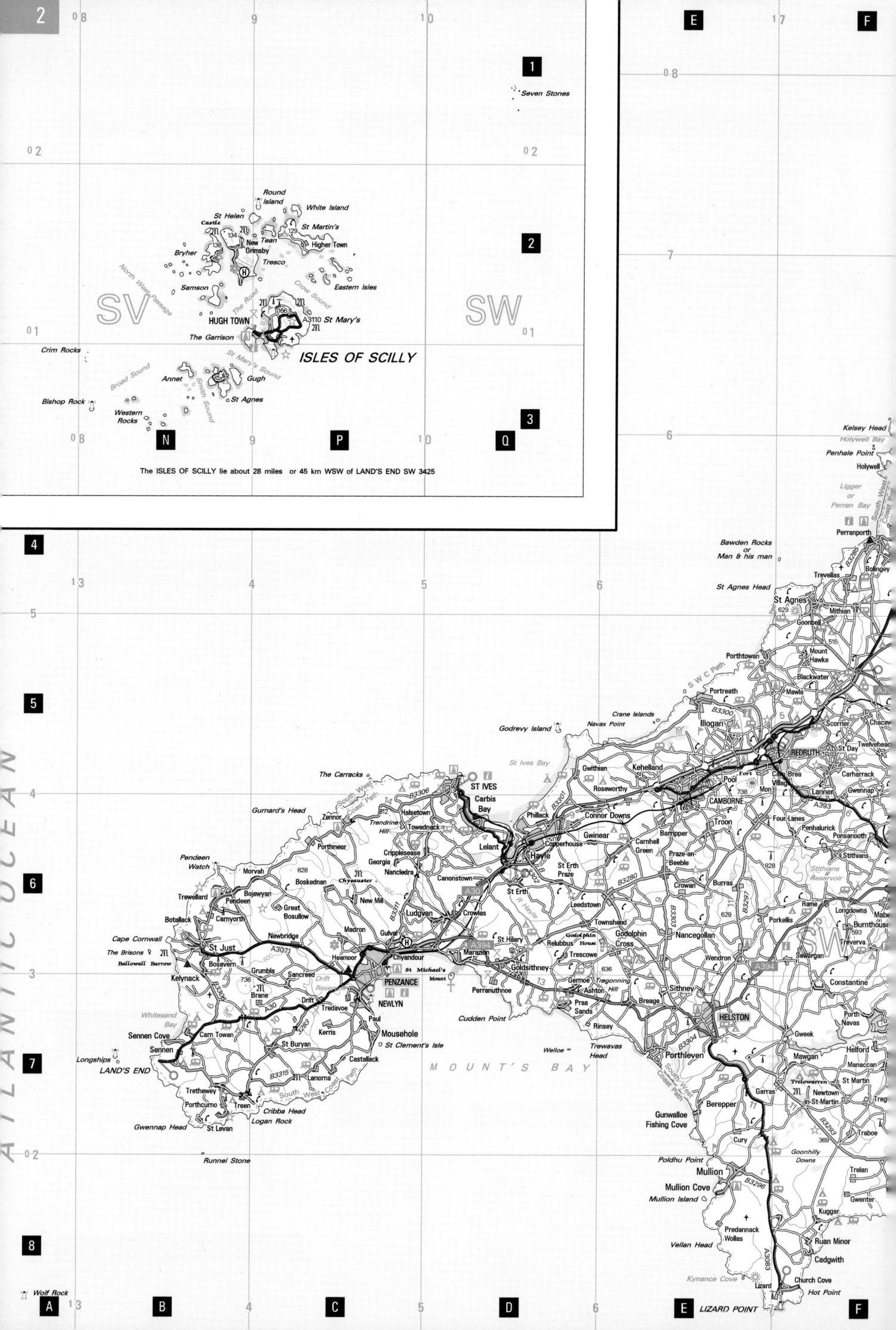

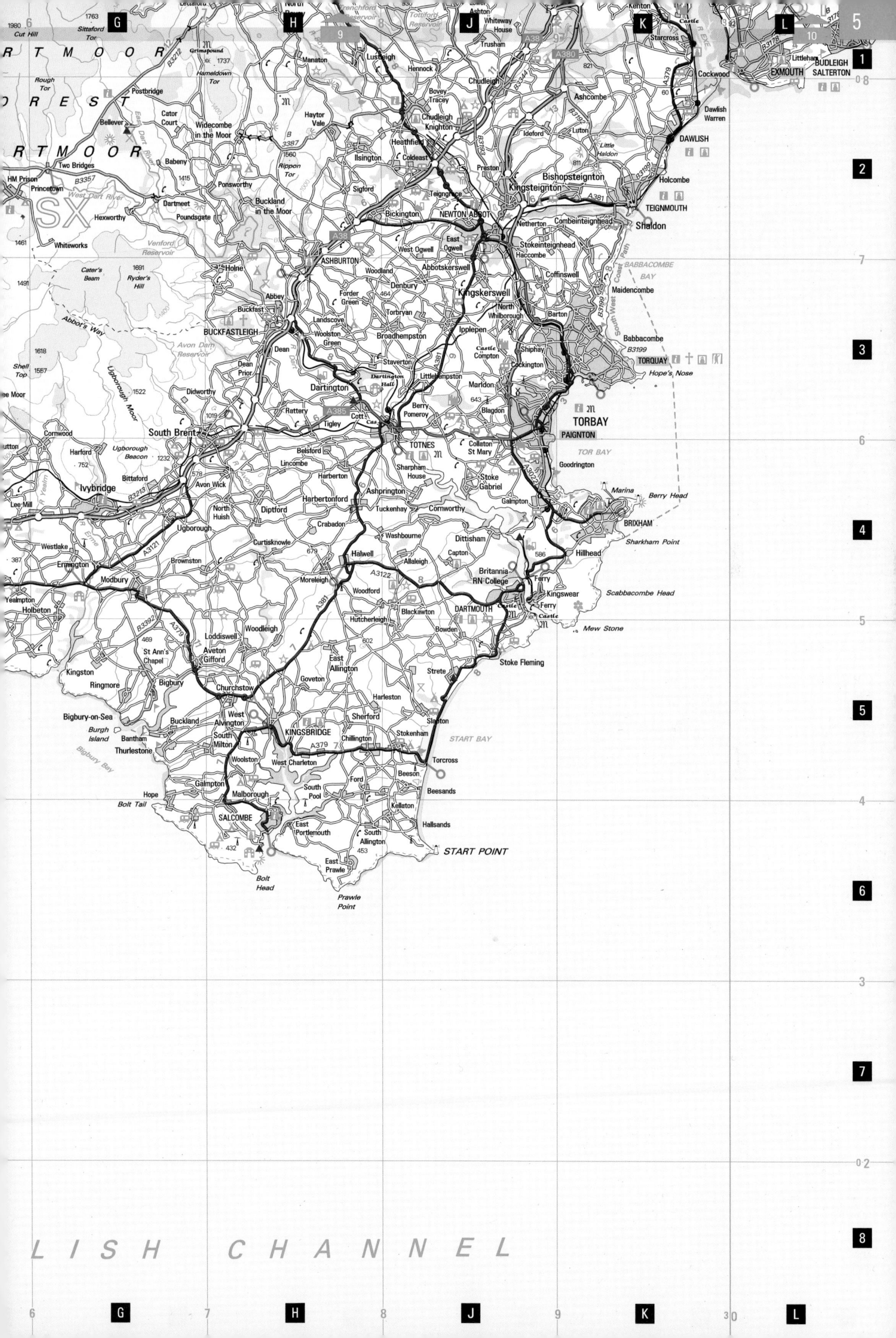

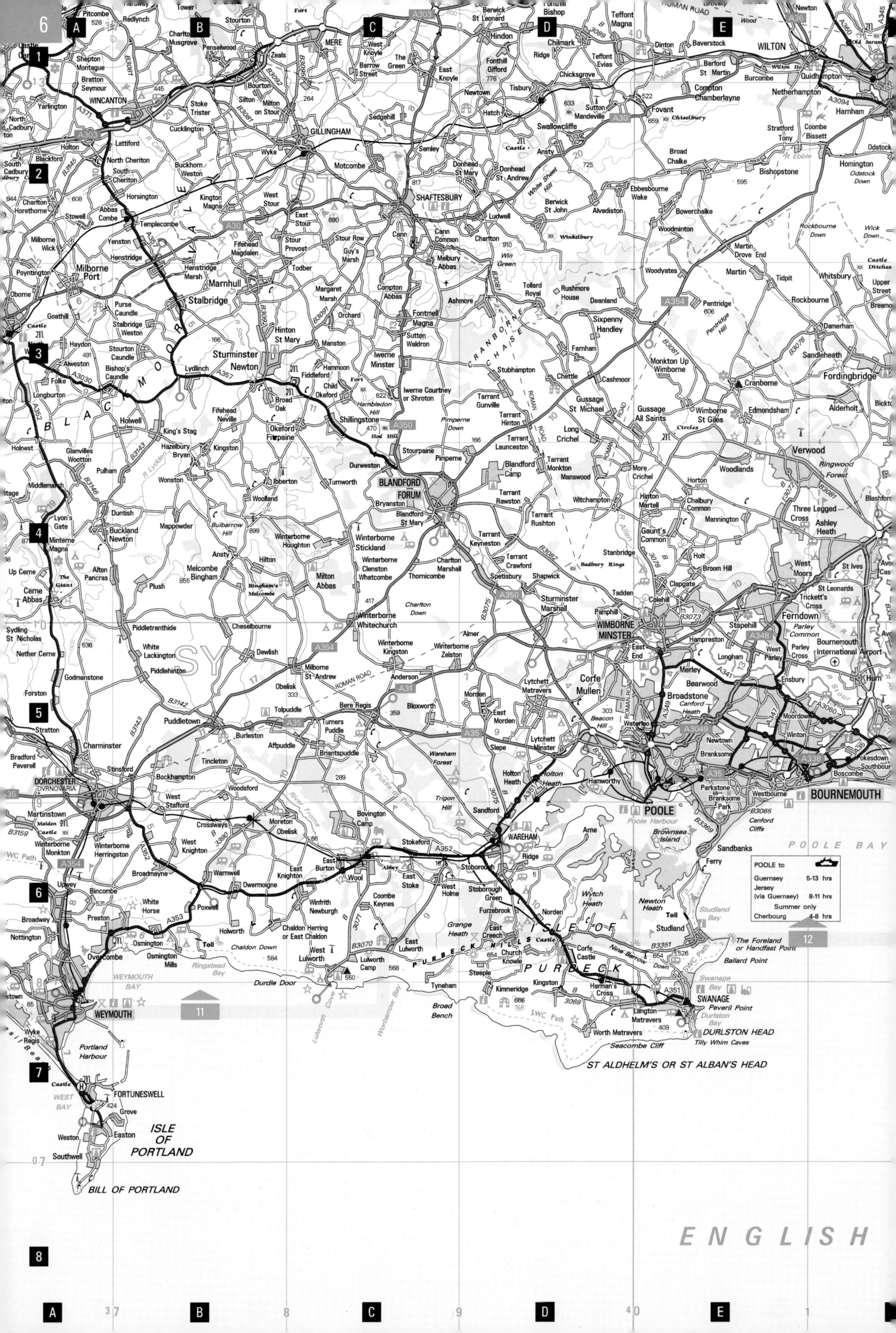

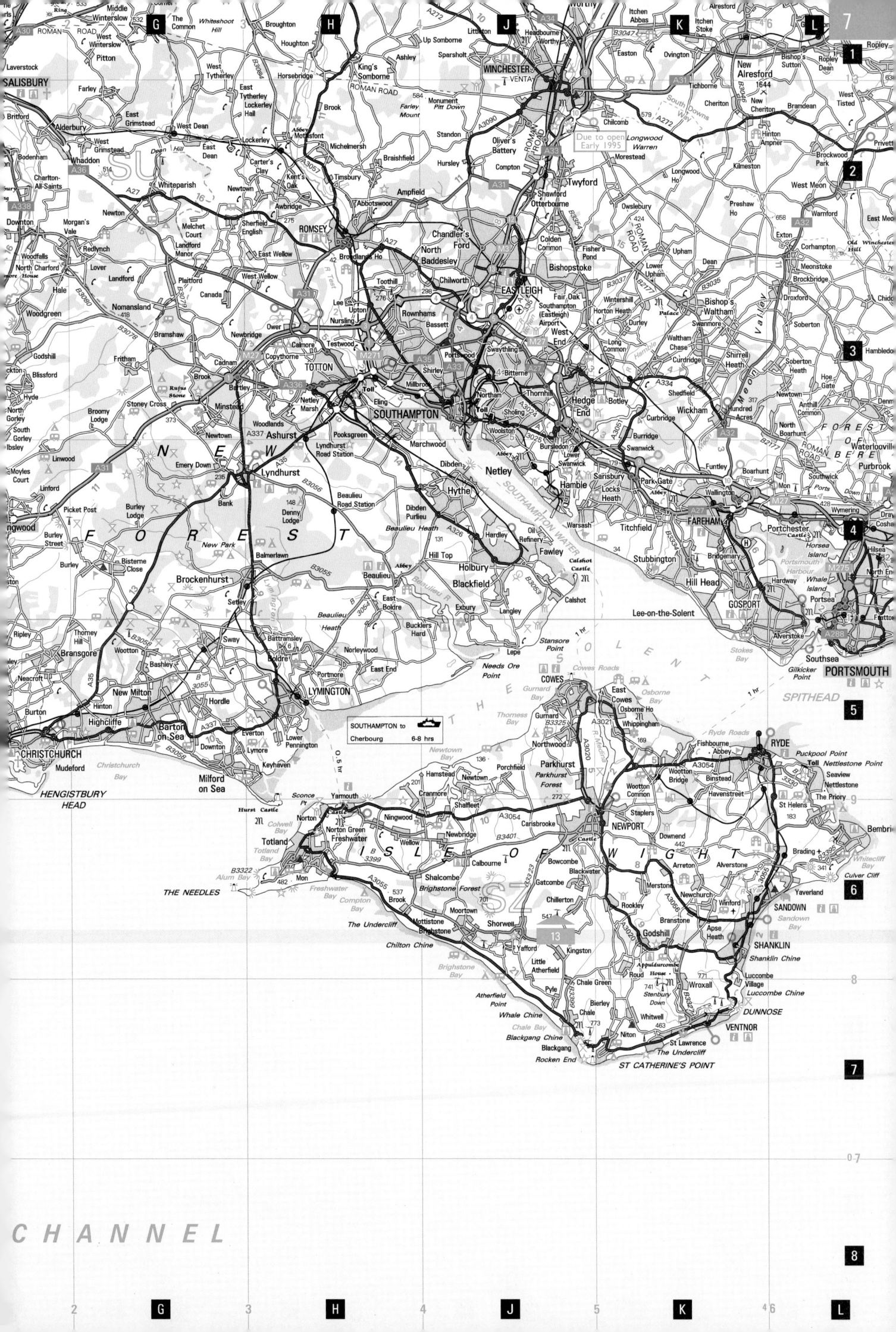

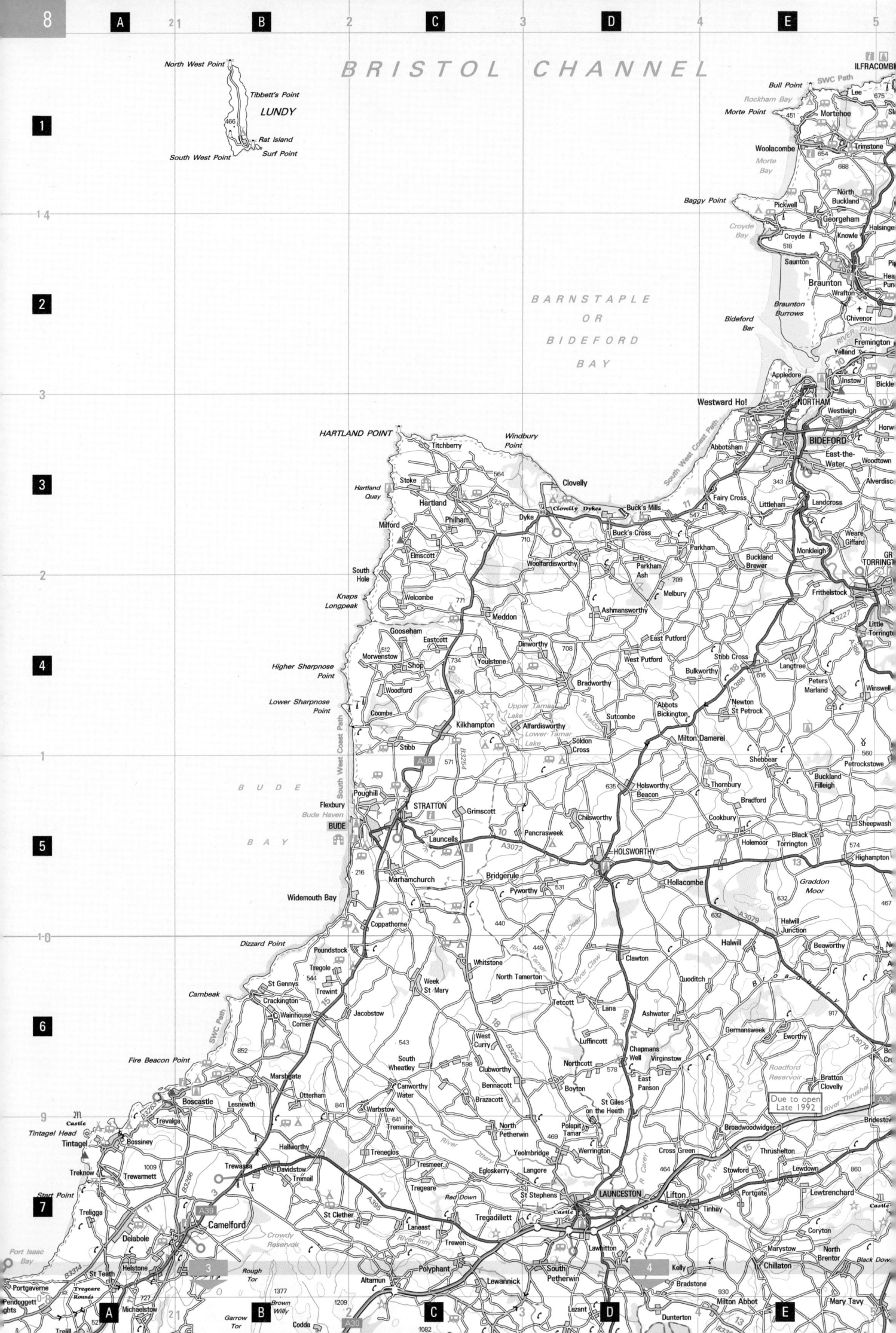

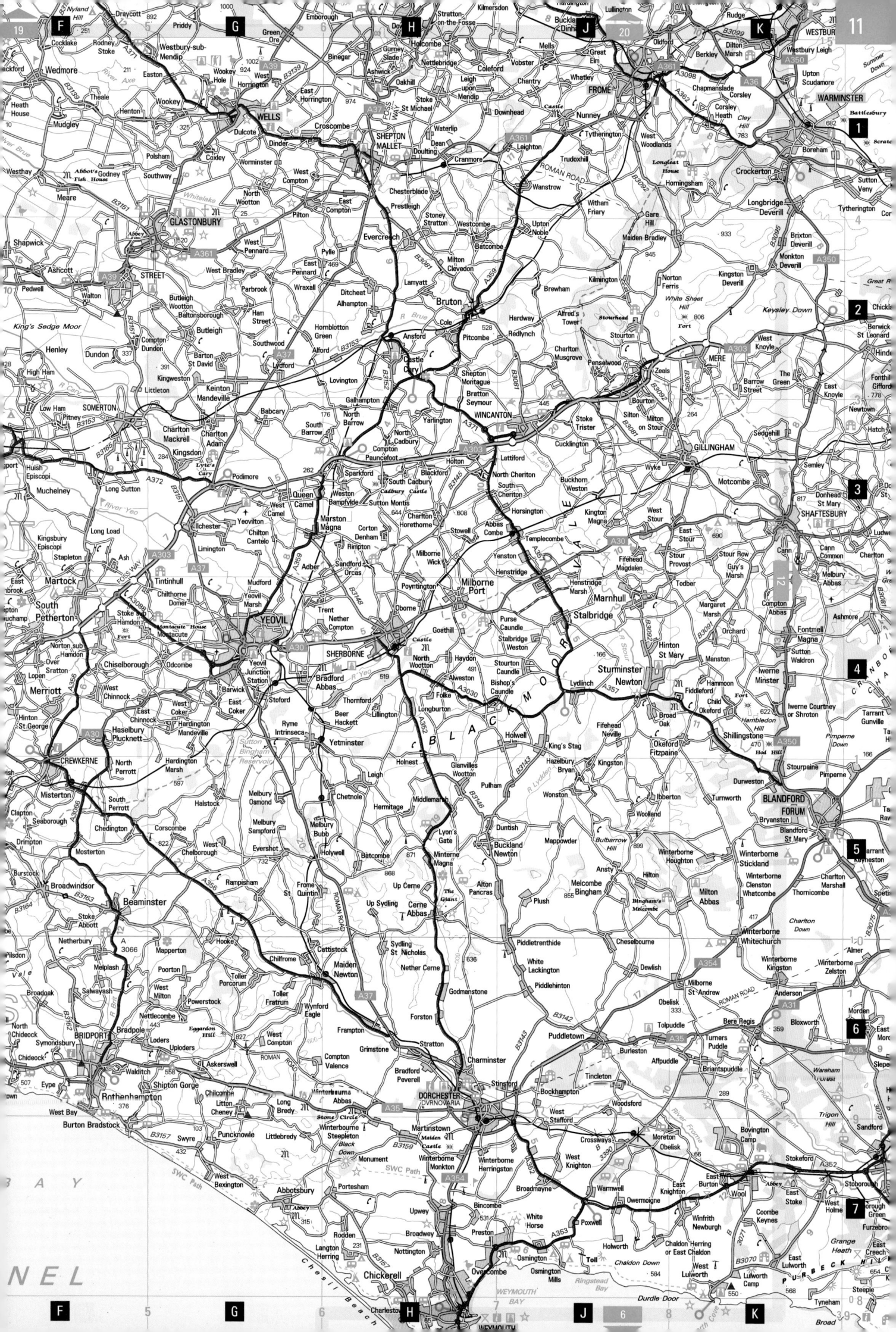

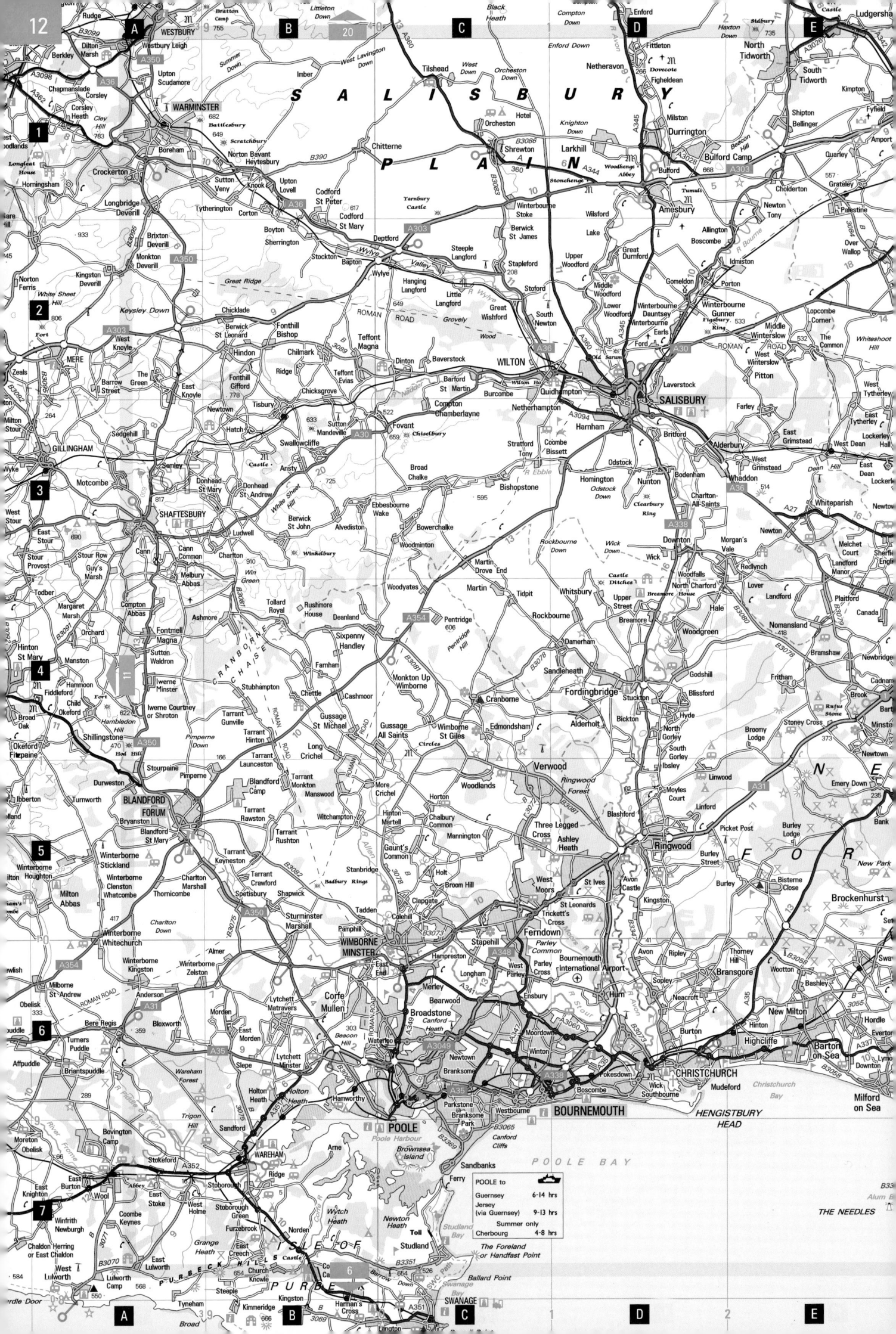

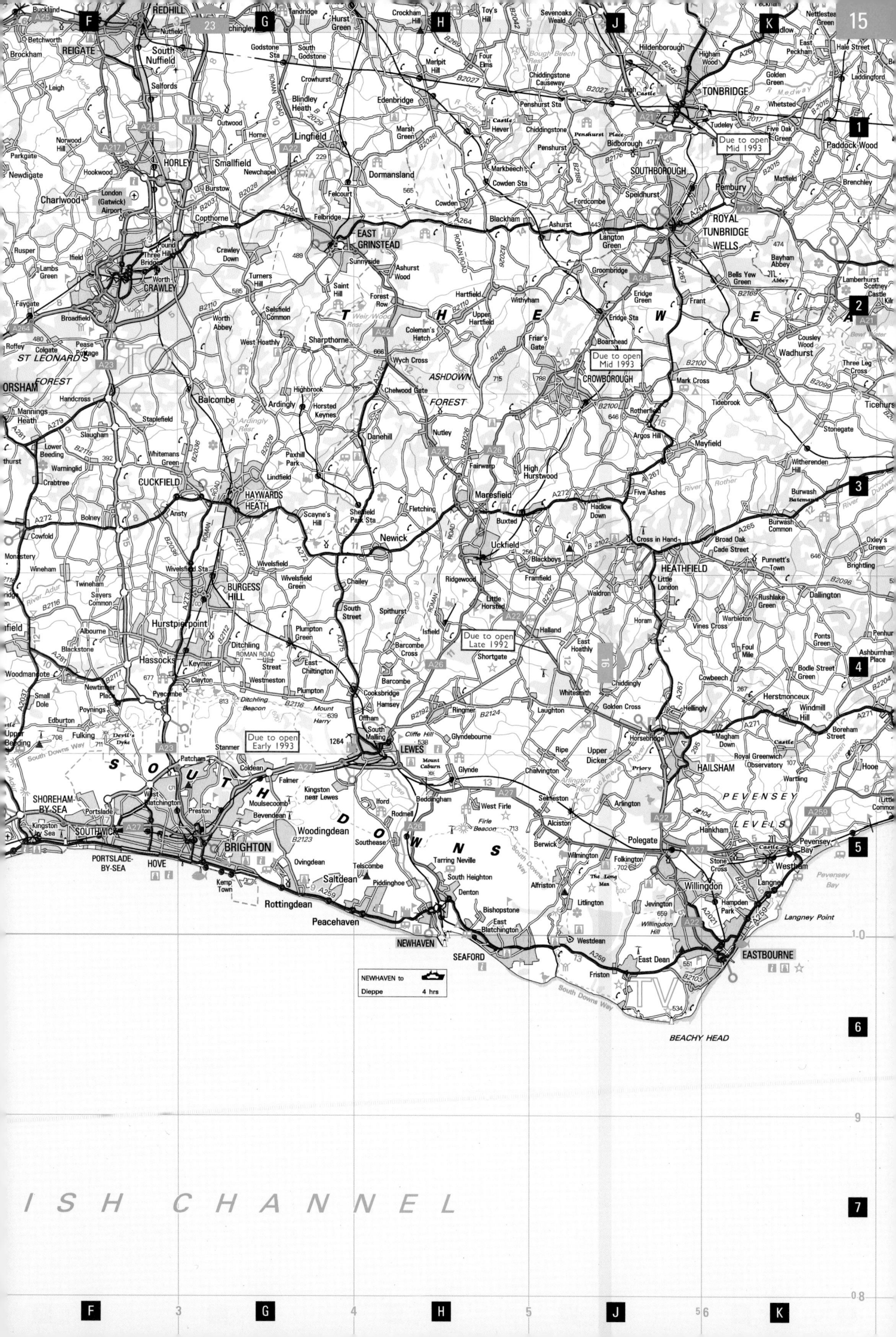

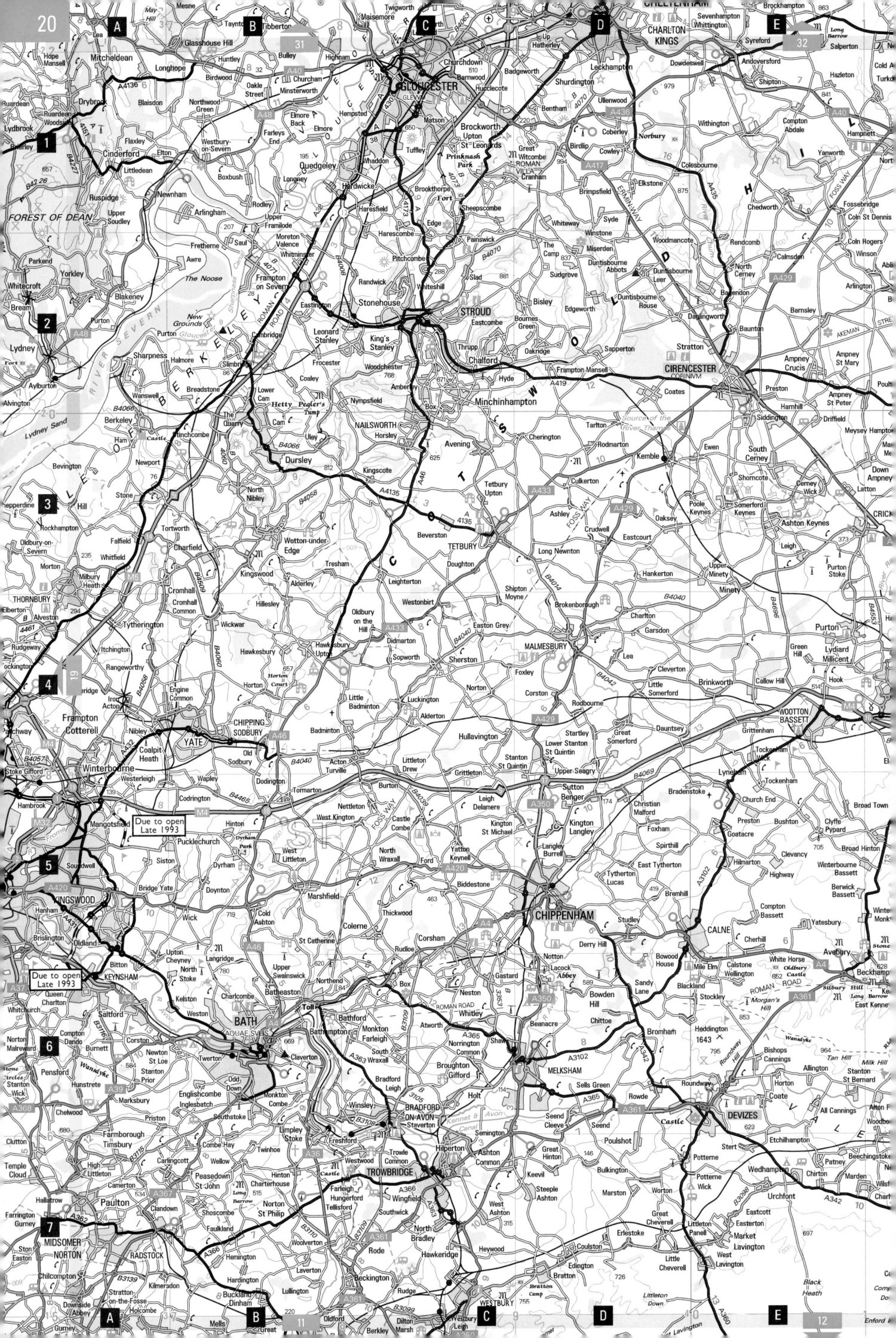

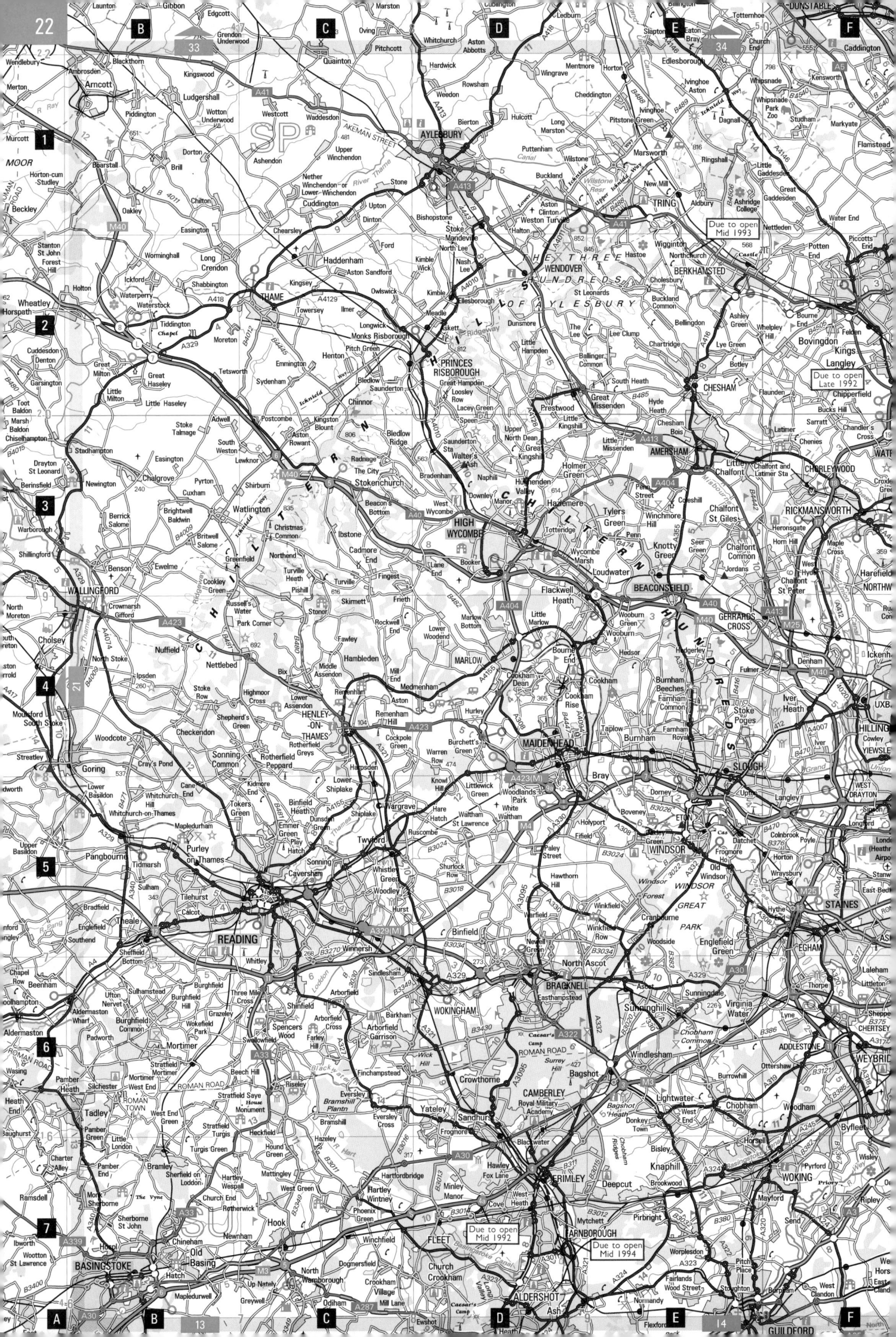

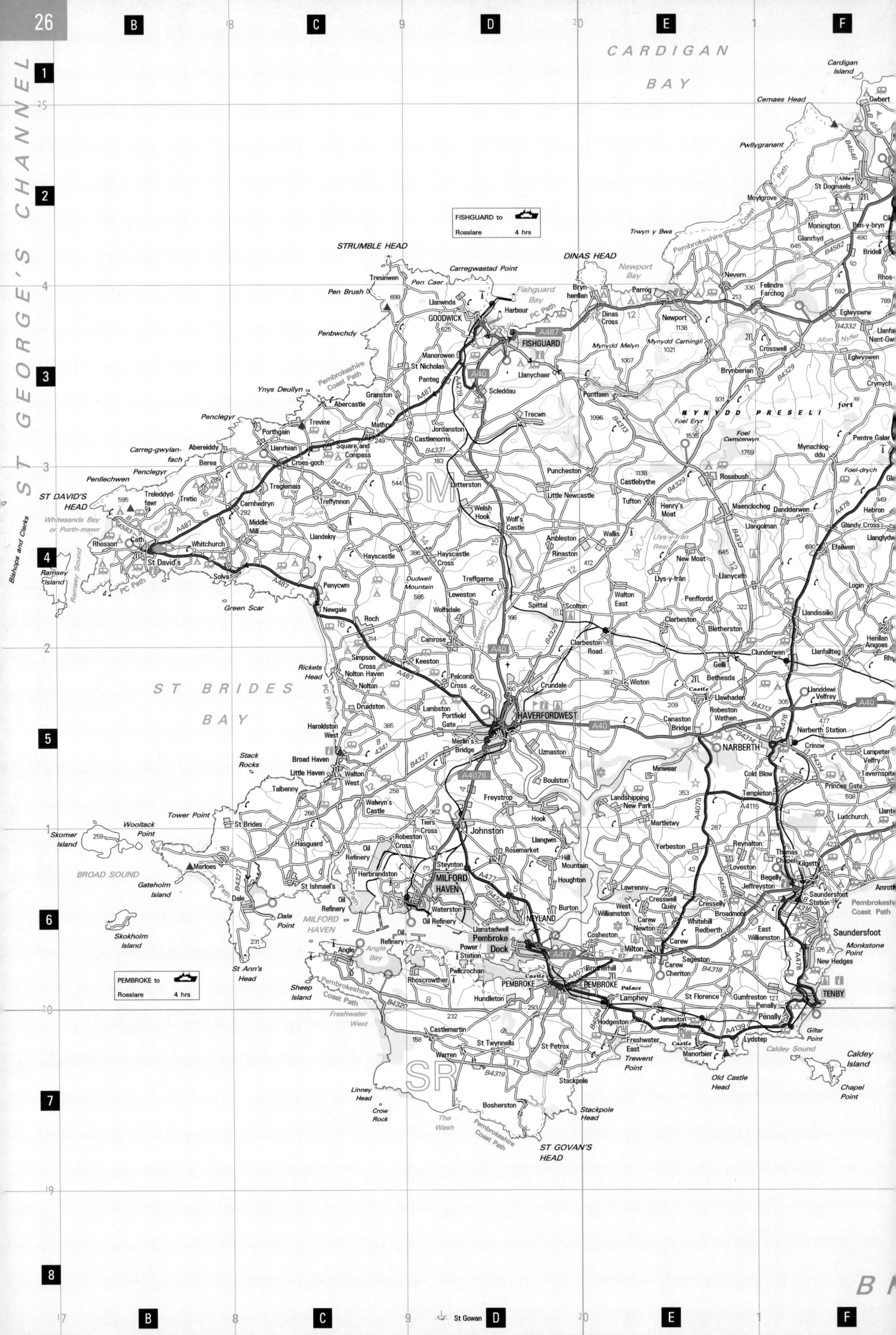

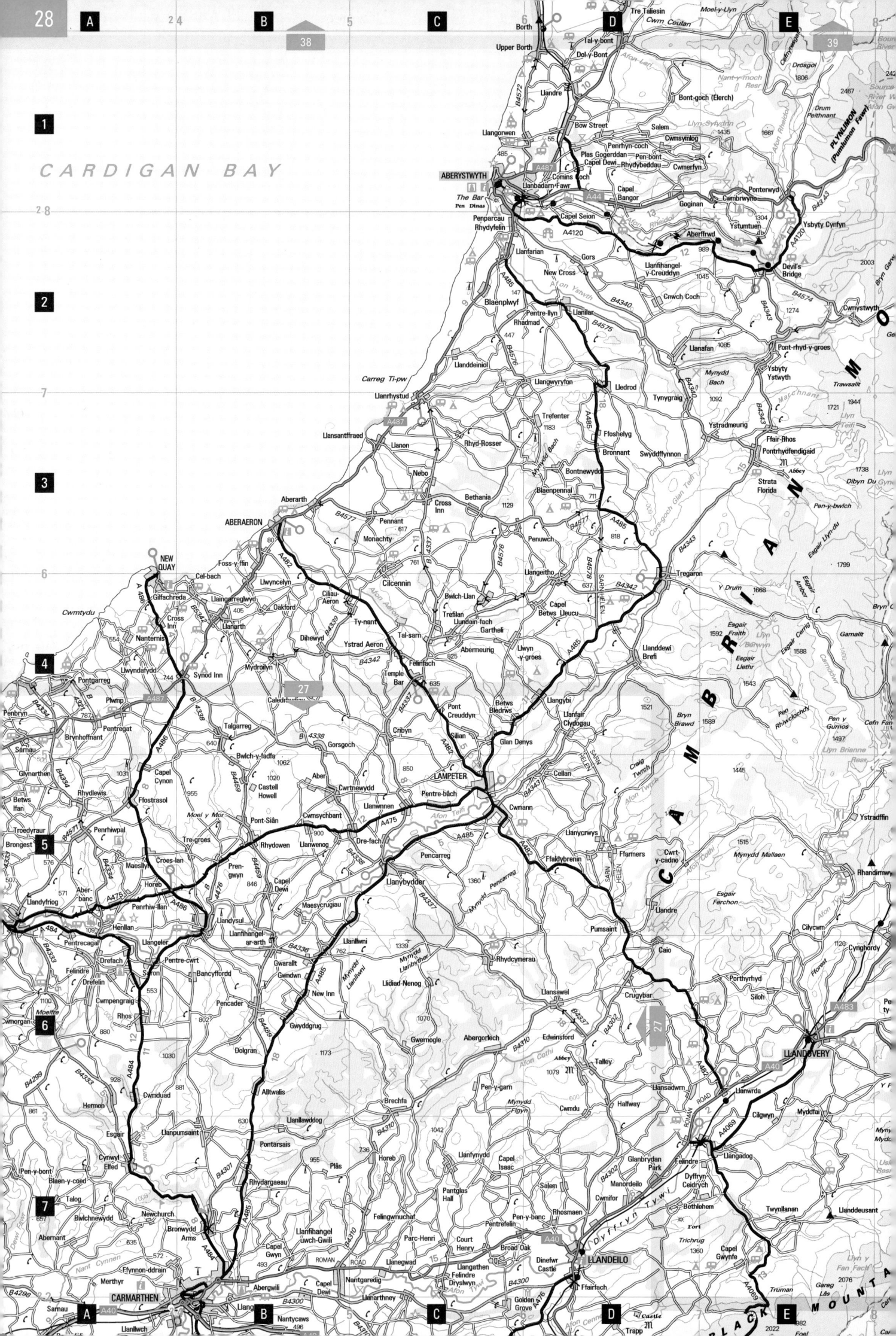

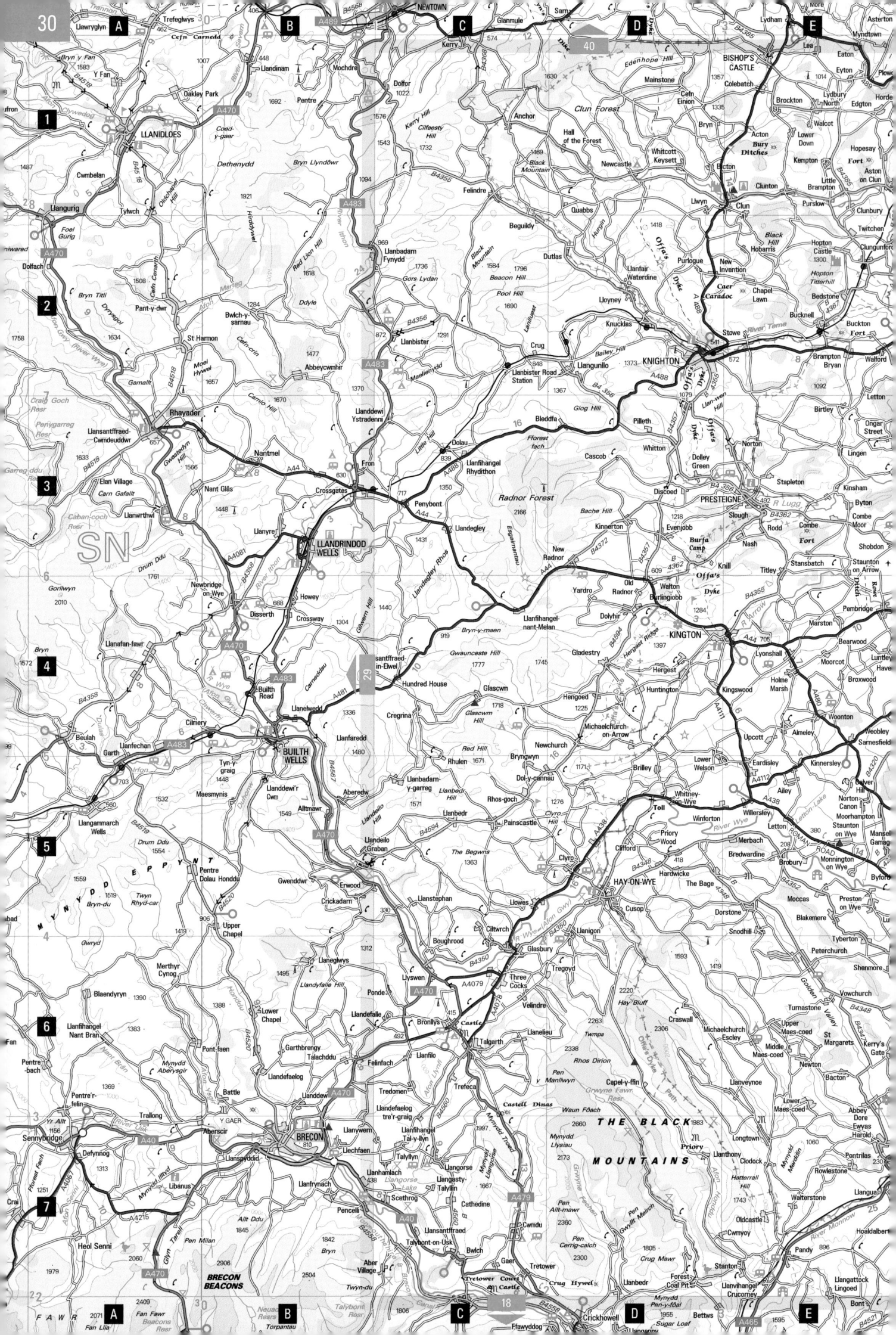

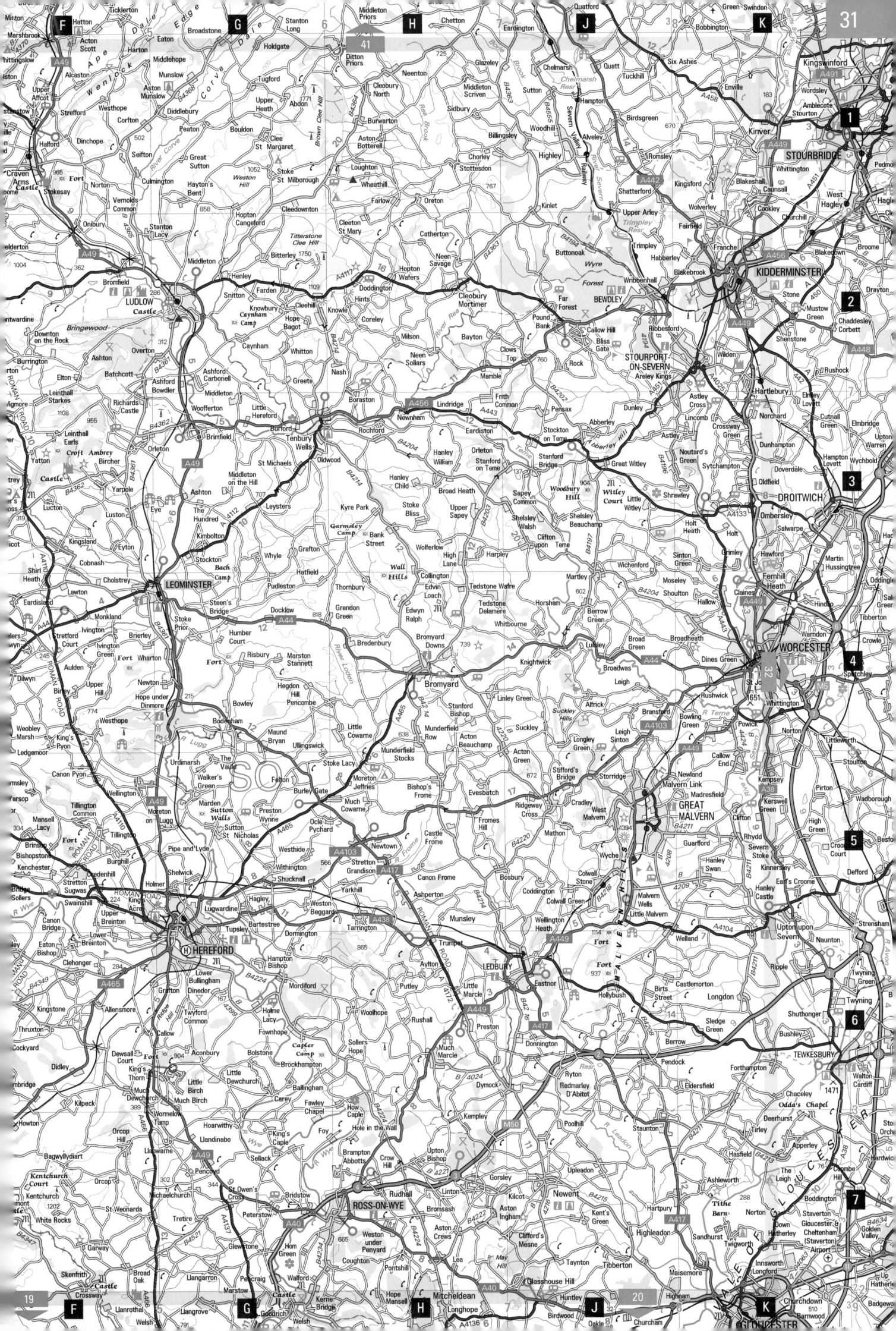

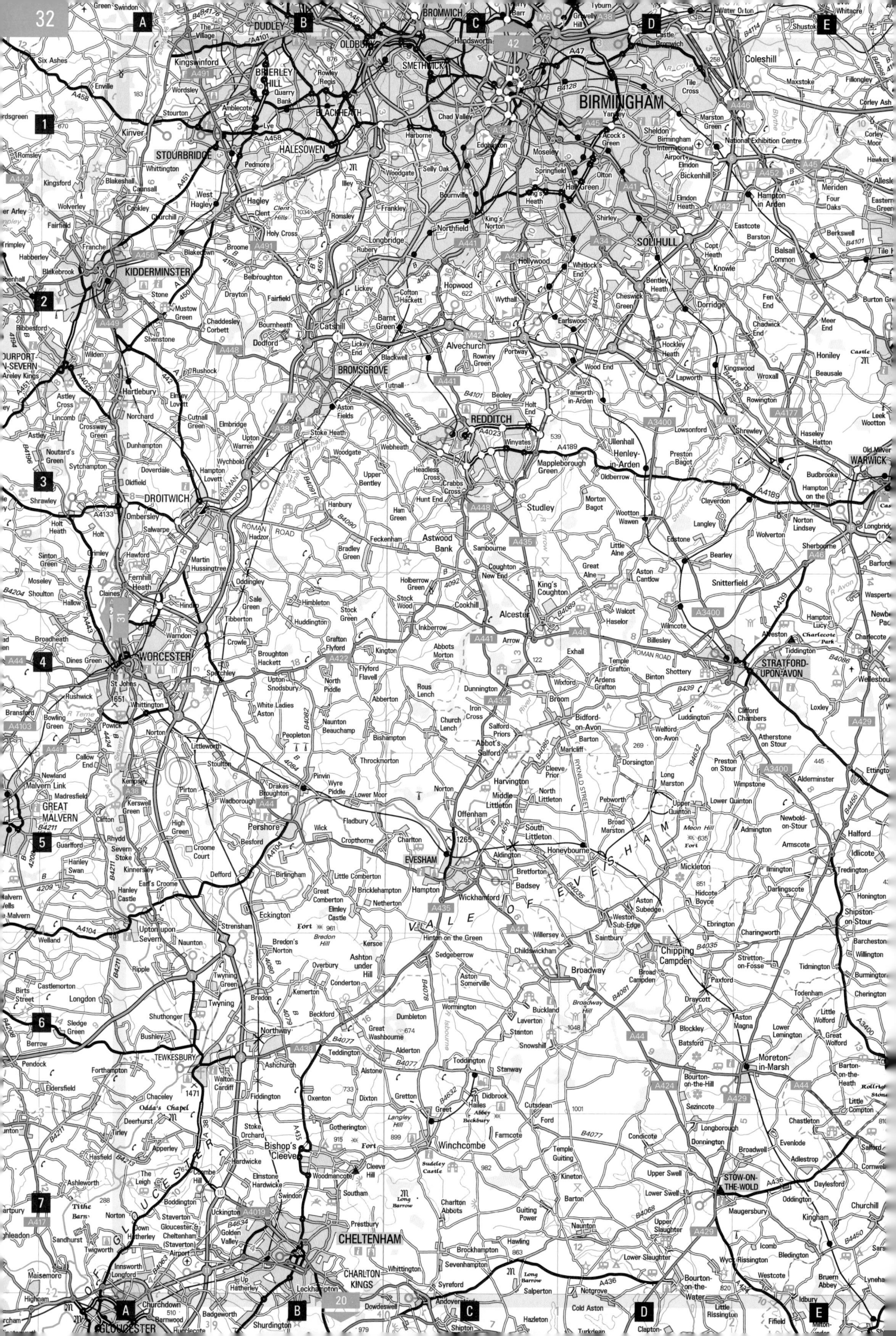

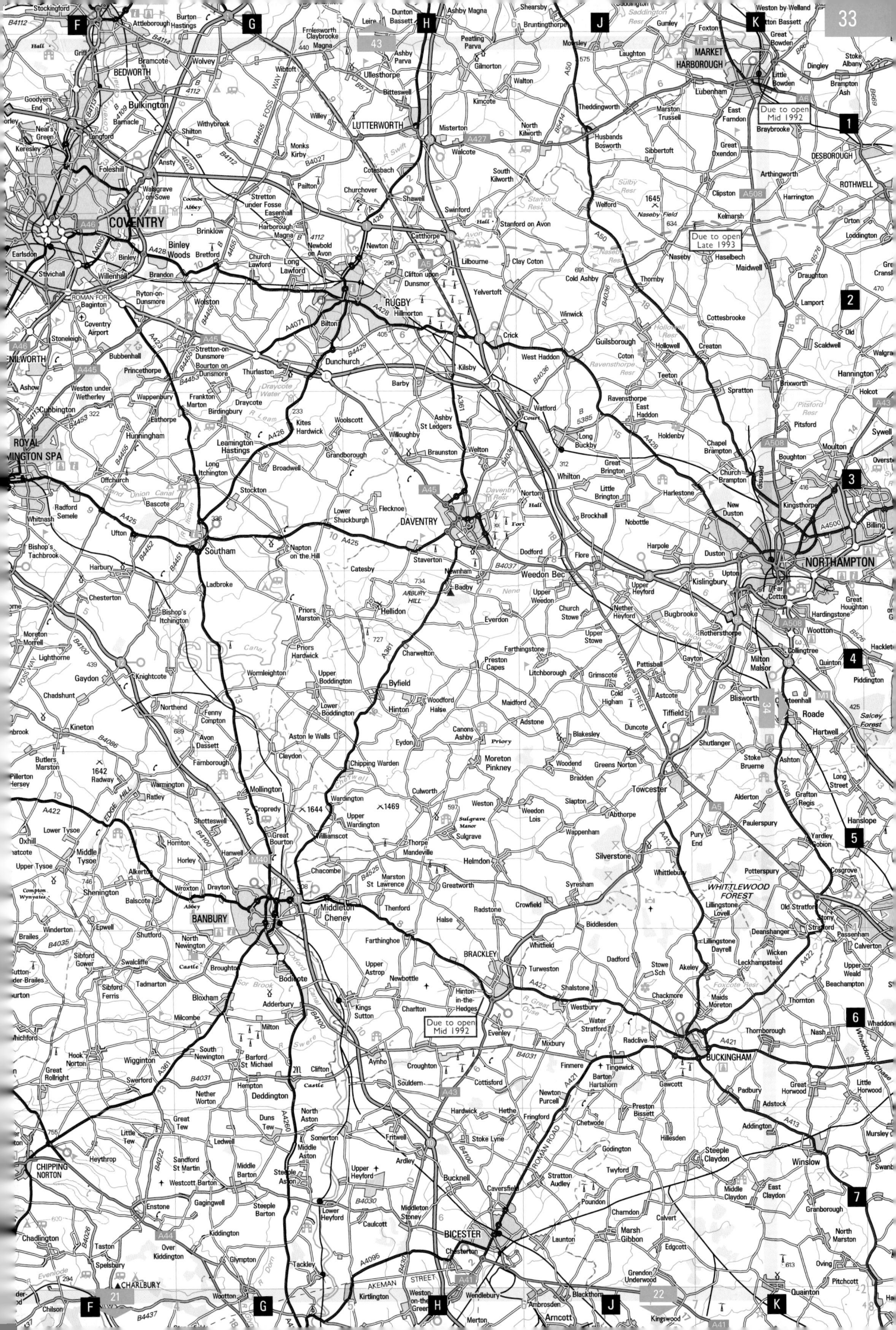

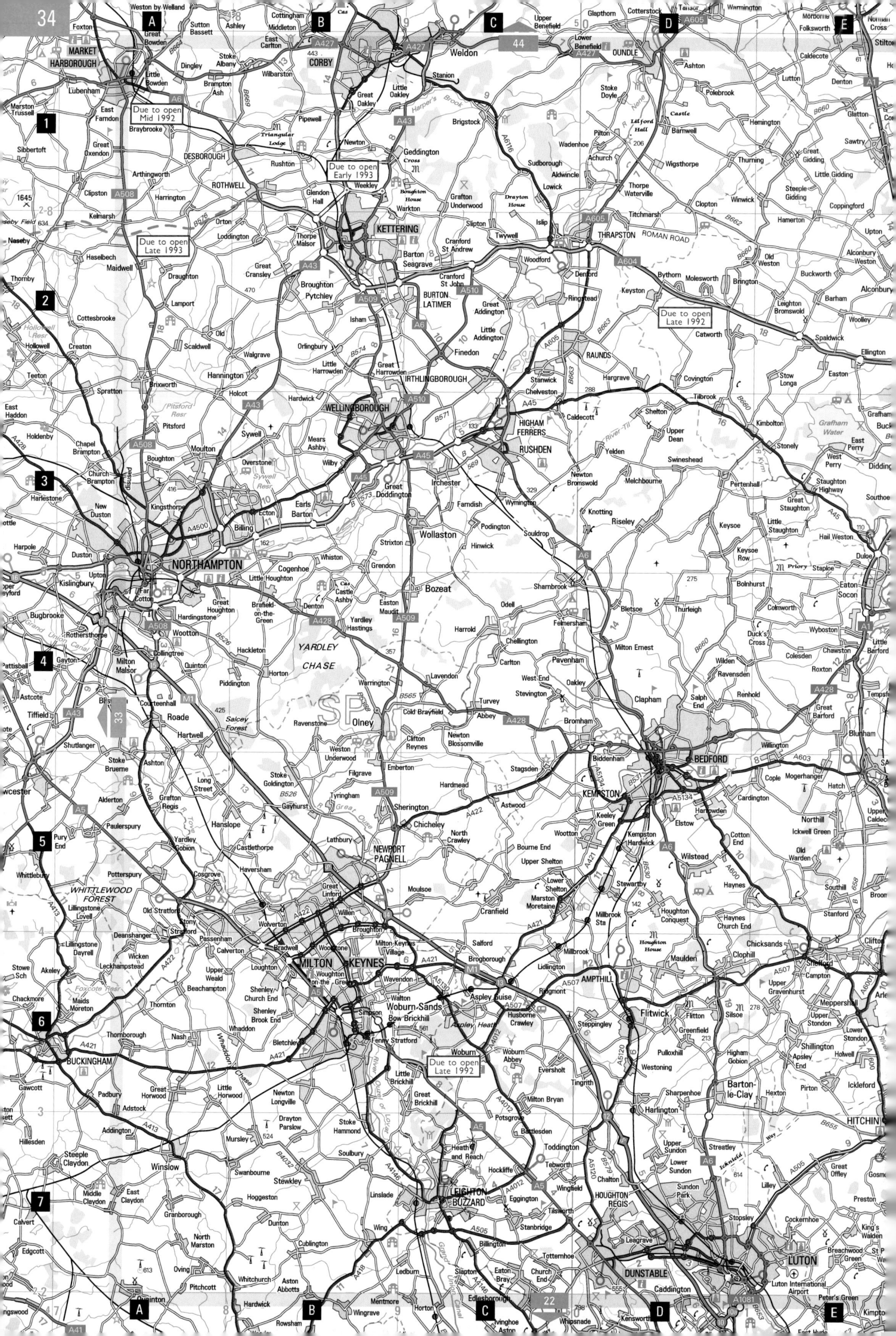

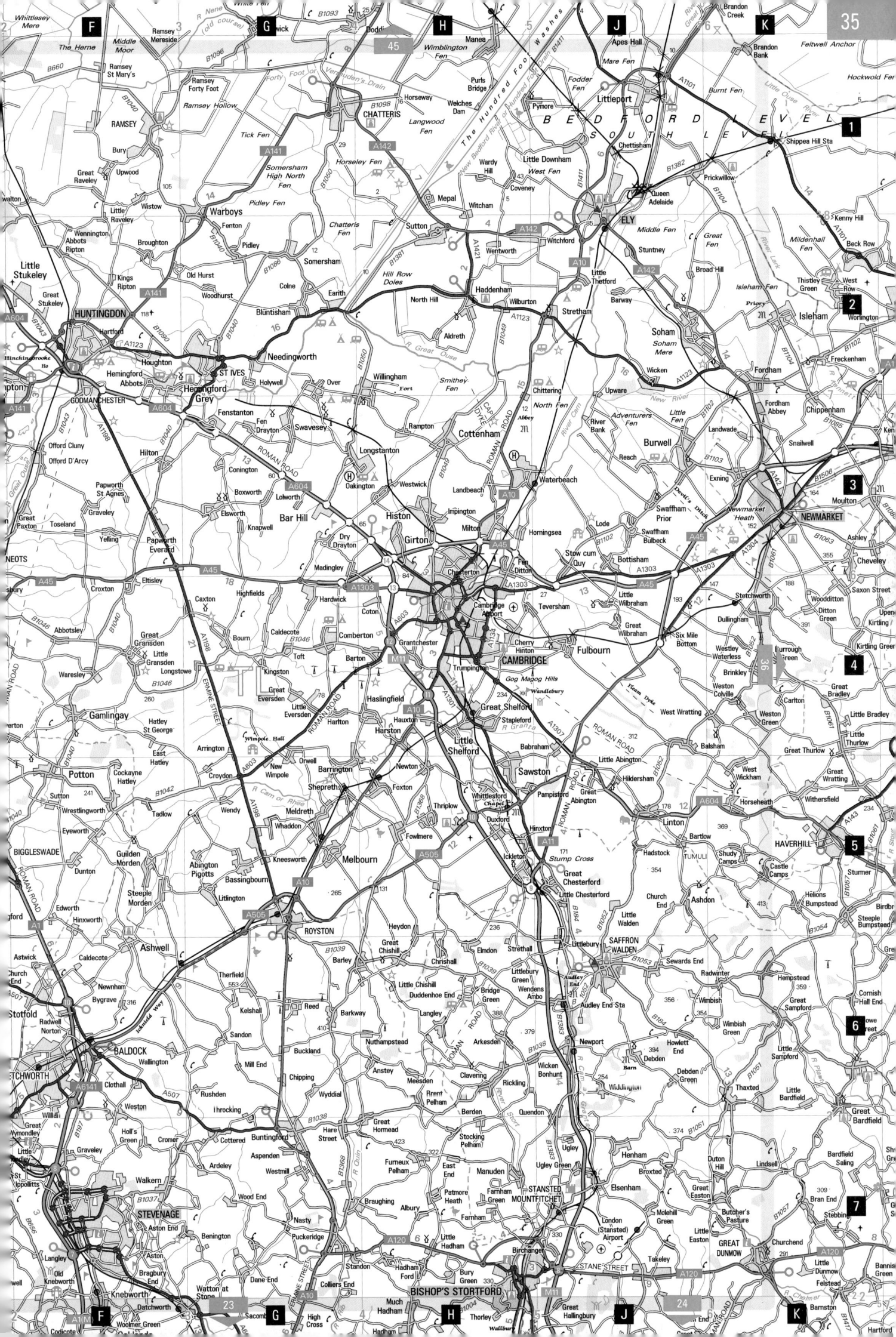

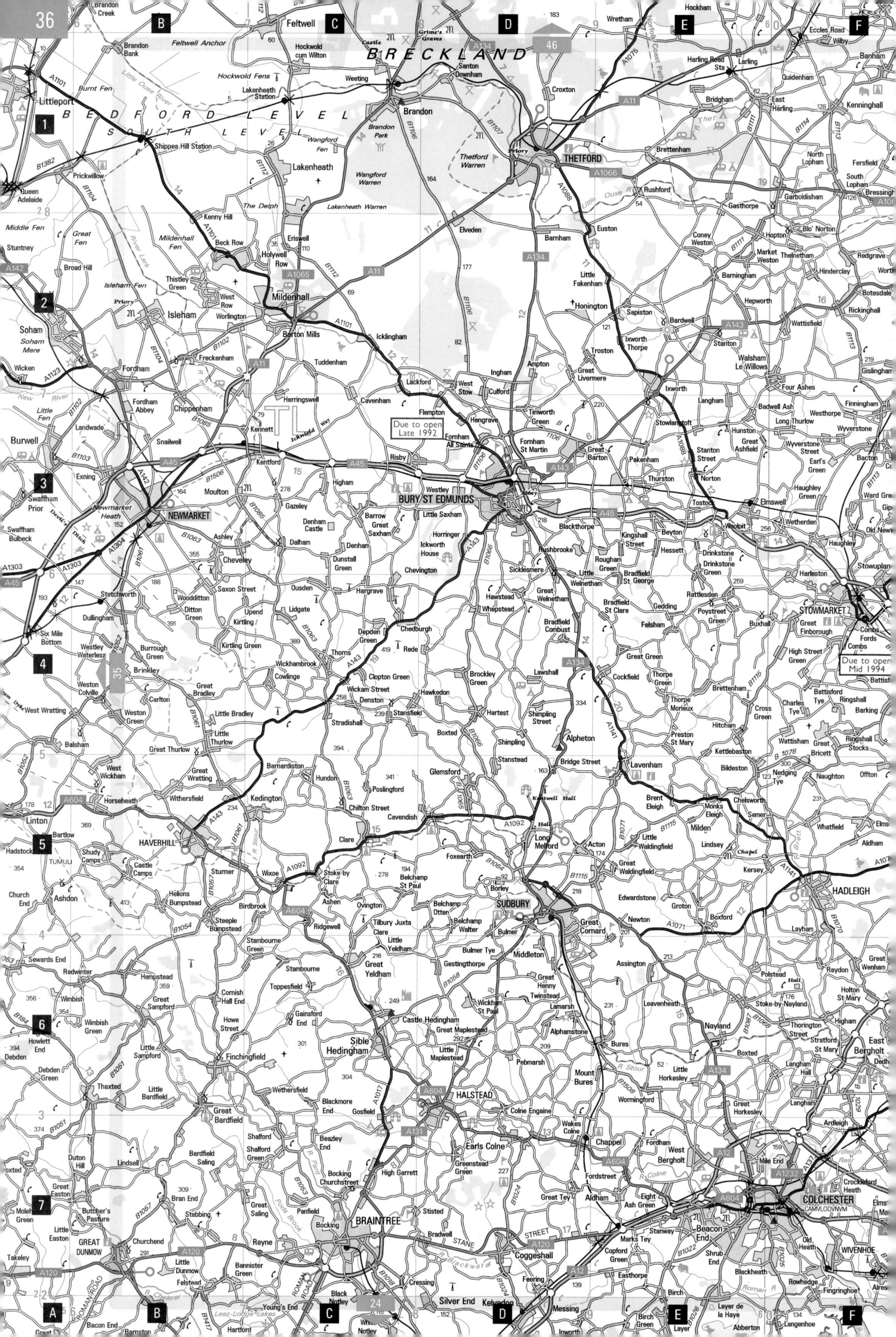

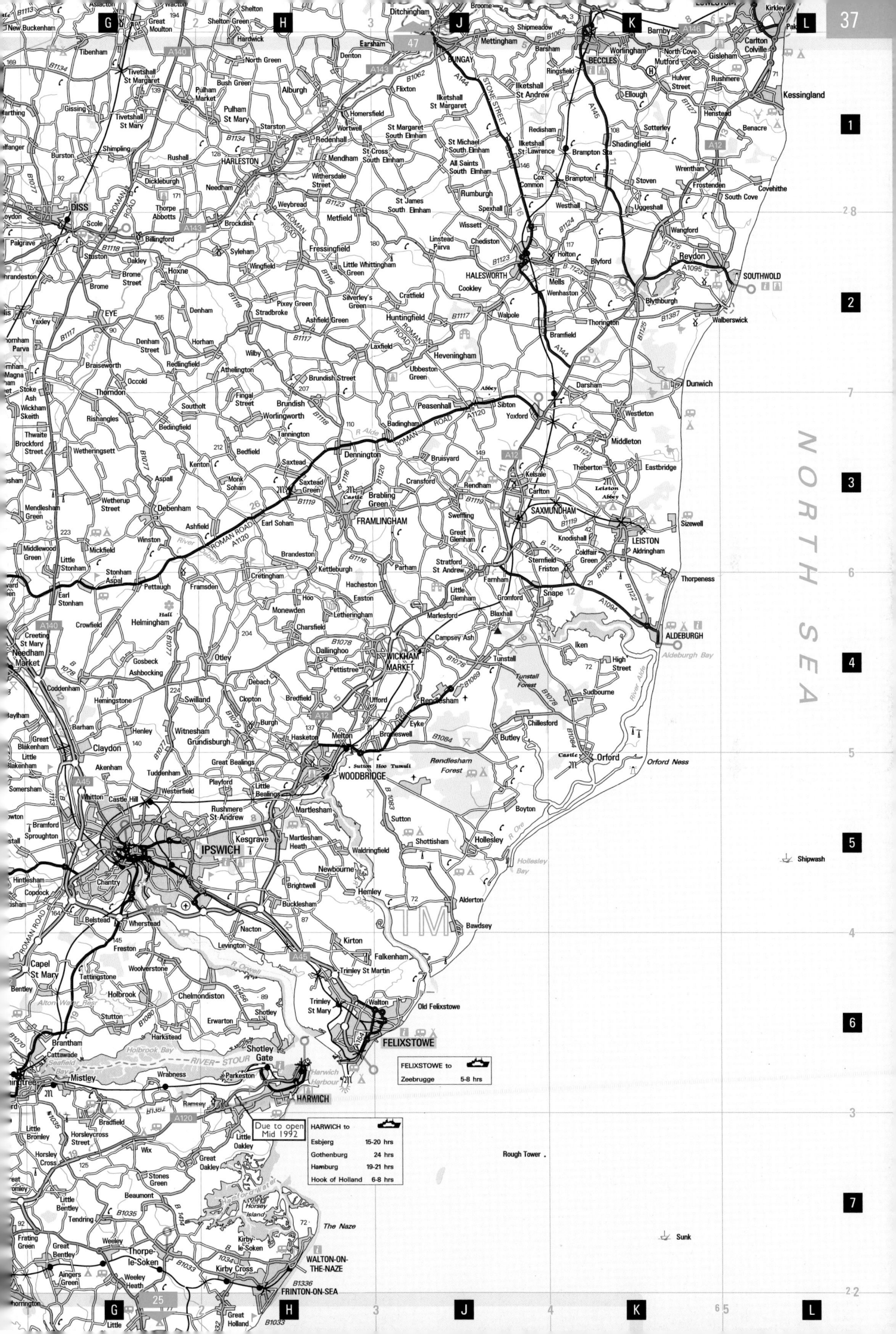

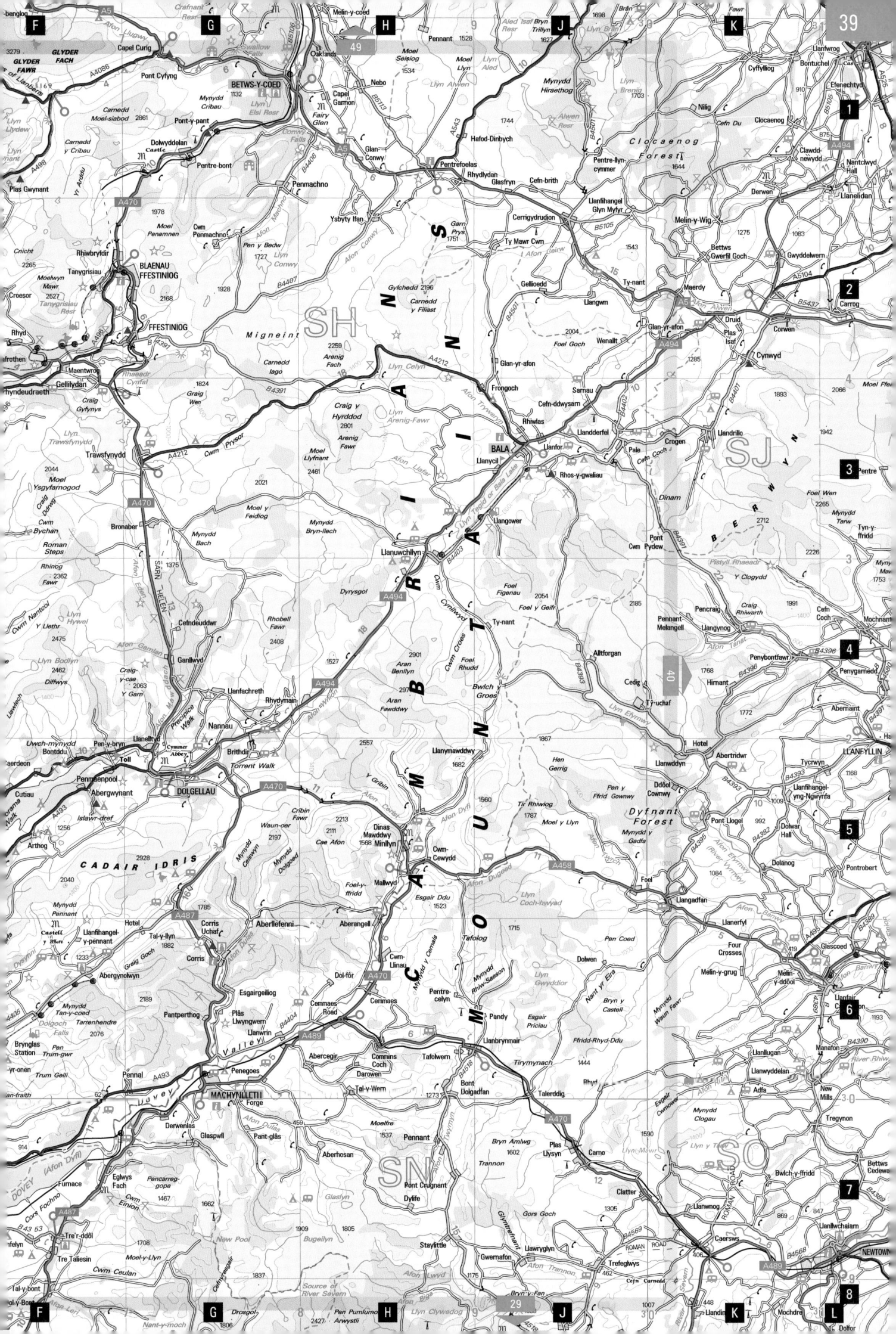

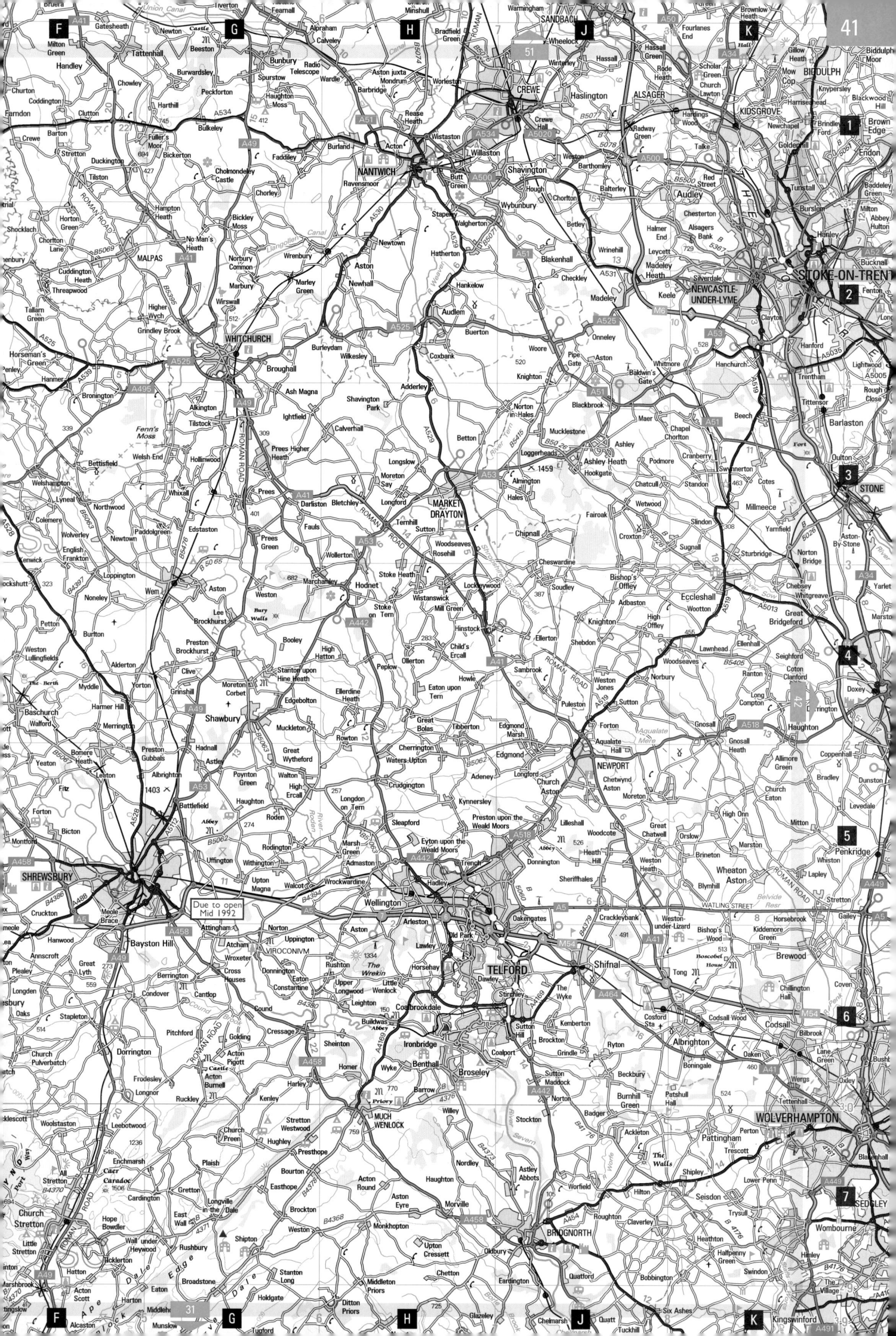

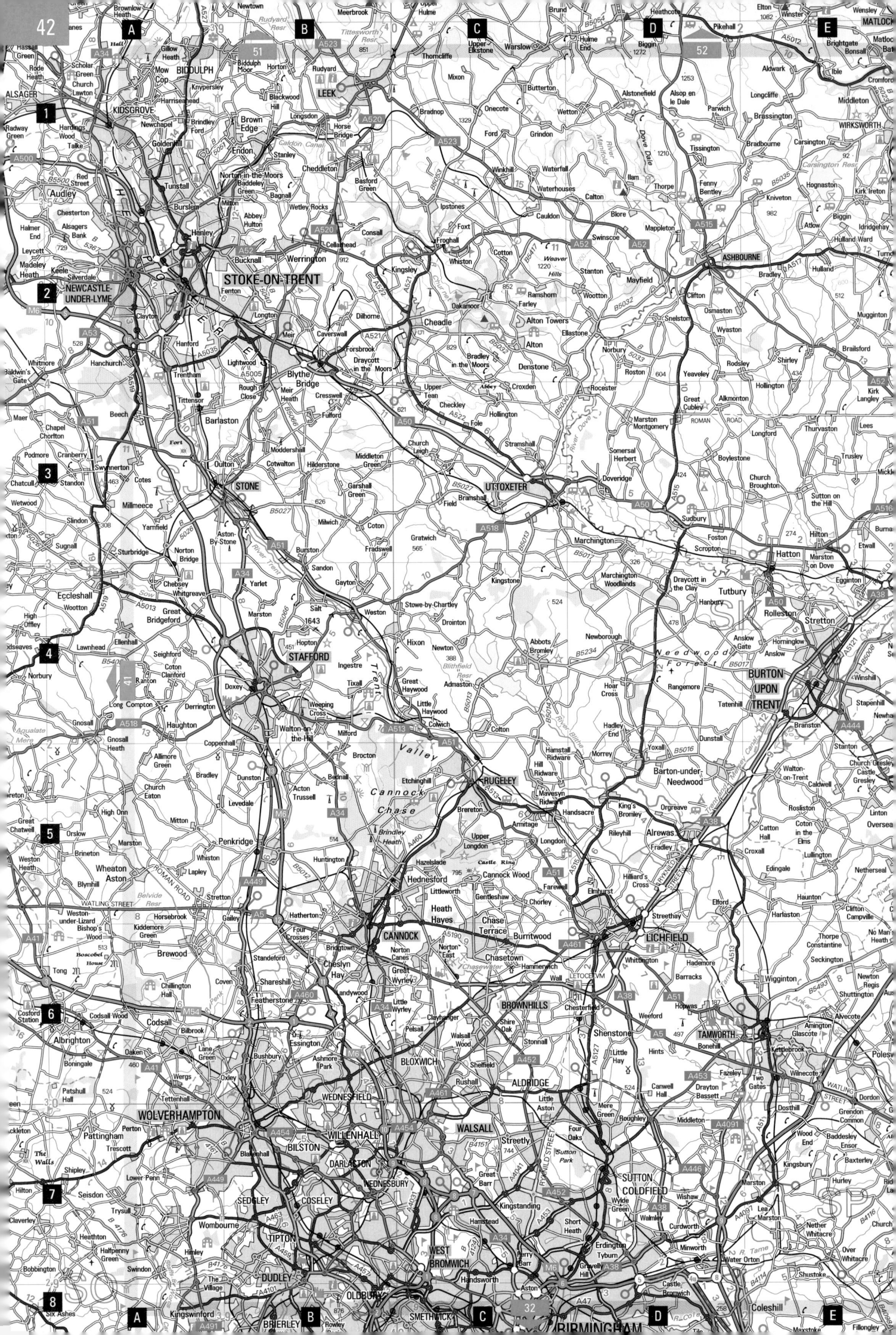

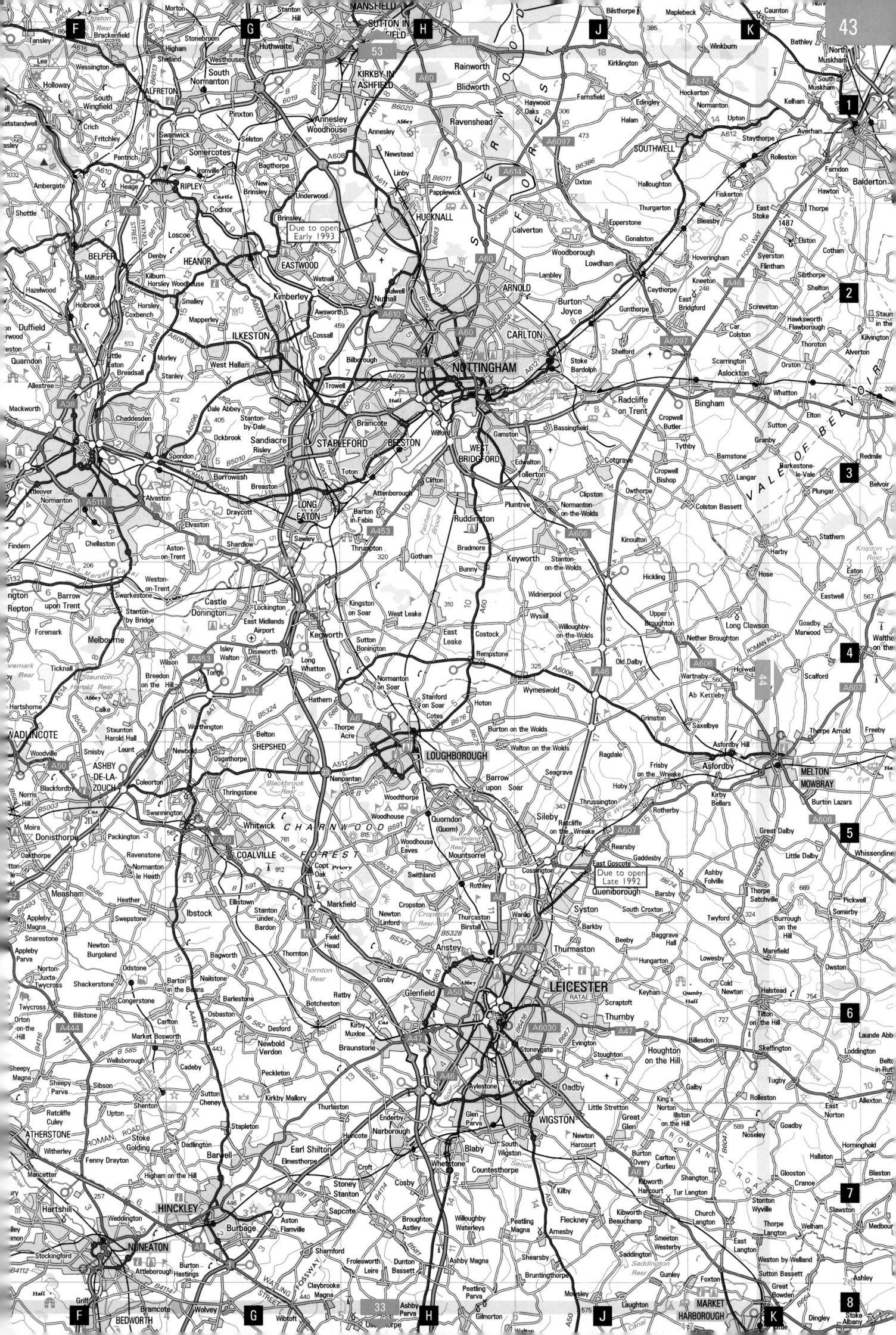

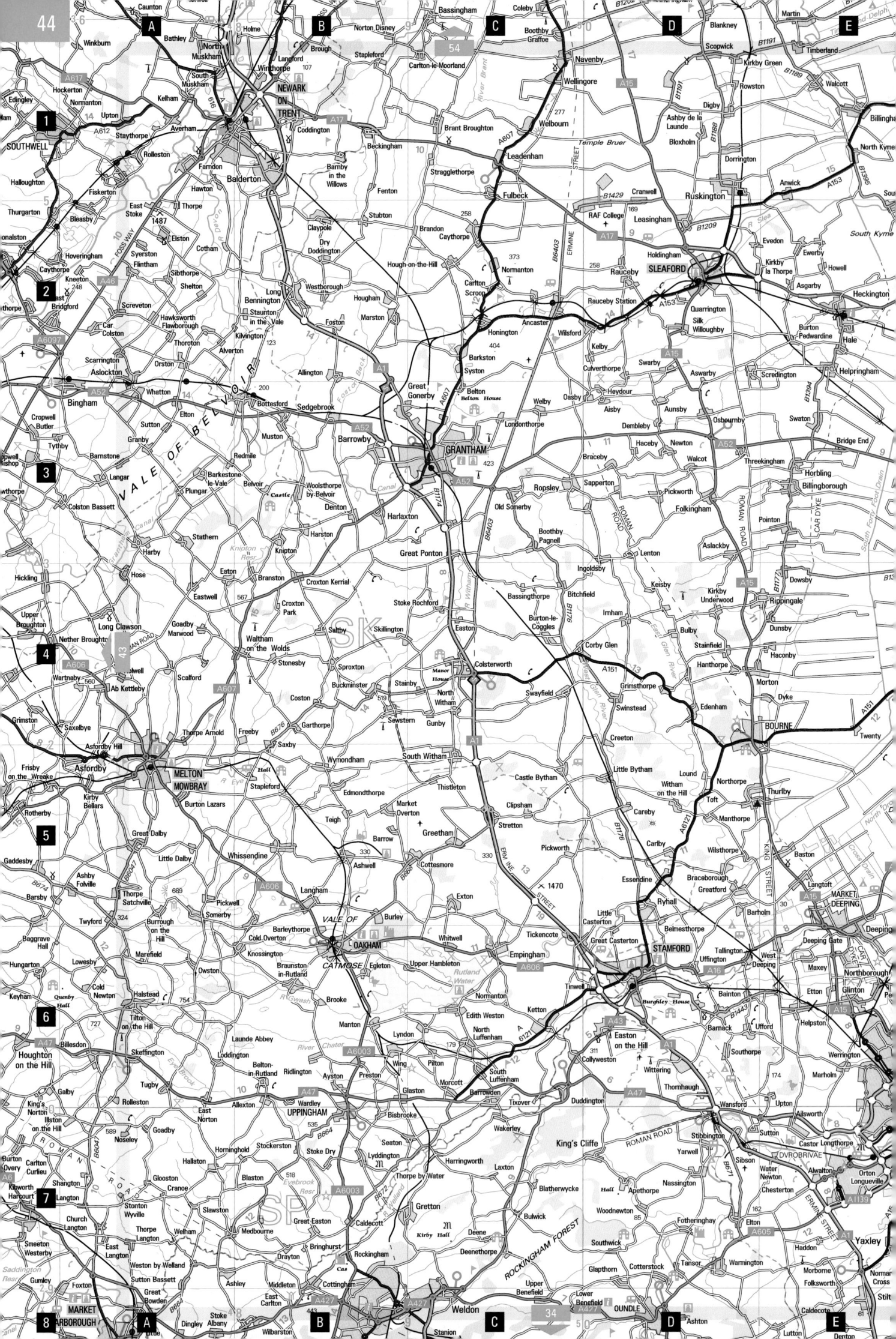

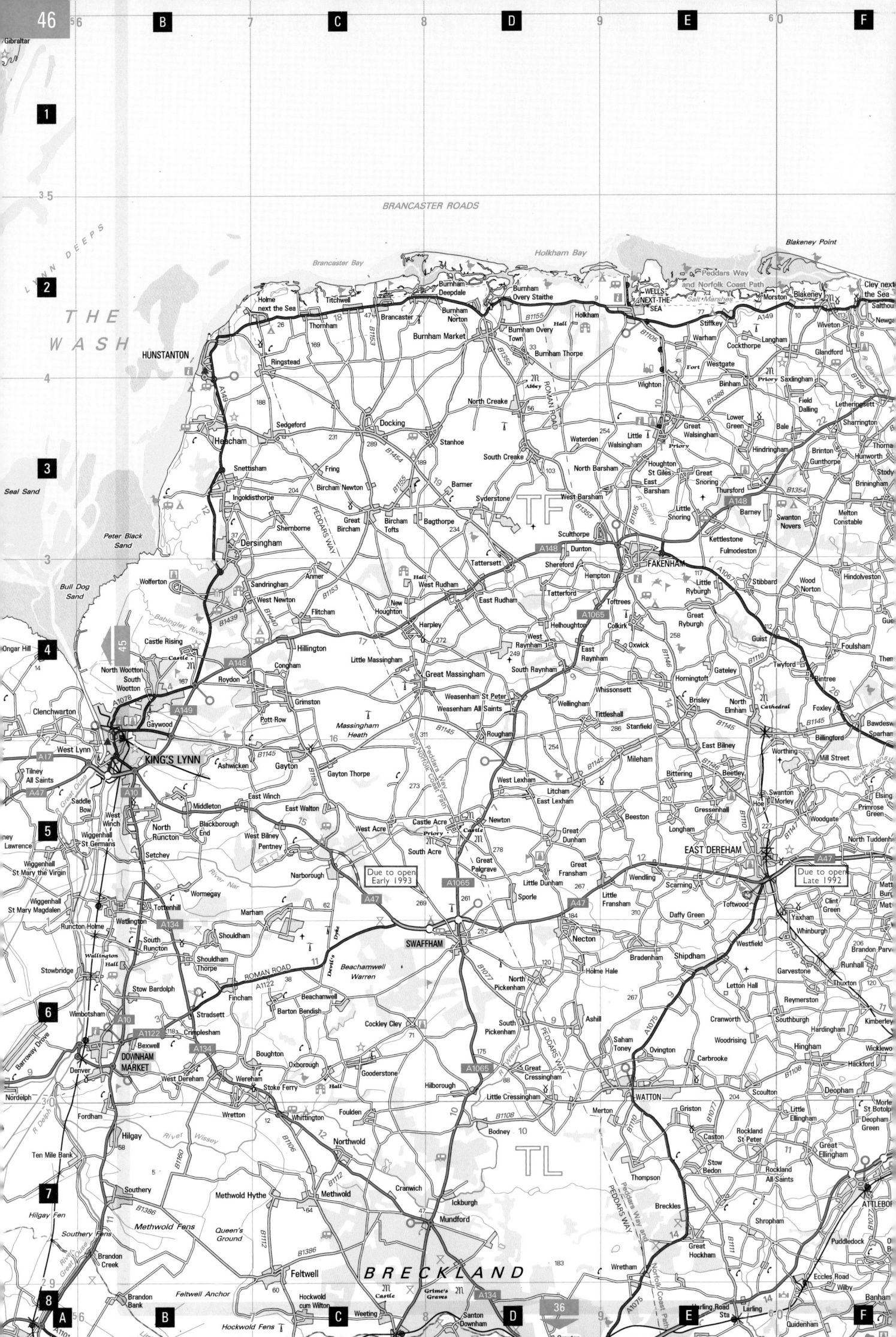

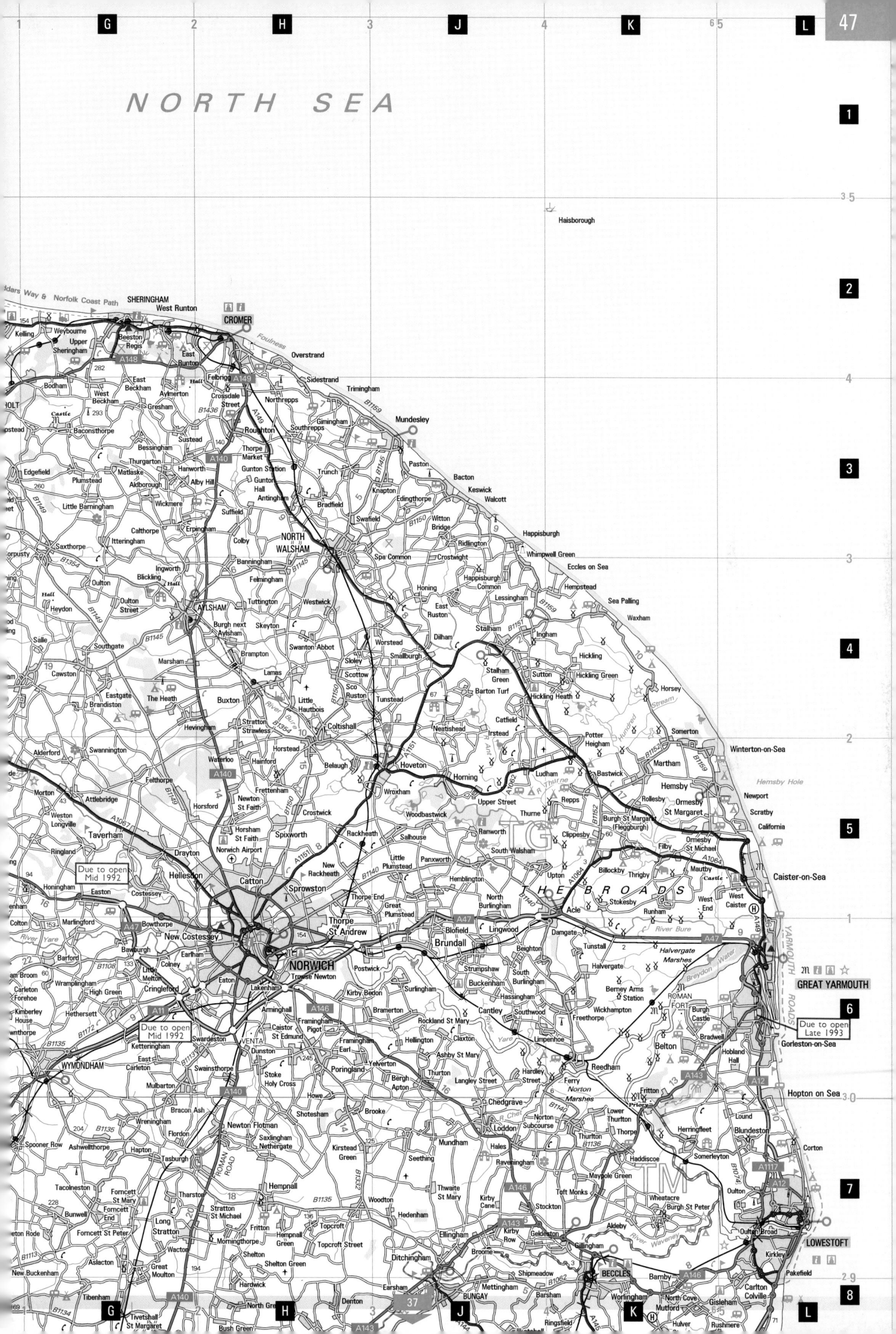

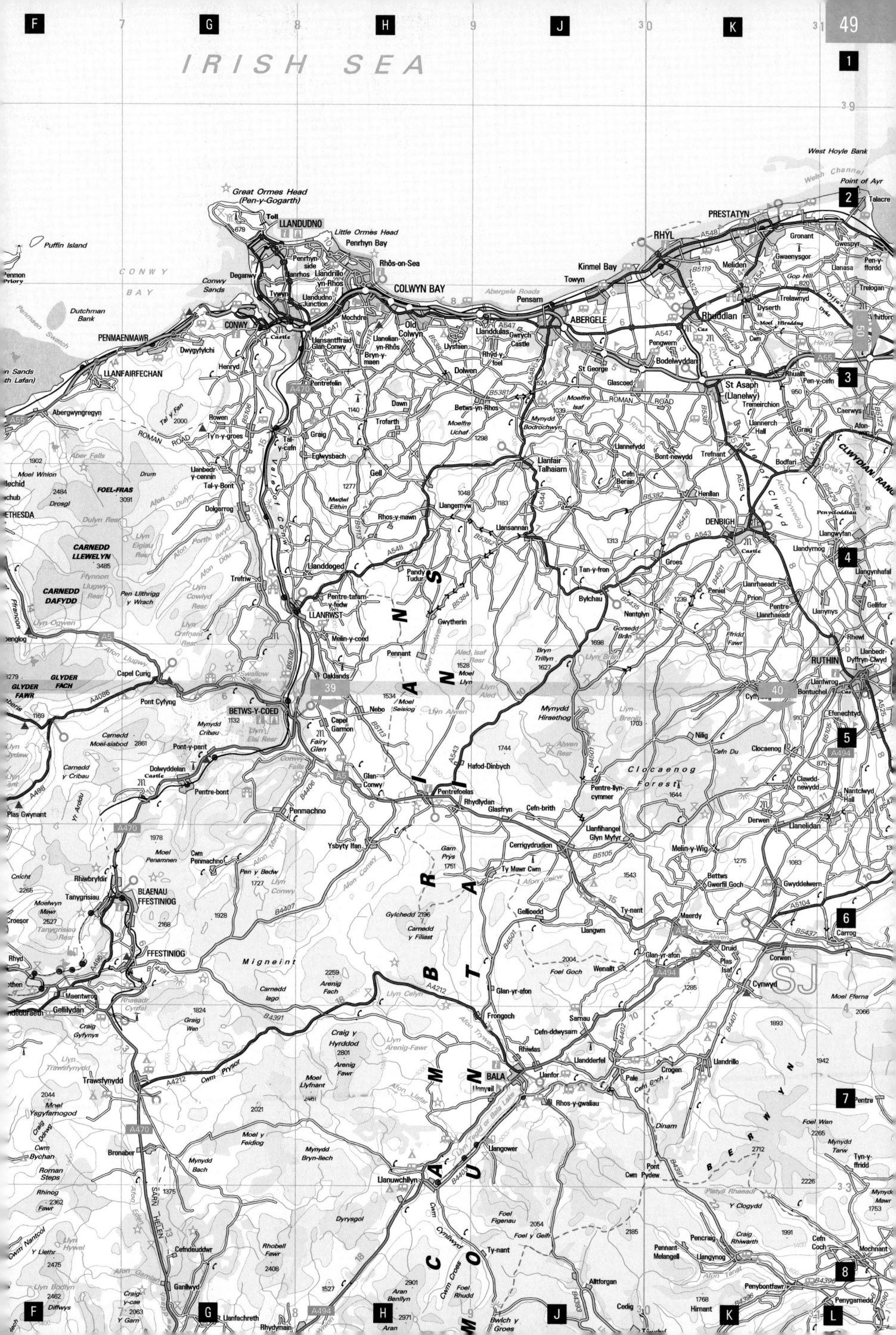

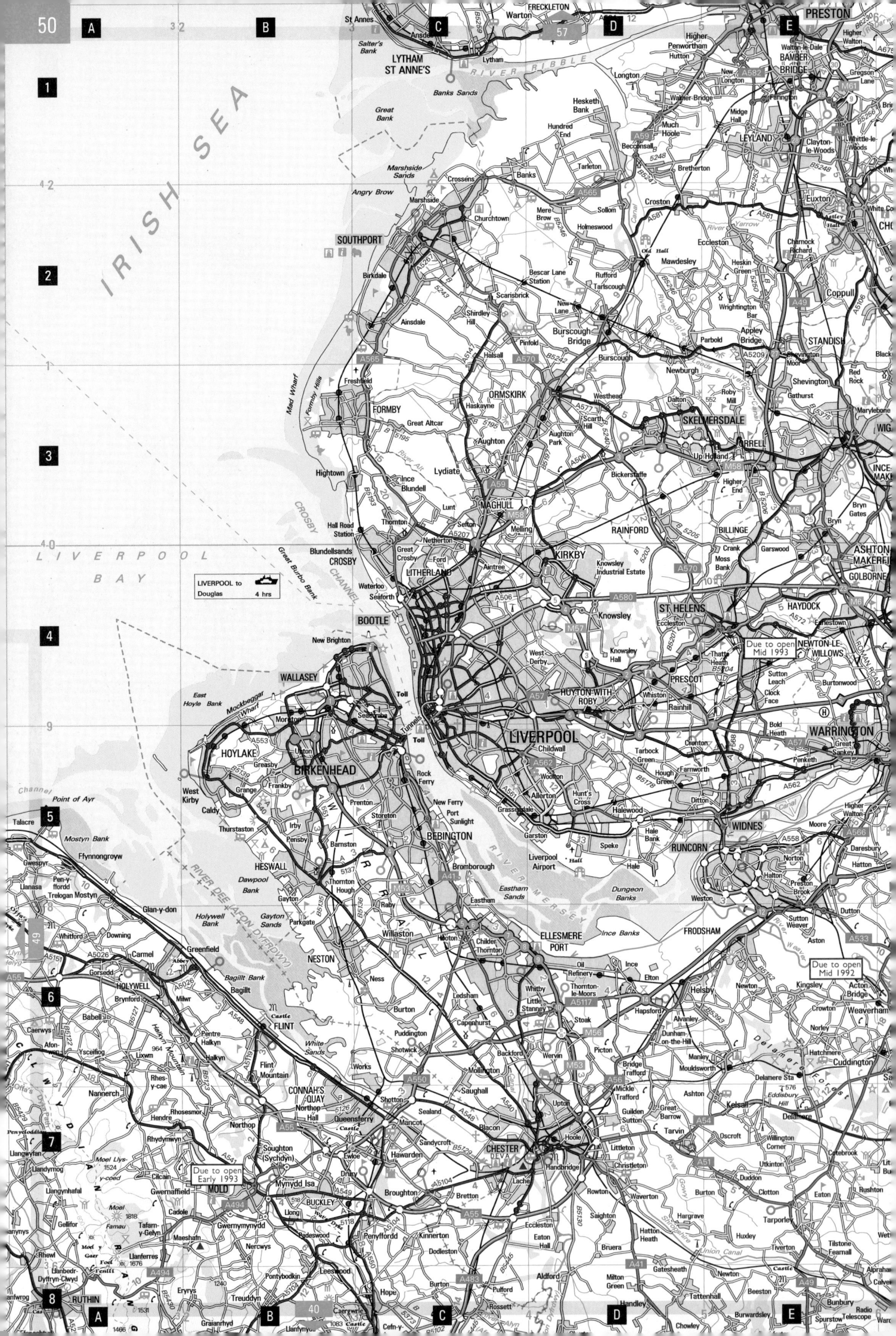

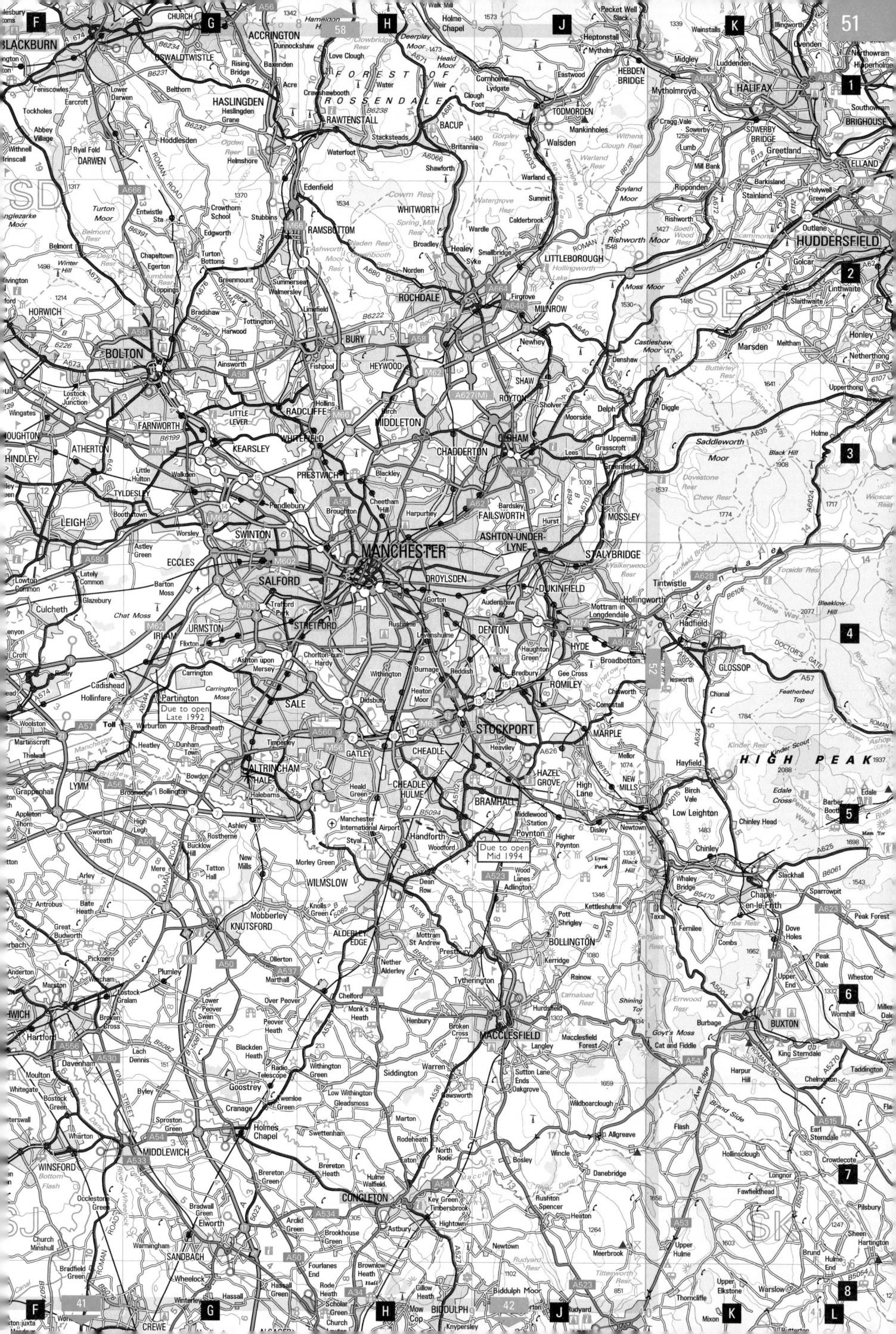

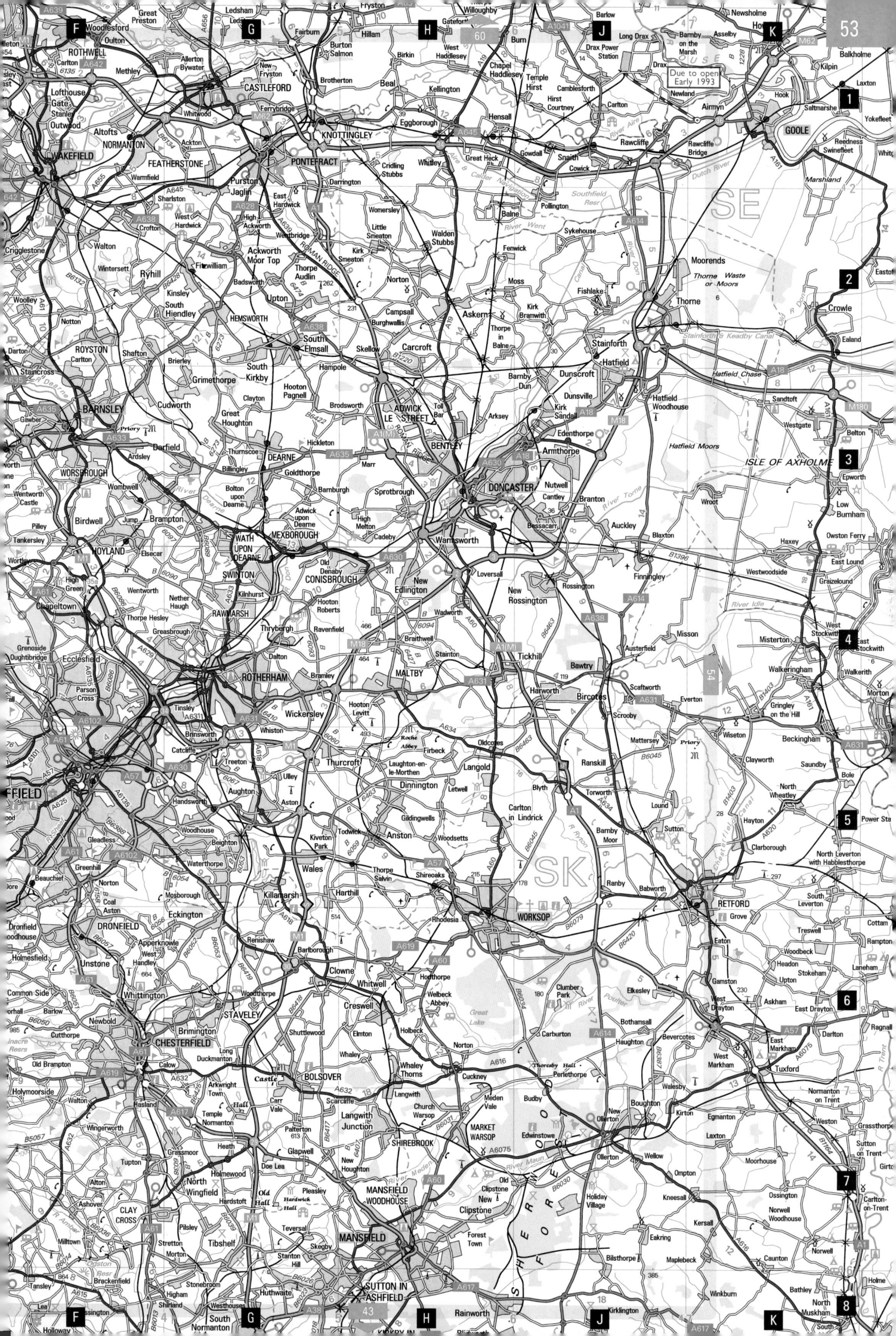

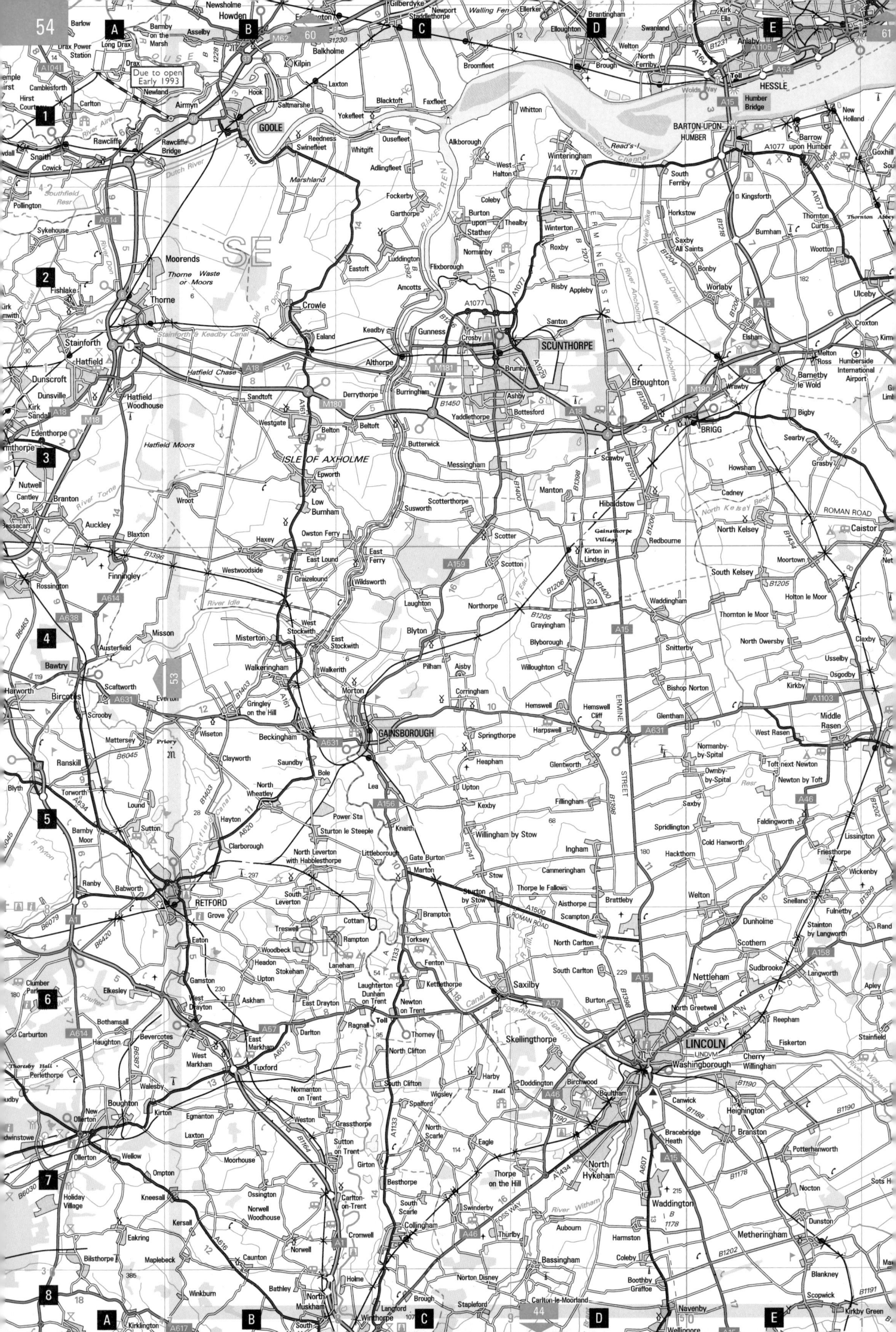

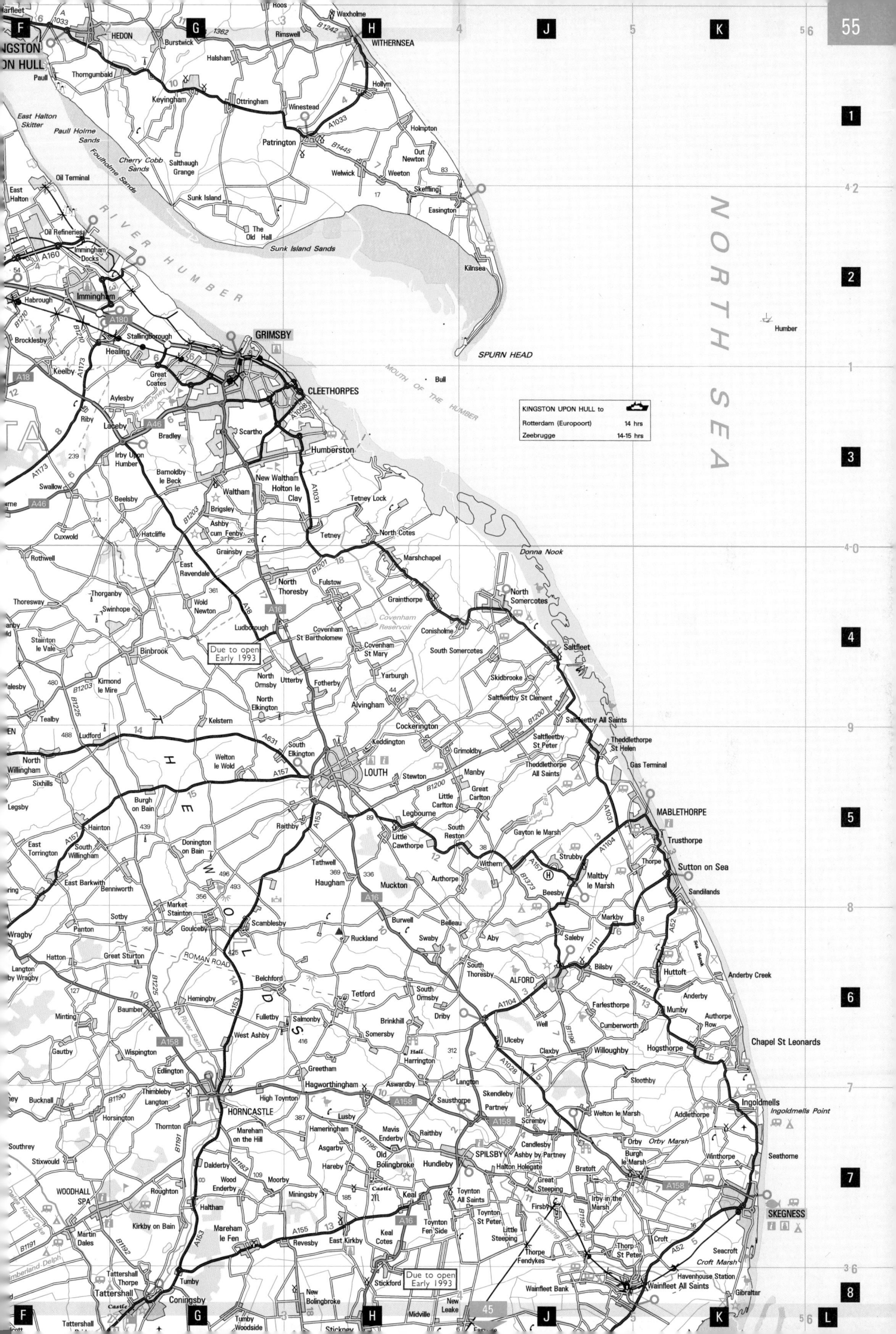

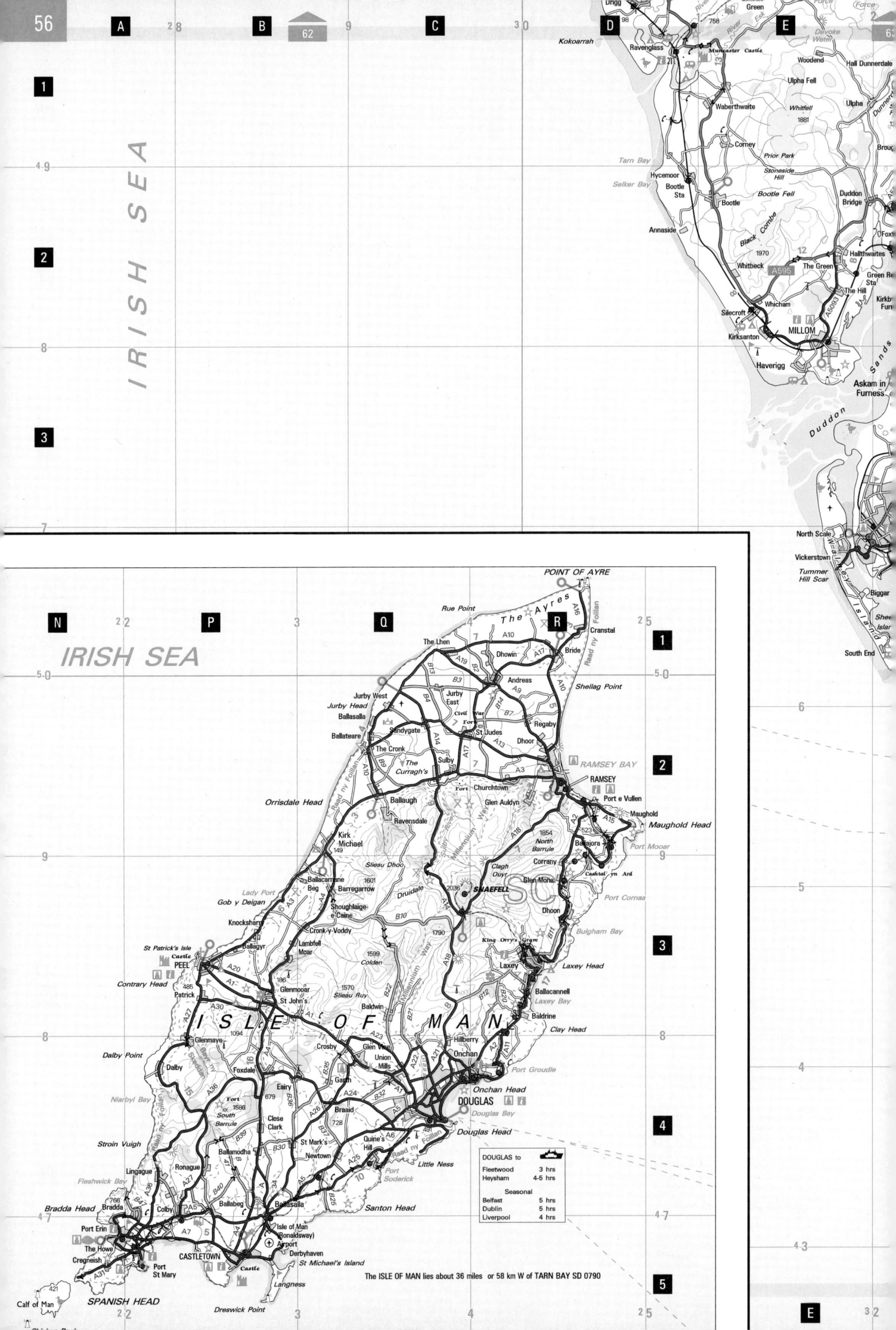

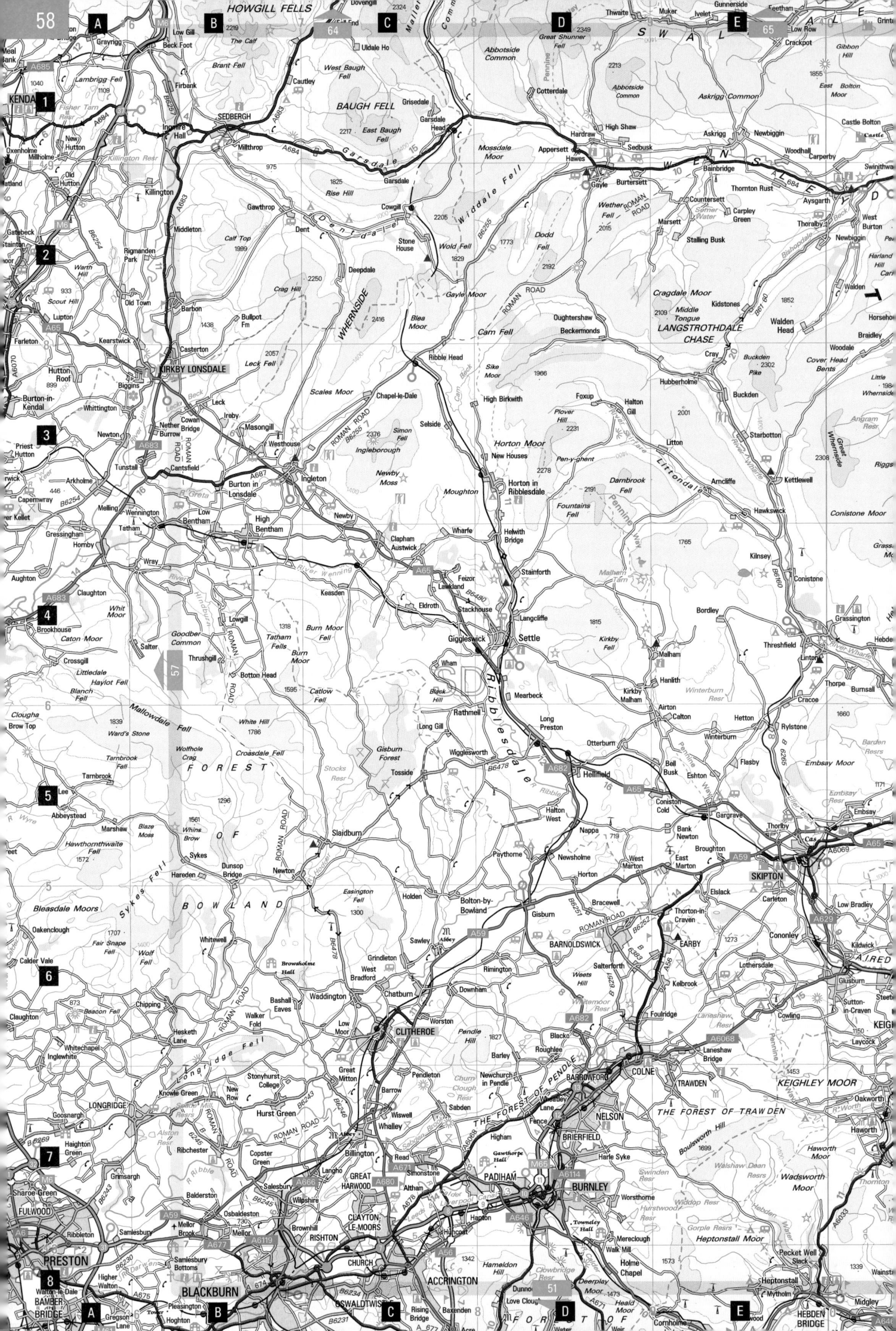

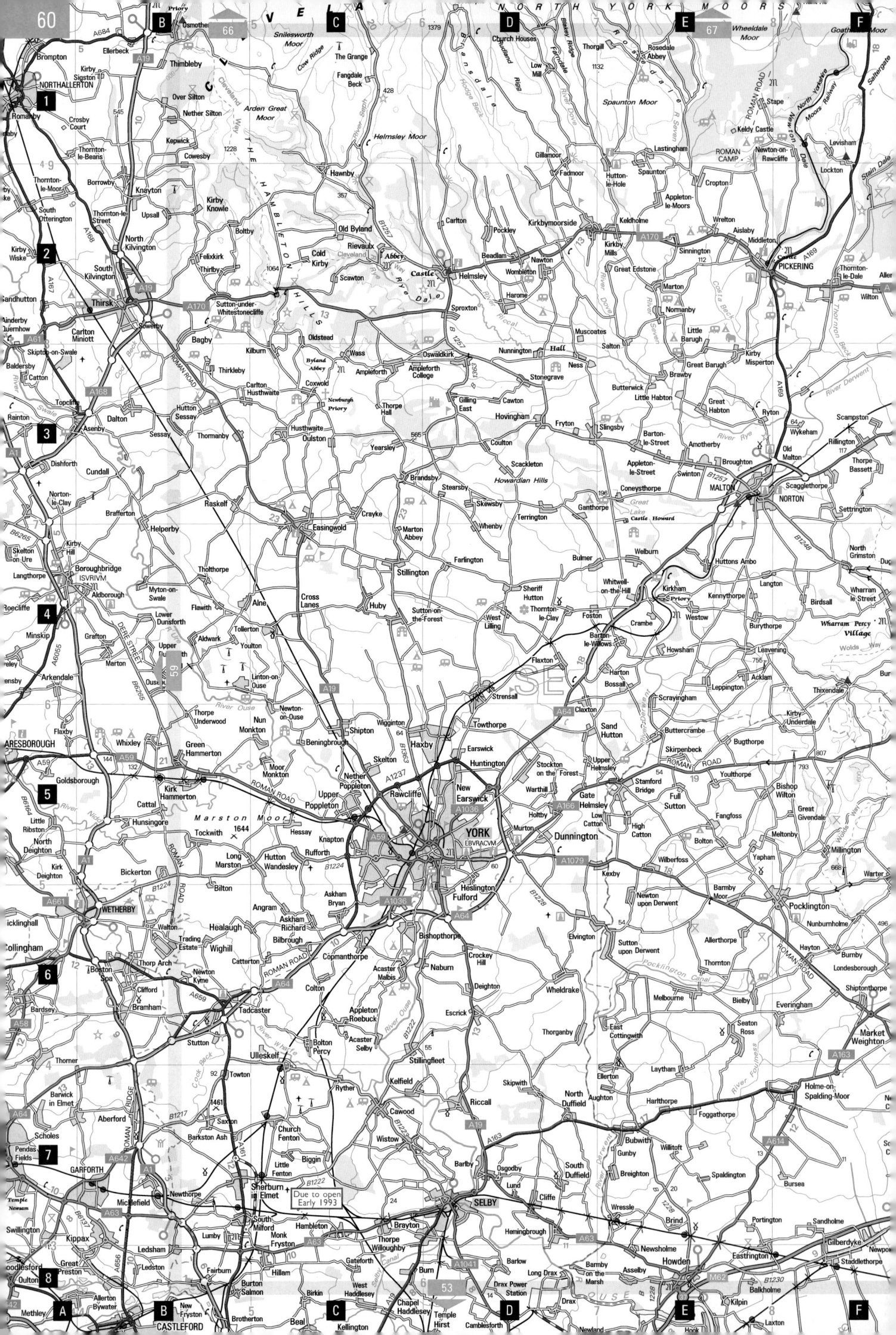

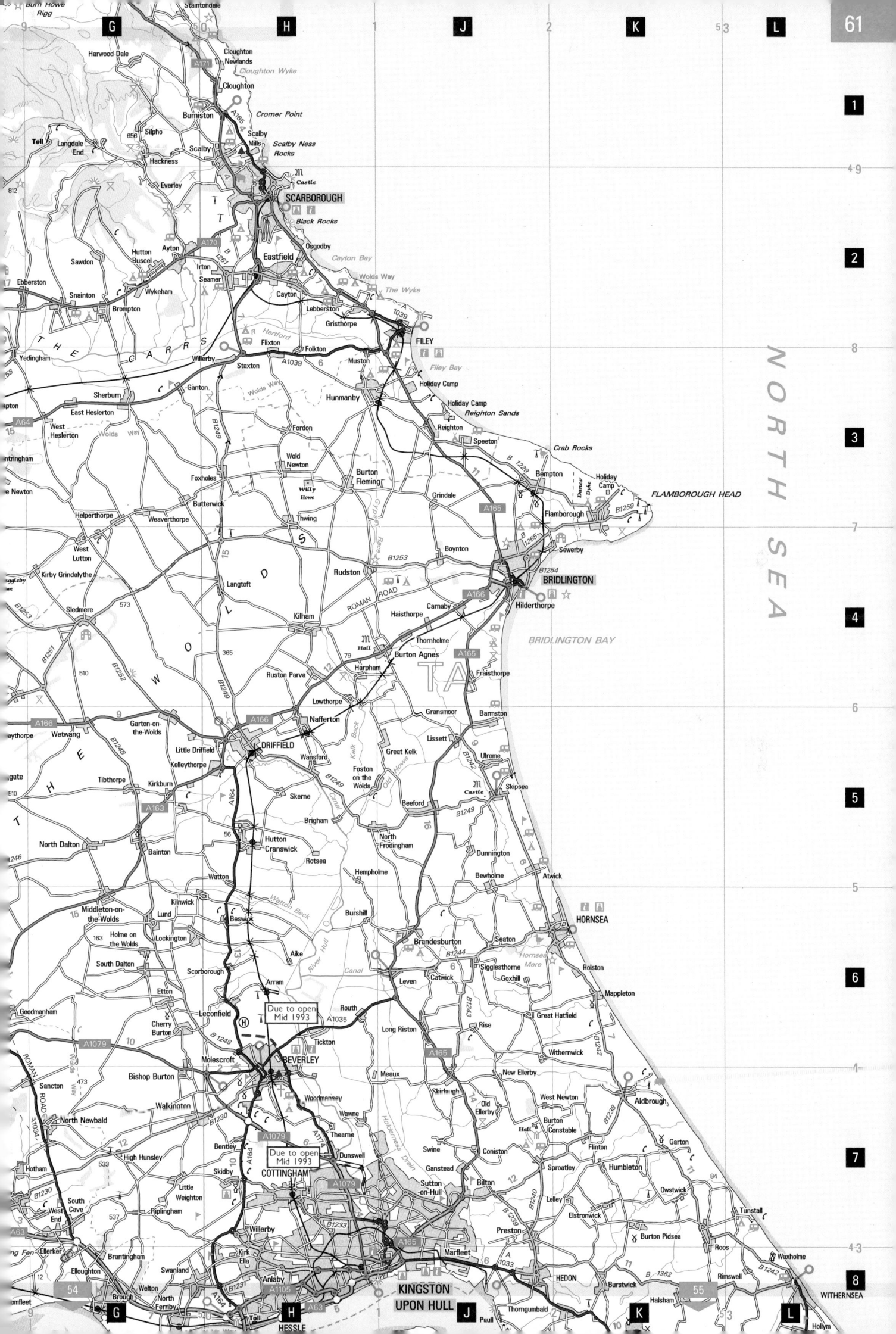

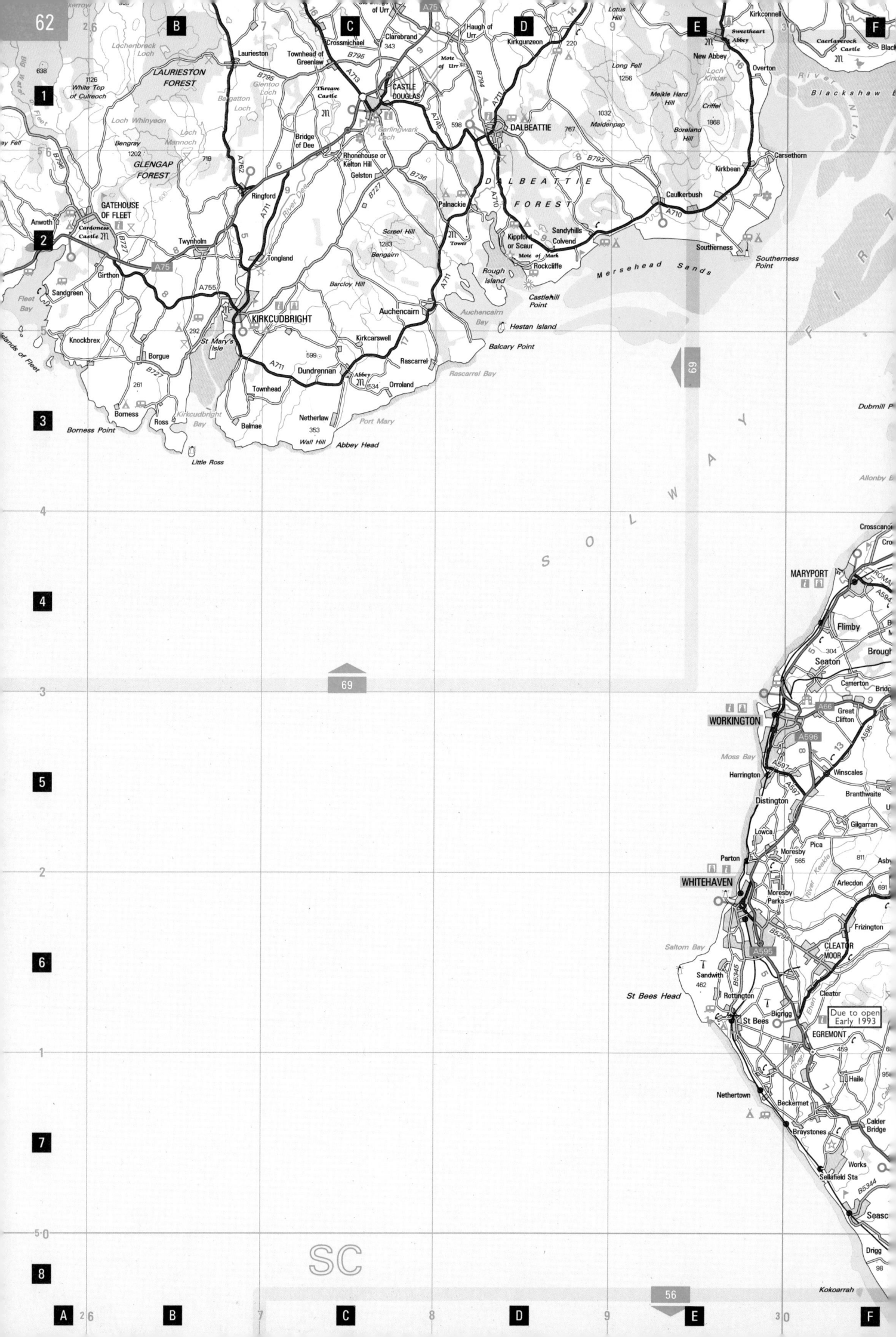

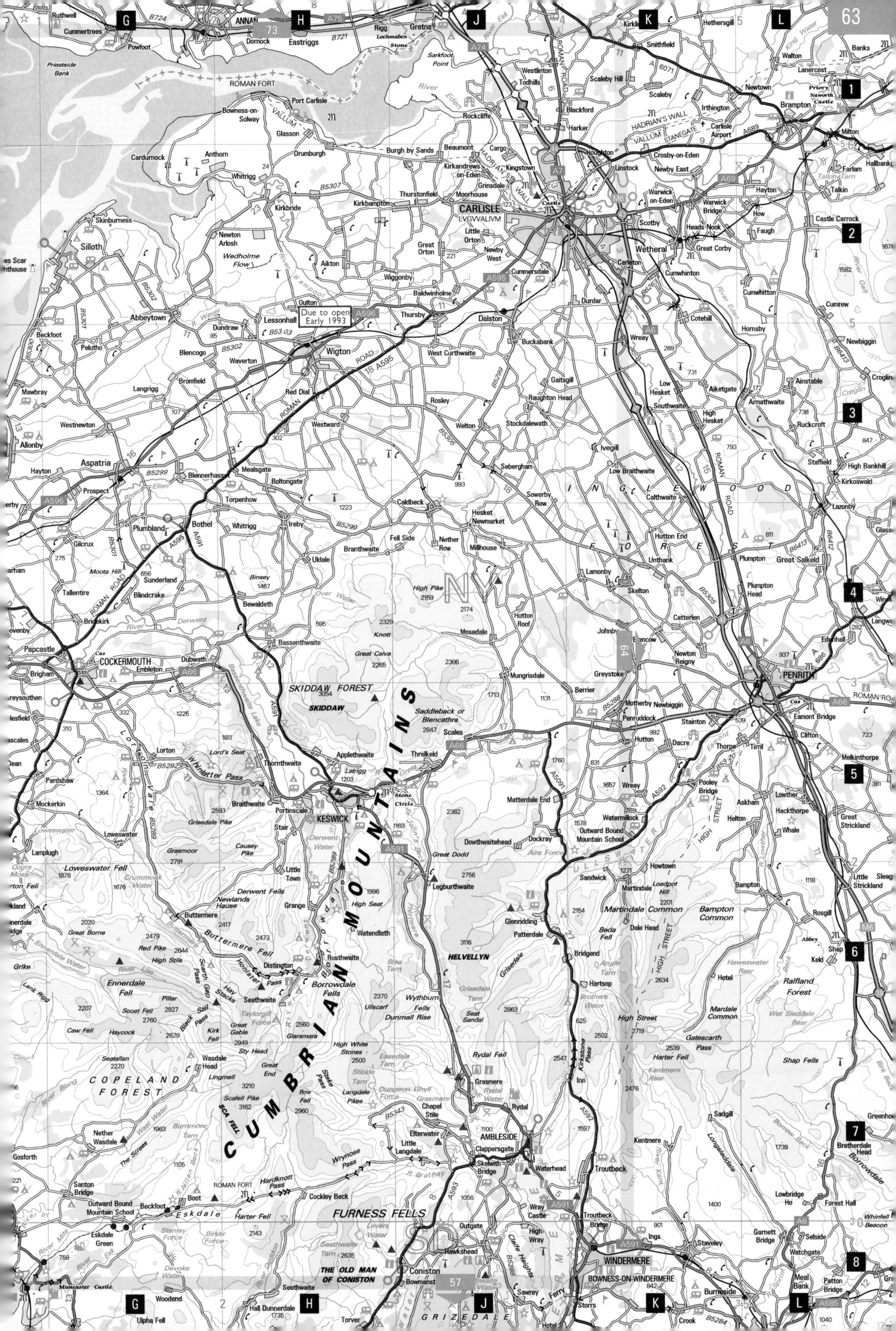

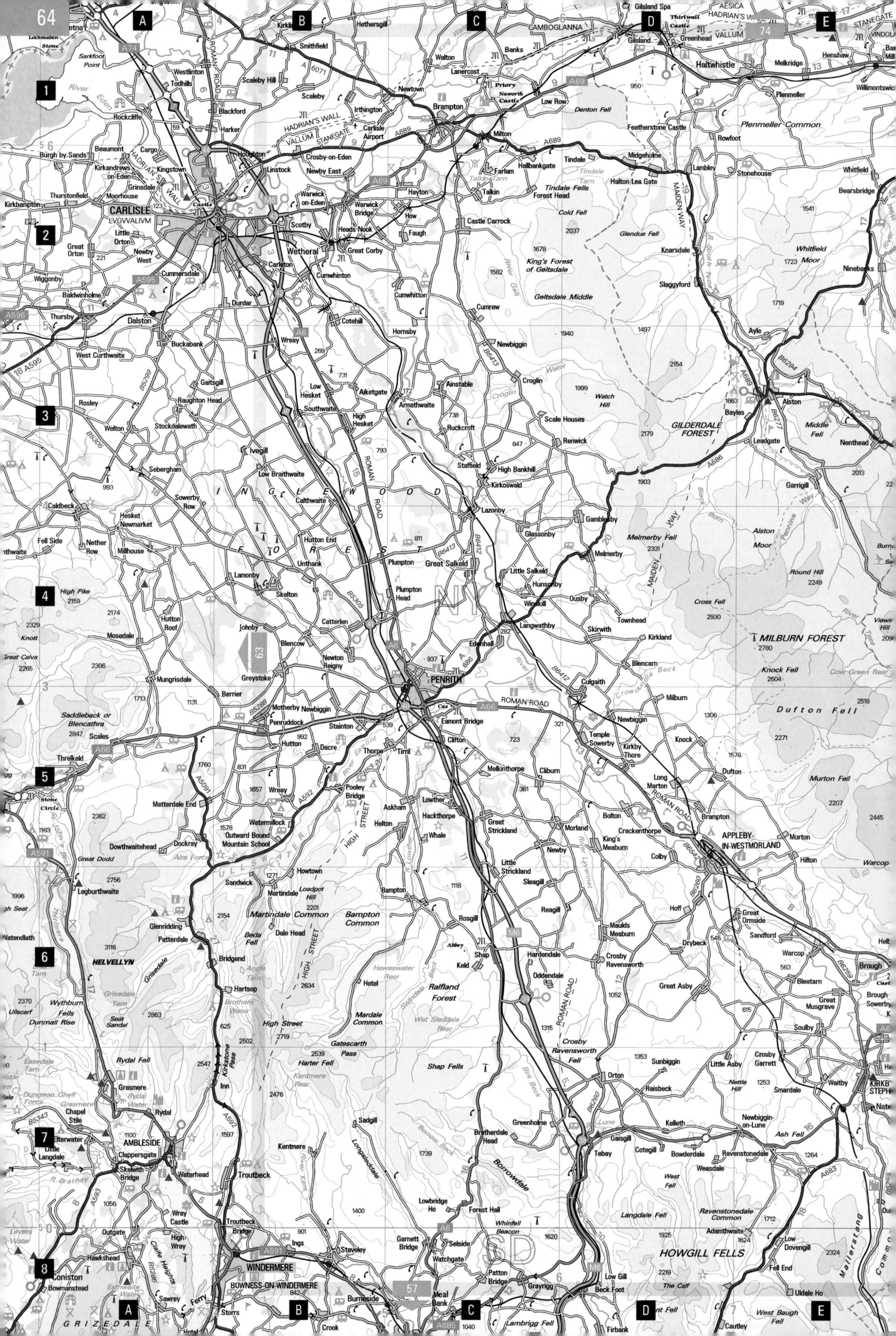

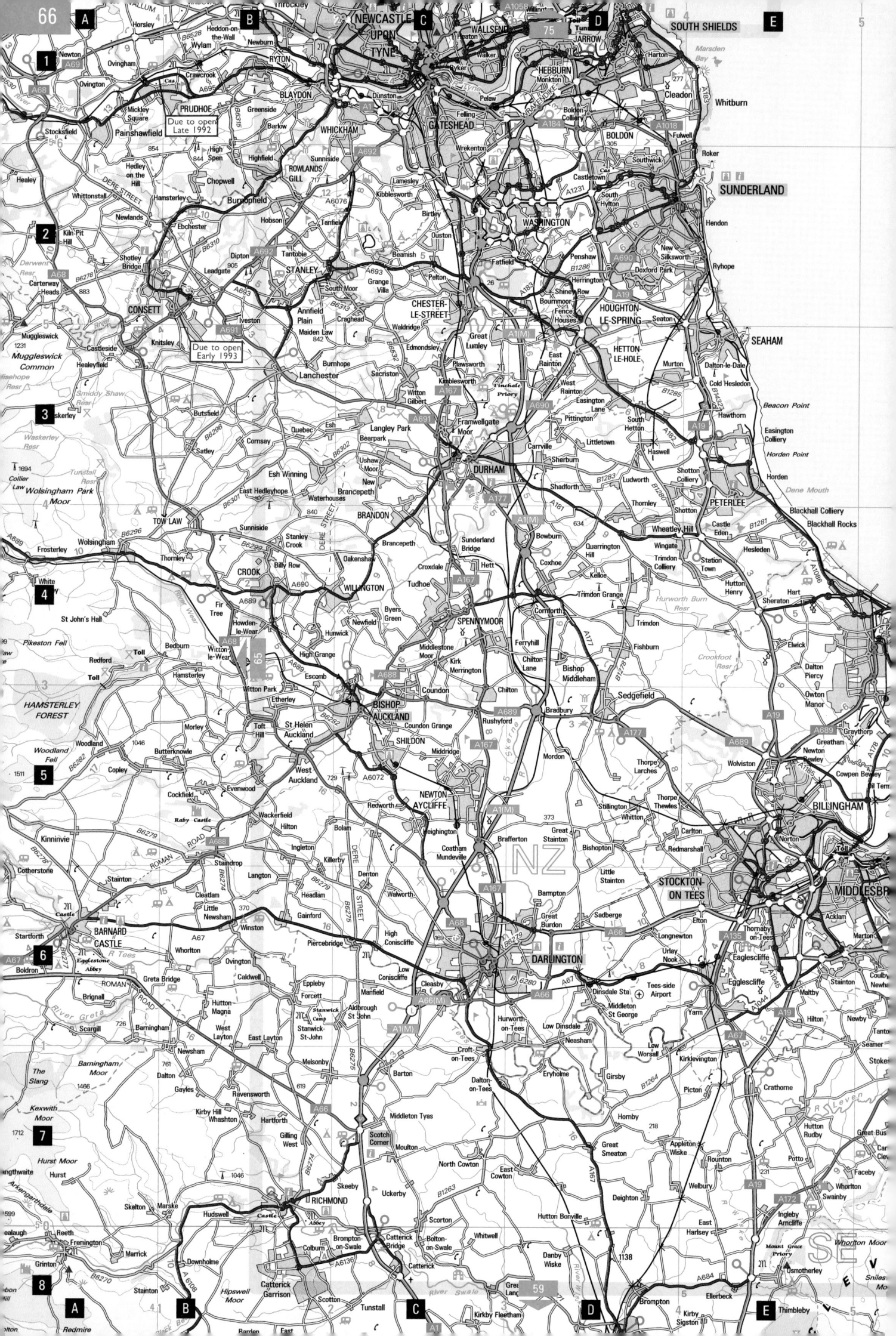

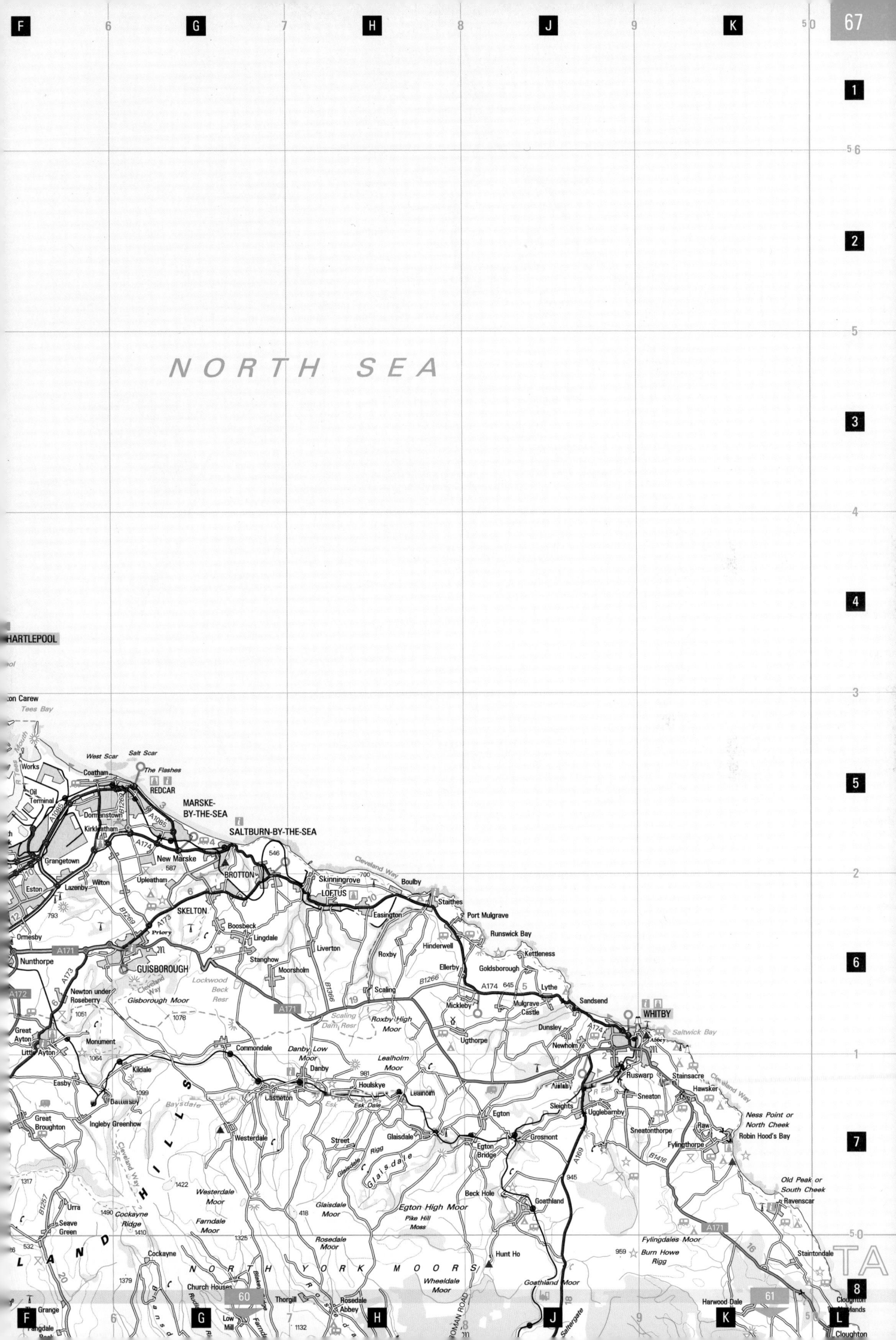

NORTH SEA

HARTLEPOOL

Seaton Carew
Tees Bay
West Scar   Salt Scar
Coatham   The Flashes
Works   REDCAR
Oil
Terminal   MARSKE-
Dormanstown   BY-THE-SEA
Kirkleatham   SALTBURN-BY-THE-SEA
Grangetown   New Marske
Eston   Upleatham   BROTTON   Cleveland Way
Wilton   546   Skinningrove   Boulby
Lazenby   Priory   LOFTUS   Staithes
Ormesby   793   SKELTON   Easington   Port Mulgrave
Nunthorpe   Boosbeck   Roxby   Runswick Bay
Newton under   Lingdale   Liverton   Hinderwell   Kettleness
Roseberry   Stanghow   Ellerby   Goldsborough
Great   Gisborough Moor   Moorsholm   Scaling   A174 645 5 Lythe
Ayton   Monument   Lockwood   Scaling   Mickleby   Mulgrave   Sandsend
Little Ayton   1064   Beck Resr   Roxby High   Castle   WHITBY
Easby   Kildale   1078   Commondale   Moor   Ugthorpe   Dunsley   Saltwick Bay
Battersby   1099   Danby Low   Lealholm   Newholm   Abbey
Great   Baysdale Beck   Moor   Danby   Moor   Aislaby   Ruswarp   Stainsacre
Broughton   Castleton   981   Sneaton   Hawsker
Ingleby Greenhow   Houlskye   Lealholm   Sleights   Ness Point or
Westerdale   Esk Dale   Egton   Ugglebarnby   North Cheek
1317   Street   Glaisdale   Grosmont   Sneatonthorpe   Raw   Robin Hood's Bay
Westerdale   Rigg   Egton   Fylingthorpe
1422   Moor   Bridge   945   B1416
Urra   Farndale   418   Glaisdale   Beck Hole   Old Peak or
1490   Moor   Moor   Egton High Moor   Goathland   South Cheek
Cockayne   1410   Pike Hill   Ravenscar
Seave   Moss
Green   532   1325   Rosedale
Moor
CLEVELAND HILLS   Goathland Moor   Fylingdales Moor
Cockayne   NORTH YORK MOORS   Hunt Ho   959   Burn Howe   Staintondale
1379   Wheeldale   Rigg
Church Houses   Moor   Harwood Dale   Cloughton
Thorgill   Rosedale   Newlands
Low   Abbey   ROMAN ROAD   Saltergate   Cloughton
Grange   Mill   1132
Fangdale   North York Moors
Beck

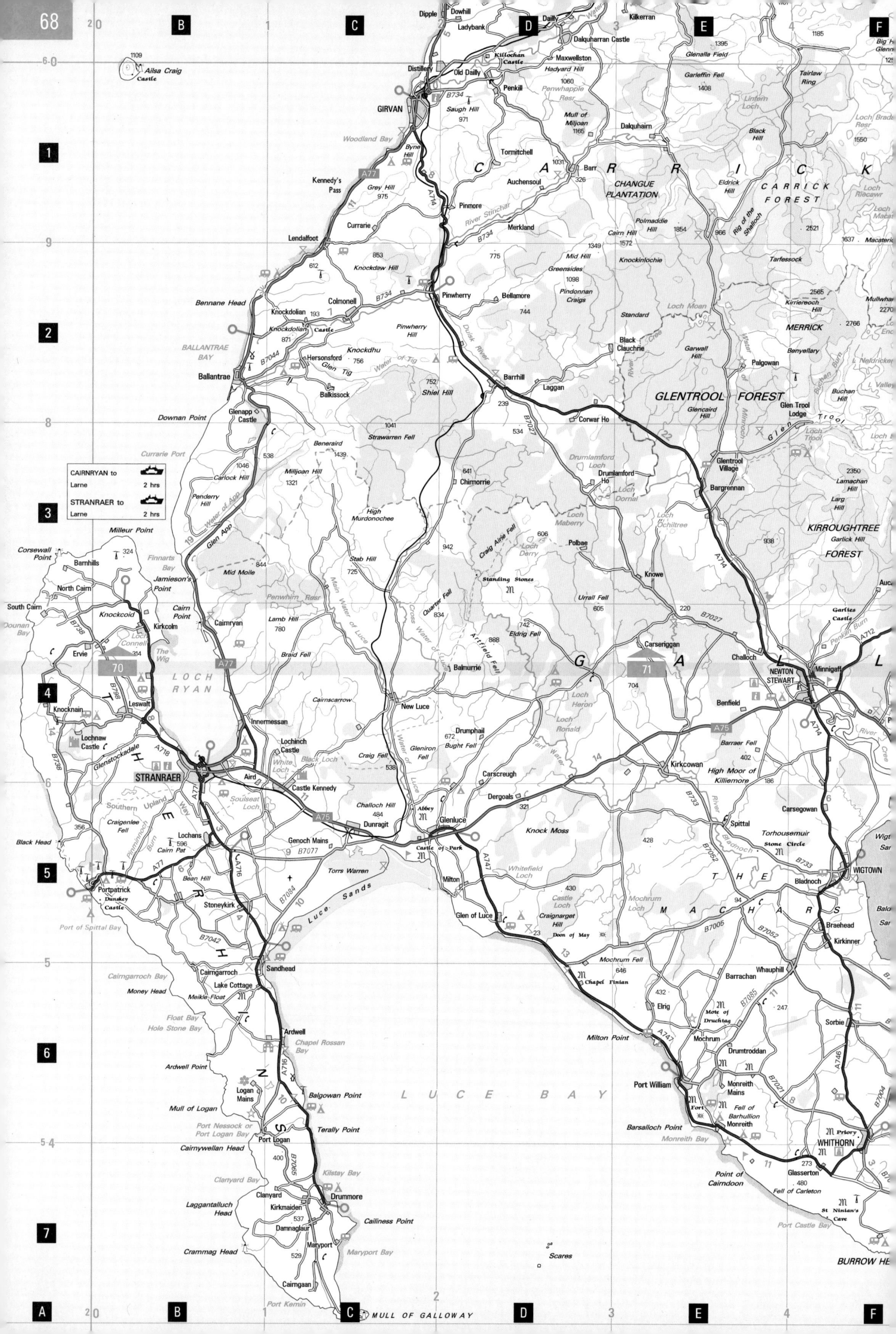

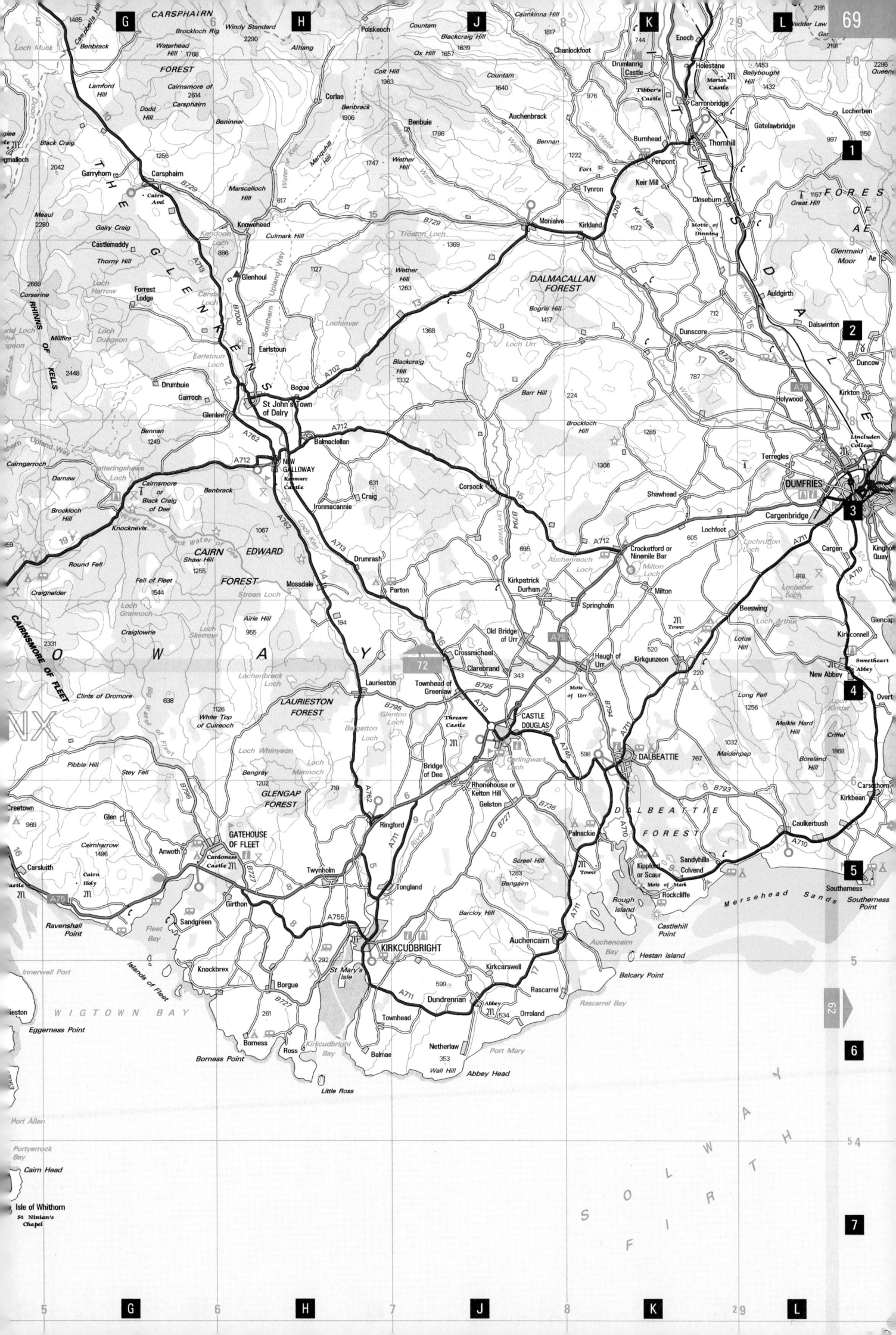

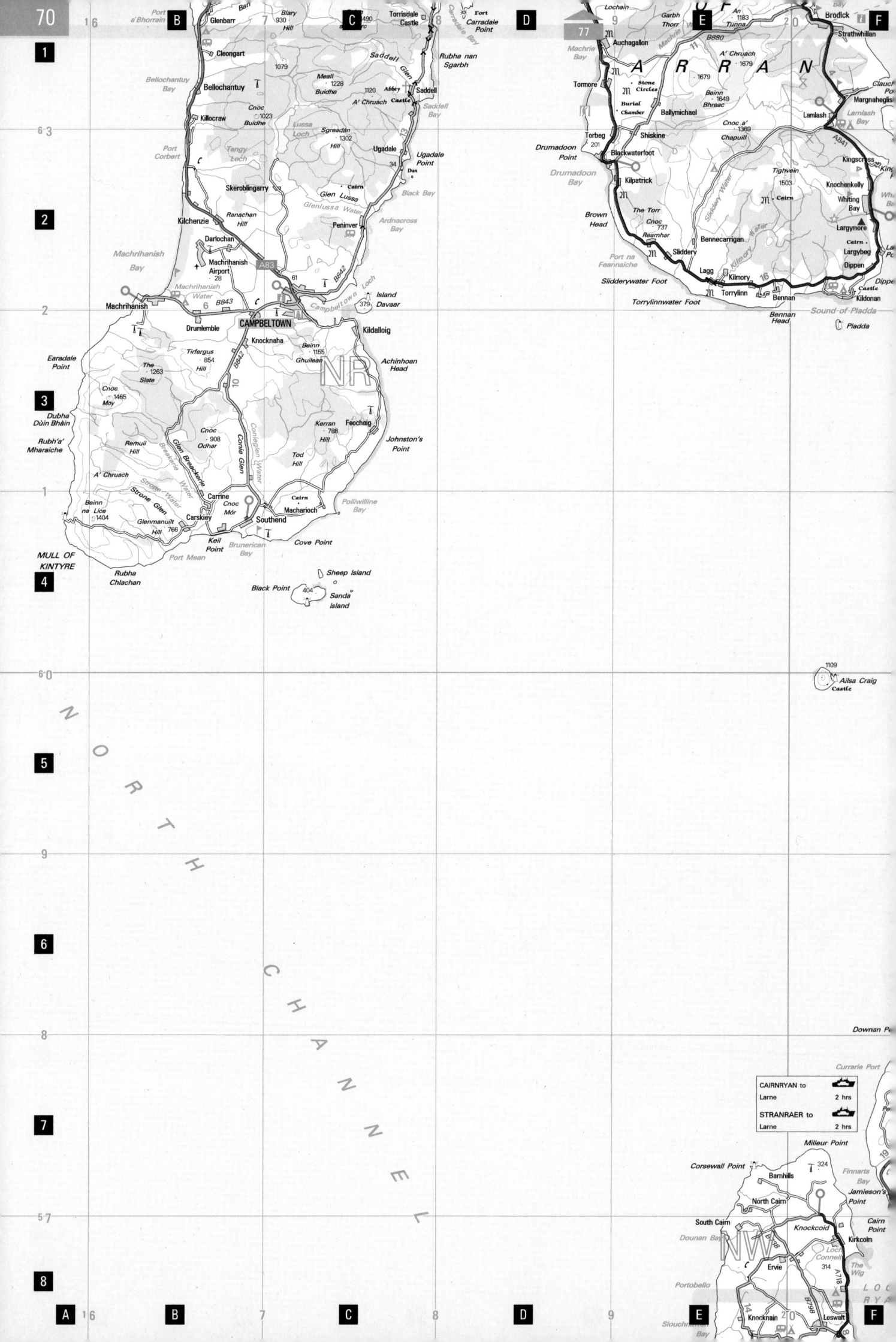

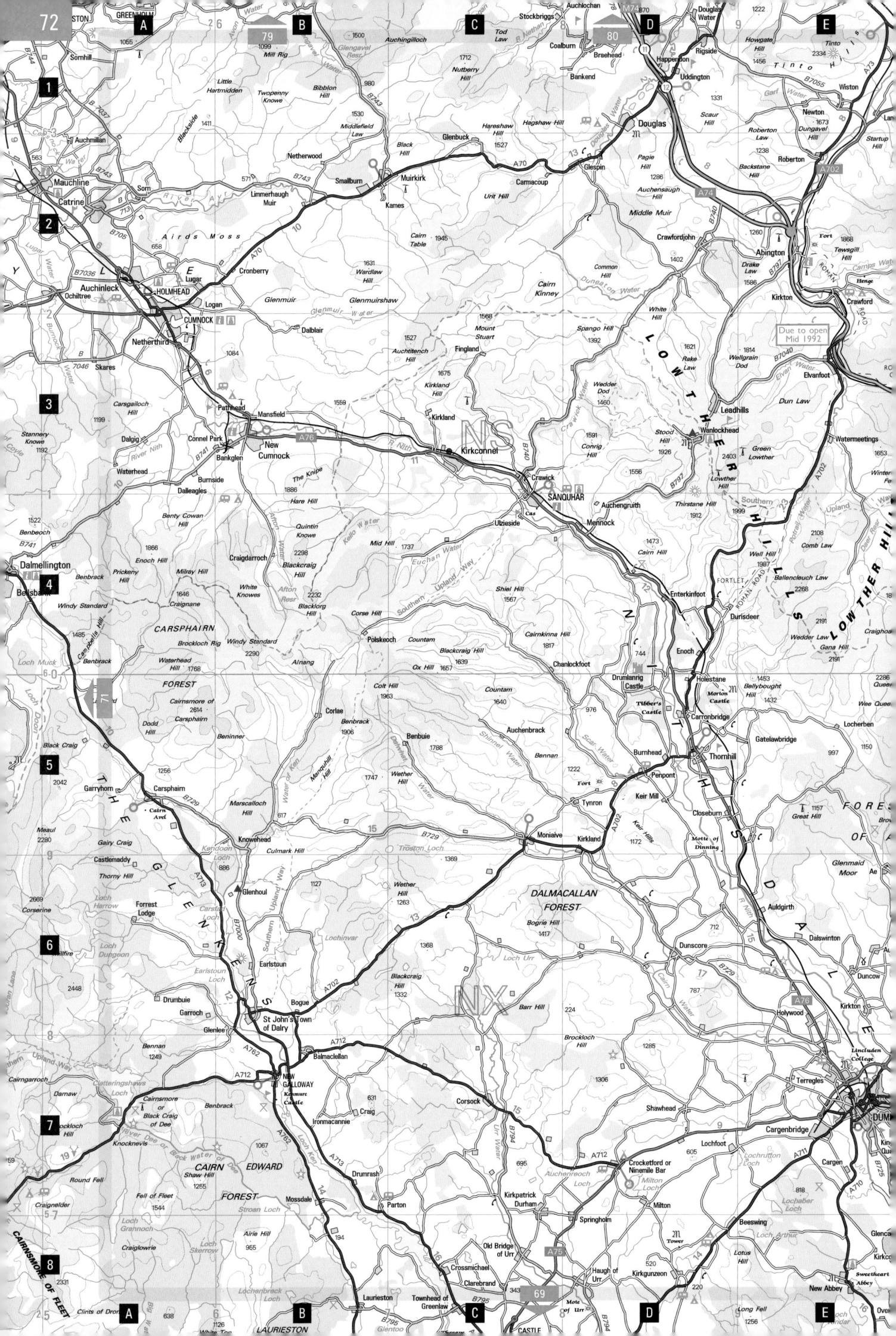

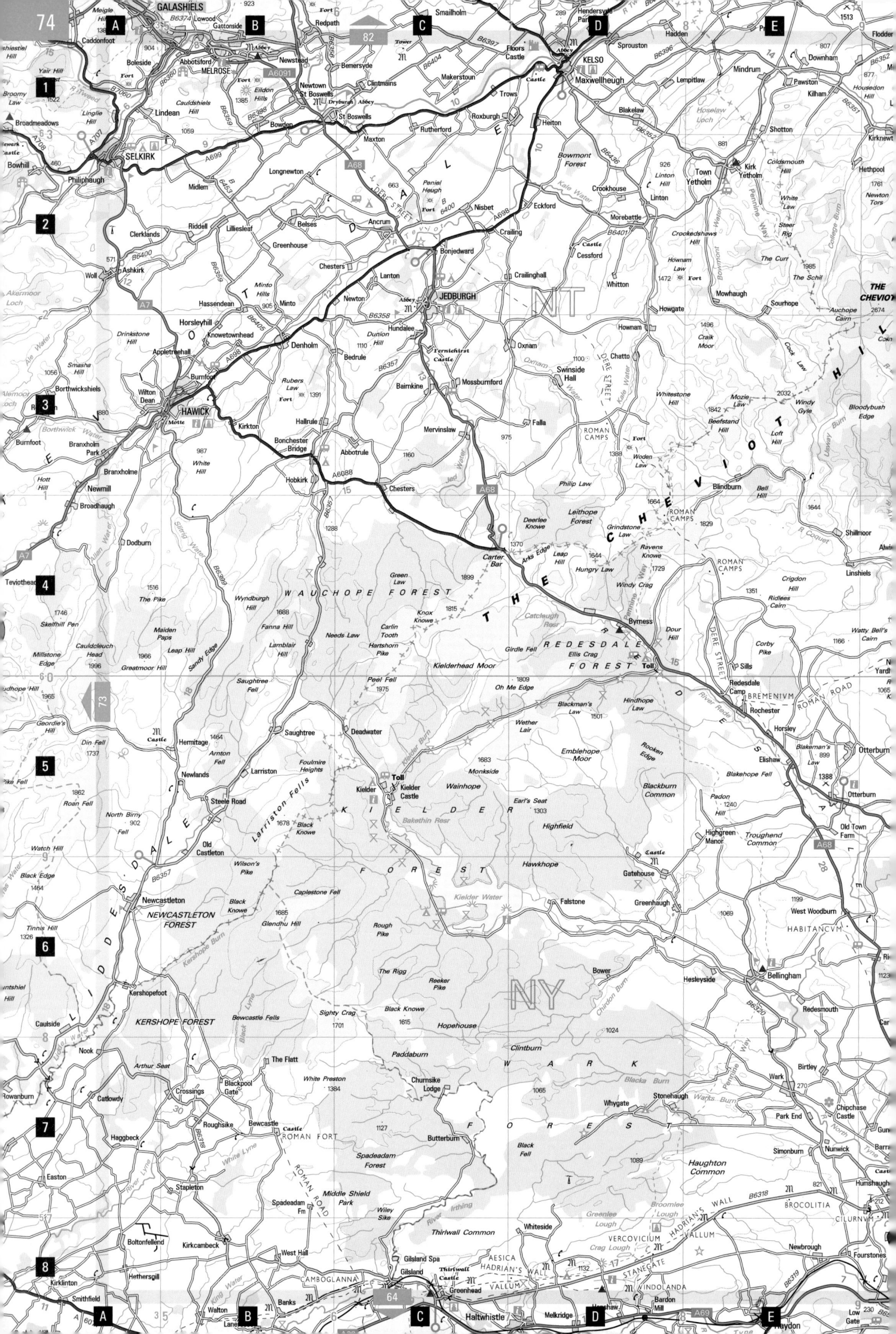

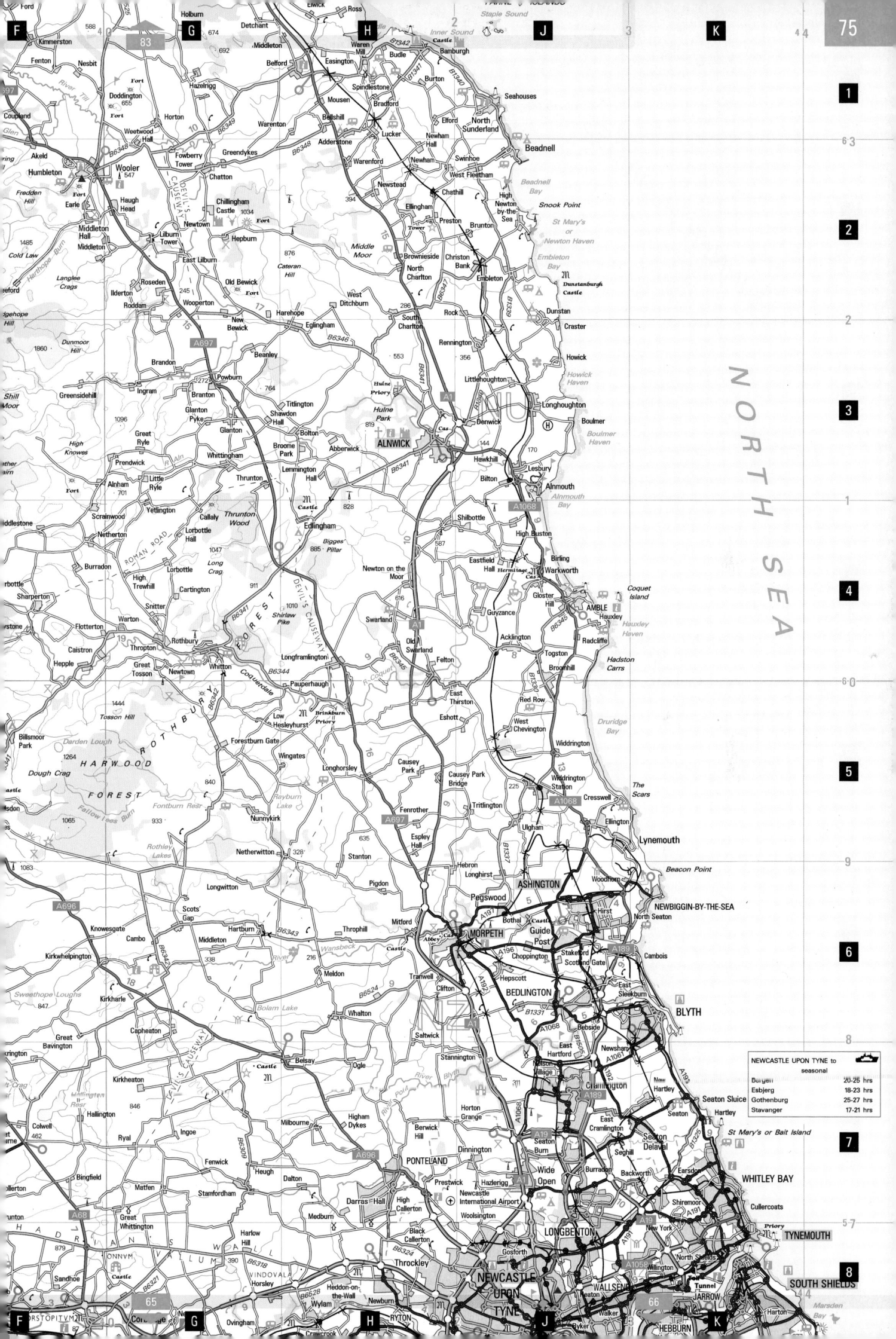

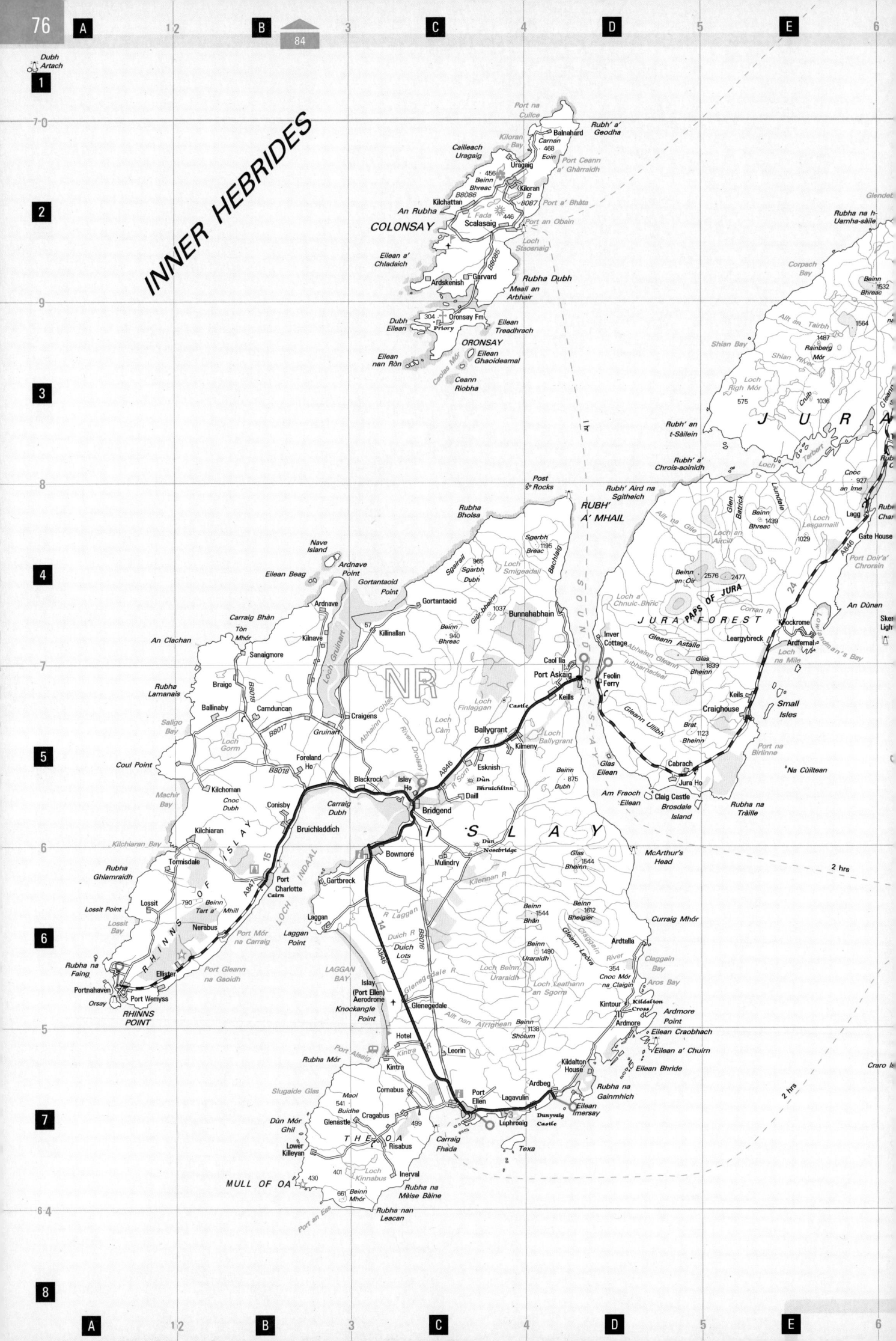

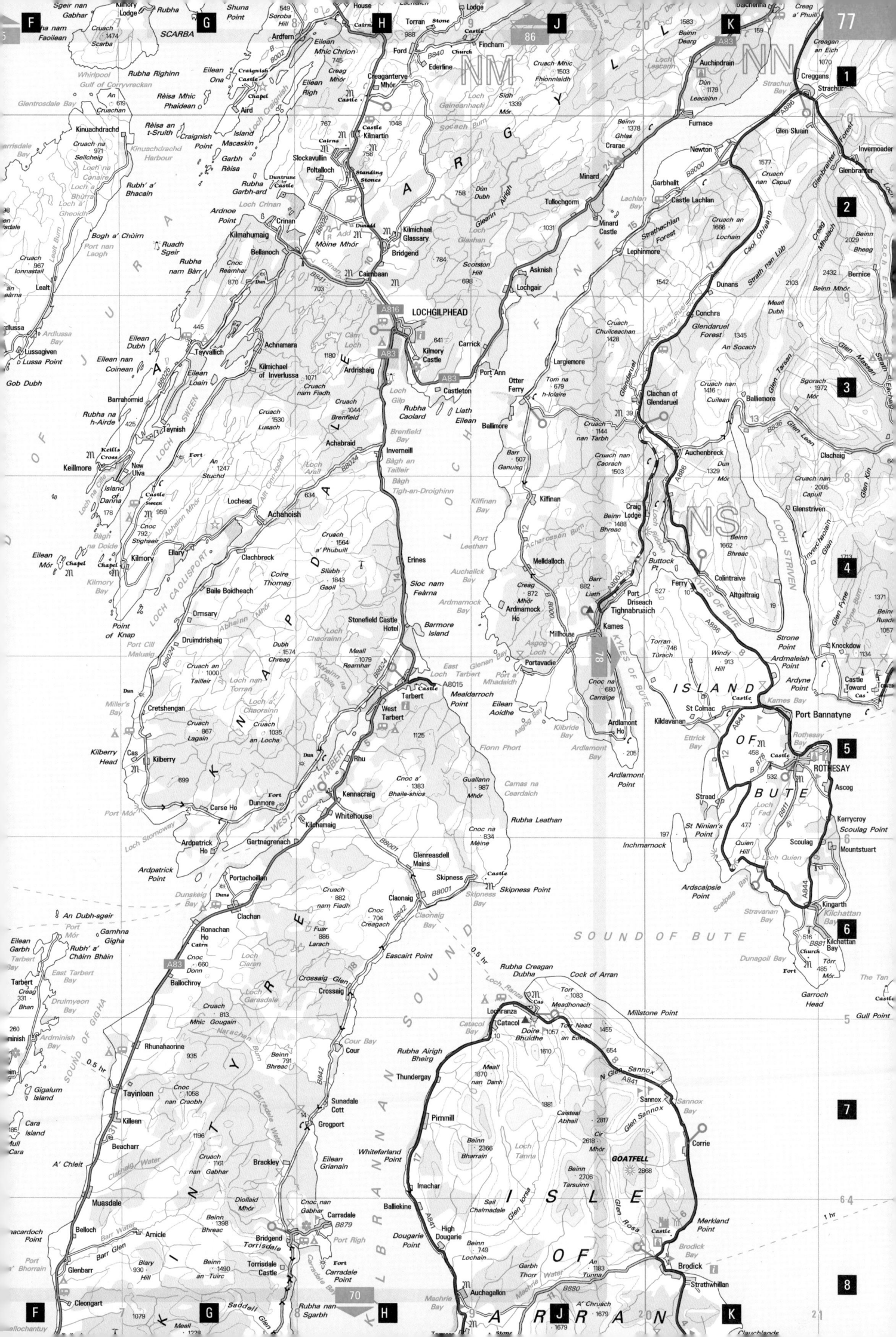

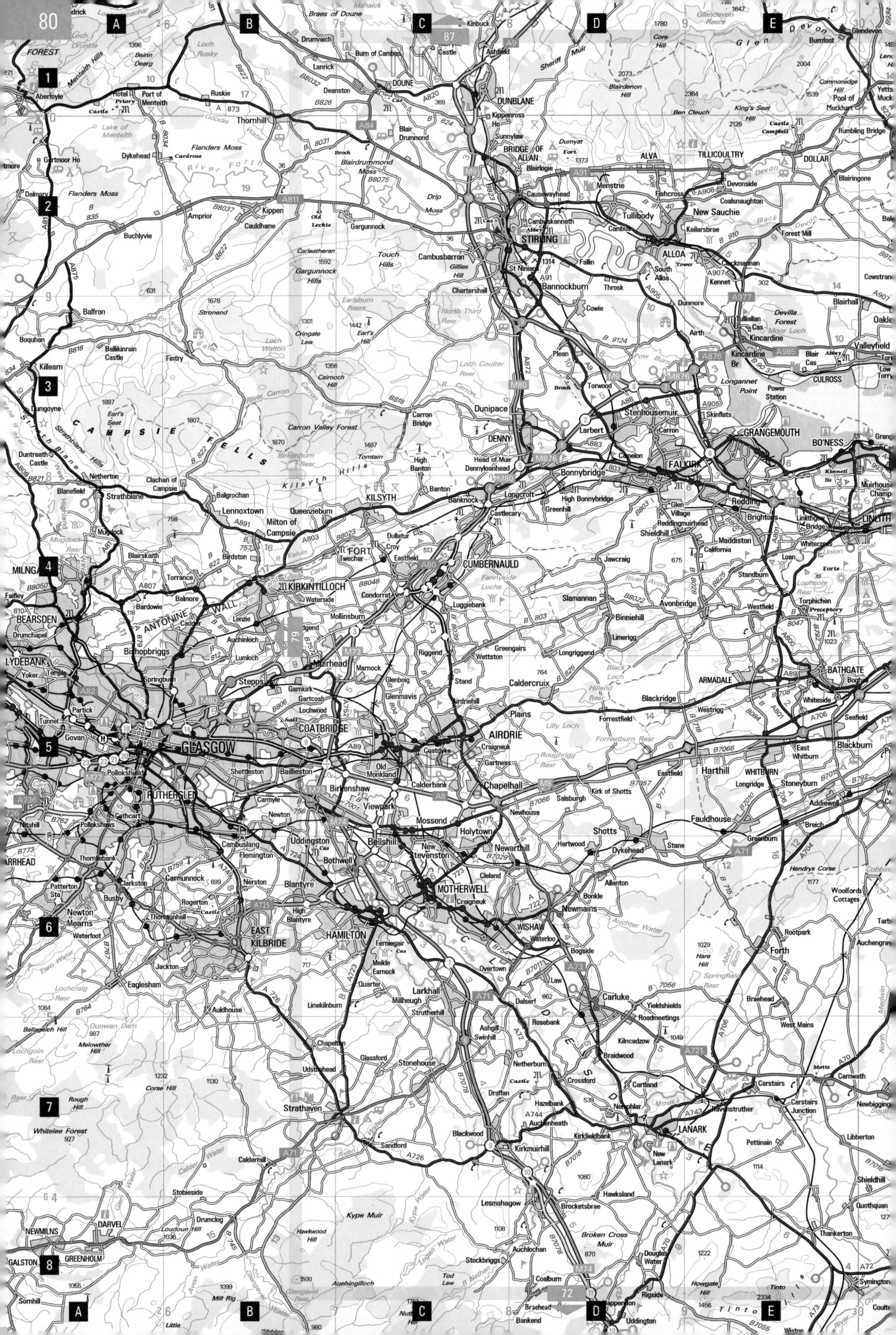

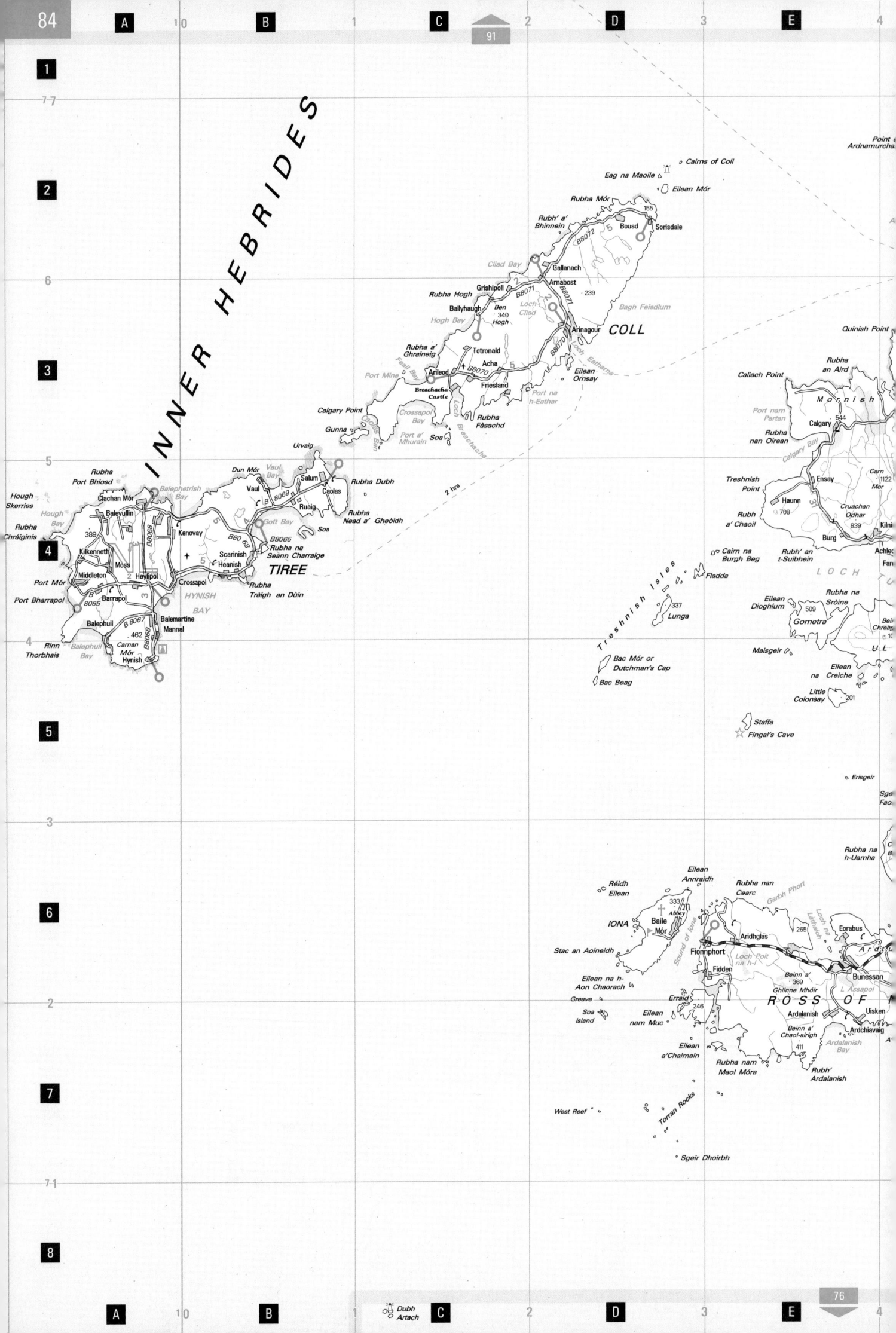

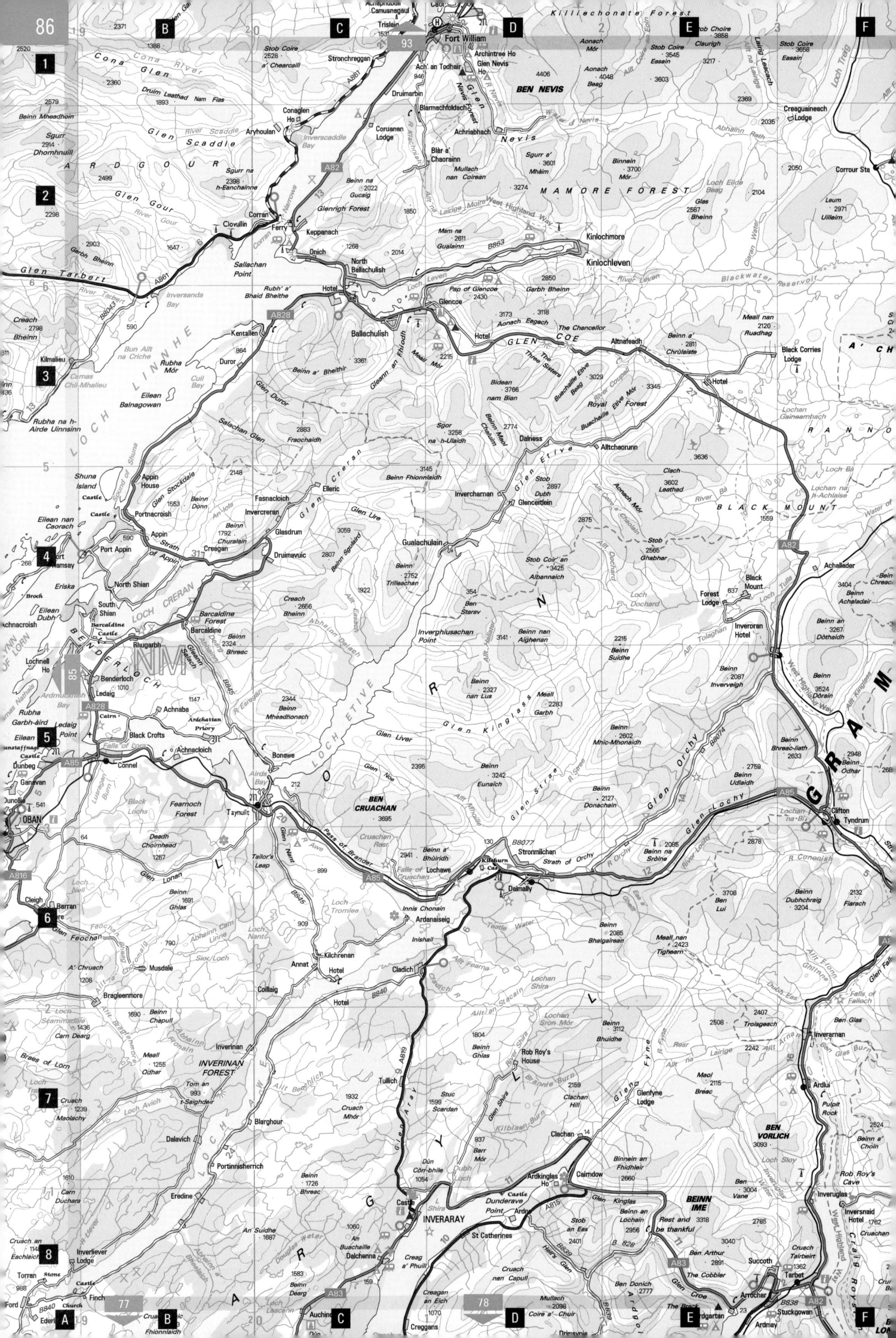

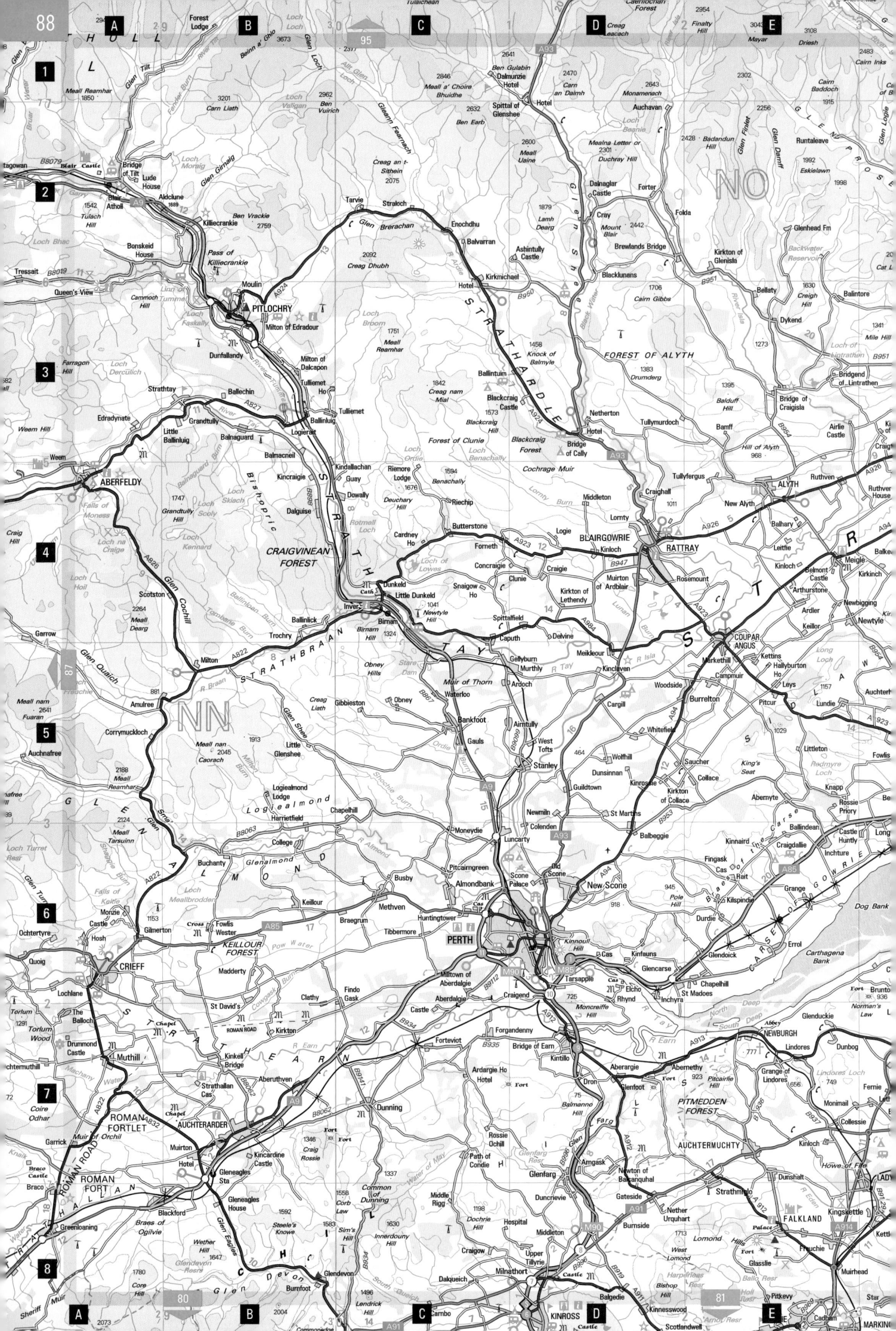

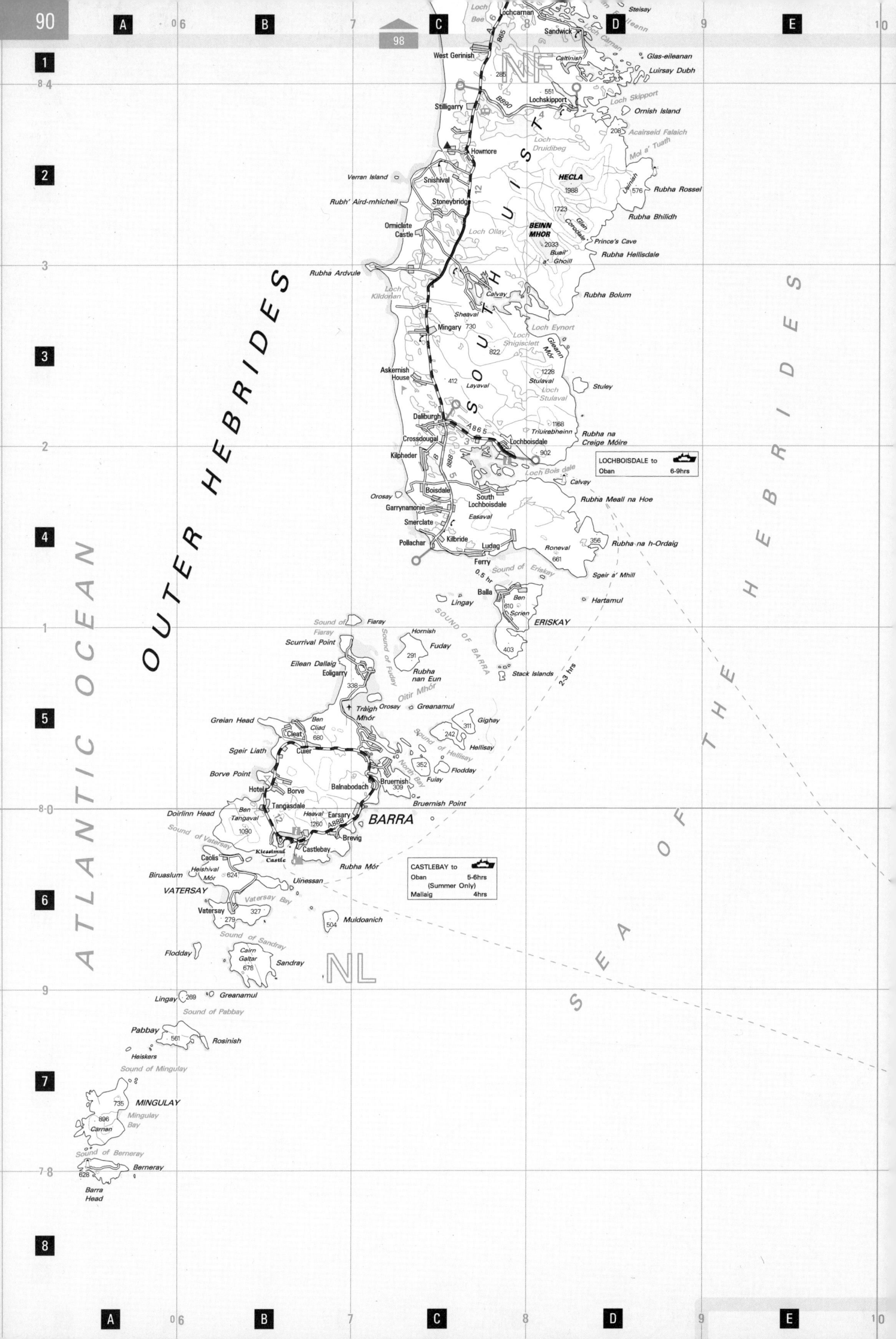

LOCHBOISDALE to
Oban   6-9hrs

CASTLEBAY to
Oban   5-6hrs
(Summer Only)
Mallaig   4hrs

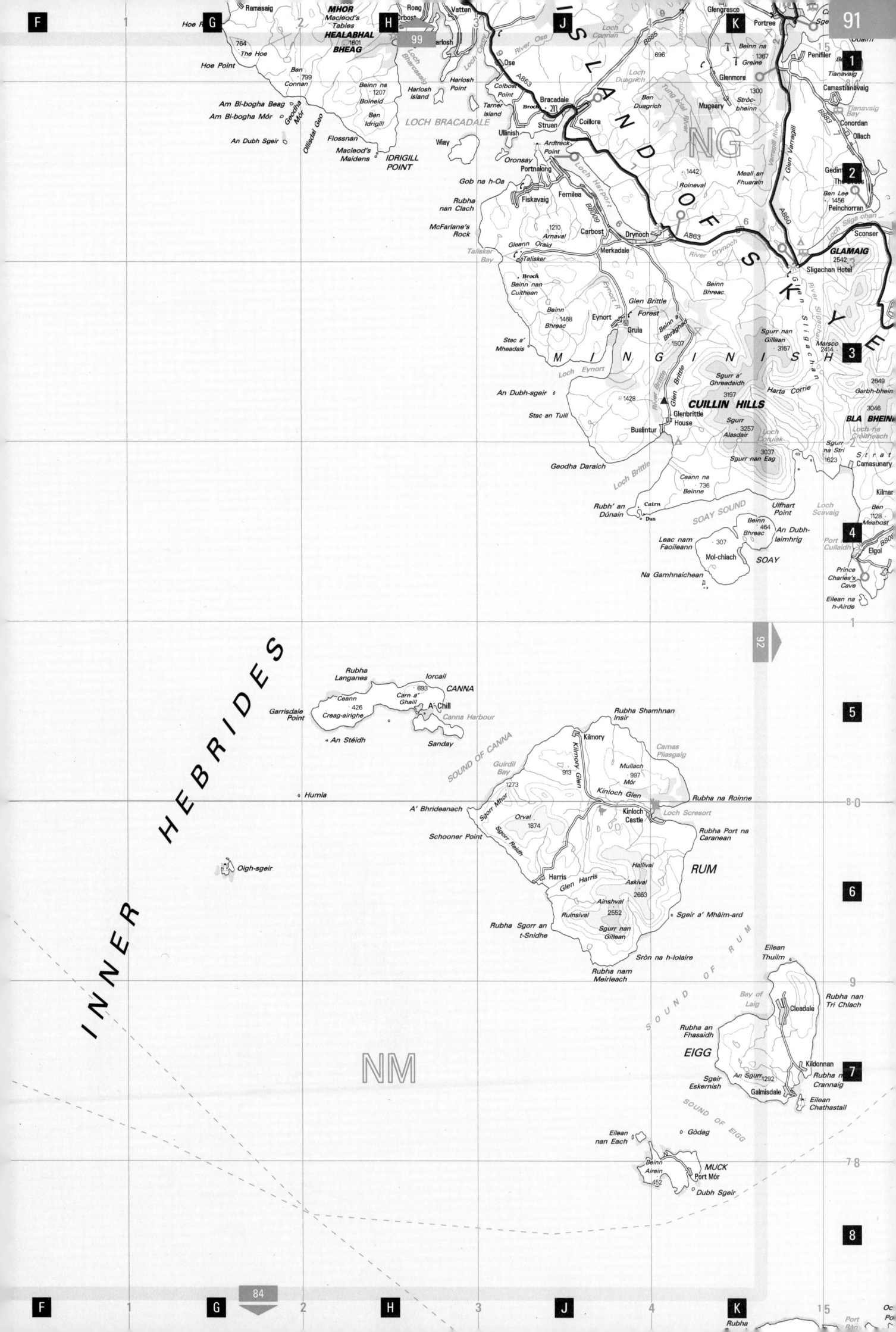

ISLAND OF SKYE

NG

INNER HEBRIDES

CANNA

RUM

EIGG

MUCK

SOAY

CUILLIN HILLS

MINGINISH

NM

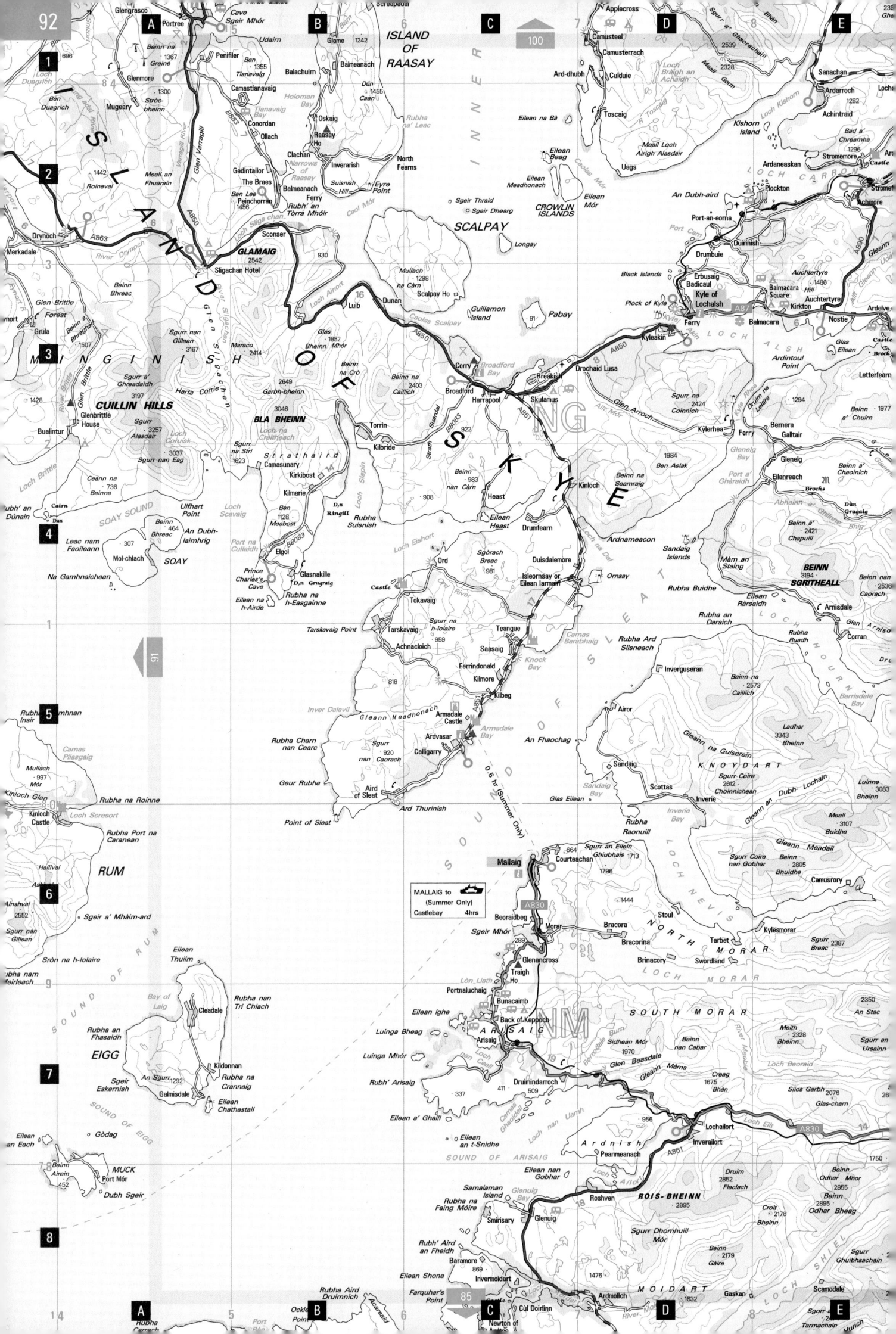

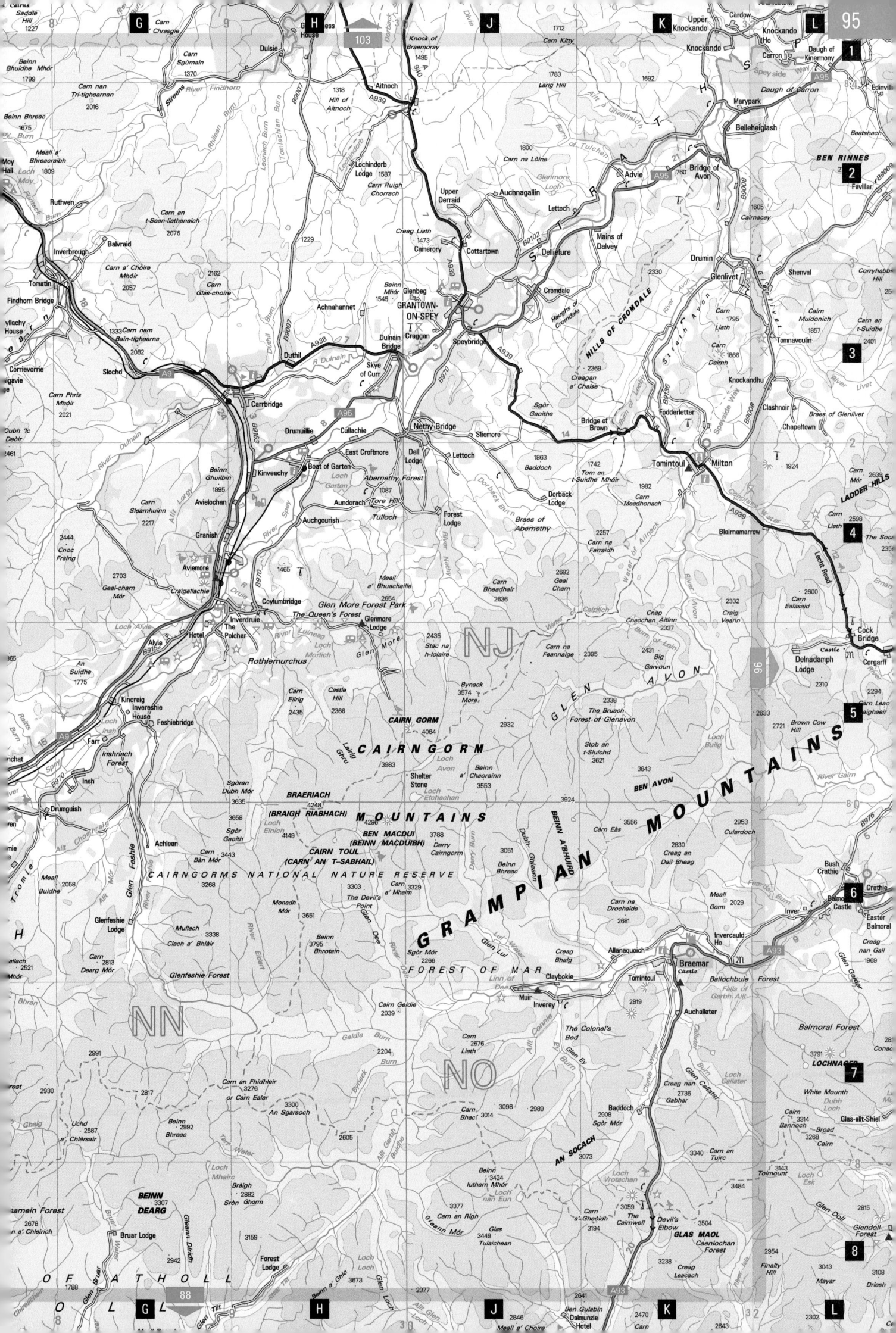

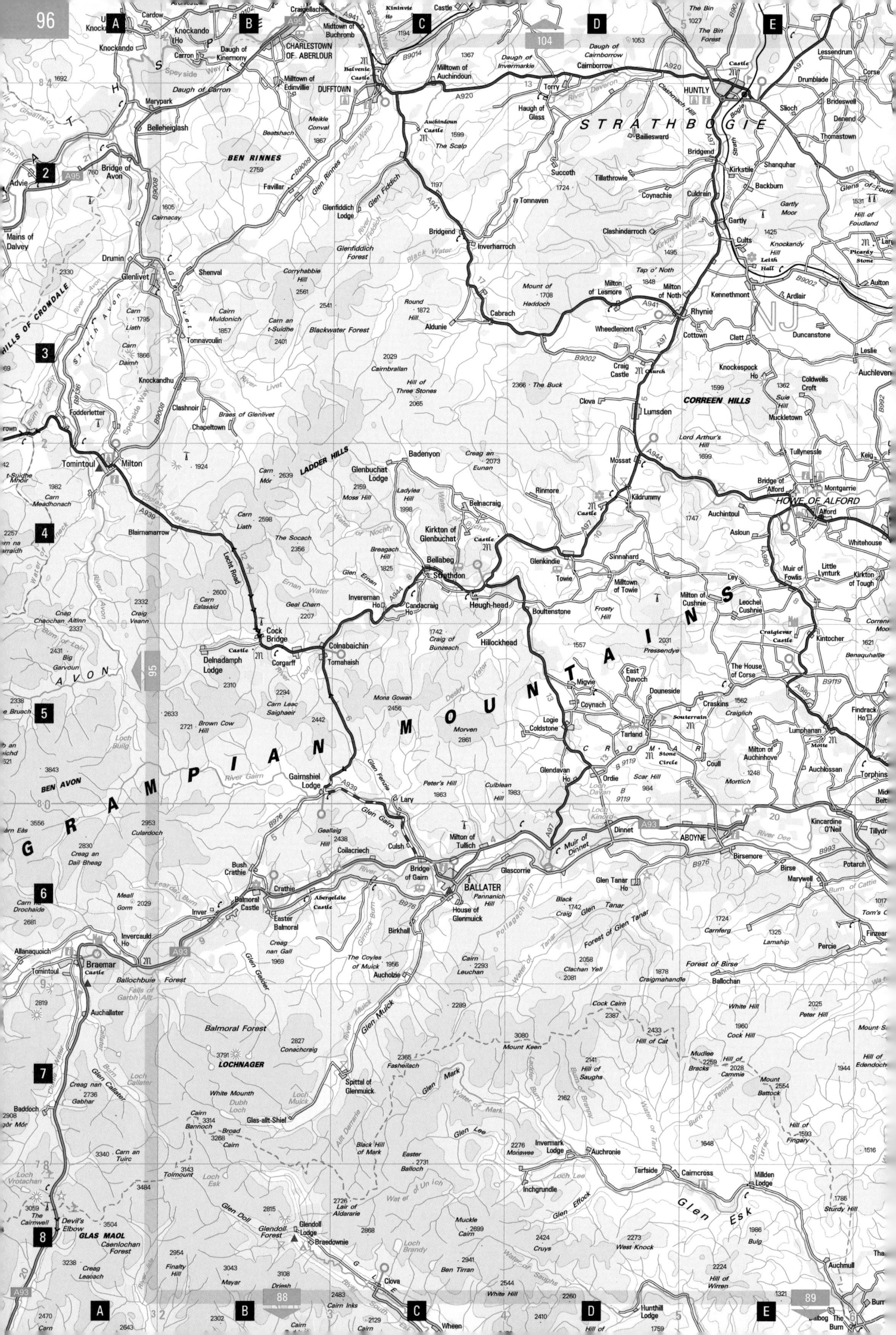

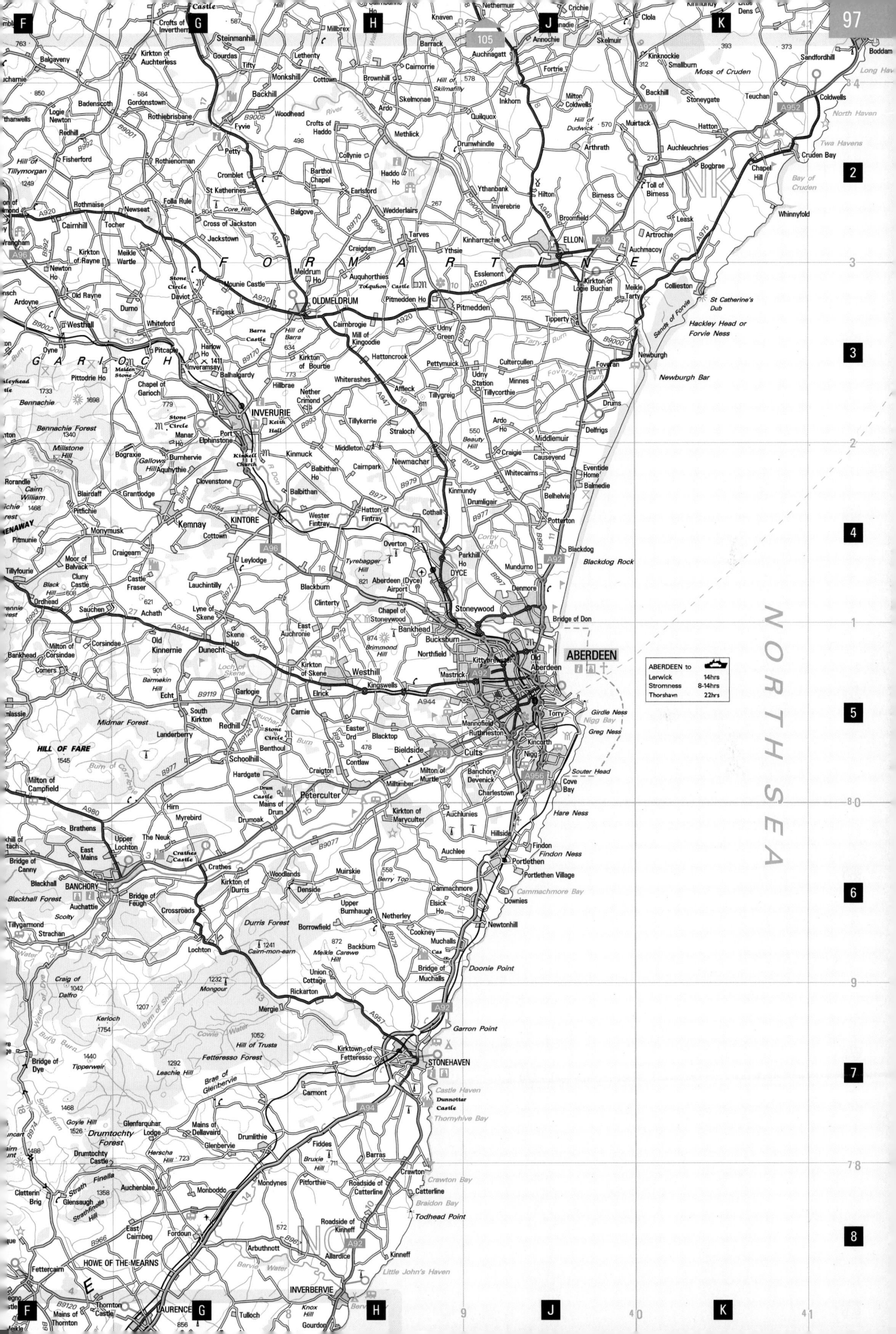

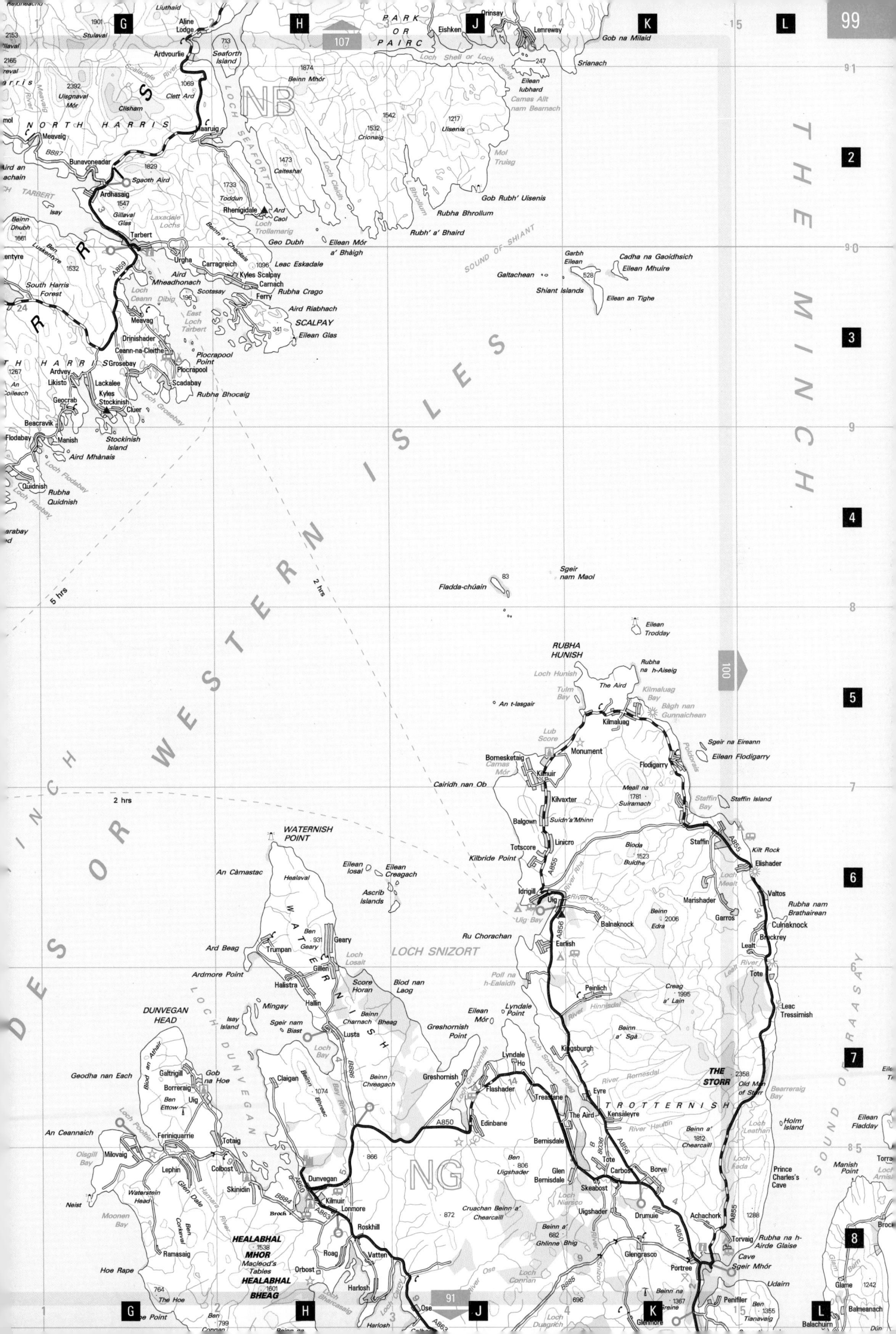

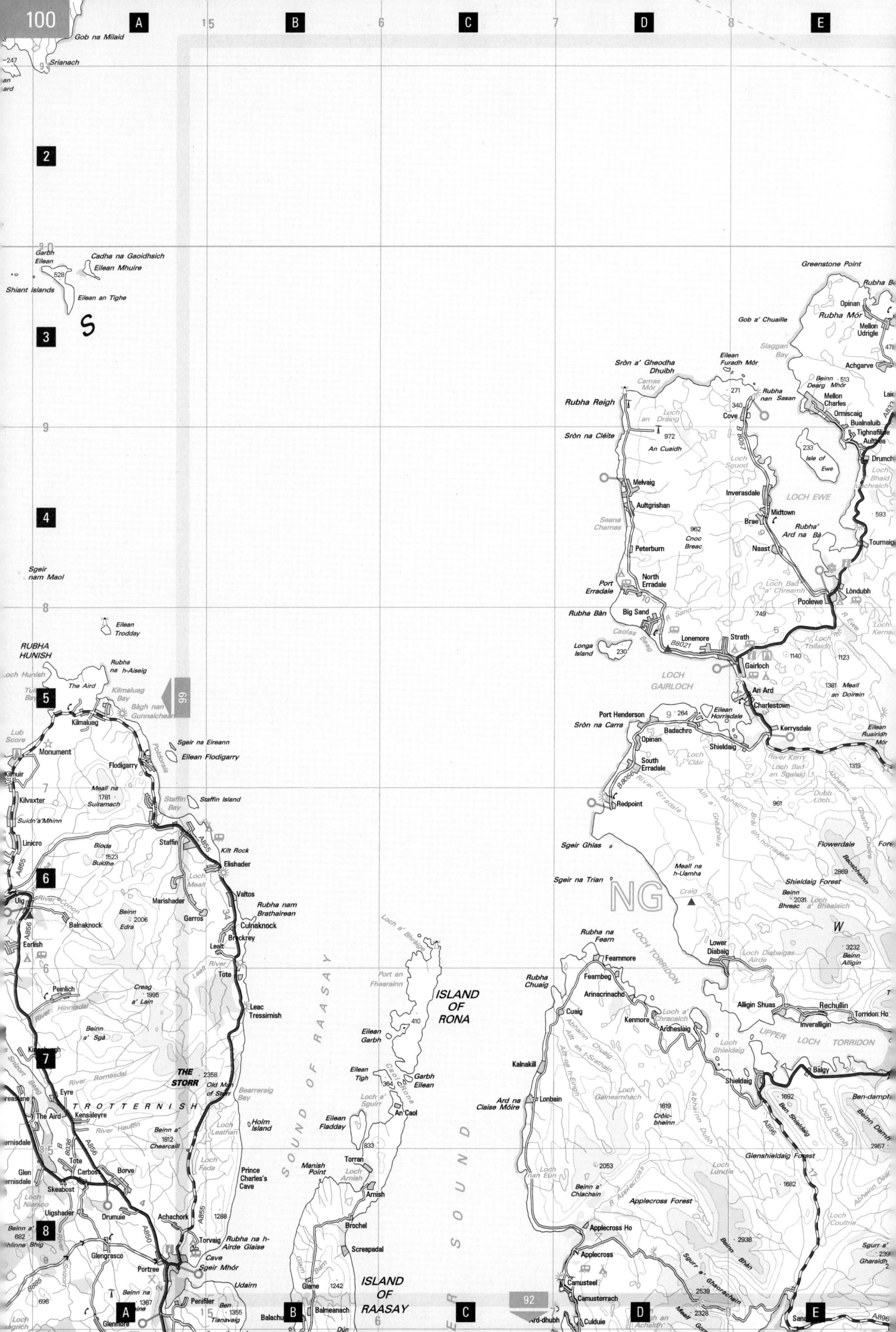

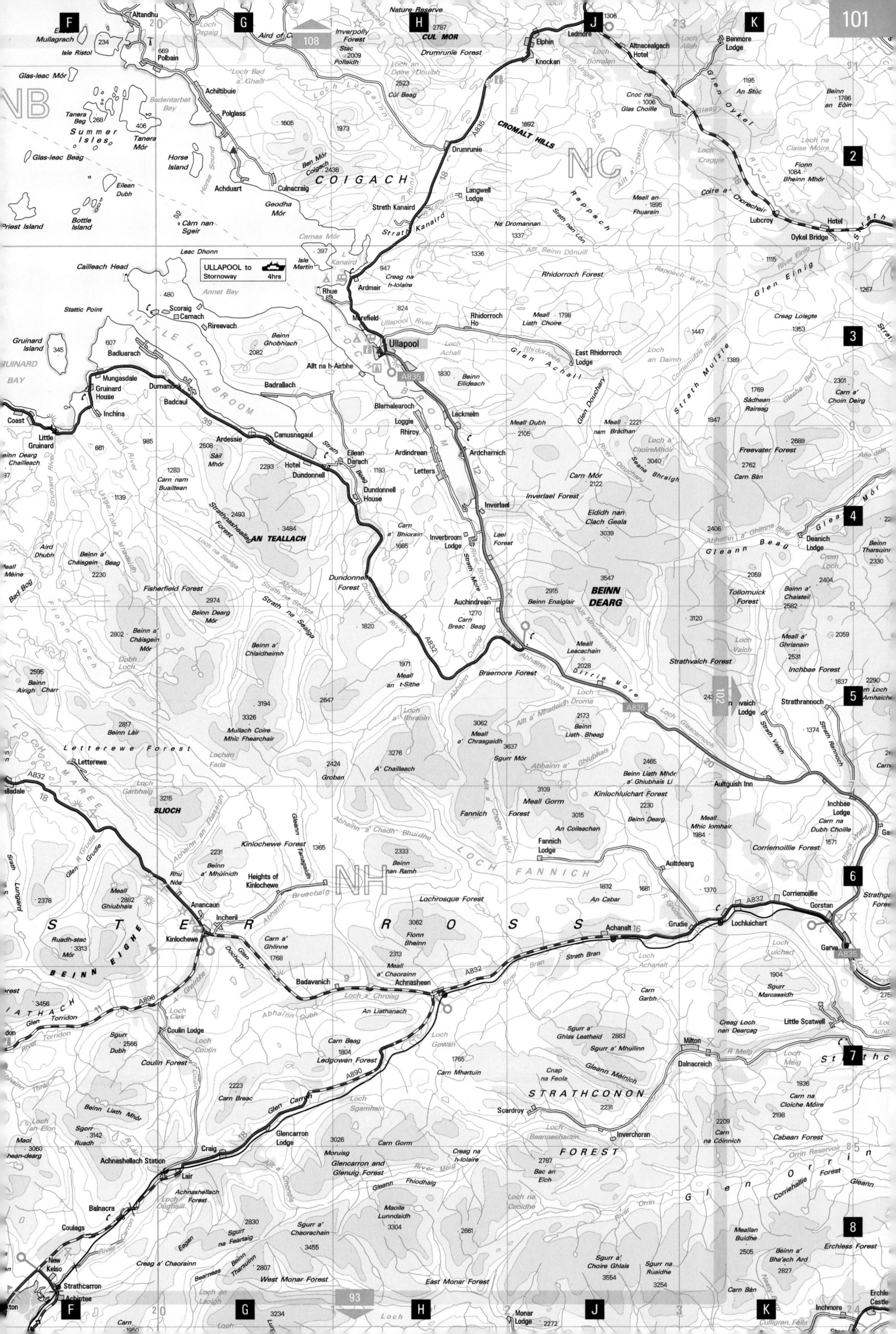

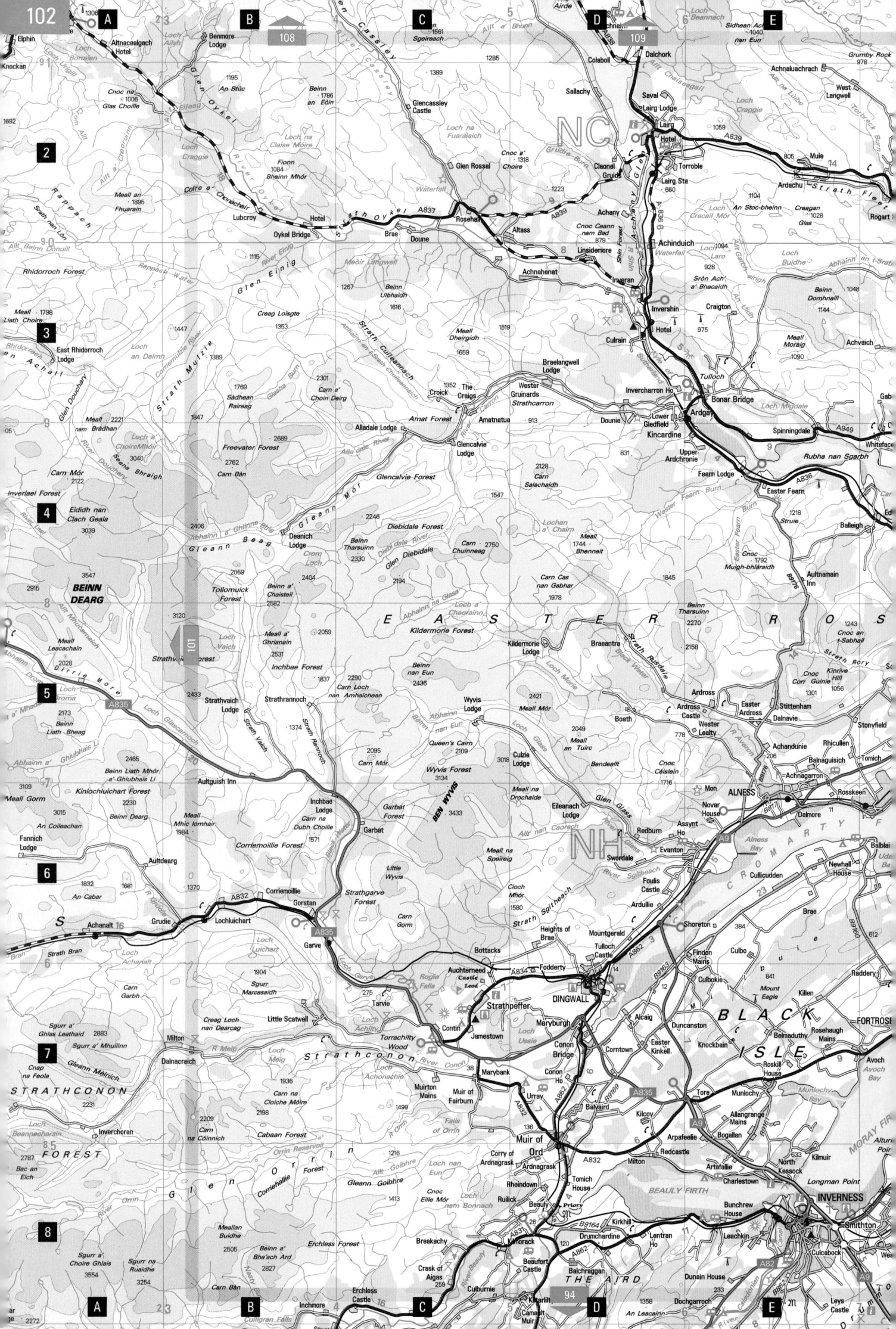

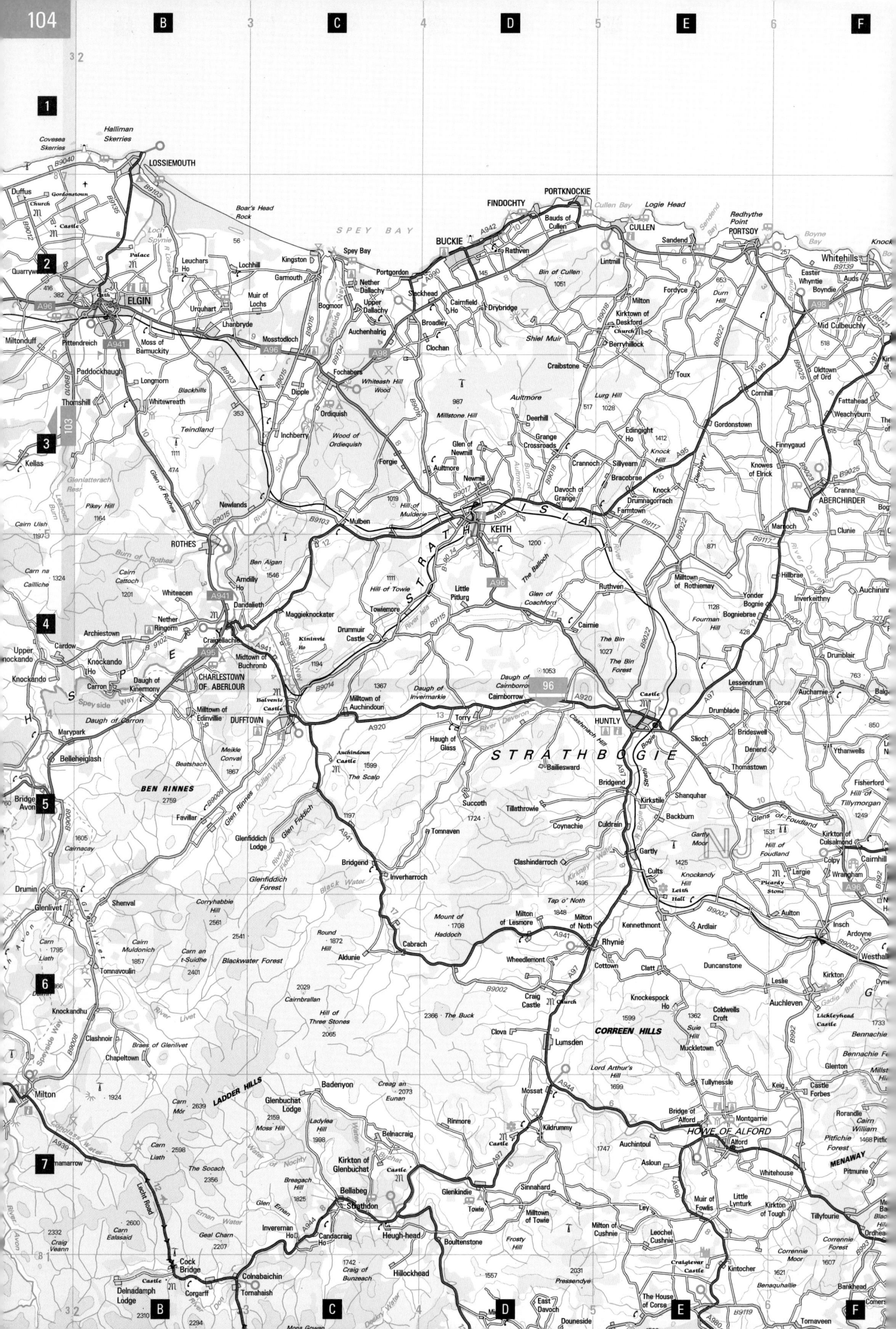

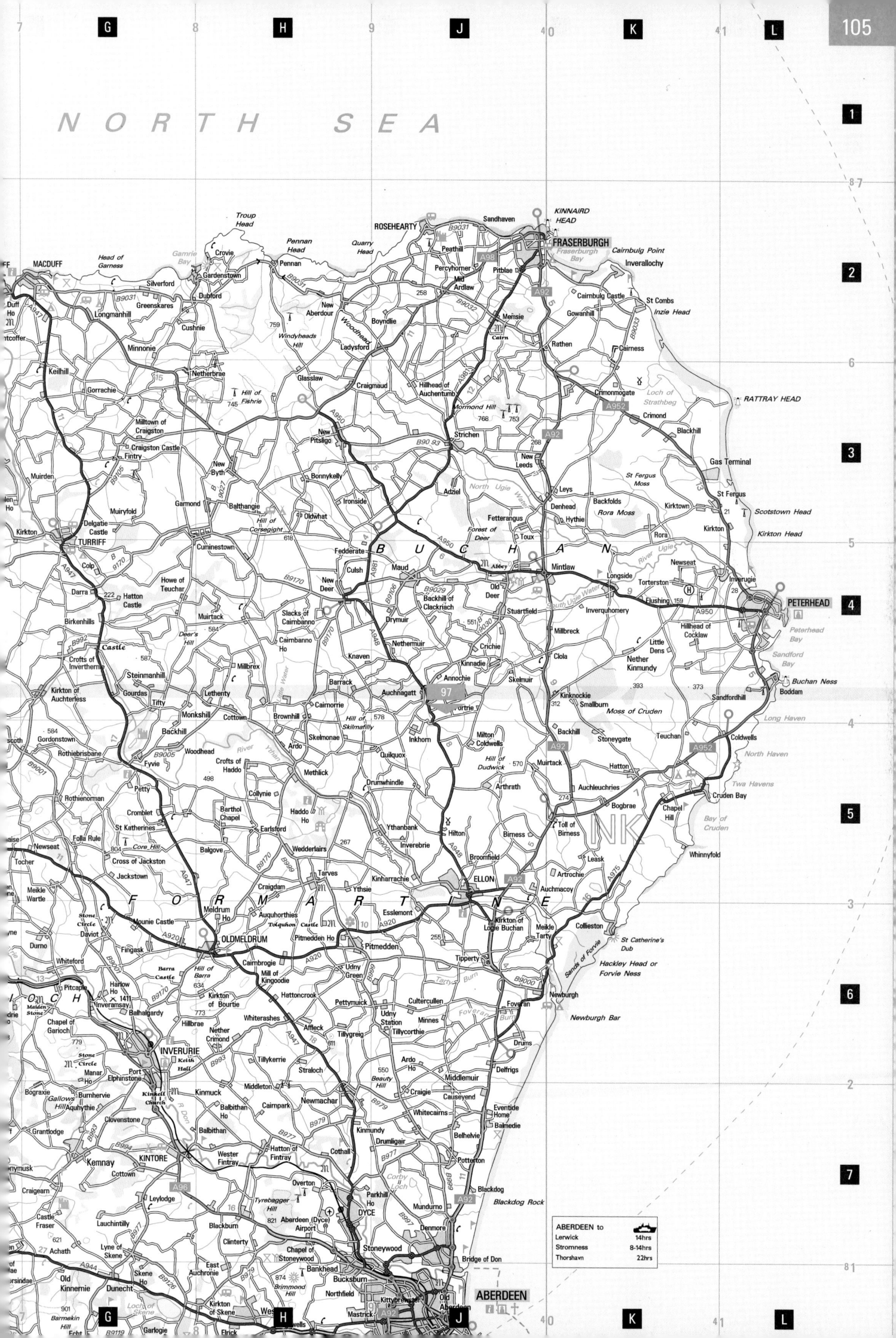

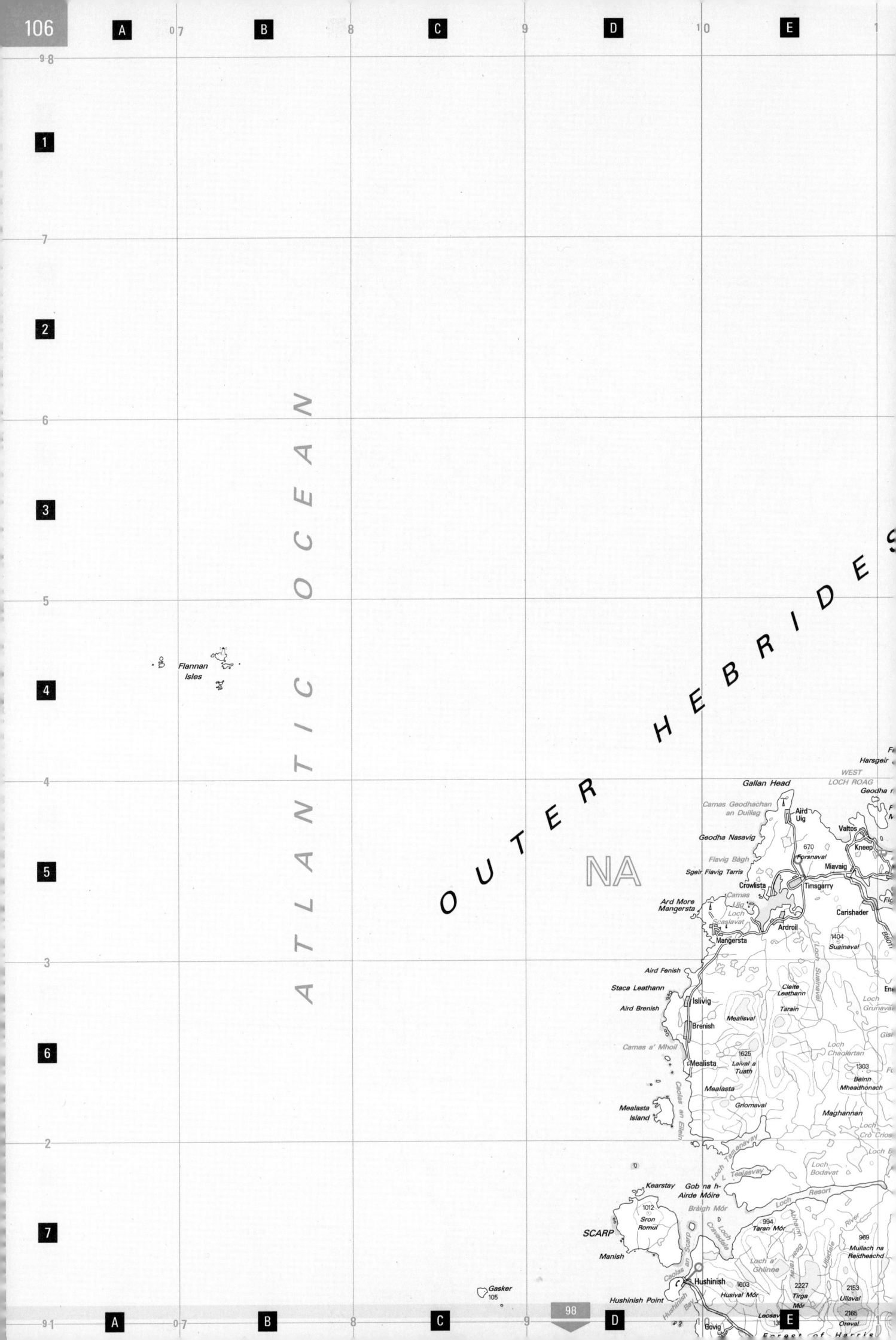

ATLANTIC OCEAN

OUTER HEBRIDES

NA

Flannan
Isles

Gasker
105

SCARP

Manish

Kearstay

Sron
Romul

1012

Gob na h-
Airde Móire

Bràigh Mór

Taran Mór
994

Mullach na
Reidheachd
969

Hushinish
Hushinish Point

Govig

1603
Husival Mór

Tirga
Mór
2227

Ullaval
2153

Oreval

Leaosaval
Forest of Harris

Gallan Head

Camas Geodhachan
an Duilisg

Aird
Uig

WEST
LOCH ROAG

Geodha
Harsgeir

Geodha Nasavig

Valtos

Fiavig Bàgh

670

Forsnaval

Kneep

Sgeir Fiavig Tarris

Miavaig

Crowlista

Timsgarry

Ard More
Mangersta

Camas
Uig
Loch
Scaslavat

Carishader

Ardroil

1404
Suainaval

Mangersta

Aird Fenish

Staca Leathann

Aird Brenish

Islivig

Cleite
Leathann

Tarain

Loch
Grunava

Mealisval

Brenish

Camas a' Mhoil

Mealista

1625

Laival a
Tuath

Loch
Chaolartan

1303

Beinn
Mheadhonach

Loch
Mealasta

Griomaval

Maghannan

Mealasta
Island

Loch
Crò Crios

Loch B

Loch Tamanavay

L. Taalasvay

Loch
Bodavat

Loch
Resort

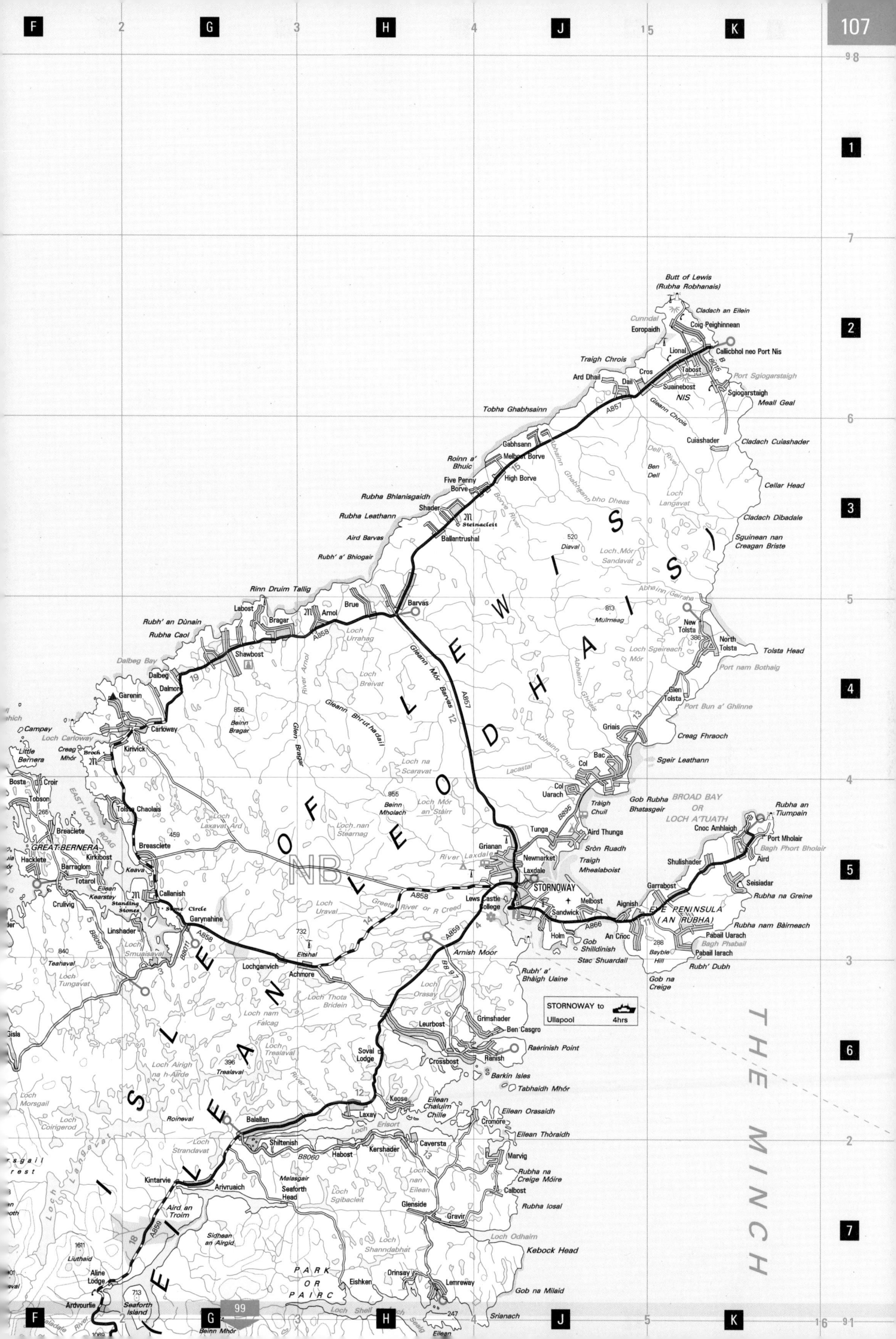

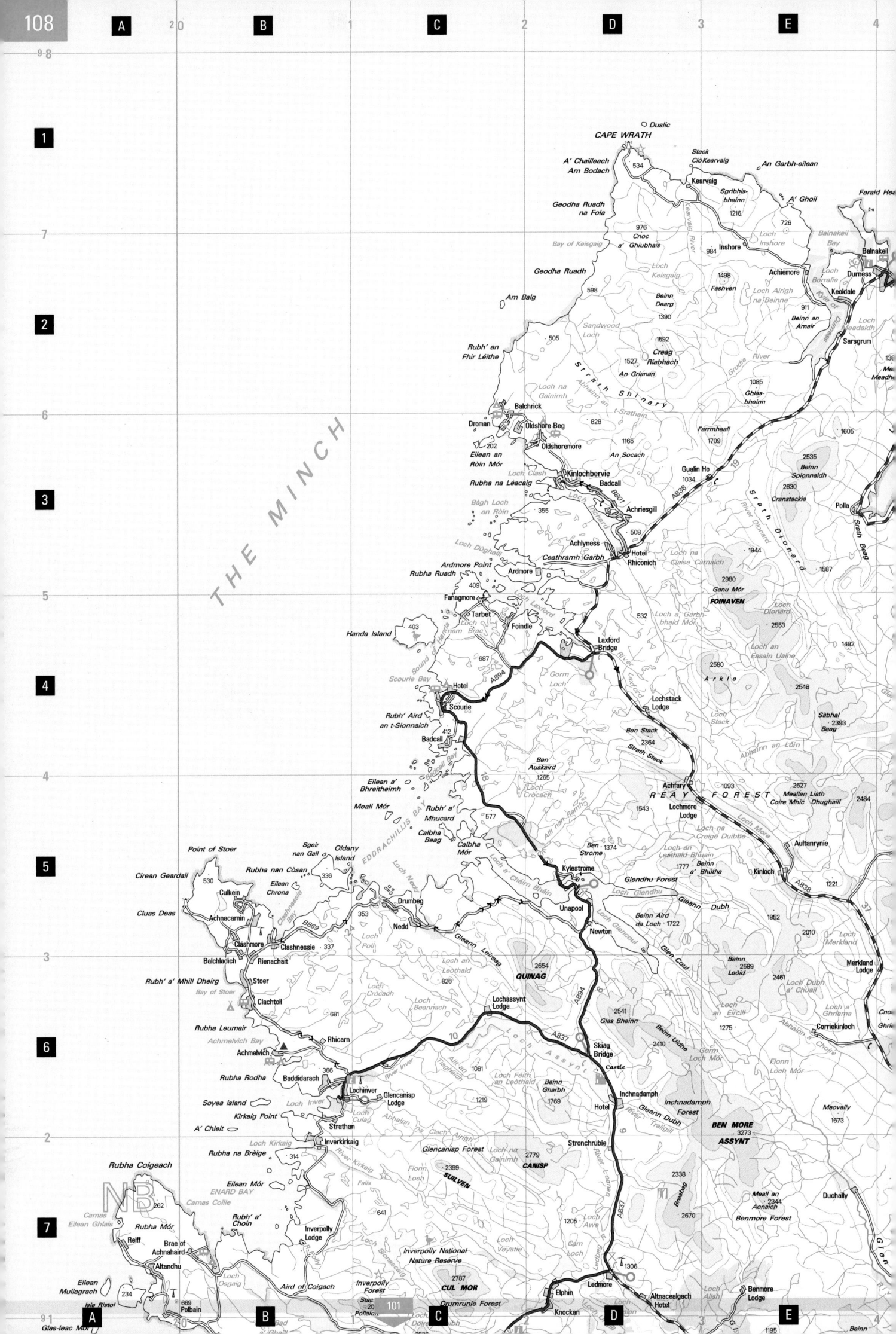

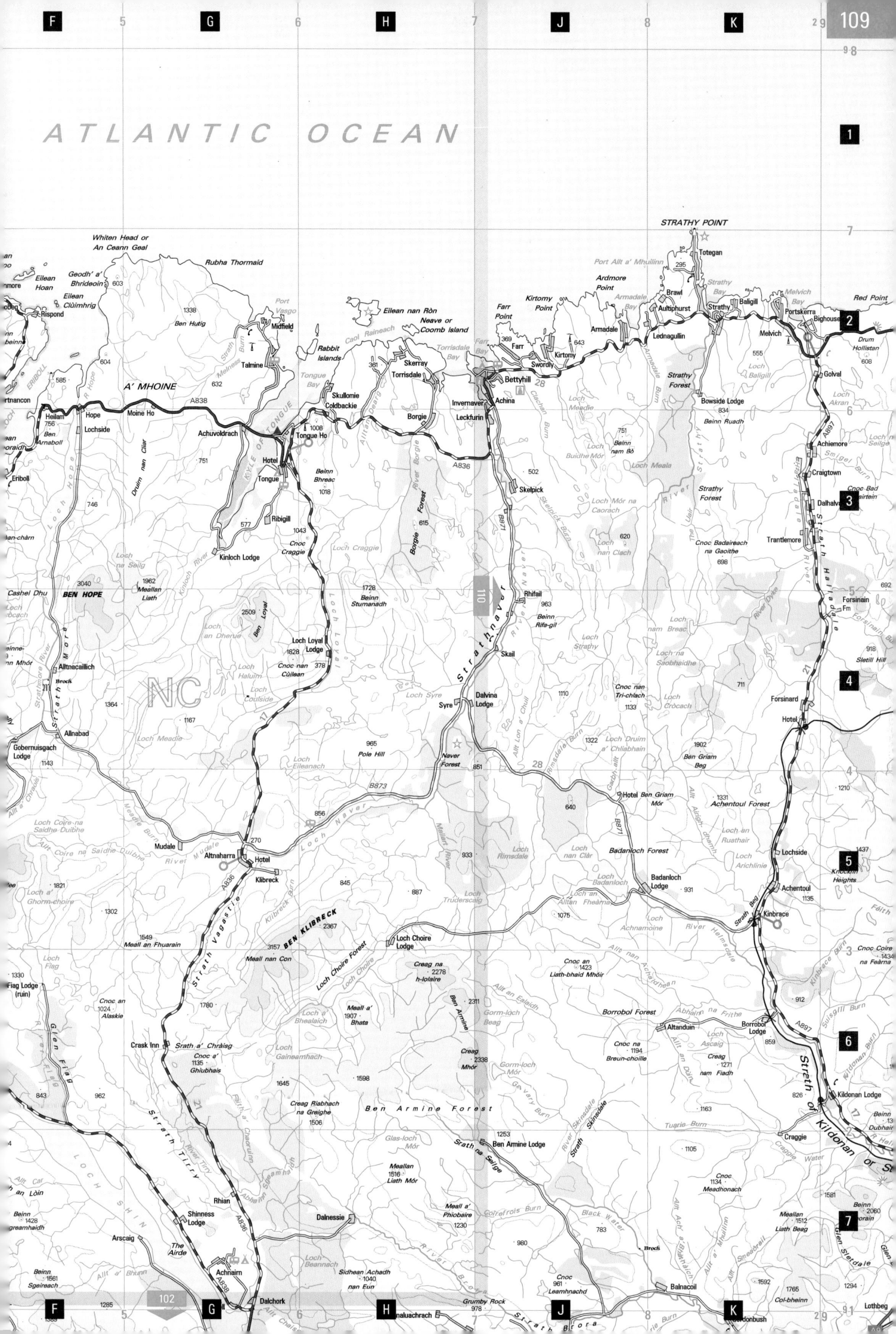

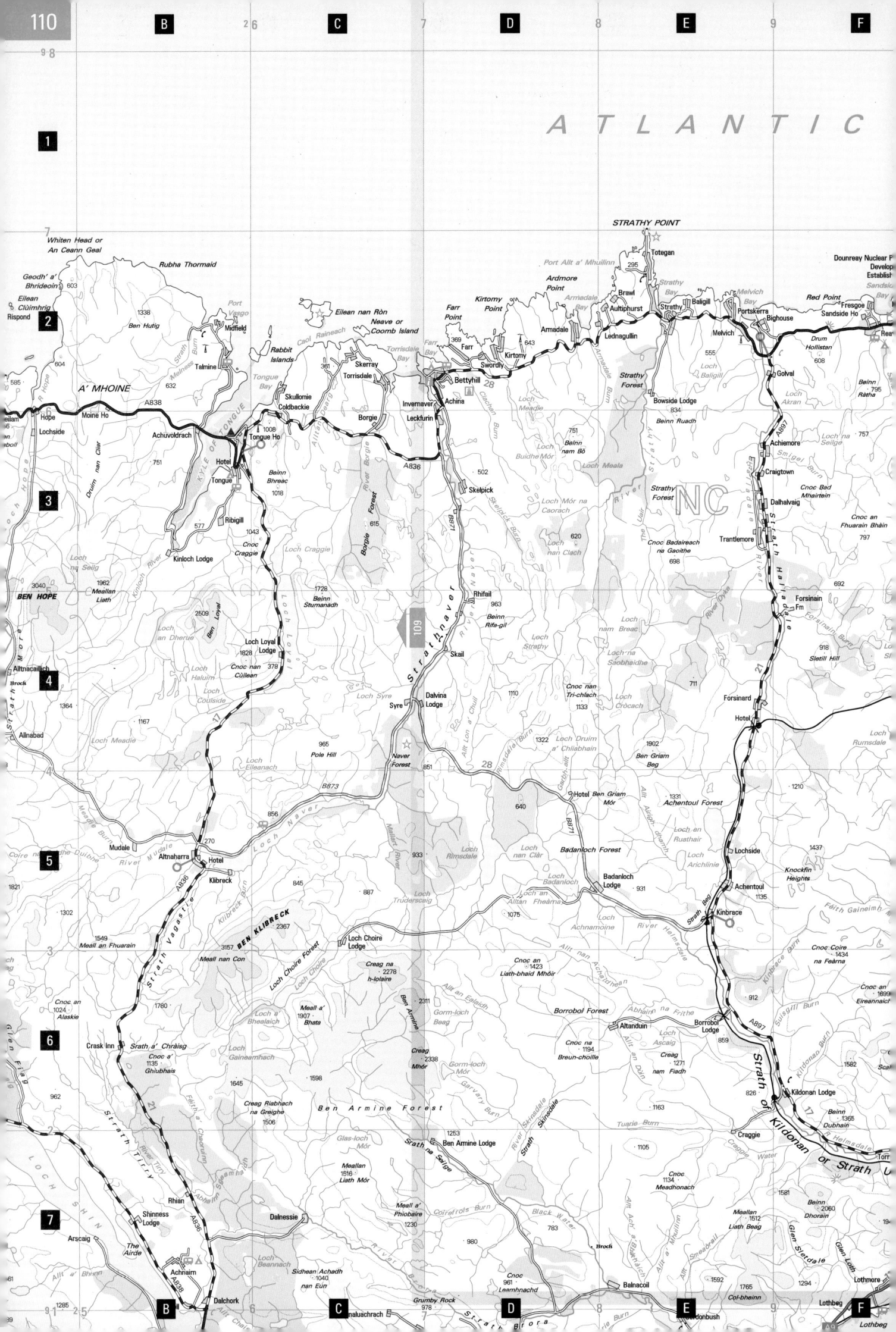

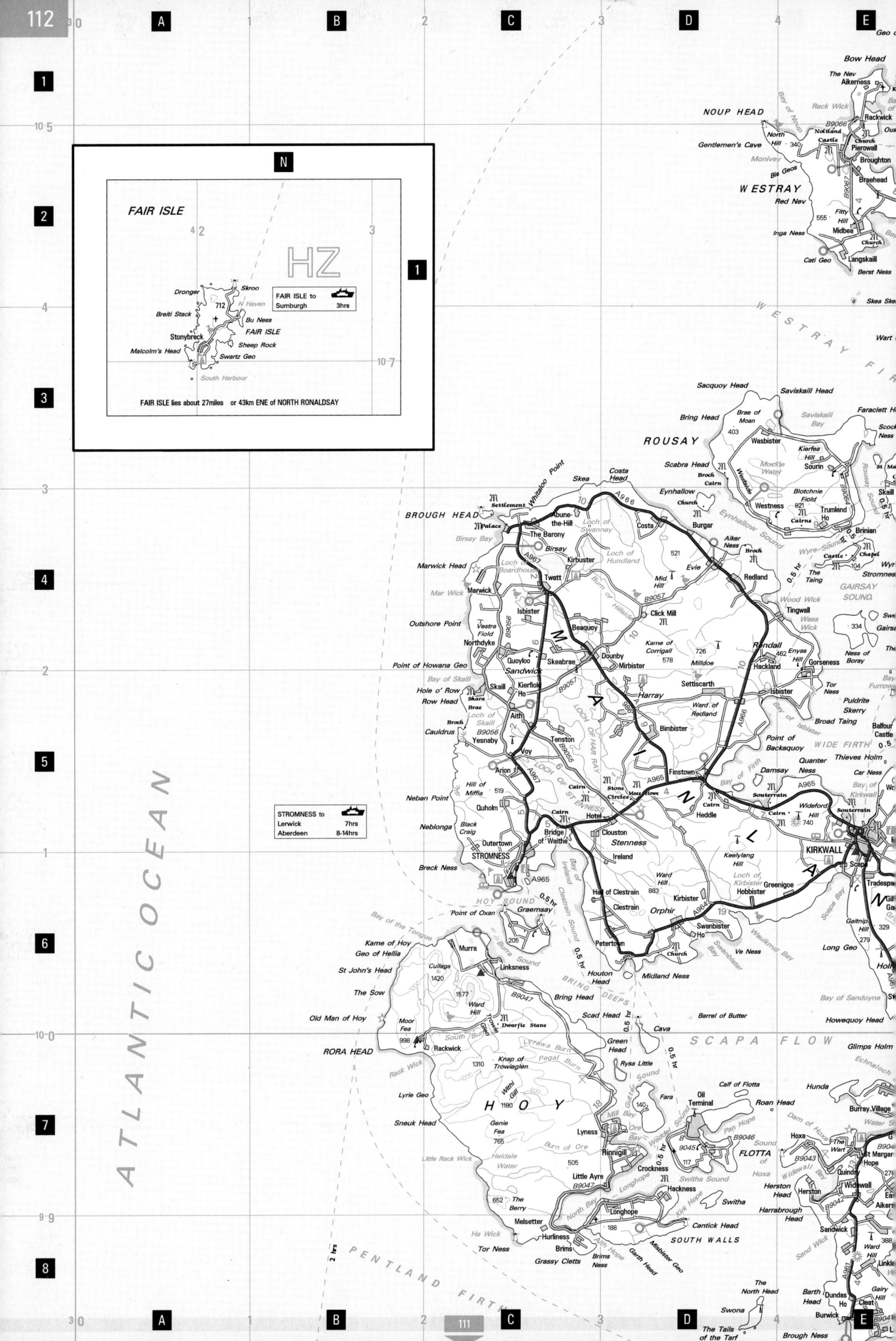

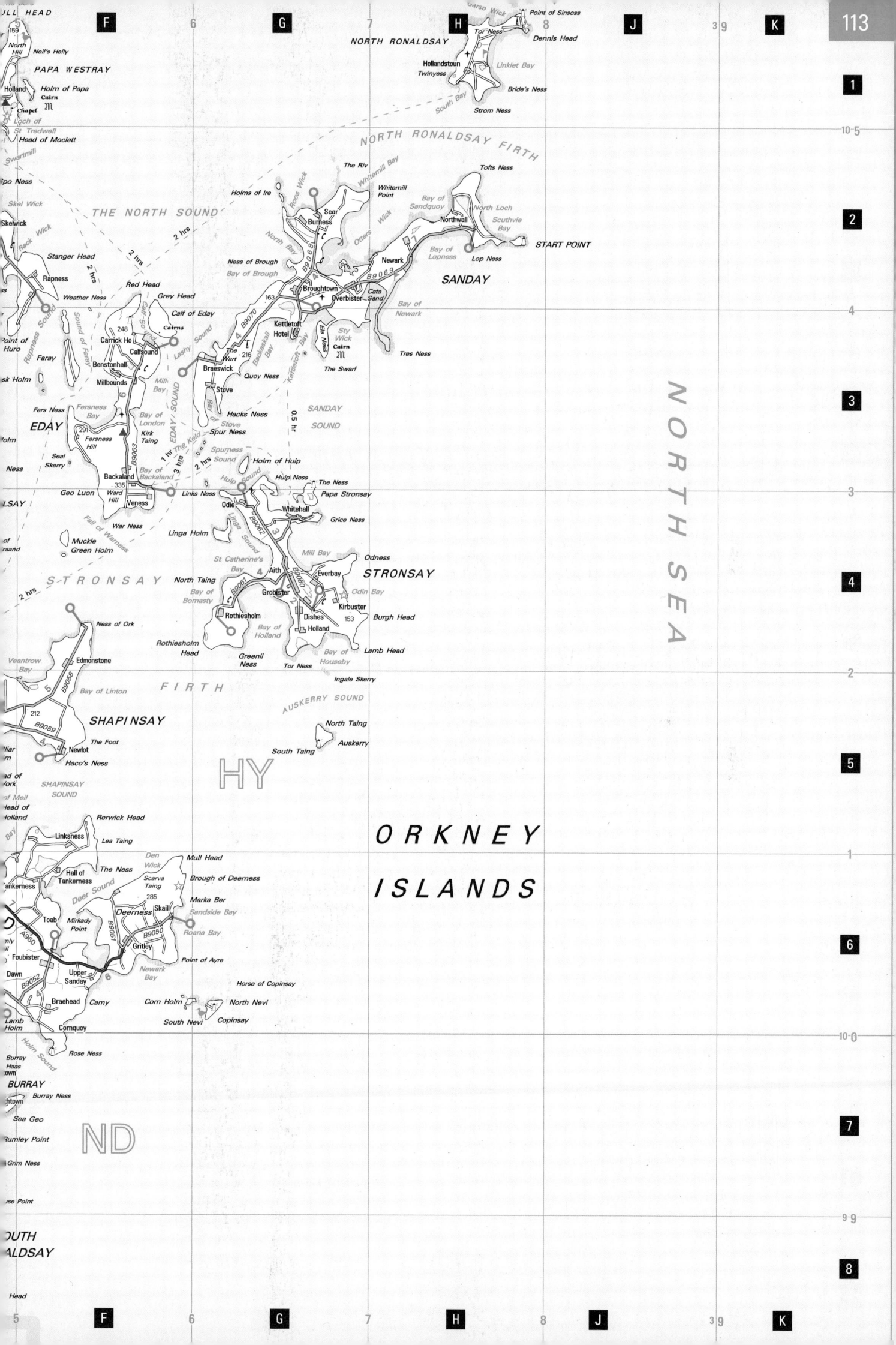

A 3 9 B 4 0 C 1 D E

ESHA NESS · Braehoulland · Burnside
Scraada · Sae Breck · Tangwick · Hillswick
2 205 · The Bruddans · Ness of Hillswick
Isle of Stenness · Stenness
Skerry of Eshaness · Dore Holm · The Drongs · Baa Taing
Isle of Nibon

ST MAGNUS BAY

Lang Head

Eg

116

Erne Stac

Strom Ness

MUCKLE ROE

Murbie Stacks

Swarbacks Head

Ve Skerries

Cribbie · North Ness · Vementry · Cairn
Fogla Skerry · Virda Field · PAPA STOUR · Gruna
285 · Isle of West Burrafirth · Brindister
Biggings · Holm of Melby · West Burrafirth · Noonsbrough
Sound of Papa · Melby-Ho · Garth · Unifirth
Quilva Taing · Sandness · A971 · West Burrafirth · Sulma Water
Pund Head · Sandness Hill · 817 · Burga Water · Loch of Voxterby

SHETLAND ISLANDS

Bay of Deepdale
Dale · Burn of Dale · 567 · Stoulbrough Hill · Bridge of Walls
Mu Ness · 12 · 246 · Stam
Voe of Dale · A971 · Browland
Wats Ness · Mid Walls · Walls
Skarpigarth · Burraland · Gruting
Braga Ness · Valla Sound · Ward of Culswick
Uskie Geo · Vaila Hall · Culswick
Vaila · 268 · 390
Strom Ness · Broch · Housa Water · West Ske
The Nev · Westerwick · 355
Giltarump · Wester Wick · Sil Wick
West Moulie Geo

ATLANTIC OCEAN

HT
Da Logat · Strem Ness
The Kame · Harrier
Da Scrodhurdins · 1373 · Ham · Head o' da Taing
Wester Hoevdi · The Sneug · 600 · FOULA
Wick of Mucklabrek · Hametoun
Hellabrick's Wick · Hesti Geo
South Ness

A 3 9 B 4 0 C 1 D 2 E

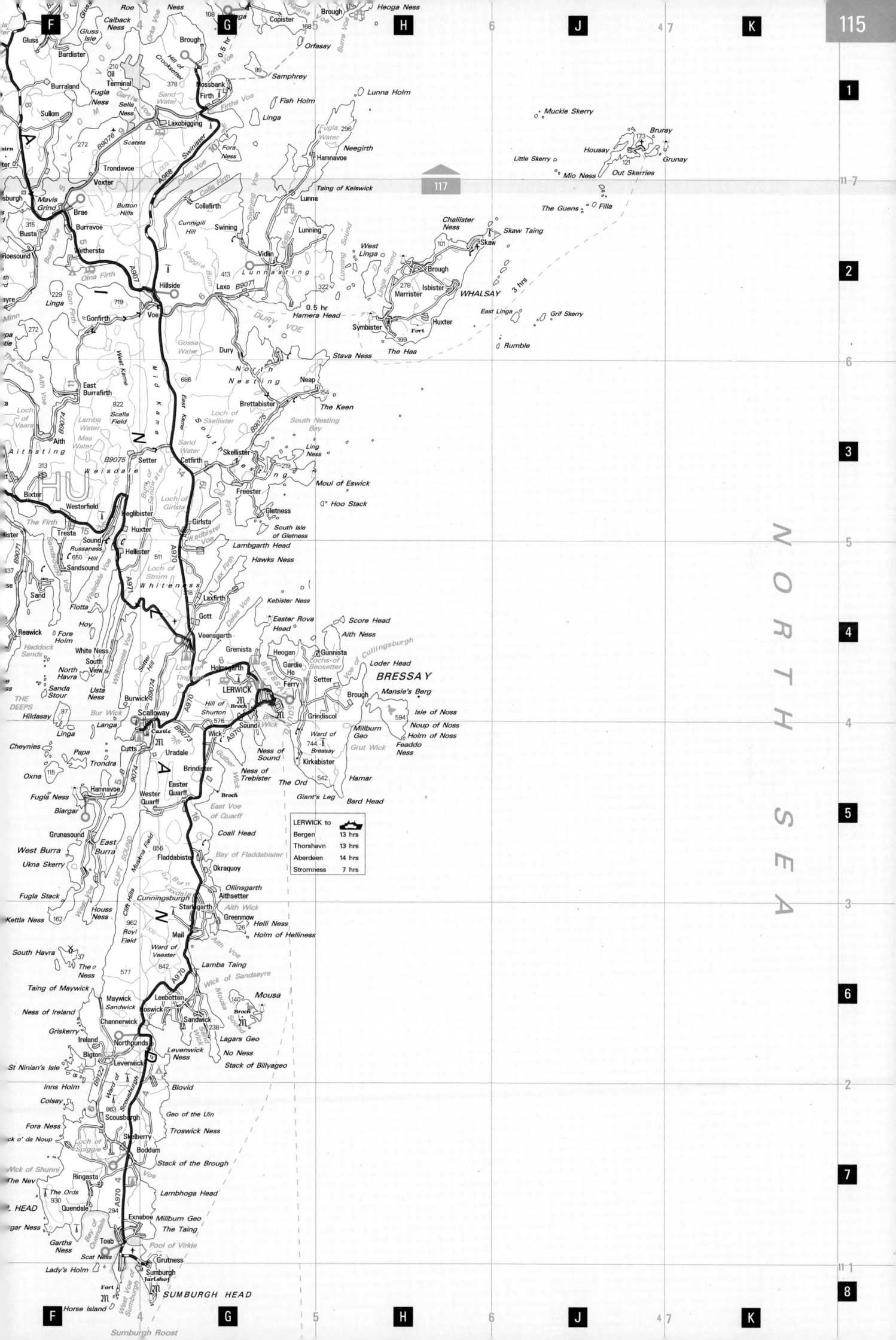

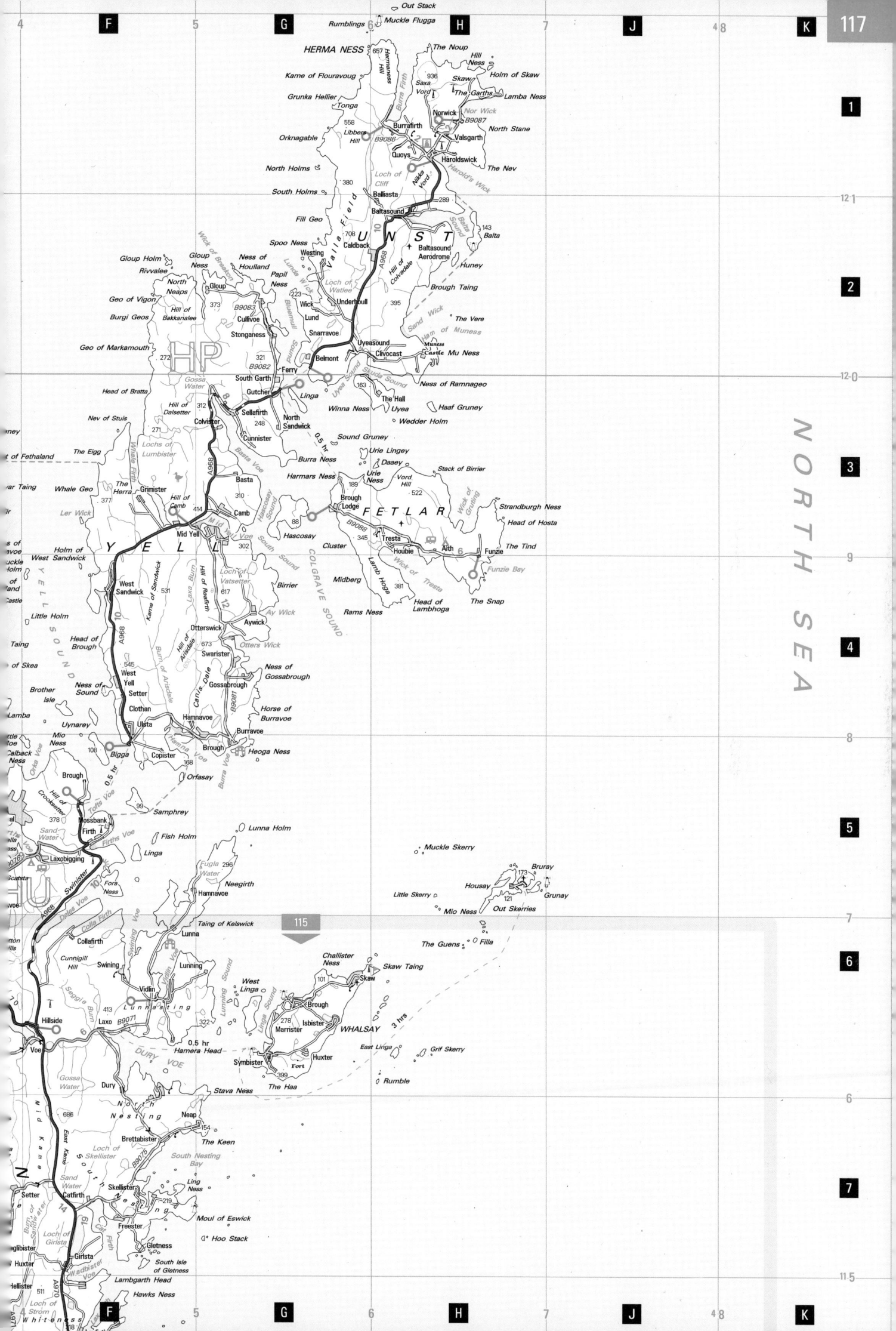

NORTH SEA

HERMA NESS

UNST

YELL

FETLAR

WHALSAY

LONDON AREA

Legend to urban area mapping
Scale 1 : 85000 or about 1 inch to 1⅓ miles

🚉 Principal British Rail station	
● Other British Rail station	
⊖ Underground/Metro station	
→ Selected one-way traffic routes	
✝ Church	

Motorway	
Primary Route	
Main Road	
Secondary Road	
Minor Road	

Dual Carriageway
Dual Carriageway
Dual Carriageway
Dual Carriageway

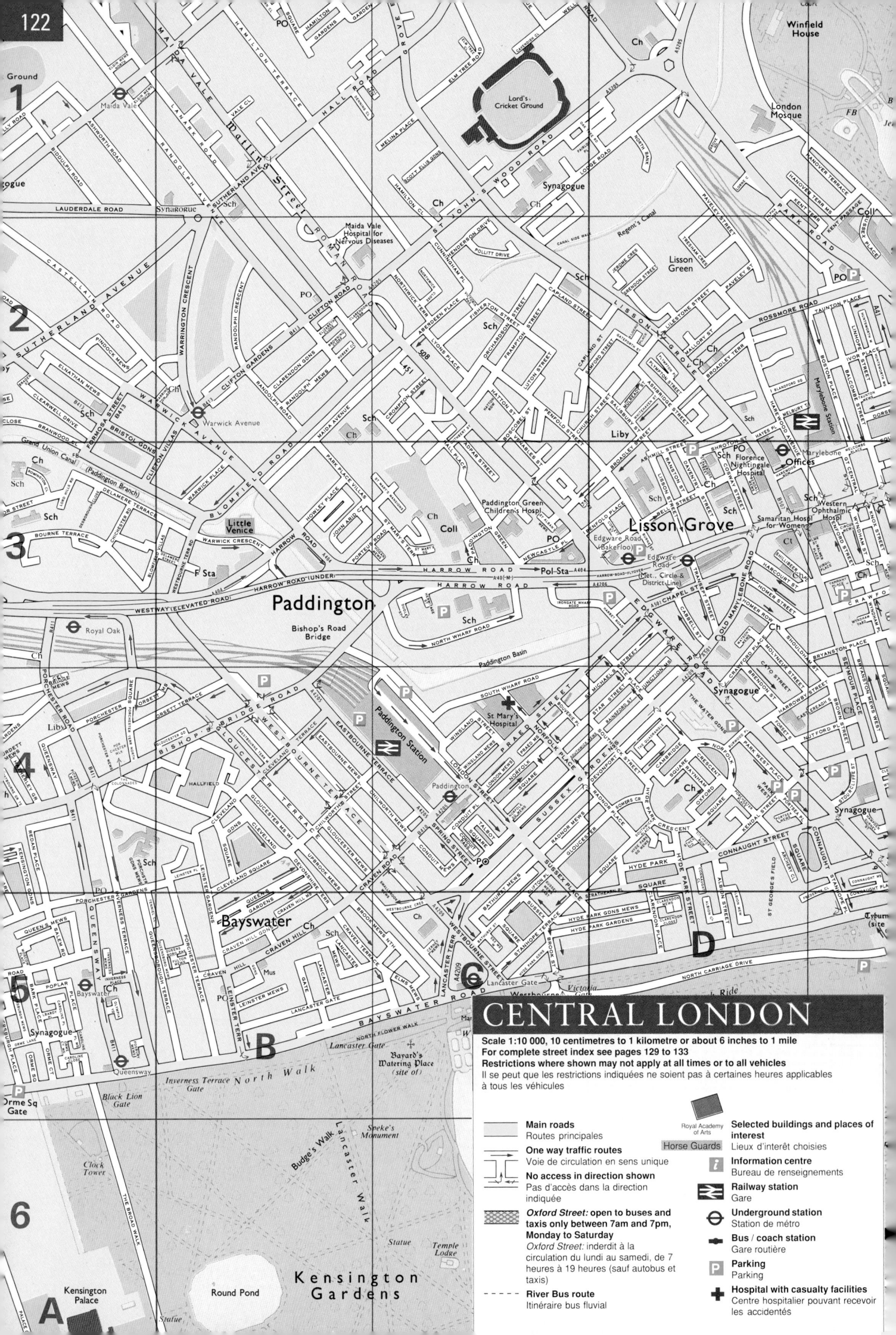

CENTRAL LONDON

Scale 1:10 000, 10 centimetres to 1 kilometre or about 6 inches to 1 mile
For complete street index see pages 129 to 133
Restrictions where shown may not apply at all times or to all vehicles
Il se peut que les restrictions indiquées ne soient pas à certaines heures applicables
à tous les véhicules

Main roads	Selected buildings and places of interest
Routes principales	
One way traffic routes	Lieux d'intérêt choisies
Voie de circulation en sens unique	Information centre
No access in direction shown	Bureau de renseignements
Pas d'accès dans la direction indiquée	Railway station
	Gare
Oxford Street: open to buses and taxis only between 7am and 7pm, Monday to Saturday	Underground station
Oxford Street: interdit à la circulation du lundi au samedi, de 7 heures à 19 heures (sauf autobus et taxis)	Station de métro
	Bus / coach station
	Gare routière
	Parking
	Parking
River Bus route	Hospital with casualty facilities
Itinéraire bus fluvial	Centre hospitalier pouvant recevoir les accidentés

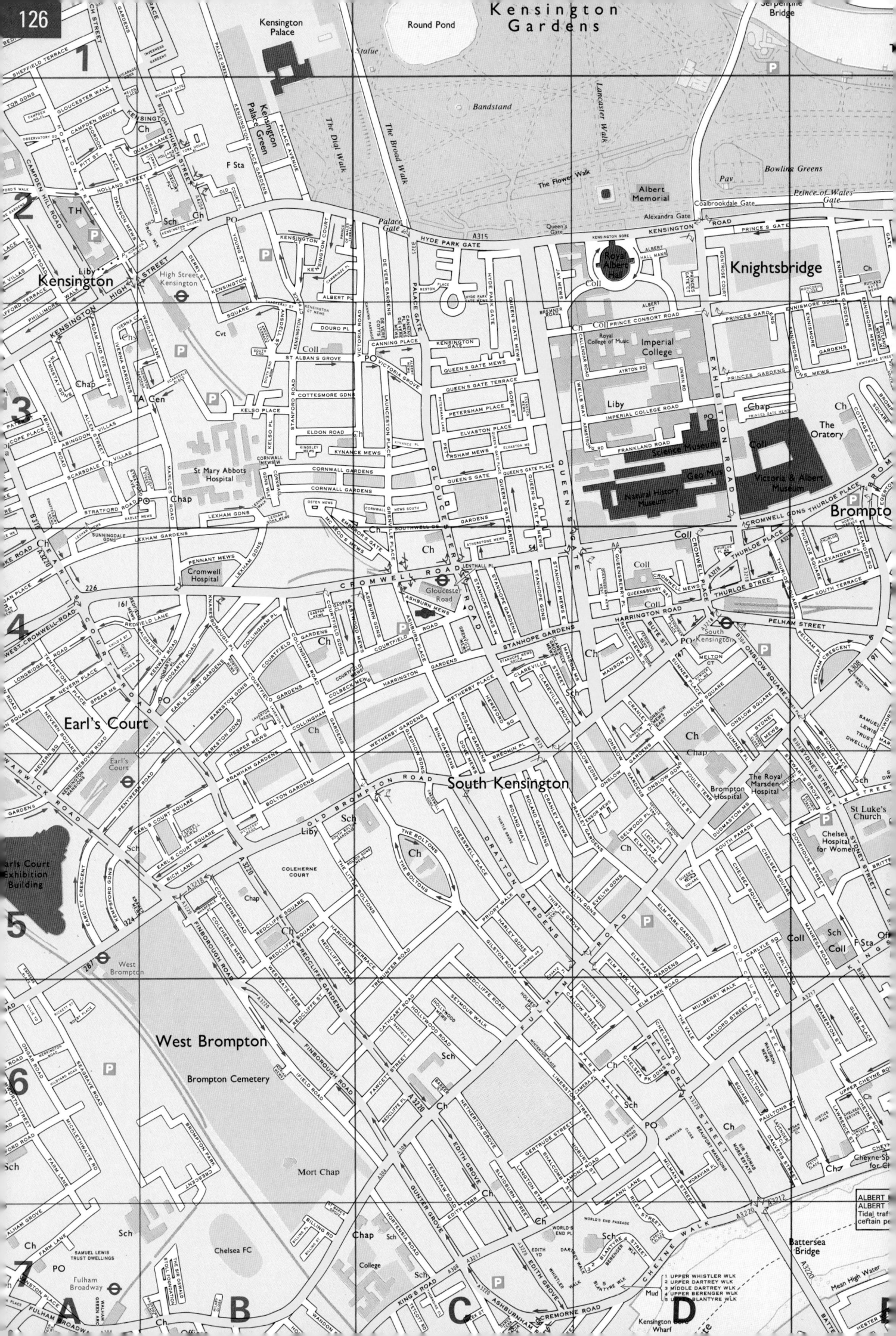

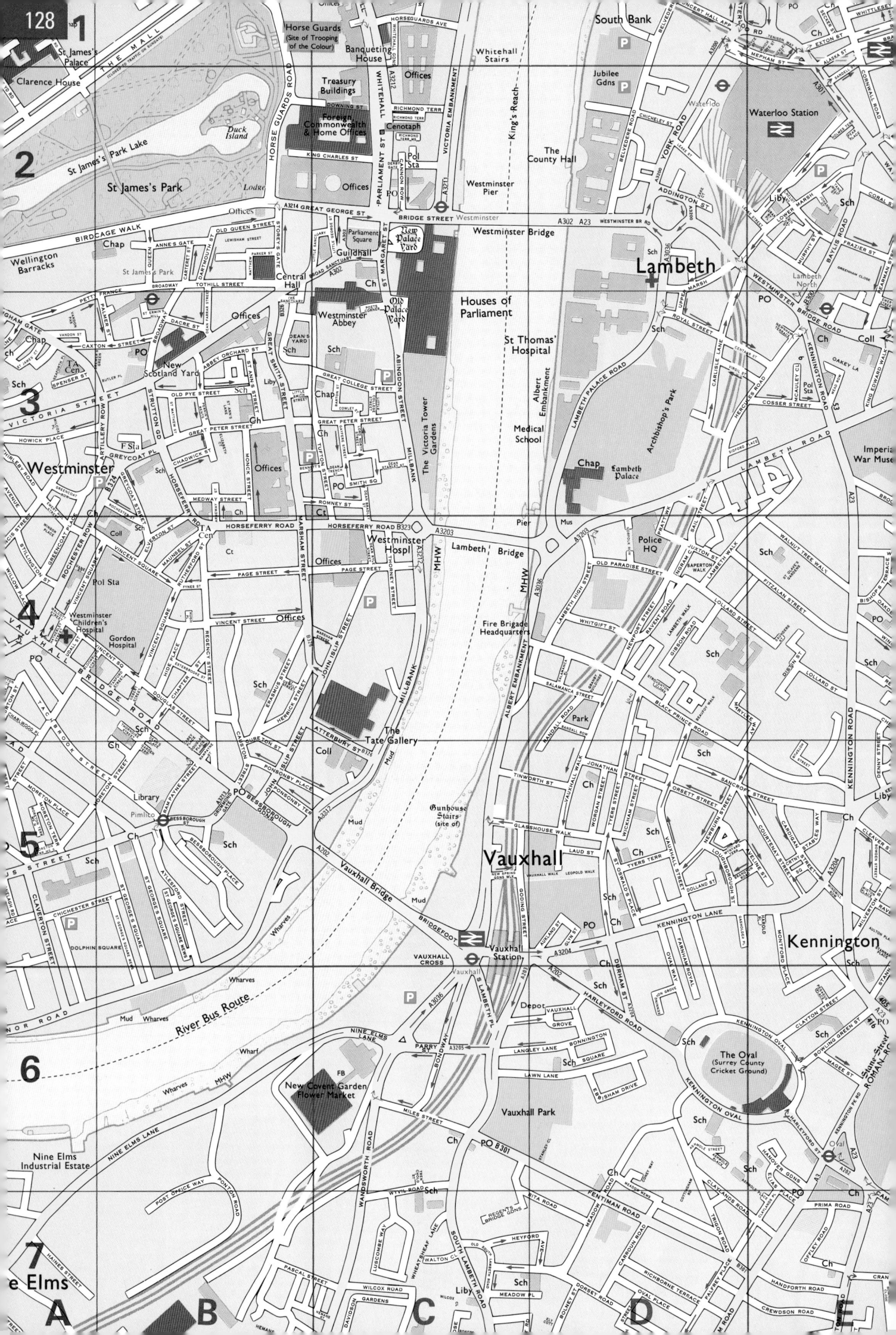

CENTRAL LONDON

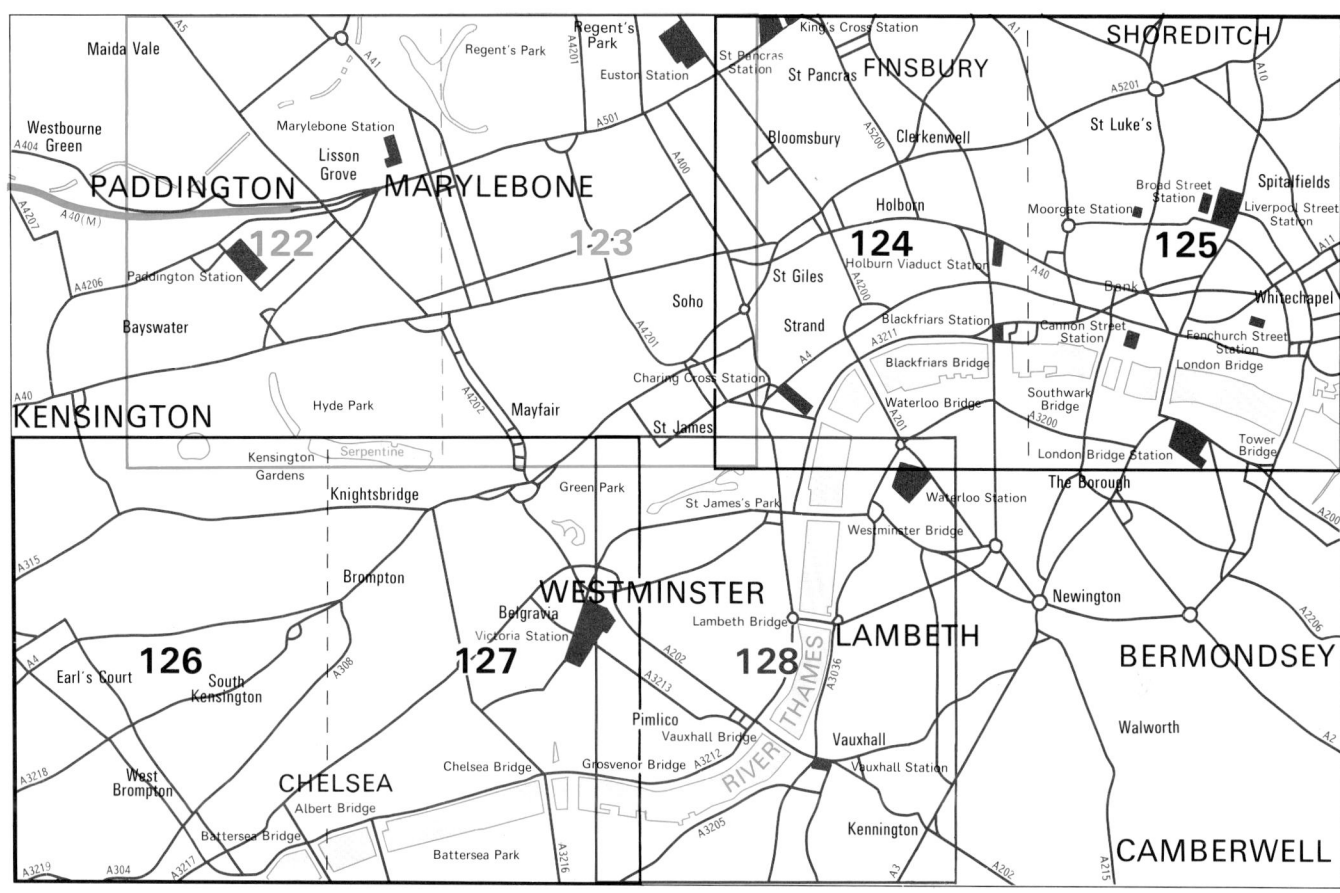

Entries preceded by an asterisk indicate that only the first two letters of the road name have been shown on the map

A

Abbey Orchard St.	128	B3
Abchurch La.	125	G5
Abchurch Yd.	125	G5
Abercorn Cl.	122	B1
Aberdeen Pl.	122	C2
Abingdon Rd.	126	A3
Abingdon St.	128	C3
Abingdon Villas	126	A3
Acacia Wlk.	126	C7
Achilles Way	123	F6
Acton St.	124	C1
Adam and Eve Ct.	123	H4
Adam and Eve Mews	126	A3
Adam St.	124	B5
Adams Ct.	125	G4
Adam's Row	123	F5
Addington St.	128	D2
Addle Hill	125	E4
Addle St.	125	F3
Adelaide St.	124	B5
Adeline Pl.	124	A3
Adelphi Terr.	124	B5
Adpar St.	122	C3
Adrian Mews	126	B6
Agar St.	124	B5
Agdon St.	124	E2
Air St.	123	H5
Airlie Gdns.	126	A1
Alaska St.	124	D6
Albany Courtyard	123	H5
Albany St.	123	G1
Albemarle St.	123	H5
Albemarle Way	124	E2
Albert Bridge	127	E6
Albert Bridge Rd.	127	F7
Albert Ct.	126	D2
Albert Emb.	128	C4
Albert Hall Mans.	126	D2
Albert Mews	126	C3
Albert Pl.	126	B2
Albion Bldgs.	125	F3
Albion Cl.	122	D5
Albion Mews	122	D5
Albion Est.	123	E3
Albion Pl.	125	G3
Albion St.	122	D5
Aldermanbury	125	F4
Aldermanbury Sq.	125	F3
Alderman's Wlk.	125	H3
Alderney St.	127	H5
Aldersgate St.	125	F3
Aldford St.	123	F6
Aldgate	125	H4
Aldgate Ave.	125	J4
Aldgate High St.	125	J4
Aldwych	124	C4
Alexander Ct.	126	E4
Alexander Sq.	126	E4
Alfred Mews	123	J3
Alfred Pl.	123	J3
Alie St.	125	J4
All Souls Pl.	123	G3
Allen St.	126	A3
Allhallows La.	125	G5
Allington St.	127	H3
Allsop Pl.	123	E2

Alma Sq.	122	B1
Alpha Cl.	122	D2
Alpha Pl.	127	E6
Ambrosden Ave.	127	J3
Amen Cnr.	124	E4
Amen Ct.	124	E4
America Sq.	125	J5
America St.	125	F6
Ampton Pl.	124	C1
Ampton St.	124	C1
Amwell St.	124	D1
Anchor Yd.	125	F2
Anderson St.	127	F5
Andrew Borde St.	124	A4
Andrews Crosse	124	D4
Angel Ct.	125	G4
Angel Ct.	123	H4
Angel Ct.	128	A1
Angel Pas.	125	G5
Angel St.	125	F4
Anhalt Rd.	126	E7
Anhalt Rd.	127	E7
Ann La.	126	D6
Anning St.	125	H2
Ann's Cl.	127	G2
Ansdell St.	126	B3
Ansdell Terr.	126	B3
Apollo Pl.	126	D7
Apothecary St.	124	E4
Apple Tree Yd.	123	H6
Apple Tree Yd.	128	A1
Appold St.	125	H3
Apsley Way	127	G2
Aquinas St.	124	D6
Arcade The	125	H3
Archer St.	123	J5
Archery Cl.	122	D4
Arches The	124	B6
Archibald Mews	123	G5
Argon Mews	126	A7
Argyle Sq.	124	B1
Argyle St.	124	B1
Argyle Wlk.	124	B1
Argyll Rd.	126	A2
Argyll St.	123	H4
Arlington St.	123	H6
Arlington St.	128	A1
Arlington Way	124	D1
Armstrong Rd.	126	C3
Arne St.	124	B4
Arneway St.	128	B3
Arnold Circ.	125	J1
Arthur St.	125	G5
Artillery La.	125	H3
Artillery Pas.	125	H3
Artillery Row	128	B3
Artizan St.	125	H4
Arundel St.	124	C5
Ascalon St.	128	A7
Ashbridge St.	122	D2
Ashburn Gdns.	126	C4
Ashburn Mews	126	C4
Ashburn Pl.	126	C4
Ashburnham Rd.	126	C7
Ashby St.	124	E1
Ashentree Ct.	124	D4
Ashford St.	125	H1
Ashland Pl.	123	F3
Ashley Pl.	127	J3
Ashmill St.	122	D3
Ashmole Pl.	128	D6

Ashmole St.	128	D6
Ashworth Rd.	122	A1
Aske St.	125	H1
Astell St.	127	E5
Astwood Mews	126	C4
Atherstone Mews	126	C4
Atterbury St.	128	C4
Attneave St.	124	D1
Auckland St.	128	D5
Audley Sq.	123	F6
Augustus St.	123	J1
Austin Friars	125	G4
Austin Friars Sq.	125	G4
Austin St.	125	J1
Ave Maria La.	125	E4
Aveline St.	128	E5
Avery Farm Row	127	H4
Avery Row	123	G5
Aybrook St.	123	F3
Aylesbury St.	124	E2
Aylesford St.	128	B5
Ayrton Rd.	126	D3

B

Babmaes St.	123	J5
Bache's St.	125	G1
Back Alley	125	H4
Back Hill	124	D2
Bainbridge St.	124	A4
Baird St.	125	F2
Baker St.	123	E3
Bakers Hall Ct.	125	H5
Baker's Mews	123	F4
Baker's Row	124	D2
Balcombe St.	122	E2
Balderton St.	123	F4
Baldwin St.	125	G1
Baldwin's Gdns.	124	D3
Balfour Mews	123	F6
Balfour Pl.	123	F5
Ball Ct.	125	G4
Baltic St.	125	F2
Banbury Ct.	124	B5
Bank End	125	F5
Bankside	125	F5
Banner St.	125	F2
Barge House St.	124	D6
Barge House St.	128	E1
Bark Pl.	122	A5
Barker St.	126	C6
Barkston Gdns.	126	B4
Barley Mow Pas.	125	E3
Barlow Pl.	123	G5
Barnard's Inn	124	D3
Barnby St.	123	H1
Barnwood Ct.	122	A2
Baroness Rd.	125	J1
Barrett St.	123	F4
Barter St.	124	B3
Bartholomew Cl.	125	F3
Bartholomew La.	125	G4
Bartholomew Pl.	125	F3
Bartlett Ct.	124	D4
Barton St.	128	C3
Basil St.	127	F2
Basil St.	127	F2
Basing House Yd.	125	H1

Basing Pl.	125	H1
Basinghall Ave.	125	G4
Basinghall St.	125	G3
Bassishaw Highwalk	125	G3
Bastwick St.	125	F2
Bateman St.	123	J4
Bateman's Bldgs.	123	J4
Bateman's Row	125	H2
Bath Ct.	124	D2
Bath Pl.	125	H1
Bath St.	125	G1
Bathurst Mews	122	C5
Bathurst St.	122	C5
Battersea Bridge Rd.	126	E7
Battersea Bridge Rd.	127	E7
Battersea Park Rd.	127	J7
Battersea Park Rd.	128	A7
Battle Bridge La.	125	H6
Bayley St.	123	J3
Baylis Rd.	128	E2
Bayswater Rd.	122	C5
Beak St.	123	H5
Bear Alley	124	E4
Bear Gdns.	125	F6
Bear La.	124	E6
Bear St.	124	A5
Beauchamp Pl.	127	E3
Beauchamp St.	124	D3
Beaufort Gdns.	127	E3
Beaufort Mansions	126	D6
Beaufort St.	126	D6
Beaufoy Wlk.	128	D4
Beaumont Mews	123	F3
Beaumont Pl.	123	H2
Beaumont St.	123	F3
Bedale St.	125	G6
Bedford Ave.	124	A3
Bedford Ct.	124	B5
Bedford Gdns.	126	A1
Bedford Pl.	124	B3
Bedford Row	124	C3
Bedford Sq.	124	A3
Bedford St.	124	B5
Bedford Way	124	A2
Bedfordbury	124	B5
Beech St.	125	F3
Beeston Pl.	127	H3
Belgrave Mews N.	127	G3
Belgrave Mews S.	127	G3
Belgrave Mews W.	127	G3
Belgrave Pl.	127	G3
Belgrave Rd.	127	J4
Belgrave Sq.	127	G3
Belgrave St.	123	J6
Belgrove St.	124	B1
Bell Inn Yd.	125	G4
Bell La.	125	H3
Bell St.	122	D3
Bell Wharf La.	125	F5
Bell Yd.	124	D4
Belvedere Rd.	128	D2
Bendall Mews	122	D3
*Bengal Ct.	125	G4
Benjamin St.	124	E3
Bennet St.	123	H6
Bennett St.	128	A1
Bennett's Hill	125	F5
Bennett's Yd.	128	B3
Bentinck Mews	123	F4
Bentinck St.	123	F4
Berenger Wlk.	126	D7

Berkeley Gdns.	126	A1
Berkeley Mews	123	E4
Berkeley Sq.	123	G5
Berkeley St.	123	G6
Bernard St.	124	B2
Berners Mews	123	H3
Berners Pl.	123	H4
Berners St.	123	H4
Berry Pl.	124	E1
Berry St.	125	F2
Berwick St.	123	H4
Bessborough Gdns.	128	B5
Bessborough Pl.	128	B5
Bessborough St.	128	B5
Bethnal Green Rd.	125	J2
Betterton St.	124	B4
Bevenden St.	125	G1
Bevin Way	124	D1
Bevis Marks	125	H4
Bickenhall St.	123	E3
Bidborough St.	124	B1
Biddulph Rd.	122	A1
Billing Pl.	126	B7
Billing Rd.	126	B7
Billing St.	126	B7
Billiter Sq.	125	H4
Billiter St.	125	H4
Bina Gdns.	126	C4
Bingham Pl.	123	F3
Binney St.	123	F4
Birchin La.	125	G4
Bird St.	123	F4
Birdcage Wlk.	128	B2
Birkenhead St.	124	B1
Bishop's Bridge Rd.	122	B4
Bishop's Ct.	124	E4
Bishop's Ct.	124	D4
Bishop's Terr.	128	E3
Bishopsgate	125	H4
Bishopsgate Church Yd.	125	H4
Black Friars La.	124	E4
Black Prince Rd.	128	D4
Black Prince Rd.	128	E4
Blackall St.	125	H2
Blackfriars Bridge	124	E5
Blackfriars Ct.	124	E5
Blackfriars Pas.	124	E5
Blackfriars Rd.	124	E6
Blackfriars Underpass	124	E5
Blacklands Terr.	127	F4
Blandford Sq.	122	D2
Blandford St.	123	F3
Blantyre St.	126	D7
Blantyre Wlk.	126	D7
Bleeding Heart Yd.	124	D3
Blenheim St.	123	G4
Blithfield St.	126	B3
Blomfield Rd.	122	B3
Blomfield St.	125	G3
Blomfield Villas	122	B3
Bloomburg St.	128	A4
Bloomfield Pl.	123	G5
Bloomfield Terr.	127	G5
Bloomsbury Ct.	124	B3
Bloomsbury Pl.	124	B3
Bloomsbury Sq.	124	B3
Bloomsbury St.	124	A3
Bloomsbury Way	124	A3
Blore Ct.	123	J5
Blossom St.	125	H2
Blue Ball Yd.	123	H6

Blue Ball Yd.	128	A1
Bolney St.	128	D7
Bolsover St.	123	G2
Bolt Ct.	124	D4
Bolton Gdns.	126	B5
Bolton Gdns.	126	C5
Bolton Gdns Mews	126	C5
Bolton St.	123	G6
Bolton The	126	C5
Bond Ct.	125	G4
Bondway	128	C6
Bonhill St.	125	G2
Bonnington Sq.	128	D6
Boot St.	125	H1
Booth's Pl.	123	H3
Borer's Pas.	125	H4
Boscobel Pl.	127	G4
Boscobel St.	122	C2
Boston Pl.	122	E2
Boswell Ct.	124	B3
Boswell St.	124	B3
Botolph Alley	125	H5
Botolph La.	125	H5
Boundary Pas.	125	J2
Boundary St.	125	J2
Bourchier St.	123	J5
Bourdon Pl.	123	G5
Bourdon St.	123	G5
Bourlet Cl.	123	G3
Bourne St.	127	G4
Bourne Terr.	122	A3
Bouverie Pl.	122	C4
Bouverie St.	124	D4
Bow Churchyard	125	F4
Bow La.	125	F4
Bow St.	124	B4
Bowden St.	128	E5
Bowl Ct.	125	H2
Bowland Yd.	127	F2
Bowling Green La.	124	D2
Bowling Green St.	128	E6
Bowling Green Wlk.	125	H1
Boyce St.	124	D6
Boyle St.	123	H5
Brackley St.	125	F3
Brad St.	124	D6
Braden St.	122	A3
Bradmead	127	J7
Bradwood St.	125	J4
Braidwood St.	125	H6
Bramerton St.	126	E6
Bramham Gdns.	126	B5
Brandon Mews	125	G3
Brangton Rd.	128	D5
Bray Pl.	127	F4
Bread St.	125	F4
Bream's Bldgs.	124	D4
Brechin Pl.	126	C4
Bremner Rd.	126	C3
Bressenden Pl.	127	J3
Brewer St.	123	H5
Brewer's Green	128	B3
Brewhouse Yd.	124	E2
Brick Ct.	124	D4
Brick La.	125	J2
Brick St.	123	G6
Bride La.	124	E4
Bridewell Pl.	124	E4
Bridford Mews	123	G3

Bridge Pl.....127 H4
Bridge St.....128 C2
Bridgefoot.....128 C5
Bridgewater Sq.....125 F3
Bridgewater St.....125 F3
Bridle La.....123 H5
Brinton Wlk.....124 E6
Briset St.....124 E2
Bristol Gdns.....122 A2
Bristol Mews.....122 A2
Britannia St.....124 C1
Britannia Wlk.....125 E5
Britannia Wlk.....125 G1
Britten St.....126 E5
Britton St.....124 E2
*Britton's Ct.....124 D4
Broad Ct.....124 B4
Broad Sanctuary.....128 C2
Broad St Bldgs.....125 H3
Broad St Bldgs.....125 H3
Broad Walk The.....122 A6
Broad Walk The.....126 B1
Broad Yd.....124 E2
Broadbent St.....123 G5
Broadley St.....122 D3
Broadley Terr.....122 D2
Broadstone Pl.....123 F3
Broadway.....128 B2
Broadwick St.....123 H4
Broken Wharf.....125 F5
Brompton Arcade.....127 F2
Brompton Park Cres.....126 B6
Brompton Pl.....126 E3
Brompton Rd.....126 E3
Brompton Sq.....126 E3
Brook Dri.....128 E3
Brook Gate.....123 E5
Brook Mews N.....122 C5
Brook St.....123 G5
Brook St.....122 C5
Brooke St.....124 D3
Brookes Ct.....124 D3
*Brooke's Market.....124 D3
Brown Hart Gdns.....123 F5
Brown St.....122 E4
Browning Cl.....122 B2
Browning Mews.....123 F3
Brownlow Mews.....124 C2
Brownlow St.....124 C3
Brown's Bldgs.....125 H4
Brune St.....125 J3
Brunswick Gdns.....126 A1
Brunswick Mews.....123 E4
Brunswick Pl.....125 G1
Brunswick Sq.....124 B2
Brushfield St.....125 J3
Bruton La.....123 G5
Bruton Pl.....123 G5
Bruton St.....123 G5
Bryanston Mews E.....122 E3
Bryanston Mews W.....122 E3
Bryanston Pl.....122 E3
Bryanston Sq.....122 E4
Bryanston St.....123 E4
Brydges Pl.....124 B5
Buckingham Arc.....124 B5
Buckingham Gate.....127 J3
Buckingham Mews.....127 J3
Buckingham Palace Rd.....127 H4
Buckingham Pl.....127 J3
Buckingham St.....124 B6
Buckinghamsbury.....125 G4
Buckley St.....124 D6
Bucknall St.....124 A4
Budge Row.....125 G4
Bull Inn Ct.....124 B5
Bull Wharf La.....125 F5
Bull's Gdn.....127 E4
Bulls Head Pas.....125 H4
Bulmer Mews.....126 A1
Bulstrode Pl.....123 F3
Bulstrode St.....123 F4
Bunhill Row.....125 G2
Bunhouse Pl.....127 G5
Burdett Mews.....122 A4
Burgon St.....124 E4
Burleigh St.....124 C5
Burlington Arc.....123 H5
Burlington Gdns.....123 H5
Burne St.....122 D3
Burnsall St.....127 E5
Burrell St.....124 E6
Bursar St.....125 H6
Burton Mews.....127 G4
Burton Pl.....124 A1
Burton St.....123 J2
Burwood Pl.....122 D4
Bury Ct.....125 H4
Bury Pl.....124 B3
Bury St.....125 H4
Bury St.....123 H6
Bury St.....128 A1
Bury Wlk.....126 E5
Bush La.....125 G5
Bute St.....126 D4
Butler Pl.....128 B3
Buttesland St.....125 G1
Buxton Ct.....125 F1
Byng Pl.....123 J2
Byward St.....125 H6
Bywater St.....127 F5
Bywell Pl.....123 H3

C

Cabbell St.....122 D3
Cadogan Gate.....127 F4
Cadogan Gdns.....127 F4
Cadogan La.....127 G3
Cadogan Pl.....127 F3
Cadogan Pl.....127 G4
Cadogan Sq.....127 F4
Cadogan Sq.....127 F4
Caesar St.....125 J1
Cahill St.....125 F2
Cale St.....126 E5
Callcott St.....126 A1
Callendar Rd.....126 D3
Callow St.....126 D6
Calthorpe St.....124 C2
Calvert Ave.....125 J1
Calvert's Bldgs.....125 G6
Calvin St.....125 J2
Cambridge Circ.....124 A4
Cambridge Gate.....123 G2
Cambridge Gate Mews.....123 G2
Cambridge Pl.....126 B2
Cambridge Sq.....122 D4
Cambridge Sq.....127 J5
Cambridge Terr.....123 G1
Cambridge Terr Mews.....123 G1
Camera Pl.....126 D6
Camlet St.....125 J2
Camomile St.....125 H4
Campden Gr.....126 A2
Campden Hill Gdns.....126 A1
Campden Hill Rd.....126 A2
Campden House Cl.....126 A2
Campden St.....126 A1
Camperdown St.....125 J4

Candover St.....123 H3
Canning Pas.....126 C3
Canning Pl.....126 C3
Canning Pl Mews.....126 C3
Cannon Row.....128 C2
Cannon St.....125 F5
Canvey St.....125 F6
Capener's Cl.....127 G2
Capland St.....122 C2
Capper St.....123 H2
Carburton St.....123 G2
Cardigan St.....128 E5
Cardinal Cap Alley.....125 F6
Cardington St.....123 H1
Carey La.....125 F4
Carey Pl.....128 B4
Carey St.....124 C4
Carlisle Ave.....125 J4
Carlisle La.....128 D3
Carlisle Pl.....127 J3
Carlisle St.....123 J4
Carlos Pl.....123 G5
Carlton Gdns.....123 J6
Carlton Gdns.....128 B1
Carlton House Terr.....123 J6
Carlton House Terr.....128 B1
Carlton St.....123 J5
Carlyle Sq.....126 D6
Carmel Ct.....126 B2
Carmelite St.....124 D5
*Carnaby Ct.....123 H4
Carnaby St.....123 H5
Caroline Cl.....122 A5
Caroline Gdns.....125 H1
Caroline Pl.....122 A5
Caroline Pl Mews.....122 A5
Caroline Terr.....127 G4
Carpenter St.....123 G5
Carriage Dri E.....127 G7
Carriage Dri N.....127 F7
Carrington St.....123 G6
Carroun Rd.....128 D7
Carter La.....125 E4
Carteret St.....128 B2
Carthusian St.....125 F3
Carting La.....124 B5
Cartwright Gdns.....124 B1
Castellain Rd.....122 A2
Castle Baynard St.....124 E5
Castle Baynard St.....125 F5
Castle Ct.....125 G4
Castle La.....127 J3
Castle Yd.....125 E6
Castlereagh St.....122 E4
Cathcart Rd.....126 C6
Cathedral Pl.....125 F4
Cathedral St.....125 G6
Catherine Pl.....127 J3
Catherine St.....124 C5
Catherine Wheel Alley.....125 H3
Catherine Wheel Yd.....123 H6
Catherine Wheel Yd.....128 A1
Cato St.....122 D4
Catton St.....124 C3
Causton St.....128 B5
Cavaye Pl.....126 C5
Cavendish Ave.....122 C1
Cavendish Cl.....122 C1
Cavendish Mews N.....123 G3
Cavendish Mews S.....123 G3
Cavendish Pl.....123 G4
Cavendish Sq.....123 G4
Caversham St.....127 F6
Caxton St.....128 B3
Cayton Pl.....125 G1
Cayton St.....125 G1
Cecil Ct.....124 B5
Celbridge Mews.....122 A4
Centaur St.....128 D3
Central St.....125 F1
Cerney Mew.....122 C5
Chadwell St.....124 D1
Chadwick St.....128 B3
Chagford St.....122 E2
Chamber St.....125 J5
Chambord St.....125 J1
Chance St.....125 J2
Chancel St.....124 E6
Chandos Pl.....124 B5
Chandos St.....123 G3
Change Alley.....125 G4
Chapel Pl.....123 G4
Chapel St.....122 D3
Chapel St.....127 G2
Chapone Pl.....123 J4
Chapter House Ct.....125 F4
Chapter St.....128 B4
Charing Cross.....124 B6
Charing Cross Rd.....124 A4
Charles II Pl.....123 J6
Charles II St.....128 B1
Charlotte Mews.....123 H3
Charlotte Pl.....123 H3
Charlotte Rd.....125 H1
Charlotte St.....123 H3
Charlwood Pl.....128 A4
Charlwood St.....127 J5
Chart St.....125 G1
Charterhouse Bldgs.....125 F2
Charterhouse Mews.....125 E3
Charterhouse Sq.....125 E3
Charterhouse St.....124 E3
Charterhouse St.....125 E3
Chatham Ave.....125 G1
Cheapside.....125 F4
Chelsea Bridge.....127 H6
Chelsea Bridge Rd.....127 G5
Chelsea Emb.....127 F6
Chelsea Estate.....126 E6
Chelsea Manor Gdns.....127 E5
Chelsea Manor St.....127 E5
Chelsea Park Gdns.....126 D6
Chelsea Sq.....126 D5
Cheltenham Terr.....127 F5
Chenies Mews.....123 J2
Chenies St.....123 J3
Cheniston Gdns.....126 B3
Chequer St.....125 F2
Cherry Tree Wlk.....125 F2
Chesham Cl.....127 G3
Chesham Mews.....127 G3
Chesham Pl.....127 G3
Chesham St.....127 G3
Chester Cl.....127 H3
Chester Cl N.....123 G1
Chester Cl S.....123 G1
Chester Gate.....123 G1
Chester Mews.....127 H3
Chester Pl.....123 G1
Chester Row.....127 G4
Chester Sq.....127 H4
Chester Sq Mews.....127 H3
Chester St.....127 H3
Chester Terr.....123 G1
Chester Way.....128 E4
Chesterfield Gdns.....123 G6
Chesterfield Hill.....123 G6

Chesterfield St.....123 G6
Cheval Pl.....127 E3
Cheyne Ct.....127 F6
Cheyne Gdns.....127 E6
Cheyne Mews.....127 E6
Cheyne Row.....126 E6
Cheyne Wlk.....126 D6
Cheyne Wlk.....126 E6
Chicheley St.....122 A3
Chichester Rents.....124 D4
Chichester St.....128 A5
Child's Pl.....126 A4
Child's Wlk.....126 A4
Chiltern St.....123 F3
Chilworth Mews.....122 B4
Chilworth St.....122 B4
China St.....124 B4
Chiswell St.....125 G3
Chitty St.....123 H3
Christchurch St.....127 F6
Christchurch Terr.....127 F6
Christina St.....125 H2
Christopher Pl.....124 A1
Christopher St.....125 G2
Church Ct.....124 D4
Church Entry.....124 E4
Church Pl.....123 H5
Church St.....122 D2
Churchill Gdns.....127 J5
Churchill Gdns Rd.....127 J6
Churchway.....123 J1
Churton Pl.....127 J4
Churton St.....127 J4
Circus Mews.....122 E3
Circus Pl.....125 G3
Circus Rd.....122 C1
City Rd.....125 E1
City Rd.....125 G2
Clabon Mews.....127 F4
Clapham Rd.....128 D7
Clare Market.....124 C4
Clarence Gdns.....123 G1
Clarendon Cl.....122 D5
Clarendon Gdns.....122 B2
Clarendon Gr.....123 J1
Clarendon Mews.....122 D5
Clarendon Pl.....127 H5
Clarendon St.....127 J5
Clarendon Terr.....122 B2
Clareville Gr.....126 C4
Clareville Grove Mews.....126 C4
Clareville St.....126 C4
Clarges Mews.....123 G6
Clarges St.....123 G6
Clarkes Mews.....123 F3
Clark's Pl.....125 H4
Claverton St.....128 A5
Clay St.....123 E3
Claylands Pl.....128 E7
Claylands Rd.....128 D6
Clayton St.....128 E6
Clearwell Dri.....122 A2
Cleaver St.....128 E5
Clements Inn.....124 C4
Clements Inn Pas.....124 C4
Clement's La.....125 G5
Clenston Mews.....122 E4
Clere Pl.....125 G2
Clere St.....125 G2
Clerkenwell Cl.....124 D2
Clerkenwell Green.....124 D2
Clerkenwell Rd.....124 E2
Cleveland Gdns.....122 B4
Cleveland Mews.....123 H3
Cleveland Pl.....123 H6
Cleveland Row.....123 H6
Cleveland Row.....128 A1
Cleveland Sq.....122 B4
Cleveland St.....123 H3
Cleveland Terr.....122 B4
Clifford St.....123 H5
Clifford's Inn Pas.....124 D4
Clifton Gdns.....122 B2
Clifton Pl.....122 C4
Clifton Rd.....122 B2
Clifton St.....125 H2
Clifton Villas.....122 B3
Clink St.....125 G6
Clipstone Mews.....123 H3
Clipstone St.....123 H3
Cliveden Pl.....127 G4
Cloak La.....125 G5
Cloth Ct.....125 E3
Cloth Fair.....125 E3
Cloth St.....125 F3
Clothier St.....125 H4
Clover Mews.....127 F6
Club Row.....125 J2
Coach and Horses Yd.....123 H5
Cobb St.....125 J3
Cobb's Ct.....124 E4
Cobourg St.....123 H1
Cock Hill.....125 H3
Cock La.....124 E3
Cockpit Yd.....124 C3
Cockspur Ct.....124 A6
Cockspur St.....124 A6
Coin St.....124 D6
Colbeck Mews.....126 C4
Colchester St.....125 J4
Coldbath Sq.....124 D2
Coleherne Mews.....126 B5
Coleherne Rd.....126 B5
Coleman St.....125 G4
Coleman St Bldgs.....125 G4
Coley St.....124 C2
College Ct.....127 F5
College Hill.....125 F5
College St.....125 F5
Collingham Gdns.....126 B4
Collingham Pl.....126 B4
Collingham Rd.....126 B4
Colombo St.....124 E6
Colonnade.....124 B2
Colonnades The.....122 A4
Columbia Rd.....125 J1
Colville Pl.....123 J3
Commercial St.....125 J3
Compton Cl.....123 G1
Compton Pas.....124 E2
Compton Pl.....124 B2
Compton St.....124 E2
Concert Hall App.....124 C6
Conduit Ct.....124 B5
Conduit Mews.....122 C4
Conduit Pas.....122 C4
Conduit Pl.....122 C4
Conduit St.....123 G5
Coney Way.....128 D6
Connaught Cl.....122 D4
Connaught Mews.....122 E4
Connaught Pl.....122 E4
Connaught Sq.....122 E4
Connaught St.....122 D4
Constitution Hill.....127 H2
Conway St.....123 H2

Cooper's Row.....125 J5
Cope Pl.....126 A3
Copthall Ave.....125 G4
Copthall Bldgs.....125 G4
Copthall St.....125 G4
Coptic St.....124 B3
Coral St.....128 E3
Coram St.....124 B2
Corbet Ct.....125 G4
Corbet Pl.....125 J3
Cork St.....123 H5
Cork St Mews.....123 H5
Corlett St.....122 D3
Cornhill.....125 G4
Cornwall Gdns.....126 B3
Cornwall Gdns Wlk.....126 B3
Cornwall Mews S.....126 C3
Cornwall Mews W.....126 B3
Cornwall Rd.....124 D6
Cornwall Terr Mews.....123 E2
Coronet St.....125 H1
Corporation Row.....124 E2
Corsham St.....125 G1
Cosmo Pl.....124 B3
Cosser St.....128 E3
Cosway St.....122 D3
Cottage Pl.....126 E3
Cottesmore Gdns.....126 B3
Cottingham Rd.....128 D7
Cotton's Gdns.....125 H1
Coulson St.....127 F5
Counter Ct.....125 G6
Counter St.....125 H6
Courtenay Sq.....128 E5
Courtenay St.....128 E5
Courtfield Gdns.....126 B4
Courtfield Mews.....126 C4
Courtfield Rd.....126 C4
Cousin La.....125 G5
Covent Gdn.....124 B5
Coventry St.....123 J5
Cowcross St.....124 E3
Cowley St.....128 C3
Cowper St.....125 G2
Cowper's Ct.....125 G4
Craig's Ct.....124 B6
Cramer St.....123 F3
Cranbourn Alley.....124 A5
Cranbourn St.....124 A5
Crane Ct.....124 D4
Cranley Gdns.....126 D5
Cranley Mews.....126 C5
Cranley Pl.....126 D4
Cranmer Ct.....127 E4
Cranmer Rd.....128 E7
Cranwood St.....125 G1
Craven Hill.....122 B5
Craven Hill Gdns.....122 B5
Craven Hill Mews.....122 B5
Craven Pas.....124 B6
Craven Rd.....122 C4
Craven St.....124 B6
Craven Terr.....122 B5
Crawford Mews.....122 E3
Crawford Pas.....124 D2
Crawford Pl.....122 D3
Crawford St.....122 E3
Creechurch La.....125 H4
Creechurch Pl.....125 H4
Creed La.....124 E4
Cremorne Rd.....126 D7
Crescent.....125 J5
Crescent Pl.....126 E4
Crescent Row.....125 F2
Cresswell Gdns.....126 C5
Cresswell Pl.....126 C5
Crestfield St.....124 B1
Crewdson Rd.....128 E7
Cringle St.....127 J7
Cripplegate St.....125 F3
Crispin St.....125 J3
Cromer St.....124 B1
Crompton St.....122 C2
Cromwell Gdns.....126 D3
Cromwell Mews.....126 D4
Cromwell Pl.....126 D4
Cromwell Rd.....126 C4
*Crooked Billet Yd.....125 H1
Crosby Sq.....125 H4
Cross Key St.....125 F2
Cross Keys Cl.....123 F3
Cross La.....125 H5
Crosswall.....125 J5
Crown Ct.....125 F4
Crown Ct.....124 B4
Crown Office Row.....124 D5
Crown Pas.....123 H6
Crown Pas.....128 A1
Cruickshank St.....124 D1
Crutched Friars.....125 H5
Cubbit St.....124 C1
Culford Gdns.....127 F4
Cullum St.....125 H5
Culross St.....123 F5
Culworth St.....122 D1
Cumberland Gate.....123 E5
Cumberland Gdns.....124 D1
Cumberland Market.....123 G1
Cumberland St.....127 H5
Cumberland Terr.....123 G1
Cundy St.....127 G4
Cunningham Pl.....122 C2
Cureton St.....128 B4
Cursitor St.....124 D4
Curtain Pl.....125 H2
Curtain Rd.....125 H2
Curzon Gate.....123 F6
Curzon Pl.....123 F6
Curzon St.....123 G6
Cuthbert St.....122 C2
Cutler St.....125 H4
Cutlers Gdns.....125 H4
Cygnet St.....125 J2
Cypress Pl.....123 H2
Cyrus St.....124 E2

D

Dacre St.....128 B3
Dallington St.....124 E2
Damer Terr.....126 C7
Dane St.....124 C3
Dansey Pl.....123 J5
Danube St.....127 E5
Danvers St.....126 D6
D'arblay St.....123 H4
Dartmouth St.....128 B2
Dartrey Wlk.....126 C7
David Mews.....123 F3
Davidson Gdns.....128 C7
Davies Mews.....123 G5
Davies St.....123 G5
De Vere Cotts.....126 C3
De Vere Mews.....126 C3
De Walden St.....123 F3
Dean Bradley St.....128 C3
Dean Farrar St.....128 B3
Dean Ryle St.....128 C4

Dean St.....123 J4
Dean Stanley St.....128 C3
Dean Trench St.....128 C3
Deanery Mews.....123 F6
Deanery St.....123 F6
Dean's Ct.....125 E4
Dean's Mews.....123 G4
Dean's Pl.....128 B4
Dean's Yd.....128 B3
Delamere Terr.....122 A3
Delaware Rd.....122 A2
Dell's Mews.....127 J4
Denbigh Pl.....127 J5
Denbigh St.....127 J5
Denman St.....123 J5
Denmark St.....124 A4
Denning Cl.....122 B1
Denny Cres.....128 E5
Denny St.....128 E5
Denyer St.....127 E4
Derby Gate.....128 C2
Derby St.....123 F6
Dereham Pl.....125 H1
Dering St.....123 G4
Derry St.....126 B2
Desborough Cl.....122 A3
Devereux Ct.....124 D4
Devonport St.....122 D4
Devonshire Cl.....123 G3
Devonshire Mews N.....123 G3
Devonshire Mews S.....123 G3
Devonshire Mews W.....123 G3
Devonshire Pl.....123 F2
Devonshire Pl Mews.....123 F2
Devonshire Row.....125 H3
Devonshire Row Mews.....123 G2
Devonshire Sq.....125 H4
Devonshire St.....123 G3
Devonshire Terr.....122 B4
Diadem Ct.....123 J4
Dial Walk The.....126 B2
Diana Pl.....123 G2
Dilke St.....127 F6
Dingley Pl.....125 F1
Dingley Rd.....125 F1
Diss St.....125 J1
Distaff La.....125 F5
Distin St.....128 E4
Doby Ct.....125 F5
Dolben St.....124 E6
Dolland St.....128 D5
Dombey St.....124 C3
Domingo St.....125 F2
Dominion St.....125 G3
Donne Pl.....127 E4
Doon St.....124 D6
Doric Way.....123 J1
Dorrington St.....124 D3
Dorset Cl.....122 E3
Dorset Mews.....127 H3
Dorset Pl.....128 B5
Dorset Rd.....128 D7
Dorset Rise.....124 E4
Dorset Sq.....122 E2
Dorset St.....123 F3
Doughty Mews.....124 C2
Doughty St.....124 C2
Douglas St.....128 B5
Douglas St.....128 B5
Douro Pl.....126 B3
Dove Mews.....126 C4
Dove Wlk.....127 G5
Dovehouse St.....126 E5
Dover St.....123 H6
Dover St.....123 H6
Dover Yd.....123 H6
Dowgate Hill.....125 G5
Down St.....123 G6
Down St Mews.....123 G6
Downing St.....128 C2
D'Oyley St.....127 G4
Dragon Yd.....124 B4
Drake St.....124 C3
Drapers Gdns.....125 G4
Draycott Ave.....127 E4
Draycott Pl.....127 F4
Draycott Terr.....127 F4
Drayson Mews.....126 A2
Drayton Gdns.....126 C5
Drummond Cres.....123 J1
Drummond Gate.....128 B5
Drummond St.....123 H2
Drury Lane.....124 B4
Dryden St.....124 B4
Drysdale Pl.....125 H1
Drysdale St.....125 H1
Ducal St.....125 J1
Duchess Mews.....123 G3
Duchess St.....123 G3
Duchy St.....124 D6
Duck La.....123 J4
Dudley St.....122 C3
Dudmaston Mews.....126 D5
Dufferin Ave.....125 G2
Dufferin St.....125 G2
Dufour's Pl.....123 H4
Duke of Wellington Pl.....127 G2
Duke of York St.....123 H6
Duke St.....123 F4
Duke St Hill.....125 G6
Duke St St James's.....123 H6
Duke St St James's.....128 A1
Dukes La.....126 B2
Duke's Mews.....123 F4
Duke's Pl.....125 H4
Duke's Rd.....124 A1
Duke's Yd.....123 F5
Duncannon St.....124 B5
Dunn's Pas.....124 B4
Dunraven St.....123 E5
Dunstable Mews.....123 F3
Dunster Ct.....125 H5
Duplex Ride.....127 F2
Durham House St.....124 B5
Durham Pl.....127 F5
Durham St.....128 D6
Durweston Mews.....123 E3
Durweston St.....122 E3
Dyott St.....124 A4
Dyott St.....124 A4
Dysart St.....125 H2

E

Eagle Ct.....124 E3
Eagle Pl.....123 H5
Eagle St.....124 C3
Eardley Cres.....126 A5
Earl St.....125 H3
Earlham St.....124 A4
Earl's Court Gdns.....126 B4
Earl's Court Rd.....126 A3
Earl's Court Sq.....126 B5

Earlstoke St.....124 E1
Earnshaw St.....124 A4
Easleys Mews.....123 F4
East Harding St.....124 E3
East Pas.....125 F3
East Poultry Ave.....124 E3
East Rd.....125 G1
East Smithfield.....125 J5
Eastbourne Mews.....122 B4
Eastbourne Terr.....122 B4
Eastcastle St.....123 H4
Eastcheap.....125 H5
Easton St.....124 D2
Eaton Cl.....127 G4
Eaton Gate.....127 G4
Eaton La.....127 H3
Eaton Mews N.....127 H3
Eaton Mews S.....127 H3
Eaton Mews W.....127 H3
Eaton Pl.....127 G3
Eaton Row.....127 H3
Eaton Sq.....127 H3
Eaton Terr.....127 G4
Eaton Terr Mews.....127 G4
Ebbisham Dr.....128 D6
Ebenezer St.....125 G1
Ebor St.....125 J2
Ebury Bridge.....127 H5
Ebury Bridge Rd.....127 G5
Ebury Mews.....127 H4
Ebury Mews E.....127 H3
Ebury Sq.....127 H4
Ebury St.....127 G4
Eccleston Bridge.....127 H4
Eccleston Mews.....127 G3
Eccleston Pl.....127 H4
Eccleston Sq.....127 H4
Eccleston Sq Mews.....127 J4
Eccleston St.....127 H4
Edge St.....126 A1
Edgware Rd.....122 D3
Edith Gr.....126 C6
Edith Terr.....126 C7
Edith Yd.....126 C7
Edwards Mews.....123 F4
Effie Rd.....126 A7
Egerton Cres.....127 E4
Egerton Gdns.....126 E3
Egerton Gdns Mews.....127 E3
Egerton Pl.....127 E3
Egerton Terr.....127 E3
Elcho St.....127 E7
Elder St.....125 J2
Eldon Rd.....126 B3
Eldon St.....125 H3
Elgin Ave.....122 A1
Elgin Mews N.....122 A1
Elgin Mews S.....122 A1
Elias Pl.....128 E6
Elizabeth Bridge.....127 H4
Elizabeth Cl.....122 C2
Elizabeth St.....127 H4
Elliots Ct.....124 E4
Elliott's Row.....124 E4
Ellis St.....127 G4
Elm Ct.....124 D5
Elm Park Gdns.....126 D5
Elm Park La.....126 D5
Elm Park Rd.....126 D6
Elm Pl.....126 C5
Elm St.....124 C2
Elm Tree Cl.....122 C1
Elm Tree Rd.....122 C1
Elms Mews.....122 B5
Elnathan Mews.....122 A2
Elvaston Mews.....126 C3
Elvaston Pl.....126 C3
Elverton St.....128 B4
Ely Cottages.....128 E7
Ely Pl.....124 D3
Elystan Pl.....127 F5
Elystan St.....127 E4
Embankment Gdns.....127 F6
Embankment Pl.....124 B6
Emerald St.....124 C3
Emerson St.....125 F6
Emery Hill St.....128 A3
Emery St.....128 E3
Empress Pl.....126 A5
Endell St.....124 B4
Endsleigh Gdns.....123 J2
Endsleigh Pl.....123 J2
Endsleigh St.....123 J2
Enford St.....122 E3
English Grounds.....125 H6
Ennismore Gdns.....126 E3
Ennismore Gdns Mews.....126 E3
Ennismore Mews.....126 E3
Ennismore St.....126 E3
Ensor Mews.....126 D5
Epworth St.....125 G2
Erasmus St.....128 B4
Errol St.....125 G2
Essex Ct.....124 D4
Essex St.....124 D4
Essex Villas.....126 A2
Esterbrooke St.....128 B4
Europa Pl.....125 F1
Euston Gr.....123 J2
Euston Rd.....123 H2
Euston Sq.....123 J1
Euston St.....123 H1
Evelyn Gdns.....126 D5
Evelyn Yd.....123 J4
Ewer St.....125 F6
Excel Ct.....123 J5
Exchange Bldgs.....125 H4
Exchange Sq.....125 H3
Exeter St.....124 B5
Exhibition Rd.....126 D3
Exmouth Market.....124 D2
Exmouth Mews.....123 H1
Exton St.....124 D6
Eyre St Hill.....124 D2

F

Fairchild Pl.....125 H2
Fairchild St.....125 H2
Fairholt St.....127 E3
Fairlop Pl.....122 D1
Falcon Cl.....124 E6
Falcon Ct.....124 D4
Falconberg Ct.....123 J4
Falconberg Mews.....123 J4
Fann St.....125 F2
Fanshaw St.....125 H1
Fareham St.....123 J4
Farm La.....126 A7
Farm St.....123 G5
Farmer St.....126 A1
Farnell Mews.....126 B5
Farnham Pl.....125 F6
Farnham Royal.....128 D5
Farringdon La.....124 D2
Farringdon Rd.....124 D2
Farringdon St.....124 E4
Fashion St.....125 J3
Faulkner's Alley.....124 E3

Fawcett St......126 C6
Featherstone St......125 G2
Fen Ct......125 H4
Fenchurch Ave......125 H4
Fenchurch Bldgs......125 H4
Fenchurch St......125 H5
Fentiman Rd......128 D7
Fernsbury St......124 D1
Fernshaw Rd......126 C6
Fetter La......124 D4
Field Ct......124 C3
Field St......124 C1
Finborough Rd......126 B6
Finch La......125 G4
* Finck St......128 D2
Finsbury Ave......125 G3
Finsbury Circ......125 G3
Finsbury St......125 G3
Finsbury Market......125 H3
Finsbury Pavement......125 G3
Finsbury Sq......125 G3
Finsbury St......125 G3
First St......127 E4
Fish St Hill......125 G5
Fisher St......124 C3
Fisherton St......122 C2
Fitzalan St......128 E4
Fitzhardinge St......123 F4
Fitzmaurice Pl......123 G6
Fitzroy Ct......123 H2
Fitzroy Mews......123 H2
Fitzroy Sq......123 H2
Fitzroy St......123 H2
Flaxman Ct......123 J4
Flaxman Terr......123 A1
Fleet La......124 E4
Fleet Sq......124 C1
Fleet St......124 D4
Flitcroft St......124 A4
Flood St......127 E6
Flood Wlk......127 E6
Floral St......124 B5
Flower and Dean St......125 J3
Fluer De Lis St......125 J2
Foley St......123 H3
Folgate St......125 J3
Fore St......125 G3
Fore St Ave......125 G3
Formosa St......122 A2
Forset St......122 D4
Fort St......125 H4
Fortune St......125 F2
Fosbury Mews......122 A5
Foster La......125 F4
Foubert's Pl......123 H4
Foulis Terr......126 D5
Founders Ct......125 G4
Foundry Mews......123 H2
Fountain Ct......124 D5
Fournier St......125 J3
Fox & Knot St......125 E3
Fox's Yd......125 J2
Frampton St......122 C2
Francis St......127 J3
Frankland Rd......126 D3
Franklin's Row......127 F5
Frazier St......128 E2
Frederic Mews......127 G2
Frederick Cl......122 E5
Frederick Row......124 E1
Frederick St......124 C1
Frederick's Pl......125 G4
French Ordinary Ct......125 H5
French Pl......125 H1
Friar St......124 E4
Friday St......125 F5
Friend St......124 E1
Frith St......123 J4
Frying Pan Alley......125 J3
Fulham Bwy......126 A7
Fulham Rd......126 C6
Fullwood's Mews......125 G1
Fulton Mews......122 B5
Fulwood Pl......124 C3
Furnival St......124 D3
Fynes St......128 B4

G
Gage St......124 B3
Galen Pl......124 B3
Galway St......125 F1
Gambia St......124 E6
Ganton St......123 H4
Garbutt Pl......123 F3
Gard St......125 E1
Garden Ct......124 D5
Garden Rd......122 B1
Garden Terr......128 B5
Garden Wlk......125 H2
Gardeners La......125 F5
Garlick Hill......125 F5
Garnault Mews......124 D1
Garnault Pl......124 D1
Garrett St......125 F2
Garrick St......124 B5
Garrick Yd......124 B5
Gascoigne Pl......125 J1
Gasholder Pl......128 D5
Gaspar Cl......126 B4
Gaspar Mews......126 B4
Gate Mews......127 E2
Gate St......124 C4
Gateforth St......122 D2
Gatesborough St......125 H2
Gateways The......127 E4
Gatliff Rd......127 H5
Gayfere St......128 C3
Gee St......125 F2
Gees Ct......123 F4
George Ct......124 B5
George Inn Yd......125 G6
George Mews......123 H1
George St......123 E4
George Yd......125 G4
George Yd......123 F5
Georgina Gdns......125 J1
Gerald Mews......127 G4
Gerald Rd......127 G4
Gerrard Pl......124 A5
Gerrard St......123 J5
Gertrude St......126 C6
Gibbon's Rents......125 H6
Gilbert Pl......124 B3
Gilbert St......123 F4
Gildea St......123 G3
Gillingham Mews......127 J4
Gillingham Row......127 J4
Gillingham St......127 J4
Gilston Rd......126 C5
Giltspur St......124 E3
Glasgow Terr......127 J5
Glasshouse St......123 H5
Glasshouse Wlk......128 D5
Glasshouse Yd......125 F2
Glebe Pl......126 E6
Gledhow Gdns......126 C4
Glendower Pl......126 D4
Glentworth St......123 E2

Globe Yd......123 G4
Gloucester Ct......125 H5
Gloucester Gdns......122 B4
Gloucester Mews......122 B4
Gloucester Mews W......122 B4
Gloucester Pl......123 E3
Gloucester Pl Mews......123 E3
Gloucester Rd......126 C4
Gloucester Sq......122 D4
Gloucester Sq......127 J5
Gloucester Terr......122 B4
Gloucester Way......124 D1
Gloucester Wlk......126 A2
Glyde Mews......127 E3
Glyn St......128 D5
Godfrey St......127 E5
Goding St......128 C5
Godliman St......125 F4
Golden La......125 F2
Golden Sq......123 H5
Goldsmith St......125 F4
Goodge Pl......123 H3
Goodge St......123 J3
Goodwins Ct......124 B5
Goodman's Yd......125 J5
Gophir La......125 G5
Gordon Pl......126 A2
Gordon Sq......123 J2
Gordon St......123 J2
Gore St......126 C3
Goring St......125 J4
Gosfield St......123 H3
Goslett Yd......123 J4
Gosset St......125 J1
Goswell Pl......125 E1
Goswell Rd......125 E1
Gough Sq......124 D4
Gough St......124 C2
Goulston St......125 J4
Gower Mews......123 J3
Gower Pl......123 J2
Gower St......123 J2
Gracechurch St......125 G5
Grafton Mews......123 H2
Grafton Pl......123 J1
Grafton St......123 G5
Grafton Way......123 H2
Graham Terr......127 G4
Granby Bldgs......128 D4
Granby Pl......128 E2
Grand Ave......124 E3
Grange Ct......124 C4
Grantham Pl......123 G6
Grantully Rd......122 A1
Granville Pl......123 F4
Granville Sq......124 C1
Granville St......124 C1
Grape St......124 B4
Gravel La......125 J4
Grayfriars Pas......125 E4
Gray's Inn Pl......124 C3
Gray's Inn Rd......124 C2
Gray's Inn Sq......124 D3
Gray's Yd......123 F4
Great Bell Alley......125 G4
Great Castle St......123 G4
Great Castle St......123 H4
Great Central St......123 J4
Great Chapel St......123 J4
Great College St......128 C3
Great Cumberland Mews......122 E4
Great Cumberland Pl......123 E4
Great Eastern St......125 H2
Great George St......128 C2
Great Guildford St......125 F6
Great James St......124 C3
Great Marlborough St......123 H4
Great Maze Pond......125 G6
Great New St......124 D4
Great Newport St......124 B5
Great Ormond St......124 C2
Great Percy St......124 D1
Great Peter St......128 B3
Great Portland St......123 G3
Great Pulteney St......123 H5
Great Queen St......124 B4
Great Russell St......124 A4
Great Russell St......124 B3
Great Scotland Yd......128 B6
Great Smith St......128 B3
Great St Helen's......125 H4
Great St Thomas Apostle......125 F5
Great Suffolk St......125 E6
Great Sutton St......125 E2
Great Swan Alley......125 G4
Great Titchfield St......123 H3
Great Tower St......125 H5
Great Trinity La......125 F5
Great Turnstile......124 C3
Great Winchester St......125 G4
Great Windmill St......123 J5
Greek St......123 J4
Green Arbour Ct......124 E4
Green Dragon Ct......125 G6
Green St......123 F5
Green Terr......124 D1
Greencoat Pl......128 A4
Greencoat Row......128 A3
Greenhill's Rents......124 E3
Greens Ct......123 J5
Greenwell St......123 G2
Gregory Pl......126 B2
Grendon St......122 D2
Grenville Mews......126 C4
Grenville Pl......126 C4
Grenville St......124 B2
Gresham St......125 F4
Gresse St......123 J4
Grey Eagle St......125 J2
Greycoat Pl......128 B3
Greycoat St......128 B3
Greyhound Ct......124 D5
Greystoke Pl......124 D4
Grindal St......128 E2
Grocers' Hall Ct......125 G4
Groom Pl......127 G3
Grosvenor Bridge......127 H6
Grosvenor Cottages......127 G4
Grosvenor Cres......127 G2
Grosvenor Cres Mews......127 G2
Grosvenor Gdns......127 H3
Grosvenor Gdns Mews E......127 H3
Grosvenor Gdns Mews N......127 H3
Grosvenor Gdns Mews S......127 H3
Grosvenor Hill......123 G5
Grosvenor Pl......127 H2
Grosvenor Sq......123 F5
Grosvenor St......123 G5
Grotto Pas......123 F3
Grove End Rd......122 C1
Grove Gdns......123 D1
Guildhall Bldgs......125 G4
Guildhall Yd......125 F4
Guildhouse St......127 J4
Guilford Pl......124 C2
Guilford St......124 C2
Guinness Ct......125 F1

Guinness Trust Bldgs......127 F4
Gun St......125 J3
Gunter Gr......126 C7
Gunthorpe St......125 J4
Guthrie St......126 E5
Gutter La......125 F4
Gwynne Pl......124 C1

H
Haberdasher Pl......125 H1
Haberdasher St......125 H1
Haines St......128 A7
Half Moon Ct......125 F3
Half Moon St......123 G6
Halfmoon Pas......125 J4
Halford Rd......126 A6
Halkin Arc......127 G3
Halkin Mews......127 G3
Halkin Pl......127 G3
Halkin St......127 G2
Hall Gate......122 C1
Hall Pl......122 C3
Hall Rd......122 B1
Hall St......124 E1
Hallam Mews......123 G3
Hallam St......123 G3
Hallon Gdns......125 J3
Halsey St......127 F4
Ham Yd......123 J5
Hamilton Cl......122 C1
Hamilton Gdns......122 B1
Hamilton Mews......127 H2
Hamilton Pl......127 G1
Hamilton Terr......122 B1
Hammett St......125 J5
Hampden Gurney St......122 E4
Hampstead Rd......123 H1
Hanbury St......125 J3
Hand Ct......124 C3
Handel St......124 B2
Handforth Rd......128 E7
Hanover Gdns......128 E6
Hanover Pl......124 B4
Hanover Sq......123 G4
Hanover St......123 G4
Hanover Terr......122 E1
Hanover Terr Mews......122 E1
Hans Cres......127 F3
Hans Pl......127 F3
Hans Rd......127 F3
Hans St......127 F3
Hanson St......123 H3
Hanway Pl......123 J4
Hanway St......123 J4
Harbet Rd......122 D3
Harcourt St......122 D3
Harcourt Terr......126 C5
Hardwick St......124 D1
Hare Ct......124 D4
Harewood Ave......122 D2
Harewood Pl......123 G4
Harewood Row......122 D3
Harley Gdns......126 C5
Harley Pl......123 G3
Harley St......123 G3
Harleyford Rd......128 D6
Harleyford St......128 E6
Harold Pl......128 E5
Harp Alley......124 E4
Harp La......125 H5
Harp La......125 H5
Harpur St......124 C3
Harriet St......127 F2
Harriet Wlk......127 F2
Harrington Gdns......126 C4
Harrington Rd......126 D4
Harrington St......123 H1
Harrison St......124 B1
Harrow Pl......125 J4
Harrow Rd......122 B3
Harrow Rd Fly......122 D3
Harrowby St......122 D4
Hart St......125 H5
Hartington Rd......128 C7
Hartshorn Alley......125 H4
Harvey's Bldgs......124 B5
Hasker St......127 E4
Hastings St......124 B1
Hatfields......124 D6
Hatherley Gr......122 A4
Hatherley St......128 A4
Hatton Gdn......124 D3
Hatton Pl......124 D3
Hatton Row......122 C2
Hatton St......122 C2
Hatton Wall......124 D3
Haunch of Venison Yd......123 G4
Hay Hill......123 G5
Haydon St......125 J5
Haydon Wlk......125 J4
Hayes Pl......122 D2
Haymarket......123 J5
Haymarket Arc......123 J5
Hayne St......124 E3
Hay's La......125 H6
Hay's Mews......123 G5
Hayward's Pl......124 E2
Headfort Pl......127 G2
Hearn St......125 H2
Heathcote St......124 C1
Heddon St......123 H5
Helmet Row......125 F2
Hemans St......128 C7
Hemans St Estate......128 B7
Hemus Pl......127 E5
Henderson Dri......122 C2
Heneage La......125 H4
Heneage St......125 J3
Henniker Mews......126 D6
Henrietta Mews......124 B2
Henrietta Pl......123 G4
Henrietta St......124 B5
Herbal Hill......124 D2
Herbert Cres......127 F3
Herbrand St......124 B2
Hercules Rd......128 E3
Hereford Sq......126 C4
Hermit St......124 E1
Hermitage St......122 C3
Herrick St......128 B4
Hertford Pl......123 H2
Hertford St......123 G6
Hesper Mews......126 B4
Hester Rd......126 E7
Hewett St......125 H2
Heyford Ave......128 D7
Hide Pl......128 B4
High Holborn......124 C3
High Timber St......125 F5
Hilary Cl......126 B7
Hildyard Rd......126 A6
Hill St......123 G6
Hillgate Pl......126 A1
Hillgate St......126 A1
Hills Pl......123 H4
Hind Ct......124 D4
Hinde Mews......123 F4

Hinde St......123 F4
Hobart Pl......127 H3
Hobury St......126 D6
Hocker St......125 J1
Hogarth Ct......125 H5
Hogarth Pl......126 B4
Hogarth Rd......126 B4
Holbein Mews......127 G5
Holbein Pl......127 G4
Holborn......124 C3
Holborn Mews......127 G5
Holborn Pl......124 C3
Holborn Viaduct......124 E3
Holford Pl......124 C1
Holford St......124 D1
Holland Pl......126 B2
Holland St......126 A2
Hollen St......123 J4
Holles St......123 G4
Holly Mews......126 C5
Hollywell Row......125 H2
Hollywood Mews......126 C6
Hollywood Rd......126 C6
Holmead Rd......126 B7
Holmes Pl......126 C6
Holmes Terr......128 E2
Holsworthy Sq......124 C2
Holyrood St......125 H6
Holywell La......125 H2
Homer Row......122 D3
Homer St......122 D3
Honduras St......125 F2
Honey La......125 F4
Honey La......125 F4
Hooper's Ct......127 F2
Hop Gdns......124 B5
Hopkins St......123 J4
Hopton St......124 E6
Hornton Pl......126 A2
Hornton St......126 A2
Horse and Dolphin Yd......123 J5
Horse Guards Rd......130 B2
Horse Shoe Alley......125 F6
Horse Shoe Yd......123 G5
Horseferry Rd......128 B4
Horseguards Ave......124 B6
Horselydown La......125 J6
Hortensia Rd......126 C7
Hosier La......124 E3
Hotspur St......128 E5
Houghton St......124 C4
Houndsditch......125 H4
Howard St......124 C3
Howick Pl......128 A3
Howie St......126 E7
Howland Mews E......123 H3
Howland St......123 H3
Howley Pl......122 B3
Hoxton Market......125 H1
Hoxton Sq......125 H1
Hudson's Pl......127 J4
Huggin Ct......125 F5
Huggin Hill......125 F5
Hugh Mews......127 H4
Hugh Pl......128 B4
Hugh St......127 H4
Hull St......125 F1
Hungerford Bridge (foot)......124 C6
Hungerford La......124 B6
Hunter St......124 B2
Huntley St......123 J2
Hunt's Ct......124 A5
Huntsworth Mews......122 E2
Hutton St......124 D4
Hyde Park Cnr......127 G2
Hyde Park Cres......122 D4
Hyde Park Gate......126 C2
Hyde Park Gate......126 C2
Hyde Park Gate Mews......126 C2
Hyde Park Gdns......122 D5
Hyde Park Gdns Mews......122 D5
Hyde Park Sq......122 D4
Hyde Park Sq Mews......122 D4
Hyde Park St......122 D4

I
Idol La......125 H5
Ifield Rd......126 B6
Imperial College Rd......126 D3
India St......125 J4
Ingestre Pl......123 H5
Inglebert St......124 D1
Ingram Cl......128 D4
Inigo Pl......124 B5
Inner Circ......123 F1
Inner Temple La......124 D4
Insurance St......124 D1
Inverness Gdns......126 B1
Inverness Mews......122 A5
Inverness Pl......122 A5
Inverness Terr......122 A5
Ireland Yd......124 E4
Irongate Wharf Rd......122 C3
Ironmonger La......125 G4
Ironmonger Pas......125 F1
Ironmonger Row......125 F1
Irving St......124 A5
Isabella St......124 E6
Iverna Ct......126 B3
Iverna Gdns......126 B3
Ives St......127 E4
Ivor Pl......122 E2
Ivybridge La......124 B5
Ixworth Pl......126 E4

J
Jacob's Well Mews......123 F4
James St......123 F4
James St......124 B5
Jameson St......126 A1
Jason Ct......123 F4
Jay Mews......126 C2
Jerdan Pl......126 A7
Jermyn St......123 H5
Jerome Cres......122 D2
Jerome St......125 J3
Jerusalem Pas......124 E2
Jervis Ct......123 G4
Jewry St......125 J4
Joan St......124 E6
Jockey's Fields......124 C3
Johanna St......128 E2
John Adam St......124 B5
John Aird St......122 B3
John Carpenter St......124 E5
John Islip St......128 C4
John Prince's St......123 G4
John St......124 C2
John's Mews......124 C2
Johnsons Ct......124 D4
Johnson's Pl......127 J5
Joiner St......125 G6
Jonathan St......128 D5
Jones St......123 G5
Jubilee Pl......127 E5
Judd St......124 B1

Juer St......127 E7
Junction Mews......122 D4
Junction Pl......122 C4
Justice Wlk......126 E6
Juxon St......128 D4

K
Kean St......124 C4
Keats Pl......125 G3
Keeley St......124 C4
Kelso Pl......126 B3
Kemble St......124 C4
Kemp's Ct......123 J4
Kempsford Gdns......126 A5
Kenchester Cl......128 C7
Kendal St......122 D4
Kendall Pl......123 F3
Kendrick Mews......126 D4
Kendrick Pl......126 D4
Kennington Gr......128 D6
Kennington La......128 D5
Kennington Oval......128 D6
Kennington Park Rd......128 E6
Kennington Rd......128 E3
Kenrick Pl......123 F3
Kensington Church Ct......126 B2
Kensington Church St......126 A1
Kensington Church Wlk......126 B2
Kensington Ct......126 B3
Kensington Court Mews......126 B3
Kensington Court Pl......126 B3
Kensington Ct......126 B2
Kensington Gate......126 C3
Kensington Gdns Sq......122 A4
Kensington Gore......126 C2
Kensington High St......126 A3
Kensington Mall......126 A1
Kensington Mansions......126 A5
Kensington Palace Gdns......126 B2
Kensington Palace Gdns......126 B1
Kensington Pl......126 A1
Kensington Rd......126 D2
Kensington Sq......126 B3
Kent Pas......122 E1
Kent Terr......122 D1
Kent Yd......127 E2
Kentish Bldgs......125 G6
Kenton St......124 B2
Kenway Rd......126 B4
Keppel Row......125 F6
Keppel St......124 A3
Kibworth St......128 D7
Kiffen St......125 G2
Kimbolton Row......126 E4
King Charles St......128 C2
King Edward St......125 F4
King Edward Wlk......128 E3
King John Ct......125 H2
King Sq......125 F1
King St......123 H6
King St......124 B5
King St......128 A1
King William St......125 G5
Kinghorn St......125 F3
Kingly Ct......123 H5
Kingly St......123 H5
King's Arms Yd......125 G4
King's Bench Wlk......124 D4
King's Cross......124 B1
King's Cross Bridge......124 B1
King's Cross Rd......124 C1
King's Head Yd......125 G6
King's Mews......124 C2
King's Rd......127 G3
King's Rd......127 G3
King's Scholars' Pas......127 J4
Kingscote St......124 E5
Kingsley Mews......126 B3
Kingsway......124 C4
Kinnerton Pl N......127 F2
Kinnerton Pl S......127 F2
Kinnerton St......127 G2
Kinnerton St......127 G2
Kirby St......124 D3
Kirkman Pl......123 J3
Kirtling St......127 J7
Kirton Gdns......125 J1
Knaresborough Pl......126 B4
Knightrider St......125 E5
Knightsbridge......127 E2
Knightsbridge......127 F2
Knightsbridge Green......127 F2
Knox St......122 E3
Kramer Mews......126 B5
Kynance Mews......126 C3
Kynance Pl......126 C3

L
Lackington St......125 G3
Lamb St......125 J3
Lambeth Bridge......128 D4
Lambeth High St......128 D4
Lambeth Hill......125 F5
Lambeth Mews......128 D5
Lambeth Palace Rd......128 D3
Lambeth Rd......128 E3
Lambeth Wlk......128 D4
Lamb's Bldgs......125 G2
Lamb's Conduit Pas......124 C2
Lamb's Conduit St......124 C2
Lamb's Pas......125 G2
Lamont Rd......126 D6
Lamont Rd Pas......126 D6
Lanark Pl......122 B2
Lanark Rd......122 B1
Lancashire Ct......123 G5
Lancaster Gate......122 B5
Lancaster Mews......122 C5
Lancaster Pl......124 C5
Lancaster Terr......122 C5
Lancelot Pl......127 F2
Lancing St......123 J1
Landon Pl......127 F3
Lanfranc St......128 E3
Langham Pl......123 G3
Langham St......123 G3
Langley Ct......124 B5
Langley La......128 D6
Langley St......124 B4
Langthorn St......125 G4
Langton Cl......124 C2
Langton St......126 C6
Lanhill Rd......122 A1
Lansdowne Rd......126 A1
Lansdowne Terr......124 B2
Laud St......128 D5
Lauderdale Rd......122 A1
Launcelot St......128 E2
Laurence Pountney Hill......125 G5
Laurence Pountney La......125 G5
Lavender Cl......126 D6
Laverton Mews......126 B4

Laverton Pl......126 B4
Lavington St......125 E6
Lawn La......128 D6
Lawrence La......125 F4
Lawrence St......126 E6
Laxton Pl......123 G2
Laystall St......124 D2
Lazenby Ct......124 B5
Leadenhall Ave......125 H4
Leadenhall Market......125 H4
Leadenhall Pl......125 H4
Leadenhall St......125 H4
Leake Ct......128 D2
Leake St......128 D2
Leather La......124 D3
Lecky St......126 D5
Leeke St......124 C1
Lees Pl......123 F5
Leicester Ct......124 A5
Leicester Pl......124 A5
Leicester Sq......124 A5
Leicester St......123 J5
Leigh Pl......124 D3
Leigh St......124 B1
Leinster Gdns......122 B4
Leinster Mews......122 B5
Leinster Pl......122 B4
Leinster Terr......122 B5
Lennox Gdns......127 F3
Lennox Gdns Mews......127 F3
Lenthal Pl......126 C4
Leo St......124 E2
Leonard St......125 G2
Leopards Ct......124 D3
Leopold Wlk......128 D5
Lever St......125 F1
Leverett St......127 E4
Leverington Pl......125 G1
Lewisham St......128 B2
Lexham Gardens Mews......126 B3
Lexham Gdns......126 B3
Lexham Mews......126 A3
Lexham Wlk......126 B3
Lexington St......123 H5
Leyden St......125 J3
Ligonier St......125 J2
Lilac Ct......128 D4
Lilestone St......122 D2
Lillie Rd......126 A6
Lillie Yd......126 A6
Lily Pl......124 D3
Lime St......125 H4
Lime St Pas......125 H4
Limerston St......126 D6
Lincoln St......127 F4
Lincoln's Inn Fields......124 C4
Lindsey St......125 E3
Linhope St......122 E2
Lisle St......124 A5
Lisson Gr......122 C2
Lisson St......122 D3
Litchfield St......123 J5
Little Albany St......123 G2
Little Argyll St......123 H4
Little Boltons The......126 C5
Little Britain......125 F3
Little Chester St......127 H3
Little College La......125 G5
Little College St......128 C3
Little Essex St......124 D5
Little George St......128 C2
Little Marlborough St......123 H4
Little New St......124 D4
Little Newport St......124 A5
Little Portland St......123 H4
Little Russell St......124 B3
Little Sanctuary......128 C2
Little Smith St......128 B3
Little Somerset St......125 J4
Little St James' St......123 H6
Little St James's St......128 A1
Little Titchfield St......123 H3
Little Trinity La......125 F5
Liverpool St......125 H3
Livonia St......123 H4
Lizard St......125 F1
Lloyd Baker St......124 D1
Lloyd Sq......124 D1
Lloyd St......124 D1
Lloyd's Ave......125 H5
Lloyd's Row......124 E1
Lodge Rd......122 D1
Logan Mew......126 A4
Logan Pl......126 A4
Lollard St......128 D4
Lollard St......128 D4
Lombard Ct......125 G5
Lombard La......124 D4
Lombard St......125 G5
Lombardy Pl......122 A5
London Bridge......125 G5
London Bridge St......125 G6
London Mews......122 C4
London St......122 C4
London St......125 H4
London Wall......125 F3
Long Acre......124 B4
Long La......125 G6
Long St......125 J1
Longford St......123 G2
Longmoore St......127 J4
Longridge Rd......126 A4
Long's Ct......124 A5
Lord Hills Rd......122 A3
Lord North St......128 C3
Lordship Pl......126 E6
Lorenzo St......124 C1
Lorne Cl......122 D1
Lothbury......125 G4
Lots Rd......126 C7
Loughborough St......128 D5
Lovat La......125 H5
Love La......125 F4
Lowdes Ct......123 H4
Lower Belgrave St......127 H3
Lower Grosvenor Pl......127 H3
Lower James St......123 H5
Lower John St......123 H5
Lower Marsh......128 E2
Lower Sloane St......127 G5
Lower Thames St......125 G5
Lowndes Cl......127 G3
Lowndes Pl......127 G3
Lowndes Sq......127 F2
Lowndes St......127 G3
Loxham St......124 B1
Lucan Pl......126 E4
Lucerne Mews......126 A1
Ludgate Bwy......124 E4
Ludgate Circ......124 E4
Ludgate Hill......124 E4
Ludgate Sq......124 E4
Ludlow St......125 F2
Luke St......125 H2
Lumley Ct......124 B5
Lumley St......123 F4
Lupus St......127 H5
Luscombe Way......128 C7
Luton St......122 C2
Luxborough St......123 F3

Lyall Mews....127 G3
Lyall Mews W....127 G3
Lyall St....127 G3
Lygon Pl....127 H3
Lyons Pl....122 C2

M

Mabledon Pl....124 A1
Mac Farren Pl....123 F2
Macclesfield Rd....125 F1
Macclesfield St....123 J5
Macklin St....124 B4
Mackworth St....123 H1
Maddox St....123 H5
Magdalen St....125 H6
Magee St....128 E6
Magpie Alley....124 D4
Maida Ave....122 B2
Maida Vale....122 B1
Maiden La....123 B5
Maidstone Bldgs....125 G6
Mail Coach Yd....125 H1
Makins St....127 E4
Malet Pl....123 J2
Malet St....124 A3
Mall The....123 J6
Mallord St....126 D6
Mallory St....122 D2
Mallow St....125 G2
Malta St....124 E2
Maltravers St....124 D5
Manchester Sq....123 F4
Manchester St....123 F3
Mandeville Pl....123 F4
Manette St....123 J4
Manningford Cl....124 E1
Manor St Estate....127 E6
Manresa Rd....126 E5
Mansell St....125 J4
Mansfield Mews....123 G3
Mansfield St....123 G3
Mansion House Pl....125 G4
Mansion House St....125 G4
Manson Mews....126 D4
Manson Pl....126 D4
Maple Pl....123 H3
Maple St....123 H2
Marble Arch....123 E5
Marchmont St....124 B2
Margaret Ct....123 H4
Margaret St....123 H4
Margaretta Terr....126 E6
Margery St....124 D1
Mark La....125 H6
Mark Sq....125 H2
Mark St....125 H2
Market Ct....123 H4
Market Mews....123 G6
Market Pl....123 H4
Markham Pl....127 F5
Markham Sq....127 F5
Markham St....127 E5
*Marlborough Ct....123 H4
Marlborough Flats....127 E4
Marlborough Rd....123 H6
Marlborough St....124 E4
Marloes Rd....126 B3
Marshall St....123 H4
Marsham St....128 B4
Martin La....125 G5
Martlett Ct....123 B4
Marylebone High St....123 F3
Marylebone La....123 F4
Marylebone Mews....123 G3
Marylebone Pas....123 H4
Marylebone Rd....123 E3
Marylebone St....123 F3
Marylee Way....128 D4
Mason's Arms Mews....123 G5
Mason's Ave....125 G4
Mason's St....125 F1
Mason's Yd....123 H6
Mason's Yd....128 A1
Matthew Parker St....128 B2
Maunsel St....128 B4
Mayfair Pl....123 G6
Mays Ct....124 B5
McAuley St....128 E3
McLeod's Mews....126 B4
Mead Row....128 E3
Meadow Mews....128 D6
Meadow Pl....128 C7
Meadow Rd....128 D7
Meard St....123 H4
Mecklenburgh Pl....124 C2
Mecklenburgh Sq....124 C2
Medway St....128 B3
Meek St....126 C7
Melbourne Pl....124 C4
Melbury Terr....122 D2
Melcombe Pl....122 E3
Melcombe St....122 E2
Melina Pl....122 C1
Melon Pl....126 A2
Melton Ct....126 D4
Melton St....123 J1
Memel Ct....125 F2
Memel St....125 F2
Mepham St....124 D6
Mercer St....124 B4
Meredith St....124 E1
Merlin St....124 D1
Merrington Rd....126 A6
Meymott St....124 E6
Micawber St....125 F1
Micklethwaite Rd....126 A6
Middle Dartrey Wlk....126 D7
Middle St....125 F3
Middle Temple La....124 D5
Middle Yd....125 H6
Middlesex Pas....125 E3
Middlesex St....125 J4
Middleton Bldgs....123 H3
Midford Pl....123 H2
Midhope St....124 B1
Midland Rd....124 B1
Milborne Gr....126 C5
Miles Pl....122 C3
Miles St....128 C6
Milford La....124 D5
Milford La....124 D5
Milk St....125 F4
Mill St....123 H4
Millbank....128 C4
Millman Mews....124 C2
Millman St....124 C2
Mills Ct....125 H1
Milman's St....126 D6
Milner St....127 F4
Milroy Wlk....124 E6
Milton Ct....125 G3
Milton St....125 G3
Milverton St....128 E5
Mincing La....125 H5
Minera Mews....127 G4
Minories....125 J5
Mitchell St....125 F2
Mitre Ct....124 C4
Mitre Ct....124 D4

Mitre Sq....125 H4
Mitre St....125 H4
Modern Ct....124 E4
Molyneux St....122 D3
Monck St....128 B3
Moncorvo Cl....126 E2
Monkwell Sq....125 F3
Monmouth St....124 B4
Montagu Mansions....123 E3
Montagu Mews N....123 E4
Montagu Mews S....123 E4
Montagu Mews W....123 E4
Montagu Pl....127 F3
Montagu Row....123 E3
Montagu Sq....123 E4
Montagu St....123 E4
Montague Cl....125 G6
Montague Pl....127 F3
Montague Pl....124 B3
Montclare St....125 J2
Montford Pl....128 E5
Montpelier Mew....127 E3
Montpelier Pl....127 E3
Montpelier Sq....127 E2
Montpelier St....127 E2
Montpelier Terr....127 E2
Montpelier Wlk....127 E3
Montreal Pl....124 C5
Montrose Ct....126 D2
Montrose Pl....127 G2
Monument St....125 G5
Moor La....125 G3
Moor La....125 G3
Moor Pl....125 G3
Moor St....124 A4
Moore St....127 F4
Moorfields....125 G3
Moorfields Highwalk....125 G3
Moorgate....125 G3
Moorgate....125 G4
Mora St....125 F1
Moravian Cl....126 D6
Moravian Pl....126 D6
Moreland St....125 E1
Moreton Pl....128 A5
Moreton St....128 B5
Moreton Terr....128 A5
Moreton Terr Mews N....128 A5
Moreton Terr Mews S....128 A5
Morgans La....125 H6
Morpeth Terr....127 J4
Mortimer Market....123 H2
Mortimer St....123 H3
Morton Mews....126 B4
Morwell St....123 J3
Moscow Pl....122 A5
Moscow Rd....122 A5
Mossop St....127 E4
Motcomb St....127 G3
Mount Mills....125 E1
Mount Pleasant....124 D2
Mount Row....123 G5
Mount St....123 F5
Moxon St....123 F3
Mulberry Wlk....126 D6
Mulready St....122 D2
Mumford Ct....125 F4
Mundy St....125 H1
Munster Sq....123 G2
Murphy St....124 D7
Muscovy St....125 H5
Museum St....124 B4
Myddelton Pas....124 D1
Myddelton Sq....124 D1
Myddelton St....124 D1
Mylne St....124 D1

N

Nantes Pas....125 J3
Nassau St....123 H3
Navarre St....125 J2
Neal St....124 B4
Neal's Yd....124 B4
Neathouse Pl....127 J4
Nelson Pl....125 F1
Netherton Gr....126 C6
Netley St....123 H1
Nevern Pl....126 A4
Nevern Rd....126 A4
Nevern Sq....126 A4
Neville St....126 D5
Neville Terr....126 D5
New Bond St....123 G5
New Bridge St....124 E4
New Broad St....125 H3
New Burlington Mews....123 H5
New Burlington Pl....123 H5
New Burlington St....123 H5
New Cavendish St....123 G3
New Change....125 F4
New Charles St....124 E1
New Compton St....124 B4
New Coventry St....124 A5
New Fetter La....124 D4
New Goulston St....125 J4
New Inn Bwy....125 H2
New Inn Pas....124 C4
New Inn Sq....125 H2
New Inn St....125 H2
New Inn Yd....125 H2
New London St....125 H5
New North Pl....125 H2
New North St....124 C3
New Oxford St....124 B4
New Quebec St....123 E4
New Row....124 B5
New Spring Gdns Wlk....128 C5
New Sq....124 C4
New St....125 H3
New St Sq....124 D4
New Turnstile....124 C3
New Union St....125 G3
Newburgh St....123 H4
Newburn St....128 D5
Newbury St....125 F3
Newcastle Cl....124 E4
Newcastle Ct....125 F5
Newcastle Pl....122 C3
Newcastle Row....124 D2
Newcombe St....126 A1
Newgate St....125 E4
Newman Pas....123 H3
Newman St....123 H3
Newman's Ct....125 G4
Newman's Row....124 C3
Newnham Terr....128 E3
Newport Ct....124 A5
Newport Pl....124 A5
Newton St....124 B4
Nicholas La....125 G5
Nicholson St....124 E6
Nile St....125 G1
Nine Elm Ind Estate....127 J6
Noble St....125 F4
Noel St....123 H4
Norfolk Cres....122 D4
Norfolk Pl....122 C4
Norfolk Row....128 D4

Norfolk Sq....122 C4
Norfolk Sq Mews....122 C4
Norman St....125 F1
Norris St....123 J5
North Audley St....123 F5
North Bank....122 D1
North Carriage Dri....122 D5
North Cres....123 J3
North Folgate....125 H3
North Gower St....123 H1
North Mews....124 C2
North Row....123 F5
North Tenter St....125 J4
North Terr....126 E3
North Wharf Rd....122 C3
Northampton Bldgs....124 D2
Northampton Rd....124 D2
Northampton Sq....124 E1
Northburgh St....125 E2
Northcourt....123 H3
Northington St....124 C2
Northumberland Alley....125 H4
Northumberland Ave....124 B6
Northumberland St....124 B6
Northwick Cl....122 C2
Northwick Terr....122 C2
Norwich St....124 D4
Notting Hill Gate....126 A1
Nottingham Ct....124 B4
Nottingham Pl....123 F3
Nottingham St....123 F3
Nun Ct....125 G4
Nutford Pl....122 D4

O

Oak Tree Rd....122 D1
Oakden St....128 E4
Oakey La....128 E4
Oakfield St....126 C6
Oakley Gdns....127 E6
Oakley St....127 E6
Oat La....125 F4
Observatory Gdns....126 A2
Odhams Wlk....124 B4
Offley Rd....128 E7
Ogle St....123 H3
Old Bailey....124 E4
Old Barge House Alley....124 D6
Old Barrack Yd....127 G2
Old Bldgs....124 D4
Old Bond St....123 H5
Old Broad St....125 H4
Old Brompton Rd....126 B5
Old Brompton Rd....126 D4
Old Burlington St....123 H5
Old Castle St....125 J4
Old Cavendish St....123 G4
Old Change Ct....125 F4
Old Church St....126 D5
Old Compton St....124 A4
Old Court Pl....126 B2
Old Fish St Hill....125 F5
Old Gloucester St....124 B3
Old Jewry....125 G4
Old Manor Yd....126 B4
Old Market Sq....125 J1
Old Marylebone Rd....122 D3
Old Nichol St....125 J2
Old North St....124 C3
Old Paradise St....128 D4
Old Park La....127 H1
Old Pye St....128 B3
Old Quebec St....123 E4
Old Queen St....128 B2
Old Seacoal La....124 E4
Old South Lambeth Rd....128 C7
Old St....125 G2
Old St....125 G2
Oldbury Pl....123 F3
Oliver's Yd....125 G2
Olympia Yd....122 A5
Omeara St....125 F6
Ongar Rd....126 A6
Onslow Mews....126 D4
Onslow Mews E....126 D4
Onslow Mews W....126 D4
Onslow Sq....126 D4
Onstow Gdns....126 D5
Orange St....124 A5
Orange Yd....123 J4
Oratory La....126 E5
Orchard St....123 F4
Orchardson St....122 C2
Orde Hall St....124 C3
Orme Ct....122 A5
Orme Ct Mews....122 A5
Orme La....122 A5
Orme Sq....122 A5
Ormond Cl....124 B3
Ormond Mews....124 B2
Ormond Yd....123 H6
Ormond Yd....128 A1
Ormonde Gate....127 F5
Ormonde Pl....127 G4
Orsett St....128 D5
Orsett Terr....122 B4
Osbert St....128 B4
Osnaburgh St....123 G2
Osnaburgh Ter....123 G2
Ossington Bldgs....123 F3
Ossulston St....124 A1
Osten Mews....126 B3
Oswin St....125 E3
Outwich St....125 H4
Outer Circ....123 F2
Oval Pl....128 D7
Oval Way....128 D6
Ovington Gdns....127 E3
Ovington Mews....127 E3
Ovington Sq....127 E3
Ovington St....127 F4
Owen's Ct....124 E1
Owen's Row....124 E1
Oxendon St....123 J5
Oxford Circ....123 H4
Oxford Circus Ave....123 H4
Oxford St....125 G5
Oxford Sq....122 D4
Oxford St....123 G4

P

Padbury Ct....125 J1
Paddington Green....122 C3
Paddington St....123 F3
Page St....128 B4
Paget St....124 E1
Pakenham St....124 C2
Palace Ave....126 B2
Palace Gate....126 C2
Palace Gdns Mews....126 A1
Palace Gdns Terr....126 B1
Palace Green....126 A6
Palace Green....126 B1
Palace Mews....127 G4
Palace Pl....127 J3
Palace St....127 J3
Palfrey Pl....128 D7

Palissy St....125 J1
Pall Mall....123 J6
Pall Mall....128 B1
Pall Mall E....124 A6
Pall Mall Pl....128 B1
Pall Mall Pl....123 H6
Palmer St....128 A3
Pancras La....125 G4
Panton St....123 J5
Panyer Alley....125 F4
Parade The....127 F7
Paradise Wlk....127 F6
Pardon St....125 E2
Paris Gdn....124 E6
Park Cl....127 F2
Park Cres....123 G2
Park Cres Mews E....123 G2
Park Cres Mews W....123 G2
Park La....123 F5
Park Mansions Arc....127 F2
Park Pl....123 H6
Park Pl....123 A1
Park Pl Villas....122 B3
Park Rd....122 E2
Park Rd....122 D1
Park Road....122 D2
Park Sq E....123 G2
Park Sq Mews....123 G2
Park Sq W....123 G2
Park St....125 F6
Park St....123 F5
Park West....122 D4
Park West Pl....122 D4
Park Wlk....126 D6
Parker Mews....124 B4
Parker St....124 B4
Parkgate Rd....126 E7
Parliament St....128 C2
Parry St....128 C6
Pascal St....128 B7
Passing Alley....124 E2
Passmore St....127 G5
Pater St....126 A3
Paternoster Row....125 F4
Paternoster Sq....125 F4
Paton St....125 F1
Paul St....125 H2
Paultons Sq....126 D6
Paultons St....126 D6
Paveley St....122 D1
Paveley St....122 D2
Paveley Way....127 E7
Pavilion Rd....127 F3
Pavilion St....127 F3
Peabody Ave....127 H5
Peabody Estate....125 E6
Peabody Estate....127 J4
Pear Pl....128 E2
Pear Tree Ct....124 D2
Pear Tree St....125 F2
Pearman St....128 E2
Peartree St....125 F2
Peel Pass....126 A1
Peel St....126 A1
Peerless St....125 G1
Pegasus Pl....128 E6
Pelham Cres....126 E4
Pelham Pl....126 E4
Pelham St....126 E4
Pemberton Row....124 D4
Pembroke Cl....127 G2
Pembroke Pl....126 A4
Penfold Pl....122 D3
Penfold St....122 C2
Pennant Mews....126 B4
Penton Rise....124 C1
Penywern Rd....126 A5
Pepys St....125 H5
Percival St....124 E1
Percy Circ....124 C1
Percy Mews....123 J3
Percy Pass....123 J3
Percy St....123 J3
Perkins Rents....128 B3
Perry's Pl....123 J4
Peter St....123 J5
Peter's Hill....125 F5
Peter's La....124 E3
Petersham La....126 C3
Petersham Mews....126 C3
Petersham Pl....126 C3
Peto Pl....123 G2
Petty France....128 A3
Petyt Pl....126 E6
Petyward....127 E4
Phene St....127 E6
Philbeach Gdns....126 A5
Phillimore Wlk....126 A3
Philpot St....125 H5
Phipp St....125 H2
Phoenix Pl....124 C2
Phoenix St....124 A4
Piccadilly....123 H6
Piccadilly....128 A1
Piccadilly Arc....123 H6
Piccadilly Circ....123 J5
Piccadilly Pl....123 H5
Pickard St....125 E1
Pickering Mews....122 A4
Pickering Pl....123 H6
Pickering St....122 A4
Picton Pl....123 F4
Pilgrim St....124 E4
Pilgrimage St....125 G6
Pimlico Rd....127 G5
Pimlico Wlk....125 H1
Pindar St....125 H3
Pindock Mews....122 A2
Pine Apple Ct....127 J3
Pine St....124 D2
Pitfield St....125 H1
Pitt St....126 A2
Pitt's Head Mews....123 F6
Platina St....125 G2
Playhouse Yd....124 E4
Pleydell St....124 D4
Plough Ct....125 G5
Plough Pl....124 D4
Plough Yd....125 H2
Plumber's Pl....124 D2
Plumtree Ct....124 E4
Plympton Pl....122 D2
Plympton St....122 D2
Poets Corner....128 C3
Poland St....123 H4
Pollen St....123 H4
Pollitt Dri....122 C2
Pomell Way....125 J4
Pond Pl....126 E5
Ponsonby Pl....128 B5
Ponsonby Terr....128 B5
Pont St....127 F3
Pont St Mews....127 F3
Ponton Rd....128 B7
Pooles Bldgs....124 D2
*Pope's Head Alley....125 G4
Poplar Pl....122 A5

Poppins Ct....124 E4
Porchester Gdn Mews....122 A4
Porchester Gdns....122 A5
Porchester Mews....122 A4
Porchester Pl....122 D4
Porchester Rd....122 A4
Porchester Sq....122 A4
Porchester Terr....122 B5
Porchester Terr N....122 A4
Porchester Wlk....122 A4
Porter St....123 F3
Porteus Rd....122 B3
Portland Mews....123 H4
Portland Pl....123 G3
Portman Cl....123 F4
Portman Mews S....123 F4
Portman Sq....123 F4
Portman St....123 F4
Portman Towers....123 E4
Portpool La....124 D3
Portsea Pl....122 D4
Portsea St....122 D4
Portsmouth St....124 C4
Portsoken St....125 J5
Portugal St....124 C4
Post Office Ct....125 G4
Post Office Way....128 B6
Potters Fields....125 H6
Poultry....125 G4
Powis Pl....124 B2
Praed Mews....122 C4
Praed St....122 C4
Pratt Wlk....128 D4
Prescot St....125 J5
President St....125 F1
Price's St....125 E6
Prideaux Pl....124 C1
*Priest's Ct....125 F4
Prima Rd....128 E7
Primrose Hill....124 D4
Primrose St....125 H3
Prince Consort Rd....126 D3
Prince of Wales Pas....123 H1
Prince of Wales Terr....126 C2
Princelet St....125 J3
Princes Arc....123 H6
Princes Ct....128 A1
Princes Gate....126 D2
Princes Gate Ct....126 D2
Princes Gate Mews....126 D3
Princes Gdns....126 D3
Prince's St....125 G4
Princes St....123 G4
Princeton St....124 C3
Printer St....124 D4
Printing House Yd....125 H1
Priory Wlk....126 C5
Procter St....124 C3
Providence Ct....123 F5
Provost St....125 G1
Prudent Pas....125 F4
Pudding La....125 G5
Puddle Dock....124 E5
Pugh's Pl....123 H4
Puma Ct....125 J3
Pump Ct....124 D4

Q

Quadrangle The....122 D4
Quadrant Arc....123 H5
Quaker St....125 J2
Quality Ct....124 D4
Quebec Mews....123 E4
Queen Anne Mews....123 G3
Queen Anne St....123 G3
Queen Anne's Gate....128 B2
Queen Sq....124 B3
Queen Sq Pl....124 B2
Queen St....125 G6
Queen St....123 G6
Queen Victoria St....125 F5
Queenhithe....125 F5
Queen's Elm Sq....126 D5
Queen's Gate....126 C3
Queen's Gate Gdns....126 C3
Queen's Gate Mews....126 C3
Queen's Gate Pl....126 C3
Queen's Gate Pl Mews....126 C3
Queen's Gate Terr....126 C3
Queen's Gdns....122 B5
Queen's Head Yd....125 G6
Queen's Mews....122 A5
Queen's Wlk....123 H6
Queen's Wlk....128 A1
*Queen's Yd....123 H2
Queensberry Mews W....126 D4
Queensberry Pl....126 D4
Queensberry Way....126 D4
Queensborough Mews....122 B5
Queensborough Pas....122 B5
Queensborough Terr....122 B5
Queenstown Rd....127 H7
Queensway....122 A5

R

Rabbit Row....126 A1
Radley Mews....126 B3
Radnor Mews....122 C4
Radnor Pl....122 D4
Radnor St....125 F1
Radnor Wlk....127 F5
Radstock St....126 E7
Railway App....125 G6
Railway St....124 B1
Rainsford St....122 D4
Ralston St....127 F5
Ramillies Pl....123 H4
Ramillies St....123 H4
Rampayne St....128 B5
Randall Pl....128 D4
Randall Row....128 D4
Randolph Ave....122 B1
Randolph Cres....122 B2
Randolph Mews....122 B2
Randolph Rd....122 B2
Ranelagh Gr....127 G5
Ranelagh Rd....128 A5
Ranston St....122 D2
Raphael St....127 F2
Rathbone Pl....123 J4
Rathbone St....123 H3
Raven Rd....128 D4
Ravenscroft....125 J2
Ravent Rd....128 D4
Ravey St....125 H2
Rawlings St....127 E4
Rawstone Pl....124 E1
Rawstorne St....124 E1
Ray St....124 D2
Raynham....122 D4
Red Lion Ct....124 D4
Red Lion Sq....124 C3
Red Lion St....124 C3
Red Lion Yd....123 F6
Red Pl....123 F5

Redan Pl....122 A4
Redanchop Cl....126 E6
Redburn St....127 F6
Redchurch St....125 J2
Redcliffe Gdns....126 B6
Redcliffe Mews....126 B5
Redcliffe Pl....126 C6
Redcliffe Rd....126 C6
Redcliffe Sq....126 B5
Redcliffe St....126 B6
Redcross Way....125 F6
Redesdale St....127 F5
Redfield La....126 B4
Redfield Mews....126 A4
Redhill St....123 G1
Redvers St....125 H1
Reece Mews....126 D4
Reeves Mews....123 F5
Regency St....128 B4
Regent Pl....123 H5
Regent Sq....124 B1
Regent St....123 J5
Regent St....123 H5
Regnart Bldgs....123 H2
Relton Mews....127 E3
Rembrandt Cl....127 G5
Remnant St....124 C4
Rennie St....124 E6
Reston Pl....126 C2
Rex Pl....123 F6
Rhoda St....125 J2
Rich La....126 B5
Richard's Pl....127 E4
Richardson's Mews....123 H2
Richbell Pl....124 C3
Richborne Terr....128 D7
Richmond Bldgs....123 J4
Richmond Mews....123 J4
Richmond Terr....128 C2
Richmond Terr Mews....128 C2
Rickett St....126 A6
Ridgmount Gdns....123 J3
Ridgmount Pl....123 J3
Ridgmount St....123 J3
Riding House St....123 H3
Rifle Pl....128 E6
Riley St....126 D7
Rising Sun Ct....125 E3
Rita Rd....128 D7
River St....124 D1
Rivington Pl....125 H1
Rivington St....125 H1
Robert Adam St....123 F4
Robert Cl....122 B2
Robert St....123 H1
Robert St....124 A4
Roberts Mews....127 G3
Robinson St....127 F6
Rochelle St....125 J1
Rochester Row....128 A4
Rochester St....128 B3
Rochester Wlk....125 G6
Rodmarton St....123 E3
Roger St....124 C2
Roland Gdns....126 C5
Roland Way....126 C5
Rolls Bldgs....124 D4
Rolls Pas....124 D4
Romilly St....124 A4
Romney St....128 C3
Rood La....125 H5
Ropemaker St....125 G3
Rosary Gdns....126 C4
Roscoe St....125 F2
Rose Alley....125 F6
Rose and Crown Ct....125 F4
Rose and Crown Yd....128 A1
Rose St....124 B5
Roseberry Sq....124 D2
Rosebery Ave....124 D2
Rosemoor St....127 F4
Rosetta St....128 C7
Rosoman Pl....124 D2
Rosoman St....124 D2
Rossmore Rd....122 D2
Rotherham Wlk....124 E6
Roupell St....124 D6
Rowington Cl....122 A3
Roxby Pl....126 A6
Royal Arc....123 H5
Royal Ave....127 F5
Royal Exchange Ave....125 G4
Royal Exchange Bldgs....125 G4
Royal Hospital Rd....127 F5
Royal Mint St....125 J5
Royal Opera Arc....123 J6
Royal Opera Arc....128 B1
Royal St....128 D3
Rufus St....125 H1
Rugby St....124 C2
Rupert Ct....123 J5
Rupert St....123 J5
Russell Ct....123 H6
Russell Pl....128 B5
Russell Sq....124 B3
Russell St....124 B5
Russia Ct....125 F4
Russia Row....125 F4
Rutherford St....128 B4
Rutland Gate....126 E2
Rutland Gate Mews....126 E2
Rutland Gdns....127 E2
Rutland Mews....126 E3
Rutland Mews E....127 E2
Rutland Mews S....126 E3
Rutland Mews W....126 E3
Rutland Pl....125 F3
Rutland St....127 E3
Ryder Ct....123 H6
Ryder St....123 H6
Ryder Yd....123 H6
Ryder Yd....128 A1
Rysbrack St....127 F3

S

Sackville St....123 H5
Saffron Hill....124 D3
Saffron St....127 F2
Sage Way....124 C1
Sail St....128 D3
St Alban's Gr....126 B3
St Alban's Mews....122 C3
St Alban's St....123 J5
St Alphage Gdn....125 F3
St Alphage Highwalk....125 F3
St Andrew St....124 D3
St Andrew's Hill....124 E4
St Andrew's Pl....123 G2
St Anne's Ct....123 J4
St Ann's La....128 B3
St Ann's St....128 B3
St Anselm's Pl....123 G5
St Barnabas St....127 G5
St Benet's Pl....125 G5

St Botolph St.....125 J4
St Bride St.....124 E4
St Bride's Ave.....124 E4
St Bride's Pas.....124 E4
St Chad's Pl.....124 C1
St Chad's St.....124 B1
St Christopher's Pl.....123 F4
St Clare St.....125 J4
St Clement's Ct.....125 G5
St Clement's La.....124 C4
St Cross St.....124 D3
St Dunstan's Alley.....125 H5
St Dunstan's Ct.....124 D4
St Dunstan's Hill.....125 H5
St Dunstan's Hill.....125 H5
St Ermin's Hill.....128 B3
St George St.....123 G5
St George's Dri.....127 J5
St Georges Field.....122 D4
St George's La.....125 G5
St George's Sq.....128 B5
St Giles Circ.....123 J4
St Giles High St.....124 A4
St Giles Pl.....124 A4
St Helena St.....124 D1
St Helen's Pl.....125 H4
St James' Ct.....128 A3
St James's App.....125 H2
St James's Market.....123 J5
St James's Pas.....125 H4
St James's Pl.....123 H6
St James's Pl.....128 A1
St James's Row.....124 E2
St James's Sq.....123 J6
St James's Sq.....128 B1
St James's Sq.....123 H6
St James's St.....128 A1
St James's Wlk.....124 E2
St John St.....124 E2
St John's La.....124 E3
St John's Path.....124 E2
St John's Pl.....124 E2
St John's Sq.....124 E2
St John's Wood Rd.....122 C1
St Katharine's Way.....125 J5
St Katherine's Row.....125 H5
St Leonard's Terr.....127 F5
St Loo Ave.....127 E6
St Luke's St.....126 E5
St Margaret St.....128 C2
St Margaret's Ct.....125 G6
St Mark's Gr.....126 B7
St Martin's La.....124 B5
St Martin's La.....125 B5
St Martin's Le Grand.....124 F4
St Martin's Pl.....124 B5
St Martin's St.....124 A5
St Mary at Hill.....125 H5
St Mary Axe.....125 H4
St Mary's Mansions.....122 C3
St Mary's Sq.....122 C3
St Mary'S Terr.....122 C3
St Matthew St.....128 B3
St Michael's Alley.....125 G4
St Michael's St.....122 D4
St Mildred's Ct.....125 G4
St Olave's Ct.....125 G4
St Olave's Gdns.....128 E4
St Oswald's Pl.....128 D5
St Oswuld St.....128 B4
St Paul's Church.....125 F4
St Paul's Church Yd.....125 F4
St Peter's Alley.....125 G4
St Petersburgh Mews.....122 A5
St Stephen's Row.....125 G4
St Swithin's La.....125 G5
St Thomas St.....125 G6
St Vincent St.....123 F3
Salamanca Pl.....128 D4
Salamanca St.....128 D4
Salamanca St.....128 D4
Sale Pl.....122 D4
Salem Rd.....122 A5
Salisbury Ct.....124 E4
Salisbury Pl.....122 E3
Salisbury Sq.....124 D4
Salisbury St.....122 D2
Salters Hall Ct.....125 G5
Samford St.....122 D2
Samuel Lewis Trust
  Dwellings.....126 E4
Samuel Lewis Trust
  Dwellings.....126 A7
Sancroft St.....128 E5
Sanctuary St.....128 B3
Sandell St.....128 E2
Sandland St.....124 C3
Sandwich St.....124 B1
Sandy's Row.....125 H3
Sans Wlk.....124 E2
Saperton Wlk.....128 D4
Saracen's Head Yd.....125 J4
Sarah St.....125 H1
Sardinia St.....124 C4
Saunders St.....128 E4
Savage Gdns.....125 H5
Saville Row.....123 H6
Savona St.....128 A7
Savoy Bldgs.....124 C5
Savoy Ct.....124 B5
Savoy Hill.....124 C5
Savoy Pl.....124 C5
Savoy Row.....124 C5
Savoy Steps.....124 C5
Savoy St.....124 C5
Savoy Way.....124 C5
Scala St.....123 H3
Scarborough St.....125 J4
Scarsdale Pl.....126 B3
Scarsdale Villas.....126 A3
School App.....125 H1
Sclater St.....125 J2
Scoresby St.....124 E6
Scotland Pl.....124 B6
Scotswood St.....124 D2
Scott Ellis Gdns.....122 C1
Scott's Yd.....125 G5
Scrutton St.....125 H2
Seacoal La.....124 E4
Seaford St.....124 B1
Seaforth Pl.....128 A3
Seagrave Rd.....126 A6
Searles Cl.....127 E7
Sebastion St.....124 E1
Secker St.....124 D6
Sedding St.....127 G4
Seddon St.....124 C1
Sedley Pl.....123 G4
Seething La.....125 H5
Sekforde St.....124 E2
Selwood Pl.....126 D5
Selwood Terr.....126 D5
Semley Pl.....127 H4
Senior St.....122 A3
Serjeants' Inn.....124 D4
Serle St.....124 C4
Sermon La.....125 F4
Serpentine Rd.....122 E6
Serpentine Rd.....127 F1
Seven Dials.....126 B4

Seville St.....127 F2
Seward St.....125 F1
Seymour Mews.....123 F4
Seymour Pl.....122 E4
Seymour St.....123 E4
Seymour Wlk.....126 C6
Shacklewell St.....125 J1
Shad Thames.....125 J6
Shaftesbury Ave.....123 J5
Shaftesbury Mews.....126 A3
Shafto Mews.....127 F3
Shafts Ct.....125 H4
Shalcomb St.....126 C6
Shand St.....125 H6
Shaver's Pl.....123 J5
Shawfield St.....127 E5
Sheba St.....125 J2
Sheffield St.....124 C4
Sheffield Terr.....126 A1
Shelton St.....124 B4
Shepherd Cl.....123 F5
Shepherd Market.....123 G6
Shepherd St.....123 G6
Shepherdess Pl.....125 G1
Shepherds Pl.....123 F5
Sheraton St.....123 J4
Sherborne La.....125 G5
Sherlock Mews.....123 F3
Sherwood St.....123 J5
Shillibeer Pl.....122 D3
Ship Tavern Pas.....125 H5
Shipwright Yd.....125 H6
Shoe La.....124 D4
Shoreditch High St.....125 H2
Shorter St.....125 J5
Shorts Gdns.....124 B4
Shouldham St.....122 D3
Shropshire Pl.....123 J2
Shroton St.....122 D3
Sicilian Ave.....124 B3
Siddons La.....123 E2
Sidford Pl.....128 D3
Sidmouth St.....124 C1
Sidney Gr.....124 E1
Silbury St.....125 G1
Silk St.....125 F3
Silver St.....123 H5
Singer St.....125 G1
Sir Thomas More Estate.....126 D6
Sise La.....125 G4
Skin Market Pl.....125 F6
Skinner Pl.....127 G4
Skinner St.....124 D2
Skinners La.....125 F5
Slaidburn St.....126 C6
Sleaford St.....127 J7
Sleaford St.....128 A7
Slingsby Pl.....124 B5
Sloane Ave.....127 E4
Sloane Ct E.....127 G5
Sloane Ct W.....127 G5
Sloane Gdns.....127 G4
Sloane Sq.....127 G4
Sloane St.....127 F3
Sloane Terr.....127 G4
Smallbrook Mews.....122 C4
Smart's Pl.....124 B4
Smith Sq.....128 C3
Smith St.....127 F5
Smith Terr.....127 F5
Smithfield St.....124 E3
Smith's Ct.....123 H5
Smith's Pl.....123 J5
Snow Hill.....124 E3
Snowden St.....125 H2
Soho Sq.....123 J4
Soho St.....123 J4
Soley Mews.....124 D1
Somers Cres.....122 D4
South Audley St.....123 F6
South Bolton Gdns.....126 B5
South Carriage Dri.....127 F2
South Carriage Dri.....127 E2
South Cres.....123 J3
South Eaton Pl.....127 G4
South End.....126 B3
South End Row.....126 B3
South Lambeth Pl.....128 C6
South Lambeth Rd.....128 C7
South Molton La.....123 G4
South Molton St.....123 G4
South Parade.....126 D5
South Pl.....125 G3
South Pl Mews.....125 G3
South Sq.....124 D3
South St.....123 F6
South Tenter St.....125 J5
South Terr.....126 E4
South Wharf Rd.....122 C4
South Yd.....125 G3
Southampton Bldgs.....124 D3
Southampton Pl.....124 B3
Southampton Row.....124 B3
Southampton St.....124 B5
Southwark Bridge.....125 F5
Southwark St.....125 F6
Southwell Gdns.....126 C4
Southwick Mews.....122 C4
Southwick Pl.....122 D4
Southwick St.....122 D4
Southwick Yd.....122 D4
Spafield St.....124 D2
Spanish Pl.....123 F4
Spear Mews.....126 A4
Speedy Pl.....124 B1
Spencer Pl.....124 E1
Spenser St.....128 A3
Spital Sq.....125 H3
Spital Yd.....125 H3
Sprimont Pl.....127 F5
Spring Gdns.....124 A6
Spring Gdns.....128 B1
Spring Mews.....123 E3
Spring St.....122 C4
Stable Yd Rd.....127 J2
Stables Way.....128 E5
Stacey St.....124 A4
Stackhouse St.....127 F3
Stadium St.....126 C7
Staff St.....125 G1
Stafford Pl.....127 J3
Stafford Pl.....123 H6
Stafford St.....123 H6
Stafford St.....128 A1
Stafford St.....126 A2
Stag Pl.....127 J3
Stainer St.....125 G6
Staining La.....125 F4
Stalbridge St.....122 D3
Stamford St.....124 D6
Stanbrook Ct.....128 B2
Stanbrook Ct.....128 B1
Standard Pl.....125 H1
Stanford Rd.....126 B3
Stanford St.....128 B4
Stanhope Gate.....123 F6
Stanhope Mews E.....126 C4
Stanhope Mews S.....126 C4
Stanhope Mews W.....126 C4
Stanhope Pl.....122 E5

Stanhope Row.....123 G6
Stanhope St.....123 H1
Stanhope Terr.....122 C5
Stanley Cl.....128 D6
Stannary Pl.....128 E5
Stannary St.....128 E5
Staple Inn Bldgs.....124 D3
Star Alley.....125 H5
Star St.....122 D4
Starcross St.....123 H1
Stationers Hall Ct.....124 E4
Stedham Pl.....124 B4
Stephen Mews.....123 J3
Stephen St.....123 J3
Stephenson Way.....123 H2
Sterling St.....127 E3
Stew La.....125 F5
Steward St.....125 H3
Stewart's Gr.....126 E5
Stillington St.....128 A4
Stone Bldgs.....124 C3
Stonecutter St.....124 E4
Stonehouse Ct.....125 H4
Stoney La.....125 J4
Stoney St.....125 G6
Store St.....123 J3
Storey's Gate.....128 B2
Stothard Pl.....125 H3
Stourcliffe St.....122 E4
Stourton St.....124 D5
Strand.....124 C5
Strand La.....124 C5
Stratford Pl.....123 G4
Stratford Pl.....123 G4
Stratford Rd.....126 A3
Strathearn Pl.....122 D5
Strathmore Gdns.....126 A1
Stratton St.....123 G6
Streatham St.....124 B4
Stroughton Cl.....128 D4
Strout's Pl.....125 J1
Strutton Ground.....128 B3
Strype St.....125 J3
Studio Pl.....127 F2
Stukeley St.....124 B4
Suffolk La.....125 G5
Suffolk Pl.....123 J6
Suffolk Pl.....128 B1
Suffolk St.....123 J6
Sugar Bakers Ct.....125 H4
Sugar Loaf Ct.....125 F5
Summers St.....124 D2
Sumner Bldgs.....125 F6
Sumner Pl.....126 D4
Sumner Place Mews.....126 D4
Sumner St.....125 F6
Sun Ct.....125 G4
Sun St.....125 H3
Sun St Pas.....125 H3
Sunningdale Gdns.....126 A3
Surrey St.....124 C5
Sussex Gdns.....122 C4
Sussex Mews E.....122 C4
Sussex Mews W.....122 C5
Sussex Pl.....125 H4
Sussex Pl.....122 E2
Sussex Pl.....122 C4
Sussex Sq.....122 C5
Sussex St.....127 H5
Sutherland Ave.....122 A2
Sutherland Pl.....122 A4
Sutherland Row.....127 H5
Sutherland St.....127 H5
Sutton Dwellings.....126 E5
Sutton Row.....123 J4
Suttons Way.....125 G2
Swallow Pas.....123 G4
Swallow St.....123 H5
Swan Ct.....127 E5
Swan La.....125 G5
Swan Wlk.....127 F6
Swanfield St.....125 J1
Swinton Pl.....124 C1
Swinton St.....124 C1
Sycamore St.....125 F2
Sydney Cl.....126 D4
Sydney Mews.....126 D4
Sydney Pl.....126 E4
Sydney St.....126 E5
Symons St.....127 F4

T
Tabernacle St.....125 G2
Tachbrook Mews.....127 J4
Tachbrook St.....128 A4
Tadema Rd.....126 C7
Talbot Ct.....125 G5
Talbot Sq.....122 C4
Talbot Yd.....125 G6
Tallis St.....124 D5
Tamworth St.....126 A6
Tankerton St.....124 B1
Tanswell St.....128 E2
Taunton Mews.....122 E2
Taunton Pl.....122 E2
Tavistock Pl.....124 B2
Tavistock Sq.....124 B2
Tavistock St.....124 B5
Tavistock St.....124 C4
Taviton St.....123 J2
Tedworth Gdns.....127 F5
Tedworth Sq.....127 F5
Telegraph St.....125 G4
Temple Ave.....124 D5
Temple La.....124 D4
Templeton Pl.....126 A4
Tenison Ct.....123 H5
Tenison Way.....124 D6
Tenniel Cl.....122 A5
Tenter Ground.....125 J3
Tenterden St.....123 G4
Terminus Pl.....127 H3
Terrace The.....124 D4
Tetcott Rd.....126 C7
Thackeray St.....126 B3
Thanet St.....124 B1
Thavie's Inn.....124 D4
Thayer St.....123 F4
The Sir Oswald Stoll
  Foundation.....126 B7
Theed St.....124 D6
Theobald's Rd.....124 C3
Thirleby Rd.....127 J3
Thistle Gr.....126 C5
Thoresby St.....125 F1
Thorndike Cl.....126 C7
Thorndike St.....128 B4
Thorney St.....128 C4
Thornhaugh Mews.....124 A2
Thornhaugh St.....124 A2
Thornton Pl.....122 E3
Thrale St.....125 F6
Thrawl St.....125 J3
Threadneedle St.....125 G4

Three Kings Yd.....123 G5
Three Nun Ct.....125 F4
Throgmorton Ave.....125 G4
Throgmorton St.....125 G4
Thurloe Cl.....126 E4
Thurloe Pl.....126 D4
Thurloe Place Mews.....126 D4
Thurloe Sq.....126 E4
Thurloe St.....126 D4
Tilney Ct.....125 F2
Tilney St.....123 F6
Timber St.....125 F2
Tinworth St.....128 D5
Tisbury Ct.....123 J5
Titchborne Row.....122 D4
Tite St.....127 F6
Tokenhouse Yd.....125 G4
Tolmers Sq.....123 H2
Tomlinson Cl.....125 J1
Tompion St.....124 E1
Tonbridge St.....124 B1
Tooley St.....125 H6
Topham St.....124 D2
Tor Gdns.....126 A2
Torrington Pl.....123 J3
Torrington Sq.....124 A2
Tothill St.....128 B2
Tottenham Ct Rd.....123 J3
Tottenham Mews.....123 H3
Tottenham St.....123 H3
Tower Bridge.....125 J6
Tower Bridge App.....125 J5
Tower Bridge Rd.....125 J6
Tower Ct.....124 B4
Tower Hill.....125 J5
Tower Royal.....125 F5
Tower St.....124 B4
Toynbee St.....125 J3
Tradescant Rd.....128 C7
Trafalgar Sq.....124 A6
Trafalgar Sq.....128 B1
Trafalgar St.....124 B6
Transept St.....122 D3
Trebeck St.....123 G6
Trebovir Rd.....126 A4
Tregunter Rd.....126 C5
Trenchold St.....128 C6
Tresham Cres.....122 D2
Treveris St.....124 E6
Trevor Pl.....127 E2
Trevor Sq.....127 E2
Trevor St.....127 E2
Trigon Rd.....128 D7
Trinity Pl.....125 J5
Trinity Sq.....125 J5
Triton Sq.....123 H2
Trump St.....125 F4
Tryon St.....127 F5
Tuck's Ct.....124 D4
Tudor St.....124 D5
Tufton St.....128 C3
Turks Row.....127 F5
Turnagain La.....124 E4
Turnmill St.....124 E3
Turpentine La.....127 H5
Turville St.....125 J2
Tweezer's Alley.....124 D5
Twyford St.....124 C4
Tyburn Way.....123 E5
Tyers Gate.....125 H6
Tyers St.....128 D5
Tyers Terr.....128 D5
Tyne St.....125 J4
Tysoe St.....124 D1

U
Udall St.....128 A4
Ulster Pl.....123 G2
Undershaft.....125 H4
Underwood Row.....125 F1
Underwood St.....125 F1
Unicorn Pas.....125 H6
Union Ct.....125 H4
Union St.....125 F6
Union Wlk.....125 J1
University St.....123 H2
Unwin Rd.....126 D3
Upbrook Mews.....122 B4
Upper Belgrave St.....127 G3
Upper Berenger Wlk.....126 D7
Upper Berkeley St.....123 E4
Upper Blantyre Wlk.....126 D7
Upper Brook St.....123 F5
Upper Cheyne Row.....126 E6
Upper Dartrey Wlk.....126 D7
Upper Grosvenor St.....123 F5
Upper Ground.....124 D6
Upper Harley St.....123 G2
Upper James St.....123 H5
Upper John St.....123 H5
Upper Marsh.....128 D2
Upper Montague St.....122 E3
Upper St Martin's La.....124 B5
Upper Tachbrook St.....127 J4
Upper Thames St.....125 F5
Upper Whistler Wlk.....126 D7
Upper Wimpole St.....123 F3
Upper Woburn Pl.....124 A1
Uverdale Rd.....126 C7
Uxbridge St.....126 A1

V
Vale Cl.....122 B1
Vale The.....126 D6
Vandon Pas.....128 A3
Vandon St.....128 A3
Vandy St.....125 H2
Vane St.....128 A4
Vanston Pl.....126 A6
Varndell St.....123 H1
Vauxhall Bridge.....128 C5
Vauxhall Bridge Rd.....128 A4
Vauxhall Cross.....128 C5
Vauxhall Gr.....128 D6
Vauxhall St.....128 D5
Vauxhall Wlk.....128 D5
Venables St.....122 C3
Vere St.....123 G4
Vernon Pl.....124 B3
Vernon Rise.....124 C1
Vernon Sq.....124 C1
Verulam St.....124 D3
Vestry St.....125 G1
Viaduct St.....124 E4
Vicarage Gate.....126 B2
Vicarage Gate.....126 B1
Vicarage Gdns.....126 A1
Victoria Arc.....127 H3
Victoria Ave.....125 H3
Victoria Bldgs.....127 H3
Victoria Emb.....124 C5
Victoria Emb.....128 C2
Victoria Gdns.....126 A1
Victoria Gr.....126 C3

Victoria Pas.....122 C2
Victoria Rd.....126 C3
Victoria Sq.....127 H3
Victoria St.....128 A3
Vigo St.....123 H5
Villiers St.....124 B6
Vince St.....125 G1
Vincent Sq.....128 B4
Vincent St.....128 B4
Vine Hill.....124 D2
Vine St.....125 J5
Vine St.....123 H6
Vine St.....123 H5
Vinery Villas.....122 D1
Vineyard Wlk.....124 D2
Virgil Pl.....122 E3
Virgil St.....128 D3
Virginia Rd.....125 J1
Viscount St.....125 F3

W
Waithman St.....124 E4
Wakefield St.....124 B1
Wakley St.....124 E1
Walbrook.....125 G4
Walcot Sq.....128 E4
Walcott St.....128 A4
Waldron Mews.....126 D6
Walham Gr.....126 A7
Walham Green Arc.....126 A7
Walker's Ct.....123 J5
Wallgrave Rd.....126 B4
Walmer Pl.....122 E3
Walmer St.....122 E3
Walnut Tree Wlk.....128 E4
Walpole St.....127 F5
Walton Pl.....127 F3
Walton St.....127 E4
Wandon Rd.....126 B7
Wandsworth Rd.....128 C7
Wansdown Pl.....126 B7
Wardens Gr.....125 F6
Wardour Mews.....123 H4
Wardour St.....123 J4
Wardrobe Pl.....124 E4
Wardrobe Terr.....125 E5
Warner St.....124 D2
Warner Yd.....124 D2
Warren Mews.....123 H2
Warren St.....123 H2
Warrington Cres.....122 B2
Warrington Gdns.....122 B2
Warwick Ave.....122 B2
Warwick Cres.....122 B3
Warwick Ct.....124 C3
Warwick House St.....124 A6
Warwick La.....124 E4
Warwick Pl.....122 B3
Warwick Pl N.....127 J4
Warwick Row.....127 H3
Warwick Sq.....127 J4
Warwick Sq Mews.....127 J4
Warwick St.....123 H5
Warwick Way.....127 J4
Warwick Yd.....125 F2
Water Gdns The.....122 D4
Water St.....124 D5
Watergate.....124 D5
Watergate Wlk.....124 B6
Waterloo Bridge.....124 C5
Waterloo Pl.....123 J6
Waterloo Pl.....128 B1
Waterloo Rd.....128 E2
Waterson St.....125 H1
Watling Ct.....125 F4
Watling St.....125 F4
Watson's Mews.....122 D3
Waverton St.....123 G6
Weaver's La.....125 H6
Weighhouse St.....123 F4
Weir's Pas.....124 A1
Welbeck Ct.....123 G4
Welbeck Way.....123 G4
Well Ct.....125 F4
Well St.....125 F4
Wellesley Pl.....123 J1
Wellesley Terr.....125 F1
Wellington Bldgs.....127 G5
Wellington Pl.....122 D1
Wellington Rd.....122 D1
Wellington Sq.....127 F5
Wellington St.....124 C5
Wells Mews.....123 H4
Wells St.....123 H3
Wells Way.....126 D3
Wentworth Dwellings.....125 J4
Wentworth St.....125 J3
Wesley St.....123 F3
West Carriage Dri.....122 D6
West Central St.....124 B4
West Cromwell Rd.....126 A4
West Eaton Pl.....127 G4
West Eaton Pl Mews.....127 G4
West Halkin St.....127 G3
West Harding St.....124 D4
West Mall.....126 A1
West Mews.....127 J4
West Poultry Ave.....124 E3
West Rd.....127 F6
West Smithfield.....124 E3
West St.....124 A4
West Tenter St.....125 J4
Westbourne Cres.....122 C5
Westbourne Gdns.....122 A4
Westbourne Gr Terr.....122 A4
Westbourne St.....122 C5
Westbourne Terr.....122 B4
Westbourne Terr Mews.....122 B4
Westbourne Terr Rd.....122 B3
Westgate Terr.....126 B5
Westland Pl.....125 G1
Westminster Bridge.....128 C2
Westminster Bridge Rd.....128 E3
Westminster Bldgs.....128 E3
Westmoreland Pl.....127 H5
Westmoreland St.....123 F3
Westmoreland Terr.....127 H5
Weston Rise.....124 C1
Weston St.....125 H6
Westway.....122 B3
Wetherby Gdns.....126 C4
Wetherby Mews.....126 B4
Wetherby Pl.....126 C4
Weymouth Mews.....123 G3
Weymouth St.....123 F3
Wharfedale St.....126 B5
Wharton St.....124 C1
Wheatley St.....123 F3
Wheatsheaf La.....128 C7

Wheler St.....125 J2
Whetstone Park.....124 C4
Whichcote St.....124 D6
Whidborne St.....124 B1
Whiskin St.....124 E1
Whistler Wlk.....126 C7
Whistlers Ave.....127 E7
Whitby St.....125 J2
Whitcomb Ct.....123 J5
Whitcomb St.....124 A5
White Bear Yd.....124 D2
White Hart St.....125 H3
White Hart Yd.....125 G6
White Horse Alley.....124 E3
White Horse St.....123 G6
White Kennett St.....125 H4
White Lion Hill.....125 F5
White Lion Yd.....123 G5
Whitechapel High St.....125 J3
Whitecross St.....125 G3
Whitecross St.....125 F2
Whitecross St.....125 F3
Whitefriars St.....124 D4
Whitehall.....124 B6
Whitehall Ct.....124 B6
Whitehall Gdns.....124 B6
Whitehall Pl.....124 B6
Whitehaven St.....122 D2
Whitehead's Gr.....127 E4
White's Row.....125 J3
Whitfield Pl.....123 H2
Whitfield St.....123 H3
Whitgift St.....128 D4
Whitington Ave.....125 H4
Whittaker St.....127 G4
Whittlesey St.....124 D6
Wickham St.....128 D5
Wicklow St.....124 C1
Widegate St.....125 H3
Wigmore Pl.....123 G4
Wigmore St.....123 F4
Wilbraham Pl.....127 G4
Wilcox Cl.....128 C7
Wilcox Pl.....128 A3
Wilcox Rd.....128 C7
Wild Ct.....124 C4
Wild St.....124 C4
Wilfred St.....127 J3
Wilkes St.....125 J3
Wilkes St.....125 J3
William IV St.....124 B5
William Mews.....127 F2
William Rd.....123 H1
William St.....127 F2
Willoughby St.....124 B3
Willow Pl.....128 A4
Willow St.....125 H2
Wilmington Sq.....124 D1
Wilmington St.....124 D1
Wilson St.....125 G2
Wilton Cres.....127 G2
Wilton Mews.....127 H3
Wilton Pl.....127 G2
Wilton Rd.....127 J4
Wilton Row.....127 G2
Wilton St.....127 H3
Wilton Terr.....127 G3
Wiltshire Cl.....127 F4
Wimpole Mews.....123 G3
Wimpole St.....123 G3
Winchester Mews.....123 F3
Winchester Sq.....125 G6
Winchester St.....127 H5
Winchester Wlk.....125 G6
Wincott St.....128 E4
Windmill Row.....128 E5
Windmill St.....123 J3
Windmill Wlk.....124 D6
Windsor St.....128 A4
Windsor Terr.....125 F1
Wine Office Ct.....124 D4
Winnett St.....123 J5
Winsland Mews.....122 C4
Winsland St.....122 C4
Winsley St.....123 H4
Winterton Pl.....126 C6
Withers Pl.....125 F2
Woburn Pl.....124 A2
Woburn Sq.....124 A2
Woburn Wlk.....124 A1
Wood St.....125 F4
Woodbridge St.....124 E2
Woodfall St.....127 F5
Woods Mews.....123 E5
Woodstock Mews.....123 F3
Woodstock St.....123 G4
Wootton St.....124 D6
Worfield St.....127 E7
Worgan St.....128 D5
World's End Pas.....126 C7
World's End Pl.....126 C7
Wormwood St.....125 H4
Worship St.....125 H2
Wren St.....124 C2
Wright's La.....126 B3
Wyclif St.....124 E1
Wynard Terr.....128 D5
Wyndham Mews.....122 E3
Wyndham Pl.....122 E3
Wyndham St.....122 E3
Wyndham Yd.....122 E3
Wynnstay Gdns.....126 A3
Wynyard Terr.....128 D5
Wynyatt St.....124 E1
Wythburn Pl.....122 E4
Wyvil Rd.....128 D6

Y
Yardley St.....124 D1
Yarmouth Pl.....123 G6
Yeoman's Pl.....126 E3
Yeoman's Row.....126 E3
Yeoman's St.....125 J5
York Bldgs.....124 B5
York Gate.....123 F2
York House Pl.....126 B2
York Pl.....124 B5
York Rd.....128 D2
York St.....122 E3
York Terr E.....123 F2
York Terr W.....123 F2
Yorkshire Grey Yd.....124 C3
Young St.....126 B3
Young's Bldgs.....125 F2

Z
Zoar St.....125 F6

Aberdeen

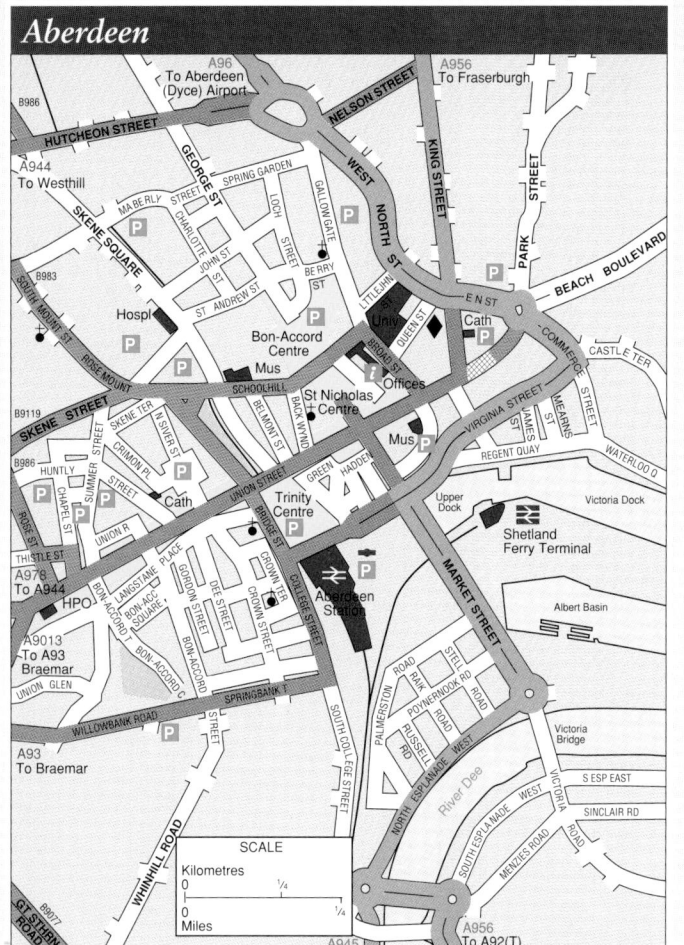

Bath

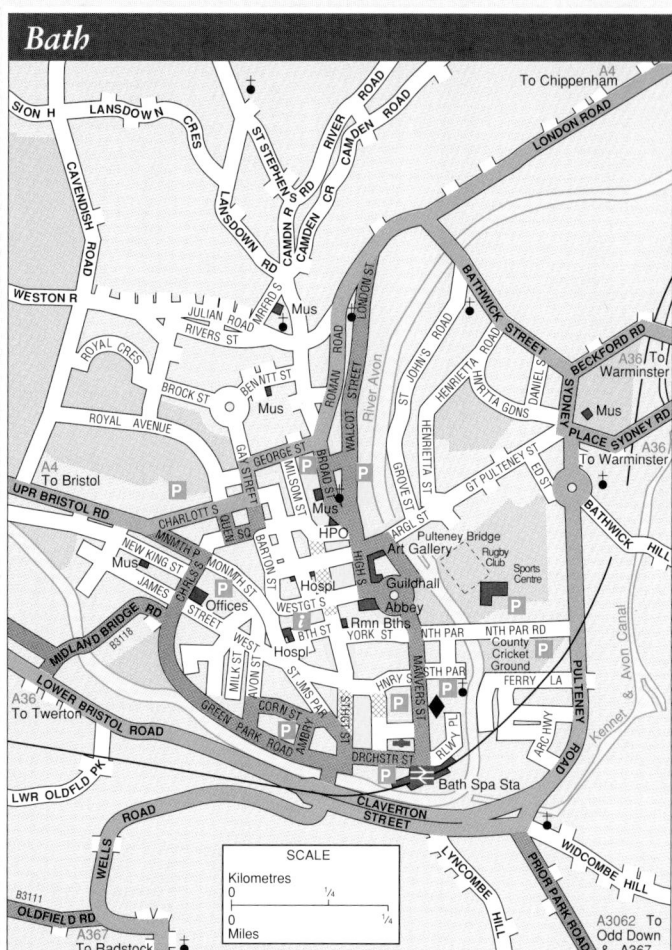

Birmingham

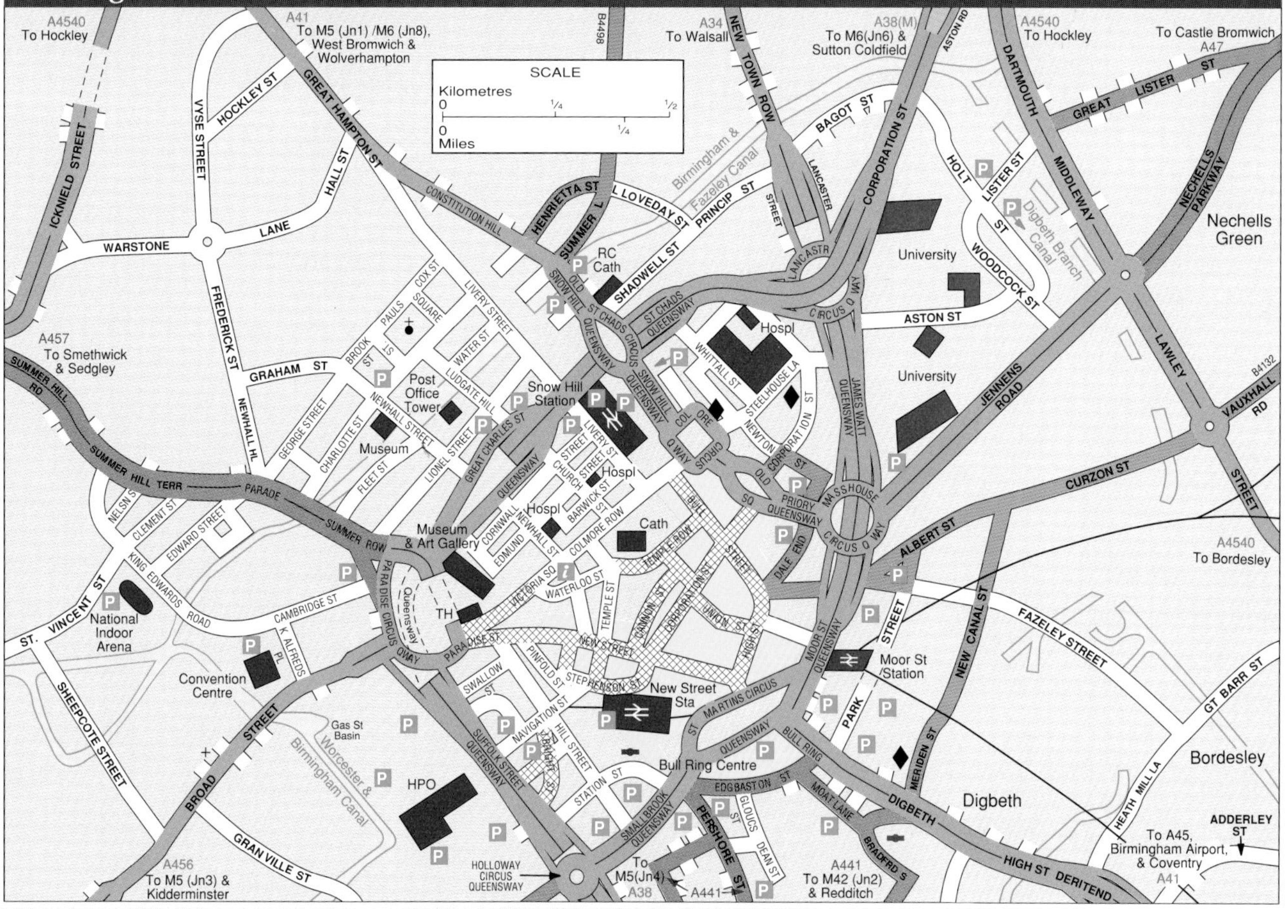

TOWN PLANS

Motorway Autoroute	**Principal shopping centre** Centre commercial	**TH** **Town Hall** Hôtel de ville	**P** **Parking** Parking
Primary route Itinéraire principal	**Main police station** Commissariat de police	**Railway station** Gare	**Underground/metro station** Station de métro
Main road Route principale	**6** **Motorway junction** Echangeur d'autoroute	**Church** Eglise	**Bus/coach station** Gare routière
Secondary road Route secondaire	**Important building** Edifice important		
Pedestrian area Zone piétonnière	**HPO** **Head Post Office** Bureau de poste principal	**i** **Information Centre** Bureau de renseignements	

Blackpool

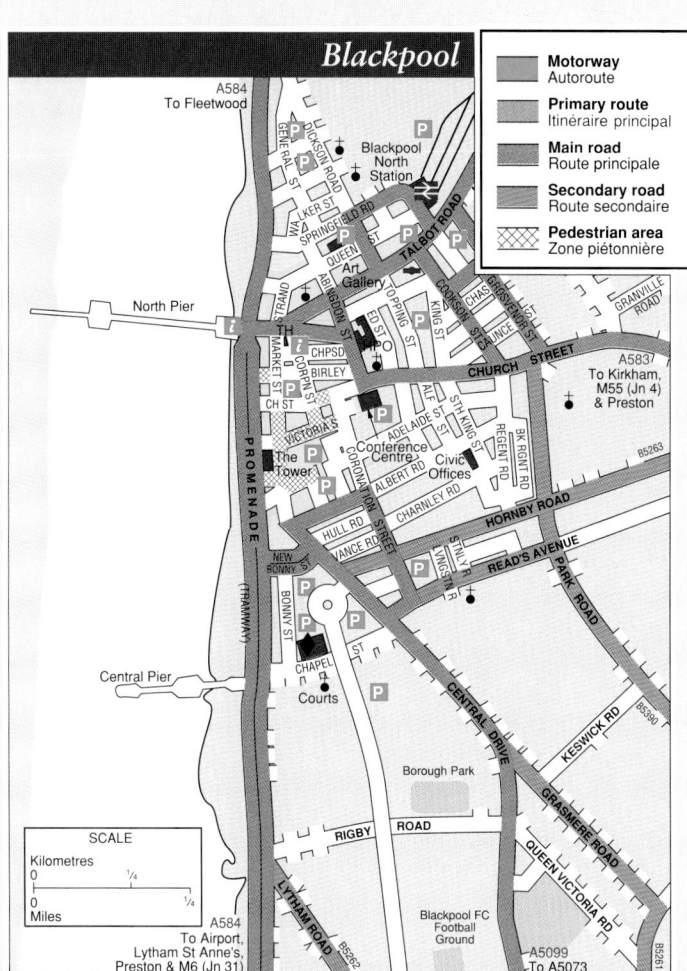

Bournemouth

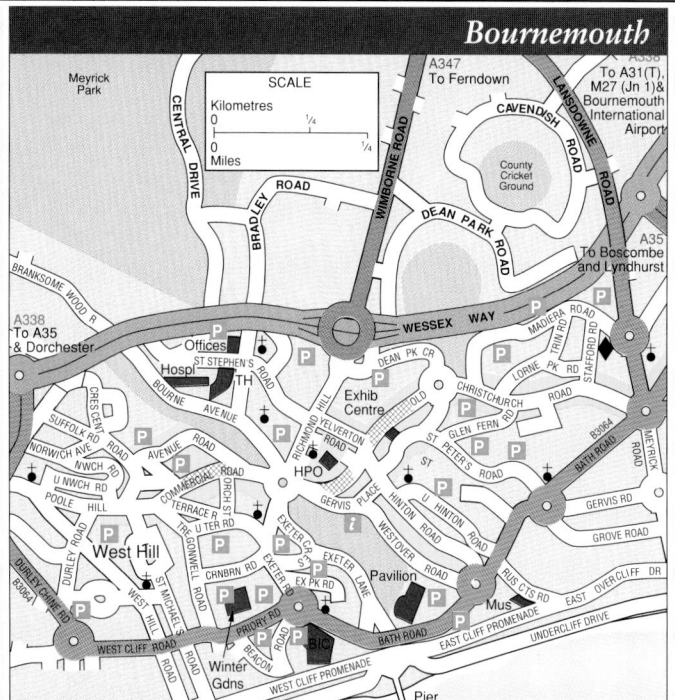

Bradford

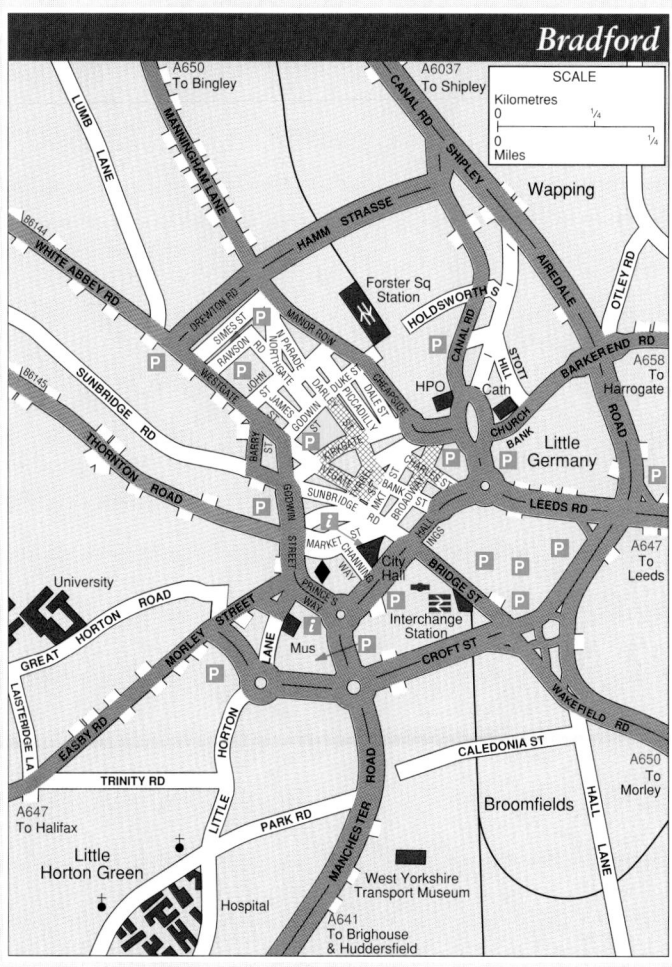

Brighton

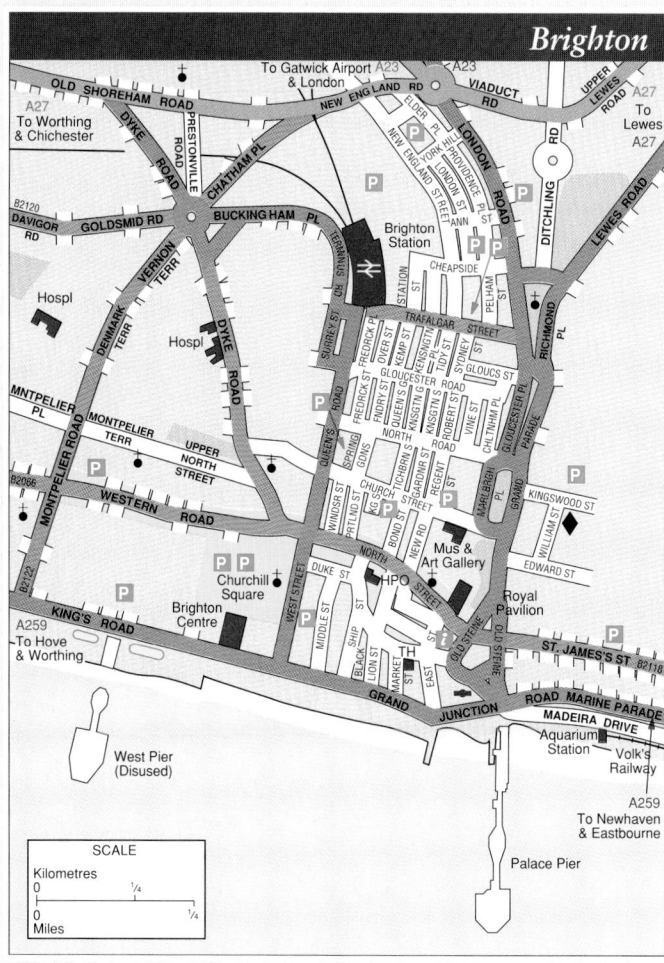

Cambridge

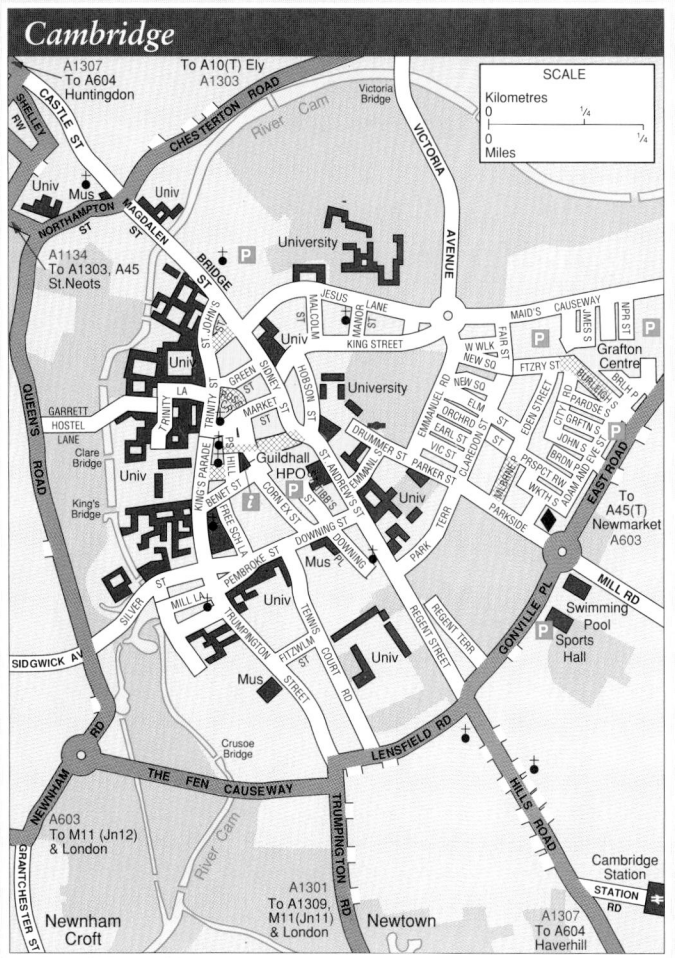

Canterbury

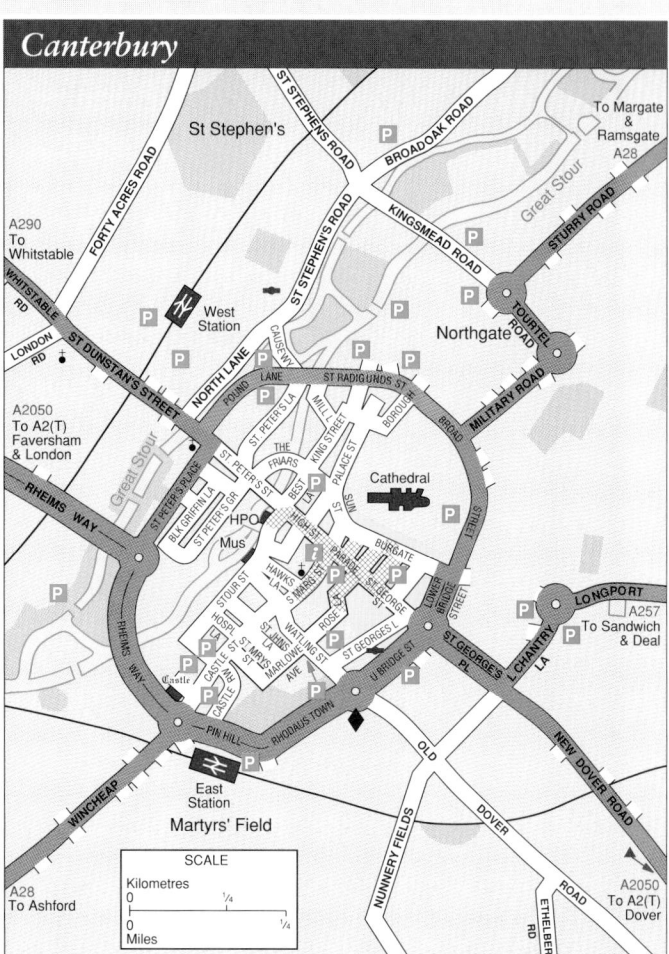

Bristol

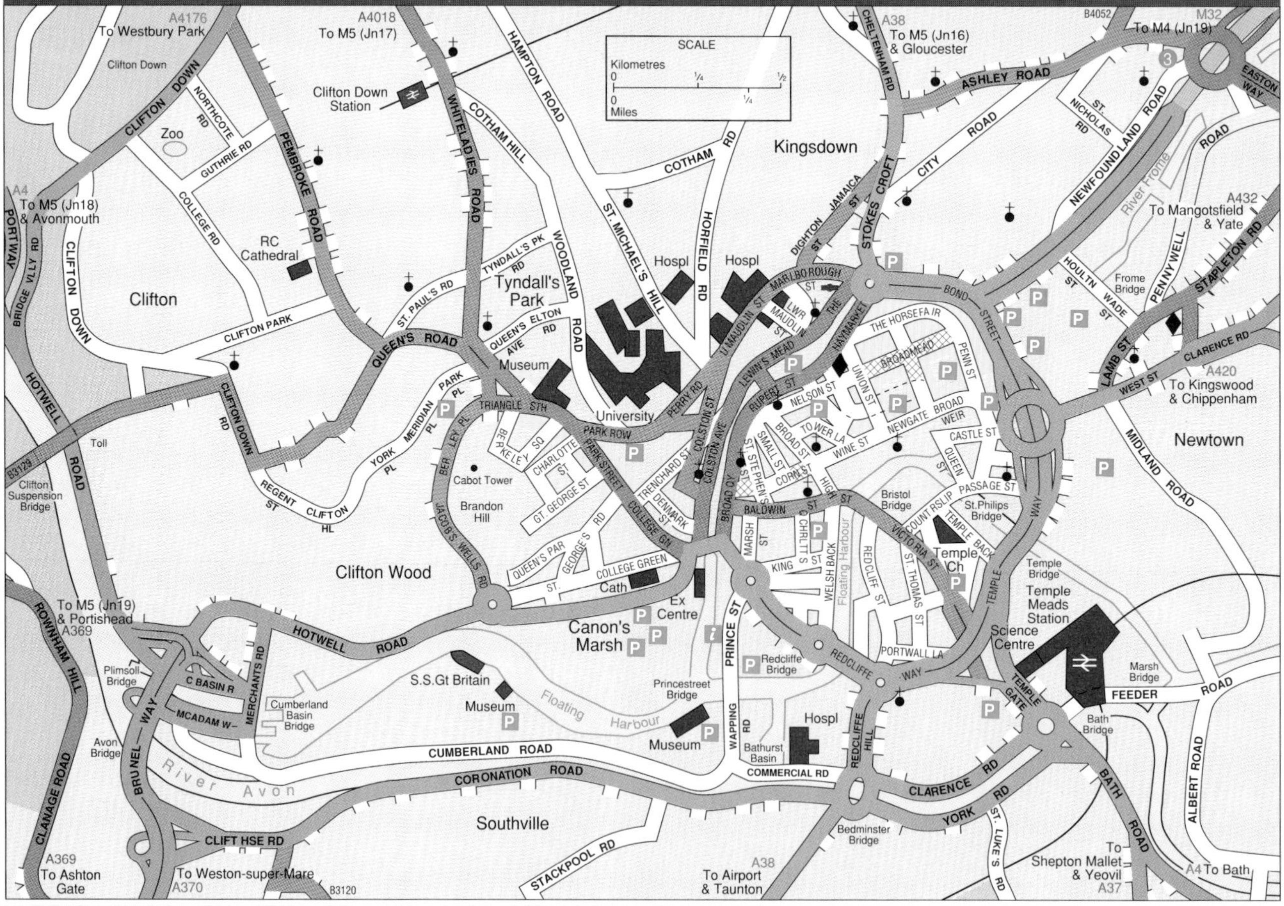

Cheltenham
SCALE
Kilometres
Miles
To M5 (Jn 10)
Tewkesbury
A4019
St.Paul's
Hospl
A435
To Racecourse
& Evesham
Pittville
EVESHAM RD
TEWKESBURY ROAD
GLOUCESTER RD
B4633
POOLE W
SWINDON RD
HIGH STREET
ST.MARGARET'S RD
WELLINGTON RD
PRESTBURY RD
PITTVILLE CIRCUS
B4632
PORTLAND ST
Mus
GT WESTERN RD
NEW ST
KNAPP RD
Library
Mus &
Art Gallery
HPO
NORTH ST
WINCHCOMBE ST
FAIRVIEW RD
ALL SAINT'S ROAD
ALBION STREET
ST JOHN AV
ST. GEORGE'S ST
JESSOP AV
CLARENCE ST
Overton
Park
Bays
Hill
ROYAL WELL LA
ROYAL WELL ROAD
PROMENADE
REGENT ST
REGENT ARCADE
HIGH STREET
HEWLETT RD
MALVERN ROAD
PARABOLA RD
BAYSHILL LA
BAYSHILL ROAD
IMPERIAL LA
IMPERIAL
TH
ORIEL RD
RODNEY RD
CAMBRAY PL
BATH ST
WELLINGTON ST
ST JAMES ST
BERKELEY ST
ROYAL PARADE M
MONTPELLIER ST
MONTPELLIER W
SQUARE
TRAFALGAR ST
VICTORIA WLK
MONTPELLIER SPA RD
Sandford
Park
LONDON ROAD
LANSDOWN CRES
LANSDOWN RD
Montpellier
MONTPELLIER TERR
BATH RD
COLLEGE ROAD
Hospl
A40
To
Oxford
A40(T)
To M5 (Jn 11)
Gloucester
A4013
To A40
SUFFOLK ROAD
SANDFORD ROAD
THIRLESTAINE ROAD
BATH ROAD
SANDFORD MILL RD
OLD
To Stroud
& Bath
A46
A40
A40

Chester
CHEYNEY ROAD
BOUVERIE ST
A540
To
Hoylake
PARKGATE RD
LIVERPOOL RD
A5116
To A41(T),
Birkenhead
& Liverpool
VICTORIA R
Leisure
Centre
Newtown
A56
To M53,M56
& Manchester
BROOK ST BRIDGE
General
Station
GARDEN LANE
HOOLE WAY
BROOK STREET
STATION ROAD
RAYMOND ST
ST-OSWALDS-WAY
CITY ROAD
STH VIEW RD
GEORGE ST
GORSE STACKS
Shropshire Union Canal
CANAL ST
ABBEY GREEN
TOWER RD
KING ST
UNION T
VICTORIA PLACE
YORK ST
BOLD SQ
HUNTER ST
Abbey
Cath
BOUGHTON
A51
To Nantwich &
Stoke on Trent
NEW CRANE STREET
CITY WALLS RD
Infmy
PRINCESS ST
Mkt
TH
FOREGATE STREET
FOREST ST
UNION ST
DEE LA
A548
To
Queensferry
Guildhall
HAMILTON P
EASTGATE ST
HPO
PRIORY PLACE
WATERGATE S
Grosvenor
Precinct
Grosvenor
Park
GROSVENOR PK TER
COMMONHALL STREET
WHITE FRIARS
CUPPIN ST
PEPPER ST
NUNS ROAD
Mus
THE GROVES
LOWER BRIDGE ST
River Dee
Queen's Park
Roodee
Chester Race Course
Exhib
Centre
Weir
Dee
Bridge
CASTLE DRIVE
GROSVENOR ROAD
Grosvenor
Bridge
HANDBRIDGE
Handbridge
RIVER LANE
OVERLEIGH ROAD
EATON ROAD
To A494(T)
Dolgellau
& Llandudno
A5104
HOUGH GREEN
WXM RD
A483
To Wrexham,
A55(T) & North Wales
SCALE
Kilometres
Miles

Cardiff
A48(T)
To Newport
& M4 (Jn29a)
England
A470
To M4 (Jn29a),
Pontypridd
& Brecon
CROWN WAY
A469
To Caerphilly
NINIAN RD
Llandaff
Cathedral
WESTERN AVENUE
MACKINTOSH PLACE
CATHAYS TERRACE
CRWYS ROAD
PEN-Y-LAN RD
MAINDY ROAD
To Rhondda
A4119
SCALE
Kilometres
Miles
ALBANY ROAD
A469
To Roath
Cathays
Pontcanna
Fields
Blackweir
A48(T)
To Cowbridge
& Bridgend
CARDIFF ROAD
Llandaff
Fields
Pontcanna
COLUM ROAD
River Taff
B4488
PENCISELY ROAD
PEN-HILL RD
Welsh
Office
Cathays
Station
SENGHENNYDD RD
RICHMOND ROAD
CITY ROAD
Roath
CHARGOT RD
ROAD
CATHEDRAL ROAD
County
Cricket
Ground
University
Univ
To
A48/M4
(Jn28)
Newport
A4161
ROMILLY RD W
ROMILLY ROAD
ROMILLY CRES
LLANDAFF ROAD
National
Sports
Centre
Univ
County Hall
National
Museum
ST ANDREWS PLACE
ST.PETER'S ST
VICTORIA PK RD E
CLIVE
WYNDHAM CRES
City
Hall
Court
Bute
Park
BOULEVARD DE NANTES
STUTTGARTER STRASSE
Univ
NEWPORT ROAD
WEST GROVE
GLOSSOP RD
Canton
St David's
Hospital
Royal
Infmy
A4161
To Fairwater
COWBRIDGE RD EAST
Castle
Mus
GREYFRIARS RD
QUEEN STREET
KNOX RD
MOIRA TERR
MOIRA PL
LANSDOWNE ROAD
GROSVENOR STREET
Cardiff
Bridge
CASTLE ST
DUKE ST
Cath
Queen
St
Station
WINDSOR RD
WELLINGTON ST
NEVILLE ST
Cardiff
R F C
Ground
St. David's
Hall
ATLAS RD
BROAD ST
Riverside
National
Stadium
Cardiff Arms
Park
HPO
World
Trade
Centre
NINIAN PARK ROAD
TUDOR STREET
WOOD ST
CENTRAL SQ
CUSTOMHSE ST
BUTE TERRACE
TYNDALL STREET
Ninian Park
Station
LECKWITH ROAD
SLOPER RD
To
Grangetown
A4119
Wales
Empire
Pool
Central
Station
To Penarth
A4160
BUTE ST
To Butetown
A470
Bute
East
Dock
A4232
To M4 (Jn33) Swansea
Sports
Stadium
Cardiff City
Football Ground
CLARE RD
B4267

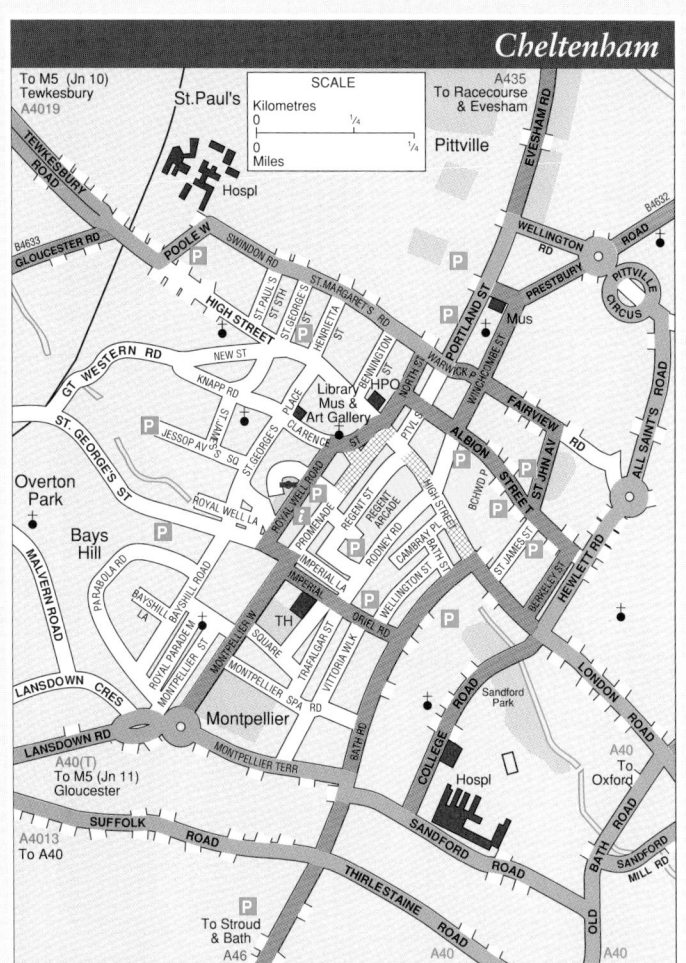

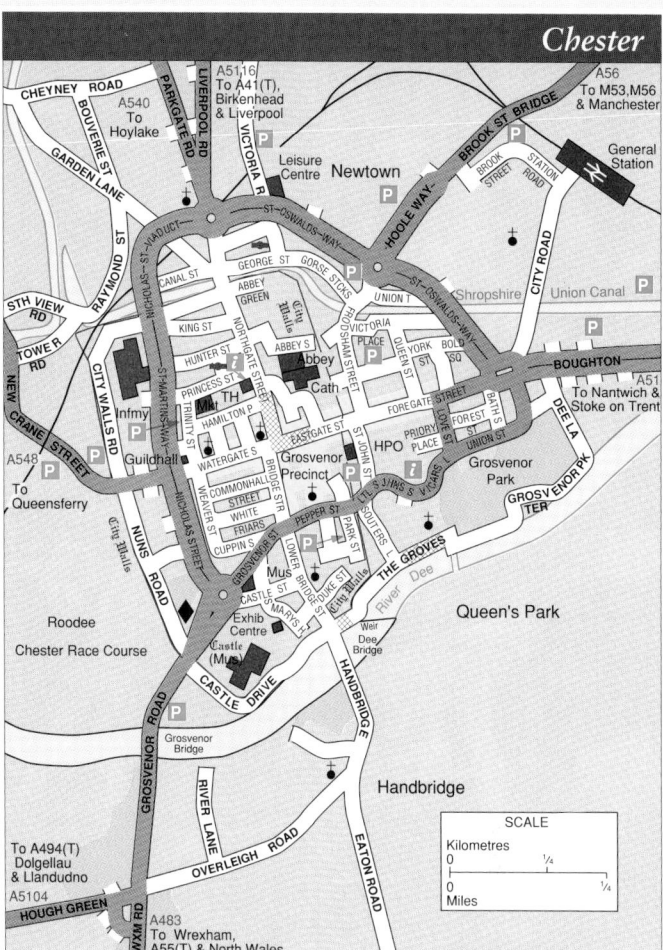

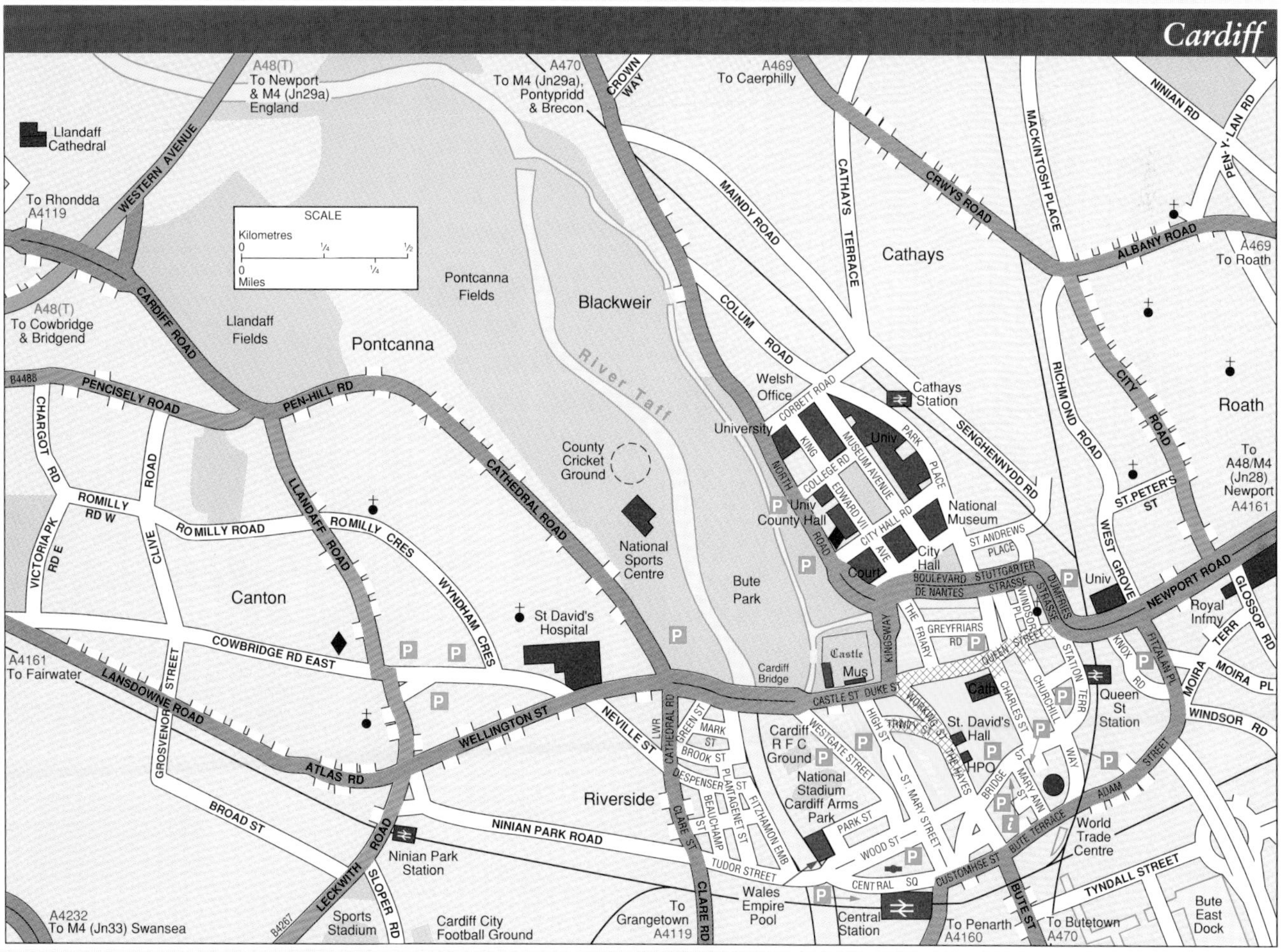

Coventry

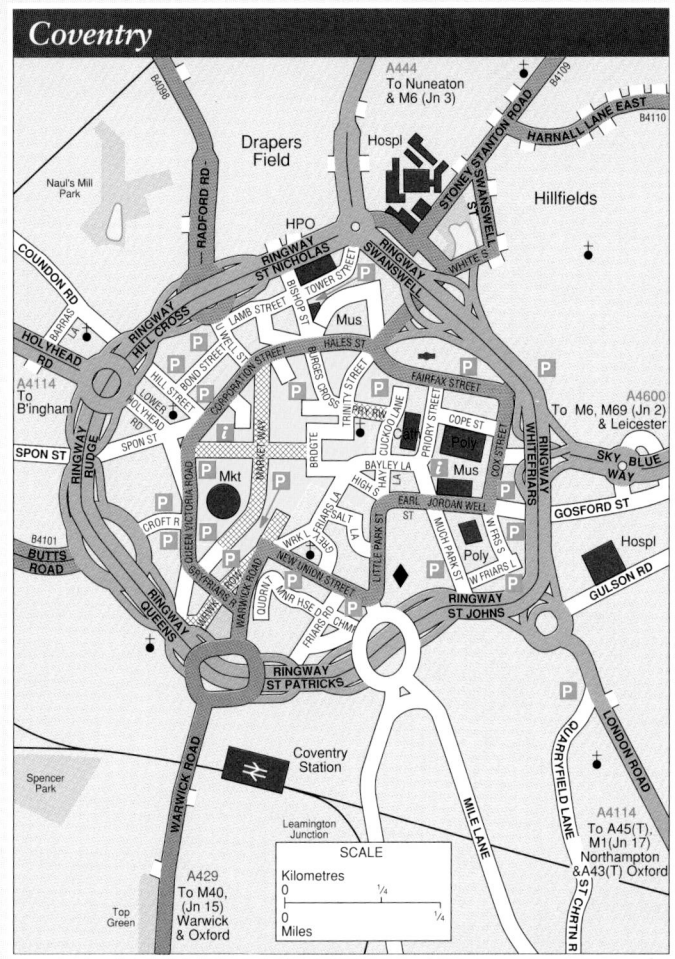

Croydon

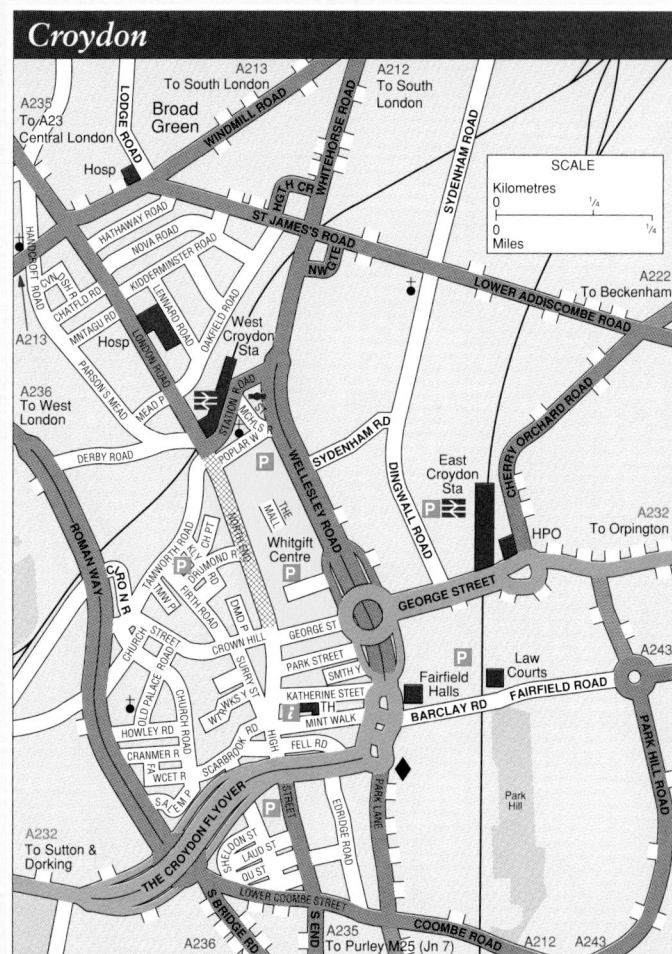

Derby

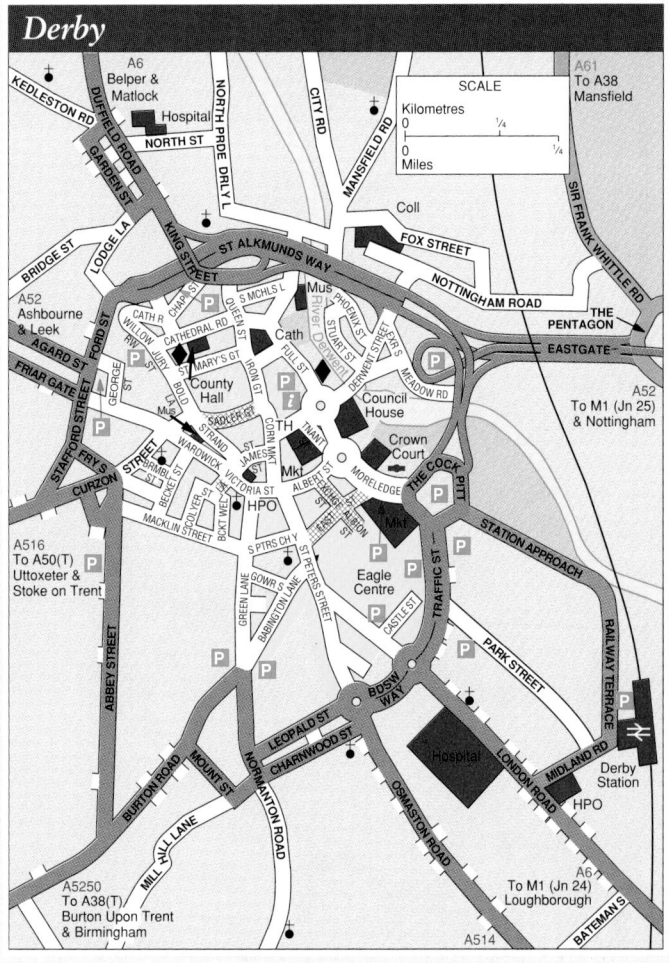

Dundee

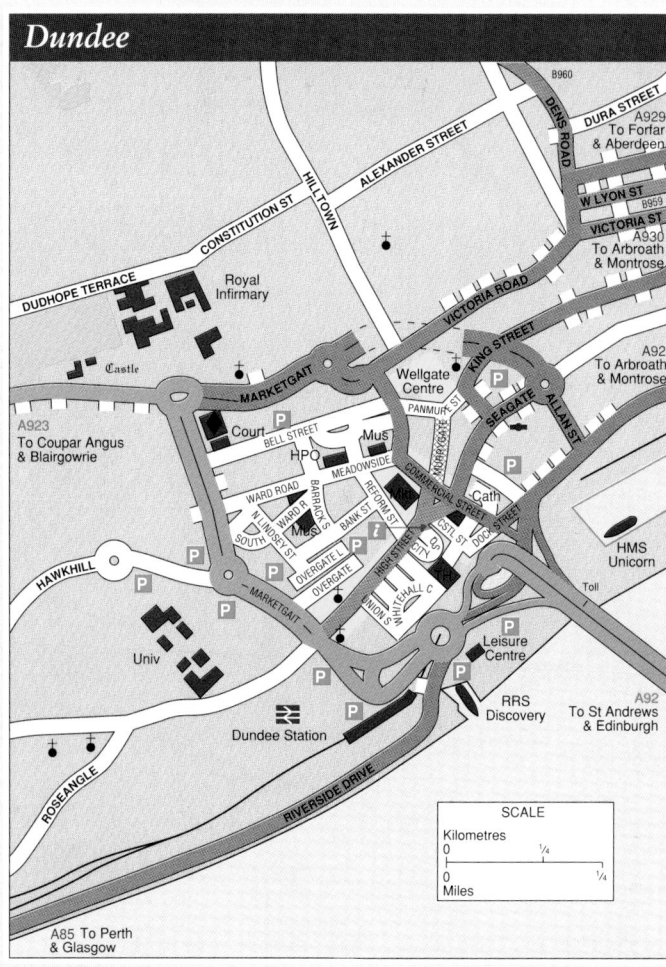

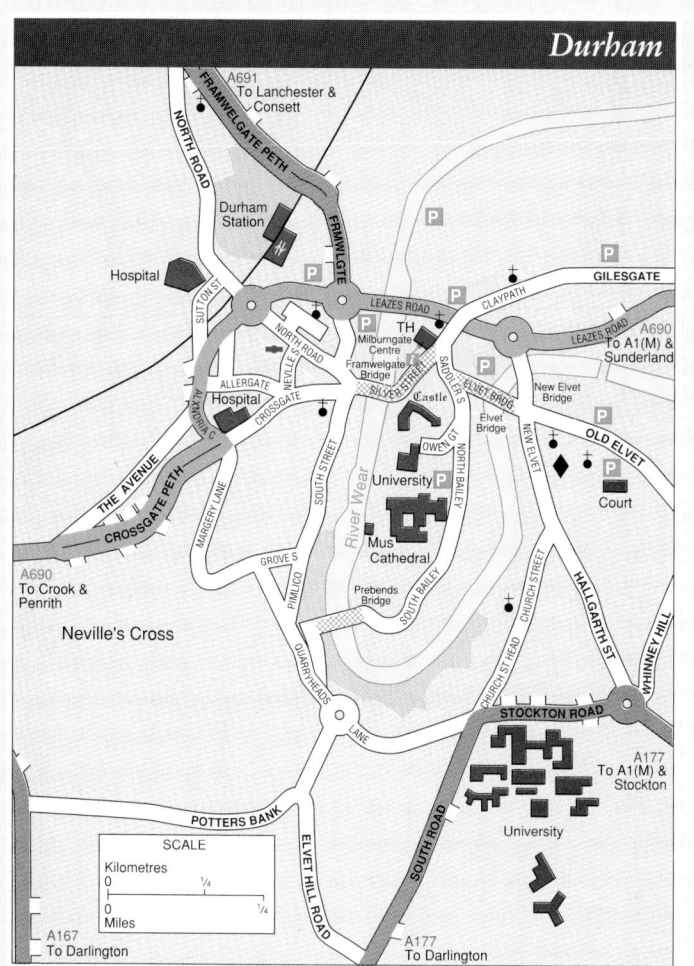

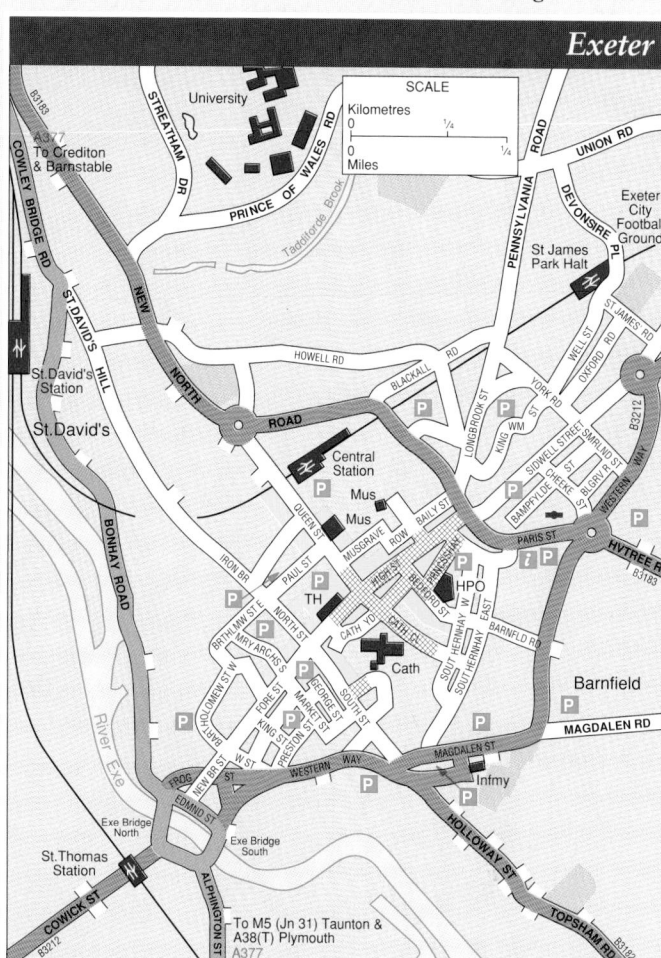

Durham

To Lanchester & Consett
A691
FRAMWELGATE PETH
NORTH ROAD
Durham Station
Hospital
SUTTON ST
NORTH RD
ALEXANDRA C
THE AVENUE
CROSSGATE PETH
A690
To Crook & Penrith
Neville's Cross
MARGERY LANE
GROVE S
PIMLICO
QUARRYHEADS
CHURCH ST HEAD
SOUTH STREET
SOUTH BAILEY
LANE
POTTERS BANK
ELVET HILL ROAD
SOUTH ROAD
A167
To Darlington
A177
To Darlington
Hospital
ALLERGATE
CROSSGATE
SILVER STREET
FRAMWLGTE
LEAZES ROAD
CLAYPATH
GILESGATE
TH
Milburngate Centre
Framwelgate Bridge
Castle
OWEN
SADDLER'S
NORTH BAILEY
ELVET BRDG
Elvet Bridge
New Elvet Bridge
LEAZES ROAD
A690
To A1(M) & Sunderland
New Elvet
OLD ELVET
Court
University
Mus Cathedral
Prebends Bridge
River Wear
CHURCH STREET
HALLGARTH ST
WHINNEY HILL
STOCKTON ROAD
A177
To A1(M) & Stockton
University

SCALE
Kilometres
0   ¼
0   ¼
Miles

Exeter

University
STREATHAM DR
PRINCE OF WALES RD
A377
To Crediton & Barnstable
COWLEY BRIDGE RD
ST DAVID'S HILL
St David's Station
St. David's
BONHAY ROAD
IRON BR
River Exe
NEW BR ST
TROB
EDMND ST
COWICK ST
B2212
St.Thomas Station
Exe Bridge North
Exe Bridge South
ALPHINGTON ST
To M5 (Jn 31) Taunton & A38(T) Plymouth
A377
Tadelorde Brook
NORTH ROAD
HOWELL RD
BLACKALL ST
QUEEN ST
MUSGRAVE
PAUL ST
NORTH ST
BRTH MW ST
MRY ARCHS
GEORGES
FORE ST
KING ST
MARKET ST
PRESTON ST
SMYTHEN ST
WESTERN WAY
MAGDALEN ST
HOLLOWAY ST
Central Station
Mus
Mus
TH
Cath
HPO
PENNSYLVANIA ROAD
DEVONSHRE PL
UNION RD
Exeter City Football Ground
St James Park Halt
ST JAMES RD
WELL ST
YORK RD
OXFORD RD
B2212
LONGBROOK ST
KING
WM
SIDWELL STREET
SMRLD ST
CHEEKE
ST
BLGRV ST
WESTERN WAY
B3183
PARIS ST
HVTREE R
B3183
Barnfield
BARNFLD RD
MAGDALEN RD
Infmy
TOPSHAM RD
B3182

SCALE
Kilometres
0   ¼
0   ¼
Miles

Edinburgh

LESLIE PL
KERR ST
B900
CIRCUS PL
HOWE ST
DUNDAS ST
New Town
DUBLIN ST
BROUGHTON ST
A900
To Leith
LONDON ROAD
Greenside
Calton
A1
To Berwick & Newcastle
MORAY
PLACE
AINSLIE
A90
To Forth Bridge & Perth
Dean Bridge
QUEENSFERRY ST
RANDOLPH CRES
ABERCROMBY PLACE
Ntnl Portrait Gallery & mus
YORK PLACE
RC Cath
HERIOT ROW
QUEEN STREET
THISTLE
HANOVER STREET
ANDREW
FREDERICK STREET
CASTLE STREET
GEORGE STREET
HILL ST
YOUNG ST
ROSE STREET
NTS
CHARLOTTE SQUARE
St. James Centre
City Observatory
Monuments
St Andrew ST
LEITH ST
REGENT ROAD
PO
Waverley Station
CALTON ROAD
Canongate Tolbooth Museum
CANONGATE
Palace of Holyroodhouse & remains of Holyrood Abbey
ABBEYHILL
ABBEY MNT
QUEENS DR
PRINCES STREET
West Princes Street Gardens
Royal Scottish Academy
Scott Mon
National Gallery
EAST MARKET ST
NEW STREET
JEFFREY
J. Knox House
Huntly House Museum
The Royal Mile
Mus
HOLYROOD ROAD
Canongate
To M8 (Jn2) Glasgow & M9 (Jn1) Stirling
A8
SHANDWICK ST
W MAITLAND ST
CANNING
W APPROACH RD
LOTHIAN ROAD
KING'S STABLES
Castle
CASTLE HILL
JOHNSTON TERRACE
Museum
MARKET STREET
BANK ST
TH
COCKBURN ST
HIGH ST
GEORGE IV BRIDGE
Cath
BLAIR ST
SOUTH BRIDGE
ST MARY'S ST
Univ
National Library
VICTORIA ST
COWGATE
Univ
CHAMBERS STREET
DRUMMOND ST
INFMY ST
PLEASANCE
Holyrood Park
Holyrood Park
QUEEN'S DRIVE
Salisbury Crags
TORPHICHEN ST
A70
To Ayr
MORRISON ST
CASTLE TERRACE
GRINDLAY ST
SPITTAL ST
BREAD ST
LADY LAWSON ST
WEST PORT
GRASSMARKET
CANDLEMAKER RW
Old Town
KEIR ST
LAURISTON PL
HERIOT PL
FORREST RD
TEVIOT PL
BRISTO P
BRISTO
POTTERROW
NICOLSON STREET
Mus
Univ
CLERK ST
ST LEONARD'S ST
University
Infirmary
FOUNTAINBRIDGE
SEMPLE ST
PONTON ST
HOME ST
MELVILLE DRIVE
GILMORE PL
A702
To Biggar & Stranraer
A700
To Newington
BUCCLEUCH ST
A7
To Galashiels & The South
St. Leonard's

SCALE
Kilometres
0   ¼   ½
0   ¼
Miles

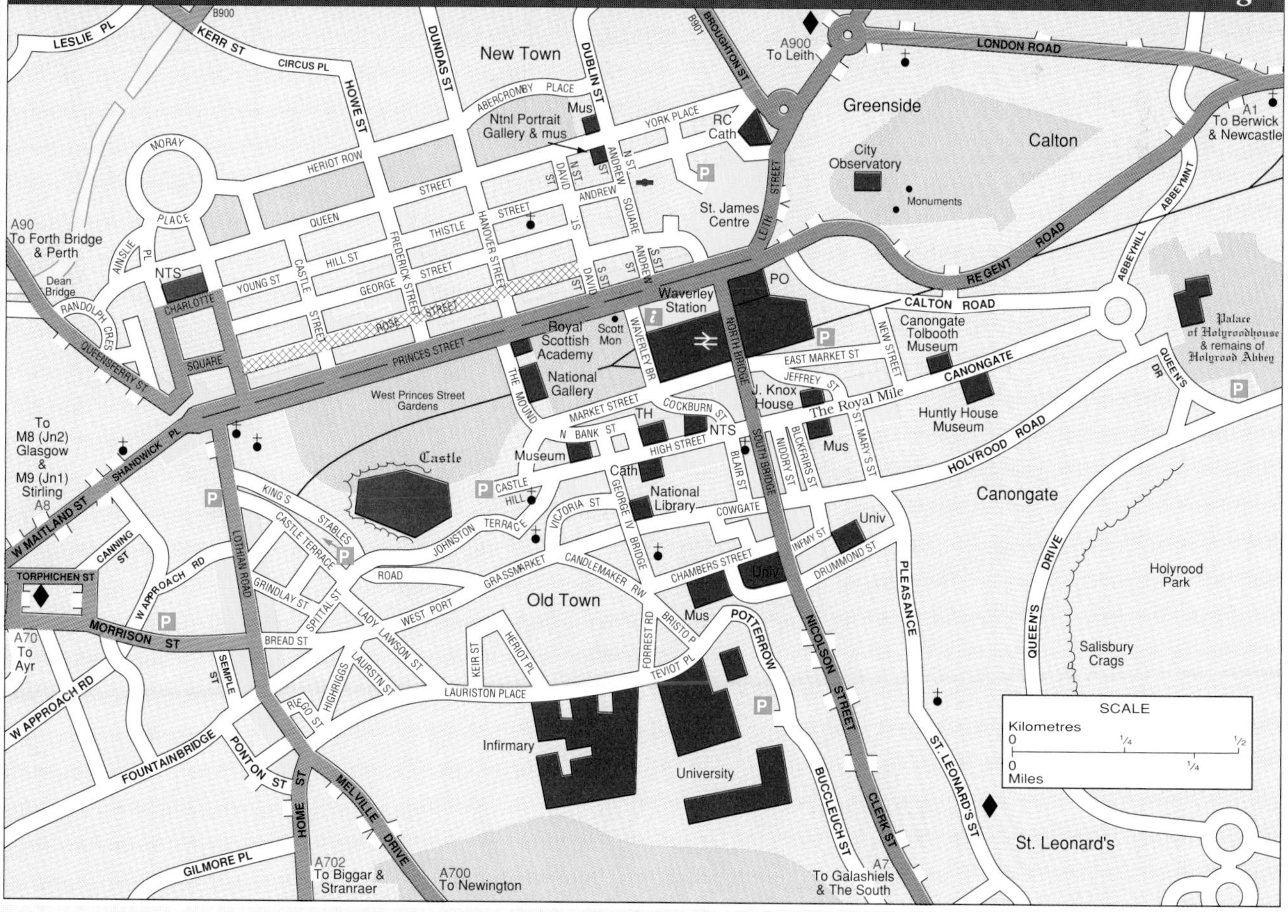

Gloucester

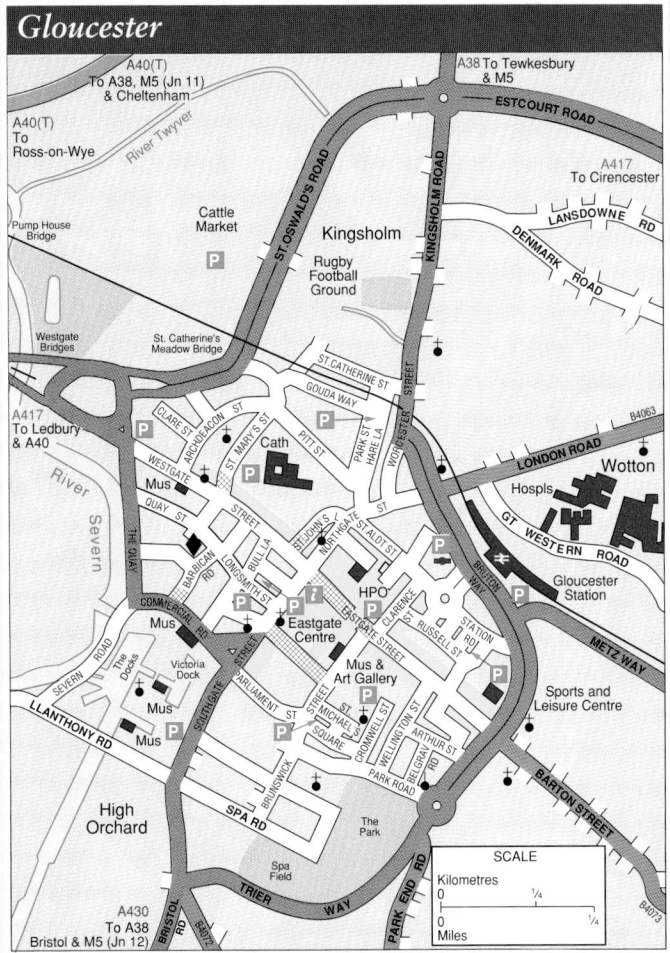

Hull

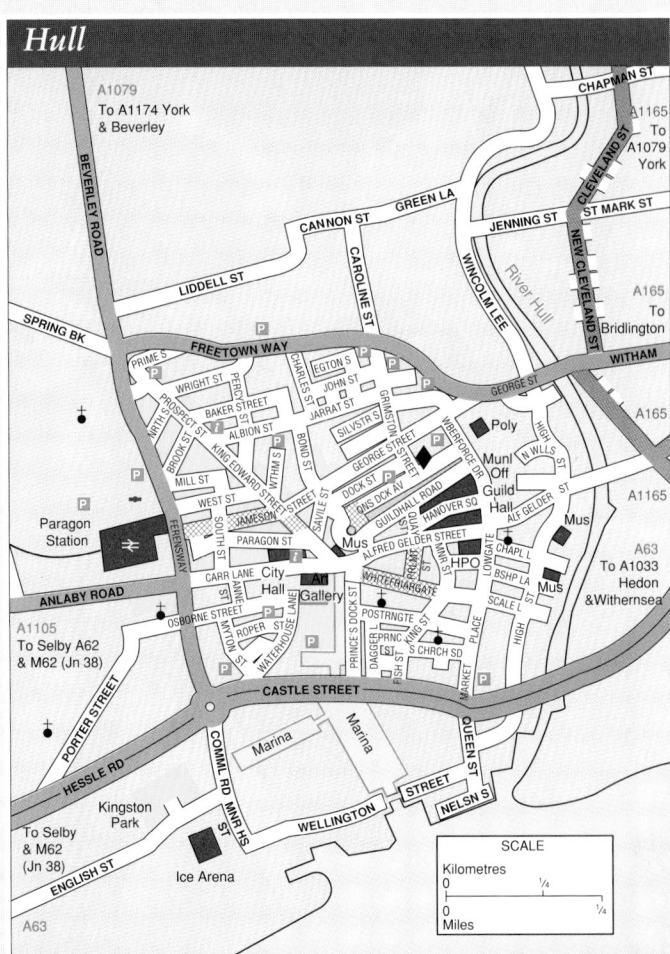

Glasgow

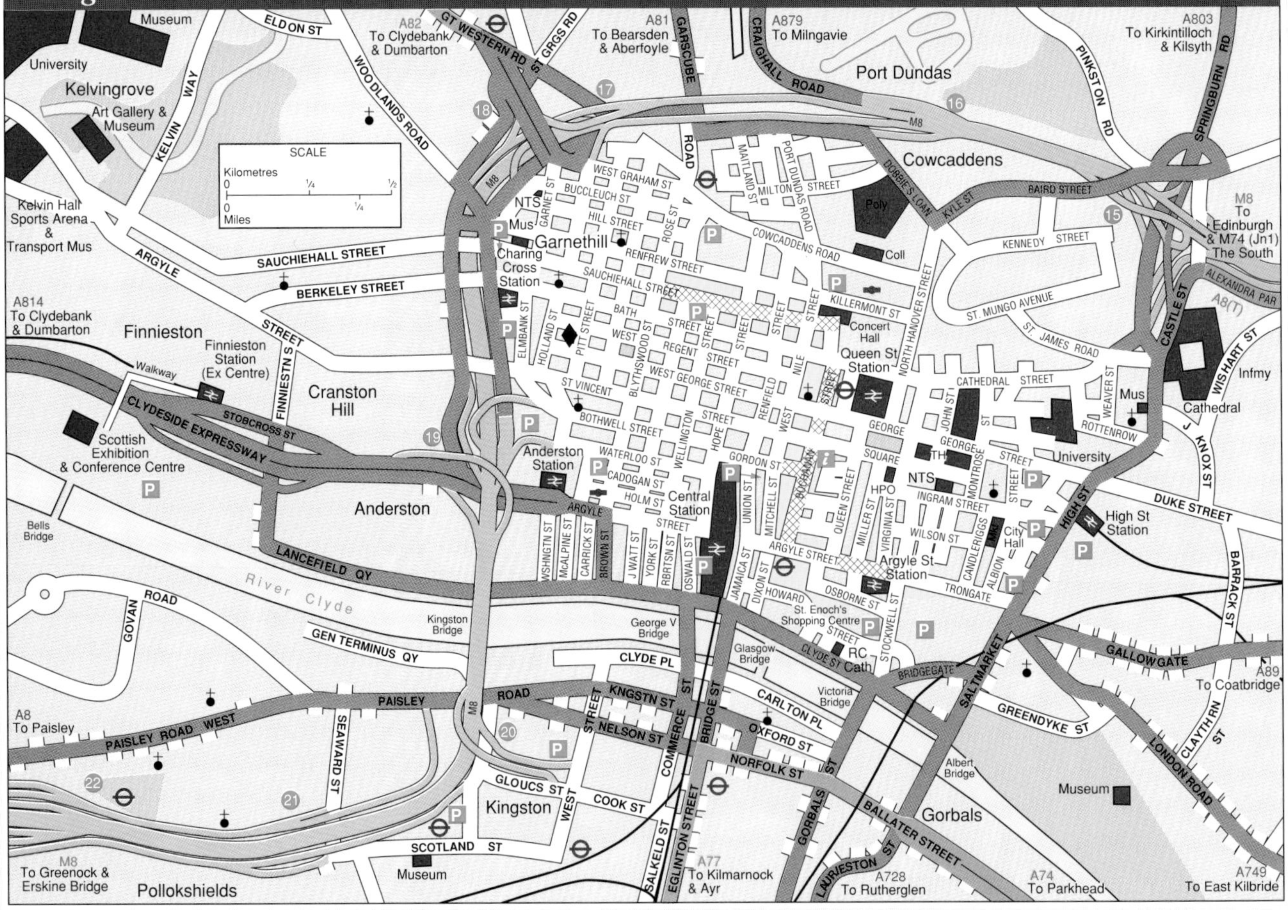

Leeds

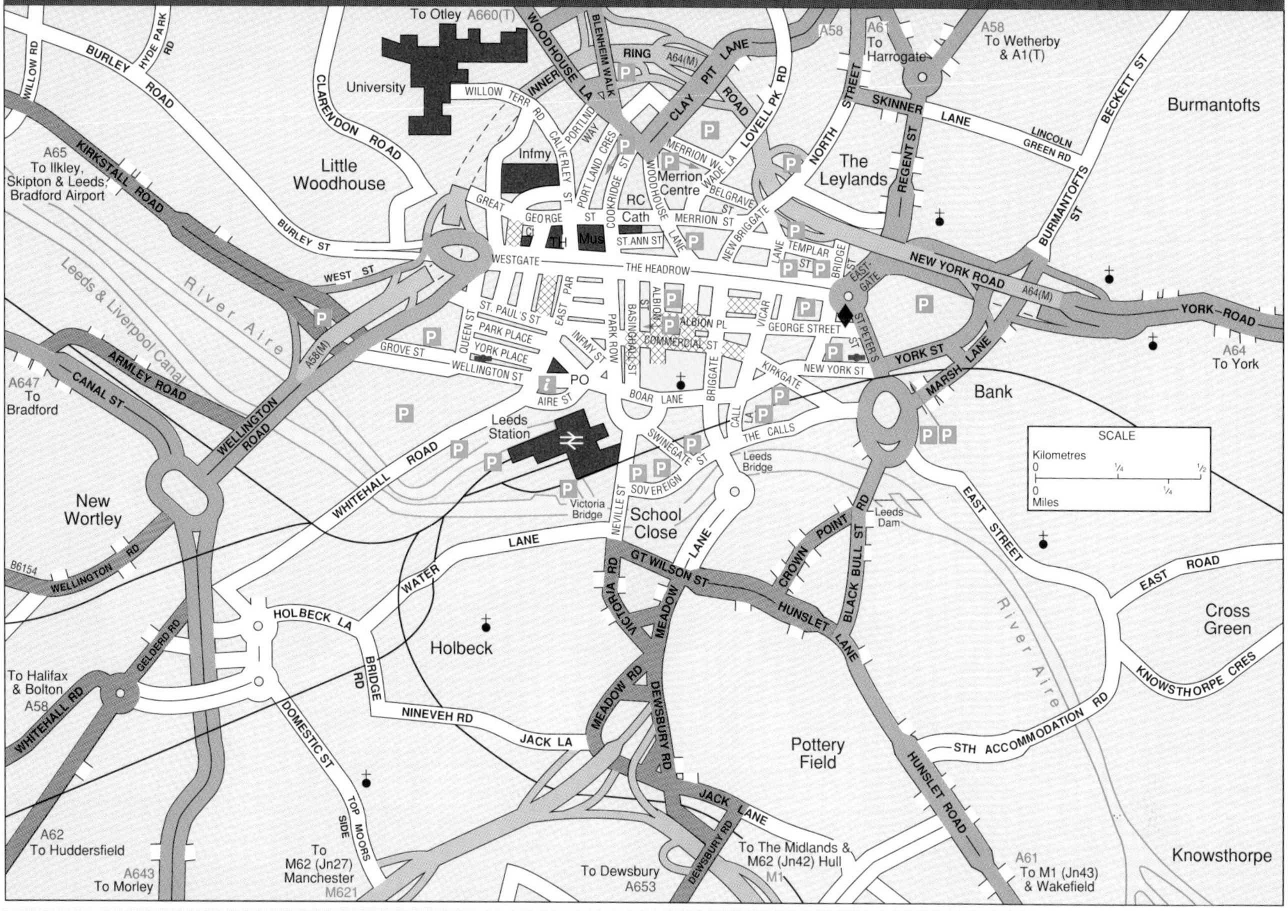

To Otley A660(T)
To Wetherby & A1(T) A58 A61
To Harrogate A64(M)
WOODHOUSE LANE
BLENHEIM WALK
RING
INNER LA
CLAY PIT RD
LOVELL PK RD
NORTH STREET
SKINNER LANE
REGENT ST
BECKETT ST
LINCOLN GREEN RD
BURMANTOFTS
Burmantofts

University
HYDE PARK
WILLOW RD
BURLEY ROAD
CLARENDON ROAD
WILLOW TERR RD
PORTLAND WAY
CALVERLEY ST
MERRION WEST
BELGRAVE
MERRION ST
NEW BRIGGATE
TEMPLAR ST
EAST ST
The Leylands

Little Woodhouse
Infmy
Merrion Centre
RC Cath
GEORGE
TH Mus
WESTGATE
ST ANN ST
NEW YORK ROAD
A64(M)

A65 KIRKSTALL ROAD
To Ilkley, Skipton & Leeds, Bradford Airport
WEST ST
THE HEADROW
ALBION PL
ALBION ST
COMMERCIAL ST
VICAR LANE
GEORGE STREET
ST PETER'S
YORK ST
NEW YORK ST
MARSH LANE
YORK ROAD
A64 To York

Leeds & Liverpool Canal
River Aire
ST PAUL'S ST
QUEEN ST
PARK PLACE
YORK PLACE
WELLINGTON ST
GROVE ST
INFMY ST
PARK ROW
BASINGHALL ST
BRIGGATE
CALL LANE
KIRKGATE
Bank

A647 To Bradford
ARMLEY ROAD
CANAL ST
A58(M)
WELLINGTON ROAD
WHITEHALL ROAD
P PO
AIRE ST
BOAR LANE
Leeds Station
THE CALLS
Leeds Bridge
EAST STREET
EAST ROAD
Cross Green

New Wortley
B6154
WELLINGTON RD
GELDERD RD
Victoria Bridge
School Close
Leeds Dam
River Aire
KNOWSTHORPE CRES

To Halifax & Bolton
A58
WHITEHALL RD
HOLBECK LA
BRIDGE RD
WATER LANE
NEVILLE ST
SWINEGATE
SOVEREIGN ST
VICTORIA RD
MEADOW RD
GT WILSON ST
CROWN POINT
BLACK BULL ST
HUNSLET LANE
EAST STREET
SCALE
Kilometres
Miles

Holbeck
NINEVEH RD
DOMESTIC ST
TOP MOORS SIDE
JACK LA
DEWSBURY RD
MEADOW LANE
Pottery Field
HUNSLET ROAD
STH ACCOMMODATION RD
Knowsthorpe

A62 To Huddersfield
A643 To Morley
M621
JACK LANE
To M62 (Jn27) Manchester
To Dewsbury A653
HUNSLET ROAD
To The Midlands & M62 (Jn42) Hull M1
A61 To M1 (Jn43) & Wakefield

Liverpool

A5036 To Crosby
A565 To Southport
A5038 To Litherland
SCOTLAND ROAD
To Ormskirk & Preston A59
FOX ST
VILLAGE ST
A580 To Manchester
Hospital
A5049 To West Derby
SHIEL ROAD
Elm Park

Kingsway (Road Tunnel)
WATERLOO ROAD
GREAT HOWARD ROAD
PALL MALL
VAUXHALL ROAD
ST ANNE STREET
EVERTON BROW
SHAW STREET
EVERTON ROAD
WEST DERBY ROAD
LOW HILL
KENSINGTON
A57 To Prescot & St Helens

LEEDS STREET
ADDISON ST
BYROM ST
Poly
HUNTER ST
NEW ISLINGTON
ISLINGTON
BRUNSWICK RD
PRESCOT ST
Hospital
HALL LANE
HOLT RD
A5047 To M62 (Jn 5) Manchester & St Helens

Hospl
Moorfields Station
Museum
Art Gallery
LONDON ROAD
PEMBROKE PLACE
WEST DERBY ST
EDGE LANE

TH
W BROWN ST
Hall
LD NELSON ST
Lime St Station
RUSSELL ST
CROWN ST
IRVINE ST
WAVERTREE ROAD
B5178

Ferry (Foot)
Royal Liver Building
James St Station
ST JOHN'S LANE
COPPERAS
St John's Centre
BROWNLOW HILL
Univ

Queensway (Mersey Tunnel)
Museum
LORD STREET
SCHOOL LA
PARADISE ST
HANOVER STREET
Clayton Square
RENSHAW ST
RANELAGH ST
Central Station
RC Cathedral
Univ
MOUNT PLEASANT
OXFORD ST
GRINFIELD ST
OVERBURY ST
Edge Hill
Edge Hill Station

Ferry (Foot)
River Mersey
Museum
Tate Gallery
Albert Dock
WAPPING
PARK LA
DUKE ST
BOLD ST
RODNEY STREET
Hospl
Univ
GROVE STREET
TUNNEL ROAD

SCALE
Kilometres
Miles
ST JAMES STREET
CHALONER ST
GT GEORGE ST
BERRY ST
UPPER DUKE ST
Cath
HOPE STREET
CATHARINE ST
Hospl
PARLIAMENT STREET
MULGRAVE ST
Princes Park
KINGSLEY RD
LODGE LANE
SMITHDOWN ROAD
A562 To Widnes & Runcorn

A5036
PARLIAMENT ST
To Widnes A561
UPPER PRINCES RD
B5175

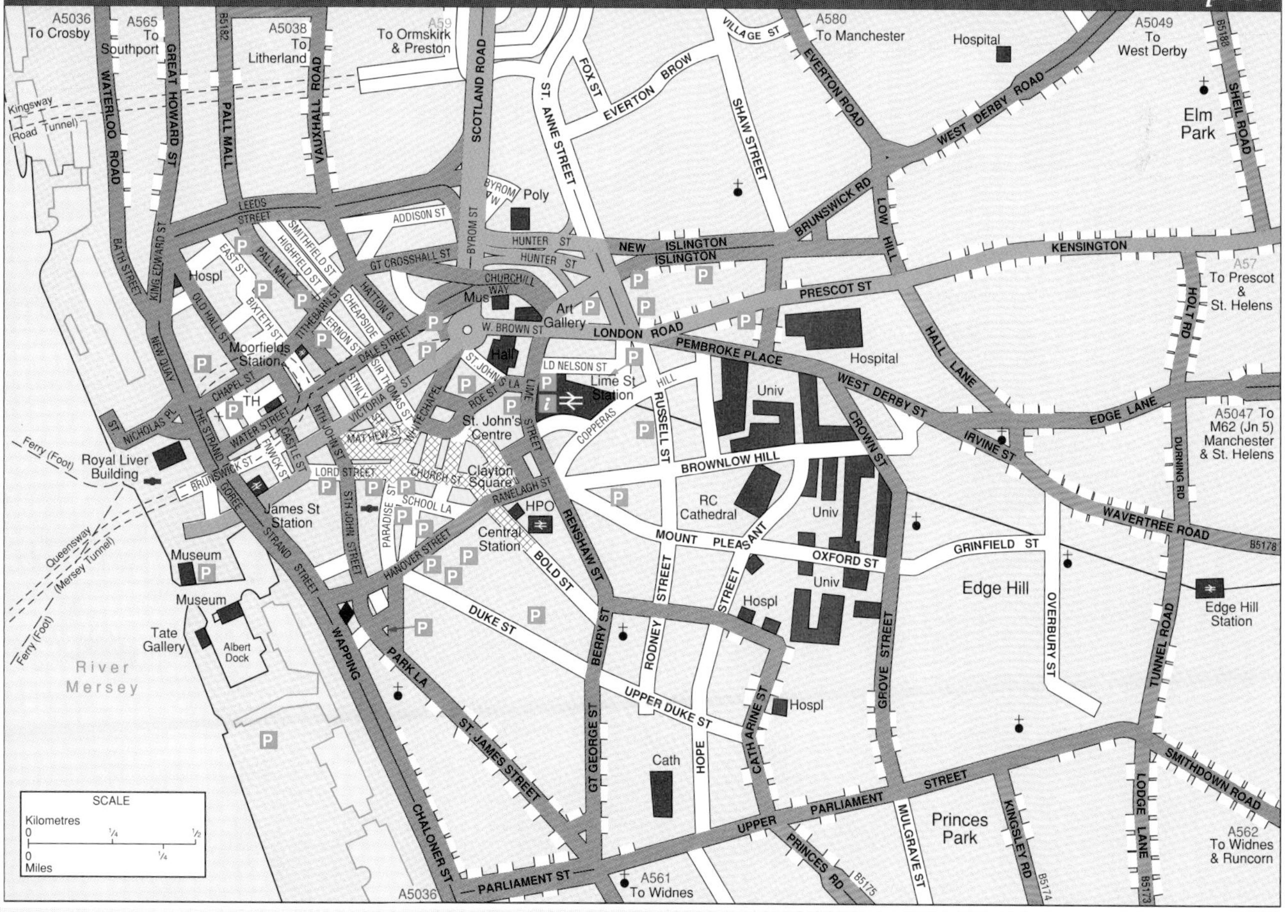

Leicester

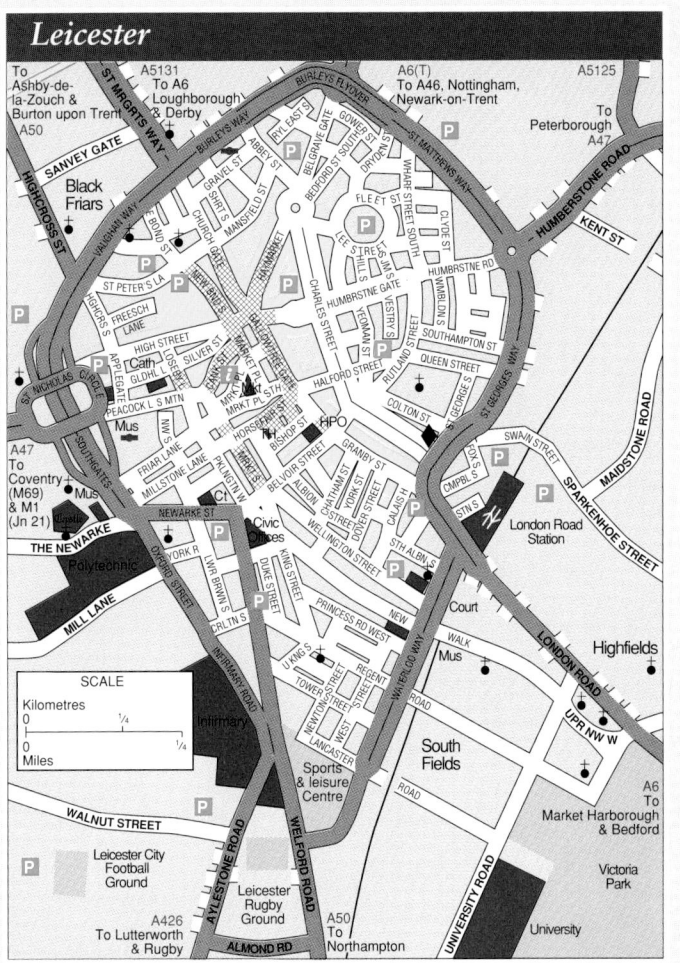

Middlesbrough

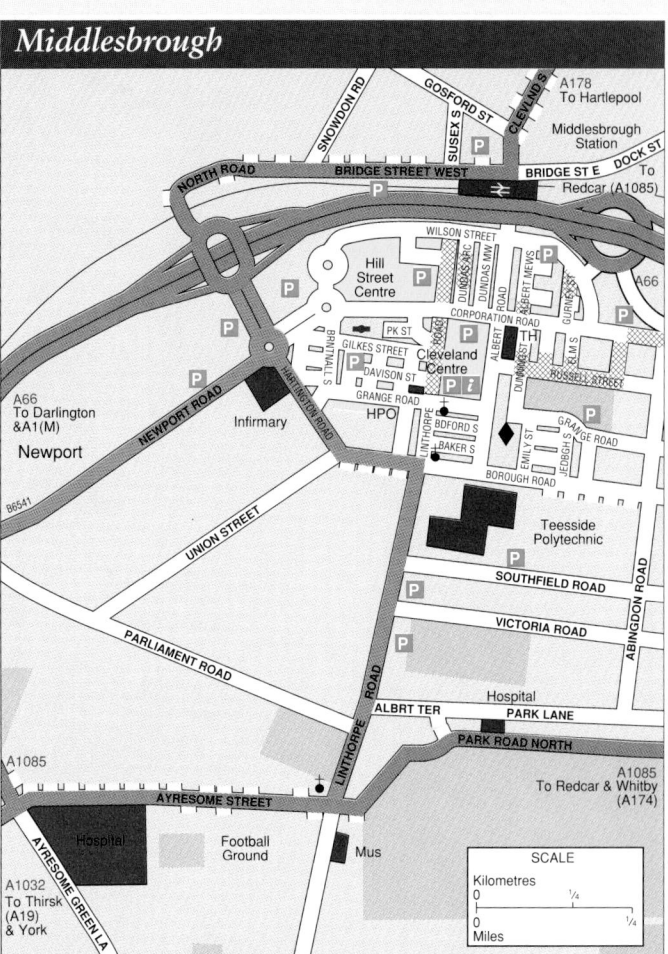

Manchester

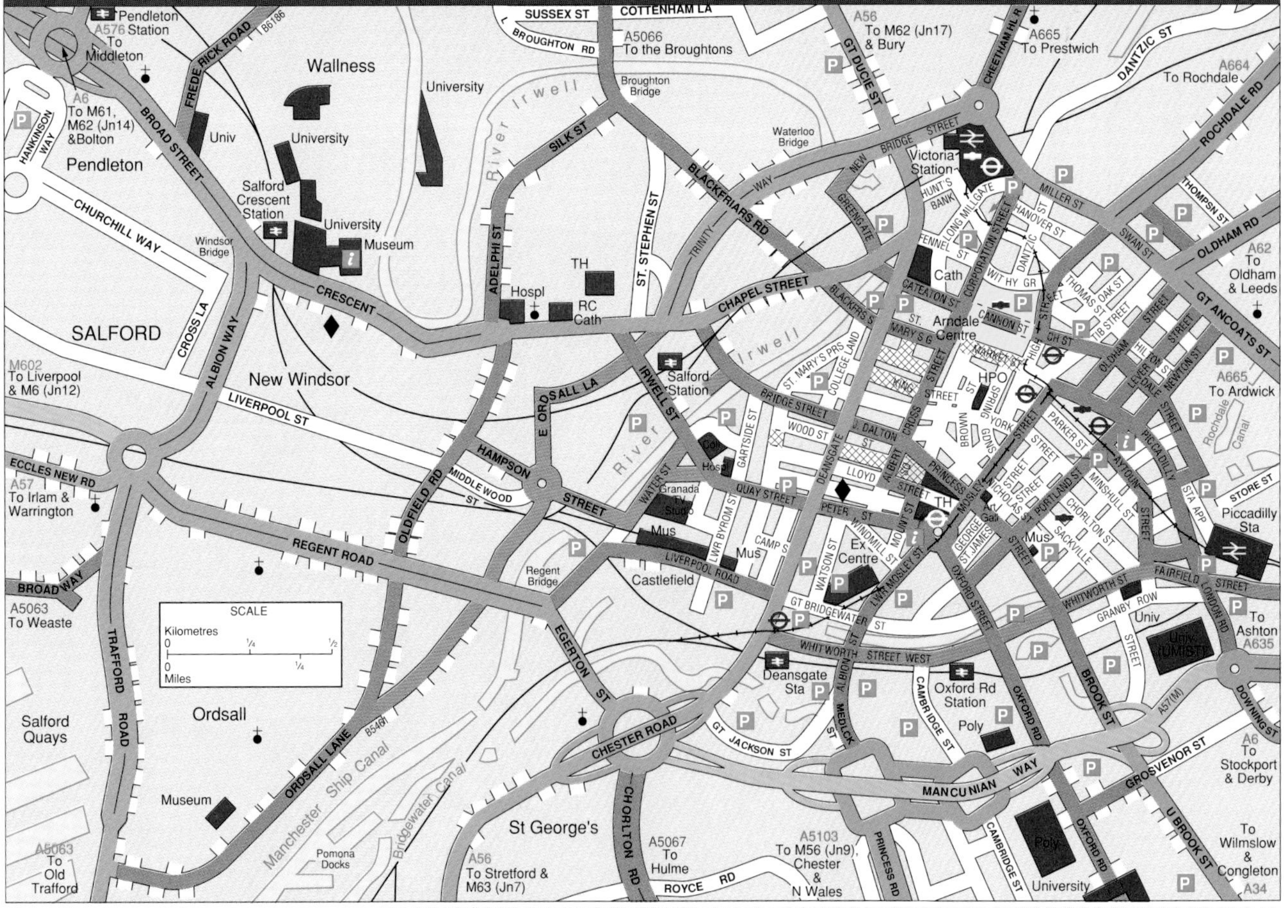

Milton Keynes
SCALE
Kilometres
Miles
To Bedford (A422)
& Wellingborough (A509)
A4146
A509
Heelands
Conniburrow
DANSTEED WAY
SAXON STREET
CONNIBURROW BLVD
Bradwell
Common
BRADWELL COMMON BLVD
PORTWAY
A4146
To M1
(Jn 14)
Luton &
Northampton
NORTH ROW
N 13TH ST
N 12TH ST
N 11TH ST
N 10TH ST
N 9TH ST
N 8TH ST
N 7TH ST
N 6TH ST
N 5 S
N 4TH ST
N 3RD
N 2ND ST
SECKLOW GATE
Munl
Offices
SAXON GATE
SILBURY BOULEVARD
Courts
UPPER 5TH ST
UPPER 4TH ST
UPR 3RD S
UPPER 2ND ST
MIDSUMMER BOULEVARD
LOW 10TH ST
LOW 9TH ST
STH 10TH ST
STH 9TH ST
STH 8TH ST
SOUTH ROW
WITAN GATE
Winter
Gardens
AVEBURY BOULEVARD
STH 7TH ST
STH 6TH ST
STH 5TH ST
LOW 4TH ST
CHILDS WAY
SAXON STREET
A509
To Rugby
& Dunstable
A5(T)
GRAFTON GATE
ELDER GATE
Central
Milton Keynes
Oldbrook
Leisure
Centre
Milton Keynes
Central Station

Oxford
SCALE
Kilometres
Miles
A4144
To A44 &
Worcester
A4165
To A423 &
A4260
Banbury
FYFIELD R
Northam
Manor
NORHAM GARDENS
Walton
Manor
WOODSTOCK ROAD
BANBURY ROAD
Univ
ST BERNARDS RD
University Parks
River Cherwell
Radcliffe
Infirmary
University Museum &
Pitt Rivers Museum
Jericho
WALTON STREET
ST GILES
PARKS ROAD
SOUTH PARKS ROAD
ST CROSS ROAD
Mus
Bodleian
Library
HOLYWELL STREET
BEAUMONT ST
BROAD STREET
To M4 (Jn 15)
& Swindon
A420
HYTHE BRDG ST
PARK END ST
GEORGE STREET
SHIP ST
QUEEN'S LANE
LONGWALL STREET
Clarendon
Centre
HIGH STREET
To A40,
M40 (Jn 8)
& London
A420
ST THOMAS
NEW ROAD
Castle
County
Hall
PARADISE S
QUEEN S
MERTON STREET
Magdalen
Bridge
HLYBSH ROW
Westgate
Shopping
Centre
PEMBROKE S
Pic
Gllry
Cath
Merton
Field
OXPENS ROAD
BREWER ST
ST ALDATES
Botanic
Gardens
A4158
To A423 &
Maidenhead
SPEEDWELL ST
THAMES STREET
Grandpont
Christ Church
Meadow
River Thames
Folly
Bridge
To A34
& Newbury
A4144

Newcastle
A187
To Blakelaw
A189
To Gosforth
A1058
To Whitley Bay
To A1(T) Berwick
Newcastle Airport
& Scotland
CLAREMONT
ROAD
GT NORTH RD
Brandling
Village
OSBORNE RD
JESMOND RD
SANDYFORD ROAD
SCALE
Kilometres
Miles
HEATON
PONTELAND RD
HUNTER'S RD
Spital
Tongues
RICHARDSON ROAD
Infirmary
Mus
Civic
Centre
HEATON PK
VIEW
Jesmond
Vale
GROVE
BARRACK
QUEEN VICTORIA RD
University
KING'S RD
Poly
City
Hall
PORTLAND RD
WARWICK ST
ROAD
STUDLEY TERR
WALTER TERR
NEW MILLS
BRIGHTON
Newcastle
United
Football
Ground
ROAD
Shieldfield
SHIELDS ROAD
Byker
Bridge
STANHOPE STREET
Eldon
Square
DURANT
NEW BRIDGE ST
Battle
Field
BYKER BANK
A187
To North Shields
& Tynemouth
WELLINGTON ST
GALLOWGATE
BLACKETT ST
Manors
Station
MELBOURNE ST
HOWARD ST
A186
To A69
Hexham &
Carlisle
WESTGATE
CORPORATION
ROAD
CITY ROAD
QUAYSIDE
St. Lawrence
ELSWICK ROAD
ELSWICK ROW
Museum
RC
Cath
Cath
Mus
PANDON
River Tyne
WALKER ROAD
To Walker
A186
NEVILLE STREET
Central
Station
FORTH
Tyne
Bridge
Swing
Bridge
Salt
Meadows
HAWKS ROAD
SALT MEADOWS RD
BEECH GR RD
GEORGE ST
WESTMORLAND ROAD
PARK RD
High Level
Bridge
Q.E.2
Bridge
GATESHEAD
HIGHWAY
GATESHEAD
SCOTSWOOD
ROAD
NELSON ST
New Redheugh
Bridge
ASKEW RD
HIGH ST
PARK LANE
PARK RD
TYNE MAIN RD
To Sunderland
A184
A695
To Blaydon
& Hexham
WATER ST
To Bensham
A6082
To Blaydon & A1(M) The South
A184
To A1(M) The South
& Chester-le-Street
A167

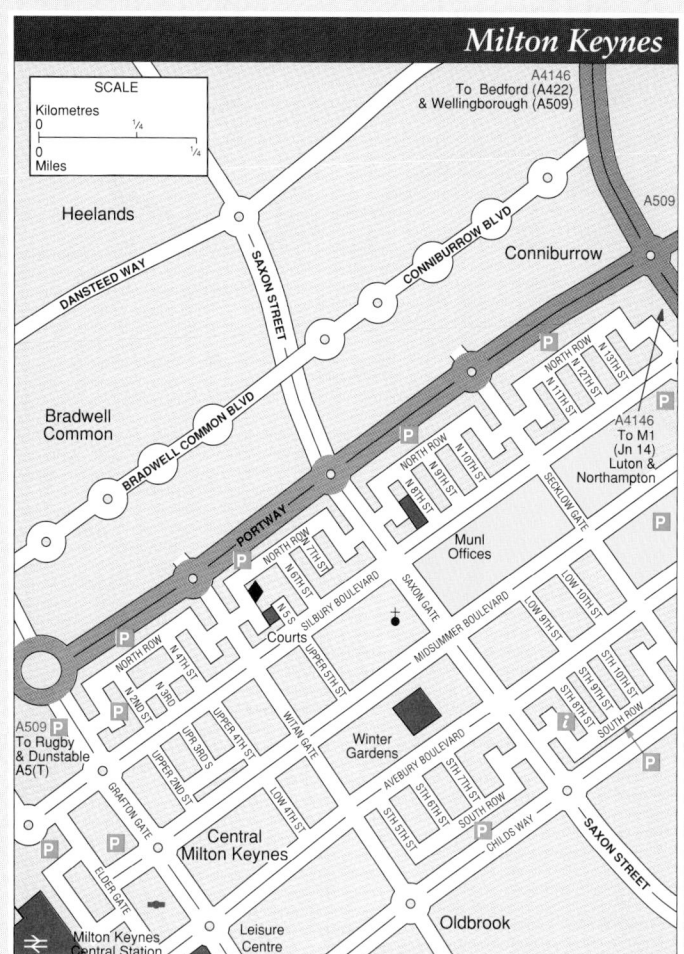

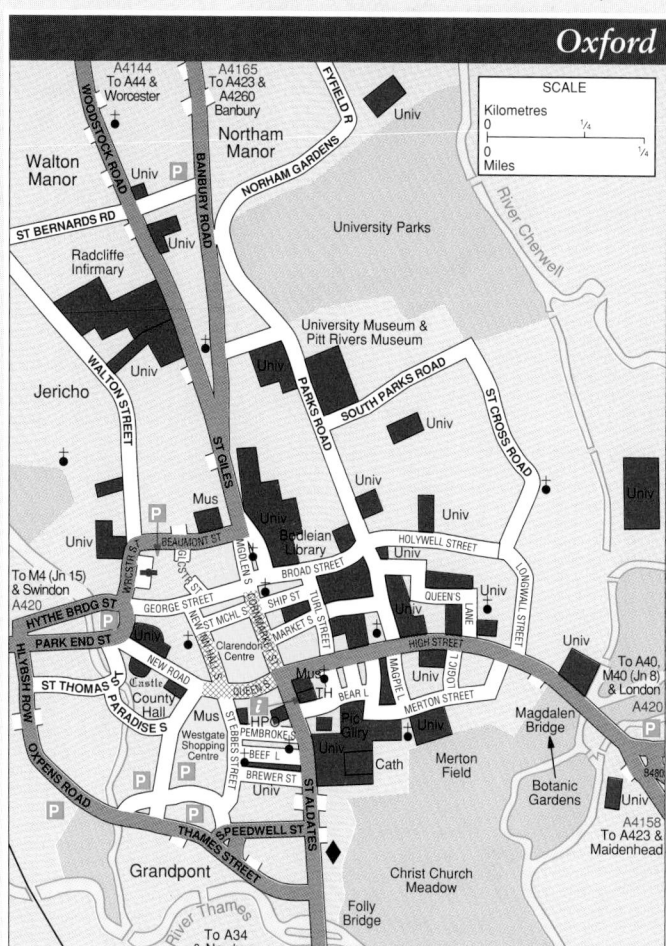

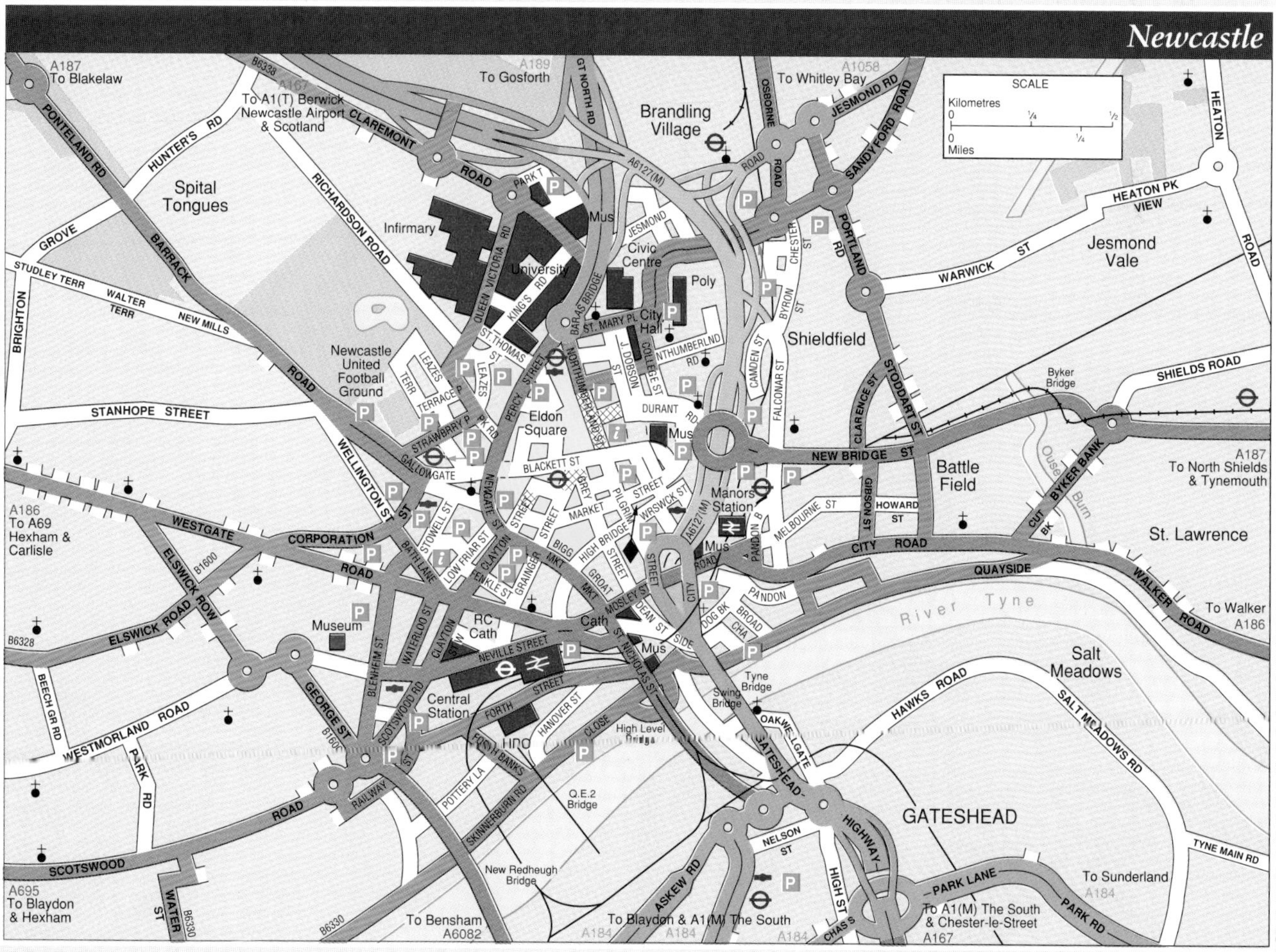

Norwich

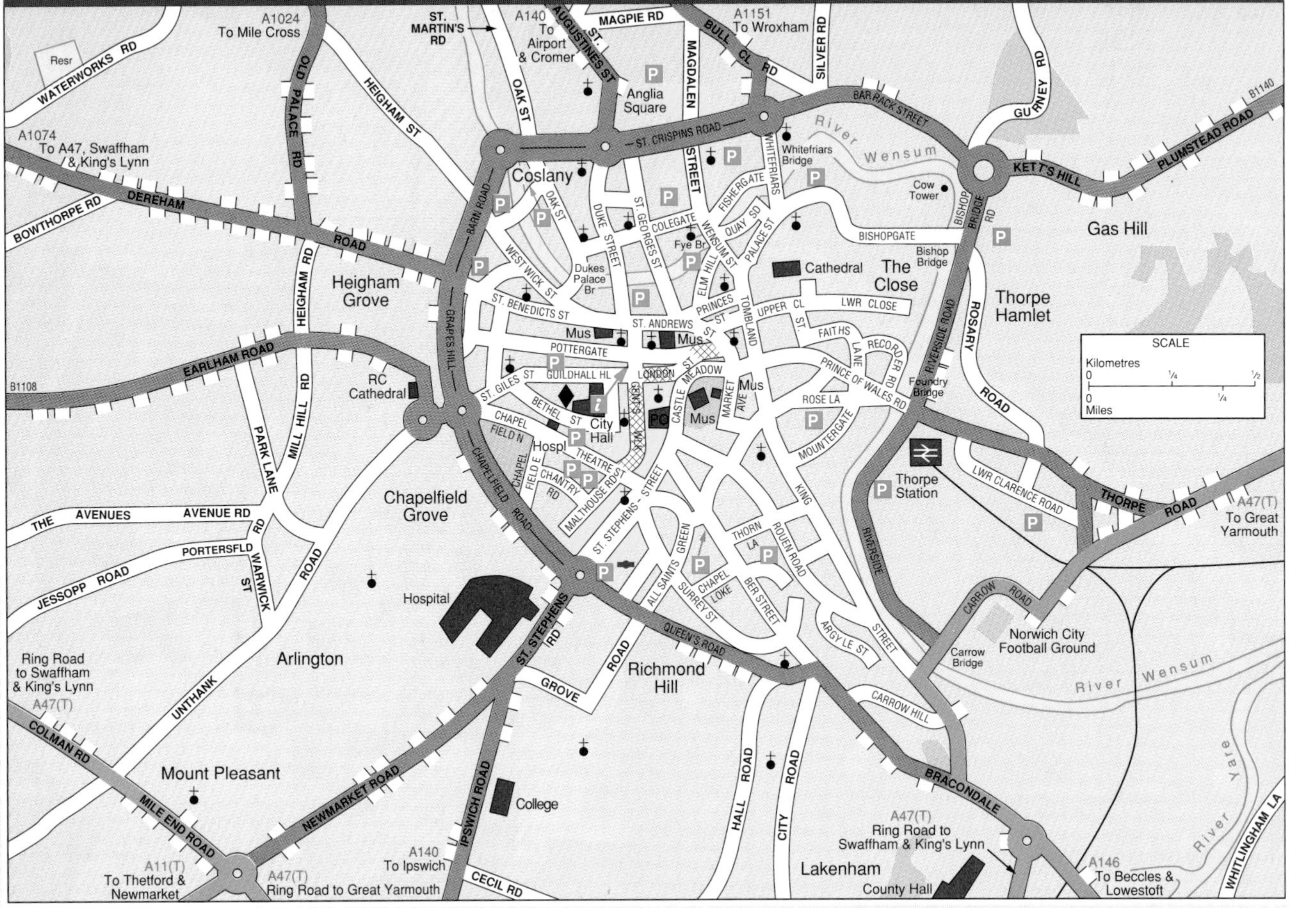

To Mile Cross A1024
ST. MARTIN'S RD
To Airport & Cromer A140
MAGPIE RD
A1151 To Wroxham
BULL CL RD
SILVER RD
WATERWORKS RD
Resr
OLD PALACE RD
HEIGHAM ST
ST. AUGUSTINES ST
OAK ST
MAGDALEN
BARRACK STREET
GURNEY RD
PLUMSTEAD ROAD
B1140

A1074 To A47, Swaffham / & King's Lynn
DEREHAM
BOWTHORPE RD
St. Crispins Road
Coslany
River Wensum
Cow Tower
KETT'S HILL
Gas Hill

B1108
EARLHAM ROAD
HEIGHAM RD
BARN ROAD
Heigham Grove
WEST WICK ST
DUKE STREET
COLEGATE
ST GEORGES ST
FISHERGATE
Whitefriars Bridge
QUAY SD
PALACE ST
Cathedral
The Close
Bishop Bridge
BISHOPGATE
Thorpe Hamlet
ROSARY ROAD

MILL HILL RD
PARK LANE
RC Cathedral
GRAPES HILL
ST. BENEDICTS ST
Mus
POTTERGATE
ST GILES
GUILDHALL HL
BETHEL ST
London ST
CASTLE MDW
Mus
MARKET
ROSE LA
Mus
PRINCE OF WALES RD
Foundry Bridge
LWR CLARENCE ROAD
THORPE ROAD
Thorpe Station
A47(T) To Great Yarmouth

THE AVENUES
AVENUE RD
WARWICK ST
Chapelfield Grove
CHAPELFIELD RD
City Hall
Hospl
Theatre
CHANTRY RD
ST. STEPHENS STREET
THORN LA
ROUEN ROAD
KING STREET
RIVERSIDE
CARROW ROAD
Norwich City Football Ground

PORTERSFLD RD
JESSOPP ROAD
A47(T)
UNTHANK
Arlington
ST STEPHENS RD
GROVE
ST STEPHENS ROAD
Richmond Hill
QUEEN'S ROAD
ARGYLE ST
SURREY STREET
BER STREET
CARROW HILL
Carrow Bridge
River Wensum

COLMAN RD
MILE END ROAD
Mount Pleasant
NEWMARKET ROAD
IPSWICH ROAD
College
HALL ROAD
CITY ROAD
BRACONDALE
A47(T) Ring Road to Swaffham & King's Lynn
WHITLINGHAM LA
River Yare

A11(T) To Thetford & Newmarket
A47(T) Ring Road to Great Yarmouth
CECIL RD
A140 To Ipswich
Lakenham
County Hall
A146 To Beccles & Lowestoft

SCALE
Kilometres
0 1/4 1/2
0 Miles 1/4

Nottingham

A6130 To Eastwood
A610
FOREST ROAD W
WAVERLEY ST
To Mansfield & Worksop A60
St. Ann's

HARTLEY
RADFORD BOULEVARD
ST. PETERS ST
ALFRETON ROAD
FOREST ROAD
Radford
PEEL ST
GILL ST
DRYDEN ST
HAMPDEN ST
MANSFIELD RD
HUNTINGDON STREET
ST. ANN'S WELL ROAD
To Newark-on-Trent A612

WOLLATON ROAD
ILKESTON ROAD
RADFORD ROAD
CROMWELL STREET
CLARENDON ST
GOLDSMITH STREET
SHAKESPEARE STREET
S SHERWOOD ST
CHAUCER
TALBOT ST
Victoria Centre
TH
BURTON
BATH ST
HPO
CARLTON ROAD

A609 To Ilkeston & Belper
LENTON BOULEVARD
CANNING CIR
WOLLATON STREET
UT PARLIAMENT ST
PARLIAMENT ST
LONG ROW
S PARADE
LOWER PARLIAMENT ST
GOOSE G
WOOLPCK LA
MANVERS STREET

The Park
RC Cath
DERBY ROAD
REGENT
OXFORD ST
R. Hood Centre
Hosp
FRIAR LA
PETER ST
ST MARY'S G
FLETCHER GT
BELLAR GT
Ice Stad
PENNYFOOT ST

New Lenton
Standard Hill
Hosp
LENTON ROAD
CASTLE GT
Mus
Broad Marsh Centre
MIDDLE CLIFF RD
Lace Market
B685

DERBY ROAD
Castle Mus
PEVERIL DR
Museum
COLLIN ST
CANAL
TRENT STREET
STATION ST
Nottingham Station
LONDON ROAD

Old Lenton
ABBEY BRIDGE
CASTLE BOULEVARD
Castle Marina
Nottingham Canal
CASTLE BRIDGE
WILFORD RD
Canal Museum
WATERWAY ST W
QUEEN'S ROAD
B686

CLIFTON BOULEVARD
Hospital
ABBEY ST
LENTON LANE
QUEEN'S DRIVE
Meadows
CATTLE MKT RD
COUNTY RD
MEADOW LANE
L BAY RD
Notts County Football Ground
A6011 To A52(T), Nottingham Airport & Grantham

A52(T) To Stapleford & Derby
University
DERBY
BEESTON R
Dunkirk
A52(T) To Grantham & A606(T) Melton Mowbray
A453(T) To East Midlands Airport & M1 (Jn24) The South
A60 To West Bridgford & Loughborough
Nottm Forest Football Ground
TRENT BRIDGE
River Trent
County Cricket Gd

A6005 To Beeston

SCALE
Kilometres
0 1/4 1/2
0 Miles 1/4

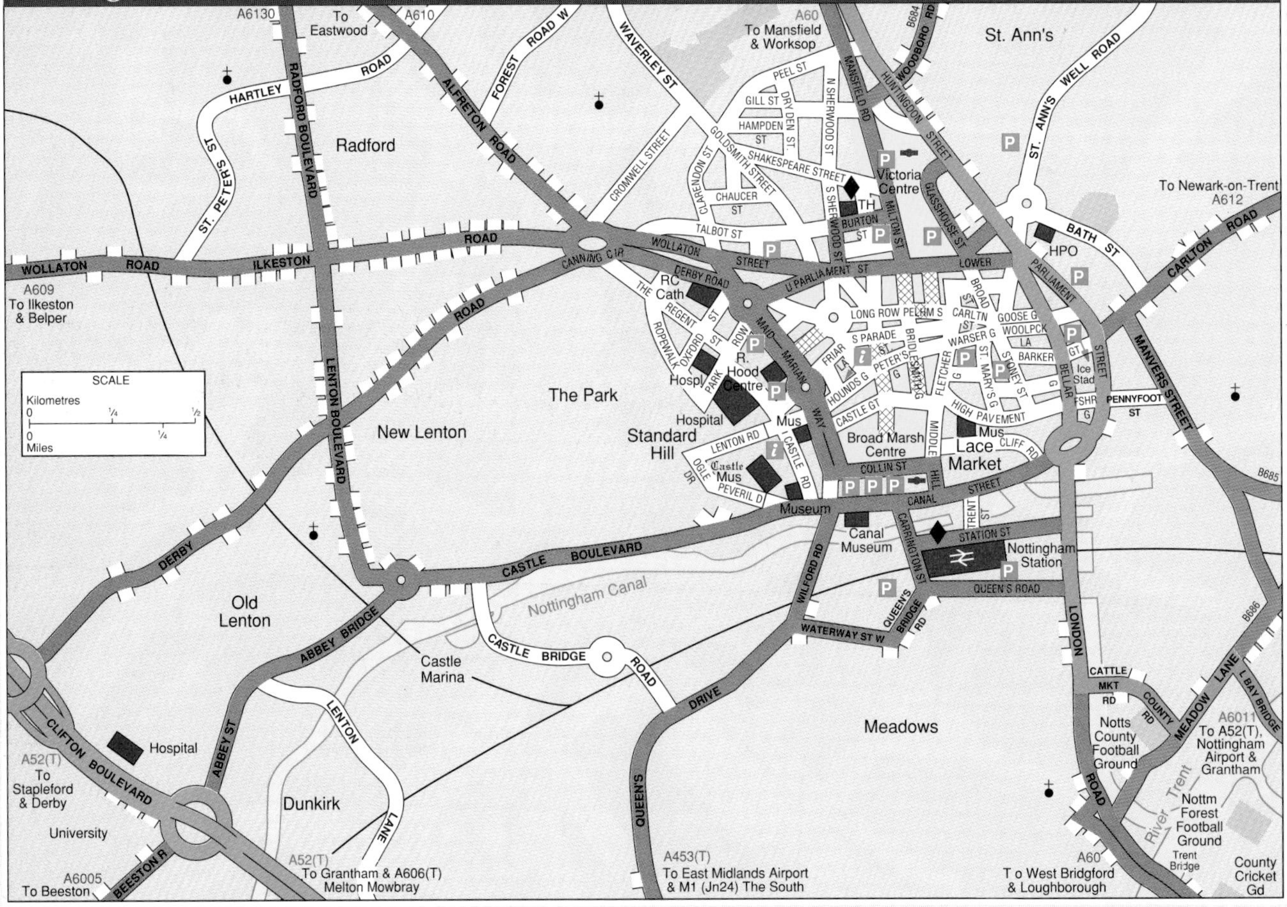

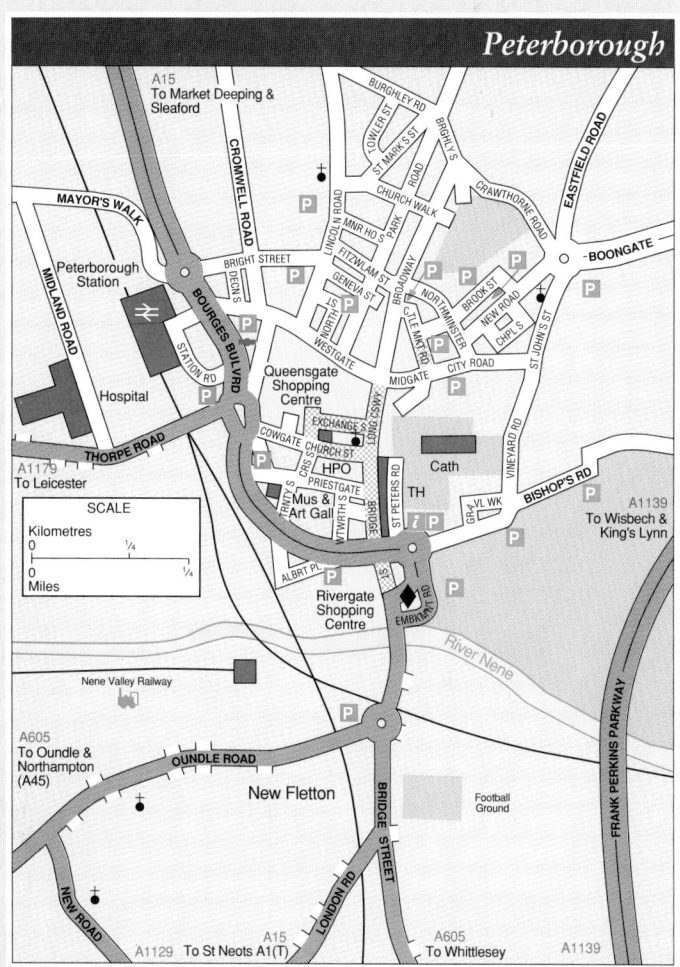

Peterborough

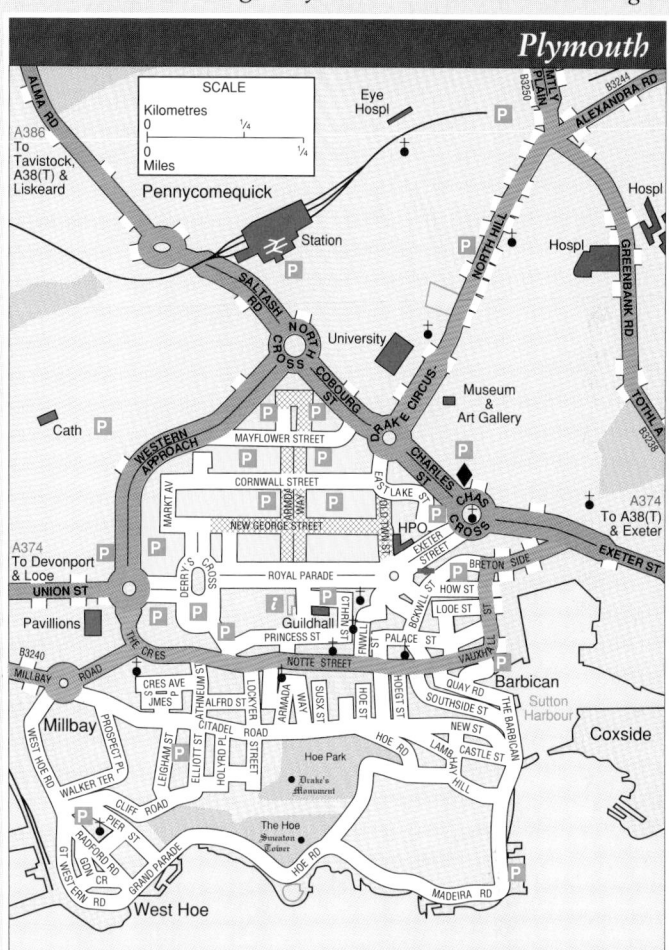

Plymouth

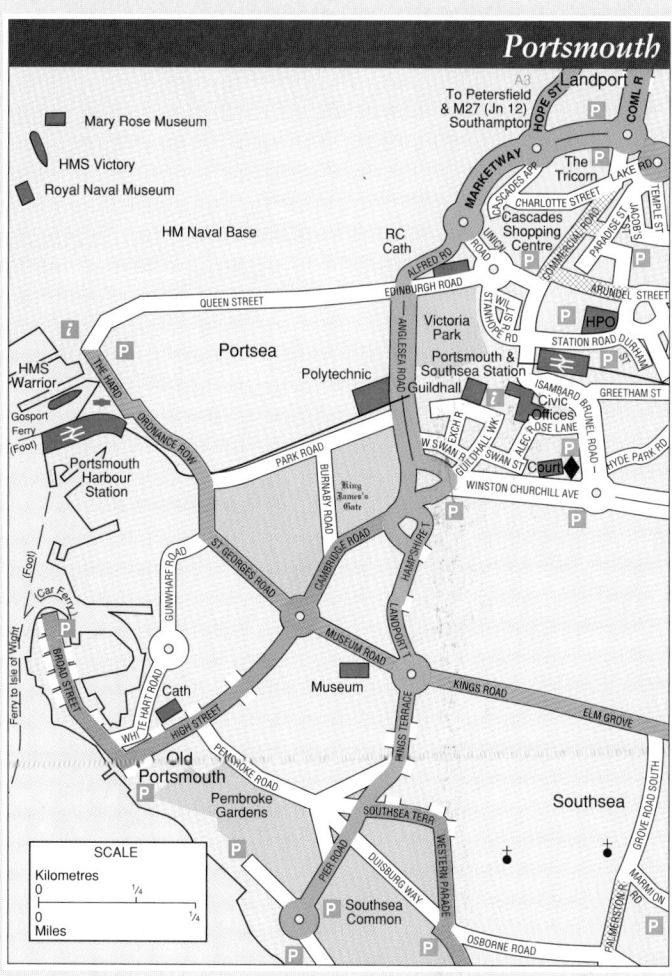

Portsmouth

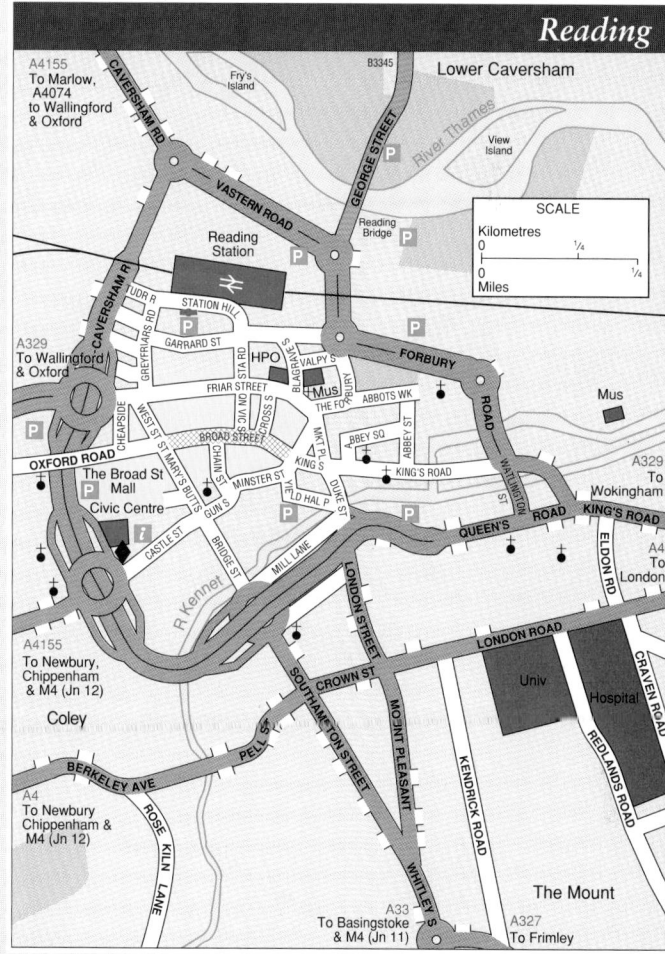

Reading

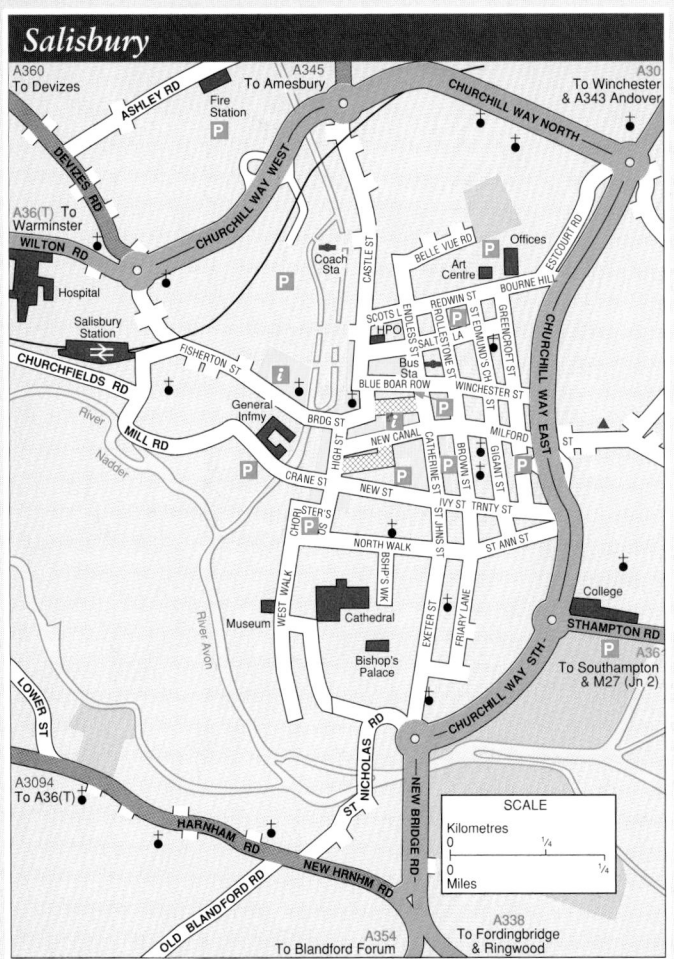

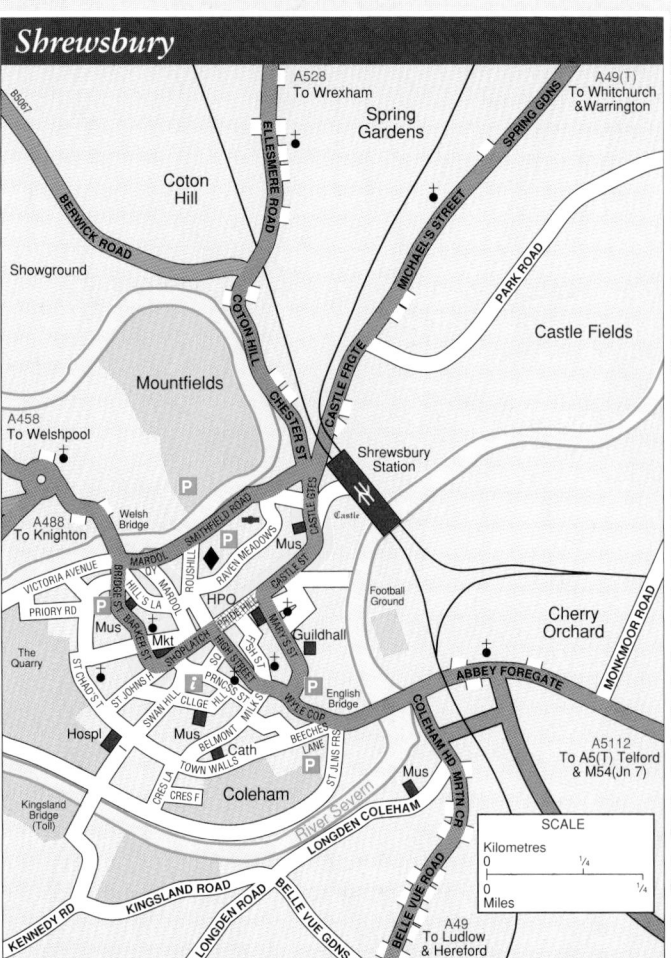

Sheffield

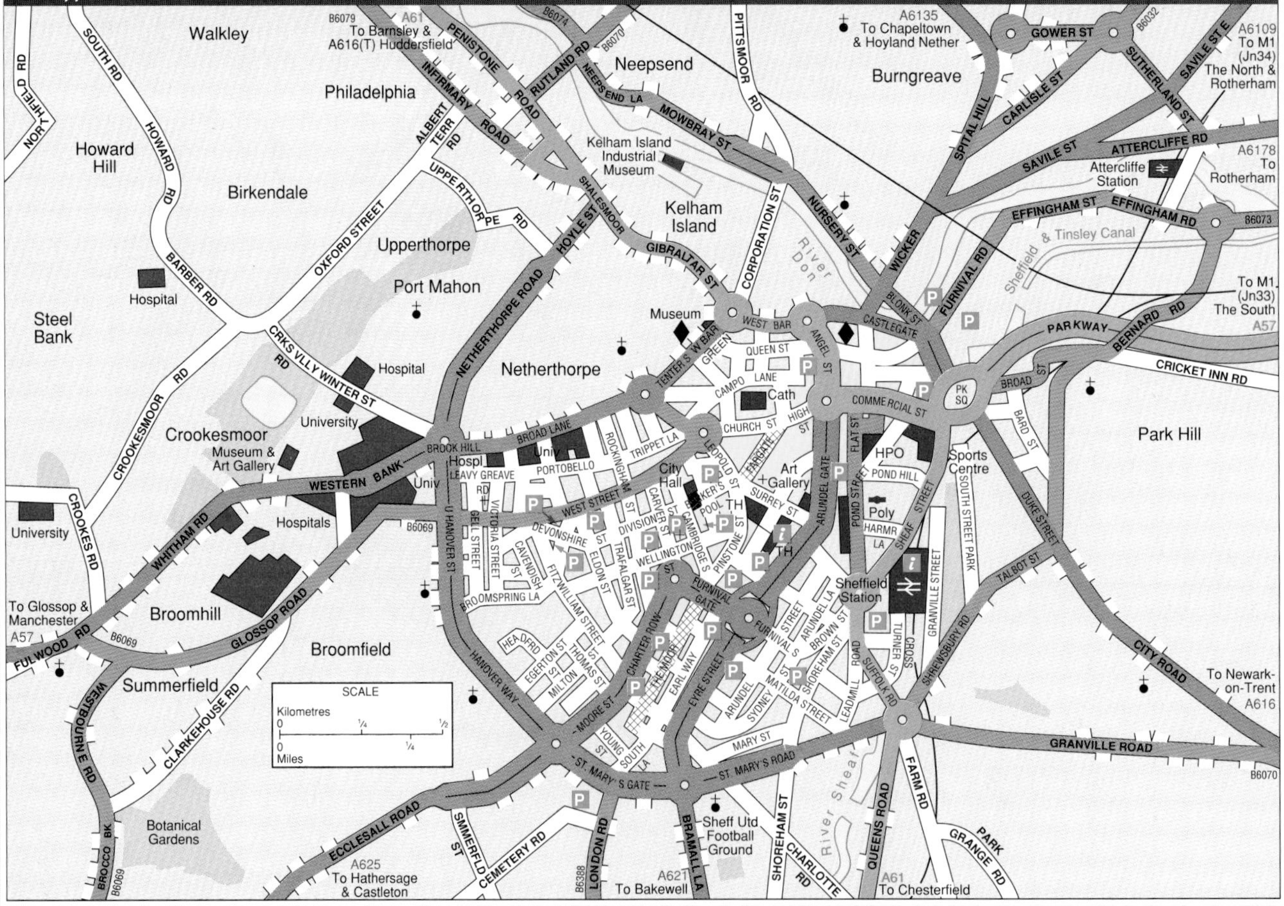

147

Southampton Stratford Swansea York

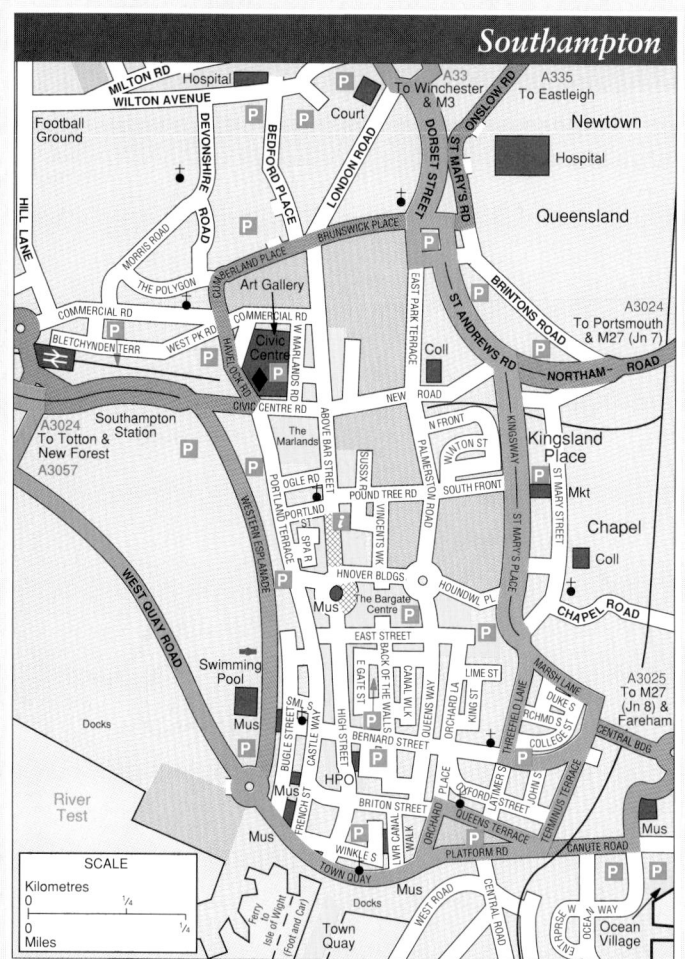

Southampton

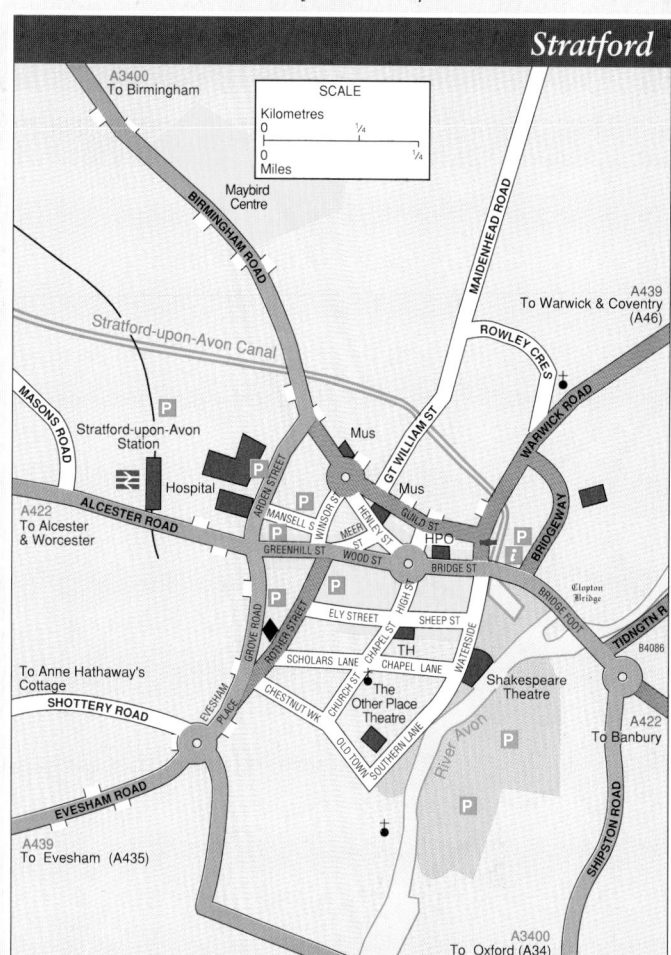

Stratford

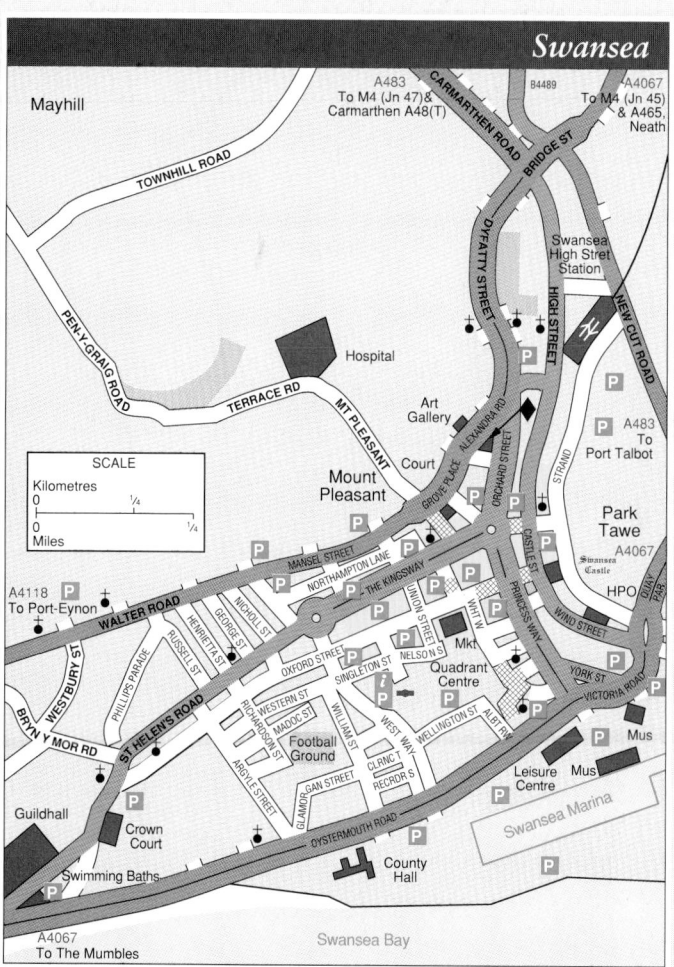

Swansea

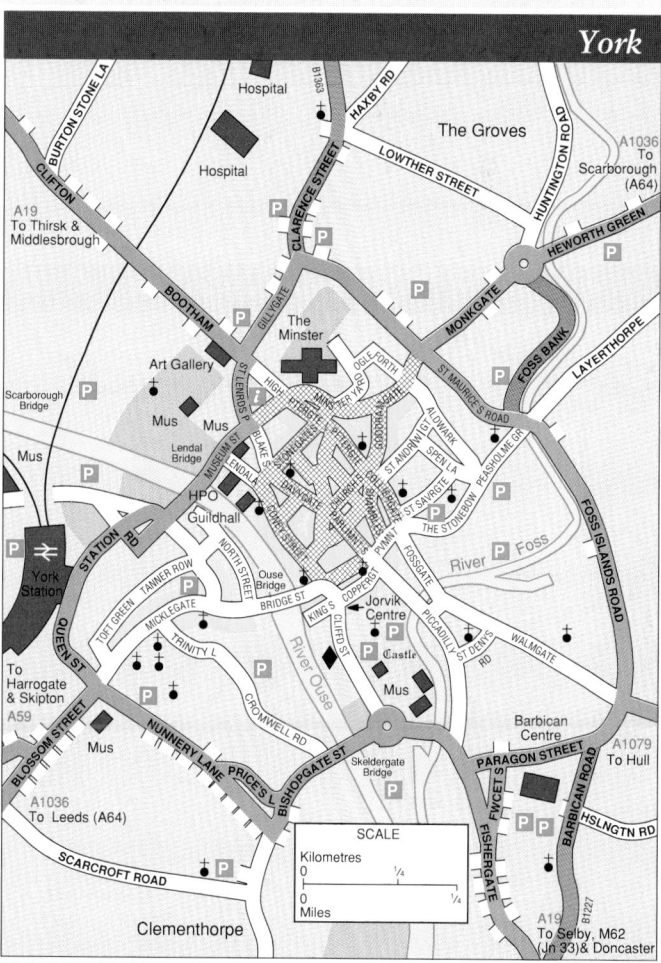

York

FERRY PORTS

Dover

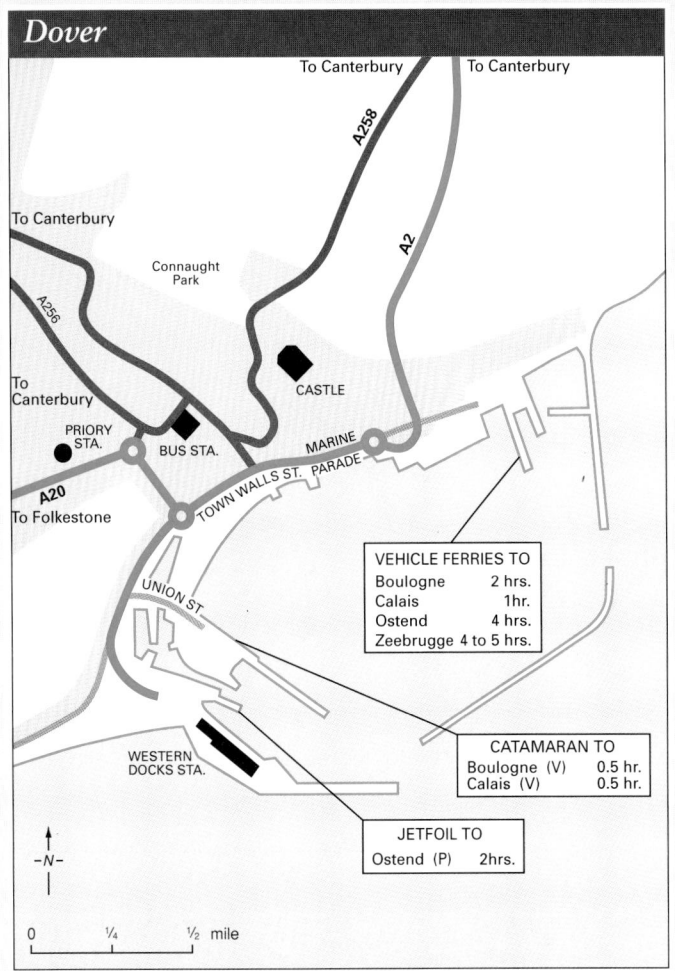

To Canterbury
To Canterbury

A258

A2

To Canterbury

Connaught Park

A256

CASTLE

To Canterbury

PRIORY STA.

BUS STA.

A20
To Folkestone

MARINE PARADE

TOWN WALLS ST.

UNION ST

WESTERN DOCKS STA.

VEHICLE FERRIES TO
Boulogne 2 hrs.
Calais 1hr.
Ostend 4 hrs.
Zeebrugge 4 to 5 hrs.

CATAMARAN TO
Boulogne (V) 0.5 hr.
Calais (V) 0.5 hr.

JETFOIL TO
Ostend (P) 2hrs.

–N–

0   ¼   ½ mile

Fishguard

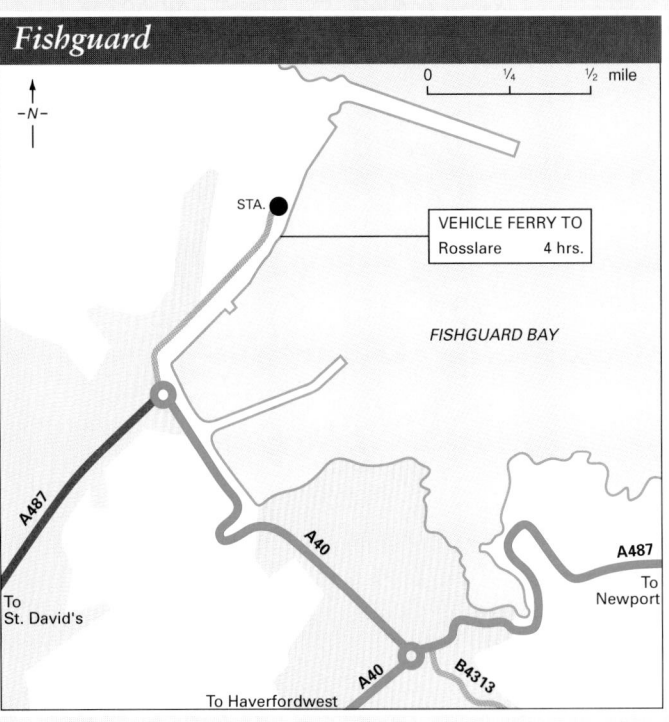

–N–

0   ¼   ½ mile

STA.

VEHICLE FERRY TO
Rosslare 4 hrs.

FISHGUARD BAY

A487

To St. David's

A40

A40   B4313

A487
To Newport

To Haverfordwest

Folkestone

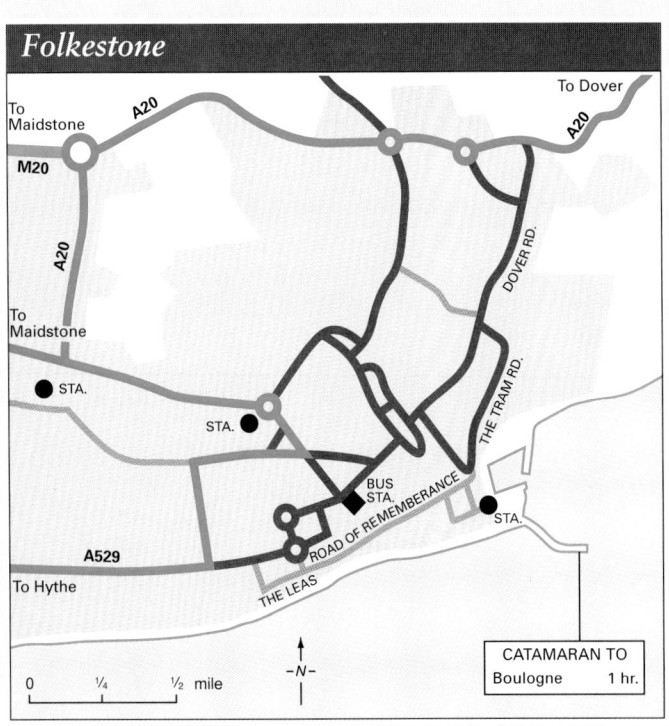

To Maidstone

A20

To Dover

A20

M20

A20

DOVER RD.

To Maidstone

THE TRAM RD.

STA.

STA.

BUS STA.

ROAD OF REMEMBERANCE

STA.

A529

To Hythe

THE LEAS

–N–

0   ¼   ½ mile

CATAMARAN TO
Boulogne 1 hr.

Harwich and Felixstowe

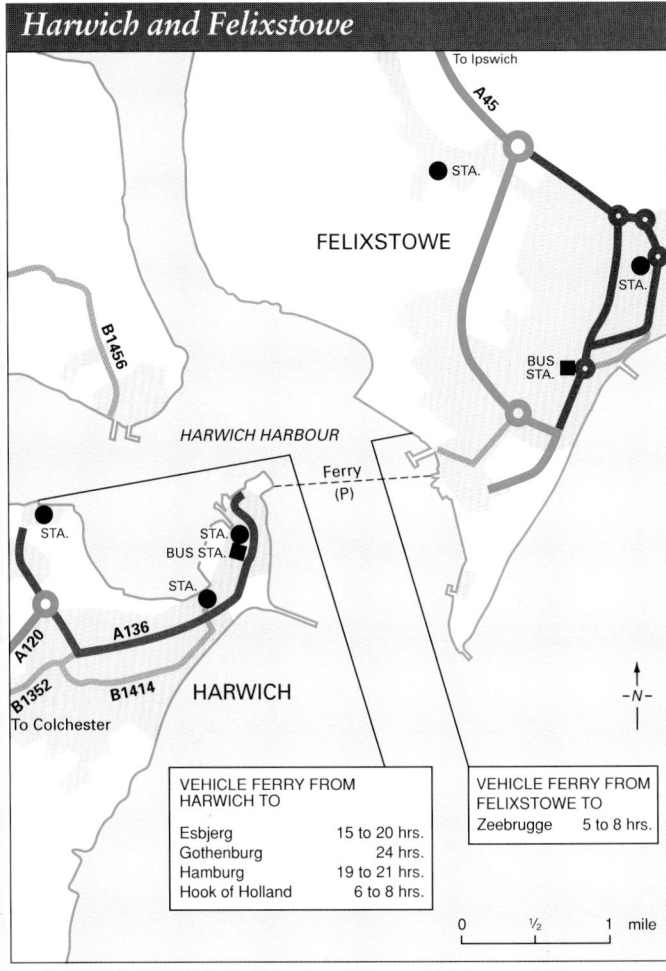

To Ipswich

A45

STA.

FELIXSTOWE

STA.

BUS STA.

B1456

HARWICH HARBOUR

Ferry (P)

STA.

STA.
BUS STA.

STA.

A120   A136

B1352   B1414

HARWICH

To Colchester

–N–

VEHICLE FERRY FROM HARWICH TO

Esbjerg 15 to 20 hrs.
Gothenburg 24 hrs.
Hamburg 19 to 21 hrs.
Hook of Holland 6 to 8 hrs.

VEHICLE FERRY FROM FELIXSTOWE TO
Zeebrugge 5 to 8 hrs.

0   ½   1 mile

Holyhead

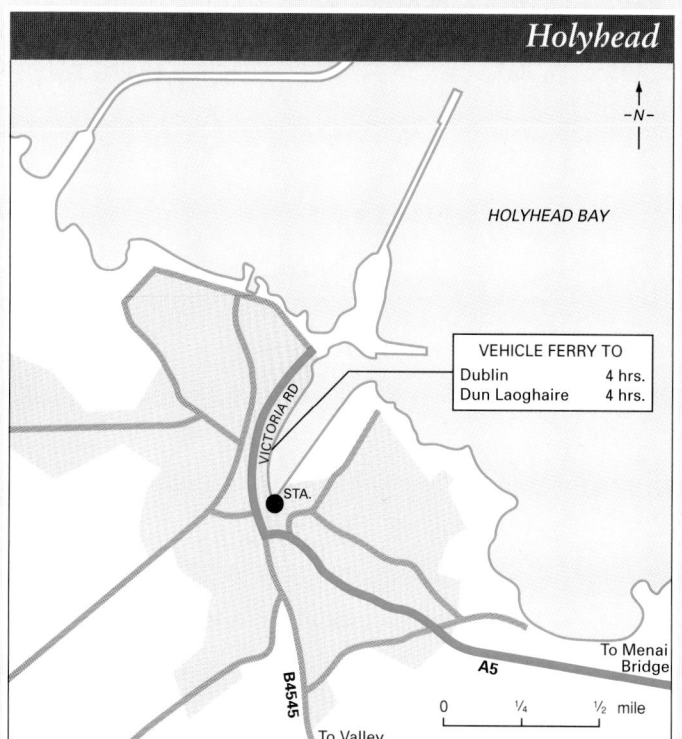

HOLYHEAD BAY

VEHICLE FERRY TO
Dublin   4 hrs.
Dun Laoghaire   4 hrs.

VICTORIA RD

STA.

To Menai Bridge

A5

B4545

To Valley

0   ¼   ½ mile

Plymouth

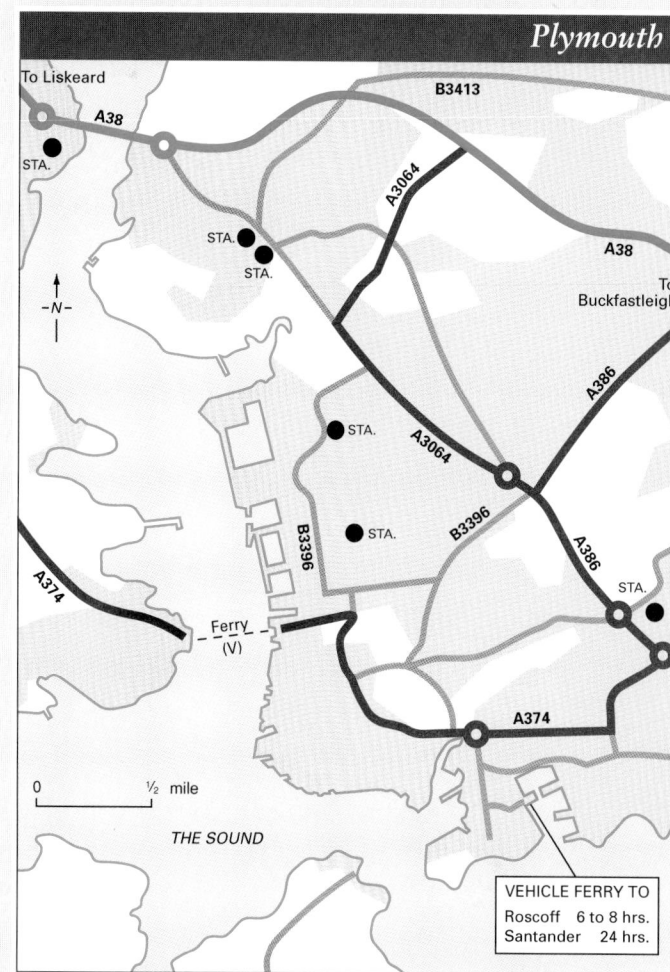

To Liskeard

A38

B3413

STA.

A3064

A38

To Buckfastleigh

STA.
STA.

A386

STA.

A3064

B3396

B3396

A386

STA.

A374

Ferry (V)

A374

THE SOUND

VEHICLE FERRY TO
Roscoff   6 to 8 hrs.
Santander 24 hrs.

0   ½ mile

Newhaven

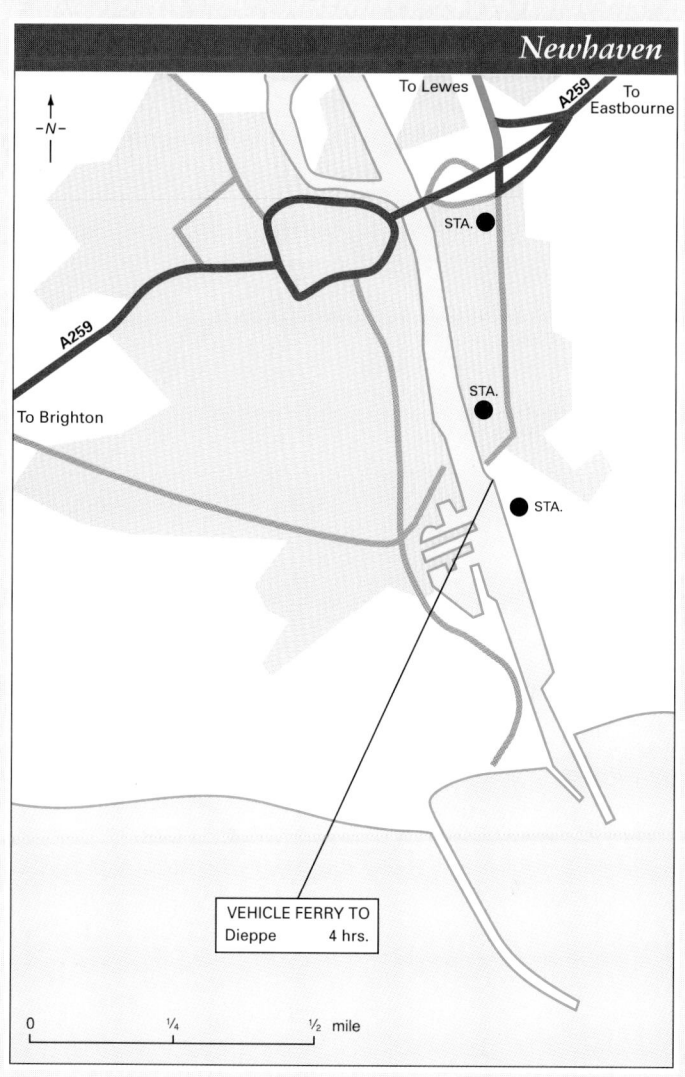

To Lewes

A259

To Eastbourne

STA.

A259

To Brighton

STA.

STA.

VEHICLE FERRY TO
Dieppe   4 hrs.

0   ¼   ½ mile

Poole

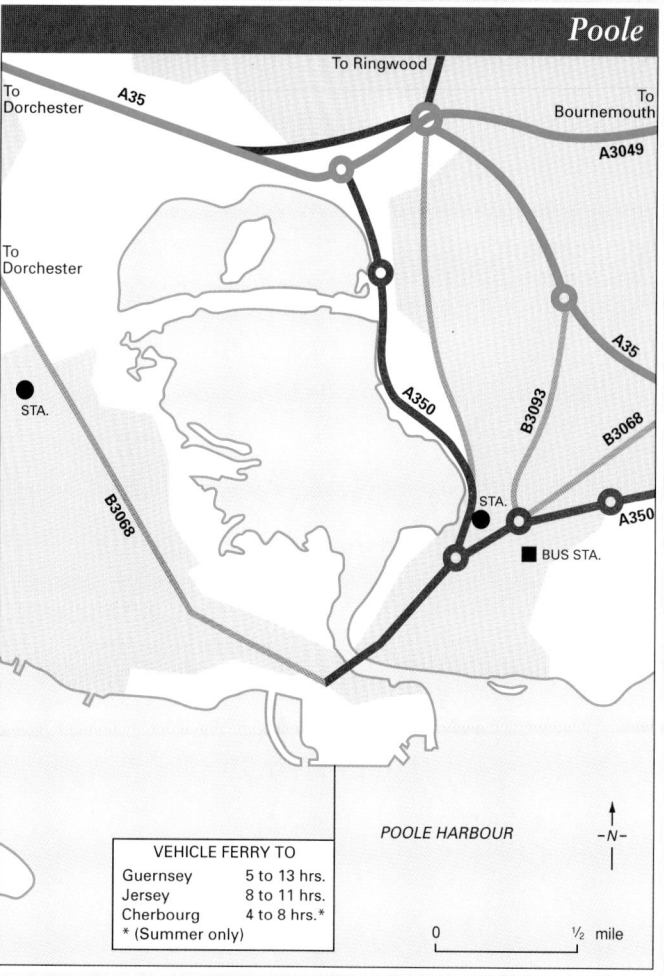

To Ringwood

To Dorchester

A35

To Bournemouth

A3049

To Dorchester

A350

B3093

A35

STA.

B3068

B3068

STA.

BUS STA.

A350

POOLE HARBOUR

VEHICLE FERRY TO
Guernsey   5 to 13 hrs.
Jersey   8 to 11 hrs.
Cherbourg 4 to 8 hrs.*
* (Summer only)

0   ½ mile

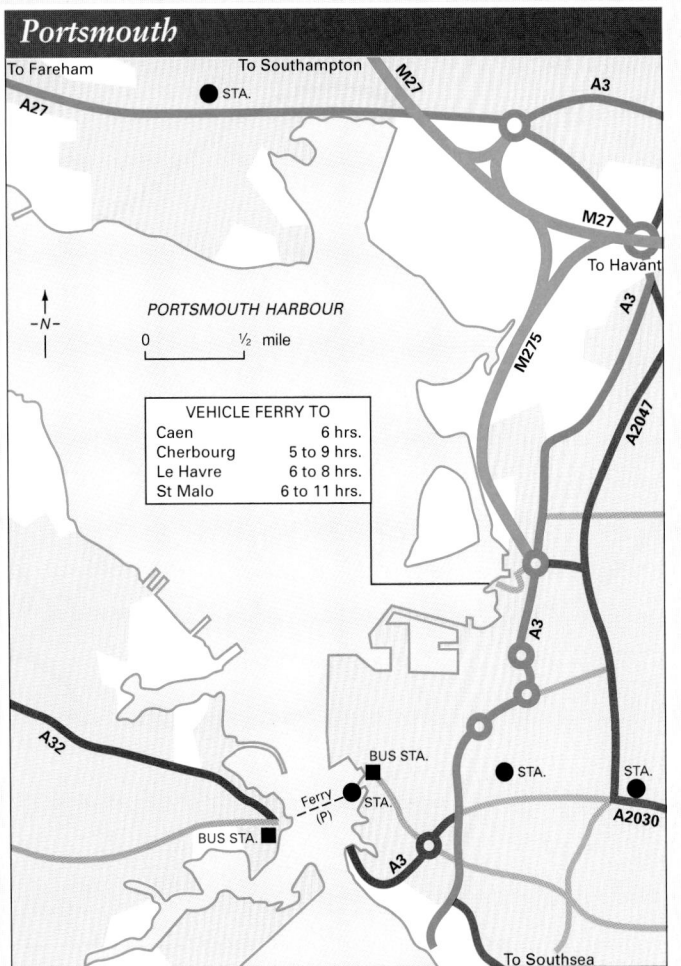

Portsmouth

To Fareham
To Southampton
STA.
A27
M27
A3
M27
To Havant
PORTSMOUTH HARBOUR
A3
–N–
0   ½ mile
M275
A3
A2047

VEHICLE FERRY TO
Caen   6 hrs.
Cherbourg   5 to 9 hrs.
Le Havre   6 to 8 hrs.
St Malo   6 to 11 hrs.

A32
BUS STA.
STA.
STA.
Ferry
(P)
STA.
A2030
BUS STA.
A3
To Southsea

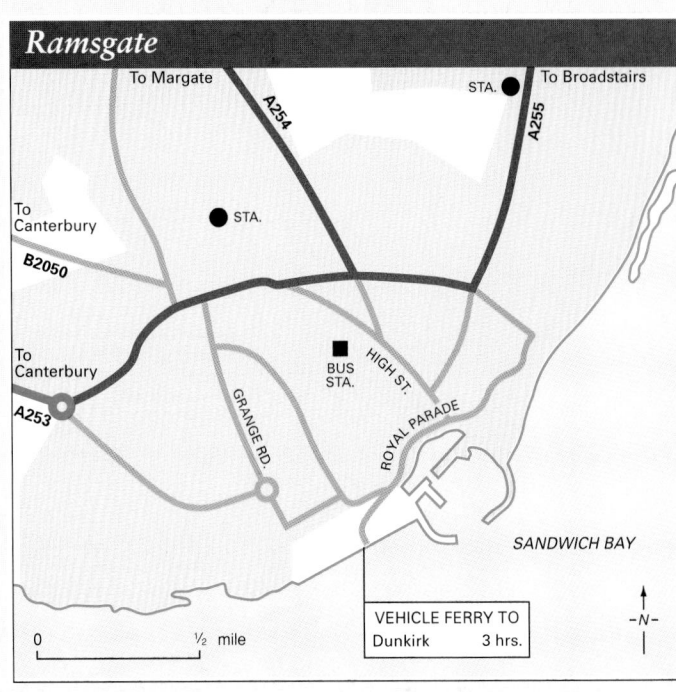

Ramsgate

To Margate
A254
STA.
To Broadstairs
A255
To Canterbury
B2050
STA.
To Canterbury
BUS STA.
HIGH ST.
A253
GRANGE RD.
ROYAL PARADE
SANDWICH BAY
0   ½ mile

VEHICLE FERRY TO
Dunkirk   3 hrs.

–N–

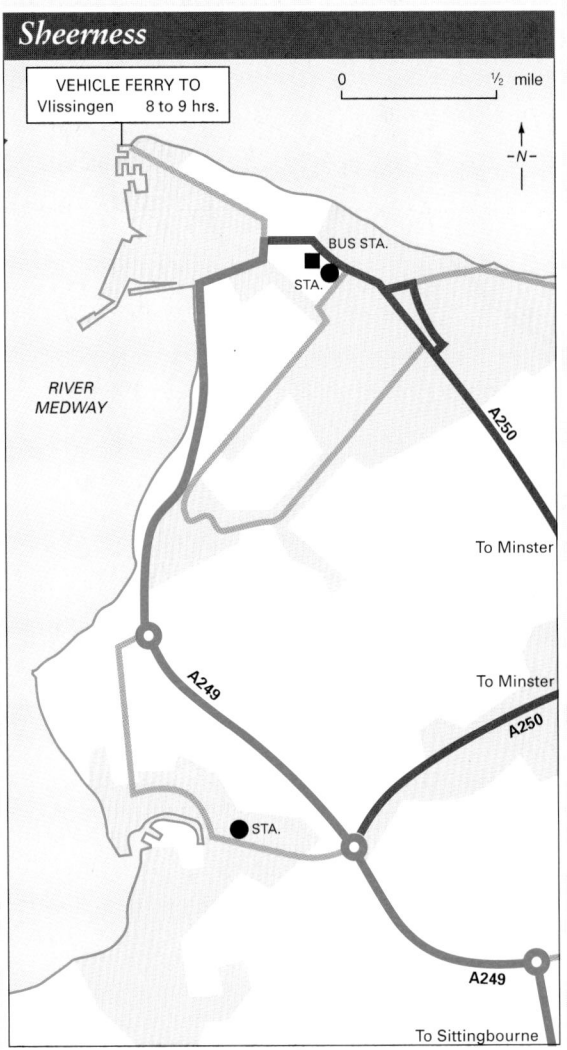

Sheerness

VEHICLE FERRY TO
Vlissingen   8 to 9 hrs.
0   ½ mile
–N–
BUS STA.
STA.
RIVER MEDWAY
A250
To Minster
A249
To Minster
A250
STA.
A249
To Sittingbourne

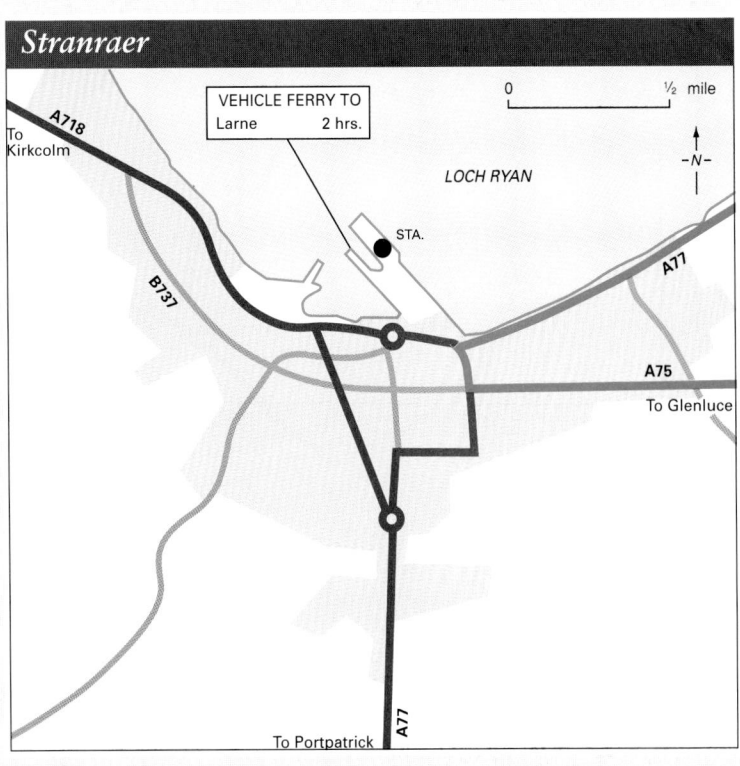

Stranraer

VEHICLE FERRY TO
Larne   2 hrs.
0   ½ mile
A718
To Kirkcolm
LOCH RYAN
STA.
–N–
A77
B737
A75
To Glenluce
A77
To Portpatrick

CHANNEL TUNNEL

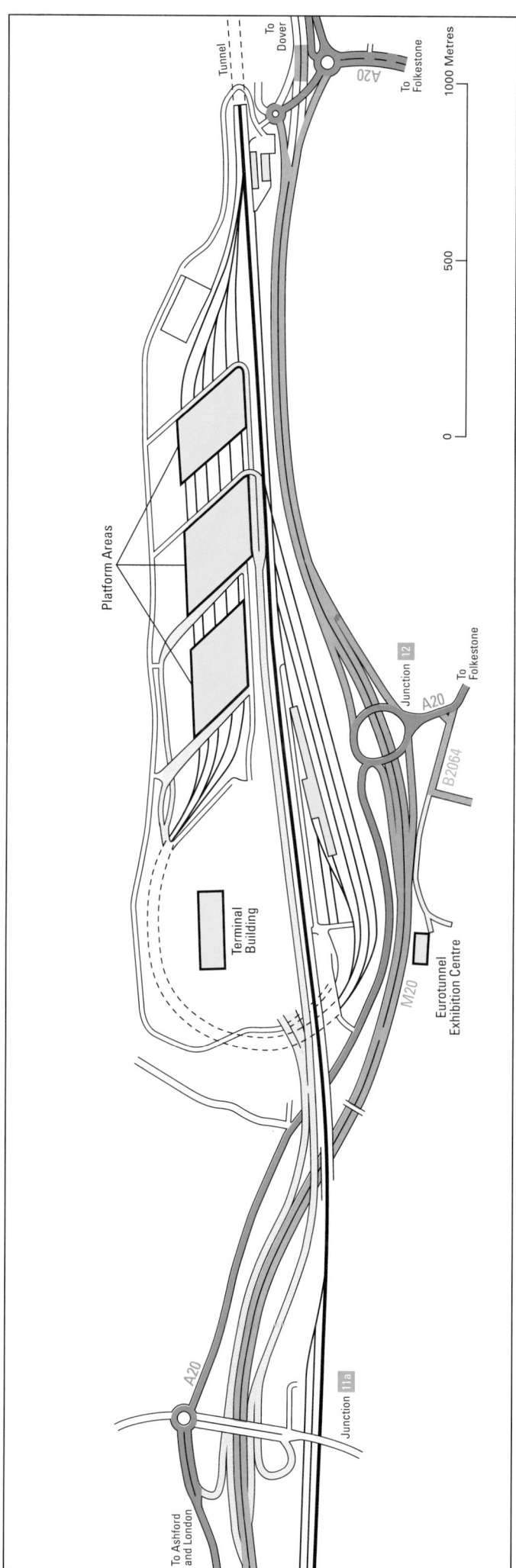

Scheduled to open in the Summer of 1993, the Channel Tunnel will provide a new link between between Great Britain and the rest of Europe. It will run between Folkestone and Calais, where the terminals will give direct access to each country's motorway network.

The tunnel system consists of three tunnels at a depth of 25 to 45 metres beneath the sea bed. There are two running tunnels 7.6 metres in diameter each containing a single railway track with shuttles running in one direction only. At 375m intervals they are linked by cross passages to a central service tunnel.

Eurotunnel will operate two types of shuttle service between the terminals: a passenger vehicle service for cars, coaches and motorcycles and a separate shuttle service for freight vehicles. In addition there will be through passenger and freight trains operated by British Rail and the French and Belgian railways.

Access to the Folkestone terminal will be from junction 11a of the M20. Travellers simply drive to the terminal, buy tickets at the toll booth and take the next available shuttle; there is no need to make reservations although tickets may be purchased in advance if passengers wish. At the Folkestone terminal is a passenger amenity building with restaurants, duty free shops, toilets and bureaux de change.

Passport and custom checks for both Britain and France will be completed before departure. The journey from platform to platform will be 35 minutes or, from motorway to motorway about an hour. Passengers stay with their vehicles during the journey but are free to walk around on the shuttle. Once in France there are no further frontier controls and the Calais terminal located at Sangatte will allow direct access to the motorway network.

AIRPORTS

Aberdeen

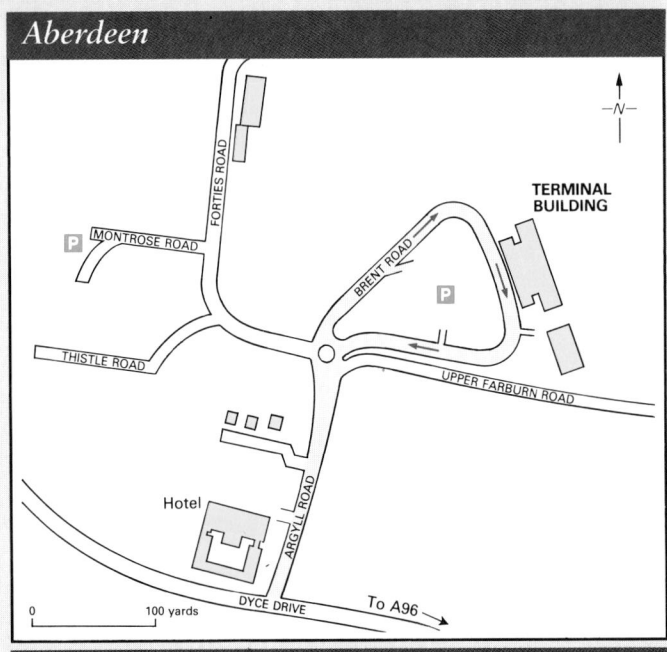

Birmingham International

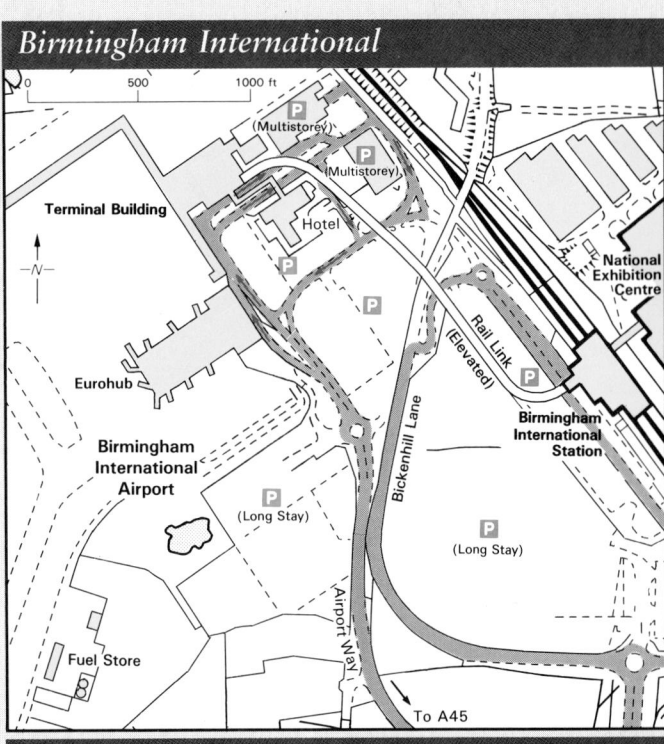

East Midlands

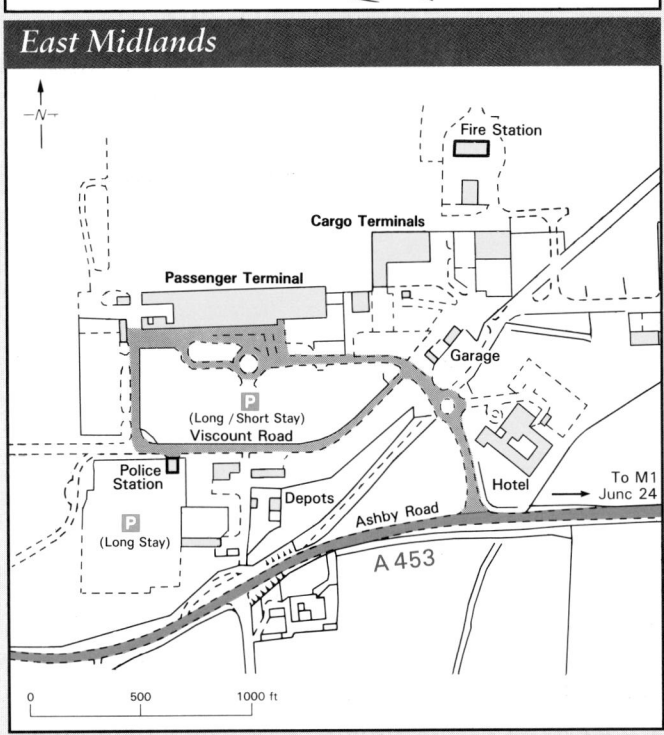

Edinburgh

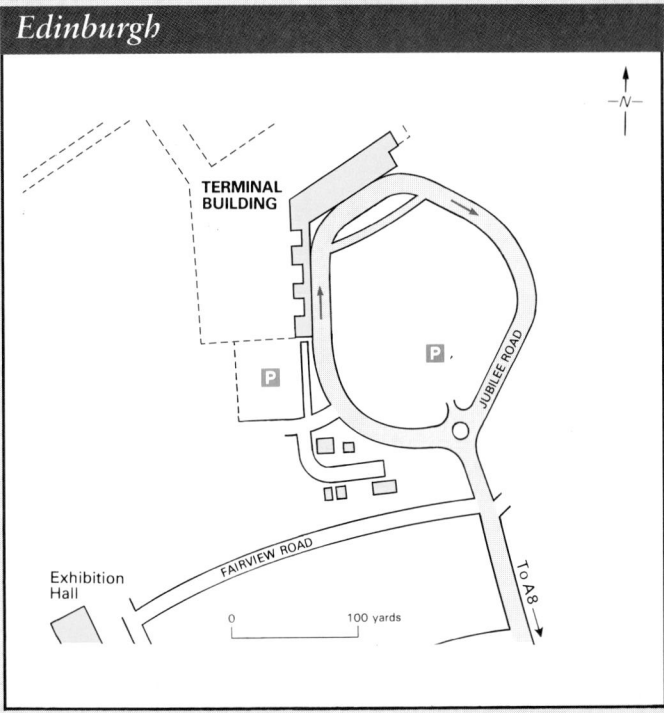

Glasgow

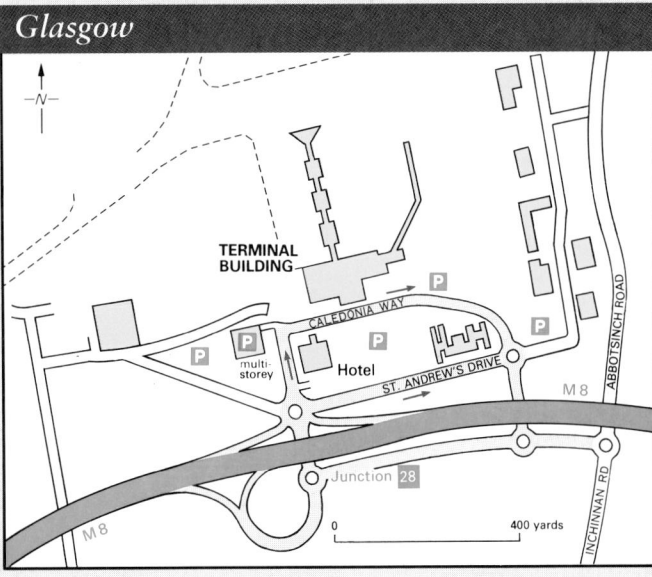

Stansted

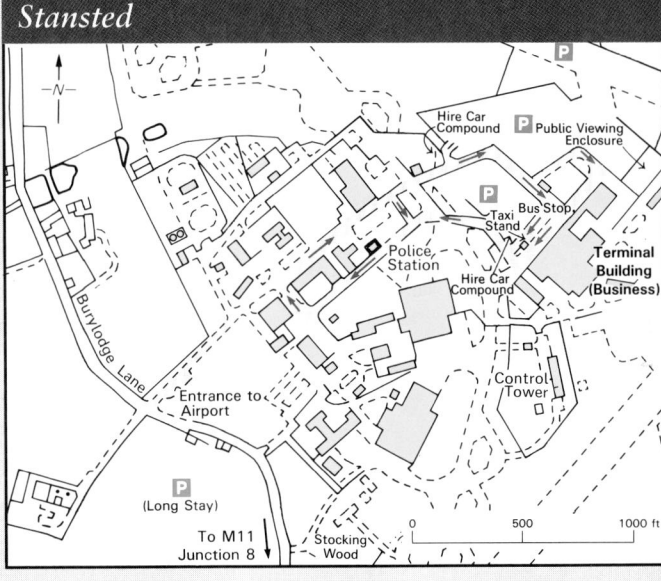

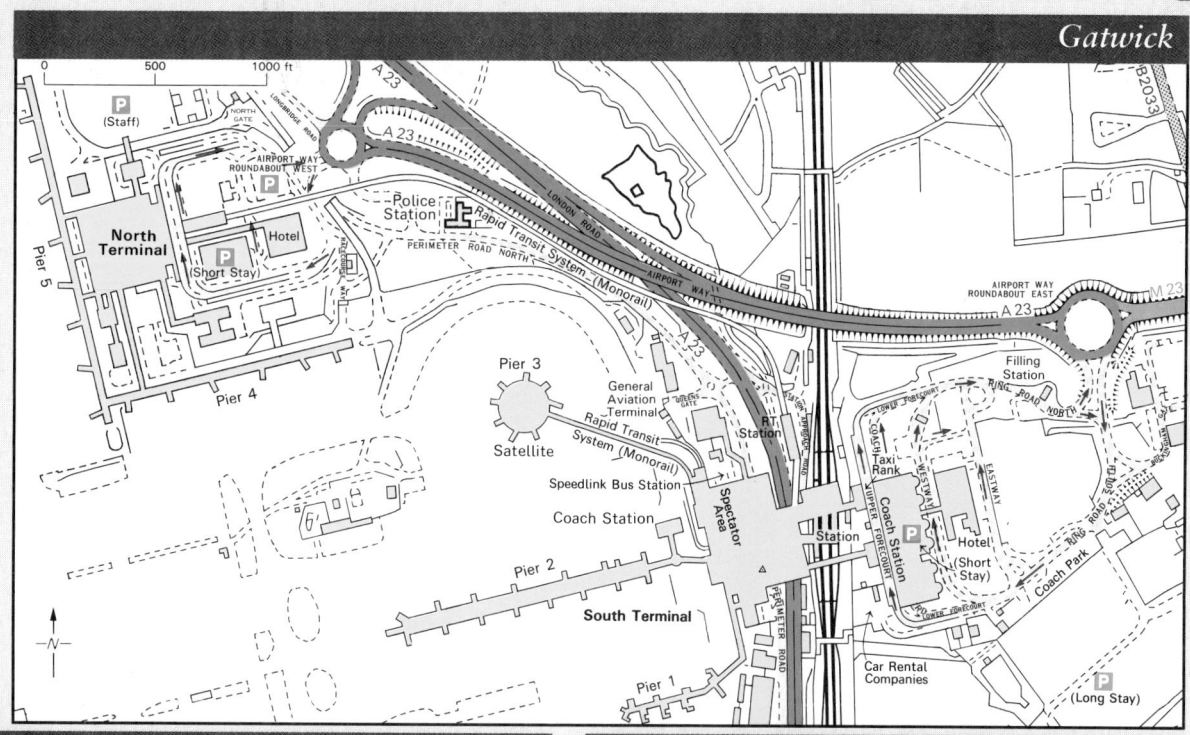

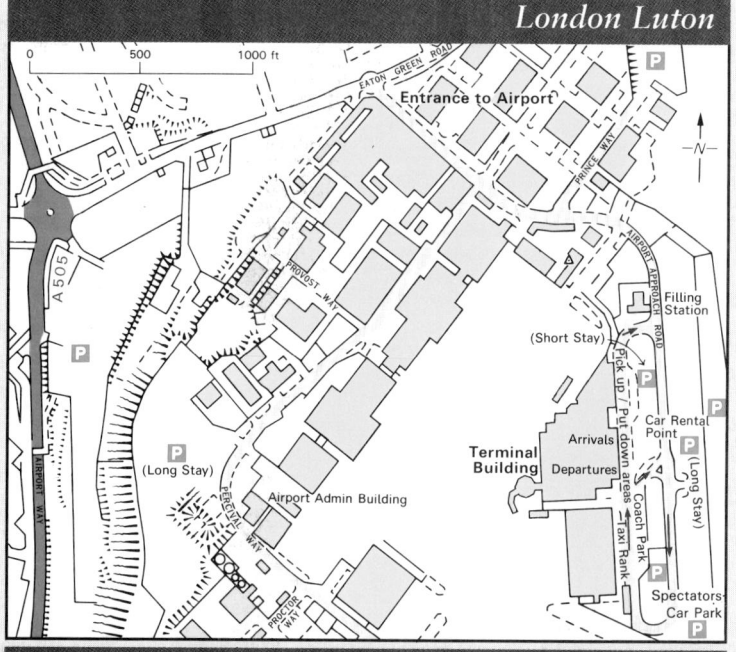

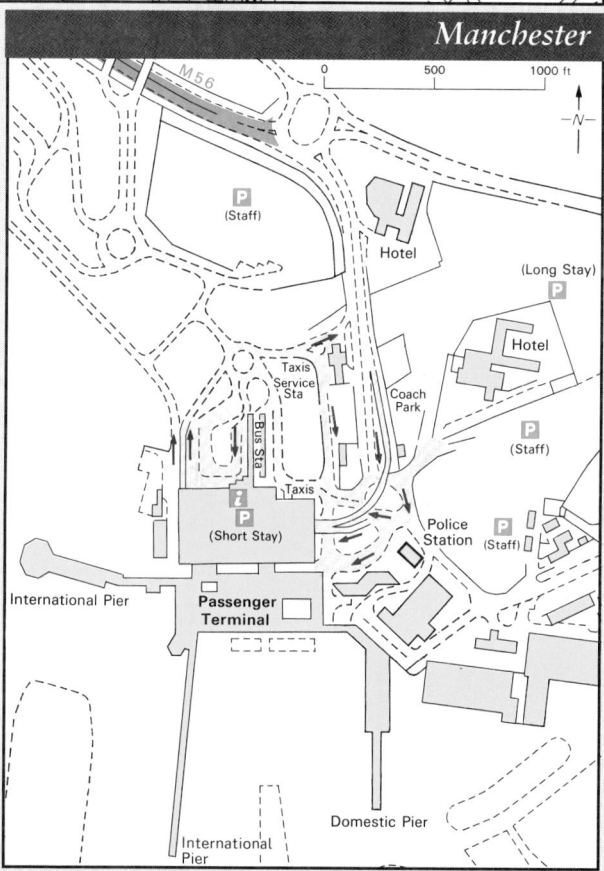

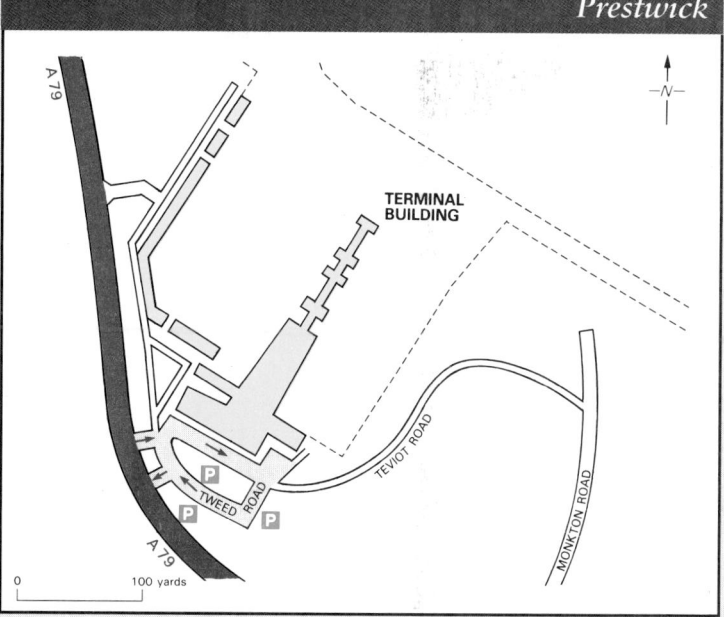

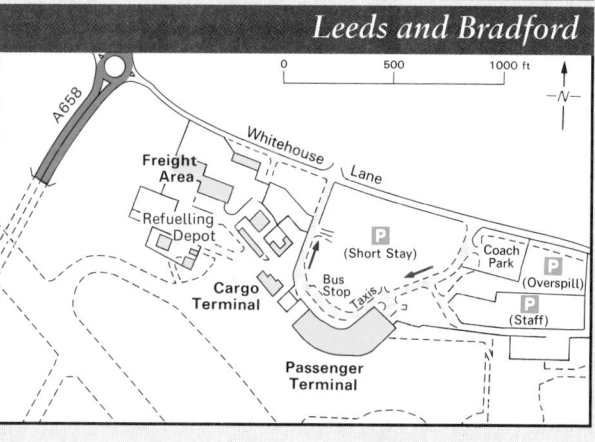

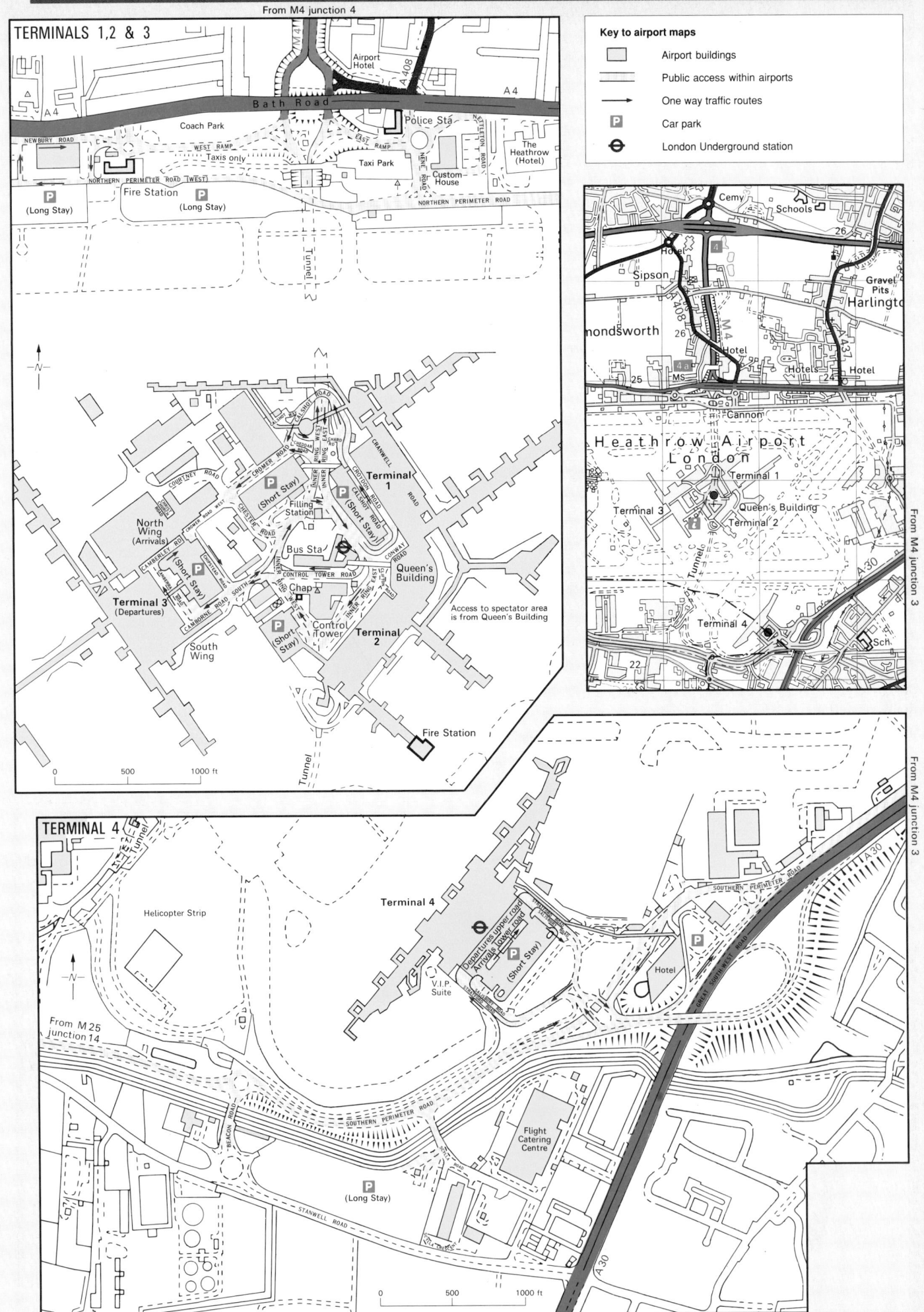

TERMINALS 1,2 & 3

From M4 junction 4

Key to airport maps

Airport buildings

Public access within airports

One way traffic routes

P — Car park

London Underground station

Airport Hotel

Police Sta

Bath Road

Coach Park

WEST RAMP

EAST RAMP

Taxis only

Taxi Park

Custom House

The Heathrow (Hotel)

NEWBURY ROAD

NORTHERN PERIMETER ROAD (WEST)

Fire Station

P (Long Stay)

P (Long Stay)

NORTHERN PERIMETER ROAD

Tunnel

Cemy

Schools

Hotel

Sipson

Gravel Pits

Harlington

mondsworth

Cannon

Hotel

Hotel

Hotel

Hotels

Heathrow Airport London

Terminal 1

Terminal 3

Queen's Building

Terminal 2

Terminal 4

Sch.

From M4 junction 3

CALSHOT ROAD

CRANWELL

Terminal 1

North Wing (Arrivals)

P (Short Stay)

P (Short Stay)

Filling Station

CROYDON ROAD

CALSHOT ROAD

INNER RING WEST

INNER RING EAST

CROMER ROAD

COURTNEY ROAD

CHESTER ROAD

CAMBERLEY RD

CAMBORNE ROAD

Bus Sta

CONWAY ROAD

Queen's Building

CONTROL TOWER ROAD

Chap

Control Tower

Terminal 2

Terminal 3 (Departures)

P (Short Stay)

South Wing

P (Short Stay)

Access to spectator area is from Queen's Building

Fire Station

Tunnel

0   500   1000 ft

From M4 junction 3

TERMINAL 4

Tunnel

Helicopter Strip

Terminal 4

Departures upper road

Arrivals lower road

P (Short Stay)

V.I.P. Suite

Hotel

SOUTHERN PERIMETER ROAD

From M25 junction 14

BEACON ROAD

SOUTHERN PERIMETER ROAD

GREAT SOUTH WEST ROAD

A30

Flight Catering Centre

P (Long Stay)

STANWELL ROAD

0   500   1000 ft

INDEX

How to use this Index

For each entry the Atlas page number is listed and an alpha-numeric map reference is given for the grid square in which the name appears.
For example:

Barnstaple......... **9** F2

Barnstaple will be found on page 9, square F2

If you want to give a National Grid Reference to a place or feature all the information you need is contained on the Atlas map pages. Grid lines appear at 10 kilometre (km) intervals and each carries a reference number (eg 9) in blue. Those 10 km grid lines which fall at the top and bottom and outside edges of each Atlas map page carry an additional smaller reference number (eg [29]). This smaller number is the reference of the preceding 100 km grid line.

All 100 km grid lines appear in dark blue and carry a two-figure reference number (eg [20]) in blue. The reference letters of the relevant 100 km grid square (eg SS, ST etc) are also printed in blue on every Atlas map page spread.

Thus Barnstaple on page 9 of this Atlas has a National Grid Reference accurate to the nearest 10 km of SS53 where:

SS are the reference letters of the 100 km grid in which Barnstaple lies

5 and **3** are the references for the grid lines running north/south and east/west respectively and which intersect to form the south west corner of the 10 km grid square in which Barnstaple falls.

Barnstaple can be pinpointed more precisely by breaking the 10 km grid square into 10 sub squares of 1 km x 1 km and constructing a four-figure

reference SS 5533. The second and fourth figures in the number identify within the 10 km grid square SS53 the imaginary 1 km grid line intervals running north/south and east/west respectively and which intersect to form the south west corner of the 1 km grid square in which the centre of Barnstaple lies. The numbering sequence runs east and north from the south west corner of the country.

A leaflet on the National Grid references system is available from the Information Section, Ordnance Survey, Romsey Road, Maybush, Southampton SO9 4DH.

County names showing abbreviations used in this index

England

Avon	Avon
Bedfordshire	Beds
Berkshire	Berks
Buckinghamshire	Bucks
Cambridgeshire	Cambs
Cheshire	Ches
Cleveland	Cleve
Cornwall	Corn
Cumbria	Cumbr
Derbyshire	Derby
Devon	Devon
Dorset	Dorset
Durham	Durham
East Sussex	E. Susx
Essex	Essex
Gloucestershire	Glos
Greater London	G. Lon
Greater Manchester	G. Man
Hampshire	Hants
Hereford & Worcester	H.& W
Hertfordshire	Herts
Humberside	Humbs
Isle of Wight	I. of W
Kent	Kent
Lancashire	Lancs
Leicester	Leic
Lincolnshire	Lincs
Merseyside	Mers
Norfolk	Norf
North Yorkshire	N. Yks
Northamptonshire	Northnts
Northumberland	Northum
Nottinghamshire	Notts
Oxfordshire	Oxon
Shropshire	Shrops
Somerset	Somer
South Yorkshire	S. Yks
Staffordshire	Staffs
Suffolk	Suff
Surrey	Surrey
Tyne and Wear	T. & W
Warwickshire	Warw
West Midlands	W. Mids
West Sussex	W. Susx
West Yorkshire	W. Yks
Wiltshire	Wilts

Wales

Clwyd	Clwyd
Dyfed	Dyfed
Gwent	Gwent
Gwynedd	Gwyn
Mid Glamorgan	M. Glam
Powys	Powys
South Glamorgan	S. Glam
West Glamorgan	W. Glam

Other Areas

Isle of Man	I. of M
Isles of Scilly	I. Scilly

Scotland Regions

Borders	Border
Central	Central
Dumfries & Galloway	D. & G.
Fife	Fife
Grampian	Grampn
Highland	Highl
Lothian	Lothn
Strathclyde	Strath
Tayside	Tays

Scotland Island Areas

Orkney	Orkney
Shetland	Shetld
Western Isles	W. Isles

Abbas Combe   Aird Uig

A

Abbas Combe...............11 J3
Abberton, H. & W........32 B4
Abberton, Essex..........25 G1
Abberwick....................75 H3
Abbess Roding.............24 B1
Abbey...........................10 C4
Abbeycwmhir..............29 H2
Abbey Dore..................30 E6
Abbey Hulton...............42 B2
Abbey St Bathans........82 F5
Abbeystead...................57 J5
Abbeytown...................63 G2
Abbey Village...............51 F1
Abbots Bickington..........8 D4
Abbots Bromley...........42 C4
Abbotsbury..................11 G7
Abbotsham....................8 E3
Abbotskerswell..............5 J3
Abbots Langley............23 F2
Abbots Leigh...............19 K5
Abbotsley....................35 F4
Abbots Morton.............32 C4
Abbots Ripton..............35 F2
Abbot's Salford...........32 C4
Abbotswood................13 F3
Abbotts Ann................13 F1
Abdon.........................31 G1
Aber............................27 J2
Aberaeron...................28 B3
Aberaman...................18 E2
Aberangell..................39 H5
Abergie......................88 D7
Aberarth.....................28 B3
Aber-banc...................27 H2
Aberbargoed...............18 F2
Aberbeeg....................19 G2
Abercanaid.................18 E2

Abercarn....................19 G3
Abercastle..................26 C3
Abercegir....................39 H6
Aberchalder...............94 B5
Aberchirder...............104 F3
Abercraf.....................18 C1
Abercych....................27 G2
Abercynon..................18 E3
Aberdalgie..................88 C6
Aberdare....................18 E2
Aberdaron...................38 A4
Aberdeen....................97 J5
Aberdour....................81 G3
Aberdulais..................18 B3
Aberdyfi.....................38 F7
Aberedw.....................29 H5
Abereiddy...................26 B3
Abererch....................38 C3
Aberfan.......................18 E2
Aberfeldy...................88 A4
Aberffraw...................48 C4
Aberffrwd...................28 D2
Aberford.....................59 K7
Aberfoyle....................79 H1
Abergavenny..............19 H1
Abergele.....................49 J3
Abergorlech................27 K3
Abergwesyn................29 F4
Abergwili....................27 J4
Abergwynant...............39 F5
Abergwynfi..................18 C3
Abergwyngregyn.........49 F3
Abergynolwyn.............39 F6
Aberhosan..................39 H7
Aberkenfig..................18 C4
Aberlady.....................82 C4
Aberlemno..................89 H3
Aberllefenni................39 G6
Abermeurig.................28 C4
Abermule....................40 C7

Aber-nant, M. Glam......18 E2
Abernant, Dyfed..........27 H4
Abernethy...................88 D7
Abernyte.....................88 E5
Aberporth...................27 G1
Abersoch....................38 C4
Abersychan.................19 G2
Abertillery..................19 G2
Abertridwr, Powys.......40 B5
Abertridwr, M. Glam.....18 F4
Abertysswg.................18 F2
Aberuthven.................88 B7
Aber Village................30 C7
Aberyscir....................29 H7
Aberystwyth................28 C1
Abingdon....................21 J3
Abinger Common.........14 E1
Abington.....................72 E2
Abington Pigotts.........35 G5
Ab Kettleby.................43 K4
Ablington....................20 F2
Abney.........................52 D6
Aboyne.......................96 E6
Ahram........................50 F3
Abriachan...................94 D2
Abridge......................23 K3
Abthorpe....................33 J5
Abune-the-Hill...........112 C4
Aby.............................55 J6
Acaster Malbis...........60 C6
Acaster Selby.............60 C6
Accrington..................58 C8
Achachork...................99 K6
Achahoish...................77 G4
Achanalt...................101 J6
Achandunie...............102 E5
Ach' an Todhair...........86 C1
Achaphubuil...............93 G8
Acharacle....................85 H2
Acharn........................87 K4

Achath.........................97 G4
Achfary.....................108 D5
Achgarve...................100 E3
Achiemore...................110 E3
Achiltibuie.................101 G2
Achina.......................110 D2
Achinduich.................102 D3
Achingills..................111 H2
Achintee......................93 F1
Achintraid...................92 E2
Achleck.......................84 F4
Achluachrach................93 K7
Achlyness...................108 D3
Achmelvich................108 B6
Achmore, Highld..........92 E2
Achmore, W. Isles.......107 H6
Achnacarnin................111 G5
Achnacarry..................93 H7
Achnacloich.................92 B5
Achnaconeran.............94 C4
Achnacroish................85 K4
Achnagarron..............102 E5
Achnahanat................102 D3
Achnahannet...............95 H3
Achnairn...................109 G7
Achnamara...................77 G3
Achnasaul....................93 H7
Achnasheen................101 H7
Achreamie..................111 G2
Achriesgill.................108 D3
Achurch......................34 D1
Ackergill...................111 K3
Acklam, N. Yks............60 E4
Acklam, Cleve.............66 E6
Ackleton......................41 J7
Acklington...................75 J4
Ackton........................53 G1
Ackworth Moor Top......53 G2
Acle............................47 K5
Acock's Green.............32 D1

Acol............................25 K6
Acomb........................75 F8
Aconbury....................31 G6
Acre............................51 G1
Acrefair......................40 D2
Acton, Suff..................36 D5
Acton, Shrops..............30 E1
Acton, Ches.................41 H1
Acton, G. Lon..............23 H4
Acton Beauchamp.......31 H4
Acton Bridge...............50 E6
Acton Burnell..............41 G6
Acton Green................31 H4
Acton Pigott...............41 G6
Acton Round...............41 H7
Acton Scott.................41 F8
Acton Trussell.............42 B5
Acton Turville..............20 C4
Adamthwaite...............64 E8
Adbaston....................41 J4
Adber.........................11 G3
Adderbury...................33 G6
Adderley.....................41 H3
Adderstone..................75 H1
Addiewell....................80 E5
Addingham..................59 F6
Addington, Bucks........34 A7
Addington, Kent...........24 C7
Addlestone..................22 F6
Addlethorpe.................55 K7
Adeney........................41 J5
Adfa...........................40 B6
Adforton......................30 F2
Adisham......................25 J7
Adlestrop....................32 E7
Adlingfleet..................54 C1
Adlington, Lancs..........50 F2
Adlington, Ches...........51 J5
Admaston, Staffs.........42 C4
Admaston, Shrops.......41 H5

Admington...................32 E5
Adstock......................33 K6
Adstone......................33 H4
Advie..........................95 K2
Adwell.........................22 B3
Adwick le Street...........53 H3
Adwick upon Dearne....53 G3
Adziel........................105 J3
Ae...............................72 E6
Affleck........................97 H3
Affpuddle....................11 K6
Afon-wen.....................50 A6
Agglethorpe................59 F2
Aignish......................107 J5
Aike............................61 H6
Aikerness...................112 E1
Aikers........................112 E7
Aiketgate.....................64 B3
Aikton.........................63 H2
Ailey...........................30 E5
Ailsworth.....................44 E7
Ailwonth......................44 E7
Ainderby Quernhow......59 J2
Ainderby Steeple.........59 J1
Aingers Green.............37 G7
Ainsdale.....................50 C2
Ainstable.....................64 C3
Ainsworth....................51 G2
Aintree........................50 C4
Aird, D. & G.................68 B4
Aird, Strath..................77 G1
Aird, W. Isles.............107 K5
Aird Mhanais................99 G4
Aird Mheadhonach.......99 G3
Aird of Sleat................92 B5
Aird Riabhach..............99 H3
Airdrie........................80 C5
Airdriehill....................80 C5
Aird, The.....................99 K7
Aird Thunga...............107 J5
Aird Uig.....................106 E5

Airmyn.....54 B1	All Stretton.....41 F7	Anlaby.....61 H8	Ardross.....102 E5	Ashley, Northnts.....34 A2	Atherington.....9 F3
Airntully.....88 C5	Alltforgan.....39 J4	Anmer.....46 C4	Ardrossan.....78 E7	Ashley, Cambs.....36 B3	Atherstone.....43 H3
Airor.....92 D5	Alltmawr.....29 H5	Anna.....73 G8	Ardshealach.....85 H2	Ashley, Glos.....20 D3	Atherstone on Stour.....32 E4
Airth.....80 D3	Allt na h-Airbhe.....101 H3	Annaside.....56 D2	Ardsley.....53 F3	Ashley, Hants.....13 F2	Atherton.....51 F3
Airton.....58 E5	Allt-nan-Sugh.....93 F3	Annat, Strath.....86 C6	Ardsley East.....53 F1	Ashley, Devon.....9 G4	Atlow.....42 E2
Aisby, Lincs.....54 C4	Alltwalis.....27 J3	Annat, Highld.....100 E7	Ardtalnaig.....87 K5	Ashley, Ches.....51 G5	Attadale.....93 F2
Aisby, Lincs.....44 D3	Alltwen.....18 B2	Anna Valley.....13 F1	Ardtoe.....85 H1	Ashley, Staffs.....41 J3	Attenborough.....43 H3
Aiskew.....59 H2	Almeley.....30 E4	Annbank.....71 K2	Ardtornish.....85 J4	Ashley Green.....22 E2	Attleborough, Norf.....46 F7
Aislaby, N. Yks.....60 E2	Almer.....12 B6	Annesley.....43 H1	Ardullie.....102 D6	Ashley Heath, Dorset.....12 D5	Attleborough, Warw.....43 F7
Aislaby, N. Yks.....67 J7	Almington.....41 J3	Annesley Woodhouse.....43 G1	Ardvasar.....92 C5	Ashley Heath, Staffs.....41 J3	Attlebridge.....47 G5
Aisthorpe.....54 D5	Almondbank.....88 C6	Annfield Plain.....66 B2	Ardvey, W. Isles.....99 F4	Ash Magna.....41 G3	Atwick.....61 J5
Aith, Shetld.....115 F3	Almondbury.....52 D2	Annochie.....105 J4	Ardvey, W. Isles.....99 G3	Ashmansworth.....21 J7	Atworth.....20 C6
Aith, Orkney.....113 G4	Almondsbury.....19 L4	Annscroft.....41 F6	Ardvourlie.....99 G1	Ashmansworthy.....8 D4	Aubourn.....54 D7
Aithsetter.....115 G5	Alne.....60 B4	Ansdell.....57 G8	Ardwell.....68 C6	Ash Mill.....9 H3	Auchagallon.....70 D1
Akeld.....75 F2	Alness.....102 E6	Ansford.....11 H2	Areley Kings.....31 K2	Ashmore.....12 B4	Aucharnie.....97 F1
Akeley.....33 K6	Alnham.....75 F3	Ansley.....43 F7	Argos Hill.....16 C3	Ashmore Park.....42 B6	Auchattie.....97 F6
Akenham.....37 G5	Alnmouth.....75 J3	Anslow.....42 E4	Aridhglas.....84 E6	Ashorne.....33 F4	Auchenblae.....97 G8
Albaston.....4 E2	Alnwick.....75 H3	Anslow Gate.....42 D4	Arinacrinachd.....100 D7	Ashover.....53 F7	Auchenbrack.....72 C5
Alberbury.....40 E5	Alphamstone.....36 D6	Anstey, Herts.....35 H6	Arinagour.....84 D3	Ashow.....33 F2	Auchencairn.....69 J3
Albourne.....15 F5	Alpheton.....36 D4	Anstey, Leic.....43 H6	Arisaig.....92 C3	Asherton.....31 H5	Auchencrow.....83 G5
Albrighton, Shrops.....41 F5	Alphington.....9 K7	Anston.....53 H5	Arivruaich.....107 G7	Ashperton.....31 H5	Auchengray.....80 E6
Albrighton, Shrops.....41 K6	Alport.....52 E7	Anstruther.....82 D1	Arkendale.....59 J4	Ashprington.....5 J4	Auchenhalrig.....104 C2
Alburgh.....37 H1	Alpraham.....50 E8	Ansty, Wilts.....12 B3	Arkesden.....35 H6	Ash Priors.....10 C3	Auchenheath.....80 D7
Albury, Surrey.....14 D1	Alresford.....36 F7	Ansty, Warw.....33 F1	Arkholme.....57 J3	Ashreigney.....9 G4	Auchentiber.....79 F7
Albury, Herts.....35 H7	Alrewas.....42 D5	Ansty, W. Susx.....15 F3	Arkley.....23 H3	Ashtead.....23 G7	Auchgourish.....95 H4
Alby Hill.....47 G3	Alsager.....41 J1	Ansty, Dorset.....11 J5	Arksey.....53 H3	Ash Thomas.....10 B4	Auchindrain.....78 C1
Alcaig.....102 D7	Alsagers Bank.....41 K2	Anthill Common.....13 J4	Arkwright Town.....53 G6	Ashton, Northnts.....34 A4	Auchindrean.....101 H4
Alcaston.....31 F1	Alsop en le Dale.....42 D1	Anthorn.....63 G2	Arlecdon.....62 F6	Ashton, Northnts.....34 D1	Auchininna.....104 F4
Alcester.....32 C4	Alston.....64 E3	Antingham.....47 H3	Arlesey.....35 E6	Ashton, Ches.....50 E7	Auchinleck.....72 A2
Alciston.....15 J5	Alstone.....32 B6	Antony.....4 D4	Arleston.....41 H5	Ashton, Corn.....2 E7	Auchinloch.....79 J4
Alcombe.....10 A1	Alstonefield.....42 D1	Antrobus.....51 F6	Arley, Warw.....42 E7	Ashton, H. & W.....31 G3	Auchinroer.....97 K2
Alconbury.....34 E2	Alswear.....9 H3	Anwick.....44 E1	Arley, Ches.....51 F5	Ashton Common.....20 C7	Auchleuchries.....96 F3
Alconbury Weston.....34 E2	Altandhu.....108 A7	Anwoth.....69 G5	Arlingham.....20 B1	Ashton in Makerfield.....50 E4	Auchleven.....80 D8
Aldborough, Norf.....47 G3	Altarnun.....4 C1	Apes Hall.....45 J7	Arlington, E. Susx.....16 C5	Ashton Keynes.....20 E3	Auchlochan.....96 E5
Aldborough, N. Yks.....59 K4	Altass.....102 D2	Apethorpe.....44 D7	Arlington, Glos.....20 F2	Ashton under Hill.....32 B6	Auchlyne.....87 H6
Aldbourne.....21 G5	Alterwall.....111 J2	Apley.....54 F6	Arlington, Devon.....9 G1	Ashton-under-Lyne.....51 J4	Auchmillan.....71 L2
Aldbrough.....61 K7	Altham.....58 C7	Apperknowle.....53 F6	Armadale, Highld.....110 D2	Ashton upon Mersey.....51 G4	Auchmithie.....89 J4
Aldbrough St John.....66 C6	Althorne.....24 F3	Apperley.....32 A7	Armadale, Lothn.....80 D5	Ashurst, W. Susx.....14 E4	Auchnacree.....89 G2
Aldbury.....22 E1	Althorpe.....54 C3	Appersett.....58 D1	Armathwaite.....64 C3	Ashurst, Hants.....13 F4	Auchnagallin.....95 J2
Aldclune.....88 A2	Altnaharra.....109 G5	Appin.....86 B4	Arminghall.....47 H6	Ashurst, Kent.....15 J2	Auchnagatt.....97 J1
Aldeburgh.....37 K4	Altofts.....53 F1	Appleby.....54 D2	Armitage.....42 C5	Ashurst Wood.....15 H2	Auchterarder.....88 B7
Aldeby.....47 K7	Alton, Staffs.....42 C2	Appleby-in-Westmorland.....64 D5	Armscote.....32 E5	Ashwater.....8 D6	Auchteraw.....94 B5
Aldenham.....23 D3	Alton, Derby.....53 F7	Appleby Magna.....43 F5	Armthorpe.....53 J3	Ashwell, Leic.....44 B5	Auchterderran.....81 H2
Alderbury.....12 D3	Alton, Hants.....13 K2	Appleby Parva.....43 F6	Arncliffe.....58 E3	Ashwell, Herts.....35 F6	Auchtermuchty.....88 E7
Alderford.....47 G5	Alton Pancras.....11 H5	Applecross.....100 D8	Arncott.....22 B1	Ashwellthorpe.....47 G7	Auchterneed.....102 C7
Alderholt.....12 D4	Alton Priors.....20 F6	Appledore, Devon.....10 B4	Arncroach.....89 H8	Ashwick.....11 H1	Auchtertool.....81 H2
Alderley.....20 B3	Altrincham.....51 G5	Appledore, Devon.....8 E2	Arne.....12 B7	Ashwicken.....46 C5	Auchtertyre.....92 E3
Alderley Edge.....51 H6	Altrua.....93 J6	Appledore, Kent.....17 G3	Arnesby.....43 J7	Askam in Furness.....56 F3	Auchtubh.....87 H6
Aldermaston.....21 K6	Alva.....80 D2	Appleford.....21 K3	Arnisdale.....92 E4	Askern.....53 H2	Auckengill.....111 K2
Alderminster.....32 E5	Alvanley.....50 D6	Appleshaw.....13 F1	Arnish.....100 B8	Askerswell.....11 G6	Auckley.....53 J3
Aldershot.....22 D7	Alvaston.....43 F3	Appleton.....21 J2	Arniston Engine.....81 J5	Askett.....22 D2	Audenshaw.....51 J4
Alderton, Northnts.....34 A5	Alvechurch.....32 C2	Appleton-le-Moors.....60 E2	Arnol.....107 H4	Askham, Notts.....54 B6	Audlem.....41 H2
Alderton, Wilts.....20 C4	Alvecote.....42 E6	Appleton-Le-Street.....60 E3	Arnold.....43 H2	Askham, Cumbr.....64 C5	Audley.....41 J1
Alderton, Glos.....32 C6	Alvediston.....12 B3	Appleton Roebuck.....60 C6	Arnprior.....79 J2	Askham Bryan.....60 C6	Auds.....104 F2
Alderton, Shrops.....41 F4	Alveley.....31 J1	Appleton Thorn.....51 F5	Arnside.....57 H3	Askham Richard.....60 C6	Aughton, Lancs.....50 C4
Alderton, Suff.....37 J5	Alverdiscott.....8 F3	Appleton Wiske.....66 D7	Arpafeelie.....102 E7	Asknish.....77 J2	Aughton, Humbs.....60 E7
Alderwasley.....43 F1	Alverstoke.....13 J6	Appletreehall.....74 B3	Arrad Foot.....57 G2	Askrigg.....58 E1	Aughton, S. Yks.....53 G5
Aldfield.....59 H4	Alverstone.....13 H7	Appletreewick.....59 F4	Arram.....61 H6	Askwith.....59 G6	Aughton, Lancs.....57 J4
Aldford.....50 D8	Alverton.....44 A2	Appley.....10 B3	Arrathorne.....59 H1	Aslackby.....44 D3	Aughton Park.....50 D3
Aldham, Essex.....36 E7	Alves.....103 K6	Appley Bridge.....50 E3	Arreton.....13 H7	Aslacton.....47 G7	Auldearn.....103 H7
Aldham, Suff.....36 F5	Alvescot.....21 G2	Apse Heath.....13 H7	Arrington.....35 G4	Aslockton.....44 A2	Aulden.....31 F4
Aldingbourne.....14 C5	Alveston, Warw.....32 E4	Apsley End.....34 E6	Arrochar.....78 E1	Asloun.....96 E4	Auldhame.....82 D3
Aldingham.....57 F3	Alveston, Avon.....19 L4	Aquahorthies.....97 H3	Arrow.....32 C4	Aspall.....37 G3	Auldhouse.....79 J6
Aldington, H. & W.....32 C5	Alvie.....95 G5	Aquhythie.....97 G4	Artafallie.....102 E8	Aspatria.....63 G3	Ault a' Chruinn.....93 F3
Aldington, Kent.....17 H2	Alvingham.....55 H4	Arabella.....103 G5	Arthington.....59 H6	Aspenden.....35 G7	Aultbea.....100 E4
Aldington Frith.....17 H2	Alvington.....19 L2	Arbirlot.....89 J4	Arthingworth.....34 A1	Aspley Guise.....34 C6	Aultdearg.....101 J6
Aldochlay.....79 F2	Alwalton.....44 E7	Arboll.....103 G4	Arthog.....39 F5	Aspull.....50 F3	Aultgrishan.....100 D4
Aldreth.....35 H2	Alweston.....11 H4	Arborfield.....22 C6	Arthrath.....97 J2	Asselby.....60 E8	Aultiphurst.....110 E2
Aldridge.....42 C6	Alwinton.....74 F4	Arborfield Cross.....22 C6	Arundel.....14 D5	Assington.....36 E6	Aultmore.....104 D3
Aldringham.....37 K3	Alyth.....88 E4	Arborfield Garrison.....22 C6	Asby.....62 F5	Astbury.....51 H7	Ault-na-goire.....94 D3
Aldsworth.....21 F1	Amatnatua.....102 C3	Arbroath.....89 J4	Ascog.....78 D5	Astcote.....33 J4	Aultnamain Inn.....102 E4
Aldunie.....96 C3	Ambergate.....43 F1	Arbuthnott.....97 H8	Ascot.....22 E6	Asterley.....40 E6	Aundorach.....95 H4
Aldwark, N. Yks.....60 B4	Amber Hill.....45 F2	Archiestown.....104 B4	Ascott-under-Wychwood.....21 H1	Asterton.....40 F7	Aunsby.....44 D3
Aldwark, Derby.....42 E1	Amberley, Glos.....20 C2	Arclid Green.....51 G7	Asenby.....59 J3	Asthall.....21 G1	Auquhorthies.....97 H3
Aldwick.....14 C6	Amberley, W. Susx.....14 D4	Ardachu.....102 E2	Asfordby.....43 K5	Asthall Leigh.....21 H1	Aust.....19 K4
Aldwincle.....34 D1	Amble.....75 J4	Ardalanish.....84 E7	Asfordby Hill.....43 K5	Astley, Warw.....43 F8	Austerfield.....53 J4
Aldworth.....21 K5	Amblecote.....32 A1	Ardanaiseig.....86 C6	Asgarby, Lincs.....44 E2	Astley, Shrops.....41 G5	Austrey.....42 E6
Alexandria.....79 F3	Ambleside.....63 J7	Ardaneaskan.....92 E2	Asgarby, Lincs.....55 H7	Astley, H. & W.....31 J3	Austwick.....58 C4
Alfardisworthy.....8 C4	Ambleston.....26 E4	Ardarroch.....92 E2	Ash, Kent.....24 B6	Astley Abbots.....41 J7	Authorpe.....55 J5
Alfington.....10 C6	Ambrosden.....21 L1	Ardbeg.....76 D7	Ash, Surrey.....22 D7	Astley Cross.....31 K3	Authorpe Row.....55 K6
Alfold.....14 D2	Amcotts.....54 C2	Ardcharnich.....101 H4	Ash, Somer.....11 F3	Astley Green.....51 G4	Avebury.....20 E6
Alford, Grampn.....96 E4	Amersham.....22 E3	Ardchiavaig.....84 E7	Ash, Kent.....25 J7	Aston, Berks.....22 C4	Aveley.....24 B4
Alford, Somer.....11 F2	Amesbury.....12 D1	Ardchyle.....87 H6	Ashampstead.....21 K5	Aston, W. Mids.....42 C8	Avening.....20 C3
Alford, Lincs.....55 J6	Amhuinnsuidhe.....98 F2	Ardclach.....103 H8	Ashbocking.....37 G4	Aston, Derby.....52 D5	Averdaron.....38 A4
Alfreton.....43 G1	Amington.....42 E6	Ard Dhail.....107 J2	Ashbourne.....42 D2	Aston, Ches.....50 E6	Averffraw.....48 C4
Alfrick.....31 J4	Amisfield.....73 F6	Ard-dhubh.....92 D1	Ashbrittle.....10 B3	Aston, H. & W.....31 F2	Averham.....44 A1
Alfriston.....15 J5	Amlwch.....48 D1	Arddleen.....40 D5	Ashburton.....5 H3	Aston, Herts.....35 F7	Aveton Gifford.....5 G5
Alhampton.....11 H2	Amlwch Port.....48 D1	Ardechive.....93 H6	Ashbury, Devon.....8 F6	Aston, Shrops.....41 G4	Avielochan.....95 H4
Alkborough.....54 C1	Ammanford.....27 L5	Ardeley.....35 G7	Ashbury, Oxon.....21 G4	Aston, S. Yks.....53 G5	Aviemore.....95 G4
Alkerton.....33 F5	Amotherby.....60 E3	Ardelve.....92 E3	Ashby.....54 D3	Aston, Ches.....41 H2	Avington.....21 H6
Alkham.....17 K1	Ampfield.....13 G3	Arden.....79 F3	Ashby by Partney.....55 J7	Aston, Oxon.....21 H2	Avoch.....102 F7
Alkington.....41 G3	Ampleforth.....60 C3	Ardens Grafton.....32 D4	Ashby cum Fenby.....55 G3	Aston, Shrops.....41 H6	Avon.....12 D6
Alkmonton.....42 D3	Ampney Crucis.....20 E2	Ardentinny.....78 D3	Ashby de la Launde.....44 D1	Aston, Staffs.....41 J2	Avonbridge.....80 E4
Allaleigh.....5 J4	Ampney St Mary.....20 E2	Ardeonaig.....87 J5	Ashby-de-la-Zouch.....43 F5	Aston Abbotts.....34 B7	Avon Dassett.....33 G4
Allanaquoich.....95 K6	Ampney St Peter.....20 E2	Ardersier.....103 F7	Ashby Folville.....43 K5	Aston Botterell.....31 H1	Avonmouth.....19 K5
Allanton, Strath.....80 D6	Amport.....13 F1	Ardessie.....101 G4	Ashby Magna.....43 H7	Aston-by-Stone.....42 B3	Avon Wick.....5 H5
Allanton, Border.....83 G6	Ampthill.....34 D6	Ardfern.....85 K8	Ashby Parva.....33 H1	Aston Cantlow.....32 D3	Awbridge.....13 F3
Allardice.....97 H8	Ampton.....36 D2	Ardgay.....102 D3	Ashby St Ledgers.....33 H3	Aston Clinton.....22 D1	Awkley.....19 K4
All Cannings.....21 F6	Amroth.....26 F6	Ardgowan.....78 E4	Ashby St Mary.....47 J6	Aston Crews.....31 H7	Awliscombe.....10 C5
Allendale Town.....65 F2	Amulree.....88 B5	Ardhasaig.....99 G2	Ashchurch.....32 B6	Aston End.....35 F7	Awre.....20 B2
Allenheads.....65 F3	Anaheilt.....85 K2	Ardheslaig.....100 D7	Ashcombe.....5 K2	Aston Eyre.....41 H7	Awsworth.....43 G2
Allensmore.....31 F6	Anancaun.....101 G6	Ardindrean.....101 H4	Ashcott.....11 F2	Aston Fields.....32 B3	Axbridge.....19 J7
Aller.....63 F4	An Ard.....100 E5	Ardingly.....15 G3	Ashdon.....35 J5	Aston Flamville.....43 G7	Axford, Wilts.....21 G5
Allerby.....63 F4	An Caol.....100 C7	Ardington.....21 J4	Asheldham.....25 F2	Aston Ingham.....31 H7	Axford, Hants.....13 J1
Allerford.....9 K1	Ancaster.....44 C2	Ardivachar.....98 C8	Ashen.....36 C5	Aston juxta Mondrum.....41 H1	Axminster.....10 D6
Allerston.....61 F2	Anchor.....30 C1	Ardivachar Point.....98 C8	Ashendon.....22 C1	Aston le Walls.....33 G4	Axmouth.....10 D6
Allerthorpe.....60 E6	An Cnoc.....107 J5	Ardlair.....96 E3	Ashfield, Central.....80 C1	Aston Magna.....32 E6	Ayburton.....19 L2
Allerton.....50 D5	Ancroft.....83 J7	Ardleigh.....36 F7	Ashfield, Suff.....37 H3	Aston Munslow.....31 G1	Ayle.....64 E3
Allerton Bywater.....53 G1	Ancrum.....74 C2	Ardler.....88 E4	Ashfield Green.....37 H2	Aston on Clun.....30 E1	Aylesbeare.....10 B6
Allesley.....32 E1	Ancton.....14 C5	Ardley.....33 H7	Ashford, Devon.....9 F2	Aston-on-Trent.....43 G4	Aylesbury.....22 D1
Allestree.....43 F3	Anderby.....55 K6	Ardlui.....86 F7	Ashford, Surrey.....22 F5	Aston Rogers.....40 E6	Aylesby.....55 G3
Allexton.....44 B6	Anderby Creek.....55 K6	Ardlussa.....77 F3	Ashford, Kent.....17 H1	Aston Rowant.....22 C2	Aylesford.....24 D7
Allgreave.....51 J7	Anderson.....12 A6	Ardmair.....101 H3	Ashford Bowdler.....31 G2	Aston Sandford.....22 C2	Aylesham.....25 J7
Allhallows-on-Sea.....24 E5	Anderton.....51 F6	Ardminish.....77 F7	Ashford Carbonell.....31 K6	Aston Somerville.....32 C6	Aylestone.....43 H6
Allhallows.....24 E5	Andover.....13 F1	Ardmolich.....85 J1	Ashford Hill.....21 K6	Aston Subedge.....32 D5	Aylmerton.....47 G3
Alligin Shuas.....100 E7	Andover Down.....13 F1	Ardnacroish.....85 K4	Ashford in the Water.....52 D7	Aston Tirrold.....21 K4	Aylsham.....47 G4
Allimore Green.....42 A5	Andoversford.....20 E1	Ardnadam.....78 D3	Ashgill.....80 C7	Aston Upthorpe.....21 K4	Aylton.....31 H6
Allington, Lincs.....44 B2	Andreas.....56 R2	Ardnagrask.....102 D8	Ashill, Devon.....10 B4	Astwick.....35 F6	Aymestrey.....31 F3
Allington, Wilts.....12 E2	Angersleigh.....10 C4	Ardnarff.....92 E2	Ashill, Norf.....46 D6	Astwood.....34 C5	Aynho.....33 H6
Allington, Wilts.....20 D4	Angle.....26 C6	Ardnastang.....85 K2	Ashill, Somer.....10 E4	Astwood Bank.....32 C3	Ayot St Lawrence.....23 H1
Allithwaite.....57 G3	Angmering.....14 D5	Ardo.....97 H2	Ashington.....24 E3	Aswarby.....44 D3	Ayot St Peter.....23 H1
Alloa.....80 D2	Angram, N. Yks.....60 C6	Ardoyne.....97 F3	Ashington, W. Susx.....14 E4	Aswardby.....55 H6	Ayr.....71 J2
Allonby.....63 F3	Angram, N. Yks.....65 F8	Ardrishaig.....77 H3	Ashington, Northum.....75 J6	Atcham.....41 G6	Aysgarth.....58 F2
Alloway.....71 J3	Ankerville.....103 G5	Ardroil.....106 E5	Ashkirk.....74 A2	Athelington.....37 H2	Ayside.....57 G2
All Saints South Elmham.....37 J1				Ashleworth.....31 K7	

Ayston....44 B6
Aythorpe Roding....24 B1
Ayton, N. Yks....61 G2
Ayton, Border....83 H5
Aywick....117 G4
Azerley....59 H3

B

Babbacombe....5 K3
Babbinswood....40 E3
Babcary....11 G3
Babel....29 F6
Babell....50 A6
Babraham....35 J4
Babworth....53 J5
Bac....107 J4
Backaland....113 F3
Backbarrow....57 G2
Backburn, Grampn....96 E2
Backburn, Grampn....97 H6
Backfolds....105 K3
Backford....50 C6
Backhill, Grampn....97 G2
Backhill, Grampn....97 K2
Backhill of Clackriach....105 J4
Backhill of Trustach....97 F6
Backies....103 G2
Backlass....111 J3
Backmuir of New Gilston....89 G8
Back of Keppoch....92 C7
Backwell....19 J6
Backworth....75 K7
Bacon End....24 C1
Baconsthorpe....47 G3
Bacton, H. & W....30 E6
Bacton, Suff....36 F3
Bacton, Norf....47 J3
Bacup....51 H1
Badachro....100 D5
Badbury....21 F4
Badby....33 H4
Badcall, Highld....108 C4
Badcall, Highld....108 D3
Badcaul....101 G3
Baddeley Green....42 B1
Baddesley Ensor....42 E7
Baddidarach....108 B6
Badenscoth....97 G2
Badger....41 J7
Badgers Mount....23 K6
Badgeworth....20 D1
Badgworth....19 H7
Badicaul....92 D3
Badingham....37 J3
Badlesmere....25 G7
Badluarach....101 F3
Badminton....20 C4
Badninish....103 F3
Badrallach....101 G3
Badsey....32 C5
Badsworth....53 G2
Badwell Ash....36 E3
Bagby....60 B2
Bagendon....20 E2
Bage, The....30 D5
Bagillt....50 B6
Baginton....33 F2
Baglan....18 B3
Bagley....40 F4
Bagnall....42 B1
Bagshot, Surrey....22 E6
Bagshot, Wilts....21 H6
Bagthorpe, Norf....46 C3
Bagthorpe, Notts....43 G1
Bagworth....43 G6
Bagwyllydiart....31 F7
Baildon....59 G7
Baile....98 E4
Bailebeag....94 D4
Baile Boidheach....77 G4
Baile Mor....84 D6
Baillieston....79 J5
Bail Uachdraich....98 D6
Bainbridge....58 E1
Bainton, Cambs....44 D6
Bainton, Humbs....61 G5
Bairnkine....74 C3
Bakers End....23 J1
Baker Street....24 C4
Bakewell....52 E7
Bala....39 J3
Balachuirn....92 B1
Balaglas....98 D7
Balallan....107 G6
Balbeg....94 C3
Balbeggie....88 D6
Balbithan....97 G4
Balblair....102 F6
Balcherry....103 G4
Balchladich....108 B5
Balchraggan....102 D8
Balchrick....108 C2
Balcombe....15 G2
Balcurvie....81 J1
Baldersby....59 J3
Balderstone....58 B7
Balderton....44 B1
Baldhu....2 F5
Baldinnie....89 G7
Baldock....35 F6
Baldrine....56 R3
Baldwin....56 Q3
Baldwinholme....63 J2
Baldwin's Gate....41 J2
Bale....46 F3
Balemartine....84 A4
Balephuil....84 A4
Balerno....85 G5
Balevullin....84 A4
Balfield....89 H2
Balfour....112 E5

Balfron....79 H3
Balgaveny....97 F1
Balgedie....88 D8
Balgonar....80 F2
Balgove....97 H2
Balgowan....94 E6
Balgown....99 J6
Balgrochan....79 J4
Balgy....100 E7
Balhalgardy....97 G3
Baligill....110 E2
Balintore....103 G5
Balintraid....103 F5
Balivanich....98 C7
Balkholme....60 E8
Balkissock....71 G6
Ball....40 E4
Balla....90 C4
Ballabeg....56 P4
Ballacannell....56 R3
Ballacarnane Beg....56 Q3
Ballachulish....86 C3
Ballagyr....56 P3
Ballajora....56 R2
Ballamodha....56 P4
Ballantrae....71 F6
Ballantrushal....107 H3
Ballasalla, I. of M....56 P5
Ballasalla, I. of M....56 Q2
Ballater....96 C6
Ballaugh....56 Q2
Balleigh....102 F4
Ballencrieff....82 C4
Ball Hill....21 J6
Balliasta....117 H2
Balliekine....77 H8
Ballig....56 P3
Ballinaby....76 B5
Ballinger Common....22 C2
Ballingham....31 G6
Ballingry....81 G2
Ballinluig....88 B3
Ballintuim....88 D3
Balloch, Strath....79 F3
Balloch, Highld....103 F8
Ballochan....96 E6
Balls Cross....14 C3
Ballygown....85 K4
Ballygrant....76 C5
Ballymichael....70 E1
Balmacara....92 E3
Balmacara Square....92 E3
Balmaclellan....72 B7
Balmae....69 H6
Balmaha....79 G2
Balmartin....98 C5
Balmedie....97 J4
Balmerino....89 F6
Balmer Lawn....13 F5
Balmore....79 J4
Balmullo....89 G6
Balnabodach....90 C5
Balnacra....101 F8
Balnaguard....88 B3
Balnaguisich....102 E5
Balnahard....85 F5
Balnain....94 C2
Balnakeil....108 E2
Balnaknock....99 K6
Balnapaling....103 F6
Balne....53 H2
Balquhidder....87 H6
Balranald....98 C6
Balsall Common....32 E2
Balscote....33 F5
Balsham....35 J4
Baltasound....117 H2
Balterley....41 J1
Balthangie....105 H3
Baltonsborough....11 G2
Balvaird....102 D7
Balvicar....85 J7
Balvraid....95 G2
Bamber Bridge....50 E1
Bamburgh....75 H1
Bamford....52 E5
Bampton, Cumbr....64 C6
Bampton, Oxon....21 H2
Bampton, Devon....9 K3
Banavie....93 H8
Banbury....33 G5
Banchory....97 G6
Banchory-Devenick....97 J5
Bancffosfelen....27 H5
Bancyffordd....27 J3
Banff....105 F2
Bangor....48 E3
Bangor-is-y-coed....40 E2
Banham....36 F1
Bank....12 E5
Bankend, Strath....72 D1
Bankend, D. & G....73 F8
Bankfoot....88 C5
Bankglen....72 A3
Bankhead, Grampn....97 F5
Bankhead, Grampn....97 H4
Bank Newton....58 E5
Banknock....80 C4
Banks, Lancs....50 C1
Banks, Cumbr....64 C1
Bankshill....73 G6
Bank Street....31 H3
Banningham....47 H4
Bannister Green....36 B7
Bannockburn....80 D2
Banstead....23 H7
Bantham....5 G5
Banton....80 C4
Banwell....19 H7
Bapchild....24 F6
Bapton....12 B2
Baramore....92 C8
Barassie....71 J1
Barbaraville....103 F5

Barber Booth....52 D5
Barbon....57 K2
Barbridge....50 F7
Barbrook....9 H1
Barby....33 H2
Barcaldine....86 B4
Barcheston....32 E6
Barcombe....15 H4
Barcombe Cross....15 H4
Barden....59 G1
Bardfield Saling....36 B7
Bardney....54 F7
Bardowie....79 H4
Bardrainney....79 F4
Bardsea....57 G3
Bardsey....59 J6
Bardwell....36 E2
Barford, Warw....32 E3
Barford, Norf....47 K6
Barford St Martin....12 C2
Barford St Michael....33 G6
Barfrestone....25 J7
Bargoed....18 F3
Bargrennan....71 J7
Barham, Cambs....34 E2
Barham, Suff....37 G4
Barham, Kent....25 J7
Bar Hill....35 G3
Barholm....44 D5
Barkby....43 J6
Barkestone-le-Vale....44 A3
Barkham....22 C6
Barking, Suff....36 F4
Barking, G. Lon....23 K4
Barkingside....23 K4
Barkisland....52 C2
Barkston....44 C2
Barkston Ash....60 B7
Barkway....35 G6
Barkwith....55 F5
Barlaston....42 A3
Barlavington....14 C4
Barlborough....53 G6
Barlby....60 D7
Barlestone....43 G6
Barley, Lancs....58 D6
Barley, Herts....35 G6
Barleythorpe....44 B6
Barling....24 F4
Barlow, N. Yks....60 D8
Barlow, Derby....53 F6
Barlow, T. & W....65 J1
Barmby Moor....60 E6
Barmby on the Marsh....60 D8
Barmer....46 D3
Barmouth....38 F5
Barmpton....66 D6
Barmston....61 J5
Barnack....44 D6
Barnacle....33 F1
Barnard Castle....65 H6
Barnard Gate....21 J1
Barnardiston....36 C5
Barnburgh....53 G3
Barnby....47 K8
Barnby Dun....53 J3
Barnby in the Willows....44 B1
Barnby Moor....53 J5
Barnes....23 H5
Barnet....23 H3
Barnetby le Wold....54 E3
Barney....46 E3
Barnham, W. Susx....14 C5
Barnham, Suff....36 D2
Barnham Broom....47 F6
Barnhill....103 K7
Barningham, Suff....36 E2
Barningham, Durham....65 H6
Barnoldby le Beck....55 G3
Barnoldswick....58 D6
Barns Green....14 E3
Barnsley, Glos....20 E2
Barnsley, S. Yks....53 F3
Barnstaple....9 F2
Barnston, Mers....50 B5
Barnston, Essex....24 C1
Barnstone....43 K3
Barnt Green....32 C2
Barnton....51 F6
Barnwell....34 D1
Barnwood....20 C1
Barony, The....112 C4
Barr....71 H5
Barrachan....68 E6
Barrack....105 H4
Barraglom....107 F5
Barrahormid....77 G3
Barran....85 K6
Barrapol....84 A4
Barras, Cumbr....65 F6
Barras, Grampn....97 H7
Barrasford....75 F7
Barravullin....85 K8
Barregarrow....56 Q3
Barrhead....79 H6
Barrhill....71 H6
Barrington, Somer....10 E4
Barrington, Cambs....35 G5
Barripper....2 E6
Barrmill....79 F6
Barrock....111 J1
Barrow, Leic....44 B5
Barrow, Suff....36 C3
Barrow, Lancs....58 C7
Barrow, Shrops....41 H6
Barroway Drove....45 J6
Barrowby....44 B3
Barrowden....44 C6
Barrowford....58 D7
Barrow Gurney....19 K6
Barrow-in-Furness....56 E4
Barrow Street....11 K2
Barrow upon Humber....54 E1

Barrow upon Soar....43 H5
Barrow upon Trent....43 F4
Barry, S. Glam....18 F6
Barry, Tays....89 H5
Barry Island....18 F6
Barsby....43 J5
Barsham....47 J8
Barston....32 E2
Bartestree....31 G5
Bartford St Martin....12 C2
Barthol Chapel....97 H2
Barthomley....41 J1
Bartley....13 F4
Bartlow....35 J5
Barton, N. Yks....66 C7
Barton, Warw....32 D4
Barton, Glos....32 D7
Barton, Ches....41 F1
Barton, Cambs....35 H4
Barton, Lancs....57 J7
Barton, Devon....5 K3
Barton Bendish....46 C6
Barton Hartshorn....33 J6
Barton in Fabis....43 H3
Barton in the Beans....43 F6
Barton-le-Clay....34 D6
Barton-le-Street....60 E3
Barton-le-Willows....60 E4
Barton Mills....36 C2
Barton Moss....51 G4
Barton on Sea....12 E6
Barton-on-the-Heath....32 E6
Barton Seagrave....34 B2
Barton Stacey....13 G1
Barton St David....11 G2
Barton Turf....47 J4
Barton-under-Needwood....42 D5
Barton-upon-Humber....54 E1
Barvas....107 H4
Barway....35 J2
Barwell....43 G6
Barwick....11 G4
Barwick in Elmet....59 K7
Baschurch....41 F4
Bascote....33 G3
Basford Green....42 B1
Bashall Eaves....58 C6
Bashley....12 E6
Basildon....24 D4
Basingstoke....22 B7
Baslow....52 E6
Bason Bridge....10 E1
Bassaleg....19 G4
Bassenthwaite....63 H4
Bassett....13 G4
Bassingbourn....35 G5
Bassingfield....43 J3
Bassingham....54 D8
Bassingthorpe....44 C4
Basta....117 G3
Baston....44 E5
Bastwick....47 K5
Batchcott....31 F2
Batcombe, Somer....11 H2
Batcombe, Dorset....11 H5
Bate Heath....51 F6
Bath....20 B6
Bathampton....20 B6
Bathealton....10 B3
Batheaston....20 B6
Bathford....20 B6
Bathgate....80 E5
Bathley....54 B8
Bathpool....4 C2
Batley....52 E1
Batsford....32 D6
Battersby....67 F7
Battersea....23 H5
Battisford....36 F4
Battisford Tye....36 F4
Battle, E. Susx....16 E4
Battle, Powys....29 H6
Battlefield....41 G5
Battlesbridge....24 D3
Battlesden....34 C7
Battleton....9 K3
Battramsley....13 F6
Bauds of Cullen....104 D2
Baughurst....21 K6
Baulking....21 H3
Baumber....55 G6
Baunton....20 E2
Baverstock....12 C2
Bawburgh....47 G6
Bawdeswell....46 F4
Bawdrip....10 E2
Bawdsey....37 J5
Bawtry....53 J4
Baxenden....51 G1
Baxterley....42 E7
Baycliff....57 F3
Baydon....21 G5
Bayford....23 J2
Bayham Abbey....16 D2
Bayles....64 E3
Baylham....37 G4
Bayston Hill....41 F6
Bayton....31 H2
Beachamwell....46 C6
Beachampton....22 C3
Beachans....103 J8
Beachborough....17 G3
Beachley....19 K3
Beacon End....36 D6
Beacon's Bottom....22 C3
Beaconsfield....22 E3
Beacravik....99 G3
Beadlam....60 D2
Beadnell....75 J2
Beaford....9 F4
Beal, N. Yks....53 H1
Beal, Northum....83 J7
Beaminster....11 F5

Beamish....66 C2
Beamsley....59 F5
Bean....24 B5
Beanacre....20 D6
Beanley....75 G3
Beaquoy....112 C4
Beare Green....14 E1
Bearley....32 D3
Bearpark....66 C3
Bearsbridge....64 E2
Bearsden....79 H4
Bearsted....24 D7
Bearwood....12 C6
Bearwood, H. & W....30 E4
Beattock....73 F4
Beauchamp Roding....24 B1
Beauchief....53 F5
Beaufort....18 F1
Beaulieu....13 F5
Beauly....102 D8
Beaumaris....48 F3
Beaumont, Essex....37 G7
Beaumont, Cumbr....63 J2
Beausale....32 E2
Beaworthy....8 E6
Beazley End....36 C7
Bebington....50 C5
Bebside....75 J6
Beccles....47 K7
Becconsall....50 D1
Beckbury....41 J6
Beckenham....23 J6
Beckermet....62 F7
Beckermonds....58 D2
Beckfoot, Cumbr....63 F3
Beckfoot, Cumbr....63 G7
Beckford....32 B6
Beckhampton....20 E6
Beck Hole....67 J7
Beckingham, Lincs....44 B1
Beckingham, Notts....54 B4
Beckington....20 C7
Beckley, E. Susx....16 F3
Beckley, Oxon....21 K1
Beck Row....36 B2
Beck Side....57 F2
Beckton....23 K4
Beckwithshaw....59 H5
Becontree....23 K4
Bedale....59 H2
Bedburn....65 J4
Beddau....18 E4
Beddgelert....38 E2
Beddingham....15 H5
Beddington....23 J6
Bedfield....37 H3
Bedford....34 D5
Bedhampton....13 K5
Bedingfield....37 G3
Bedlington....75 J6
Bedlinog....18 E2
Bedmond....23 F2
Bednall....42 B5
Bedrule....74 C3
Bedstone....30 E2
Bedwas....19 F4
Bedworth....33 F1
Bedworth Heath....33 F1
Beeby....43 J6
Beech, Staffs....42 A3
Beech, Hants....13 J2
Beech Hill....22 B6
Beechingstoke....20 E7
Beedon....21 J5
Beeford....61 J5
Beeley....52 E7
Beelsby....55 G3
Beenham....21 K6
Beer....10 D7
Beer Crocombe....10 E3
Beer Hackett....11 G4
Beesands....5 J5
Beesby....55 J5
Beeson....5 J5
Beeston, Beds....34 E5
Beeston, Norf....46 E5
Beeston, Ches....50 E8
Beeston, Notts....43 H3
Beeston, W. Yks....59 H7
Beeston Regis....47 G2
Beeswing....72 D8
Beetham....57 H3
Beetley....46 E5
Begbroke....21 J1
Begelly....26 F6
Beguildy....30 C2
Beighton, S. Yks....53 G5
Beighton, Norf....47 J6
Beith....79 F6
Bekesbourne....25 J7
Belaugh....47 H5
Belbroughton....32 B2
Belchamp Otten....36 D5
Belchamp St Paul....36 C5
Belchamp Walter....36 D5
Belchford....55 G6
Belford....75 H1
Belhelvie....97 J4
Bellabeg....96 C4
Bellanoch....77 G2
Bell Busk....58 E5
Belleau....55 J6
Bellehiglash....95 K2
Bellerby....59 G1
Bellever....5 G2
Bellingdon....22 E2
Bellingham....74 E6
Belloch....77 F8
Bellochantuy....70 B1
Bellsbank....71 K4
Bellshill, Strath....80 C6
Bellshill, Northum....75 H1
Bellsmyre....79 G4
Bellspool....81 G8

Bellsquarry....81 F5
Bells Yew Green....16 D2
Belmesthorpe....44 D5
Belmont....51 F2
Belnacraig....96 C4
Belowda....3 H3
Belper....43 F2
Belsay....75 H7
Belses....74 B2
Belsford....5 H4
Belstead....37 G5
Belston....71 J2
Belstone....9 G6
Belthorn....51 G1
Beltinge....25 J6
Beltoft....54 C3
Belton, Humbs....54 B3
Belton, Lincs....44 C3
Belton, Leic....43 G4
Belton, Norf....47 K6
Belton-in-Rutland....44 B6
Belvedere....23 K5
Belvoir....44 B3
Bembridge....13 J7
Bemersyde....74 B1
Bempton....61 J3
Benacre....37 L1
Ben Casgro....107 J6
Benderloch....86 B5
Benenden....16 F2
Bengate....47 J4
Benholm....89 L2
Benington, Lincs....45 G2
Benington, Herts....35 G1
Benllech....48 E2
Benmore, Strath....78 D3
Benmore, Central....87 G6
Bennacott....8 C6
Bennan....70 E2
Bennecarrigan....70 E2
Benniworth....55 G5
Benover....16 E1
Benson....22 B3
Benthall....41 H6
Bentham....20 D1
Benthoul....97 H5
Bentley, Hants....14 A1
Bentley, H. & W....32 B3
Bentley, Warw....42 E7
Bentley, Suff....37 G6
Bentley, S. Yks....53 H3
Bentley, Humbs....61 H7
Bentley Heath....32 D2
Bentpath....73 J5
Bentworth....13 J1
Benwick....45 G7
Beoley....32 C3
Beoraidbeg....92 C6
Bepton....14 B4
Berden....35 H7
Berea....26 B4
Bere Alston....4 E3
Bere Ferrers....4 E3
Berepper....2 E7
Bere Regis....11 K6
Bergh Apton....47 J6
Berinsfield....21 K3
Berkeley....20 A3
Berkhamsted....22 E2
Berkley....11 K1
Berkswell....32 E2
Bermondsey....23 J5
Bernera....92 E3
Bernisdale....99 K7
Berrick Salome....22 B3
Berriedale....111 H6
Berrier....63 K5
Berriew....40 C6
Berrington, Shrops....41 G6
Berrington, Northum....83 J7
Berrow....19 G7
Berrow, H. & W....31 J6
Berrow Green....31 J4
Berry Hill....19 K1
Berryhillock....104 E2
Berrynarbor....9 F1
Berry Pomeroy....5 J3
Bersham....40 E2
Bersted....14 C5
Berwick....15 J5
Berwick Bassett....20 F5
Berwick Hill....75 H7
Berwick St James....12 C2
Berwick St John....12 B3
Berwick St Leonard....12 B2
Berwick-upon-Tweed....83 H6
Berwyn....40 C2
Besford....32 B5
Bessacarr....53 J3
Bessels Leigh....21 J2
Bessingham....47 G3
Besthorpe, Notts....54 C7
Besthorpe, Norf....46 F7
Beswick....61 H6
Betchworth....23 H7
Bethania, Dyfed....28 C3
Bethania, Gwyn....39 F1
Bethel....38 E4
Bethersden....17 G1
Bethesda, Dyfed....26 E5
Bethesda, Gwyn....49 F4
Bethlehem....28 D7
Bethnal Green....23 J4
Betley....41 J2
Betsham....24 C5
Betteshanger....25 K7
Bettiscombe....10 E6
Bettisfield....41 F3
Betton, Shrops....40 E6
Betton, Shrops....41 H3
Bettws, Gwent....19 G1
Bettws, Gwent....19 G3
Bettws Cedewain....40 C7

158 Bettws Gwerfil Goch Bradwell, Derby

Bettws Gwerfil Goch 40 B2
Bettws Newydd 19 H2
Bettyhill 110 D2
Betws, M. Glam 18 D4
Betws, Dyfed 27 L5
Betws Bledrws 27 K1
Betws Garmon 38 E1
Betws Ifan 27 H2
Betws-y-Coed 39 G1
Betws-yn-Rhos 49 J3
Beulah, Dyfed 27 G2
Beulah, Powys 29 G4
Bevendean 15 G5
Bevercotes 53 J6
Beverley 61 H7
Beverston 20 C3
Bevington 20 A3
Bewaldeth 63 H4
Bewcastle 74 B7
Bewdley 31 J2
Bewerley 59 G4
Bewholme 61 J5
Bexhill 16 E5
Bexley 23 K5
Bexleyheath 23 K5
Bexwell 46 B6
Beyton 36 E3
Bibury 20 F2
Bicester 33 H7
Bickenhall 10 D4
Bickenhill 32 D1
Bicker 45 F3
Bickerstaffe 50 D3
Bickerton, Ches 41 G1
Bickerton, N. Yks 59 K5
Bickington, Devon 9 F2
Bickington, Devon 5 H2
Bickleigh, Devon 4 F3
Bickleigh, Devon 9 K5
Bickleton 8 F2
Bickley 23 K6
Bickley Moss 41 G2
Bicknacre 24 D2
Bicknoller 10 C2
Bicknor 24 E7
Bickton 12 D4
Bicton, Shrops 30 D1
Bicton, Shrops 41 F5
Bidborough 16 C1
Biddenden 16 F2
Biddenham 34 D4
Biddestone 20 C5
Biddisham 19 H7
Biddlesden 33 J5
Biddlestone 75 F4
Biddulph 42 A1
Biddulph Moor 51 J8
Bideford 8 E3
Bidford-on-Avon 32 D4
Bielby 60 E6
Bieldside 97 H5
Bierley 7 K7
Bierton 22 D1
Bigbury 5 G5
Bigbury-on-Sea 5 G5
Bigby 54 E3
Biggar, Cumbr 56 E4
Biggar, Strath 81 F8
Biggin, N. Yks 60 C7
Biggin, Derby 52 D8
Biggin, Derby 42 E2
Biggings 114 D2
Biggin Hill 23 K7
Biggins 57 K3
Biggleswade 35 E5
Bighton 13 J2
Bignor 14 C4
Big Sand 100 D5
Bigton 115 F6
Bilberry 3 J3
Bilborough 43 H2
Bilbrook 42 A6
Bilbrough 60 C6
Bilbster 111 J3
Bildeston 36 E5
Billericay 24 C3
Billesdon 43 K6
Billesley 32 D4
Billing 34 B3
Billingborough 44 E3
Billinge 50 E3
Billingford, Norf 46 F4
Billingford, Suff 37 G2
Billingham 66 E5
Billinghay 44 E1
Billingley 53 G3
Billingshurst 14 D3
Billingsley 31 J1
Billington, Lancs 58 C7
Billington, Beds 34 C7
Billockby 47 K5
Billy Row 66 B4
Bilsborrow 57 J6
Bilsby 55 J6
Bilsington 17 H2
Bilsthorpe 53 J7
Bilston, W. Mids 42 B7
Bilston, Lothn 81 H5
Bilstone 43 F6
Bilting 17 H1
Bilton, N. Yks 60 B5
Bilton, Warw 33 G2
Bilton, Northum 75 J3
Bilton, Humbs 61 J7
Bimbister 112 D5
Binbrook 55 G4
Bincombe 11 H7
Binegar 11 H1
Binfield 22 D5
Binfield Heath 22 C5
Bingfield 75 F7
Bingham 43 K3
Bingley 59 G7
Binham 46 E3
Binley, W. Mids 33 F2
Binley, Hants 21 J7
Binley Woods 33 F2
Binniehill 80 D4
Binstead 13 H6
Binsted 14 A1
Binton 32 D4
Bintree 46 F4
Binweston 40 E6
Birch, Essex 25 F1
Birch, G. Man 51 H3
Bircham Newton 46 C3
Bircham Tofts 46 C3
Birchanger 35 J7
Bircher 31 F3
Birch Green 25 F1
Birchgrove 18 B3
Birchington 25 J6
Birchover 52 E7
Birch Vale 52 C5
Birchwood 54 D7
Bircotes 53 J4
Birdbrook 36 C5
Birdham 14 B5
Birdingbury 33 G3
Birdlip 20 D1
Birdsall 60 F4
Birdsgreen 31 J1
Birdston 79 J4
Birdwell 53 F3
Birdwood 20 B1
Birgham 83 F8
Birkdale 50 C2
Birkenhead 50 C5
Birkenhills 105 G4
Birkenshaw, Strath 80 B5
Birkenshaw, W. Yks 59 H8
Birkhall 96 C6
Birkhill 89 F5
Birkin 53 H1
Birley 31 F4
Birling, Kent 24 C6
Birling, Northum 75 J4
Birlingham 32 B5
Birmingham 32 C1
Birnam 88 C4
Birness 97 J2
Birse 96 E6
Birsemore 96 E6
Birstall 43 H6
Birstall Smithies 52 E1
Birstwith 59 H5
Birtley, T. & W 66 C2
Birtley, H. & W 30 E3
Birtley, Northum 74 E7
Birts Street 31 J6
Bisbrooke 44 B7
Bishampton 32 B4
Bishop Auckland 66 C5
Bishopbriggs 79 J4
Bishop Burton 61 G7
Bishop Middleham 66 D4
Bishop Monkton 59 J4
Bishop Norton 54 D4
Bishopsbourne 25 H7
Bishops Cannings 20 E6
Bishop's Castle 30 E1
Bishop's Caundle 11 H4
Bishop's Cleeve 32 B7
Bishop's Frome 31 H5
Bishop's Itchington 33 F4
Bishops Lydeard 10 C3
Bishop's Nympton 9 H3
Bishop's Offley 41 J4
Bishop's Stortford 35 H7
Bishop's Sutton 13 J2
Bishop's Tachbrook 33 F3
Bishop's Tawton 9 F2
Bishopsteignton 5 K2
Bishopstoke 13 G4
Bishopston 27 K8
Bishopstone, Wilts 12 C3
Bishopstone, Bucks 22 D1
Bishopstone, H. & W 31 F5
Bishopstone, Wilts 21 G4
Bishopstone, E. Susx 15 H5
Bishop Sutton 19 K7
Bishop's Waltham 13 H4
Bishopswood, Somer 10 D4
Bishop's Wood, Staffs 41 K6
Bishopsworth 19 K6
Bishop Thornton 59 H4
Bishopthorpe 60 C6
Bishopton, Durham 66 D5
Bishopton, Strath 79 G4
Bishop Wilton 60 E5
Bishton 19 H4
Bisley, Glos 20 D2
Bisley, Surrey 22 E7
Bispham 57 G6
Bissoe 2 F5
Bisterne Close 12 E5
Bitchfield 44 C4
Bittadon 9 F1
Bittaford 5 G4
Bittering 46 E5
Bitterley 31 G2
Bitterne 13 G4
Bitteswell 33 H1
Bitton 20 A6
Bix 22 C4
Bixter 115 F3
Blaby 43 H7
Blackacre 73 F5
Blackadder 83 G6
Blackawton 5 J4
Blackborough 10 B5
Blackborough End 46 B5
Black Bourton 21 G2
Blackboys 15 J3
Blackbrook 41 J3
Blackburn, Lancs 58 B8
Blackburn, Lothn 80 E5
Blackburn, Grampn 97 H4
Black Callerton 75 H8
Black Clauchrie 71 H6
Black Crofts 86 B5
Blackden Heath 51 G6
Blackdog, Grampn 97 J4
Black Dog, Devon 9 J5
Blackfield 13 G5
Blackford, Tays 88 A8
Blackford, Somer 11 F1
Blackford, Somer 11 H3
Blackford, Cumbr 63 J1
Blackfordby 43 F5
Blackgang 7 J7
Blackhall 97 F6
Blackhall Rocks 66 E4
Blackham 15 J2
Blackhaugh 82 C8
Blackheath, W. Mids 32 B1
Blackheath, Essex 36 F7
Blackhill 105 K3
Blackland 20 E6
Blackley 51 H3
Blacklunans 88 D2
Black Marsh 40 E7
Blackmill 18 D4
Blackmoor 14 A2
Blackmore 24 C2
Blackmore End 36 C6
Black Mount 86 E4
Blackness 81 F4
Blacknest 14 A1
Black Notley 36 C7
Blacko 58 D6
Black Pill 27 L7
Blackpool 57 G7
Blackpool Gate 74 B7
Blackridge 80 D5
Blackrock, Strath 76 C5
Blackrock, Gwent 19 G1
Black Rocks 61 H2
Blackrod 50 F2
Blackshaw 62 F1
Blackstone 15 F4
Blackthorn 22 B1
Blackthorpe 36 E3
Blacktoft 54 C1
Blacktop 97 H5
Black Torrington 8 E5
Blackwater, Hants 22 D6
Blackwater, Corn 2 F5
Blackwater, I. of W 13 H7
Blackwaterfoot 70 D2
Blackwell, H. & W 32 B2
Blackwell, Derby 52 D6
Blackwood, Strath 80 C7
Blackwood, Gwent 19 F3
Blackwood Hill 42 B1
Blacon 50 C7
Bladerstone 57 K7
Bladnoch 68 F5
Bladon 21 J1
Blaenannerch 27 G2
Blaenau Ffestiniog 39 G2
Blaenavon 19 G2
Blaendyryn 29 G6
Blaenffos 27 F3
Blaengarw 18 D3
Blaengwrach 18 C2
Blaengwynfi 18 C3
Blaenpennal 28 D3
Blaenplwyf 28 C2
Blaenporth 27 G2
Blaenrhondda 18 D3
Blaenwaun 27 G4
Blagdon, Devon 5 J3
Blagdon, Avon 19 K7
Blagdon Hill 10 D4
Blaich 93 G8
Blaina 19 G2
Blair Atholl 88 A2
Blairdaff 97 F4
Blairgowrie 88 D4
Blairhall 80 F3
Blairingone 80 E2
Blairlogie 80 D2
Blairmore 78 D3
Blairskaith 79 H4
Blaisdon 20 B1
Blakebrook 31 K2
Blakedown 32 A2
Blakelaw 74 D1
Blakemere 30 E5
Blakeney, Glos 20 A2
Blakeney, Norf 46 F2
Blakenhall, W. Mids 42 B7
Blakenhall, Ches 41 J2
Blakeshall 31 K1
Blakesley 33 J4
Blanchland 65 G2
Blandford Camp 12 B5
Blandford Forum 12 A5
Blandford St Mary 12 A5
Bland Hill 59 H5
Blanefield 79 H4
Blankney 54 E7
Blantyre 80 B6
Blarmachfoldach 86 C2
Blarnalearoch 101 H3
Blashford 12 D5
Blaston 44 B7
Blatherwycke 44 C7
Blawith 57 F2
Blaxhall 37 J4
Blaxton 53 J3
Blaydon 66 B1
Bleadon 19 H7
Blean 25 H6
Bleasby 43 K2
Bleatarn 64 E6
Blebocraigs 89 G7
Bleddfa 30 D3
Bledington 32 E7
Bledlow 22 C2
Bledlow Ridge 22 C3
Blegbie 82 C5
Blencarn 64 D4
Blencogo 63 G3
Blencow 64 B4
Blendworth 13 K4
Blennerhasset 63 G3
Bletchingdon 21 K1
Bletchingley 23 J7
Bletchley, Bucks 34 B6
Bletchley, Shrops 41 H3
Bletherston 26 E4
Bletsoe 34 D4
Blewbury 21 K4
Blickling 47 G4
Blidworth 43 H1
Blindcrake 63 G4
Blindley Heath 15 G1
Blisland 3 K2
Blissford 12 D4
Bliss Gate 31 J2
Blisworth 33 K4
Blockley 32 D6
Blofield 47 J6
Blo' Norton 36 F2
Blore 42 D2
Bloxham 33 G6
Bloxholm 44 D1
Bloxwich 42 C6
Bloxworth 12 A6
Blubberhouses 59 G5
Blue Anchor 10 B1
Blue Bell Hill 24 D6
Blundellsands 50 C4
Blundeston 47 L7
Blunham 34 E4
Blunsdon St Andrew 21 F4
Bluntisham 35 G2
Blyborough 54 D4
Blyford 37 K2
Blymhill 41 K5
Blyth, Notts 53 J5
Blyth, Northum 75 K6
Blyth Bridge 81 G7
Blythburgh 37 K2
Blythe 82 D7
Blythe Bridge 42 B2
Blyton 54 C4
Boarhills 89 H7
Boarhunt 13 J5
Boarshead 15 J2
Boarstall 22 B1
Boasley Cross 8 F6
Boath 102 D5
Boat of Garten 95 H4
Bobbing 24 E6
Bobbington 41 K7
Bocaddon 4 B4
Bockhampton 11 J6
Bocking 36 C7
Bocking Churchstreet 36 C7
Boddam, Shetld 115 F7
Boddam, Grampn 105 L4
Boddington 32 A7
Bodedern 48 C2
Bodelwyddan 49 K3
Bodenham, Wilts 12 D3
Bodenham, H. & W 31 G4
Bodewryd 48 D1
Bodfari 49 K3
Bodffordd 48 D3
Bodham 47 G2
Bodiam 16 E3
Bodicote 33 G6
Bodieve 3 H2
Bodle Street Green 16 D4
Bodmin 3 J3
Bodney 46 D7
Boduan 38 C3
Bogallan 102 E7
Bogbrae 97 K2
Bogend 71 J1
Boghall 80 E5
Bogmoor 104 C2
Bogniebrae 104 E4
Bognor Regis 14 C6
Bograxie 97 G4
Bog, The 40 E7
Bogton 104 F3
Bohenie 93 J7
Bohortha 3 G6
Bohuntine 93 J7
Boisdale 90 C4
Bojewyan 2 B6
Bolam 66 B5
Bold Heath 50 E5
Boldon 66 D1
Boldre 13 F6
Boldron 65 H6
Bole 54 C5
Bolehill 42 E1
Boleside 74 A1
Bolham 9 K4
Bolham Water 10 C4
Bolingey 2 F4
Bollington, Ches 51 G5
Bollington, Ches 51 J6
Bolney 15 F3
Bolnhurst 34 D4
Bolsover 53 G6
Bolsterstone 52 E4
Bolstone 31 G6
Boltby 60 B2
Bolton, Lothn 82 D4
Bolton, Cumbr 64 D5
Bolton, Humbs 60 E5
Bolton, G. Man 51 G3
Bolton, Northum 75 H3
Bolton Abbey 59 F5
Bolton-by-Bowland 58 C6
Boltonfellend 74 A8
Boltongate 63 H3
Bolton-le-Sands 57 H4
Bolton-on-Swale 66 C8
Bolton Percy 60 C6
Bolton upon Dearne 53 G3
Bolventor 4 B2
Bomere Heath 41 F5
Bonar Bridge 102 E3
Bonawe 86 C5
Bonby 54 E2
Boncath 27 G3
Bonchester Bridge 74 B3
Bondleigh 9 G5
Bonehill 42 D6
Bo'Ness 80 E3
Bonhill 79 F4
Boningale 41 K6
Bonjedward 74 C2
Bonkle 80 D6
Bonnington, Northnts 81 G5
Bonnington, Kent 17 H2
Bonnybridge 80 D3
Bonnykelly 105 H3
Bonnyrigg and Lasswade 81 J5
Bonnyton 89 J3
Bonsall 52 E8
Bont 19 H1
Bontddu 39 F5
Bont Dolgadfan 39 H6
Bont-goch or Elerch 28 D1
Bontnewydd, Gwyn 48 D4
Bont-newydd, Clwyd 49 K3
Bontuchel 40 B1
Bonvilston 18 E5
Booker 22 D3
Booley 41 G4
Boosbeck 67 G6
Boot 63 G7
Boothby Graffoe 54 D8
Boothby Pagnell 44 C3
Boothstown 51 G3
Booth Wood Reservoir 56 E2
Bootle, Mers 50 C4
Bootle, Cumbr 56 E2
Boraston 31 H2
Borden 24 E6
Bordley 58 E4
Bordon Camp 14 A2
Boreham, Wilts 12 A1
Boreham, Essex 24 D2
Boreham Street 16 D4
Borehamwood 23 G3
Boreland 73 G5
Borgie 109 H3
Borgue, D. & G 69 H6
Borgue, Highld 111 H6
Borley 36 D5
Bornesketaig 99 J5
Borness 69 H6
Boroughbridge 59 J4
Borough Green 24 C7
Borras Head 40 E1
Borreraig 99 G7
Borrowash 43 G3
Borrowby 59 K2
Borth 38 F7
Borthwickbrae 73 K3
Borthwickshiels 73 K3
Borth-y-Gest 38 E3
Borve, W. Isles 90 B5
Borve, W. Isles 98 E4
Borve, W. Isles 98 F3
Borve, Highld 99 K8
Borwick 57 J3
Bosavern 2 B6
Bosbury 31 H5
Boscastle 8 A6
Boscombe, Dorset 12 D6
Boscombe, Wilts 12 E2
Bosham 14 B5
Bosherston 26 D7
Boskednan 2 C6
Bosley 51 J7
Bossall 60 E4
Bossiney 8 A7
Bossingham 17 J1
Bosta 107 F4
Bostock Green 51 F7
Boston 45 G2
Boston Spa 59 K6
Boswinger 3 H5
Botallack 2 B6
Botany Bay 23 H3
Botcheston 43 G6
Botesdale 36 F2
Bothal 75 J6
Bothamsall 53 J6
Bothel 63 G4
Bothenhampton 11 F6
Bothwell 80 C6
Botley, Bucks 22 E2
Botley, Hants 13 H4
Botley, Oxon 21 J2
Botolphs 15 E5
Bottacks 102 C6
Bottesford, Leic 44 B3
Bottesford, Humbs 54 C3
Bottisham 35 J3
Bottomcraig 89 F6
Botusfleming 4 E3
Botwnnog 38 B3
Boughrood 30 C6
Boughspring 19 K3
Boughton, Northnts 34 A3
Boughton, Norf 46 B6
Boughton, Notts 53 J7
Boughton Aluph 17 H1
Boughton Lees 17 H1
Boughton Malherbe 17 F1
Boughton Monchelsea 24 D7
Boughton Street 25 G7
Boulby 67 H6
Bouldon 31 G1
Boulmer 75 J3
Boulston 26 D5
Boultham 54 D7
Bourn 35 G4
Bourne 44 D4
Bourne End, Beds 34 C5
Bourne End, Bucks 22 D4
Bourne End, Herts 22 F2
Bournemouth 12 C6
Bournes Green 20 D2
Bourneville 32 C1
Bournheath 32 B2
Bournmoor 66 D2
Bourton, Oxon 21 G4
Bourton, Shrops 41 G7
Bourton, Avon 19 H6
Bourton, Dorset 11 J2
Bourton on Dunsmore 33 G2
Bourton-on-the-Hill 32 D6
Bourton-on-the-Water 32 D7
Boveney 22 E5
Boverton 18 D6
Bovey Tracey 5 J2
Bovingdon 22 F2
Bovington Camp 11 K7
Bow, Devon 9 H5
Bow, G. Lon 23 J4
Bowbank 65 G5
Bow Brickhill 34 C6
Bowburn 66 D4
Bowcombe 13 G7
Bowd 10 C6
Bowden, Border 74 B1
Bowden, Devon 5 J5
Bowden Hill 20 D6
Bowderdale 64 D7
Bowdon 51 G5
Bowerchalke 12 C3
Bowermadden 111 J2
Bowers Gifford 24 D4
Bowershall 81 F2
Bowertower 111 J2
Bowes 65 G6
Bowhill 73 K2
Bowland 82 C7
Bowland Bridge 57 H2
Bowley 31 G4
Bowlhead Green 14 C2
Bowling 79 G4
Bowling Bank 40 E2
Bowling Green 31 K4
Bowmanstead 57 G1
Bowmore 76 C6
Bowness-on-Solway 63 H1
Bowness-on-Windermere 57 H1
Bowsden 83 H7
Bow Street 28 D1
Bowthorpe 47 G6
Box, Glos 20 C2
Box, Wilts 20 C6
Boxbush 20 B1
Boxford, Suff 36 E5
Boxford, Berks 21 J5
Boxgrove 14 C5
Boxley 24 D7
Boxted, Suff 36 D4
Boxted, Essex 36 E6
Boxworth 35 G3
Boylestone 42 D3
Boyndie 104 F2
Boyndlie 105 J2
Boynton 61 J4
Boyton, Wilts 12 B2
Boyton, Corn 8 D6
Boyton, Suff 37 J5
Bozeat 34 C4
Braaid 56 Q4
Brabling Green 37 H3
Brabourne 17 J1
Brabourne Lees 17 H1
Brabster 111 K2
Bracadale 91 J2
Braceborough 44 D5
Bracebridge Heath 54 D7
Braceby 44 D3
Bracewell 58 D6
Brackenfield 53 F8
Brackletter 93 H7
Brackley, Strath 77 G7
Brackley, Northnts 33 H6
Bracknell 22 D6
Braco 87 L8
Bracobrae 104 E3
Bracon Ash 47 G7
Bracora 92 D6
Bracorina 92 D6
Bradbourne 42 E1
Bradbury 66 D5
Bradda 56 N4
Bradden 33 J5
Braddock 3 K3
Bradenham, Bucks 22 D3
Bradenham, Norf 46 E6
Bradenstoke 20 E5
Bradfield, Essex 37 G6
Bradfield, Norf 47 H3
Bradfield, Berks 21 L5
Bradfield Combust 36 D4
Bradfield Green 51 F8
Bradfield St Clare 36 E4
Bradfield St George 36 E3
Bradford, Devon 8 E5
Bradford, W. Yks 59 G7
Bradford, Northum 75 H1
Bradford Abbas 11 G4
Bradford Leigh 20 C6
Bradford-on-Avon 20 C6
Bradford-on-Tone 10 C3
Bradford Peverell 11 H6
Brading 14 B7
Bradley, Staffs 42 A5
Bradley, Derby 42 E2
Bradley, Humbs 55 G3
Bradley, Hants 13 J1
Bradley Green 32 B3
Bradley in the Moors 42 C2
Bradmore 43 H3
Bradninch 10 A5
Bradnop 42 C1
Bradpole 11 F6
Bradshaw 51 G2
Bradstone 4 D1
Bradwall Green 51 G7
Bradwell, Bucks 34 B6
Bradwell, Derby 52 D5

Bradwell, Essex............36 D7
Bradwell, Norf.............47 L6
Bradwell Grove............21 G2
Bradwell-on-Sea...........25 G2
Bradwell Waterside........25 F2
Bradworthy.................8 D4
Brae, Shetld............115 F2
Brae, Highld............100 E4
Brae, Highld............102 E6
Braeantra...............102 D5
Braefield................94 C2
Braehead, Orkney........112 E2
Braehead, Strath.........72 D1
Braehead, Strath.........80 E6
Braehead, D. & G.........68 F5
Braehead, Tays...........89 J3
Braehoulland............116 D5
Braemar..................95 K6
Braemore................111 G5
Brae of Achnahaird......108 B7
Brae Roy Lodge...........94 B6
Braeside.................78 E4
Braes, The...............92 B2
Braeswick...............113 G3
Brafferton, Durham.......66 C5
Brafferton, N. Yks.......59 K3
Brafield-on-the-Green....34 B4
Bragar..................107 G4
Bragbury End.............35 F7
Braides..................57 H5
Braidley.................58 F2
Braidwood................80 D7
Brailes..................33 H6
Brailsford...............42 E2
Braintree................36 C7
Braiseworth..............37 G2
Braishfield..............13 F3
Braithwaite..............63 H5
Braithwell...............53 H4
Bramber..................15 E4
Bramcote.................43 H3
Bramdean.................13 J3
Bramerton................47 H6
Bramfield, Herts.........23 H1
Bramfield, Suff..........37 K2
Bramford.................37 G5
Bramhall.................51 H5
Bramham..................59 K6
Bramhope.................59 H6
Bramley, Hants...........22 B7
Bramley, Surrey..........14 D1
Bramley, S. Yks..........53 G4
Brampford Speke...........9 K6
Brampton, Cumbr..........64 C1
Brampton, Lincs..........54 C6
Brampton, Cumbr..........64 D5
Brampton, Cambs..........35 F2
Brampton, S. Yks.........53 G3
Brampton, Norf...........47 H4
Brampton, Suff...........37 K1
Brampton Abbots..........31 H7
Brampton Ash............34 A1
Brampton Bryan...........30 E2
Bramshall................42 C3
Bramshaw.................12 E4
Bramshott................14 B2
Brancaster...............46 C2
Brancepeth...............66 C4
Branchill...............103 J7
Branderburgh............104 B1
Brandesburton............61 J6
Brandeston...............37 H3
Brandiston...............47 G4
Brandon, Suff............36 C1
Brandon, Lincs...........44 C2
Brandon, Durham..........66 C4
Brandon, Warw............33 G2
Brandon, Northum.........75 G3
Brandon Bank.............35 K1
Brandon Creek............45 K7
Brandon Parva............46 F6
Brandsby.................60 C3
Brane.....................2 C7
Bran End.................36 B7
Branksome................12 C6
Branksome Park...........12 C6
Branscombe...............10 C7
Bransford................31 J4
Bransgore................12 D6
Branston, Leic...........44 B4
Branston, Staffs.........42 E4
Branston, Lincs..........54 E7
Branstone................13 J7
Brant Broughton.........44 C1
Brantham.................36 E6
Branthwaite..............62 F5
Branthwaite..............63 H4
Brantingham..............61 G8
Branton, Northum.........75 G3
Branton, S. Yks..........53 J3
Branxholme...............73 K3
Branxholm Park...........73 K3
Branxton.................83 G8
Brassington..............42 E1
Brasted..................23 K7
Brasted Chart............23 K7
Brathens.................97 F6
Bratoft..................55 J7
Brattleby................54 D5
Bratton..................20 D7
Bratton Clovelly..........8 E6
Bratton Fleming...........9 G2
Bratton Seymour..........11 H3
Braughing................35 G7
Braunston................33 H3
Braunstone...............43 H6
Braunston-in-Rutland.....44 B4
Braunton..................8 E2
Brawby...................60 E3
Brawl...................110 E2
Brawlbin...............111 G3
Bray.....................22 E5
Braybrooke...............34 A1
Brayford..................9 G2
Bray Shop.................4 D2

Braystones...............62 F7
Brayton..................60 D7
Brazacott.................8 C6
Breachwood Green.........34 E7
Breaclete...............107 F5
Breadsall................43 H7
Breadstone...............20 B2
Breage....................2 E7
Breakachy...............102 C8
Breakish.................92 C3
Bream....................19 L2
Breamore.................12 D4
Brean....................19 G7
Brearton.................59 J4
Breasclete..............107 G5
Breaston.................43 G3
Brechfa..................27 K3
Brechin..................89 H2
Breckles.................46 E7
Breckrey................100 B6
Bredbury.................51 J4
Brede....................16 F4
Bredenbury...............31 H4
Bredfield................37 H4
Bredgar..................24 E6
Bredhurst................24 D6
Bredon...................32 B6
Bredon's Norton..........32 B6
Bredwardine..............30 E5
Breedon on the Hill......43 G4
Breich...................80 D6
Breighton................60 E7
Bremhill.................20 D5
Brenchley................16 D1
Brendon...................9 H1
Brenish.................106 D6
Brent Eleigh.............36 E5
Brentford................23 G5
Brent Knoll..............19 H7
Brent Pelham.............35 H6
Brentwood................24 B3
Brenzett.................17 H3
Brereton.................42 C5
Brereton Green...........51 G7
Brereton Heath...........51 H7
Bressingham..............37 F1
Bretby...................42 E4
Bretford.................33 G2
Bretforton...............32 C5
Bretherdale Head.........64 C7
Bretherton...............50 D1
Brettabister............115 G3
Brettenham, Norf.........36 E1
Brettenham, Suff.........36 E4
Bretton..................50 C7
Brevig...................90 B6
Brewham..................11 J2
Brewlands Bridge.........88 D2
Brewood..................42 A6
Briantspuddle............11 K6
Brickendon...............23 J2
Bricket Wood.............23 G2
Bricklehampton...........32 B5
Bride....................56 R1
Bridekirk................63 G4
Bridell..................26 F2
Bridestowe...............8 F7
Brideswell...............96 E2
Bridford..................9 J7
Bridge...................25 H7
Bridge End...............44 E3
Bridgefoot, Tays.........89 F5
Bridgefoot, Cumbr........62 F5
Bridge Green.............35 H6
Bridgemary...............13 H5
Bridgend, Strath.........80 B4
Bridgend, Grampn.........96 C2
Bridgend, Strath.........76 C5
Bridgend, M. Glam........18 D4
Bridgend, Grampn.........96 E2
Bridgend, Lothn..........81 F4
Bridgend, Fife...........89 F7
Bridgend, Strath.........77 G8
Bridgend, Strath.........77 H2
Bridgend, Tays...........89 H2
Bridgend, Cumbr..........63 J6
Bridgend of Lintrathen...88 E3
Bridge of Alford.........96 E4
Bridge of Allan..........80 C2
Bridge of Avon...........95 K2
Bridge of Brown..........95 K3
Bridge of Cally..........88 D3
Bridge of Canny..........97 F6
Bridge of Dee............69 J4
Bridge of Don............97 J4
Bridge of Dun............89 J3
Bridge of Dye............97 F7
Bridge of Earn...........88 D7
Bridge of Feugh..........97 G6
Bridge of Forss.........111 G2
Bridge of Gairn..........96 C6
Bridge of Muchalls.......97 H6
Bridge of Orchy..........86 E5
Bridge of Walls.........114 E3
Bridge of Weir...........79 F5
Bridgerule................8 C5
Bridges..................40 E7
Bridge Sollers...........31 F5
Bridge Street............36 D5
Bridgetown................9 K2
Bridge Trafford..........50 D6
Bridge Yate..............20 A5
Bridgham.................36 E1
Bridgnorth...............41 J7
Bridgtown................42 B6
Bridgwater...............10 E2
Bridlington..............61 J4
Bridport.................11 F6
Bridstow.................31 G7
Brierfield...............58 D7
Brierley, H. & W.........31 F4
Brierley, S. Yks.........53 G2
Brierley, Glos...........19 L1
Brierley Hill............32 B1

Brigg....................54 E3
Brigham, Cumbr...........63 F4
Brigham, Humbs...........61 H5
Brighouse................52 D1
Brighstone...............13 G7
Brightgate...............52 E8
Brighthampton............21 H2
Brightling...............16 D3
Brightlingsea............25 G1
Brighton, E. Susx........15 G5
Brighton, Corn............3 H4
Brightons................80 E4
Brightwalton.............21 J5
Brightwell...............37 H5
Brightwell Baldwin.......22 B3
Brightwell-cum-Sotwell...21 K3
Brignall.................65 H6
Brig o' Turk.............87 H8
Brigsley.................55 G3
Brigsteer................57 H2
Brigstock................34 C1
Brill....................22 B1
Brilley..................30 D5
Brimfield................31 G3
Brimington...............53 G6
Brimpsfield..............20 D1
Brimpton.................21 K6
Brims...................112 C8
Brinacory................92 D6
Brington.................34 D2
Brinian.................112 E4
Briningham...............46 F3
Brinkhill................55 H6
Brinkley.................35 K4
Brinklow.................33 G2
Brinkworth...............20 E4
Brinscall................51 F1
Brinsley.................43 G2
Brinsop..................31 F5
Brinsworth...............53 G4
Brinton..................46 F3
Brisley..................46 E4
Brislington..............19 L5
Bristol..................19 K5
Briston..................46 F3
Britannia................51 H1
Britford.................12 D3
Brithdir.................39 G5
Briton Ferry.............18 B3
Britwell Salome..........22 B3
Brixham...................5 K4
Brixton, Devon............4 F4
Brixton, G. Lon..........23 J5
Brixton Deverill.........12 A2
Brixworth................34 A2
Brize Norton.............21 H2
Broad Blunsdon...........21 F3
Broadbottom..............51 J4
Broadbridge..............14 B5
Broadbridge Heath........14 D3
Broad Campden............32 D6
Broad Chalke.............12 C3
Broadclyst...............10 A6
Broadford................92 C3
Broad Green..............31 J4
Broad Haven..............26 C5
Broadheath, G. Man.......51 G5
Broad Heath, H. & W......31 H3
Broadheath, H. & W.......31 K4
Broadhembury.............10 C5
Broadhempston.............5 J3
Broad Hill...............35 J2
Broad Hinton.............20 F5
Broad Laying.............21 J6
Broadley, Grampn........104 C2
Broadley, Lancs..........51 H2
Broadley Common..........23 K2
Broad Marston............32 D5
Broadmayne...............11 J7
Broadmeadows.............73 K1
Broadmere................13 J1
Broad Oak, E. Susx.......16 D3
Broad Oak, E. Susx.......16 F3
Broadoak, Dorset.........11 F6
Broad Oak, H. & W........31 F7
Broad Oak, Kent..........25 H6
Broad Oak, Dorset........11 J4
Broadstairs..............25 K6
Broadstone, Dorset.......12 C6
Broadstone, Shrops.......41 G8
Broad Street.............24 E7
Broad Town...............20 E5
Broadwas.................31 J4
Broadwater...............14 E5
Broadway, H. & W.........32 D6
Broadway, Somer..........10 E4
Broadwell, Glos..........32 E7
Broadwell, Oxon..........21 G2
Broadwell, Warw..........33 G3
Broadwell, Glos..........19 K1
Broadwey.................11 H7
Broadwindsor.............11 F5
Broadwoodkelly...........9 G5
Broadwoodwidger..........8 E7
Brobury..................30 E5
Brochel.................100 B8
Brockbridge..............13 J4
Brockdish................37 H2
Brockenhurst.............12 E5
Brocketsbrae.............80 D8
Brockford Street.........37 G3
Brockhall................33 J3
Brockham.................15 E1
Brockhampton, Glos.......32 C7
Brockhampton, H. & W.....31 G6
Brockholes...............52 D2
Brocklesby...............55 F2
Brockley.................19 J6

Brockley Green...........36 D4
Brockton, Shrops.........30 E1
Brockton, Shrops.........40 E6
Brockton, Shrops.........41 G7
Brockton, Shrops.........41 J6
Brockweir................19 K2
Brockwood Park...........13 J3
Brockworth...............20 C1
Brocton..................42 B5
Brodick..................78 C8
Brodsworth...............53 H3
Brogborough..............34 C6
Brokenborough............20 D4
Broken Cross, Ches.......51 F6
Broken Cross, Ches.......51 H6
Bromborough.............50 C5
Bromcote.................33 G1
Brome....................37 G2
Brome Street.............37 G2
Bromeswell...............37 J4
Bromfield, Shrops........31 F2
Bromfield, Cumbr.........63 G3
Bromham, Beds............34 D4
Bromham, Wilts...........20 D6
Bromley..................23 K6
Bromley Green............17 H2
Brompton, Kent...........24 D6
Brompton, N. Yks.........61 G2
Brompton, N. Yks.........59 J1
Brompton-on-Swale........66 C8
Brompton Ralph...........10 B2
Brompton Regis............9 K2
Bromsash.................31 H7
Bromsgrove...............32 B2
Bromyard.................31 H4
Bromyard Downs...........31 H4
Bronaber.................39 G3
Brongton.................41 F3
Bronllys.................30 C6
Bronnant.................28 D3
Bronwydd Arms............27 J4
Brongarth................40 D3
Bronygarth...............40 D3
Bronwydd Arms............27 J4
Bronygarth...............40 D3
Brook, Surrey............14 C2
Brook, Hants.............12 E4
Brook, Hants.............13 F3
Brook, I. of W...........13 F7
Brook, Kent..............17 H1
Brooke, Leic.............44 B6
Brooke, Norf.............47 H7
Brookfield...............79 G5
Brookhouse...............57 J4
Brookhouse Green.........51 H7
Brookland................17 G3
Brookmans Park...........23 H2
Brooks...................40 C7
Brook Street.............24 B3
Brookthorpe..............20 C1
Brookwood................22 E7
Broom, Warw..............32 C4
Broom, Beds..............34 E5
Broome, H. & W...........32 B2
Broome, Shrops...........30 F1
Broome, Norf.............47 J7
Broomedge................51 G5
Broome Park..............75 H3
Broomer's Corner.........14 E3
Broomfield, Essex........24 D1
Broomfield, Somer........10 D2
Broomfield, Kent.........24 E7
Broomfield, Kent.........25 H6
Broomfield, Grampn.......97 J2
Broomfleet...............54 C1
Broom Hill, Dorset.......12 C5
Broomhill, Northum.......75 J4
Brora...................103 H2
Broseley.................41 H6
Brotherton...............53 G1
Brotton..................67 G6
Broubster...............111 G2
Brough, Notts............54 C8
Brough, Humbs............54 D1
Brough, Shetld..........117 F5
Brough, Shetld..........117 G5
Brough, Shetld..........115 H2
Brough, Derby............52 D5
Brough, Cumbr............64 E6
Brough, Highld..........111 J1
Broughall................41 G2
Brough Sowerby...........64 E6
Broughton, Northnts......34 B2
Broughton, Bucks.........34 B5
Broughton, Orkney.......112 E2
Broughton, Clwyd.........50 C7
Broughton, Humbs.........54 D3
Broughton, M. Glam.......18 D5
Broughton, N. Yks........60 E5
Broughton, N. Yks........58 E5
Broughton, Cambs.........35 F2
Broughton, Hants.........13 F2
Broughton, Cumbr.........62 F4
Broughton, Oxon..........33 G6
Broughton, Border........81 G8
Broughton, G. Man........51 H3
Broughton, Lancs.........57 J7
Broughton Astley.........43 H7
Broughton Beck...........57 F2
Broughton Gifford........20 C6
Broughton Hackett........32 B4
Broughton in Furness.....56 F2
Broughton Mills..........57 F1
Broughton Moor...........62 F4
Broughton Poggs..........21 G2
Broughtown.............113 G2
Broughty Ferry...........89 G5
Browland................114 E3
Brown Candover...........13 H2
Brown Edge...............42 B1
Brownhill, Lancs.........58 B7
Brownhill, Grampn........97 H1
Brownhills...............42 C6
Brownieside..............75 H2
Brownlow Heath...........51 H7
Brownston.................5 G4
Brow Top.................57 J5

Broxbourne...............23 J2
Broxburn, Lothn..........82 E4
Broxburn, Lothn..........81 F4
Broxted..................35 J7
Broxwood.................30 E4
Bruan...................111 K5
Bruar...................107 H4
Bruera...................50 D7
Bruern Abbey.............32 E7
Bruernish................90 C5
Bruichladdich............76 B5
Bruisyard................37 J3
Brumby...................54 C2
Brund....................52 D7
Brundall.................47 J6
Brundish.................37 H3
Brundish Street..........37 H2
Bruntingthorpe...........43 J7
Brunton, Fife............88 F6
Brunton, Northum.........75 J2
Brushford, Devon..........9 G5
Brushford, Somer..........9 K3
Bruton...................11 H2
Bryanston................12 A5
Brydekirk................73 G7
Brymbo...................40 D1
Bryn, W. Glam............18 C3
Bryn, Shrops.............30 D1
Bryn, N. Yks.............59 J1
Bryn, G. Man.............50 E3
Bryn-coch................18 B3
Bryncroes................38 B3
Bryncrug.................38 F6
Bryneglwys...............40 C2
Brynford.................50 A6
Bryn Gates...............50 E3
Bryngwran................48 C3
Bryngwyn, Powys..........30 C5
Bryngwyn, Gwent..........19 H2
Bryn-henllan.............26 E3
Brynhoffnant.............27 H1
Brynithel................19 G2
Brynmawr.................19 F1
Brynmenyn................18 D4
Brynna...................18 D4
Brynrefail...............48 D2
Brynsadler...............18 E4
Brynsiencyn..............48 D4
Brynteg, Gwyn............48 D2
Brynteg, Clwyd...........40 E1
Bryn, The................19 H2
Bryn-y-maen..............49 H3
Bualintur................91 K3
Bualnaluib..............100 E3
Bubbenhall...............33 F2
Bubwith..................60 E7
Buccleuch................73 J3
Buchanhaven..............97 K3
Buchanty.................79 H2
Buckabank................63 J3
Buckden, Cambs...........35 E3
Buckden, N. Yks..........58 E3
Buckenham................47 J6
Buckerell................10 C5
Buckfast..................5 H3
Buckfastleigh............5 H3
Buckhaven................81 J2
Buckholm.................81 K3
Buckholt.................31 J3
Buckhorn Weston..........11 J3
Buckhurst Hill...........23 K3
Buckie..................104 D2
Buckies.................111 H2
Buckingham...............33 J6
Buckland, Glos...........32 C6
Buckland, Devon...........5 G5
Buckland, Herts..........35 G6
Buckland, Oxon...........21 H3
Buckland, Surrey.........23 H7
Buckland, Kent...........17 L1
Buckland Brewer...........8 E3
Buckland Common..........22 E2
Buckland Dinham..........20 B7
Buckland Filleigh.........8 E5
Buckland in the Moor......5 H2
Buckland Monachorum......4 E3
Buckland Newton..........11 H5
Buckland St Mary.........10 D4
Bucklebury...............21 K5
Bucklers Hard............13 G5
Bucklesham..............37 H5
Buckley..................50 B7
Bucklow Hill.............51 G5
Buckminster.............44 B4
Bucknall, Staffs.........42 B2
Bucknall, Lincs..........55 F7
Bucknell, Shrops.........30 E2
Bucknell, Oxon...........33 H7
Bucksburn................97 H5
Buck's Cross..............8 D3
Bucks Green..............14 D2
Bucks Hill...............22 E2
Bucks Horn Oak...........14 B1
Buck's Mills..............8 D3
Buckton, H. & W..........30 E2
Buckton, Northum.........83 J8
Buckworth................34 E2
Budbrooke................32 E3
Budby....................53 J6
Bude......................8 C5
Budlake..................10 A5
Budle....................83 K8
Budleigh Salterton.......10 B7
Budock Water..............3 F6
Buerton..................41 H2
Bugbrooke................33 J4
Bugle.....................3 J4
Bugthorpe................60 E5
Buildwas.................41 H6
Builth Road..............29 H3
Builth Wells.............29 H4
Bulby....................44 D4

Buldoo..................111 F2
Bulford..................12 D1
Bulford Camp.............12 D1
Bulkeley.................41 G1
Bulkington, Wilts........20 D7
Bulkington, Warw.........33 F1
Bulkworthy...............8 D4
Bulley...................20 B1
Bullwood.................78 D4
Bulmer, N. Yks...........60 D4
Bulmer, Essex............36 D5
Bulmer Tye...............36 D6
Bulphan..................24 C4
Bulverhythe..............16 E5
Bulwell..................43 H2
Bulwick..................44 C7
Bumble's Green...........23 K2
Bunacaimb................92 C7
Bunarkaig................93 H7
Bunavoneadar.............99 G2
Bunbury..................50 E8
Bundalloch...............93 E3
Bunessan.................84 E6
Bungay...................47 J8
Bunnahabhain............76 D4
Bunny....................43 H4
Buntait..................94 C2
Buntingford..............35 G7
Bunwell..................47 G7
Burbage, Derby...........52 C6
Burbage, Wilts...........21 G6
Burbage, Leic............43 G7
Burcombe.................12 C2
Burcot...................21 K3
Burdale..................60 F4
Bures....................36 E6
Burford, Oxon............21 G1
Burford, Shrops..........31 G3
Burg.....................84 E4
Burgess Hill.............15 G4
Burgh....................37 H4
Burgh by Sands...........63 J2
Burgh Castle.............47 K6
Burghclere...............21 J6
Burghead................103 K6
Burghfield...............22 B6
Burghfield Common........22 B6
Burghfield Hill..........22 B6
Burgh Heath..............23 H7
Burghill.................31 F5
Burgh le Marsh...........55 K7
Burgh next Aylsham.......47 H4
Burgh on Bain............55 G5
Burgh St Margaret or
 Fleggburgh.........47 K5
Burgh St Peter...........47 K7
Burghwallis..............53 H2
Burham...................24 D6
Buriton..................13 K3
Burland..................41 H1
Burlawn...................3 H2
Burlescombe..............10 B4
Burleston................11 J6
Burley, Leic.............44 B5
Burley, Hants............12 E5
Burleydam................41 H2
Burley Gate..............31 G5
Burley in Wharfedale.....59 G6
Burley Street............12 E5
Burlingjobb..............30 D4
Burlton..................41 F4
Burmarsh.................17 J2
Burmington...............32 E6
Burn.....................60 C8
Burnage..................51 H4
Burnaston................42 E3
Burnby...................60 F6
Burneside................57 J1
Burness.................113 G2
Burneston................59 J2
Burnett..................20 A6
Burnfoot, Border.........74 B3
Burnfoot, Border.........73 K3
Burnham, Humbs...........54 E2
Burnham, Berks...........22 E4
Burnham Deepdale.........46 D2
Burnham Green............23 H1
Burnham Market...........46 D2
Burnham Norton...........46 D2
Burnham-on-Crouch........25 F3
Burnham-on-Sea...........10 E1
Burnham Overy Staithe....46 D2
Burnham Overy Town.......46 D2
Burnham Thorpe...........46 D2
Burnhead.................72 D5
Burnhervie...............97 G4
Burnhill Green...........41 J6
Burnhope.................66 B3
Burnhouse................79 F6
Burniston................61 H1
Burnley..................58 D7
Burnmouth................83 H5
Burn of Cambus...........80 C1
Burnopfield..............66 B2
Burnsall.................58 F4
Burnside, Strath.........72 A3
Burnside, Shetld........116 D5
Burnside, Fife...........88 D8
Burnside, Lothn..........81 F4
Burnside of Duntrune.....89 G5
Burntisland.............81 H3
Burntwood................42 C6
Burnt Yates..............59 H4
Burpham, W. Susx.........14 D5
Burpham, Surrey..........22 F7
Burradon.................75 J3
Burrafirth.............117 H1
Burras....................2 E6
Burravoe, Shetld........116 E4
Burravoe, Shetld........117 G5
Burray Village..........112 E7
Burrelton................88 E5
Burridge.................13 H4
Burrill..................59 H2
Burringham...............54 C3

Burrington, H. & W..............31 F2
Burrington, Devon..................9 G4
Burrington, Avon..................19 J7
Burrough Green....................36 B4
Burrough on the Hill............44 A5
Burrowbridge......................10 E2
Burrowhill..........................22 E6
Burry Green........................27 J7
Burry Port..........................27 J6
Burscough..........................50 D2
Burscough Bridge................50 D2
Bursea..............................60 F7
Burshill..............................61 H6
Bursledon..........................13 G5
Burslem.............................42 A2
Burstall..............................37 F5
Burstock.............................11 F5
Burston, Staffs.....................42 B3
Burston, Norf.......................37 G1
Burstow..............................15 G1
Burstwick............................55 G1
Burtersett............................58 D2
Burtle.................................10 F1
Burton, Somer......................10 C1
Burton, Wilts........................20 C5
Burton, Ches.........................50 C6
Burton, Dyfed.......................26 D6
Burton, Lincs........................54 D6
Burton, Dorset.......................12 D6
Burton, Ches.........................50 E7
Burton, Northum....................75 H1
Burton Agnes.......................61 J4
Burton Bradstock...................11 F7
Burton Constable...................61 J7
Burton Fleming.....................61 H3
Burton Green, Clwyd..............50 C8
Burton Green, Warw...............32 E2
Burton Hastings....................43 G8
Burton-in-Kendal...................57 J3
Burton in Lonsdale................58 B3
Burton Joyce........................43 J2
Burton Latimer.....................34 C2
Burton Lazars.......................44 A5
Burton-le-Coggles..................44 C4
Burton Leonard......................59 J4
Burton on the Wolds...............43 H4
Burton Overy.......................43 J7
Burton Pedwardine.................44 E2
Burton Pidsea......................61 K7
Burton Salmon.....................53 G1
Burton upon Stather...............54 C2
Burton upon Trent.................42 E4
Burtonwood.........................50 E4
Burwardsley.........................41 G1
Burwarton...........................31 H1
Burwash.............................16 D3
Burwash Common..................16 D3
Burwell, Lincs.......................55 H6
Burwell, Cambs.....................35 J3
Bury, W. Susx.......................14 D4
Bury, Cambs.........................35 F1
Bury, G. Man........................51 H2
Bury, Somer..........................9 K3
Bury Green...........................35 H7
Bury St Edmunds...................36 D3
Burythorpe...........................60 E4
Busbridge............................14 C1
Busby................................79 H6
Buscot...............................21 G3
Bushbury............................42 B6
Bush Crathie........................96 B6
Bushey...............................23 G3
Bushey Heath.......................23 G3
Bush Green...........................37 H1
Bushley...............................32 A6
Bushton...............................20 E5
Busta................................115 F2
Butcher's Pasture...................35 K7
Butcombe............................19 K6
Butleigh..............................11 G2
Butleigh Wootton...................11 G2
Butlers Marston.....................33 F4
Butley................................37 J4
Butsfield.............................65 J3
Buttercrambe.......................60 E5
Butterknowle........................65 J5
Butterleigh..........................10 A5
Buttermere, Cumbr................63 G6
Buttermere, Wilts..................21 H6
Buttershaw...........................59 G8
Butterstone..........................88 C4
Butterton............................42 C1
Butterwick, Humbs.................54 C3
Butterwick, N. Yks................60 E3
Butterwick, Lincs...................45 G2
Butterwick, N. Yks................61 G3
Butt Green...........................41 H1
Buttington...........................40 D6
Buttonoak...........................31 J2
Buxhall..............................36 F4
Buxted...............................15 H3
Buxton, Derby.......................52 C6
Buxton, Norf.........................47 H4
Bwlch.................................30 C7
Bwlch-derwin.......................38 D2
Bwlchgwyn..........................40 D1
Bwlch-Llan..........................28 C4
Bwlchnewydd.......................27 H4
Bwlchtocyn..........................38 C4
Bwlch-y-cibau......................40 C5
Bwlch-y-fadfa.......................27 J2
Bwlch-y-ffridd......................40 B7
Bwlchygroes.........................27 G3
Bwlch-y-sarnau.....................29 H2
Byers Green..........................66 C4
Byfield...............................33 H4
Byfleet...............................22 F6
Byford...............................30 E5
Bygrave.............................35 F6
Byker................................66 C1
Bylchau..............................49 J4
Byley................................51 G7
Byrness, Northum..................74 D4
Byrness, Northum..................64 E7
Bythorn.............................34 D2

Byton................................30 E3
Byworth..............................14 C3

C

Cabourne............................55 F3
Cabrach.............................96 C3
Cadbury..............................9 K5
Cadbury Barton.....................9 G4
Cadder..............................79 J4
Caddington.........................22 F1
Caddonfoot.........................73 K1
Cadeby, Leic.........................43 G6
Cadeby, S. Yks.....................53 H3
Cadeleigh.............................9 K5
Cade Street..........................16 D3
Cadgwith..............................2 F8
Cadishead............................51 G4
Cadle................................27 L7
Cadley...............................21 G6
Cadmore End........................22 C3
Cadnam..............................12 E4
Cadney...............................54 E3
Cadole...............................50 B7
Caeathro.............................48 E4
Caehopkin...........................18 C1
Caerau, M. Glam....................18 C3
Caerau, S. Glam.....................18 F5
Caerdeon.............................39 F5
Caergeiliog...........................48 C3
Caergwrle............................40 E1
Caerleon..............................19 H3
Caer Llan.............................19 J2
Caernarfon...........................48 D4
Caerphilly............................18 F4
Caersws..............................40 B7
Caerwent.............................19 J3
Caerwys..............................50 A6
Caethle...............................38 F7
Caio.................................27 L3
Cairnbaan............................77 H2
Cairnborrow.........................96 D1
Cairnbrogie..........................97 H3
Cairncross, Tays.....................96 D8
Cairncross, Border..................83 G5
Cairndow.............................86 D7
Cairneyhill...........................81 F3
Cairngaan............................68 C7
Cairngarroch.........................68 B6
Cairnhill.............................97 F2
Cairnie.............................104 D4
Cairnorrie............................97 H1
Cairnryan.............................70 F8
Caister-on-Sea.......................47 L5
Caistor...............................54 F3
Caistor St Edmund.................47 H6
Caistron..............................75 F4
Caldbeck............................107 J7
Calbourne............................13 G7
Calcot................................22 B5
Caldbeck.............................63 J4
Caldbergh............................59 F2
Caldecote, Cambs...................34 E1
Caldecote, Herts....................35 F6
Caldecote, Cambs...................35 G4
Caldecott, Leic......................44 B7
Caldecott, Northnts.................34 C3
Calderbank..........................80 C5
Calder Bridge........................62 F7
Calderbrook.........................51 J2
Caldercruix...........................80 D5
Calder Mains.......................111 G3
Caldermill............................79 J7
Calder Vale..........................57 J6
Caldicot..............................19 J4
Caldwell, N. Yks....................66 B6
Caldwell, Derby.....................42 E5
Caldy................................50 B5
Caledrhydiau........................27 J1
Calfsound..........................113 F3
Calgary...............................84 E3
Califer..............................103 J7
California, Central..................80 E4
California, Norf......................47 L5
Calke................................43 F4
Callakille............................104 D5
Callaly...............................75 G4
Callander.............................87 J8
Callanish...........................107 G5
Callaughton..........................31 K5
Callestick..............................2 F4
Callichbhol neo Port Nis......107 K2
Calligarry............................92 C5
Callington.............................4 D3
Callow...............................31 F6
Callow End..........................31 K5
Callow Hill, Wilts....................20 E4
Callow Hill, H. & W...............31 J2
Callows Grave.......................31 G3
Calmore..............................12 E4
Calmsden.............................20 E2
Calne................................20 E5
Calow................................53 G6
Calshot..............................13 G5
Calstock...............................4 E3
Calstone Wellington.................20 E6
Calthorpe.............................47 G3
Calthwaite...........................64 B3
Calton..................................90 D1
Calton, Staffs........................42 D1
Calton, N. Yks......................58 E5
Calveley.............................50 E8
Calver................................52 E6
Calverhall...........................41 H3
Calver Hill..........................30 E5
Calverleigh...........................9 K4
Calverley.............................59 H7
Calvert...............................33 J7
Calverton, Bucks....................34 A6
Calverton, Notts.....................43 J2
Calvine................................87 L2
Cam...................................20 B3
Camas-luinie.........................93 F3
Camastianavaig......................92 B2

Camasunary.........................92 B4
Camault Muir.......................94 D1
Camb...............................117 G3
Camber...............................17 G4
Camberley............................22 D6
Camberwell.........................23 J5
Camblesforth........................53 J1
Cambo................................75 G6
Cambois.............................75 K6
Camborne..............................2 E5
Cambridge, Glos.....................20 B2
Cambridge, Cambs..................35 H4
Cambus...............................80 D2
Cambusbarron.......................80 C2
Cambuskenneth.....................80 D2
Cambuslang.........................79 J6
Camden Town.......................23 H4
Camelford............................8 B7
Camelon..............................80 D3
Camelsdale..........................14 B2
Camerory............................95 J2
Camerton, Avon.....................20 A7
Camerton, Cumbr...................62 F4
Cammachmore.......................97 J6
Cammeringham.....................54 D5
Campbelton..........................78 D6
Campbeltown.........................70 C2
Campsall.............................53 H2
Campsey Ash........................37 J4
Camp, The............................20 D2
Campton.............................34 E6
Camrose..............................26 D4
Camster..............................111 J4
Camusnagaul, Highld...........101 G4
Camusnagaul, Highld............93 G8
Camusory............................92 E6
Camusteel.........................100 D8
Camusterrach........................92 D1
Canada................................12 E4
Canal Foot...........................57 G3
Candlesby............................55 J7
Candy Mill............................81 F7
Cane End.............................22 B5
Canewdon............................24 E3
Canisbay...........................111 K1
Cann................................12 A3
Cann Common.......................12 A3
Cannich..............................94 B2
Cannington..........................10 D2
Cannock..............................42 B5
Cannock Wood......................42 C5
Canonbie............................73 J7
Canon Bridge.......................31 F5
Canon Frome.......................31 H5
Canon Pyon.........................31 F5
Canons Ashby.......................33 H4
Canonstown...........................2 D6
Canterbury...........................25 H7
Cantley, S. Yks.....................53 J3
Cantley, Norf........................47 J6
Cantlop...............................41 G6
Canton...............................18 F5
Cantraydoune......................103 F8
Cantraywood.......................103 F8
Cantsfield...........................57 K3
Canvey Island........................24 D4
Canwick.............................54 D7
Canworthy Water.....................8 C6
Caol.................................93 H8
Caolas................................84 B4
Caol Ila..............................76 D5
Caolis................................90 B6
Capel...............................14 E1
Capel Bangor.........................28 D1
Capel Betws Lleucu.................28 D4
Capel Carmel........................38 A4
Capel Coch...........................48 D2
Capel Curig..........................49 G5
Capel Cynon.........................27 H2
Capel Dewi...........................27 J2
Capel Garmon........................39 H1
Capel Gwyn, Gwyn.................48 C3
Capel Gwyn, Dyfed.................27 J4
Capel Gwynfe........................28 E7
Capel Hendre........................27 K5
Capel Isaac...........................27 K4
Capel Iwan...........................27 G3
Capel-le-Ferne.......................17 K2
Capel Llanilterne....................18 E4
Capel Parc............................48 D2
Capel St Mary........................37 F6
Capel-y-ffin..........................30 D6
Capenhurst..........................50 C6
Capernwray..........................57 J3
Capheaton...........................75 G6
Cappercleuch.........................73 H2
Capstone.............................24 D6
Capton.................................5 J4
Caputh................................88 C4
Carbis Bay............................2 D6
Carbost, Highld......................91 J2
Carbost, Highld......................99 K8
Carbrooke............................46 E6
Carburton............................53 J6
Car Colston..........................43 K2
Carcroft...............................53 H2
Cardenden............................81 H2
Cardeston.............................40 E5
Cardiff................................19 F5
Cardigan.............................26 F2
Cardington, Beds....................34 D5
Cardington, Shrops.................41 G7
Cardinham.............................3 K3
Cardow.............................103 K8
Cardrona..............................81 J8
Cardross..............................79 F4
Cardurnock..........................63 G2
Careby................................44 D5
Carew................................26 E6
Carew Cheriton......................26 E6
Carew Newton.......................26 E6
Carey................................31 G6
Carfrae...............................82 D5
Cargen...............................72 E7
Cargenbridge........................72 E7

Cargo..................................63 J2
Cargreen...............................4 E3
Carham...............................83 F8
Carhampton...........................10 B1
Carharrack.............................2 F5
Carisbrooke..........................13 G7
Carishader.........................106 E5
Cark..................................57 G3
Carlby................................44 D5
Carlecotes............................52 D3
Carleton, N. Yks....................58 E6
Carleton, Lancs......................57 G6
Carleton, Cumbr....................63 K2
Carleton Forehoe....................47 F6
Carleton Rode........................47 G7
Carlingcott...........................20 A7
Carlisle...............................63 K2
Carlops...............................81 G6
Carloway...........................107 G4
Carlton, Cambs......................36 B4
Carlton, Beds.........................34 C4
Carlton, N. Yks......................60 D2
Carlton, Cleve.......................66 D5
Carlton, W. Yks.....................53 F1
Carlton, N. Yks......................59 F2
Carlton, S. Yks.......................43 F6
Carlton, Leic.........................43 F6
Carlton, N. Yks......................53 J1
Carlton, Notts........................43 J2
Carlton, Suff.........................37 J3
Carlton Colville......................47 L7
Carlton Curlieu.......................43 J7
Carlton Husthwaite..................60 B3
Carlton in Cleveland................66 F7
Carlton in Lindrick..................53 H5
Carlton-le-Moorland................44 C1
Carlton Miniott......................59 K2
Carlton-on-Trent.....................54 B7
Carlton Scroop.......................44 C2
Carluke...............................80 D6
Carmacoup............................72 C2
Carmarthen...........................27 J4
Carmel, Clwyd.......................50 A6
Carmel, Gwyn.......................48 C2
Carmel, Gwyn.......................38 D1
Carmel, Dyfed.......................27 K5
Carminish............................98 F4
Carmunnock..........................79 H6
Carmyle..............................79 J5
Carmyllie.............................89 H4
Carnaby...............................61 J4
Carnach, Highld.....................101 G3
Carnach, Highld......................93 G3
Carnach, W. Isles....................99 H3
Carnbee...............................89 H8
Carnbo................................81 F1
Carn Brea Village......................2 E5
Carne...................................3 H6
Carnell................................71 K1
Carnforth.............................57 H3
Carn-gorm............................93 F3
Carnhedryn..........................26 C4
Carnhell Green.........................2 E6
Carnie.................................97 H5
Carnish...............................98 D6
Carno.................................39 J7
Carnock..............................81 F3
Carnon Downs.........................3 F5
Carn Towan............................2 B7
Carnwath.............................80 E7
Carnyorth..............................2 B6
Carperby..............................58 F2
Carpley Green.........................58 E2
Carradale.............................77 H8
Carragreich...........................99 G3
Carrbridge............................95 H3
Carreglefn............................48 C2
Carrick Castle........................78 D2
Carriden..............................81 G3
Carrington, Lincs....................45 G1
Carrington, G. Man.................51 G4
Carrington, Lothn...................81 J5
Carrog...............................40 C2
Carron, Grampn.....................96 B1
Carron, Central......................80 D3
Carronbridge........................72 D3
Carr Shield...........................65 F3
Carrutherstown......................73 G7
Carr Vale.............................53 G7
Carrville...............................66 D2
Carsaig...............................85 G6
Carsegowan..........................68 E5
Carsethorn...........................65 F2
Carshalton............................23 H6
Carsington...........................42 E1
Carskiey...............................70 B4
Carsluith.............................68 F5
Carsphairn...........................72 A5
Carstairs..............................80 E7
Carstairs Junction...................80 E7
Carswell Marsh......................21 H3
Carter's Clay.........................13 F3
Carterton.............................21 G2
Carterway Heads....................65 H2
Carthew...............................3 J4
Carthorpe.............................59 J2
Cartington...........................75 G4
Cartland..............................80 D7
Cartmel..............................57 G3
Cartmel Fell.........................57 H2
Carway...............................27 J6
Cas...................................77 G5
Cascob................................30 D3
Cashmoor.............................12 B4
Cassington...........................21 H1
Cassiobury Park......................23 F3
Castallack..............................2 C7
Castellau.............................18 E4
Castell Howell.......................27 J2
Castell-y-bwch.......................19 G3
Casterton............................57 K3
Castle Acre..........................46 D3
Castle Ashby.........................34 B4

Castlebay............................90 B6
Castle Bolton........................58 F1
Castle Bromwich....................42 D7
Castlebythe..........................26 E4
Castle Caereinion...................40 C6
Castle Camps.......................36 B5
Castle Carrock.......................64 C2
Castlecary, Strath..................80 C4
Castle Cary, Somer................11 H2
Castle Combe........................20 C5
Castlecraig, Highld................103 H6
Castlecraig, Border.................81 G7
Castle Donington...................43 G4
Castle Douglas.......................69 J4
Castle Eaton.........................21 F3
Castle Eden..........................66 E4
Castleford............................53 G1
Castle Frome.........................31 H5
Castle Gresley.......................42 E5
Castle Heaton.......................83 H7
Castle Hedingham...................36 C6
Castle Hill............................37 G5
Castle Kennedy......................68 C5
Castlemartin.........................26 D7
Castlemilk............................73 G7
Castlemorris..........................26 D3
Castlemorton........................31 J6
Castle O'er...........................73 H5
Castle Rising........................46 B4
Castle Side...........................65 H3
Castlethorpe.........................34 A5
Castleton, Derby....................52 D5
Castleton, Gwent...................19 G4
Castleton, N. Yks....................67 G7
Castleton, Strath....................77 H3
Castletown, T. & W.................66 D2
Castletown, Highld...............111 H2
Castletown, I. of M................56 P5
Caston.................................46 E7
Castor................................44 E7
Catacol..............................77 J7
Catbrain.............................19 K4
Catcliffe.............................53 G5
Catcott................................10 C2
Caterham.............................23 J7
Catfield...............................47 J4
Catfirth............................115 G3
Catforth...............................57 H7
Cathcart..............................79 H5
Cathedine............................30 C7
Catherine de Barnes...............13 K4
Catherston..........................31 H2
Catlodge..............................94 E6
Catlowdy..............................73 K7
Catmore...............................21 J4
Caton.................................57 J4
Catrine................................71 L2
Cat's Ash.............................19 H3
Catsfield...............................16 E4
Catsgore..............................11 G2
Cattal.................................59 K5
Cattawade.............................37 G6
Catterall..............................57 H6
Catterick.............................66 C8
Catterick Bridge.....................66 C8
Catterick Garrison...................66 B8
Catterlen..............................64 B4
Catterline............................97 H8
Catterton.............................60 C6
Catthorpe............................33 H2
Cattistock............................11 G6
Catton, Northum....................65 F2
Catton, Norf..........................47 H5
Catton, N. Yks.......................59 J3
Catwick...............................61 J6
Catworth.............................34 D2
Caulcott..............................33 H7
Cauldhame...........................79 J2
Cauldon...............................42 C2
Caulkerbush.........................69 L5
Caunsall..............................32 A1
Caunton...............................54 B7
Causewayhead.......................80 D2
Causeyend...........................97 J4
Causey Park Bridge................75 H5
Cautley...............................58 B1
Cavendish............................36 D5
Cavenham............................36 C3
Caversfield...........................33 H7
Caversham...........................22 C5
Caversta.............................107 H7
Caverswall...........................42 B2
Cawdor.............................103 G7
Cawood...............................60 C7
Cawsand..............................4 E4
Cawston..............................47 G4
Cawthorne...........................52 E3
Cawton...............................60 D3
Caxton................................35 G4
Caynham.............................31 G2
Caythorpe, Lincs....................44 C2
Caythorpe, Notts....................43 J2
Cayton................................61 H2
Ceann-na-Cleithe...................99 G3
Cefn Berain..........................49 J4
Cefn-brith............................39 J1
Cefn Canol...........................40 C4
Cefn-coed-y-cymmer...............18 E2
Cefn Cribwr..........................18 C4
Cefn Cross...........................18 C4
Cefn Einion..........................30 D1
Cefneithin............................27 K5
Cefn-gorwydd.......................29 H6
Cefn-mawr...........................40 D2
Cefn-y-bedd.........................40 E1
Cefn-y-pant..........................27 F4
Ceint.................................48 D3
Cellan................................27 L2
Cellarhead...........................42 B2
Cemaes...............................48 C1

Cemmaes.............................39 H6
Cemmaes Road......................39 H6
Cenarth...............................27 G2
Cennin...............................38 D2
Ceres.................................89 G7
Cerne Abbas.........................11 H5
Cerney Wick.........................20 E3
Cerrigceinwen.......................48 D3
Cerrigydrudion......................39 J2
Cessford..............................74 D2
Chaceley.............................32 A6
Chacewater...........................2 E5
Chackmore...........................33 J6
Chacombe...........................33 G5
Chadderton..........................51 J3
Chaddesden.........................43 F3
Chaddesley Corbett.................32 A2
Chaddleworth.......................21 J5
Chadlington.........................33 F7
Chadshunt...........................33 F4
Chad Valley.........................32 C1
Chadwell St Mary..................24 C5
Chadwick End.......................32 E2
Chaffcombe.........................10 E4
Chagford..............................9 H7
Chailey...............................15 G4
Chainhurst...........................16 E1
Chalbury Common..................12 C5
Chaldon..............................23 J7
Chaldon Herring or
East Chaldon......................11 J7
Chale..................................7 J7
Chale Green...........................7 J7
Chalfont Common..................22 F3
Chalfont St Giles...................22 F3
Chalfont St Peter....................22 F3
Chalford..............................20 C2
Chalgrove............................22 B3
Chalk................................24 C5
Challacombe...........................9 G1
Challoch..............................71 J8
Challock..............................25 G7
Chalton, Beds........................34 D7
Chalton, Hants......................13 K4
Chalvington..........................15 J5
Champany............................80 F4
Chandler's Cross....................22 F3
Chandler's Ford.....................13 G3
Channerwick.......................115 G6
Chantry, Suff........................37 G5
Chantry, Somer.....................11 J1
Chapel................................81 H2
Chapel Allerton, Somer...........19 J7
Chapel Allerton, W. Yks..........59 J7
Chapel Amble.........................3 H2
Chapel Brampton...................33 K3
Chapel Chorlton....................41 K3
Chapel-en-le-Frith..................52 C5
Chapelgate...........................45 H4
Chapel Haddlesey...................53 H1
Chapelhall...........................80 C5
Chapelhill, Tays....................88 C5
Chapel Hill, Lincs...................45 F1
Chapel Hill, Grampn..............97 K2
Chapel Hill, Gwent.................19 K2
Chapelknowe........................73 J7
Chapel Lawn.........................30 E2
Chapel-le-Dale.......................58 C3
Chapel of Garioch...................97 G3
Chapel of Stoneywood............97 H4
Chapel Row...........................21 K6
Chapel Stile..........................63 J7
Chapel St Leonards.................55 K6
Chapelton, Strath...................80 B7
Chapelton, Devon....................9 G4
Chapelton, Tays.....................89 J4
Chapeltown, Grampn.............96 B3
Chapeltown, S. Yks................53 F4
Chapeltown, Lancs.................51 G2
Chapmanslade........................11 K1
Chapmans Well........................8 D6
Chappel..............................36 D7
Chard................................10 E5
Chardstock...........................10 E5
Charfield.............................20 B3
Charing...............................17 G1
Charing Heath.......................17 G1
Charingworth........................32 E6
Charlbury............................21 H1
Charlcombe..........................20 B6
Charlecote...........................32 E4
Charles................................9 G2
Charleston..........................89 F4
Charlestown, Highld.............100 E5
Charlestown, Highld.............102 E8
Charlestown, Fife..................81 F3
Charlestown, Dorset...............11 H8
Charlestown, Corn...................3 J4
Charlestown, Grampn.............97 J5
Charlestown of Aberlour.......104 B4
Charles Tye..........................37 F5
Charlesworth.........................52 C4
Charlton, Wilts......................12 B3
Charlton, W. Susx..................14 B4
Charlton, H. & W..................32 C5
Charlton, Wilts......................20 D4
Charlton, Wilts......................20 D4
Charlton, Northnts..................33 H6
Charlton, G. Lon...................23 K5
Charlton Abbotts....................32 C7
Charlton Adam.......................11 G3
Charlton-All-Saints.................12 D3
Charlton Horethorne...............11 H3
Charlton Kings......................32 B7
Charlton Mackrell...................11 G3
Charlton Marshall...................12 B5
Charlton Musgrove..................11 J2
Charlton-on-Otmoor................21 K1
Charlwood...........................15 F1
Charminster.........................11 H6
Charmouth...........................10 E6
Charndon............................33 J7
Charney Bassett....................21 H3
Charnock Richard...................50 E2

Place	Ref		Place	Ref		Place	Ref		Place	Ref		Place	Ref		Place	Ref
Charsfield	37 H4		Chideock	11 F6		Church Eaton	41 K5		Claxby, Lincs	54 F4		Clowne	53 G6		Cold Brayfield	34 C4
Charter Alley	21 K7		Chidham	14 A5		Church End, Hants	22 B7		Claxby, Lincs	55 J6		Clows Top	31 J2		Coldean	15 G5
Charterhouse	19 J7		Chieveley	21 J5		Churchend, Essex	36 B7		Claxton, N. Yks	60 D4		Clubworthy	8 C6		Coldeast	5 J2
Chartershall	80 D2		Chignall Smealy	24 C1		Church End, Beds	34 C7		Claxton, Norf	47 J6		Cluer	99 G3		Colden Common	13 G3
Charterville Allotments	21 H1		Chignall St James	24 C2		Church End, Wilts	20 E5		Claybokie	95 J6		Clun	30 E1		Coldfair Green	37 K3
Chartham	25 H7		Chigwell	23 K3		Church End, Beds	35 E6		Claybrooke Magna	33 G3		Clunbury	30 E1		Cold Hanworth	54 E5
Chartham Hatch	25 H7		Chigwell Row	23 K3		Church End, Warw	42 E7		Clay Coton	33 H2		Clunderwen	26 F5		Coldharbour	14 E1
Chartridge	22 E2		Chilbolton	13 F2		Churchend, Essex	25 G3		Clay Cross	53 F7		Clunes	93 J7		Cold Hesledon	66 E3
Chart Sutton	24 D7		Chilcombe	11 G6		Church End, Cambs	45 G6		Claydon, Suff	37 G4		Clungunford	30 E2		Cold Higham	33 H5
Charwelton	33 H4		Chilcompton	19 L7		Church End, Essex	35 J5		Claydon, Oxon	33 G4		Clunie	104 F3		Coldingham	83 H5
Chase Terrace	42 C6		Chilcote	42 E5		Church Fenton	60 C7		Claygate	23 G6		Clunton	30 E1		Cold Kirby	60 C2
Chasetown	42 C6		Childer Thornton	50 C6		Church Gresley	42 E5		Claygate Cross	24 C7		Cluny	81 H2		Cold Newton	43 K6
Chastleton	32 E7		Child Okeford	11 K4		Church Hanborough	21 J1		Clayhanger, Devon	10 B3		Clutton, Ches	41 F1		Cold Norton	24 E2
Chatburn	58 C6		Childrey	21 H4		Church Houses	67 G8		Clayhanger, W. Mids	42 C6		Clutton, Avon	19 L7		Cold Overton	44 B5
Chatcull	41 J3		Child's Ercall	41 H4		Churchill, H. & W	32 A2		Clayhidon	10 C4		Clwyt-y-bont	48 E4		Coldred	17 K1
Chatham	24 D6		Childswickham	32 C6		Churchill, Devon	10 D5		Claypole	44 B2		Clydach, W. Glam	18 A2		Coldridge	9 G5
Chathill	75 H2		Childwall	50 D5		Churchill, Oxon	32 E7		Clayton, Staffs	42 A2		Clydach, Gwent	19 G1		Coldstream	83 G8
Chattenden	24 D5		Chilfrome	11 G6		Churchill, Avon	19 J7		Clayton, S. Yks	53 G3		Clydach Vale	18 D3		Coldwaltham	14 D4
Chatteris	35 G1		Chilgrove	14 B4		Churchinford	10 D4		Clayton, W. Susx	15 G4		Clydebank	79 H5		Coldwells	97 L2
Chattisham	37 F5		Chilham	25 G7		Church Knowle	6 C6		Clayton, W. Yks	59 G7		Clydey	27 G3		Coldwells Croft	96 E3
Chatto	74 D3		Chillaton	4 E1		Church Langton	43 K7		Clayton-le-Moors	58 C7		Clyffe Pypard	20 E5		Cole	11 H2
Chatton	75 G2		Chillenden	25 J7		Church Lawford	33 G2		Clayton-le-Woods	50 E1		Clynder	78 E3		Colebatch	30 E1
Chawleigh	9 H4		Chillerton	13 G7		Church Lawton	41 K1		Clayton West	52 E2		Clynelish	103 G2		Colebrook	10 B5
Chawston	34 E4		Chillesford	37 J4		Church Leigh	42 C3		Clayworth	54 B5		Clynnog-fawr	38 D2		Colebrooke	9 H5
Chawton	13 K2		Chillingham	75 G2		Church Lench	32 C4		Cleadale	92 A7		Clyro	30 D5		Coleburn	66 C8
Cheadle, Staffs	42 C2		Chillington, Somer	10 E4		Church Minshull	51 F7		Cleadon	66 D1		Clyst Honiton	10 A6		Coleby, Humbs	54 C2
Cheadle, G. Man	51 H5		Chillington, Devon	5 H5		Church Norton	14 B6		Clearbrook	5 F4		Clyst Hydon	10 B5		Coleby, Lincs	54 D7
Cheadle Hulme	51 H5		Chilmark	12 B2		Churchover	33 H1		Clearwell	19 K2		Clyst St George	10 A7		Coleford, Somer	11 H1
Cheam	23 H6		Chilson	21 H1		Church Preen	41 G7		Cleasby	66 C6		Clyst St Lawrence	10 B5		Coleford, Devon	9 H5
Chearsley	22 C1		Chilsworthy, Devon	8 D5		Church Pulverbatch	41 F6		Cleat, W. Isles	90 B5		Clyst St Mary	10 A6		Coleford, Glos	19 K1
Chebsey	42 A4		Chilsworthy, Corn	4 E2		Churchstanton	10 C4		Cleat, Orkney	112 E8		Clyth	111 J5		Colehill	12 C5
Checkendon	22 B4		Chilthorne Domer	11 G4		Church Stoke	40 D7		Cleatlam	65 J6		Cnoc Amhlaigh	107 K5		Coleman's Hatch	15 H2
Checkley, Staffs	42 C3		Chilton, Bucks	22 B1		Church Stowe	33 J4		Cleator	62 F6		Cnwch Coch	28 D2		Colemere	41 F3
Checkley, Ches	41 J2		Chilton, Durham	66 C5		Church Street	24 D5		Cleator Moor	62 F6		Coad's Green	4 C2		Colenden	88 B6
Chedburgh	36 C4		Chilton, Oxon	21 J4		Church Stretton	41 F7		Cleckheaton	52 D1		Coal Aston	53 F6		Coleorton	43 G5
Cheddar	19 J7		Chilton Cantelo	11 G3		Churchtown, Mers	50 C2		Cleedownton	31 G1		Coalbrookdale	41 H6		Colerne	20 C5
Cheddington	22 E1		Chilton Foliat	21 H5		Churchtown, Lancs	57 H6		Cleehill	31 G2		Coalburn	72 D1		Colesbourne	20 D1
Cheddleton	42 B1		Chilton Lane	66 D4		Churchtown, I. of M	56 R2		Clee St Margaret	31 G1		Coalcleugh	65 F3		Colesden	34 E4
Cheddon Fitzpaine	10 D3		Chilton Polden	10 E2		Church Village	18 E4		Cleethorpes	55 H3		Coaley	20 B2		Coleshill, Bucks	22 E3
Chedgrave	47 J7		Chilton Street	36 C5		Church Warsop	53 H7		Cleeton St Mary	31 H2		Coalpit Heath	20 A4		Coleshill, Warw	42 E8
Chedington	11 F5		Chilton Trinity	10 D2		Churt	14 B2		Cleeve	19 J6		Coalport	41 H6		Coleshill, Oxon	21 G3
Chediston	37 J2		Chilworth, Surrey	14 D1		Churton	41 F1		Cleeve Hill	32 B7		Coalsnaughton	80 E2		Colgate	15 G2
Chedworth	20 E1		Chilworth, Hants	13 G4		Churwell	59 H8		Cleeve Prior	32 C5		Coaltown of Balgonie	81 J2		Colgrain	78 F3
Chedzoy	10 E2		Chimney	21 H2		Chwilog	38 D3		Cleghorn	80 C6		Coaltown of Wemyss	81 J2		Colinsburgh	82 C1
Cheeseman's Green	17 H2		Chineham	22 B7		Chyandour	2 C6		Cleigh	85 K6		Coalville	43 G5		Colinton	81 H5
Cheetham Hill	51 H3		Chingford	23 J3		Cilan Uchaf	38 B4		Cleish	81 F2		Coalway	19 K1		Colintraive	78 C4
Cheldon	9 H4		Chinley	52 C5		Cilcain	50 A7		Cleland	80 C6		Coast	101 F3		Colkirk	46 E4
Chelford	51 H6		Chinley Head	52 C5		Cilcennin	28 C3		Clench Common	21 F6		Coatbridge	80 C5		Collafirth	116 E4
Chellaston	43 F3		Chinnor	22 C2		Cilfrew	18 B2		Clenchwarton	45 J4		Coatdyke	80 C5		Collaton St Mary	5 J3
Chellington	34 C4		Chipnall	41 J3		Cilfynydd	18 E3		Clent	32 B2		Coate	20 E6		Collessie	88 E7
Chelmarsh	31 J1		Chippenham, Cambs	36 B3		Cilgerran	27 F2		Cleobury Mortimer	31 H2		Coates, Glos	20 D2		Collier Row	23 K3
Chelmondiston	37 H6		Chippenham, Wilts	20 D5		Cilgwyn	28 E7		Cleobury North	31 H1		Coates, Cambs	45 G7		Colliers End	35 G7
Chelmorton	52 D6		Chipperfield	22 F2		Ciliau-Aeron	28 C4		Clephanton	103 G7		Coatham	67 F5		Collier Street	16 E1
Chelmsford	24 D2		Chipping, Herts	35 G6		Cilmaengwyn	18 B2		Clerklands	74 B2		Coatham Mundeville	66 C5		Collieston	97 K3
Chelsea	23 H5		Chipping, Lancs	57 K6		Cilmery	29 H4		Clestrain	112 D6		Coatsgate	73 F4		Collin	73 F7
Chelsfield	23 K6		Chipping Campden	32 D6		Cilrhedyn	27 G3		Cleughbrae	73 F7		Cobbaton	9 G3		Collingbourne Ducis	21 G7
Chelsworth	36 E5		Chipping Hill	24 E1		Ciltwrch	30 C5		Clevancy	20 E5		Coberley	20 D1		Collingbourne Kingston	21 G7
Cheltenham	32 B7		Chipping Norton	33 F7		Cilwendeg	27 G3		Clevedon	19 J5		Cobham, Kent	24 C6		Collingham, Notts	54 C7
Chelveston	34 C3		Chipping Ongar	23 L2		Cilybebyll	18 B2		Cleveley	21 H6		Cobham, Surrey	23 G6		Collingham, W. Yks	59 H6
Chelvey	19 J6		Chipping Sodbury	20 B4		Cilycwm	28 E5		Cleveleys	57 G6		Cobnash	31 F3		Collington	31 H3
Chelwood	19 L6		Chipping Warden	33 G5		Cinderford	20 A1		Cleverton	20 D4		Cockayne	67 G8		Collingtree	34 A4
Chelwood Gate	15 H3		Chipstable	10 B3		Cirencester	20 E1		Clewer	19 J7		Cockayne Hatley	35 F5		Colliston	89 J4
Cheney Longville	31 F1		Chipstead	23 H7		City Dulas	48 D2		Cley next the Sea	46 F2		Cock Bridge	96 B5		Collyweston	44 C6
Chenies	22 F3		Chirbury	40 D7		City of London	23 J4		Cliasmol	99 F2		Cockburnspath	82 F4		Colmonell	71 G6
Chepstow	19 K3		Chirk	40 D3		City, The	22 C3		Cliburn	64 C5		Cock Clarks	24 D1		Colmworth	34 E4
Cherhill	20 E5		Chirmorie	83 G6		Clachaig	78 D3		Cliddesden	13 J1		Cockenzie and Port Seton	82 C4		Colnabaichin	96 B5
Cherington, Glos	20 D3		Chirnside	83 G6		Clachan, Highld	92 B2		Cliffe, Kent	24 D5		Cockerham	57 H5		Colnbrook	22 F5
Cherington, Warw	32 E6		Chirnsidebridge	83 G6		Clachan, Strath	77 G6		Cliffe, N. Yks	60 D7		Cockerington	55 H4		Colne, Lancs	58 D6
Cheriton, Devon	10 C5		Chirton	20 E7		Clachan, Strath	85 J7		Cliff End	17 F4		Cockermouth	63 G4		Colne, Cambs	35 G2
Cheriton, Hants	13 H3		Chisbury	21 G6		Clachan, Strath	85 K4		Cliffe Woods	24 D5		Cockernhoe	34 E7		Colne Engaine	36 D6
Cheriton, W. Glam	27 J7		Chiselborough	11 F4		Clachan-a-Luib	98 D6		Clifford, H. & W	30 D5		Cockfield, Suff	36 E4		Colney	47 G6
Cheriton Bishop	9 H6		Chiseldon	21 F5		Clachan of Campsie	79 J4		Clifford, W. Yks	59 K6		Cockfield, Durham	65 J5		Colney Heath	23 H2
Cheriton Fitzpaine	9 J5		Chiselhampton	21 K3		Clachan of Glendaruel	78 B3		Clifford Chambers	32 D4		Cockfosters	23 H3		Colney Street	23 G2
Cherrington	41 H4		Chislehurst	23 K5		Clachan-Seil	85 J7		Clifford's Mesne	31 J7		Cocking	14 B4		Coln Rogers	20 E2
Cherry Burton	61 G6		Chislet	25 J6		Clachbreck	77 G4		Cliffs End	25 K6		Cockington	5 J3		Coln St Aldwyns	21 F2
Cherry Hinton	35 H4		Chiswell Green	23 G2		Clachtoll	108 B6		Clifton, Cumbr	64 C5		Cocklake	11 F1		Coln St Dennis	20 E1
Cherry Willingham	54 E6		Chiswick	23 H5		Clackmannan	80 E2		Clifton, Derby	42 D2		Cockley Beck	63 H7		Colpy	97 G2
Chertsey	22 F6		Chisworth	51 J4		Clacton-on-Sea	25 H1		Clifton, Beds	34 E6		Cockley Cley	46 C6		Colsterdale	59 G2
Cheselbourne	11 J6		Chitcomb	13 H3		Cladach Kirkibost	98 C6		Clifton, Central	86 F5		Cockpole Green	22 C4		Colsterworth	44 C4
Chesham	22 E2		Chithurst	14 B3		Claggan	85 H4		Clifton, Oxon	33 G6		Cockshutt	41 F4		Colston Bassett	43 J3
Chesham Bois	22 E3		Chittering	35 H2		Claigan	99 H7		Clifton, Notts	43 H3		Cockthorpe	46 E2		Coltfield	103 K6
Cheshunt	23 J2		Chitterne	12 B1		Claines	32 A4		Clifton, Lancs	57 H7		Cockwood	5 K1		Coltishall	47 H4
Cheslyn Hay	42 B6		Chittlehamholt	9 G3		Clandown	20 A7		Clifton, Northum	75 J6		Cockyard	31 F6		Colton, Staffs	42 C4
Chessington	23 G6		Chittlehampton	9 G3		Clanfield, Oxon	21 G2		Clifton, H. & W	31 K5		Coddenham	37 G4		Colton, N. Yks	60 C6
Chester	50 D7		Chittoe	20 D6		Clanfield, Hants	13 J4		Clifton Campville	42 E5		Coddington, Notts	44 B1		Colton, Cumbr	57 G2
Chesterblade	11 H1		Chivenor	8 F2		Clanville	13 F1		Clifton Hampden	21 K3		Coddington, Ches	41 F1		Colton, Norf	47 G6
Chesterfield, Staffs	42 D6		Chobham	22 E6		Clanyard	68 C7		Clifton Reynes	34 C4		Coddington, H. & W	31 J5		Col Uarach	107 J5
Chesterfield, Derby	53 F6		Cholderton	12 E1		Claonaig	77 H6		Clifton upon Dunsmore	33 H2		Codford St Mary	12 B2		Colvend	69 K5
Chester-le-Street	66 C2		Cholesbury	22 E2		Claonel	102 D2		Clifton upon Teme	31 J3		Codford St Peter	12 B1		Colvister	117 G3
Chesters, Border	74 C2		Chollerton	75 F7		Clapgate	12 C5		Climping	14 C5		Codicote	23 H1		Colwall Green	31 J5
Chesters, Border	74 C3		Cholsey	21 K4		Clapham, N. Yks	58 C4		Clink	59 H5		Codnor	43 G2		Colwall Stone	31 J5
Chesterton, Cambs	44 E7		Cholstrey	31 F4		Clapham, Beds	34 D4		Clint Green	46 F5		Codrington	20 B5		Colwell	75 F7
Chesterton, Warw	33 F4		Choppington	75 J6		Clapham, W. Susx	14 D5		Clintmains	74 C1		Codsall	40 D1		Colwich	42 C4
Chesterton, Cambs	35 H3		Chopwell	65 J2		Clapham, G. Lon	23 H5		Clippesby	47 K5		Codsall Wood	41 K6		Colwinston	18 D5
Chesterton, Oxon	33 H7		Chorley, Staffs	42 C5		Clappers	83 H6		Clipsham	44 C5		Coedely	18 E4		Colworth	14 C5
Chesterton, Staffs	41 K2		Chorley, Lancs	50 E2		Clappersgate	63 J7		Clipston, Notts	43 J3		Coedkernew	19 G4		Colwyn Bay	49 H3
Chestfield	25 H6		Chorley, Ches	41 G1		Clapton	11 F5		Clipston, Northnts	33 K1		Coedpoeth	40 D1		Colyford	10 D6
Cheswardine	41 J4		Chorley, Shrops	31 H1		Clapton-in-Gordano	19 J5		Clitheroe	58 C6		Coed-y-paen	19 H3		Colyton	10 D6
Cheswick	83 J7		Chorleywood, Herts	22 F3		Clapton-on-the-Hill	21 F1		Clive	41 G4		Coed Ystumgwern	38 E4		Combe, H. & W	30 E3
Cheswick Green	32 D2		Chorleywood, Bucks	22 F3		Clapworthy	9 G3		Clivocast	113 E1		Coelbren	18 C1		Combe, Berks	21 H6
Chetnole	11 H5		Chorlton	41 J1		Clarbeston	26 E4		Clocaenog	40 B1		Coffinswell	5 J3		Combe, Oxon	21 J1
Chettiscombe	9 K4		Chorlton-cum-Hardy	51 H4		Clarbeston Road	26 E4		Clochan	104 D2		Cofton Hackett	32 C2		Combe Florey	10 C2
Chettisham	35 J1		Chorlton Lane	41 F2		Clarborough	54 B5		Clock Face	50 E4		Cogenhoe	34 B3		Combe Hay	20 B7
Chettle	12 B4		Chowley	41 F1		Clardon	111 H2		Cloddymoss	103 H6		Coggeshall	36 D7		Combeinteignhead	5 K2
Chetton	41 H7		Chrishall	35 H6		Clare	36 C5		Clodock	30 E7		Coig Peighinnean	107 K2		Combe Martin	9 F1
Chetwode	33 J7		Christchurch, Dorset	12 D6		Clarebrand	72 C4		Clola	105 K4		Coilacriech	96 C6		Combe Moor	30 E3
Chetwynd Aston	41 J5		Christchurch, Cambs	45 H7		Clarencefield	73 F8		Clophill	34 D6		Coille Mhorgil	93 H5		Combe Raleigh	10 C5
Cheveley	36 B3		Christchurch, Glos	19 K1		Clarkston	79 H6		Clopton, Northnts	34 D1		Coillore	91 J2		Comberbach	51 F6
Chevening	23 K7		Christian Malford	20 D5		Clashmore, Highld	108 B5		Clopton, Suff	37 H4		Coity	18 D4		Comberton	35 G4
Chevington	36 C4		Christleton	50 D7		Clashmore, Highld	103 H4		Clopton Green	36 C4		Col	107 J4		Combe St Nicholas	10 E4
Chevington Drift	75 J5		Christmas Common	22 C3		Clashnessie	108 B5		Closeburn	72 D5		Colaboll	102 D1		Combpyne	10 D6
Chevithorne	10 A4		Christon	19 H7		Clashnoir	96 B3		Close Clark	56 P4		Colan	3 G3		Combrook	33 G4
Chew Magna	19 K6		Christon Bank	75 J2		Clatt	96 E3		Closworth	11 G6		Colaton Raleigh	10 B7		Combs, Derby	52 C6
Chew Stoke	19 K6		Christow	9 J7		Clatter	39 J7		Clothall	35 F6		Colbost	99 H8		Combs, Suff	36 F4
Chewton Mendip	19 K7		Chudleigh	5 J2		Clatworthy	10 B2		Clotton	50 E7		Colburn	66 B8		Combs Fords	36 F4
Chicheley	34 C5		Chudleigh Knighton	5 J2		Claughton, Lancs	57 J4		Clough Foot	51 J1		Colby, Cumbr	64 D5		Combwich	10 D1
Chichester	14 B5		Chulmleigh	9 G4		Claughton, Lancs	57 J6		Clousta	115 F3		Colby, Norf	47 H3		Comers	97 F5
Chickerell	11 H7		Chunal	52 C4		Claverdon	32 D3		Clouston	112 D5		Colby, I. of M	56 P4		Commins Coch	39 H6
Chicklade	12 B2		Church	58 C8		Claverham	19 J6		Clova	96 C6		Colchester	36 F7		Commondale	67 G6
Chicksands	34 E6		Churcham	20 B1		Clavering	35 H6		Clovelly	8 D3		Cold Ash	21 K5		Common Moor	4 C3
Chicksgrove	12 B3		Church Aston	41 J5		Claverley	41 J7		Clove Lodge	65 G6		Cold Ashby	33 J2		Common Side	53 F6
Chidden	13 J4		Church Brampton	33 K3		Claverton	20 B6		Clovenfords	82 C8		Cold Ashton	20 B5		Common, The	12 E2
Chiddingfold	14 C2		Church Broughton	42 E3		Clawdd-newydd	40 B1		Clovenstone	97 G4		Cold Aston	21 F1		Compstall	51 J4
Chiddingly	16 C4		Church Cove	2 F8		Clawton	8 D6		Clovullin	86 C2		Coldbackie	109 H2		Compton, W. Susx	14 A4
Chiddingstone	15 H1		Church Crookham	22 D7								Coldblow	23 L5		Compton, Surrey	14 C1
			Churchdown	32 A7													

Compton, Wilts......21 F7
Compton, Hants......13 G3
Compton, Devon......5 J3
Compton, Berks......21 K5
Compton Abbas......12 A4
Compton Abdale......20 E1
Compton Bassett......20 E5
Compton Beauchamp......21 G4
Compton Bishop......19 H7
Compton Chamberlayne......12 C3
Compton Dando......19 L6
Compton Dundon......11 F2
Compton Martin......19 K7
Compton Pauncefoot......11 H3
Compton Valence......11 G6
Comrie......87 K6
Conchra......78 C3
Conderton......32 B6
Condicote......32 D7
Condorrat......80 C4
Condover......41 F6
Coneyhurst......14 E3
Coneysthorpe......60 E3
Coney Weston......36 E2
Congerstone......43 F6
Congham......46 C4
Congleton......51 H7
Congresbury......19 J6
Conicavel......103 H7
Coningsby......45 F1
Conington, Cambs......34 E1
Conington, Cambs......35 G3
Conisbrough......53 H4
Conisby......76 B5
Conisholme......55 J4
Coniston, Humbs......61 J7
Coniston, Cumbr......63 J8
Coniston Cold......58 E5
Conistone......58 E4
Connah's Quay......50 B7
Connel......86 B5
Connel Park......72 B3
Connor Downs......2 D6
Conon Bridge......102 D7
Cononley......58 E6
Conordan......92 B2
Consall......42 B2
Consett......65 J2
Constable Burton......59 G1
Constantine......2 F7
Contin......102 C7
Conwy......49 G3
Conyer......25 F6
Cookbury......8 E5
Cookham......22 D4
Cookham Dean......22 D4
Cookham Rise......22 D4
Cookhill......32 C4
Cookley, Suff......37 J2
Cookley, H. & W......31 K1
Cookley Green......22 B3
Cookney......97 H6
Cooksbridge......15 H4
Cooksmill Green......24 C2
Coolham......14 E3
Cooling......24 D5
Coombe, Corn......8 C4
Coombe, Corn......3 H4
Coombe Bissett......12 D3
Coombe Hill......32 A7
Coombe Keynes......11 K7
Coombes......15 E5
Copdock......37 G5
Copford Green......36 E7
Copister......113 D3
Cople......34 E5
Copley......65 H5
Coplow Dale......52 D6
Copmanthorpe......60 C6
Coppathorne......8 C5
Coppenhall......42 B5
Copperhouse......2 D6
Coppingford......34 E1
Copplestone......9 H5
Coppull......50 E2
Copsale......14 E3
Copster Green......58 B7
Copt Heath......32 D2
Copt Hewick......59 J3
Copthorne......15 G2
Copt Oak......43 G5
Copythorne......13 F4
Corbridge......65 G1
Corby......34 B1
Corby Glen......44 C4
Coreley......31 H2
Corfe......10 D4
Corfe Castle......6 D6
Corfe Mullen......12 B6
Corfton......31 F1
Corgarff......96 B5
Corhampton......13 J3
Corlae......72 B5
Corley......33 F1
Corley Ash......32 E1
Corley Moor......32 E1
Cornelly......18 C4
Corney......56 E1
Cornforth......66 D4
Cornhill......104 E3
Cornhill-on-Tweed......83 G8
Cornholme......51 J1
Cornish Hall End......36 B6
Cornriggs......65 F3
Cornsay......65 J3
Corntown......102 F7
Cornwell......32 E7
Cornwood......5 G4
Cornworthy......5 J4
Corpach......93 G8
Corpusty......47 G3
Corran, Highld......86 C2
Corran, Highld......92 E5
Corrany......56 R3
Corrie......78 C7

Corrie Common......73 H6
Corriemoillie......102 B6
Corrimony......94 B2
Corringham, Lincs......54 C4
Corringham, Essex......24 D4
Corris......39 G6
Corris Uchaf......39 G6
Corry......92 C3
Corry of Ardnagrask......102 D8
Corscombe......11 G5
Corse......96 F1
Corsham......20 C5
Corsindae......97 F5
Corsley......11 K1
Corsley Heath......11 K1
Corsock......72 C7
Corston, Avon......20 A6
Corston, Wilts......20 D4
Corstorphine......81 G4
Corton, Wilts......12 B1
Corton, Suff......47 L7
Corton Denham......11 H3
Corwen......40 B2
Coryton, Essex......24 D4
Coryton, Devon......8 E7
Cosby......43 H7
Coseley......42 B7
Cosgrove......34 A5
Cosham......13 J5
Cosheston......26 E6
Cossall......43 G2
Cossington, Somer......10 E1
Cossington, Leic......43 J5
Costa......112 D4
Costessey......47 G5
Costock......43 H4
Coston......44 B4
Cote......21 J3
Cotebrook......50 E7
Cotegill......64 D7
Cotehill......64 B2
Cotes, Leic......43 H4
Cotes, Staffs......41 K3
Cotesbach......33 H1
Cotgrave......43 J3
Cothall......97 H4
Cotham......44 A2
Cothelstone......10 C2
Cotherstone......65 H6
Cothill......21 J3
Cotleigh......10 D5
Coton, Staffs......42 B3
Coton, Cambs......35 H4
Coton, Northnts......33 J2
Coton Clanford......42 A4
Coton in the Elms......42 E5
Cott......5 H3
Cottam, Notts......54 C5
Cottam, Lancs......57 J7
Cottenham......35 H3
Cotterdale......58 D1
Cottered......35 G7
Cotterstock......44 D7
Cottesbrooke......33 K2
Cottesmore......44 C5
Cottingham, Northnts......44 B7
Cottingham, Humbs......61 H7
Cottisford......33 H6
Cotton, Staffs......42 C2
Cotton, Suff......36 F3
Cotton End......34 D5
Cottown, Grampn......96 E3
Cottown, Grampn......97 G4
Cottown, Grampn......97 H1
Cotwalton......42 B3
Coughton, Warw......32 C3
Coughton, H. & W......31 G7
Coulags......101 F8
Coulby Newham......66 F6
Coull......96 E5
Coulport......78 E3
Coulsdon......23 J7
Coulston......20 D7
Coulter......73 F1
Coulton......60 D3
Cound......41 G6
Coundon......66 C5
Coundon Grange......66 C5
Countersett......58 E2
Countess Wear......9 K7
Countesthorpe......43 H7
Countisbury......9 H1
Coupar Angus......88 E4
Coupland......75 F1
Cour......77 H7
Courteachan......92 C6
Courteenhall......34 A4
Court Henry......27 K4
Courtsend......25 G3
Courtway......10 D2
Cousland......81 J5
Cousley Wood......16 D2
Cove, Hants......22 D7
Cove, Strath......78 E3
Cove, Highld......100 E3
Cove, Devon......9 K4
Cove Bay......97 J5
Covehithe......37 L1
Coven......42 B6
Coveney......35 H1
Covenham St Bartholomew......55 H4
Covenham St Mary......55 H4
Coventry......33 F2
Coverack......3 F8
Coverham......59 G2
Covington......34 D2
Cowan Bridge......58 B3
Cowbeech......16 D4
Cowbit......45 F5
Cowbridge......18 D5
Cowden......15 H1
Cowdenbeath......81 G2
Cowes......13 G6
Cowesby......60 B2
Cowfold......15 F3

Cowgill......58 C2
Cowick......53 J1
Cowie......80 D3
Cowley, Glos......20 D1
Cowley, G. Lon......22 F4
Cowley, Oxon......21 K2
Cowley, Devon......9 K6
Cowling, N. Yks......58 E6
Cowling, N. Yks......59 H2
Cowlinge......36 C4
Cowpen Bewley......66 E5
Cowplain......13 J4
Cowshill......65 F3
Cowstrandburn......81 F2
Coxbank......41 H2
Coxbench......43 F2
Cox Common......37 K1
Coxheath......24 D7
Coxhoe......66 D4
Coxley......11 G1
Coxwold......60 C3
Coychurch......18 D5
Coylumbridge......95 H4
Coynach......96 D5
Crabbs Cross......32 C3
Crabtree......15 F3
Crabtree Green......40 E2
Crackenthorpe......64 D5
Crackington......8 B6
Cracklebank......41 J5
Crackpot......58 E1
Cracoe......58 E4
Cradley......31 J5
Crafthole......4 D4
Craggan......95 J3
Cragg Vale......52 C1
Craghead......66 C2
Crai......29 F7
Craichie......89 H4
Craig, D. & G......72 B7
Craig, Highld......101 G8
Craig Castle......96 D3
Craigcefnparc......27 L6
Craigdam......97 H2
Craigearn......97 G4
Craigellachie......104 B4
Craigendoran......78 F3
Craighouse......76 E5
Craigie, Grampn......97 J4
Craigie, Strath......71 K1
Craiglockhart......81 H4
Craigmaud......105 H3
Craigmillar......81 H4
Craignant......40 D3
Craigneuk, Strath......80 C5
Craigneuk, Strath......80 C6
Craignure......85 J5
Craigo......89 J2
Craigrothie......89 F7
Craigton, Tays......88 F3
Craigton, Grampn......97 H5
Craigton, Tays......89 H5
Craigtown......110 E3
Craik......73 J4
Crail......89 J8
Crailing......74 C2
Crailinghall......74 C2
Crakehall......59 H1
Cramalt......73 G2
Crambe......60 E4
Cramlington......75 J7
Cramond......81 G4
Cramond Bridge......81 G4
Cranage......51 G7
Cranberry......41 K3
Cranborne......12 C4
Cranbourne......22 E5
Cranbrook......16 E2
Cranbrook Common......16 E2
Cranfield......34 C5
Cranford St Andrew......34 C2
Cranford St John......34 C2
Cranham, G. Lon......24 B4
Cranham, Glos......20 C1
Crank......50 E4
Cranleigh......14 D2
Cranmore, I. of W......13 F6
Cranmore, Somer......11 H1
Cranna......104 F3
Crannoch......104 D3
Cranoe......44 A7
Cransford......37 J3
Cranshaws......82 E5
Cranstal......56 R1
Crantock......3 F4
Cranwell......44 D2
Cranwich......46 C7
Cranworth......46 E6
Crapstone......4 F3
Craskins......96 E5
Crask of Aigas......102 C8
Craster......75 J3
Craswall......30 D6
Cratfield......37 J2
Crathes......96 G6
Crathie, Grampn......96 B6
Crathie, Highld......94 D6
Crathorne......66 E7
Craven Arms......31 F1
Crawcrook......65 J1
Crawford......72 E2
Crawfordjohn......72 D2
Crawick......72 C3
Crawleside......65 G3
Crawley, W. Susx......15 F2
Crawley, Hants......13 G2
Crawley, Oxon......21 H1
Crawley Down......15 G3
Crawshawbooth......51 H1
Crawton......97 H8
Cray......58 D3
Crayford......23 L5
Crayke......60 C3
Crays Hill......24 D3

Cray's Pond......22 B4
Creacombe......9 J4
Creagorry......98 C8
Creaton......33 K2
Creca......73 H7
Credenhill......31 F5
Crediton......9 J5
Creech St Michael......10 D3
Creed......3 H5
Creekmouth......23 K4
Creeting St Mary......36 F4
Creeton......44 D4
Creetown......69 F5
Creggans......78 C1
Cregneish......56 N5
Cregrina......30 C4
Creich......88 F6
Creigiau......18 E4
Cremyll......4 E4
Cressage......41 G6
Cresselly......26 E6
Cressing......36 C7
Cresswell, Staffs......42 B3
Cresswell, Northum......75 J5
Cresswell Quay......26 E6
Creswell......53 H6
Cretingham......37 H3
Cretshengan......77 G5
Crewe, Ches......41 F1
Crewe, Ches......41 J1
Crew Green......40 E5
Crewkerne......11 F5
Crews Hill......23 J3
Crianlarich......87 F6
Cribyn......27 K1
Criccieth......38 E3
Crich......43 F1
Crichie......105 J4
Crichton......81 J5
Crick, Northnts......33 H2
Crick, Gwent......19 J3
Crickadarn......29 H5
Cricket St Thomas......10 E5
Crickheath......40 D4
Crickhowell......19 G1
Cricklade......20 F3
Cridling Stubbs......53 H1
Crieff......88 A6
Criggion......40 D5
Crigglestone......53 F2
Crimond......105 K3
Crimplesham......46 B6
Crinan......77 G2
Cringleford......47 G6
Crinow......26 F5
Crippesease......2 D6
Cripp's Corner......16 E3
Crockenhill......23 L6
Crockernwell......9 H6
Crockerton......12 A1
Crocketford or Ninemile Bar......72 D7
Crockey Hill......60 D6
Crockham Hill......23 K7
Crockleford Heath......36 F7
Croeserw......18 C3
Croes-goch......26 C3
Croesor......39 F2
Croesyceiliog......19 H3
Croesyceiliog......27 J5
Croes-y-mwyalch......19 H3
Croft, Ches......51 F4
Croft, Leic......43 H7
Croft, Lincs......55 K7
Croftamie......79 G3
Crofton......53 F2
Croft-on-Tees......66 C7
Crofts of Benachielt......111 H5
Crofts of Haddo......97 H2
Crofts of Inverthernie......105 G4
Crofty......27 K7
Croggan......85 J6
Croglin......64 C3
Croick......107 F5
Croir......107 F5
Cromarty......103 F6
Cromdale......95 J3
Cromer, Herts......35 F7
Cromer, Norf......47 H2
Cromford......42 E1
Cromhall......20 A3
Cromhall Common......20 A4
Cromore......107 F3
Cromra......94 D6
Cromwell......54 B7
Cronberry......72 B2
Crondall......14 A1
Cronk, The......56 Q2
Cronk-y-Voddy......56 Q3
Cronton......50 D5
Crook, Durham......66 B4
Crook, Cumbr......57 H1
Crookham, Northum......83 H8
Crookham, Berks......21 K6
Crookham Village......22 C7
Crookhouse......74 D2
Crooklands......57 J2
Cropredy......33 G5
Cropston......43 H5
Cropthorne......32 B5
Cropton......60 E2
Cropwell Bishop......43 J3
Cropwell Butler......43 J3
Cros, W. Isles......107 K2
Crosby, Humbs......54 C2
Crosby, Mers......50 C4
Crosby, Cumbr......62 F4
Crosby, I. of M......56 Q4
Crosby Garrett......64 E7
Crosby-on-Eden......64 B2
Crosby Ravensworth......64 D6
Croscombe......11 G1
Cross, Somer......19 J7
Crossapol......84 A4
Cross Ash......19 J1
Crossbost......107 H6

Crosscanonby......62 F4
Crossdale Street......47 H3
Crossdougal......90 C3
Crossens......50 C2
Crossford, Strath......80 D7
Crossford, Fife......81 F3
Crossgates, Fife......81 G3
Crossgates, Powys......29 H3
Crossgill......57 J4
Cross Green, Devon......8 D7
Cross Green, Suff......36 E4
Crosshands, Dyfed......27 F4
Cross Hands, Dyfed......27 K5
Crosshill, Fife......81 G2
Crosshill, Strath......71 J4
Crosshouse......79 F8
Cross Houses......41 G6
Crossings......74 B7
Cross in Hand......16 C3
Cross Inn, Dyfed......28 A4
Cross Inn, Dyfed......28 C3
Cross Inn, M. Glam......18 E4
Crosskeys......19 G3
Crosskirk......111 G1
Cross Lanes, N. Yks......60 C4
Cross Lanes, Clwyd......40 E2
Crosslanes, Shrops......40 E5
Crosslee......73 J3
Crossmichael......72 C8
Crossmoor......57 H7
Cross of Jackston......97 G2
Crossroads......97 G6
Crossway......19 J1
Crossway Green......31 K3
Crossways......11 J7
Crosswell......26 F3
Crosthwaite......57 H1
Croston......50 D2
Crostwick......47 H5
Crostwight......47 J3
Croughton......33 H6
Crovie......105 H2
Crowan......2 E6
Crowborough......15 J2
Crowcombe......10 C2
Crowdecote......52 D7
Crowfield, Suff......37 G4
Crowfield, Northnts......33 J5
Crow Hill......31 H7
Crowhurst, E. Susx......16 E4
Crowhurst, Surrey......15 G1
Crowland......45 F5
Crowlas......2 D6
Crowle, Humbs......54 B2
Crowle, H. & W......32 B4
Crowmarsh Gifford......22 B4
Crownhill......4 E4
Crownthorpe......47 F6
Crowthorne......22 D6
Crowthorn School......51 G2
Crowton......50 E6
Croxall......42 D5
Croxdale......66 C4
Croxden......42 C3
Croxley Green......22 F3
Croxton, Norf......36 D1
Croxton, Humbs......54 E2
Croxton, Cambs......35 F4
Croxton, Staffs......41 J3
Croxton Kerrial......44 B4
Croxton Park......44 B4
Croy, Strath......80 C4
Croy, Highld......103 F8
Croyde......8 E2
Croydon, Cambs......35 G5
Croydon, G. Lon......23 J6
Cruckmeole......41 F6
Cruckton......41 F5
Cruden Bay......97 K2
Crudgington......41 H5
Crudwell......20 D3
Crug......30 C2
Crugmeer......3 H2
Crugybar......27 L3
Crulivig......107 F5
Crumlin......19 G3
Crundale, Dyfed......26 D5
Crundale, Kent......17 H1
Cruwys Morchard......9 J4
Crux Easton......21 J7
Crwbin......27 J5
Crymych......26 F3
Crynant......18 B2
Cuaig......100 D7
Cubbington......33 F3
Cubert......3 F4
Cublington......34 B7
Cuckfield......15 G3
Cucklington......11 J3
Cuckney......53 H6
Cuddesdon......21 K2
Cuddington, Bucks......22 C1
Cuddington, Ches......50 E6
Cuddington Heath......41 F2
Cuddy Hill......57 H7
Cudham......23 K7
Cudliptown......5 H5
Cudworth, Somer......10 E4
Cudworth, S. Yks......53 F3
Cuffley......23 J2
Culbo......102 E6
Culbokie......102 E6
Culburnie......94 C1
Culcabock......102 E8
Culcharry......103 G7
Culcheth......51 F4
Cul Doirlinn......85 H1
Culdrain......96 E2
Culduie......92 D1
Culford......36 D2
Culgaith......64 D5
Culham......21 K3
Culkein......108 B5
Culkerton......20 D3

Cullachie......95 H3
Cullen......104 E2
Cullercoats......75 K7
Cullicudden......102 E6
Cullingworth......59 F7
Cullipool......85 J7
Cullivoe......117 G2
Cullompton......10 B5
Culmington......31 F1
Culmstock......10 C4
Culnacraig......101 G4
Culnaknock......100 B6
Culrain......102 D3
Culross......80 E3
Culroy......71 J3
Culsh......105 H4
Culswick......114 E4
Cultercullen......97 J3
Cults, Grampn......96 E2
Cults, Grampn......97 H5
Culverstone Green......24 C6
Culverthorpe......44 D2
Culworth......33 H5
Cumbernauld......80 C4
Cumberworth......55 K6
Cuminestown......105 H3
Cummersdale......63 J2
Cummertrees......73 G8
Cummingstown......103 K6
Cumnock......72 B2
Cumnor......21 J2
Cumrew......64 C2
Cumwhinton......64 B2
Cumwhitton......64 C2
Cundall......59 K3
Cunninghamhead......79 F7
Cunnister......117 G3
Cupar......89 F7
Cupar Muir......89 F7
Curbar......52 E6
Curbridge, Oxon......21 H2
Curbridge, Hants......13 H4
Curdridge......13 H4
Curdworth......42 D7
Curland......10 D4
Currie......81 G5
Curry Mallet......10 E3
Curry Rivel......10 E3
Curtisden Green......16 E1
Curtisknowle......5 H4
Cury......2 E7
Cushnie......105 G2
Cushuish......10 C2
Cusop......30 D5
Cutiau......39 F5
Cutnall Green......32 A3
Cutsdean......32 C6
Cutthorpe......53 F6
Cuxham......22 B3
Cuxton......24 D6
Cuxwold......55 F3
Cwm, Gwent......19 F2
Cwm, Clwyd......49 K3
Cwmafan......18 B3
Cwmaman......18 E4
Cwmann......27 K2
Cwmavon......19 G2
Cwmbach, M. Glam......18 E2
Cwmbach, Dyfed......27 G4
Cwmbelan......29 H1
Cwmbran......19 G3
Cwmcarn......19 G3
Cwmcarvan......19 J2
Cwm-Cewydd......39 H5
Cwm-Cou......27 G2
Cwmdare......18 D2
Cwmdu, Powys......30 C7
Cwmdu, Dyfed......27 L3
Cwmduad......27 H3
Cwmfelin Boeth......27 F5
Cwmfelinfach......19 F3
Cwmfelin Mynach......27 G4
Cwmffrwd......27 J5
Cwmgwrach......18 C2
Cwm Irfon......29 F5
Cwmisfael......27 J5
Cwm-Llinau......39 H5
Cwmllynfell......18 B1
Cwmparc......18 D3
Cwmpengraig......27 H3
Cwm Penmachno......39 G2
Cwmsychbant......27 J2
Cwmsymlog......28 D1
Cwmtillery......19 G2
Cwm-twrch Isaf......18 B1
Cwm-twrch Uchaf......18 B1
Cwm-y-glo......48 E4
Cwmyoy......30 E7
Cwmystwyth......28 E2
Cwrtnewydd......27 J2
Cwrt-y-cadno......28 C3
Cwrt-y-gollen......19 G1
Cyffylliog......40 B1
Cyfronydd......30 B1
Cymmer, W. Glam......18 C3
Cymmer, M. Glam......18 E3
Cynghordy......28 D4
Cynwyd......40 B2
Cynwyl Elfed......27 H4

D

Dacre, Cumbr......64 B5
Dacre, N. Yks......59 G4
Dacre Banks......59 G4
Daddry Shield......65 F4
Dadford......33 J6
Dadlington......43 G7
Dafen......27 K6
Dagenham......23 L4
Daglingworth......20 D2

Dagnall....22 E1
Dail....107 J2
Dailly....71 H4
Dairsie or Osnaburgh....89 G7
Dalavich....86 B7
Dalbeattie....69 K4
Dalbeg....107 G4
Dalblair....72 B3
Dalby....56 P4
Dalchalloch....87 K2
Dalchenna....86 C8
Dalcreichart....93 J4
Dalderby....55 G7
Dale, Shetld....114 D3
Dale, Dyfed....26 C6
Dale Abbey....43 G3
Dale Head....64 B6
Dalgarven....78 E7
Dalgety Bay....81 G3
Dalginross....87 K6
Dalhalvaig....110 E3
Dalham....36 C3
Daliburgh....90 C3
Dalkeith....81 J5
Dallas....103 K7
Dalleagles....71 L3
Dallinghoo....37 H4
Dallington....16 D4
Dalmally....86 D6
Dalmary....79 H2
Dalmellington....71 K4
Dalmeny....81 G4
Dalmore, Highld....102 E6
Dalmore, W. Isles....107 G4
Dalnabreck....85 J2
Dalnacreich....101 K7
Dalnavie....102 E5
Dalreavoch....103 F2
Dalry....78 E7
Dalrymple....71 J3
Dalserf....80 C6
Dalston....63 J2
Dalswinton....72 E6
Dalton, Lancs....50 D3
Dalton, Northum....65 G2
Dalton, S. Yks....53 G4
Dalton, D. & G.....73 G7
Dalton, Northum....75 H7
Dalton, N. Yks....65 J7
Dalton, N. Yks....59 K3
Dalton-in-Furness....57 F3
Dalton-le-Dale....66 E3
Dalton-on-Tees....66 C7
Dalton Piercy....66 E4
Dalwhinnie....94 E7
Dalwood....10 D5
Damerham....12 D4
Damgate....47 K6
Damnaglaur....68 C7
Danbury....24 D2
Danby....67 H7
Danby Wiske....66 D8
Danderhall....81 J5
Danebridge, Staffs....51 J7
Danebridge, Ches....51 J7
Dane End....35 G7
Danehill....15 H3
Darenth....24 B5
Daresbury....50 E5
Darfield....53 G3
Dargate....25 G6
Darite....4 C3
Darlaston....42 B7
Darlingscote....32 E5
Darlington....66 C6
Darliston....41 G3
Darlton....54 B6
Darowen....39 H6
Darra....105 G4
Darras Hall....75 H7
Darrington....53 G1
Darsham....37 K3
Dartford....23 L5
Dartington....5 H3
Dartmeet....5 G2
Dartmouth....5 J4
Darton....53 F2
Darvel....79 H8
Darwen....51 F1
Datchet....22 E5
Datchworth....23 H1
Daugh of Kinermony....96 B1
Dauntsey....20 D4
Davenham....51 F6
Daventry....33 H3
Davidstow....8 B7
Davington....73 H4
Daviot, Highld....94 F2
Daviot, Grampn....97 G3
Davoch of Grange....104 D3
Dawley....41 H6
Dawlish....5 K2
Dawlish Warren....5 K2
Dawn....49 H3
Daws Heath....24 E4
Dawsmere....45 H3
Daylesford....32 E7
Ddol Cownwy....40 B5
Deal....25 K7
Dean, Cumbr....62 F5
Dean, Somer....11 H1
Dean, Devon....5 H3
Dean, Hants....13 H4
Deanburnhaugh....73 J3
Deane....21 K7
Deanland....12 B4
Dean Prior....5 H3
Dean Row....51 H5
Deans....80 F5
Deanscales....63 F5
Deanshanger....34 A6
Deanston....80 C1
Dearham....62 F4
Dearne....53 G3
Debach....37 H4

Debden....35 J6
Debden Green....35 J6
Debenham....37 G3
Dechmont....81 F4
Deddington....33 G6
Dedham....36 F6
Dedridge....81 F5
Deene....44 C7
Deenethorpe....44 C7
Deepcut....22 E7
Deepdale....58 C2
Deeping Gate....44 E6
Deeping St James....44 E6
Deeping St Nicholas....45 F5
Deerhill....104 D3
Deerhurst....32 A7
Deerness....113 F6
Defford....32 B5
Defynnog....29 G7
Deganwy....49 G3
Deighton, N. Yks....60 D6
Deighton, N. Yks....66 D7
Deiniolen....48 E4
Delabole....8 A7
Delamere....50 E7
Delfrigs....97 J3
Delliefure....95 J2
Delph....51 J3
Dembleby....44 D3
Denbigh....49 K4
Denbury....5 J3
Denby....43 F2
Denby Dale....52 E3
Denchworth....21 H3
Denford....34 C2
Dengie, Essex....25 F2
Dengie, Essex....25 F2
Denham, Suff....36 C3
Denham, Bucks....22 F4
Denham, Suff....37 G2
Denham Green....22 F4
Denham Street....37 G2
Denhead, Fife....89 G7
Denhead, Grampn....105 K3
Denholm....74 B3
Denholme....59 F7
Denmead....13 J4
Denmore....97 J4
Denne Park....14 E3
Dennington....37 H3
Denny....80 D3
Dennyloanhead....80 D3
Denshaw....51 J2
Denside....97 H6
Densole....17 K1
Denston....36 C4
Denstone....42 C2
Dent....58 C2
Den, The....78 F6
Denton, Lincs....44 B3
Denton, Northnts....34 B4
Denton, Durham....66 C6
Denton, Cambs....34 E1
Denton, N. Yks....59 G6
Denton, Norf....37 H1
Denton, E. Susx....15 H5
Denton, G. Man....51 J4
Denton, Kent....17 K1
Denton, Oxon....21 K2
Denver....45 K6
Denwick....75 J3
Deopham....46 F6
Deopham Green....46 F7
Depden Green....36 C4
Deptford, Wilts....12 C2
Deptford, G. Lon....23 J5
Derby....43 F3
Derbyhaven....56 P5
Deri....18 F2
Derrington....42 A4
Derryguaig....85 F5
Derry Hill....20 D5
Derrythorpe....54 C3
Dersingham....46 B3
Dervaig....85 F3
Derwen....40 B1
Desborough....34 B1
Desford....43 G6
Detchant....83 J8
Detling....24 D7
Deuddwr....40 D5
Devauden....19 J3
Devil's Bridge....28 E2
Devizes....20 E6
Devonport....4 E4
Devonside....80 E2
Devoran....3 F6
Dewlish....11 J6
Dewsbury....52 E1
Dhoon....56 R3
Dhoor....56 R2
Dhowin....56 R1
Dial Post....14 E4
Dibden....13 G5
Dibden Purlieu....13 G5
Dickleburgh....37 G1
Didbrook....32 C6
Didcot....21 K4
Diddington....35 E3
Diddlebury....31 G1
Didley....31 F6
Didmarton....20 C4
Didsbury....51 H4
Didworthy....5 G3
Digby....44 D1
Diggle....52 C3
Dihewyd....28 B4
Dilham....47 J4
Dilhorne....42 B2
Dilston....65 G1
Dilton Marsh....11 K1
Dilwyn....31 F4
Dinas, Gwyn....38 B3
Dinas, Dyfed....27 G3
Dinas Cross....26 E3

Dinas Mawddwy....39 H5
Dinas Powys....18 F5
Dinchope....31 F1
Dinder....11 G1
Dinedor....31 G6
Dines Green....31 K4
Dingestow....19 J1
Dingley....34 K1
Dingwall....102 D7
Dinnet....96 D6
Dinnington, Somer....10 F4
Dinnington, S. Yks....53 H5
Dinnington, T. & W.....75 J7
Dinorwig....48 E4
Dinton, Bucks....22 C1
Dinton, Wilts....12 C2
Dinwoodie Mains....73 G5
Dinworthy....8 D4
Dippen....70 F2
Dippenhall....14 B1
Dipple....104 C3
Diptford....5 H4
Dipton....65 J2
Dirleton....82 D3
Discoed....30 D3
Diseworth....43 G4
Dishes....113 G4
Disley....51 J5
Diss....37 G2
Disserth....29 H4
Distington....62 F5
Ditcheat....11 H2
Ditchingham....47 J7
Ditchling....15 G4
Dittisham....5 J4
Ditton, Ches....50 D5
Ditton, Kent....24 D7
Ditton Green....36 B4
Ditton Priors....41 H8
Dixton, Glos....32 B6
Dixton, Gwent....19 K1
Dlengrasco....99 K8
Dobwalls....4 C3
Doccombe....9 H7
Dochgarroch....94 E1
Docking....46 C3
Docklow....31 G4
Dockray....63 J5
Doddinghurst....24 B3
Doddington, Lincs....54 D6
Doddington, Northum....75 F1
Doddington, Kent....25 F7
Doddington, Shrops....31 H2
Doddington, Cambs....45 H7
Doddiscombsleigh....9 J7
Dodford, H. & W.....32 B2
Dodford, Northnts....33 J3
Dodington....20 B4
Dodleston....50 C7
Dodworth....53 F3
Doe Lea....53 G7
Dogmersfield....22 C7
Dog Village....10 A6
Dogdyke....45 F1
Dolanog....40 B5
Dolau....30 C3
Dolbenmaen....38 E2
Dolfach....29 G2
Dolfor....30 C1
Dolgarrog....49 G4
Dolgellau....39 G5
Dolgran....27 J3
Doll....103 G2
Dollar....80 E2
Dolley Green....30 D3
Dolphinholme....57 J5
Dolphinton....81 G7
Dolton....9 F4
Dolwen....49 H3
Dolwyddelan....39 G1
Dol-y-cannau....30 D5
Dolyhir....30 D4
Domgay....40 D5
Doncaster....53 H3
Donhead St Andrew....12 B3
Donhead St Mary....12 B3
Donibristle....81 G3
Donington....45 F3
Donington on Bain....55 G5
Donington, W. Susx....14 B5
Donnington, Glos....32 D7
Donnington, Shrops....41 G6
Donnington, Shrops....41 J5
Donnington, Berks....21 J6
Donnington, H. & W.....31 J6
Donyatt....10 E4
Doonfoot....71 J3
Doonholm....71 J3
Dorchester, Dorset....11 H6
Dorchester, Oxon....21 K3
Dordon....42 E6
Dore....53 F5
Dores....94 D2
Dorking....14 E1
Dormansland....15 H1
Dormanstown....67 F5
Dormington....31 G5
Dorney....22 E5
Dornie....92 E3
Dornoch....103 F4
Dornock....73 H8
Dorridge....32 D2
Dorrington, Lincs....44 D1
Dorrington, Shrops....41 F6
Dorsington....32 D5
Dorstone....30 E5
Dosthill....42 E6
Dottery....11 F6
Doublebois....4 B3
Doughton....20 C3
Douglas, Strath....72 D1
Douglas, I. of M.....56 Q4

Douglas and Angus....89 G5
Douglastown....89 G4
Douglas Water....80 D8
Doulting....11 H1
Dounby....112 C4
Doune....80 C1
Douneside....96 D5
Dounie....102 D3
Dousland....4 F3
Dove Holes....52 C6
Dovenby....63 F4
Dover....17 L1
Doverdale....32 A3
Doveridge....42 D3
Dowdeswell....20 E1
Dowland....9 F4
Dowlish Wake....10 E4
Down Ampney....20 F3
Downderry....4 D4
Downe....23 K6
Downend, I. of W.....13 H7
Downend, Berks....21 J5
Downfield....89 F5
Downgate....4 D2
Downham, Lancs....58 C6
Downham, Essex....24 D3
Downham, Northum....74 E1
Downham Market....45 K6
Down Hatherley....32 A7
Downhead....11 H1
Downholme....65 J8
Downies....97 J6
Downley....22 D3
Downs....18 F5
Downside Abbey....20 A7
Down St Mary....9 H5
Downton, Wilts....12 D3
Downton, Hants....12 E6
Downton on the Rock....31 F2
Dowsby....44 E4
Dowsdale....45 F5
Dowthwaitehead....63 J5
Doxey....42 B4
Doxford Park....66 D2
Doynton....20 B5
Draethen....19 G4
Draffan....80 C7
Drakeland Corner....4 F4
Drakemyre....78 E6
Drakes Broughton....32 B5
Draughton, Northnts....34 B1
Draughton, N. Yks....58 F5
Drax....53 J1
Draycote....33 G2
Draycott, Glos....32 D6
Draycott, Derby....43 G3
Draycott, Somer....19 J7
Draycott in the Clay....42 D4
Draycott in the Moors....42 B2
Drayton, H. & W.....32 B2
Drayton, Leic....44 B7
Drayton, Somer....10 F3
Drayton, Norf....47 G5
Drayton, Oxon....33 G5
Drayton, Oxon....21 J3
Drayton, Hants....13 J5
Drayton Bassett....42 D6
Drayton Parslow....34 B7
Drayton St Leonard....21 K3
Drefach, Dyfed....27 H3
Dre-fach, Dyfed....27 K2
Drefach, Dyfed....27 K5
Drefelin....27 H3
Dreghorn....79 F8
Drem....82 D4
Drewsteignton....9 H6
Driby....55 H6
Driffield, Glos....20 E3
Driffield, Humbs....61 H5
Drift....4 B6
Drigg....62 F8
Drighlington....59 H8
Drimnin....85 G3
Drimpton....11 F5
Drinisiadar....99 G3
Drinkstone....36 E3
Drinkstone Green....36 E3
Drointon....42 C4
Droitwich....32 A3
Droman....108 C3
Dron....88 D7
Dronfield....53 F6
Dronfield Woodhouse....53 F6
Drongan....71 K3
Droxford....13 J4
Droylsden....51 J4
Druid....40 B2
Druidston....26 C5
Druimarbin....86 C1
Druimdrishaig....77 K2
Druimindarroch....92 C7
Druimkinnerras....94 C2
Drum....81 F1
Drumbeg....108 C5
Drumblade....96 E1
Drumbuie....92 D2
Drumchapel....79 H4
Drumchardine....102 D8
Drumchork....100 E4
Drumclog....79 J8
Drumelzier....73 G1
Drumfearn....92 C4
Drumgley....89 G3
Drumguish....95 F6
Drumin....95 K2
Drumlasie....97 F3
Drumlemble....70 B3
Drumligair....97 J4
Drumlithie....97 G7
Drummoddie....64 D7
Drummond....61 G8
Drummore....61 G8
Drumnadrochit....94 D3
Drumnagorrach....104 E3
Drumoak....97 G6
Drums....97 J3
Drumsallie....93 F8

Drumsturdy....89 G5
Drumuie....99 K8
Drumuillie....95 H3
Drumwhindle....97 J2
Drury....50 B7
Drybeck....64 D6
Drybridge, Grampn....104 D2
Drybridge, Strath....79 F8
Drybrook....19 L1
Dry Doddington....44 B2
Dry Drayton....35 G3
Dryhope....73 H2
Drymen....79 G3
Drymuir....105 J4
Drynoch....91 K2
Dubford....105 G2
Dubwath....63 G4
Duchanstone....41 F1
Duck's Cross....34 E4
Duddenhoe End....35 H6
Duddleston....81 H4
Duddington....44 C6
Duddo....83 H7
Duddon....50 E7
Duddon Bridge....56 E2
Dudleston Heath....40 E3
Dudley, W. Mids....42 B7
Dudley, T. & W.....75 J7
Duffield....43 F2
Duffryn, W. Glam....18 C3
Duffryn, Gwent....19 G4
Dufftown....96 C1
Duffus....103 K6
Dufton....64 D5
Duggleby....60 F4
Duirinish....92 D2
Duisky....93 G8
Dukestown....18 F1
Dukinfield....51 J4
Dulas....48 D2
Dulford....10 B5
Dulcote....11 G1
Dull....87 L4
Dullingham....35 K4
Dulnain Bridge....95 H3
Duloe, Corn....4 C4
Duloe, Beds....34 E3
Dulsie....95 H1
Dulverton....9 K3
Dulwich....23 J5
Dumbarton....79 F4
Dumbleton....32 C6
Dumcrieff....73 G4
Dumfries....72 E7
Dumgoyne....79 H3
Dummer....13 H1
Dun....92 B3
Dunball....10 E1
Dunbar....82 E4
Dunbeath....111 H6
Dunbeg....85 K5
Dunblane....80 C1
Dunbog....88 E7
Duncanston....102 D7
Duncanston....96 E3
Dunchideock....9 J7
Dunchurch....33 G2
Duncote....33 J4
Duncow....72 E6
Duncrievie....88 D8
Duncton....14 C4
Dundee....89 G5
Dundon....11 F2
Dundonald....71 J1
Dundonnell....101 G4
Dundraw....63 H3
Dundreggan....93 K4
Dundrennan....69 J6
Dundry....19 K6
Dunecht....97 G5
Dunfermline....81 F3
Dunford Bridge....52 D3
Dunham-on-the-Hill....50 D6
Dunham on Trent....54 C6
Dunhampton....31 K3
Dunham Town....51 G5
Dunholme....54 E6
Dunino....89 H7
Dunipace....80 D3
Dunkeld....88 C4
Dunkeswell....10 C5
Dunkirk....25 G7
Dunk's Green....24 C7
Dunley....31 J3
Dunlop....79 G7
Dunmore, Central....80 D3
Dunmore, Strath....77 G5
Dunnet....111 J1
Dunnichen....89 H4
Dunning....88 C7
Dunnington, Warw....32 C4
Dunnington, N. Yks....60 D5
Dunnington, Humbs....61 J5
Dunnockshaw....51 H1
Dunollie....85 K5
Dunoon....78 D4
Dunragit....68 C5
Duns....83 F6
Dunsby....44 E4
Dunscore....72 D6
Dunscroft....53 J3
Dunsden Green....22 C5
Dunsfold....14 D2
Dunsford....9 J7
Dunshalt....88 E7
Dunsley....67 J6
Dunsmore....22 D2
Dunsop Bridge....58 B5
Dunstable....34 D7
Dunstall....42 D4
Dunstall Green....36 C3
Dunstan....75 J3
Dunster....10 A1
Dunston, Lincs....54 E7
Duns Tew....33 G7

Dunston, Staffs....42 B5
Dunston, T. & W.....66 C1
Dunston, Lincs....54 E7
Dunston, Norf....47 H6
Dunsville....53 J3
Dunswell....61 H7
Dunterton....4 D2
Duntisbourne Abbots....20 D2
Duntisbourne Leer....20 D2
Duntisbourne Rouse....20 D2
Duntish....11 H5
Duntocher....79 G4
Dunton, Bucks....34 B7
Dunton, Beds....35 F5
Dunton, Norf....46 D3
Dunton Bassett....43 H7
Dunton Green....23 L7
Dunure....71 H3
Dunvant....27 K7
Dunvegan....99 H8
Dunwich....37 K2
Durdar....63 K2
Durham....66 C3
Durisdeer....72 D4
Durleigh....10 D2
Durley, Wilts....21 G6
Durley, Hants....13 H4
Durnamuck....101 G3
Durness....108 F2
Durno....97 G3
Durran....111 H2
Durrington, Wilts....12 D1
Durrington, W. Susx....14 E5
Dursley....20 B3
Durston....10 D3
Durweston....11 K5
Dury....113 D3
Duston....33 K3
Duthil....95 H3
Dutlas....30 D2
Duton Hill....35 K7
Dutton....50 E6
Duxford....35 H5
Dwygyfylchi....49 G3
Dwyran....48 D4
Dyce....97 H4
Dye House....65 G2
Dyffryn, Gwyn....48 B3
Dyffryn, M. Glam....18 C3
Dyffryn Ardudwy....38 E4
Dyffryn Ceidrych....28 E7
Dyffryn Cellwen....18 C1
Dyke, Devon....8 D3
Dyke, Lincs....44 E4
Dyke, Grampn....103 H7
Dykehead, Strath....80 D6
Dykehead, Tays....89 F2
Dylife....39 H7
Dymchurch....17 J3
Dymock....31 J6
Dyrham....20 B5
Dysart....81 J2
Dyserth....49 K3

E

Eagland Hill....57 H6
Eagle....54 C7
Eaglescliffe....66 E6
Eaglesfield, Cumbr....63 F5
Eaglesfield, D. & G.....73 H7
Eaglesham....79 H6
Eairy....56 P4
Eakring....53 J7
Ealand....54 B2
Ealing....23 G4
Eamont Bridge....64 C5
Earby....58 E6
Earcroft....51 F1
Eardington....41 J7
Eardisland....31 F4
Eardisley....30 E5
Eardiston, Shrops....40 E4
Eardiston, H. & W.....31 H3
Earith....35 G2
Earle....75 F2
Earlestown....50 E4
Earlham....47 G6
Earlish....99 H6
Earls Barton....34 B3
Earls Colne....36 D7
Earl's Croome....32 A5
Earlsdon....33 F2
Earlsferry....82 C2
Earlsford....97 H2
Earl's Green....36 F3
Earl Shilton....43 G7
Earl Sterndale....52 C7
Earlston, Border....82 D8
Earlston, Strath....79 G8
Earl Stonham....37 G4
Earlswood, Warw....32 D2
Earlswood, Gwent....19 J3
Earnley....14 B6
Earsary....90 C6
Earsdon....75 K7
Earsham....47 J8
Earswick....60 D5
Eartham....14 C5
Easby....67 F7
Easdale....85 J7
Easebourne....14 B3
Easenhall....33 G2
Easington, Bucks....22 B1
Easington, Northum....75 H1
Easington, Humbs....55 H2
Easington, Cleve....67 H6
Easington Lane....66 D3
Easingwold....60 C4
Easole Street....25 J7
Eassie....89 F4

East Aberthaw............18 E6
East Allington...........5 H5
East Anstey..............9 J3
East Ashling............14 B5
East Auchronie..........97 H5
East Barkwith...........55 F5
East Barming............24 D7
East Barnet.............23 H3
East Barsham............46 E3
East Beckham............47 G3
East Bedfont............23 F5
East Bergholt...........36 F6
East Bilney.............46 E5
East Blatchington......15 H5
East Boldre.............13 F5
Eastbourne..............16 D6
East Brent..............19 H7
Eastbridge.............37 K3
East Bridgford.........43 J2
East Buckland...........9 G2
East Budleigh..........10 B7
East Burrafirth.......115 F3
East Burton............11 K7
Eastbury, Herts........23 F3
Eastbury, Berks........21 H5
East Calder............81 F5
East Carleton..........47 G6
East Carlton...........44 B8
East Chaldon or
  Chaldon Herring......11 J7
East Challow...........21 H4
East Chiltington.......15 G4
East Chinnock..........11 F4
East Chisenbury........21 F7
Eastchurch.............25 F5
East Clandon...........22 F7
East Claydon...........33 K7
East Coker.............11 G4
Eastcombe, Glos........20 C2
East Combe, Somer......10 C2
East Compton...........11 H1
Eastcote, W. Mids......32 D2
Eastcote, G. Lon.......23 G4
Eastcott, Corn..........8 C4
Eastcott, Wilts........20 E7
East Cottingwith.......60 E6
Eastcourt..............20 D3
East Cowes.............13 H6
East Cowton............66 D7
East Cramlington.......75 J7
East Creech............12 B7
East Croachy...........94 E3
East Davoch............96 D5
East Dean, W. Susx.....14 C4
East Dean, E. Susx.....16 C6
East Dean, Hants.......12 E3
East Dereham...........46 E5
East Down...............9 G1
East Drayton...........54 B6
East End, Dorset.......12 B6
East End, Kent.........16 F2
East End, Hants........13 F6
East End, Oxon.........21 H1
East End, Herts........35 H7
East End, Avon.........19 J5
East End, Hants........21 J6
Easter Ardross........102 E5
Easter Balmoral........96 B6
Easter Boleskine.......94 D3
Easter Compton.........19 K4
Easter Fearn..........102 E4
Eastergate.............14 C5
Easter Kinkell........102 D7
Easter Lednathie.......89 F2
Eastern Green..........32 E2
Easter Ord.............97 H5
Easter Quaff..........115 G5
Easter Skeld..........114 F4
Easterton..............20 E7
Eastertown.............19 H7
East Farleigh..........24 D7
East Farndon...........33 K1
East Ferry.............54 C4
Eastfield, Strath......80 C4
Eastfield, Strath......80 D5
Eastfield, N. Yks......61 H2
East Garston...........21 H5
Eastgate, Norf.........47 G4
Eastgate, Durham.......65 G4
East Ginge.............21 J4
East Goscote...........43 J5
East Grafton...........21 G6
East Grimstead.........12 E3
East Grinstead.........15 G2
East Guldeford.........17 G3
East Haddon............33 J3
East Hagbourne.........21 K4
East Halton............55 F2
Eastham, Mers..........50 C5
East Ham, G. Lon.......23 K4
Easthampstead.........22 D6
East Hanney............21 J3
East Hanningfield......24 D2
East Hardwick..........53 G2
East Harling...........36 E1
East Harlsey...........66 E8
East Harptree..........19 K7
East Hartford..........75 J7
East Harting...........14 A4
East Hatley............35 F4
East Hauxwell..........59 G1
East Haven.............89 H5
East Heckington........45 E2
East Hedleyhope........65 J3
East Hendred...........21 J4
East Heslerton.........61 G3
East Hoathly...........15 J4
Easthope...............41 G7
Easthorpe..............36 E7
East Horrington........11 G1
East Horsley...........23 F7
East Huntspill.........10 E1
East Hyde..............23 G1
East Ilsley............21 J4
Eastington, Glos.......20 B2

Eastington, Glos.......21 F1
Eastington, Devon.......9 H5
East Kennett...........20 F6
East Keswick...........59 J6
East Kilbride..........79 J6
East Kirkby............55 H7
East Knighton..........11 K7
East Knoyle............12 A2
East Lambrook..........11 F4
East Lamington........103 F5
East Langdon...........17 L1
East Langton...........43 K7
East Langwell.........102 F2
East Lavington........14 C4
East Layton............66 B7
Eastleach Martin......21 G2
Eastleach Turville.....21 F2
East Leake.............43 H4
Eastleigh, Hants.......13 G4
East Leigh, Devon.......9 G5
East Lexham............46 D5
East Lilburn...........75 G2
East Linton............82 D4
East Liss..............14 A3
East Lound.............54 B4
East Lulworth..........12 A7
East Mains.............97 F6
East Malling...........24 C7
East Marden............14 B4
East Markham...........54 B6
East Marton............58 E5
East Meon..............13 J3
East Mersea............25 G1
East Molesey...........23 G6
East Morden............12 B6
East Morton............59 G6
Eastney................13 J6
Eastnor................31 J6
East Norton............44 A6
East Oakley............21 K7
Eastoft................54 C2
East Ogwell............5 J2
Easton, Dorset.........6 A7
Easton, Lincs.........44 C4
Easton, Cambs.........34 E2
Easton, Somer.........11 G1
Easton, Norf..........47 G5
Easton, Hants.........13 H2
Easton, Suff..........37 H4
Easton, Devon..........9 H7
Easton, Cumbr.........73 K7
Easton Grey...........20 C4
Easton-in-Gordano.....19 K5
Easton Maudit.........34 B4
Easton on the Hill....44 D6
Easton Royal..........21 G6
East Ord..............83 H6
East Panson............8 D6
East Peckham..........16 D1
East Pennard..........11 G2
East Perry............34 E3
East Portlemouth.......5 H6
East Prawle............5 H6
East Preston..........14 D5
East Putford...........8 D4
East Quantoxhead......10 C1
East Rainton..........66 D3
East Ravendale........55 G4
East Raynham..........46 D4
Eastrea...............45 F7
Eastriggs.............73 H8
Eastrington...........60 E7
East Rudham...........46 D4
East Runton...........47 G2
East Ruston...........47 J4
Eastry................25 K7
East Saltoun..........82 C5
Eastside, Orkney.....112 E7
East Sleekburn........75 J6
East Stockwith........54 B4
East Stoke, Notts.....44 A2
East Stoke, Dorset....12 A7
East Stour............11 J3
East Stourmouth.......25 J6
East Stratton.........13 H2
East Studdal..........17 L1
East Taphouse..........4 B3
East-the-Water.........8 E3
East Tilbury..........24 C5
East Tisted...........13 K2
East Torrington.......55 F5
East Tuddenham........46 F5
East Tytherley........12 E3
East Tytherton........20 D5
East Village...........9 J5
Eastville.............45 H1
East Wall.............41 G7
East Walton...........46 C5
Eastwell..............44 A4
East Wellow...........12 E4
Eastwell Park.........17 H1
East Wemyss...........81 J2
East Whitburn.........80 E5
Eastwick..............23 K1
East Williamston......26 E6
East Winch............46 B5
East Wittering........14 A6
East Witton...........59 G2
Eastwood, Essex.......24 E4
Eastwood, Notts.......43 G2
Eastwood, W. Yks......51 J1
East Woodhay..........21 J6
East Worldham.........13 K2
Eathorpe..............33 F3
Eaton, Leic...........44 A4
Eaton, Notts..........54 B6
Eaton, Ches...........50 E7
Eaton, Shrops.........40 E8
Eaton, Shrops.........41 G2
Eaton, Norf...........47 H6
Eaton, Ches...........51 H7
Eaton, Oxon...........21 J2
Eaton Bishop..........31 F6
Eaton Bray............34 C7

Eaton Constantine.....41 G6
Eaton Hastings........21 G3
Eaton Socon...........34 E4
Eaton upon Tern.......41 H4
Ebberston.............61 F2
Ebbesbourne Wake......12 B3
Ebbw Vale.............19 F2
Ebchester.............65 J2
Ebford................10 A7
Ebrington.............32 D5
Ecchinswell...........21 J7
Ecclaw................82 F5
Ecclefechan...........73 G7
Eccles, Kent..........24 D6
Eccles, Border........82 F7
Eccles, G. Man........51 G4
Ecclesfield...........53 F4
Eccleshall............41 K4
Ecclesmachan..........81 F4
Eccles on Sea.........47 K4
Eccles Road...........46 F7
Eccleston, Mers.......50 D4
Eccleston, Ches.......50 D7
Eccleston, Lancs......50 E2
Eccup.................59 H6
Echt..................97 G5
Eckford...............74 D2
Eckington, H. & W.....32 B5
Eckington, Derby......53 G6
Ecton.................34 B3
Edale.................52 D5
Edburton..............15 F4
Edderton.............102 F4
Eddleston.............81 H7
Edenbridge............15 H1
Edenfield.............51 H2
Edenhall..............64 C4
Edenham...............44 D4
Eden Park.............23 J6
Edensor...............52 E6
Edenthorpe............53 J3
Edern.................38 B3
Edgbaston.............32 C1
Edgcott...............33 J7
Edge, Glos............20 C2
Edge, Shrops..........40 E6
Edgebolton............41 G4
Edge End..............19 K1
Edgefield.............47 F3
Edgefield Street......47 F3
Edgeworth.............20 D2
Edgmond...............41 J5
Edgmond Marsh.........41 J4
Edgton................30 E1
Edgware...............23 H3
Edgworth..............51 G2
Edinbane..............99 J7
Edinburgh.............81 H4
Edingale..............42 E5
Edingley..............43 J1
Edingthorpe...........47 J3
Edington, Wilts.......20 D7
Edington, Somer.......10 E2
Edithmead.............10 E1
Edith Weston..........44 C6
Edlesborough..........22 E1
Edlingham.............75 H4
Edlington.............55 G6
Edmondsham............12 C4
Edmondsley............66 C3
Edmondthorpe..........44 B5
Edmonstone...........113 F4
Edmonton..............23 J3
Edmundbyers...........65 H2
Ednam.................82 F8
Edney Common..........24 D2
Edradynate............80 E4
Edrom.................83 G6
Edstaston.............41 G3
Edstone...............32 D3
Edvin Loach...........31 H4
Edwalton..............43 H3
Edwardstone...........36 E5
Edwinsford............27 L3
Edwinstowe............53 J7
Edworth...............35 F5
Edwyn Ralph...........31 H4
Edzell................89 J2
Efail Isaf............18 E4
Efailnewydd...........38 C3
Efailwen..............26 F4
Efenechtyd............40 C1
Effingham.............23 G7
Effirth..............115 F3
Efford.................9 J5
Egerton, Kent.........17 G1
Egerton, G. Man.......51 G2
Egerton Forstal.......17 F1
Eggborough............53 H1
Eggesford.............9 G4
Eggington.............34 C7
Egginton..............42 E4
Egglescliffe..........66 E6
Eggleston.............65 G5
Egham.................22 F5
Egleton...............44 B5
Eglingham.............75 H3
Egloshayle............3 J2
Egloskerry............8 C7
Eglwysbach............49 H3
Eglwys-Brewis.........18 E6
Eglwys Fach...........39 F7
Eglwyswen.............26 F3
Eglwyswrw.............26 F3
Egmanton..............54 B7
Egmere................62 F6
Egremont..............67 J7
Egton.................67 J7
Egton Bridge..........67 J7
Eight Ash Green.......36 E7
Eilanreach............92 E4
Eilean Darach........101 H4
Eilean Glas...........99 H3
Eilean Iarmain or Isleornsay..92 C4
Eishken..............107 H7
Eisingrug.............38 E7
Elan Village..........29 G3
Elberton..............19 L4

Elburton...............4 F4
Elcombe...............21 F4
Eldersfield...........31 K6
Elderslie.............79 G5
Eldroth...............58 C4
Eldwick...............59 G6
Elerch or Bont-goch...28 D1
Elford, Staffs........42 D5
Elford, Northum.......75 H1
Elgin................104 B2
Elgol.................92 B4
Elham.................17 J1
Elie..................82 C1
Eling..................13 F4
Elim..................48 C2
Elishader............100 B6
Elishaw...............74 E5
Elkesley..............53 J6
Elkstone..............20 D1
Elland................52 D1
Ellary................77 G4
Ellastone.............42 D2
Ellemford.............82 F5
Ellenhall.............41 K4
Ellen's Green.........14 D2
Ellerbeck.............59 K1
Ellerby...............67 H6
Ellerdine Heath.......41 H4
Ellerker..............61 G8
Ellerton, Humbs.......60 E7
Ellerton, Shrops......41 J4
Ellesborough..........22 D2
Ellesmere.............40 F3
Ellesmere Port........50 C6
Ellingham, Northum....75 H2
Ellingham, Norf.......47 J7
Ellingstring..........59 G2
Ellington, Cambs......34 E2
Ellington, Northum....75 J5
Ellisfield............13 J1
Ellistown.............43 G5
Ellon.................97 J2
Ellough...............37 J1
Elloughton............54 D1
Ellwood...............19 K2
Elm...................45 H6
Elmbridge.............32 B3
Elmdon, W. Mids.......32 D1
Elmdon, Essex.........35 H6
Elmdon Heath..........32 D1
Elmesthorpe...........43 G7
Elmhurst..............42 D5
Elmley Castle.........32 B5
Elmley Lovett.........32 A3
Elmore................20 B1
Elmore Back...........20 B1
Elm Park..............23 L4
Elmscott...............8 C3
Elmsett...............36 F5
Elmstead Market.......36 F7
Elmsted...............17 J1
Elmstone..............25 J6
Elmstone Hardwicke....32 B7
Elmswell..............36 E3
Elmton................53 H6
Elphin...............108 D7
Elphinstone...........81 J4
Elrick................97 H5
Elrig.................68 E6
Elsdon................75 F5
Elsecar...............53 F3
Elsenham..............35 J7
Elsfield..............21 K1
Elsham................54 E2
Elsing................46 F5
Elslack...............58 E6
Elson.................81 F7
Elsrickle.............81 F7
Elstead...............14 C1
Elsted................14 B4
Elston................44 A2
Elstone................9 G4
Elstow................34 D5
Elstree...............23 G3
Elstronwick...........61 K7
Elswick...............57 H7
Elsworth..............35 G3
Elterwater............63 J7
Eltham................23 K5
Eltisley..............35 F4
Elton, Notts..........44 A3
Elton, Glos...........20 B1
Elton, Ches...........50 D6
Elton, Cambs..........44 D7
Elton, Cleve..........66 E6
Elton, Derby..........52 E7
Elton, H. & W.........31 F2
Elvanfoot.............72 E3
Elvaston..............43 G3
Elveden...............36 D2
Elvingston............82 C4
Elvington, N. Yks.....60 E6
Elvington, Kent.......25 J7
Elwick, Cleve.........66 E4
Elwick, Northum.......83 K8
Elworth...............51 G7
Elworthy..............10 B2
Ely, S. Glam..........18 F5
Ely, Cambs............35 J1
Emberton..............34 B5
Embleton, Cumbr.......63 G4
Embleton, Northum.....75 J2
Embo.................103 G3
Emborough.............19 L7
Embsay................58 F5
Emery Down............12 E5
Emley.................52 E2
Emmer Green...........22 C5
Emmington.............22 C2
Emneth................45 H6
Emneth Hungate........45 J6
Empingham.............44 C6
Empshott..............14 A2
Emsworth..............13 K5
Enaclete.............107 F6
Enborne...............21 J6

Enchmarsh.............41 G7
Enderby...............43 H7
Endmoor...............57 J2
Endon.................42 B1
Enfield...............23 J3
Enford................21 F7
Engine Common.........20 A4
Englefield............22 B5
Englefield Green......22 E5
English Bicknor.......19 K1
Englishcombe..........20 B6
English Frankton......41 F4
Enham-Alamein.........13 F1
Enmore................10 D2
Ennerdale Bridge......62 F6
Enochdhu..............88 C2
Ensbury...............12 C6
Ensdon................41 F5
Ensis..................9 F3
Enstone...............33 F7
Enterkinfoot..........72 D4
Enville...............31 K1
Eochar................98 C8
Eoligarry.............90 C5
Eorabus...............84 E6
Eoropaidh............107 K2
Epperstone............43 J2
Epping................23 J2
Epping Green, Herts...23 H2
Epping Green, Essex...23 K2
Eppleby...............66 B6
Epsom.................23 H6
Epwell................33 F5
Epworth...............54 B3
Erbistock.............40 F2
Erbusaig..............92 D3
Erdington.............42 D7
Eredine...............86 B8
Ericstane.............73 F3
Eridge Green..........16 C2
Eriswell..............36 C2
Erith.................23 L5
Erlestoke.............20 D7
Ermington..............5 G4
Erpingham.............47 G3
Errogie...............94 D3
Errol.................88 E6
Erskine...............79 G4
Erskine Bridge........79 H4
Erwarton..............37 H6
Erwood................29 H5
Eryholme..............66 D7
Eryrys................50 B8
Escomb................66 B4
Escrick...............60 D6
Esgairgeiliog.........39 G6
Esh...................66 B3
Esher.................23 G6
Eshott................75 J5
Eshton................58 E5
Esh Winning...........66 B3
Eskadale..............94 C2
Eskbank...............81 J4
Eskdale Green.........63 G7
Eskdalemuir...........73 H5
Esknish...............76 C5
Esprick...............57 H7
Essendine.............44 D5
Essendon..............23 H2
Essich................94 C3
Essington.............42 B6
Esslemont.............97 J3
Eston.................67 F6
Etal..................83 H8
Etchilhampton.........20 E6
Etchingham............16 E3
Etchinghill, Staffs...42 C5
Etchinghill, Kent.....17 J2
Etherley..............66 B5
Eton..................22 E4
Etteridge.............94 E6
Ettersgill............65 F5
Ettington.............32 E5
Etton, Cambs..........44 E6
Etton, Humbs..........61 G6
Ettrick...............73 H3
Ettrickbridge.........73 J2
Etwall................42 F3
Euston................36 D2
Euxton................50 E2
Evanton..............102 E6
Evedon................44 D2
Evelix...............103 F3
Evenjobb..............30 D3
Evenley...............33 H6
Evenlode..............32 E7
Evenwood..............65 J5
Everbay..............113 G4
Evercreech............11 H2
Everdon...............33 H4
Everingham............60 F6
Everleigh.............21 G7
Everley...............67 J8
Eversholt.............34 C6
Evershot..............11 G5
Eversley..............22 C6
Eversley Cross........22 C6
Everton, Hants........12 E6
Everton, Beds.........35 F4
Everton, Notts........53 J4
Evertown..............73 J7
Evesbatch.............31 H5
Evesham...............32 C5
Evington..............43 J2
Ewden Village.........52 E4
Ewell.................23 H6
Ewell Minnis..........17 K1
Ewelme................22 B3
Ewen..................20 E3
Ewenny................20 D5
Ewerby................44 D2
Ewes..................73 J5
Ewhurst...............14 D1
Ewhurst Green.........16 E3
Ewloe.................50 C7

Eworthy................8 E6
Ewshot................14 B1
Ewyas Harold..........30 E7
Exbourne...............9 G5
Exbridge...............9 K3
Exbury................13 G5
Exelby................59 H2
Exeter.................9 K6
Exford.................9 J2
Exhall................32 D4
Exminster..............9 K7
Exmouth................5 L1
Exnaboe..............115 H7
Exning................35 K3
Exton, Devon..........10 A7
Exton, Leic...........44 C5
Exton, Hants..........13 J3
Exton, Somer...........9 K2
Eyam..................52 E6
Eydon.................33 H4
Eye, H. & W...........31 F3
Eye, Cambs............45 F6
Eye, Suff.............37 G2
Eyemouth..............83 H5
Eyeworth..............35 F5
Eyhorne Street........24 E7
Eyke..................37 J4
Eynesbury.............34 E4
Eynort................91 J3
Eynsford..............23 L6
Eynsham...............21 J2
Eype..................11 F6
Eyre..................99 K7
Eythorne..............17 K1
Eyton, Shrops.........30 E1
Eyton, H. & W.........31 F3
Eyton upon the Weald Moors..41 H5

F

Faccombe..............21 H7
Faceby................66 E7
Faddiley..............41 G1
Fadmoor...............60 D2
Faerdre...............18 A2
Faifley...............79 H4
Failand...............19 K5
Failford..............71 K2
Failsworth............51 H3
Fairbourne............38 F5
Fairburn..............53 G1
Fairfield.............32 B2
Fairford..............21 F2
Fairlands.............22 E7
Fairlie...............78 E4
Fairlight.............16 F4
Fairmile..............10 B5
Fairmilehead..........81 H5
Fair Oak, Hants.......13 G4
Fairoak, Staffs.......41 J3
Fairseat..............24 C6
Fairstead.............24 D1
Fairwarp..............15 H3
Fairy Cross............8 E3
Fakenham..............46 E3
Fala..................82 C5
Fala Dam..............82 C5
Falahill..............81 J6
Faldingworth..........54 E5
Falfield..............20 A3
Falkenham.............37 H6
Falkirk...............80 D3
Falkland..............88 E8
Falla.................74 D3
Fallin................80 D2
Falmer................15 G5
Falmouth...............3 G4
Fanagmore............108 C4
Fangdale Beck.........60 C1
Fangfoss..............60 E5
Fanmore...............84 F4
Fans..................82 E7
Farcet................45 F7
Far Cotton............34 A4
Farden................31 G2
Farewell..............42 C5
Far Forest............31 J2
Faringdon.............21 G3
Farington.............50 E1
Farleigh, Surrey......23 J6
Farleigh, Avon........19 J6
Farleigh Hungerford...20 C7
Farleigh Wallop.......13 J1
Farlesthorpe..........55 J6
Farleton..............57 J2
Farley, Staffs........42 C2
Farley, Wilts.........12 E3
Farley, Shrops........40 E6
Farley Green..........14 D1
Farley Hill...........22 B6
Farleys End...........20 B1
Farlington............60 D4
Farlow................31 H1
Farmborough...........20 A6
Farmcote..............32 C7
Farmoor...............21 J2
Farmtown.............104 D2
Farnborough, Hants....22 D7
Farnborough, Warw.....33 G5
Farnborough, G. Lon...23 K6
Farncombe.............14 C1
Farndish..............34 C3
Farndon, Notts........44 A1
Farndon, Ches.........41 F1
Farnell...............89 J3
Farnham, Surrey.......14 B1
Farnham, Dorset.......12 B4
Farnham, Essex........35 H6
Farnham, Suff.........37 J3
Farnham, N. Yks.......59 J4

Farnham Common Gee Cross 165

Farnham Common 22 E4
Farnham Green 35 H7
Farnham Royal 22 E4
Farningham 23 L6
Farnley 59 H6
Farnley Tyas 52 D2
Farnsfield 43 J1
Farnworth, Ches 50 E5
Farnworth, G. Man 51 G3
Farr, Highld 110 D2
Farr, Highld 94 E2
Farringdon 10 B6
Farrington Gurney 19 L7
Farsley 59 H7
Farthinghoe 33 H6
Farthingstone 33 J4
Farway 10 C6
Fascadale 85 G1
Fasnacloich 86 C4
Fassfern 93 G8
Fatfield 66 D2
Fattahead 104 F3
Faugh 64 C2
Fauldhouse 80 E5
Faulkbourne 24 D1
Faulkland 20 B7
Fauls 41 G3
Faversham 25 G6
Favillar 96 B2
Fawfieldhead 52 C7
Fawkham Green 24 B6
Fawler 21 H1
Fawley, Bucks 22 C4
Fawley, Hants 13 G5
Fawley, Berks 21 H4
Fawley Chapel 31 G7
Faxfleet 54 C1
Faygate 15 F2
Fazeley 42 E6
Fearby 59 G2
Fearnan 87 K4
Fearnbeg 100 D7
Fearnhead 51 F4
Fearnmore 100 D6
Featherstone, Staffs 42 B6
Featherstone, W. Yks 53 G1
Feckenham 32 C3
Fedderate 105 H4
Feering 36 D7
Feetham 65 G8
Feizor 58 C4
Felbridge 15 G2
Felbrigg 47 H3
Felcourt 15 G1
Felden 22 F2
Felindre, Powys 30 C1
Felindre, Dyfed 28 E7
Felindre, Dyfed 27 H3
Felindre, W. Glam 27 L6
Felindre Farchog 26 F3
Felinfach 29 H6
Felinfoel 27 K6
Felington 83 H7
Felingwmuchaf 27 K4
Felixkirk 60 B2
Felixstowe 37 H6
Fell End 64 E8
Felling 66 C1
Fell Side 63 J4
Felmersham 34 C4
Felmingham 47 H4
Felpham 14 C6
Felsham 36 E4
Felstead 36 B7
Feltham 23 G5
Felthorpe 47 G5
Felton, H. & W. 31 G5
Felton, Northum 75 H4
Felton, Avon 19 K6
Felton Butler 40 E5
Feltwell 46 C7
Fence 58 D7
Fence Houses 66 D2
Fencote 59 H1
Fen Ditton 35 H3
Fen Drayton 35 G3
Fen End 32 E2
Feniscowles 51 F1
Feniton 10 C6
Fenny Bentley 42 D1
Fenny Bridges 10 C6
Fenny Compton 33 G4
Fenny Drayton 43 F7
Fenny Stratford 34 B6
Fen Pitton 35 H3
Fenrother 75 H5
Fenstanton 35 G3
Fenton, Staffs 42 A2
Fenton, Lincs 44 B1
Fenton, Lincs 54 C6
Fenton, Northum 75 F1
Fenton, Cambs 35 G2
Fenwick, Strath 79 G7
Fenwick, Northum 75 G7
Fenwick, S. Yks 53 H2
Fenwick, Northum 83 J7
Feochaig 70 C3
Feock 3 G6
Feolin Ferry 76 D5
Feriniquarrie 99 G7
Fern 89 G2
Ferndale 18 E3
Ferndown 12 C5
Ferness 103 H8
Fernham 21 G3
Fernhill Heath 32 A4
Fernhurst 14 B3
Ferniegair 80 C6
Fernilea 91 J2
Fernilee 52 C6
Ferrensby 59 J4
Ferrindonald 92 C5
Ferring 14 D5
Ferrybridge 53 G1
Ferryden 89 K3
Ferryhill 66 C4
Ferryside 27 H5
Fersfield 36 F1
Fersit 94 B8
Ferwig 26 F2
Feshiebridge 95 G5
Fetcham 23 G7
Fetterangus 105 J3
Fettercairn 97 F8
Fewston 59 G5
Ffairfach 27 L4
Ffaldybrenin 27 L2
Ffarmers 27 L2
Ffawyddog 19 G1
Ffestiniog 39 G2
Fforest 27 K6
Fforest-fach 27 L7
Ffostrasol 27 H2
Ffrith 40 D1
Ffynnon-ddrain 27 J4
Ffynnongroyw 50 A5
Fidden 84 E6
Fiddington, Glos 32 B6
Fiddington, Somer 10 D1
Fiddleford 11 K4
Fiddlers Hamlet 23 K2
Field 42 C3
Field Broughton 57 G2
Field Dalling 46 F3
Field Head 43 G6
Fifehead Magdalen 11 J3
Fifehead Neville 11 J4
Fifield, Berks 22 E5
Fifield, Oxon 21 G1
Figheldean 12 D1
Filby 47 K5
Filey 61 J2
Filgrave 34 B5
Filkins 21 G2
Filleigh, Devon 9 G3
Filleigh, Devon 9 H4
Fillingham 54 D5
Fillongley 32 E1
Filton 19 L5
Fimber 61 F4
Fincham 46 B6
Finchdean 13 K4
Finchampstead 22 C6
Finchingfield 36 B6
Finchley 23 H3
Findern 43 F3
Findhorn 103 J6
Findochty 104 D2
Findon, W. Susx 14 E5
Findon, Grampn 97 J6
Finedon 34 C2
Fingal Street 37 H3
Fingask 97 G3
Fingest 22 C3
Finghall 59 G2
Fingland 72 C3
Fingringhoe 36 F7
Finmere 33 J6
Finningham 36 F3
Finningley 53 J4
Finnygaud 104 F3
Finsbay 99 F4
Finsbury 23 J4
Finsthwaite 57 G2
Finstock 21 H1
Finstown 112 D5
Fintry, Grampn 105 G3
Fintry, Strath 79 J3
Finzean 96 F6
Fionnphort 84 E6
Firbank 57 K1
Firbeck 53 H5
Firgrove 51 J2
Firsby 55 J7
Firth 117 F5
Fir Tree 65 J4
Fishbourne, W. Susx 14 B5
Fishbourne, I. of W. 13 H6
Fishburn 66 D4
Fishcross 80 E2
Fisherford 97 F2
Fisher's Pond 13 G3
Fisherstreet 14 C2
Fisherton, Highld 103 F7
Fisherton, Strath 71 H3
Fishguard 26 D3
Fishlake 53 J2
Fishpool 51 H3
Fishtoft 45 G2
Fishtoft Drove 45 G2
Fishwick 83 H6
Fiskavaig 91 J2
Fiskerton, Lincs 54 E6
Fiskerton, Notts 43 K1
Fittleton 12 D1
Fittleworth 14 D4
Fitton End 45 H5
Fitz 41 F5
Fitzhead 10 C3
Fitzwilliam 53 G2
Fiunary 85 H4
Five Ashes 16 C3
Fivehead 10 E3
Five Oak Green 16 D1
Five Oaks 14 D3
Five Penny Borve 107 J3
Five Roads 27 J6
Flackwell Heath 22 D4
Fladbury 32 B5
Fladdabister 115 G5
Flagg 52 D7
Flamborough 61 K3
Flamstead 22 F1
Flansham 14 C5
Flasby 58 E5
Flash 52 C7
Flashader 99 J7
Flaunden 22 F2
Flawborough 44 A2
Flawith 60 B4
Flax Bourton 19 K6
Flaxby 59 J5
Flaxfleet 54 C1
Flaxley 20 A1
Flaxpool 10 C2
Flaxton 60 D4
Fleckney 43 J7
Flecknoe 33 H3
Fleet, Hants 22 D7
Fleet, Lincs 45 G4
Fleet Hargate 45 G4
Fleetwood 57 G6
Fleggburgh or
Burgh St Margaret 47 K5
Flemingston 18 E5
Flemington 79 J6
Flempton 36 D2
Fletching 15 H3
Flexbury 8 C5
Flexford 22 E7
Flicham 46 C4
Flimby 62 F4
Flimwell 16 E2
Flint 50 B6
Flintham 44 A2
Flint Mountain 50 B6
Flinton 61 K7
Flitcham 46 C4
Flitton 34 D6
Flitwick 34 D6
Flixborough 54 C2
Flixton, G. Man 51 G4
Flixton, N. Yks 61 H3
Flixton, Suff 37 J1
Flockton 52 E2
Flodabay 99 F4
Flodden 83 H8
Flookburgh 57 G3
Flordon 47 G7
Flore 33 J3
Flotterton 75 F4
Flowton 37 F5
Flushing, Corn 3 G6
Flushing, Grampn 105 K4
Flyford Flavell 32 B4
Fobbing 24 D4
Fochabers 104 C3
Fochriw 18 F2
Fockerby 54 C2
Fodderty 102 D7
Foel 39 J5
Foggathorpe 60 E7
Fogo 82 F7
Foindle 108 C4
Folda 88 D2
Fole 42 C3
Foleshill 33 F1
Folke 11 H4
Folkestone 17 K2
Folkingham 44 D3
Folkington 16 C5
Folksworth 44 E8
Folkton 61 H3
Folla Rule 97 G2
Follifoot 59 J5
Folly Gate 9 F6
Fonthill Bishop 12 B2
Fonthill Gifford 12 B2
Fontmell Magna 12 A4
Fontwell 14 C5
Foolow 52 D6
Foots Cray 23 K5
Forcett 66 B6
Ford, Staffs 42 C1
Ford, Bucks 22 C2
Ford, Mers 50 C4
Ford, Wilts 20 C5
Ford, Glos 32 C7
Ford, W. Susx 14 D5
Ford, Shrops 41 F5
Ford, Strath 77 H1
Ford, Devon 5 H5
Ford, Northum 83 H8
Fordcombe 15 J1
Fordell 81 G3
Forden 40 D6
Ford End 24 C1
Forder Green 5 H3
Fordham, Cambs 36 B2
Fordham, Essex 36 E7
Fordham, Norf 45 K7
Fordingbridge 12 D4
Fordon 61 H3
Fordoun 97 G8
Ford Street, Somer 10 C4
Fordstreet, Essex 36 E7
Fordwells 21 H1
Fordwich 25 H7
Fordyce 104 E2
Foremark 43 F4
Forestburn Gate 75 G5
Forestfield 80 D5
Forest Gate 23 K4
Forest Green 14 E1
Forest Head 64 C2
Forest Hill 21 K2
Forest-in-Teesdale 65 F5
Forest Mill 80 E2
Forest Row 15 H2
Forestside 14 A4
Forest Town 53 H7
Forfar 89 G3
Forgandenny 88 C7
Forge Side 19 G2
Forgie 104 C3
Formby 50 B3
Forncett End 47 G7
Forncett St Mary 47 G7
Forncett St Peter 47 G7
Forneth 88 C4
Fornham All Saints 36 D3
Fornham St Martin 36 D3
Forres 103 J7
Forsbrook 42 B2
Forse 111 J5
Forsinard 110 E4
Forston 11 H6
Fort Augustus 94 B5
Forteviot 88 C7
Fort George 103 F7
Forth 80 E6
Forthampton 32 A6
Forth Road Bridge, Fife 81 G4
Forth Road Bridge, Lothn 81 G4
Fortingall 87 K4
Forton, Somer 10 E5
Forton, Shrops 41 F5
Forton, Lancs 57 H5
Forton, Staffs 41 J4
Fortrie, Grampn 104 F4
Fortrie, Grampn 97 J1
Fortrose 102 F7
Fortuneswell 6 A7
Fort William 93 H8
Forty Hill 23 J3
Forward Green 37 F4
Fosbury 21 H7
Fosdyke 45 G3
Foss 87 K3
Fossebridge 20 E1
Foss-y-ffin 28 B3
Foster Street 23 K2
Foston, Lincs 44 B2
Foston, Derby 42 D3
Foston, N. Yks 60 D4
Foston on the Wolds 61 J5
Fotherby 55 H4
Fotheringhay 44 D7
Foubister 113 F6
Foulden, Norf 46 C7
Foulden, Border 83 H6
Foul Mile 16 D4
Foulridge 58 D6
Foulsham 46 F4
Fountainhall 82 C7
Four Ashes 36 F2
Four Crosses, Staffs 42 B6
Four Crosses, Powys 40 B6
Four Crosses, Powys 40 D5
Four Elms 15 H1
Four Forks 10 D2
Four Gotes 45 H5
Four Lanes 2 E6
Fourlanes End 51 H8
Four Marks 13 J2
Four Mile Bridge 48 B3
Four Oaks, W. Mids 42 D7
Four Oaks, W. Mids 32 E1
Four Oaks, E. Susx 16 F3
Fourpenny 103 G3
Fourstones 74 E8
Four Throws 16 E3
Fovant 12 C3
Foveran 97 J3
Fowey 3 K4
Fowlis 88 F5
Fowlis Wester 88 B6
Fowlmere 35 H5
Fownhope 31 G6
Foxdale 56 P4
Foxearth 36 D5
Foxfield 56 F2
Foxham 20 D5
Foxhole 3 H4
Foxholes 61 H3
Fox Lane 22 D7
Foxley, Wilts 20 C4
Foxley, Norf 46 F4
Foxt 42 C2
Foxton, Cambs 35 H5
Foxton, Leic 43 K8
Foxup 58 D3
Foxwist Green 51 F7
Foy 31 G7
Foyers 94 C3
Fraddon 3 H4
Fradley 42 D5
Fradswell 42 B3
Fraisthorpe 61 J4
Framfield 15 H3
Framingham Earl 47 H6
Framingham Pigot 47 H6
Framlingham 37 H3
Frampton, Lincs 45 G3
Frampton, Dorset 11 H6
Frampton Cotterell 20 A4
Frampton Mansell 20 D2
Frampton on Severn 20 B2
Frampton West End 45 G2
Framsden 37 G4
Framwellgate Moor 66 C3
Franche 31 K2
Frankby 50 B5
Frankley 32 B1
Frankton 33 G2
Frant 16 C2
Fraserburgh 105 J2
Frating Green 37 F7
Fratton 13 J5
Freathy 4 D4
Freckenham 36 B2
Freckleton 57 H8
Freeby 44 B4
Freeland 21 J1
Freester 115 G3
Freethorpe 47 K6
Freiston 45 G2
Fremington, Devon 8 F2
Fremington, N. Yks 65 H8
Fremington, Strath 79 J6
Frenchbeer 9 G7
Frensham 14 B1
Fresgoe 110 F2
Freshfield 50 B3
Freshford 20 B6
Freshwater 13 F7
Freshwater East 26 E7
Fressingfield 37 H2
Freston 37 G6
Freswick 111 K2
Fretherne 20 B2
Frettenham 47 H5
Freuchie 88 E8
Friar's Gate 15 H2
Friday Bridge 45 H6
Fridaythorpe 60 F5
Friern Barnet 23 H3
Friesthorpe 54 E5
Frieth 22 C3
Frilford 21 J3
Frilsham 21 K5
Frimley 22 D7
Frindsbury 24 D6
Fring 46 C3
Fringford 33 J7
Frinsted 24 E7
Frinton-on-Sea 37 H7
Friockheim 89 H4
Frisby on the Wreake 43 J5
Friskney 45 H1
Friston, E. Susx 16 C6
Friston, Suff 37 K3
Fritchley 43 F1
Fritham 12 E4
Frith Bank 45 G2
Frith Common 31 H3
Frithelstock 8 E4
Frithville 45 G1
Frittenden 16 F1
Fritton, Norf 47 H7
Fritton, Norf 47 K6
Fritwell 33 H7
Frizington 62 F6
Frocester 20 B2
Frodesley 41 G6
Frodsham 50 E6
Froggatt 52 E6
Froghall 42 C2
Frogmore 22 D6
Frolesworth 43 H7
Frome 11 J1
Fromes Hill 31 H5
Frome St Quintin 11 G5
Fron, Gwyn 38 C3
Fron, Powys 40 D6
Fron, Powys 29 H3
Froncysyllte 40 D2
Frongoch 39 J3
Frostenden 37 K1
Frosterley 65 H4
Froxfield 21 G6
Froxfield Green 13 K3
Fryerning 24 C2
Fryton 60 D3
Fulbeck 44 C1
Fulbourn 35 J4
Fulbrook 21 G1
Fulford, Staffs 42 B3
Fulford, Somer 10 D3
Fulford, N. Yks 60 D6
Fulham 23 H5
Fulking 15 F4
Fuller's Moor 41 F1
Fuller Street 24 D1
Fullerton 13 F2
Fulletby 55 G6
Full Sutton 60 E5
Fullwood 79 G6
Fulmer 22 E4
Fulmodeston 46 E3
Fulnetby 54 E6
Fulstow 55 H4
Fulwell 66 D2
Fulwood, S. Yks 53 F5
Fulwood, Lancs 57 J7
Funtington 14 B5
Funtley 13 H5
Funzie 117 H3
Furnace 78 C1
Furneux Pelham 35 H7
Furzebrook 12 B7
Fyfett 10 D4
Fyfield, Essex 24 B2
Fyfield, Hants 12 E1
Fyfield, Wilts 21 F6
Fyfield, Glos 21 G2
Fyfield, Oxon 21 J3
Fylingthorpe 67 K7
Fyvie 97 G2

G

Gabhsann 107 J3
Gabroc Hill 79 G6
Gaddesby 43 J5
Gadfa 48 D2
Gaer 30 C7
Gaer-fawr 19 J3
Gaerllwyd 19 J3
Gaerwen 48 D3
Gagingwell 33 G7
Gailey 42 B5
Gainford 66 B6
Gainsborough 54 C5
Gainsford End 36 C6
Gairloch 100 E5
Gairlochy 93 H7
Gaisgill 64 D7
Gaitsgill 63 J3
Galashiels 82 C8
Galby 43 J6
Galgate 57 H5
Galhampton 11 H3
Gallatown 81 H2
Galley Common 43 F7
Galleywood 24 D2
Gallowfauld 89 G4
Galltair 92 E3
Galmisdale 92 A7
Galmpton, Devon 5 G5
Galmpton, Devon 5 J4
Galphay 59 H3
Galston 79 H8
Galtrigill 99 G7
Gamblesby 64 D4
Gamlingay 35 F4
Gamston, Notts 54 B6
Gamston, Notts 43 J3
Ganarew 19 K1
Ganllwyd 39 G4
Ganstead 61 J7
Ganthorpe 60 D3
Ganton 61 G3
Garbat 102 C6
Garbhallt 78 C2
Garboldisham 36 F1
Gardenstown 105 H2
Garderhouse 115 F4
Gare Hill 11 J1
Garelochhead 78 E2
Garenin 107 F4
Garford 21 J3
Garforth 59 K7
Gargrave 58 E5
Gargunnock 80 C2
Garlieston 69 F6
Garlogie 97 G5
Garmond 105 H3
Garmouth 104 C2
Garn 38 B3
Garnant 18 A1
Garndolbenmaen 38 D2
Garnett Bridge 64 C8
Garnkirk 79 J5
Garn-yr-erw 19 G1
Garrabost 107 K5
Garras 2 F7
Garreg 38 F2
Garreg Bank 40 D5
Garrigill 64 E3
Garros 100 A6
Garrygualach 93 H5
Garrynamonie 90 C4
Garsdale 58 C2
Garsdale Head 58 C1
Garsdon 20 D4
Garshall Green 42 B3
Garsington 21 K2
Garstang 57 H6
Garston 50 D5
Garswood 50 E4
Gartcosh 80 B5
Garth, M. Glam 18 C3
Garth, Clwyd 40 D2
Garth, Powys 29 G5
Garth, I. of M. 56 Q4
Garthbrengy 29 H6
Gartheli 28 C4
Garthmyl 40 C7
Garthorpe, Leic 44 B4
Garthorpe, Humbs 54 C2
Gartly 96 E2
Gartmore 79 H2
Gartocharn 79 G3
Garton 61 K7
Garton-on-the-Wolds 61 G5
Gartymore 111 G7
Garvald 82 D4
Garvard 76 C2
Garve 102 B6
Garvestone 46 F6
Garvock 89 K1
Garway 31 F7
Garynahine 107 G5
Gastard 20 C6
Gasthorpe 36 E1
Gatcombe 13 G7
Gatebeck 57 J2
Gate Burton 54 C5
Gateforth 60 C8
Gatehead 79 F8
Gate Helmsley 60 D5
Gatehouse of Fleet 69 H5
Gatelawbridge 72 E5
Gateley 46 E4
Gatenby 59 J2
Gateshead 66 C1
Gatesheath 50 D7
Gateside, Fife 88 D8
Gateside, Strath 79 F6
Gateside, Tays 89 G4
Gathurst 50 E3
Gatley 51 H5
Gattonside 82 D8
Gauldry 89 F6
Gaunt's Common 12 C5
Gautby 55 F6
Gavinton 82 F6
Gawber 53 F3
Gawcott 33 J6
Gawsworth 51 H7
Gawthrop 58 B3
Gawthwaite 57 F2
Gaydon 33 F4
Gayhurst 34 B5
Gayle 58 D2
Gayles 65 J7
Gay Street 14 D3
Gayton, Staffs 42 B4
Gayton, Mers 50 B5
Gayton, Norf 46 C5
Gayton, Northnts 33 K4
Gayton le Marsh 55 J5
Gayton Thorpe 46 C5
Gaywood 46 B4
Gazeley 36 C3
Geary 99 H6
Gedding 36 E4
Geddington 34 B1
Gedintailor 92 B2
Gedney 45 H4
Gedney Broadgate 45 H4
Gedney Drove End 45 H4
Gedney Dyke 45 H4
Gedney Hill 45 G5
Gedney Marsh 43 G4
Gee Cross 51 J4

Geise 111 H2
Geldeston 47 J7
Gelli 26 E5
Gellifor 50 A7
Gelligaer 18 F3
Gellilydan 39 F3
Gellioedd 39 J2
Gellywen 27 G4
Gelston 69 J5
Gentleshaw 42 C5
Geocrab 99 G3
Georgeham 8 E2
George Nympton 9 H3
Georgetown 79 G5
Georgia 2 C6
Germansweek 8 E6
Germoe 2 D7
Gerrans 3 G6
Gerrards Cross 22 F4
Geshader 106 F5
Gestingthorpe 36 D6
Geuffordd 40 D5
Geufron 29 F1
Gibraltar 55 K8
Gidea Park 23 L3
Gidleigh 9 G7
Gifford 82 D5
Giggleswick 58 D4
Gilberdyke 60 F8
Gilchriston 82 C5
Gilcrux 63 G4
Gildersome 59 H8
Gildingwells 53 H5
Gileston 18 E6
Gilfach Goch 18 D4
Gilfachreda 28 B4
Gilgarran 62 F5
Gillamoor 60 D1
Gilling East 60 D3
Gillingham, Kent 24 D6
Gillingham, Dorset 11 K3
Gillingham, Norf. 47 K7
Gilling West 66 B7
Gillow Heath 51 H8
Gills 111 K1
Gilmanscleuch 73 J2
Gilmerton, Tays. 88 A6
Gilmerton, Lothn. 81 H5
Gilmorton 33 H1
Gilsland 74 C8
Gilsland Spa 74 C8
Gilston 82 C6
Gilwern 19 G1
Gimingham 47 H3
Gipping 36 F3
Gipsey Bridge 45 F1
Girlsta 115 G3
Girsby 66 D7
Girthon 69 H5
Girton, Notts. 54 C7
Girton, Cambs. 35 H3
Girvan 71 G5
Gisburn 58 C4
Gisla 107 F6
Gisleham 37 L1
Gislingham 36 F3
Gissing 37 G1
Gittisham 10 C6
Gladestry 30 D4
Gladsmuir 82 C4
Glais 18 B2
Glaisdale 67 H7
Glame 100 B8
Glamis 89 F4
Glanaman 18 A1
Glandford 46 F2
Glandwr, Dyfed 27 F4
Glandwr, Gwent 19 G2
Glangrwyney 19 G1
Glanmule 40 C7
Glanrhyd 26 F2
Glanton 75 G3
Glanton Pyke 75 G3
Glanvilles Wootton 11 H5
Glan-y-don 50 A6
Glan-yr-afon 40 B2
Glapthorn 44 D7
Glapwell 53 G7
Glasbury 30 C6
Glascoed, Powys 40 C6
Glascoed, Gwent 19 H2
Glascoed, Clwyd 49 J3
Glascote 42 E6
Glascwm 30 C4
Glasdrum 86 C4
Glasfryn 39 J1
Glasgow 79 H5
Glasinfryn 48 E4
Glasnakille 92 B4
Glaspwll 39 G7
Glassburn 94 B2
Glasserton 68 F7
Glassford 80 C7
Glasshouse Hill 31 J7
Glasshouses 59 G4
Glasslaw 105 H3
Glasson, Cumbr. 63 H1
Glasson, Lancs. 57 H5
Glassonby 64 C4
Glaston 44 B6
Glastonbury 11 F2
Glatton 34 E1
Glazebury 51 F4
Glazeley 31 J1
Gleadless 53 F5
Gleadsmoss 51 H4
Gleaston 57 F3
Glemsford 36 D5
Glenancross 92 C6
Glenastle 76 C7
Glen Auldyn 56 R2
Glenbarr 77 F8
Glenbeg 85 G2
Glen Bernisdale 99 K8
Glenbervie 97 G7

Glenboig 80 C5
Glenborrodale 85 H2
Glenbreck 73 F2
Glenbuck 72 C2
Glenburn 79 G5
Glencaple 72 E8
Glencarse 88 D6
Glencoe 86 D3
Glencraig 81 G2
Glendevon 88 B8
Glendoebeg 94 C5
Glendon Hall 34 B1
Glenegedale 76 C6
Glenelg 92 E4
Glenfarg 88 D7
Glenfield 43 H6
Glenfinnan 93 F7
Glenforsa 88 D2
Glengarnock 78 F6
Glengrasco 99 K8
Glenkerry 73 H3
Glenkindie 96 D4
Glenlee 72 B6
Glenluce 68 C5
Glenmavis 80 C5
Glenmaye 56 P4
Glenmore 91 K1
Glenmoy 89 G2
Glen of Newmill 104 D3
Glen Parva 43 H7
Glenprosen Village 88 F2
Glenreasdell Mains 77 H6
Glenridding 63 J6
Glenrothes 81 H1
Glenside 107 H7
Glentham 54 E4
Glenton 97 F3
Glentress 81 H8
Glen Trool Lodge 71 K6
Glentrool Village 71 J7
Glentworth 54 C5
Glenuig 92 C8
Glen Village 80 D4
Glen Vine 56 Q4
Glespin 72 D2
Gletness 115 G3
Glewstone 31 G2
Glinton 44 E6
Glooston 44 A7
Glossop 52 C4
Gloster Hill 75 J4
Gloucester 20 C1
Gloup 117 G2
Glusburn 58 F6
Gluss 116 E5
Glympton 33 G7
Glynarthen 27 H2
Glyn Ceiriog 40 D3
Glyncoch 18 E3
Glyncorrwg 18 C3
Glynde 15 H5
Glyndebourne 15 H4
Glyndyfrdwy 40 C2
Glyn Neath 18 C2
Glynogwr 18 D4
Glyntaff 18 E4
Gnosall 41 K4
Gnosall Heath 41 K4
Goadby 44 A7
Goadby Marwood 44 A4
Goatacre 20 E5
Goathill 11 H4
Goathland 67 J7
Goathurst 10 D2
Gobowen 40 E3
Godalming 14 C1
Godington 33 J7
Godmanchester 35 F2
Godmanstone 11 H6
Godmersham 25 G7
Godney 11 F1
Godolphin Cross 2 C6
Godre'r-graig 18 B2
Godshill, Hants. 12 D4
Godshill, I. of W. 7 K6
Godstone 23 J7
Goff's Oak 23 J2
Gogar 81 G4
Goginan 28 D1
Golan 38 E2
Golant 3 K4
Golberdon 4 D2
Golborne 50 F4
Golcar 52 D2
Goldcliff 19 H4
Golden Cross 15 J4
Golden Green 16 D1
Golden Grove 27 K5
Goldenhill 42 A1
Golden Pot 13 K1
Golden Valley 32 B7
Golders Green 23 H4
Goldhanger 24 F2
Golding 41 G6
Goldsborough, N. Yks. 59 J5
Goldsborough, N. Yks. 67 J6
Goldsithney 2 D6
Goldthorpe 53 G3
Golspie 103 G7
Gollanfield 103 G7
Gomeldon 12 D2
Gomersal 52 E1
Gomshall 14 D1
Gonalston 43 J2
Gonfirth 115 F2
Good Easter 24 C1
Gooderstone 46 C6
Goodleigh 9 F2
Goodmanham 61 F6
Goodnestone, Kent 25 G6
Goodnestone, Kent 25 J7
Goodrich 19 K1
Goodrington 5 J4
Goodwick 26 D3

Goodworth Clatford 13 F1
Goole 54 B1
Goonbell 2 F5
Goonhavern 3 F4
Gooseham 8 C4
Goosetrey 51 G2
Goosey 21 H3
Goosnargh 57 J7
Goostrey 51 G6
Gordon 82 E7
Gordonbush 103 G2
Gordonstown, Grampn. 104 E3
Gordonstown, Grampn. 97 G2
Gorebridge 81 J5
Gorefield 45 H5
Goring 21 L4
Goring-by-Sea 14 E5
Gorleston-on-Sea 47 L6
Gorran Haven 3 J5
Gors 28 D2
Gorsedd 50 A6
Gorseinon 27 K7
Gorseness 112 E5
Gorsgoch 27 J1
Gorslas 27 K5
Gorsley 31 H7
Gorstan 102 B6
Gorton 51 H4
Gosbeck 37 G4
Gosberton 45 F3
Gosfield 36 C7
Gosforth, Cumbr. 62 F7
Gosforth, T. & W. 75 J8
Gosmore 34 E7
Gosport 13 J6
Gossabrough 117 G4
Goswick 83 J7
Gotham 43 H3
Gotherington 32 B7
Goudhurst 16 E2
Goulceby 55 G6
Gourdas 97 G1
Gourdon 89 L1
Gourock 78 E4
Govan 79 H5
Goveton 5 H5
Govig 98 F2
Govilon 19 G1
Gowanhill 105 K2
Gowdall 53 J1
Gowerton 27 K7
Gowkhall 81 F3
Goxhill, Humbs. 54 F1
Goxhill, Humbs. 61 J6
Graffham 14 C4
Grafham 34 E3
Grafton, H. & W. 31 F6
Grafton, Oxon 21 G2
Grafton, H. & W. 31 G3
Grafton, N. Yks. 59 K4
Grafton Flyford 32 B4
Grafton Regis 34 A5
Grafton Underwood 34 C1
Grafty Green 16 E1
Graianrhyd 40 D1
Graig, Gwyn. 49 H3
Graig, Clwyd. 49 K3
Graig-fechan 40 C1
Graig Penllyn 18 D5
Grain 24 E5
Grainsby 55 G4
Grainthorpe 55 H4
Graizelound 54 B4
Grampound 3 H5
Grampound Road 3 H4
Gramsdale 98 D7
Granborough 34 A7
Granby 44 A3
Grandborough 33 G3
Grandtully 88 B3
Grange, Mers. 50 B5
Grange, Cumbr. 63 H6
Grange Crossroads 104 D3
Grange Hill 23 K3
Grange Moor 52 E2
Grangemouth 80 E3
Grange-over-Sands 57 H3
Grangepans 80 F3
Grangetown 67 F5
Grange Villa 66 C2
Granish 95 G4
Gransmoor 61 J5
Granston 26 C3
Grantchester 35 H4
Grantham 44 C3
Grantley 59 H4
Grantlodge 97 G4
Granton 81 H4
Grantown-on-Spey 95 J3
Grantshouse 83 G5
Grappenhall 51 F5
Grasby 54 E3
Grasmere 63 J7
Grasscroft 51 J3
Grassendale 50 C5
Grassholme 65 G5
Grassington 58 F4
Grassmoor 53 G7
Grassthorpe 54 B7
Grateley 12 E1
Gratwich 42 C3
Graveley, Cambs. 35 F3
Graveley, Herts. 35 F7
Gravelly Hill 42 D7
Gravels 40 E6
Graveney 25 G6
Gravesend 24 C5
Gravir 107 H7
Grayingham 54 D4
Grayrigg 64 C8
Grays 24 C5
Grayshott 14 B2
Grayswood 14 C2
Graythorp 66 F5

Grazeley 22 B6
Greasbrough 53 G4
Greasby 50 B5
Great Abington 35 J5
Great Addington 34 C2
Great Alne 32 D4
Great Altcar 50 C3
Great Amwell 23 J1
Great Asby 64 D6
Great Ashfield 36 F3
Great Ayton 67 F6
Great Baddow 24 D2
Great Bardfield 36 B6
Great Barford 34 E4
Great Barr 42 C7
Great Barrington 21 G1
Great Barrow 50 D7
Great Barton 36 D3
Great Barugh 60 E3
Great Bavington 75 F6
Great Bealings 37 H5
Great Bedwyn 21 G6
Great Bentley 37 G7
Great Bircham 46 C3
Great Blakenham 37 G4
Great Bolas 41 H4
Great Bookham 23 G7
Great Bosullow 2 C6
Great Bourton 33 G5
Great Bowden 34 A1
Great Bradley 36 B4
Great Braxted 24 E1
Great Bricett 36 F4
Great Brickhill 34 C6
Great Bridgeford 42 A4
Great Brington 33 J3
Great Bromley 37 F7
Great Broughton 67 F7
Great Budworth 51 F6
Great Burdon 66 D6
Great Burstead 24 C3
Great Busby 66 F7
Great Canfield 24 B1
Great Carlton 55 J5
Great Casterton 44 D6
Great Chart 17 G1
Great Chatwell 41 J5
Great Chesterford 35 J5
Great Cheverell 20 D7
Great Chishill 35 H6
Great Clacton 25 H1
Great Clifton 62 F5
Great Coates 55 G2
Great Comberton 32 B5
Great Corby 64 B2
Great Cornard 36 D5
Great Coxwell 21 G3
Great Cransley 34 B2
Great Cressingham 46 D6
Great Crosby 50 C4
Great Cubley 42 D3
Great Dalby 44 A5
Great Doddington 34 B3
Great Dunham 46 D5
Great Dunmow 35 K7
Great Durnford 12 D2
Great Easton, Leic. 44 B7
Great Easton, Essex 35 K7
Great Eccleston 57 H6
Great Edstone 60 E2
Great Ellingham 46 F7
Great Elm 11 J1
Great Eversden 35 G4
Great Finborough 36 F4
Greatford 44 D5
Great Fransham 46 D5
Great Gaddesden 22 F1
Great Gidding 34 E1
Great Givendale 60 F5
Great Glemham 37 J3
Great Glen 43 J7
Great Gonerby 44 B3
Great Gransden 35 F4
Great Green 36 E4
Great Habton 60 E3
Great Hallingbury 23 L1
Greatham, Hants. 14 A2
Greatham, Cleve. 66 E5
Great Hampden 22 D2
Great Harrowden 34 B2
Great Harwood 58 C7
Great Haseley 22 B2
Great Hatfield 61 J6
Great Haywood 42 C4
Great Heck 53 H1
Great Henny 36 D6
Great Hinton 20 D7
Great Hockham 46 E7
Great Holland 25 J1
Great Horkesley 36 E7
Great Hormead 35 H6
Great Horwood 34 A6
Great Houghton, Northnts. 34 A4
Great Houghton, S. Yks. 53 G3
Great Hucklow 52 D6
Great Kelk 61 J5
Great Kingshill 22 D3
Great Langton 59 H1
Great Leighs 24 D1
Great Limber 55 F2
Great Linford 34 B5
Great Livermore 36 D2
Great Longstone 52 E6
Great Lumley 66 C3
Great Lyth 41 F6
Great Malvern 31 J5
Great Maplestead 36 D6
Great Marton 57 G7
Great Massingham 46 C4
Great Milton 22 B2
Great Missenden 22 D2
Great Mitton 58 C7
Great Mongeham 25 K7
Great Moulton 47 G7
Great Musgrave 64 E6

Great Ness 40 E5
Great Oakley, Northnts. 34 B1
Great Oakley, Essex 37 G7
Great Offley 34 E7
Great Ormside 64 E6
Great Orton 63 J2
Great Oxendon 33 K1
Great Palgrave 46 D5
Great Parndon 23 K2
Great Paxton 35 F3
Great Plumstead 47 J5
Great Ponton 44 C3
Great Preston 59 K8
Great Raveley 35 F1
Great Rissington 21 F1
Great Rollright 33 F6
Great Ryburgh 46 E4
Great Ryle 75 G3
Great Saling 36 C7
Great Salkeld 64 C4
Great Sampford 36 B6
Great Sankey 50 E5
Great Saxham 36 C3
Great Shefford 21 H5
Great Shelford 35 H4
Great Smeaton 66 D7
Great Snoring 46 E3
Great Somerford 20 D4
Great Stainton 66 D5
Great Stambridge 24 F3
Great Staughton 34 E3
Great Steeping 55 J7
Great Stonar 25 K7
Greatstone-on-Sea 17 H3
Great Strickland 64 C5
Great Stukeley 35 F2
Great Sturton 55 G6
Great Swinburne 75 F7
Great Tew 33 F7
Great Tey 36 D7
Great Thurlow 36 B4
Great Torrington 8 E4
Great Tosson 75 G4
Great Totham, Essex 24 E1
Great Totham, Essex 24 E1
Great Wakering 25 F4
Great Waldingfield 36 E5
Great Walsingham 46 E3
Great Waltham 24 C1
Great Warley 24 B3
Great Washbourne 32 B6
Great Welnetham 36 D4
Great Wenham 36 F6
Great Whittington 75 G7
Great Wigborough 25 F1
Great Wilbraham 35 J4
Great Wishford 12 C2
Great Witcombe 20 D1
Great Witley 31 J3
Great Wolford 32 E6
Great Worth 33 H5
Great Wratting 36 B5
Great Wymondley 35 F7
Great Wyrley 42 B6
Great Yarmouth 47 L6
Great Yeldham 36 C6
Greenburn 80 E5
Greendykes 75 G2
Greenfield, Clwyd 50 A6
Greenfield, Oxon 22 C3
Greenfield, Beds. 34 D6
Greenfield, G. Man. 51 J3
Greenfield, Highld 93 J5
Greenford 23 G4
Greengairs 80 C4
Greenham 21 J6
Green Hammerton 60 B5
Greenhaugh 74 D6
Greenhead 64 D1
Greenhill, Central 80 D4
Greenhill, S. Yks. 53 F5
Greenhill, G. Lon. 23 G4
Greenhithe 24 B5
Greenholm 79 H8
Greenholme 64 C7
Greenhouse 74 B2
Greenhow Hill 59 G4
Greenigoe 112 E6
Greenland 111 J2
Greenlaw 82 F7
Greenloaning 87 L8
Greenmount 51 G2
Greenmow 115 G6
Greenock 78 E4
Greenodd 57 G2
Green Ore 19 K7
Greenside 65 J1
Greensidehill 75 F3
Greenskares 105 G2
Greens Norton 33 J5
Greenstead Green 36 D7
Greensted 23 L2
Green Street 23 G3
Green Street Green 23 K6
Green, The, Wilts. 12 A2
Green, The, Cumbr. 56 E2
Greenwich 23 K5
Greet 32 C6
Greete 31 G2
Greetham, Leic. 44 C5
Greetham, Lincs. 55 H6
Greetland 52 C1
Gregson Lane 50 E1
Greinton 11 F2
Grendon, Northnts. 34 B3
Grendon, Warw. 42 E7
Grendon Common 42 E7
Grendon Green 31 G4
Grendon Underwood 33 J7
Grenitote 98 D5
Grenoside 53 F4
Gresford 40 E1
Gresham 47 G3

Greshornish 99 J7
Gressenhall 46 E5
Gressingham 57 J4
Greta Bridge 65 H6
Gretna 73 J8
Gretna Green 73 J8
Gretton, Northnts. 44 B7
Gretton, Glos. 32 C6
Gretton, Shrops. 41 G7
Grewelthorpe 59 H3
Greygarth 59 G3
Greysouthen 62 F5
Greystoke 64 B4
Greystone 89 H4
Greywell 22 C7
Griais 107 J4
Grianan 107 J5
Griff 33 F1
Griffithstown 19 G3
Grike 63 F6
Grimeford Village 50 F2
Grimethorpe 53 G3
Griminish 98 C7
Grimister 117 F3
Grimley 31 K3
Grimness 112 E7
Grimoldby 55 H5
Grimsargh 57 J7
Grimsby 55 G3
Grimscote 33 J4
Grimscott 8 C5
Grimshader 107 J6
Grimsthorpe 44 D4
Grimston, Norf. 46 C4
Grimston, Leic. 43 J4
Grimstone 11 H6
Grindale 61 J3
Grindiscol 115 G5
Grindleford 52 E6
Grindleton 58 C6
Grindley Brook 41 G2
Grindlow 52 D6
Grindon, Staffs. 42 C1
Grindon, Northum. 83 H1
Gringle 41 J6
Gringley on the Hill 54 B4
Grinsdale 63 J2
Grinshill 41 G4
Grinton 65 H8
Grisedale 58 C1
Gristhorpe 61 H2
Griston 46 E7
Grittenham 20 E4
Grittleton 20 C4
Grizebeck 57 F2
Grizedale 57 G1
Grobister 113 G6
Groby 43 H6
Groes, W. Glam. 18 B4
Groes, Clwyd. 49 K4
Groes-faen 18 E4
Groeslon 38 D1
Grogport 77 H7
Gromford 37 J4
Gronant 49 K2
Groombridge 15 J2
Grosebay 99 G3
Grosmont, Gwent 30 F7
Grosmont, N. Yks. 67 J7
Groton 36 E5
Grove, Dorset 6 A7
Grove, Notts. 54 B6
Grove, Oxon 21 J3
Grove, Kent 25 J6
Grove Park 23 K5
Grovesend 27 K6
Grudie 101 K6
Gruids 102 D2
Gruline 85 G4
Grumbla 2 C7
Grunasound 115 F5
Grundisburgh 37 H4
Gruting 114 E4
Guardbridge 89 G7
Guarlford 31 K5
Guestling Green 16 F4
Guestwick 46 F4
Guide Post 75 J6
Guilden Morden 35 F5
Guilden Sutton 50 D7
Guildford 14 C1
Guildtown 88 D5
Guilsborough 33 J2
Guilsfield 40 D5
Guisborough 67 G6
Guiseley 59 G6
Guist 46 E4
Guiting Power 32 C7
Gullane 82 C6
Gulval 2 C6
Gumfreston 26 F6
Gumley 43 J7
Gunby, Lincs. 44 C4
Gunby, Humbs. 60 E7
Gundleton 13 J2
Gunn 9 G2
Gunnerside 65 G8
Gunnerton 74 F7
Gunness 54 C2
Gunnislake 4 E2
Gunnista 115 H4
Gunthorpe, Norf. 46 F3
Gunthorpe, Notts. 43 J2
Gunwalloe Fishing Cove 2 D7
Gurnard 13 G6
Gurney Slade 11 H1
Gurnos 18 B2
Gussage All Saints 12 C4
Gussage St Michael 12 B4
Guston 17 L1
Gutcher 117 G3
Guthrie 89 H3
Guyhirn 45 H4
Guy's Head 45 H4
Guy's Marsh 11 K3

Guyzance...75 J4
Gwaelod-y-Garth...18 F4
Gwaenysgor...49 K2
Gwalchmai...48 C3
Gwaun-Cae-Gurwen...18 B1
Gwbert...26 F1
Gweek...2 F7
Gwehelog...19 H2
Gwenddwr...29 H5
Gwennap...2 F5
Gwenter...2 F8
Gwernaffield...50 B7
Gwernesney...19 J2
Gwernogle...27 K3
Gwernymynydd...50 B7
Gwersyllt...40 E1
Gwespyr...49 L2
Gwinear...2 D6
Gwithian...2 D5
Gwyddelwern...40 B2
Gwyddgrug...27 J3
Gwytherin...49 H4

H

Habberley, Shrops...40 E6
Habberley, H. & W...31 K2
Habost, W. Isles...107 H7
Habrough...55 F2
Haccombe...5 J2
Haceby...44 D3
Hacheston...37 J4
Hackford...46 F6
Hackforth...59 H1
Hacklete...107 F5
Hackleton...34 B4
Hackness, Orkney...112 D7
Hackness, N. Yks...61 G1
Hackney...23 J4
Hackthorn...54 D5
Hackthorpe...64 C5
Haconby...44 E4
Hadden...83 F8
Haddenham, Bucks...22 C2
Haddenham, Cambs...35 H2
Haddington...82 D4
Haddiscoe...47 K7
Haddon...44 E7
Hademore...42 D6
Hadfield...52 C4
Hadham Cross...23 K1
Hadham Ford...35 H7
Hadleigh, Essex...24 E4
Hadleigh, Suff...36 F5
Hadley...41 H5
Hadley End...42 D4
Hadlow...24 C7
Hadlow Down...15 J3
Hadnall...41 G4
Hadstock...35 J5
Hadzor...32 B3
Haffenden Quarter...17 F1
Hafod-Dinbych...39 H1
Haggbeck...74 A7
Haggerston...83 J7
Hagley, H. & W...32 B1
Hagley, H. & W...31 G5
Hagworthingham...55 H7
Haigh...50 F3
Haighton Green...57 J7
Haile...62 F7
Hailes...32 C6
Hailey, Oxon...21 H1
Hailey, Herts...23 J1
Hailsham...16 C5
Hail Weston...34 E3
Hainault...23 K3
Hainford...47 H5
Hainton...55 F5
Haisthorpe...61 J4
Halberton...10 B4
Halcro...111 J2
Hale, Hants...12 D4
Hale, Ches...50 D5
Hale, Lincs...44 E2
Hale, G. Man...51 G5
Hale Bank...50 D5
Halebarns...51 G5
Hales, Staffs...41 J3
Hales, Norf...47 J7
Halesowen...32 B1
Hales Place...25 H7
Hale Street...16 D1
Halesworth...37 J2
Halewood...50 D5
Halford, Warw...32 E5
Halford, Shrops...31 F1
Halfpenny Green...41 K7
Halfway, Powys...29 F6
Halfway, Berks...21 J6
Halfway, Dyfed...27 L3
Halfway House...40 E5
Halfway Houses...25 F5
Halifax...52 C1
Halistra...99 H7
Halket...79 G6
Halkirk...111 H3
Halkyn...50 B6
Hallam...15 J4
Hallaton...44 A7
Hallatrow...19 L7
Hallbankgate...64 C2
Hall Dunnerdale...56 F1
Hallen...19 K4
Hall Green...32 D1
Halliburton...82 E2
Hallin...99 H7
Halling...24 D6
Hallington...75 F7
Hall of the Forest...30 D1
Halloughton...43 J1

Hallow...31 K4
Hallrule...74 B3
Halls...82 E4
Hallsands...5 J6
Hallthwaites...56 E2
Hallworthy...8 B7
Hallyne...81 G7
Halmer End...41 K2
Halmore...20 A2
Halmyre Mains...81 G7
Halnaker...14 C5
Halsall...50 C2
Halse, Somer...10 C3
Halse, Northnts...33 H5
Halsetown...2 D6
Halsham...55 G1
Halsinger...8 F2
Halstead, Leic...44 A6
Halstead, Essex...36 D6
Halstead, Kent...23 K6
Halstock...11 G5
Haltham...55 G7
Haltoft End...45 G2
Halton, Bucks...22 D1
Halton, Clwyd...40 E3
Halton, Ches...50 E5
Halton, Lancs...57 J4
Halton East...58 F5
Halton Gill...58 D3
Halton Holegate...55 J7
Halton Lea Gate...64 D2
Halton West...58 D5
Haltwhistle...64 E1
Halvergate...47 K6
Halwell...5 H4
Halwill...8 E6
Halwill Junction...8 E5
Ham, Glos...20 A3
Ham, Shetld...114 B5
Ham, G. Lon...23 G5
Ham, Wilts...21 H6
Ham, Highld...111 J1
Hamble...13 G5
Hambleden...22 C4
Hambledon, Surrey...14 C2
Hambledon, Hants...13 J4
Hambleton, N. Yks...60 C7
Hambleton, Lancs...57 G6
Hambridge...10 E3
Hambrook, W. Susx...14 A5
Hambrook, Avon...19 L5
Hameringham...55 H7
Hamerton...34 E2
Hametoun...114 B5
Ham Green, H. & W...32 C3
Ham Green, Avon...19 K5
Hamilton...80 C6
Hammersmith...23 H5
Hammerwich...42 C6
Hammond Street...23 J2
Hammoon...11 K4
Hamnavoe, Shetld...115 F5
Hamnavoe, Shetld...117 G4
Hampden Park...16 D5
Hampnett...20 F1
Hampole...53 H2
Hampreston...12 C6
Hampstead...23 H4
Hampstead Norreys...21 K5
Hampsthwaite...59 H5
Hampton, H. & W...32 C5
Hampton, G. Lon...23 G6
Hampton, Shrops...31 J1
Hampton Bishop...31 G6
Hampton Heath...41 F2
Hampton in Arden...32 E1
Hampton Lovett...32 A3
Hampton Lucy...32 E4
Hampton on the Hill...32 E3
Hampton Poyle...21 K1
Hamsey...15 H4
Hamstall Ridware...42 D5
Hamstead, W. Mids...42 C7
Hamstead, I. of W...13 F6
Hamstead Marshall...21 J6
Hamsterley, Durham...65 J2
Hamsterley, Durham...65 J4
Ham Street, Somer...11 G2
Hamstreet, Kent...17 H2
Hamworthy...12 B6
Hanbury, H. & W...32 B3
Hanbury, Staffs...42 D4
Hanchurch...41 K2
Handbridge...50 D7
Handcross...15 F3
Handforth...51 H5
Handley...41 F1
Handsacre...42 C5
Handsworth, W. Mids...42 C7
Handsworth, S. Yks...53 G5
Hanford...42 A2
Hanging Langford...12 C2
Hanham...19 L5
Hankelow...41 H2
Hankerton...20 D3
Hankham...16 D5
Hanley...42 A2
Hanley Castle...31 K5
Hanley Child...31 H3
Hanley Swan...31 K5
Hanley William...31 H3
Hanlith...58 E4
Hanmer...41 F3
Hannington, Northnts...34 B2
Hannington, Wilts...21 F3
Hannington, Hants...21 K7
Hannington Wick...21 F3
Hanslope...34 B5
Hanthorpe...44 D4
Hanwell...33 G5
Hanwood...41 F6
Hanworth, Norf...47 G3
Hanworth, G. Lon...23 G5
Happendon...72 D1
Happisburgh...47 J3

Happisburgh Common...47 J4
Hapsford...50 D6
Hapton, Lancs...58 C7
Hapton, Norf...47 G7
Harberton...5 H4
Harbertonford...5 H4
Harbledown...25 H7
Harborne...32 C1
Harborough Magna...33 G2
Harbottle...75 F4
Harbury...33 F4
Harby, Leic...44 A3
Harby, Notts...54 C6
Harcombe...10 C6
Harden...59 F7
Hardendale...64 C6
Hardgate...97 G5
Hardham...14 D4
Hardhorn...57 G7
Hardingham...46 F6
Hardingstone...34 A4
Hardings Wood...41 K1
Hardington...20 B7
Hardington Mandeville...11 G4
Hardington Marsh...11 G5
Hardley...13 G5
Hardley Street...47 J6
Hardmead...34 C5
Hardraw...58 D1
Hardstoft...53 G7
Hardway, Somer...11 J2
Hardway, Hants...13 J5
Hardwick, Northnts...34 B3
Hardwick, Bucks...22 D1
Hardwick, Cambs...35 G4
Hardwick, Oxon...21 H2
Hardwick, Oxon...33 H7
Hardwick, Norf...47 H8
Hardwicke, Glos...32 B7
Hardwicke, Glos...20 C1
Hardwick, H. & W...30 D5
Hareby...55 H7
Hareden...58 B5
Harefield...22 F3
Hare Hatch...22 D5
Harehope...75 G2
Harescombe...20 C1
Haresfield...20 C1
Hare Street...35 G7
Harewood...59 J6
Harford...5 G4
Hargrave, Suff...36 C4
Hargrave, Northnts...34 D2
Hargrave, Ches...50 D7
Harker...63 J1
Harkstead...37 G6
Harlaston...42 E5
Harlaxton...44 B3
Harlech...38 E3
Harlesden...23 H4
Harleston, Suff...36 F3
Harleston, Norf...37 H1
Harleston, Devon...5 H5
Harlestone...33 K3
Harle Syke...58 D7
Harley...41 G6
Harlington...34 D6
Harlosh...91 H1
Harlow...23 K1
Harlow Hill...75 G8
Harlsey...66 E8
Harlthorpe...60 E7
Harlton...35 G4
Harman's Cross...6 D6
Harmby...59 G2
Harmer Green...23 H1
Harmer Hill...41 F4
Harmston...54 D7
Harnham...12 D3
Harnhill...20 E2
Harold Hill...23 L3
Haroldston West...26 C5
Haroldswick...117 H1
Harold Wood...23 L3
Harome...60 D2
Harpenden...23 G1
Harpford...10 B6
Harpham...61 H4
Harpley, Norf...46 C4
Harpley, H. & W...31 H3
Harpole...33 J3
Harpsdale...111 H3
Harpsden...22 C4
Harpswell...54 D5
Harpurhey...51 H3
Harpur Hill...52 C6
Harrapool...92 C3
Harrietfield...88 B6
Harrietsham...24 E7
Harrington, Northnts...34 A1
Harrington, Cumbr...62 E5
Harrington, Lincs...55 H6
Harringworth...44 C7
Harriseahead...42 A1
Harrogate...59 J5
Harrold...34 C4
Harrow...23 G4
Harrowbarrow...4 E2
Harrowden...34 D5
Harrow on the Hill...23 G4
Harston, Leic...44 B3
Harston, Cambs...35 H4
Hart...66 E4
Hartburn...75 G6
Hartest...36 D4
Hartfield...15 H2
Hartford, Cambs...35 F2
Hartford, Ches...51 F6
Hartfordbridge...22 C7
Hartford End...24 C1
Harthill...66 B7
Harthill, Strath...80 E5
Harthill, Ches...41 G1
Harthill, S. Yks...53 G5
Hartington...52 D7

Hartland...8 C3
Hartland Quay...8 C3
Hartlebury...31 K2
Hartlepool...66 F4
Hartley, Kent...24 C6
Hartley, Kent...16 E2
Hartley, Cumbr...64 E7
Hartley, Northum...75 K7
Hartley Wespall...22 B7
Hartley Wintney...22 C7
Hartlip...24 E6
Harton, T. & W...66 D1
Harton, N. Yks...60 E4
Harton, Shrops...31 F1
Hartpury...31 K7
Hartshill...32 F7
Hartshorne...43 F4
Hartsop...63 K6
Hartwell...34 A4
Hartwood...80 D6
Harvel...24 C6
Harvington...32 C5
Harwell...21 J4
Harwich...37 H6
Harwood, Durham...65 F4
Harwood, G. Man...51 G2
Harwood Dale...61 G2
Harworth...53 J4
Hascombe...14 C1
Haselbech...33 K2
Haselbury Plucknett...11 F4
Haseley...32 E3
Haselor...32 D4
Hasfield...31 K7
Hasguard...26 C6
Haskayne...50 C3
Hasketon...37 H4
Hasland...53 F7
Haslemere...14 C2
Haslingden...51 G1
Haslingden Grange...51 G1
Haslingfield...35 H4
Haslington...41 J1
Hassall...41 J1
Hassall Green...51 G8
Hassell Street...17 H1
Hassendean...74 B2
Hassingham...47 J6
Hassocks...15 G4
Hassop...52 E6
Hastigrow...111 J2
Hastingleigh...17 H1
Hastings...16 F5
Hastingwood...23 K2
Hastoe...22 E2
Haswell...66 D3
Hatch, Wilts...12 B3
Hatch, Hants...22 B7
Hatch, Beds...34 E5
Hatch Beauchamp...10 E3
Hatch End...23 G3
Hatching Green...23 G1
Hatchmere...50 E6
Hatcliffe...55 G3
Hatfield, H. & W...31 G4
Hatfield, Herts...14 B2
Hatfield, S. Yks...53 J3
Hatfield Broad Oak...23 L1
Hatfield Heath...23 L1
Hatfield Peverel...24 D1
Hatfield Woodhouse...53 J3
Hatford...21 H3
Hatherden...21 H7
Hatherleigh...9 F5
Hathern...43 H4
Hatherop...21 F2
Hathersage...52 E5
Hatherton, Staffs...42 B5
Hatherton, Ches...41 H2
Hatley St George...35 F4
Hatt...4 D3
Hattingley...13 J2
Hatton, Warw...32 E3
Hatton, Derby...42 E3
Hatton, Ches...50 E5
Hatton, G. Lon...23 F5
Hatton, Lincs...55 F6
Hatton, Shrops...41 F7
Hatton, Grampn...97 K2
Hatton, Derby...97 H3
Hatton Heath...50 D7
Hatton of Fintray...35 F4
Haugham...55 H5
Haugh Head...75 G2
Haughley...36 F3
Haughley Green...36 F3
Haugh of Glass...96 D2
Haugh of Urr...72 D8
Haughton, Staffs...42 A4
Haughton, Shrops...42 A4
Haughton, Shrops...41 G5
Haughton, Shrops...41 H7
Haughton, Notts...53 J6
Haughton Green...51 J4
Haughton Moss...41 G1
Haunton...42 E6
Hauxley...75 J4
Hauxton...35 H4
Havant...13 K5
Haven...30 F4
Havenstreet...13 H6
Haverfordwest...26 D5
Haverhill...36 B5
Haverigg...56 E3
Havering-atte-Bower...23 L3
Haversham...34 B5
Haverthwaite...57 G2
Hawarden...50 C7
Hawes...58 D2
Hawford...31 K3
Hawick...74 B3
Hawkchurch...10 E5
Hawkedon...36 C4
Hawkeridge...20 C7
Hawkerland...10 B7

Hawkesbury...20 B4
Hawkesbury Upton...20 B4
Hawkes End...32 E1
Hawkhill...75 J3
Hawkhurst...16 E2
Hawkinge...17 K1
Hawkley...13 K3
Hawkridge...9 J2
Hawkshead...63 J8
Hawksland...80 D8
Hawkswick...58 E3
Hawksworth, Notts...44 A2
Hawksworth, W. Yks...59 G6
Hawkwell...24 E3
Hawley, Hants...22 D7
Hawley, Kent...23 L5
Hawling...32 C7
Haworth...58 F7
Hawksker...67 K7
Hawstead...36 D4
Hawthorn...66 E3
Hawthorn Hill...22 D5
Hawton...44 A1
Haxby...60 C4
Haxey...54 B4
Haydock...50 E4
Haydon...11 H4
Haydon Bridge...65 F1
Haydon Wick...21 F4
Haye...4 D3
Hayes, G. Lon...23 F4
Hayes, G. Lon...23 K6
Hayfield...52 C5
Hayle...2 D6
Hayes...34 D5
Haynes Church End...34 D5
Hay-on-Wye...30 D5
Hayscastle...26 C4
Hayscastle Cross...26 D4
Hayton, Notts...54 B5
Hayton, Cumbr...64 C2
Hayton, Humbs...60 F6
Hayton, Cumbr...63 G3
Hayton's Bent...31 G1
Haytor Vale...5 H2
Haywards Heath...15 G3
Haywood Oaks...43 J1
Hazelbank...80 D7
Hazelbury Bryan...11 J5
Hazeley...22 C7
Hazel Grove...51 J5
Hazelrigg...75 G1
Hazelslade...42 C5
Hazelwood...43 F2
Hazlemere...22 D3
Hazlerigg...75 J7
Hazleton...20 E1
Heacham...46 B3
Headbourne Worthy...13 G2
Headcorn...16 F1
Headingley...59 H7
Headington...21 K2
Headless Cross...32 C3
Headley, Hants...14 B2
Headley, Surrey...23 H7
Headley, Hants...21 K6
Head of Muir...80 D3
Headon...54 B6
Heads Nook...64 B2
Heage...43 F1
Healaugh, N. Yks...60 C6
Healaugh, N. Yks...65 H8
Heald Green...51 H5
Healey, N. Yks...59 G2
Healey, Lancs...51 H2
Healey, Northum...65 H2
Healeyfield...65 H3
Healing...55 G2
Heamoor...2 C6
Heanish...84 B4
Heanor...43 G2
Heapham...54 C5
Hearthstone...73 G2
Heasley Mill...9 H2
Heast...92 C4
Heath, S. Glam...19 F5
Heathcote...52 D7
Heath End, Hants...14 B1
Heath End, Hants...21 K6
Heather...43 F5
Heathfield, E. Susx...16 C3
Heathfield, Somer...10 C3
Heathfield, Strath...78 F5
Heathfield, Devon...5 J2
Heath Hayes...42 C5
Heath Hill...41 J5
Heath House...11 F1
Heath, The...47 G4
Heathton...41 K7
Heatley...51 G5
Heaton, Lancs...57 H4
Heaton, Staffs...51 J7
Heaton, T. & W...75 J8
Heaton Moor...51 H4
Heaverham...24 B7
Heaviley...51 J5
Hebburn...66 D1
Hebden...58 F4
Hebden Bridge...51 J1
Hebden Green...51 F7
Hebron...75 H6
Heckfield...22 C6
Heckington...44 E2
Heckmondwike...52 E1
Heddington...20 D6
Heddle...112 D5
Heddon-on-the-Wall...75 H8
Hedenham...47 J7
Hedge End...13 G4
Hedgerley...22 E4

Hedging...10 E3
Hedley on the Hill...65 H2
Hednesford...42 C5
Hedon...61 J8
Hedsor...22 E4
Hegdon Hill...31 G4
Heggerscales...65 F6
Heglibister...115 F3
Heighington, Durham...66 C5
Heighington, Lincs...54 E7
Heights of Brae...102 D6
Heights of Kinlochewe...101 G6
Heiton...74 D1
Helbeck...64 E6
Hele, Devon...10 A5
Hele, Devon...9 F1
Helensburgh...78 E3
Helford...2 F7
Helhoughton...46 D4
Helions Bumpstead...36 B5
Helland...3 J2
Hellesdon...47 H5
Hellidon...33 H4
Hellifield...58 D5
Hellingly...16 C4
Hellington...47 J6
Hellister...115 F4
Helmdon...33 H5
Helmingham...37 G4
Helmsdale...111 G7
Helmshore...51 G1
Helmsley...60 D2
Helperby...59 K4
Helperthorpe...61 G3
Helpringham...44 E2
Helpston...44 E6
Helsby...50 D6
Helston...2 E7
Helstone...3 J1
Helton...64 C5
Helwith Bridge...58 D4
Hemblington...47 J5
Hemel Hempstead...22 F2
Hemingbrough...60 D7
Hemingby...55 G6
Hemingford Abbots...35 F2
Hemingford Grey...35 F2
Hemingstone...37 G4
Hemington, Somer...20 B7
Hemington, Northnts...34 D1
Hemley...37 H5
Hempholme...61 H5
Hempnall...47 H7
Hempnall Green...47 H7
Hempriggs...103 K6
Hempstead, Essex...36 B6
Hempstead, Norf...47 G3
Hempstead, Norf...47 K4
Hempsted...20 C1
Hempton, Norf...46 E4
Hempton, Oxon...33 G6
Hemsby...47 K5
Hemswell...54 D4
Hemswell Cliff...54 D5
Hemsworth...53 G2
Hemyock...10 C4
Henbury, Ches...51 H6
Henbury, Avon...19 K5
Hendon, T. & W...66 E2
Hendon, G. Lon...23 H4
Hendre...50 A7
Hendy...27 K6
Heneglwys...48 D3
Henfield...15 F4
Hengoed, Shrops...40 D3
Hengoed, Powys...30 D4
Hengoed, M. Glam...18 F3
Hengrave...36 D3
Henham...35 J7
Henley, W. Susx...14 B3
Henley, Somer...11 F2
Henley, Shrops...31 G2
Henley, Suff...37 G4
Henley-in-Arden...32 D3
Henley-on-Thames...22 C4
Henley Park...22 E7
Henllan, Dyfed...27 H2
Henllan, Clwyd...49 K4
Henllan Amgoed...26 F4
Henllys...19 G3
Henlow...34 E6
Hennock...5 J1
Henryd...49 G3
Henry's Moat...26 E4
Hensall...53 H1
Henshaw...64 E1
Henstead...37 K1
Henstridge...11 J4
Henstridge Marsh...11 J3
Henton, Oxon...22 C2
Henton, Somer...19 J7
Henwood...4 C2
Heogan...113 D4
Heol Senni...29 G7
Heol-y-Cyw...18 D4
Hepburn...75 G2
Hepple...75 F4
Hepscott...75 J6
Heptonstall...58 E8
Hepworth, W. Yks...52 D3
Hepworth, Suff...36 E2
Herbrandston...26 C6
Hereford...31 G5
Hergest...30 D4
Heriot...81 J6
Hermiston...81 G4
Hermitage, W. Susx...14 A5
Hermitage, Border...74 B5
Hermitage, Dorset...11 H5
Hermitage, Berks...21 K5
Hermitage, The...23 H7
Hermon, Gwyn...48 C4
Hermon, Dyfed...27 G3
Hermon, Dyfed...27 H3
Herne...25 H6

Herne Bay	25 H6	High Grange	66 B4	Hinton-in-the-Hedges	33 H6	Holmfirth	52 D3	Horningsham	11 K1	Huby, N. Yks	59 H6
Herner	9 F3	High Green, H. & W.	32 A5	Hinton Martell	12 C5	Holmhead	72 A2	Horningtoft	46 E4	Hucclecote	20 C1
Hernhill	25 G6	High Green, S. Yks.	53 F4	Hinton on the Green	32 C5	Holmpton	55 H1	Hornish Point	98 C8	Hucking	24 E7
Herodsfoot	4 C3	High Green, Norf.	47 G6	Hinton Parva	21 G4	Holmrook	62 F8	Hornsby	64 C2	Hucknall	43 H2
Herongate	24 C3	High Halden	17 F2	Hinton St George	11 F4	Holmsgarth	115 G4	Hornsea	61 K6	Huddersfield	52 D2
Heronsgate	22 F3	High Halstow	24 D5	Hinton St Mary	11 J4	Holne	5 H3	Hornsey	23 J4	Huddington	32 B4
Herriard	13 J1	High Ham	11 F2	Hinton Waldrist	21 H3	Holnest	11 H5	Hornton	33 F5	Hudswell	65 J7
Herringfleet	47 K7	High Hatton	41 H4	Hints, Staffs.	42 D6	Holsworthy	8 D5	Horrabridge	4 F3	Huggate	61 F5
Herringswell	36 C3	High Hesket	64 B3	Hints, Shrops.	31 H2	Holsworthy Beacon	8 D5	Horringer	36 D3	Hughenden Valley	22 D3
Herrington	66 D2	High Hoyland	52 E2	Hinwick	34 C3	Holt, Dorset	12 C5	Horse Bridge, Staffs.	42 B1	Hughley	41 G7
Hersden	25 J6	High Hunsley	61 G7	Hinxhill	17 H1	Holt, Wilts.	20 C6	Horsebridge, E. Susx	16 C4	Hugh Town	2 P2
Hersham	23 G6	High Hurstwood	15 H3	Hinxton	35 H5	Holt, Clwyd.	41 F1	Horsebridge, Hants.	13 F2	Huish, Devon	9 F4
Herstmonceux	16 D4	High Lane, H. & W.	31 H3	Hinxworth	35 F5	Holt, Norf.	46 F7	Horsebrook	42 A5	Huish, Wilts.	21 F6
Herston	112 E7	High Lane, G. Man.	51 J5	Hipperholme	52 D1	Holt, H. & W.	31 K3	Horsehay	41 H6	Huish Champflower	10 B3
Hertford	23 J1	High Laver	23 L2	Hirn	97 G5	Holtby	60 D5	Horseheath	35 K5	Huish Episcopi	11 F3
Hertford Heath	23 J1	Highleadon	31 J7	Hirnant	40 B4	Holt End	32 C3	Horsehouse	58 F2	Hulcott	22 D1
Hertingfordbury	23 J1	High Legh	51 G5	Hirst	75 J6	Holt Heath	31 K3	Horsell	22 E7	Hulland	42 E2
Hesketh Bank	50 D1	Highleigh	14 B6	Hirst Courtney	53 J1	Holton, Somer.	11 H3	Horseman's Green	41 F2	Hulland Ward	42 E2
Hesketh Lane	57 K6	Highley	31 J1	Hirwaun	18 D2	Holton, Suff.	37 K2	Horseway	35 H1	Hullavington	20 C4
Hesket Newmarket	63 J4	High Littleton	19 L7	Hiscott	9 F3	Holton, Oxon.	21 L2	Horsey	47 K4	Hullbridge	24 E3
Heskin Green	50 E2	High Melton	53 H3	Histon	35 H3	Holton cum Beckering	54 F5	Horsford	47 G5	Hulme End	52 D8
Hesleden	66 E4	Highmoor Cross	22 C4	Hitcham	36 E4	Holton le Clay	55 G3	Horsforth	59 H7	Hulme Walfield	51 H7
Heslington	60 D5	Highmoor Hill	19 J4	Hitchin	34 E7	Holton le Moor	54 E4	Horsham, W. Susx	14 E2	Hulver Street	37 K1
Hessay	60 C5	Highnam	20 B1	Hither Green	23 J5	Holton St Mary	36 F6	Horsham, H. & W.	31 J4	Humber Bridge	54 E1
Hessenford	4 D4	High Newton	57 H2	Hittisleigh	9 H6	Holwell, Herts.	34 E6	Horsham St Faith	47 H5	Humber Court	31 G4
Hessett	36 E3	High Newton-by-the-Sea	75 J2	Hixon	42 C4	Holwell, Oxon.	21 G2	Horsington, Lincs	55 F7	Humberston	55 H3
Hessle	54 E1	High Offley	41 J4	Hoaden	25 J7	Holwell, Dorset	11 J4	Horsington, Somer.	11 J3	Humbie	82 C5
Hest Bank	57 H4	High Onn	41 K5	Hoaldalbert	30 E7	Holwell, Leic.	43 K4	Horsley, Glos.	20 C3	Humbleton, Northum.	75 F2
Heston	23 G5	High Roding	24 C1	Hoar Cross	42 D4	Holwick	65 G5	Horsley, Northum.	74 E5	Humbleton, Humbs.	61 K7
Heswall	50 B5	High Salvington	14 E5	Hoarwithy	31 G7	Holworth	11 J7	Horsley, Derby	43 F2	Hume	82 C7
Hethe	33 H7	High Shaw	58 D1	Hoath	25 J6	Holybourne	13 K1	Horsley, Northum.	75 G8	Humshaugh	74 F7
Hethersett	47 G6	High Spen	65 J2	Hobarris	30 E2	Holy Cross	32 B2	Horsley Cross	37 G7	Huna	111 K1
Hethersgill	74 A8	Highsted	24 F6	Hobbister	112 D6	Holyhead	48 B2	Horsleycross Street	37 G7	Huncoat	58 C7
Hethpool	74 E2	High Street, Corn.	3 H4	Hobkirk	74 B3	Holy Island	83 K7	Horsleyhill	74 B3	Huncote	43 H7
Hett	66 C4	High Street, Suff.	37 K4	Hobson	66 B2	Holymoorside	53 F7	Horsley Woodhouse	43 F2	Hundalee	74 C3
Hetton	58 E5	High Street Green	36 F4	Hoby	43 J5	Holyport	22 D5	Horsmonden	16 E1	Hunderthwaite	65 G5
Hetton-le-Hole	66 D3	Hightae	73 F7	Hockering	46 F5	Holystone	75 F4	Horspath	21 K2	Hundleby	55 H7
Heugh	75 G7	Hightown, Mers.	50 C3	Hockerton	43 K1	Holytown	80 C5	Horstead	47 H5	Hundleton	26 D6
Heugh-head	96 C4	Hightown, Ches.	51 H7	Hockley	24 E3	Holywell, Clwyd.	50 A6	Horsted Keynes	15 G3	Hundon	36 C5
Heveningham	37 J2	High Toynton	55 G7	Hockley Heath	32 D2	Holywell, Corn.	2 F4	Horton, Staffs.	42 B1	Hundred Acres	13 H4
Hever	15 H1	High Trewhill	75 G4	Hockliffe	34 C7	Holywell, Cambs.	35 G2	Horton, Northnts.	34 B4	Hundred End	50 D1
Heversham	57 H2	Highway, Wilts.	20 E5	Hockwold cum Wilton	36 C1	Holywell, Dorset	11 G5	Horton, Avon	20 B4	Hundred House	30 C4
Hevingham	47 G4	Highway, Corn.	3 K4	Hockworthy	10 B4	Holywell Green	52 C2	Horton, Dorset	12 C5	Hundred, The	31 G3
Hewelsfield	19 K2	High Wray	63 J8	Hoddesdon	23 J2	Holywell Lake	10 C3	Horton, Lancs	58 D5	Hungarton	43 J6
Hewish, Somer.	11 F5	High Wych	23 K1	Hoddlesden	51 G1	Holywell Row	36 C2	Horton, Bucks.	22 E1	Hungerford	21 H6
Hewish, Avon	19 J6	High Wycombe	22 D3	Hodgeston	26 E7	Holywood	72 E6	Horton, Som.	10 E4	Hungerford Newtown	21 H5
Hexham	65 G1	Hilborough	46 D6	Hodnet	41 H4	Homer	41 H6	Horton, Wilts.	20 E6	Hunmanby	61 H3
Hextable	23 L5	Hildenborough	16 C1	Hodthorpe	53 H6	Homersfield	37 H1	Horton, Berks.	22 F5	Hunningham	33 F3
Hexton	34 E6	Hildersham	35 J5	Hoe	46 E5	Hom Green	31 G7	Horton, Northum.	75 G1	Hunsdon	23 K1
Hexworthy	5 G2	Hilderstone	42 B3	Hoe Gate	13 J4	Homington	12 D3	Horton, W. Glam.	27 J8	Hunsingore	59 K5
Heybridge, Essex	24 C3	Hilderthorpe	61 J4	Hoff	64 D6	Honeybourne	32 D5	Horton-cum-Studley	21 K1	Hunsonby	64 C3
Heybridge, Essex	24 E2	Hilgay	45 K7	Hoggeston	34 B7	Honeychurch	9 G5	Horton Green	41 F2	Hunspow	111 J1
Heybridge Basin	24 E2	Hill	19 L3	Hognaston	42 E1	Honey Hill	25 H6	Horton Heath	13 G4	Hunstanton	46 B2
Heybrook Bay	4 E5	Hillam	60 C8	Hogsthorpe	55 K6	Honiley	32 E2	Horton in Ribblesdale	58 D3	Hunstanworth	65 G3
Heydon, Norf.	47 G4	Hillberry	56 D4	Holbeach	45 G4	Honing	47 J4	Horton Kirby	24 B6	Hunston, W. Susx	14 B5
Heydon, Cambs.	35 H5	Hillbrae, Grampn.	104 F4	Holbeach Bank	45 G4	Honingham	47 G5	Horwich	51 F2	Hunston, Suff.	36 E3
Heydour	44 D3	Hillbrae, Grampn.	97 G3	Holbeach Drove	45 G5	Honington, Lincs.	44 C2	Horwood	8 F3	Hunstrete	19 L6
Heylipol	84 A4	Hill Brow	14 A3	Holbeach Hurn	45 G4	Honington, Suff.	36 E2	Hose	43 K4	Hunt End	32 C3
Heylor	116 D4	Hilldyke	45 G2	Holbeach St Johns	45 G5	Honington, Warw.	32 E5	Hosh	88 A6	Hunter's Quay	78 D4
Heysham	57 H4	Hill End, Fife.	81 F2	Holbeach St Marks	45 G3	Honiton	10 C5	Hostingfield	35 H4	Huntingdon	35 F2
Heyshott	14 B4	Hill End, Fife.	81 G3	Holbeach St Matthew	45 H3	Honley	52 D2	Hoswick	115 G6	Huntingfield	37 J2
Heytesbury	12 B1	Hill End, Durham.	65 H4	Holbeck	53 H6	Hoo	37 H4	Hotham	61 F7	Huntington, Staffs.	42 B5
Heythrop	33 F7	Hillerton	9 H6	Holberrow Green	32 C4	Hooe, E. Susx	16 D5	Hothfield	17 G1	Huntington, Lothn.	82 C4
Heywood, Wilts.	20 C7	Hillesden	33 J7	Holborn	23 J4	Hooe, Devon	4 F4	Hoton	43 H4	Huntington, H. & W.	30 D4
Heywood, G. Man.	51 H2	Hillesley	20 B4	Holbrook, Derby	43 F2	Hook, Humbs.	54 B1	Hough	41 J1	Huntington, N. Yks.	60 D5
Hibaldstow	54 D1	Hillfarrance	10 C3	Holbrook, Suff.	37 G6	Hook, Hants.	22 C7	Hougham	44 B2	Huntingtower	88 C2
Hickleton	53 G3	Hill Head, Hants.	13 H5	Holburn	83 J8	Hook, Dyfed.	26 D5	Hougharry	98 C5	Huntley	20 B1
Hickling, Notts.	43 J4	Hillhead, Strath.	71 K3	Holbury	13 G5	Hook, Wilts.	20 E4	Hough Green	50 D5	Huntly	96 F1
Hickling, Norf.	47 K4	Hillhead, Devon	5 K4	Holcombe, Somer.	11 H1	Hook, G. Lon.	23 G6	Hough-on-the-Hill	44 C2	Hunton, Kent	16 E1
Hickling Green	47 K4	Hillhead of Auchentumb	105 J3	Holcombe, Devon	5 K2	Hooke	11 G5	Houghton, W. Susx	14 D4	Hunton, N. Yks.	59 G1
Hickling Heath	47 K4	Hillhead of Cocklaw	105 K4	Holcombe Rogus	10 B4	Hookgate	41 J3	Houghton, Dyfed.	26 D6	Hunt's Cross	50 D5
Hidcote Boyce	32 D5	Hilliard's Cross	42 D5	Holcot	34 A3	Hook Norton	33 F6	Houghton, Cambs.	35 F2	Huntsham	10 B3
High Ackworth	53 G2	Hilliclay	111 H2	Holden	58 C6	Hookway	9 J6	Houghton, Hants.	13 F2	Huntspill	10 E1
Higham, Kent	24 D5	Hillingdon	22 F4	Holdenby	33 J3	Hookwood	15 F1	Houghton, Cumbr.	63 K2	Huntworth	10 E2
Higham, Lancs	58 D7	Hillington	46 C4	Holdgate	41 G8	Hoole	50 D7	Houghton Conquest	34 D5	Hunwick	66 B4
Higham, Suff.	36 F6	Hillmorton	33 H2	Holdingham	44 D2	Hoo St Werburgh	24 D5	Houghton-le-Spring	66 D3	Hunworth	46 F3
Higham, Derby	53 F8	Hill Mountain	26 D6	Hole in the Wall	31 H7	Hooton Levitt	53 H4	Houghton on the Hill	43 J6	Hurdsfield	51 J6
Higham Dykes	75 H7	Hillockhead	96 C5	Holemoor	8 E5	Hooton Pagnell	53 G3	Houghton Regis	34 D7	Hurley, Berks.	22 D4
Higham Ferrers	34 C3	Hill of Beath	81 G2	Holford	10 C1	Hooton Roberts	53 G4	Houghton St Giles	46 E3	Hurley, Warw.	42 E7
Higham Gobion	34 E6	Hill of Fearn	103 G5	Holker	57 G3	Hope, Clwyd.	50 C7	Houlskye	67 H7	Hurliness	79 G8
Higham on the Hill	43 F7	Hill Ridware	42 C5	Holkham	46 D2	Hope, Derby	52 D5	Hound Green	22 C7	Hurn	12 D6
Highampton	8 E5	Hillside, Shetld.	115 G2	Hollacombe, Devon	8 D5	Hope, Powys	40 D6	Houndslow	82 E7	Hursley	13 G3
Higham Wood	16 D1	Hillside, Grampn.	97 J6	Hollacombe, Devon	9 G4	Hope, Shrops.	40 E6	Houndwood	83 G5	Hurst, Berks.	22 C5
High Beach	23 K3	Hillside, Tays.	89 K2	Holland-on-Sea	25 J1	Hope Bagot	31 G2	Hounsetter	116 E4	Hurst, N. Yks.	65 H7
High Bentham	58 B4	Hillswick	116 D5	Hollandstoun	113 H1	Hope Bowdler	41 F7	Houston	79 G5	Hurst, G. Man.	51 J3
High Bickington	9 G3	Hill, The	56 F2	Hollesley	37 J5	Hopeman	103 K6	Houstry	111 H5	Hurstbourne Priors	13 G1
High Birkwith	58 D3	Hilmarton	20 E5	Hollinfare	51 F4	Hope Mansell	19 L1	Hove	15 F5	Hurstbourne Tarrant	21 H7
High Blantyre	80 B6	Hilperton	20 C7	Hollingbourne	24 E7	Hope under Dinmore	31 G4	Hoveringham	43 J2	Hurst Green, Lancs	58 B7
High Bonnybridge	80 D4	Hilsea	13 J5	Hollington, Staffs.	42 C3	Hopton, Staffs.	42 B4	Hoveton	47 J5	Hurst Green, E. Susx	16 E3
High Borve	107 J3	Hilton, Durham.	66 B5	Hollington, Derby	42 E3	Hopton, Suff.	36 E2	Hovingham	60 D3	Hurst Green, Surrey	23 J7
High Bradfield	52 E4	Hilton, Derby	42 E3	Hollington, E. Susx.	16 E4	Hopton Cangeford	31 G1	How	64 C2	Hurstpierpoint	15 F4
Highbridge, Somer.	10 E1	Hilton, Cumbr.	64 E5	Hollingworth	52 C4	Hopton Castle	30 E2	How Caple	31 H7	Hurworth-on-Tees	66 C6
Highbridge, Highld.	93 H7	Hilton, Cleve.	66 E6	Hollins	51 H3	Hopton on Sea	47 L6	Howden	60 E8	Hury	65 G6
Highbrook	15 G2	Hilton, Cambs.	35 F3	Hollinsclough	52 C7	Hopton Wafers	31 H2	Howden-le-Wear	65 J4	Husbands Bosworth	33 J1
Highburton	52 D2	Hilton, Grampn.	97 J2	Hollinwood	41 G3	Hopwas	42 D6	Howe, Norf	47 H7	Husborne Crawley	34 C6
Highbury	11 H1	Hilton, Dorset.	11 J5	Holloway	43 F1	Hopwood	32 C2	Howe, Highld	111 K2	Hushinish	106 D7
High Buston	75 J4	Hilton, Shrops.	41 J7	Holloway	33 J2	Horam	16 C4	Howe Green	24 D2	Husthwaite	60 C3
High Callerton	75 H7	Hilton of Cadboll	103 G5	Holl's Green	35 F7	Horbling	44 E3	Howell	44 E2	Hustwaite	5 H4
High Catton	60 E5	Himbleton	32 B4	Hollybush, Gwent	18 F2	Horbury	52 E2	Howe of Teuchar	105 G4	Hutcherleigh	5 H4
Highclere	21 J6	Himley	42 A7	Hollybush, Strath.	71 J3	Horden	66 E3	Howe Street, Essex	36 B6	Huthwaite	53 G8
Highcliffe	12 E6	Hincaster	57 J2	Hollybush, H. & W.	31 J6	Horderley	31 F1	Howe Street, Essex	24 C1	Huttoft	55 K6
High Cogges	21 H2	Hinckley	43 G7	Holly End	45 H6	Hordle	12 E6	Howe, The, Cumbr.	57 H2	Hutton, Cumbr.	64 B5
High Coniscliffe	66 C6	Hinderclay	36 F2	Hollym	55 H1	Hordley	40 E3	Howe, The, I. of M.	56 N5	Hutton, Essex	24 C3
High Cross, Herts.	23 J1	Hinderwell	67 H6	Hollywood	32 C2	Horeb, Dyfed.	27 H2	Howey	29 H4	Hutton, Lancs.	50 D1
High Cross, Hants.	13 K3	Hindford	40 E3	Holm	107 J5	Horeb, Dyfed.	27 K4	Howgate, Border.	74 D2	Hutton, Border.	83 H6
High Dougarie	77 H8	Hindhead	14 B2	Holmbury St Mary	14 E1	Horeth	37 H2	Howgate, Lothn.	81 H6	Hutton, Avon	19 H7
High Easter	24 C1	Hindley	51 F3	Holme, Notts.	54 C8	Horkstow	54 D2	Howick	75 J3	Hutton Bonville	66 C6
High Ellington	59 G2	Hindley Green	51 F3	Holme, W. Yks.	52 D3	Horley, Surrey	15 F1	Howle	41 H4	Hutton Buscel	61 G2
Higher Ashton	9 J7	Hindlip	32 A4	Holme, Cambs.	35 F1	Horley, Oxon.	33 G5	Howlett End	35 J6	Hutton Conyers	59 J3
Higher Ballam	57 G7	Hindolveston	46 F4	Holme, Cumbr.	57 J3	Hornblotton Green	11 G2	Howmore	98 C2	Hutton Cranswick	61 H5
High Ercall	41 G5	Hindon	12 B2	Holme Chapel	58 D8	Hornby, N. Yks.	66 D7	Hownam	74 D3	Hutton End	64 B4
Higher End	50 E3	Hindringham	46 E3	Holme Hale	46 D6	Hornby, Lancs.	57 J4	Howsham, Humbs.	54 E3	Hutton Henry	66 E4
Higher Penwortham	57 J8	Hingham	46 F6	Holme Lacy	31 G6	Horncastle	55 G7	Howsham, N. Yks.	60 E4	Hutton-le-Hole	60 E1
Higher Poynton	51 J3	Hinkley Point Power Station	10 D1	Holme Marsh	30 E4	Hornchurch	23 L4	Howton	31 F7	Hutton Magna	65 J6
Higher Tale	10 B5	Hinstock	41 H4	Holme next the Sea	46 C2	Horncliffe	83 H7	Howtown	64 B6	Hutton Roof, Cumbr.	57 J3
Higher Town	2 P2	Hintlesham	37 F5	Holme-on-Spalding Moor	60 F7	Horndean	13 K4	Howwood	79 G5	Hutton Roof, Cumbr.	63 J4
Higher Walreddon	4 E2	Hinton, Avon	20 B5	Holme on the Wolds	61 G6	Horndon on the Hill	24 C4	Hoxa	112 E7	Hutton Rudby	66 E7
Higher Walton, Lancs.	50 E1	Hinton, Hants.	12 E6	Holmer	31 G5	Horne	15 G1	Hoxne	37 G2	Huttons Ambo	60 E4
Higher Walton, Ches.	50 E5	Hinton, Shrops.	41 F6	Holmer Green	22 E3	Horn Hill	22 F3	Hoylake	50 B5	Hutton Sessay	60 B3
Higher Wych	41 F2	Hinton Ampner	13 H3	Holmes Chapel	51 G7	Horning	47 J5	Hoyland	53 F3	Hutton Wandesley	60 C5
Highfield, Strath.	78 F6	Hinton Blewett	19 K7	Holmesfield	53 F6	Horninghold	44 B7	Hoyland Swaine	52 E3	Huxley	50 D7
Highfield, T. & W.	65 J2	Hinton Charterhouse	20 B7	Holmeswood	50 D2	Horninglow	42 E4	Hubberholme	58 E3	Huyton-with-Roby	50 D4
Highfields	35 G4			Holmewood	53 G7	Horningsea	35 H3	Hubbert's Bridge	45 F2	Hycemoor	56 F2
High Garrett	36 C7									Hyde, Glos.	20 C2
										Hyde, Hants.	12 D4

Hyde, G. Man....51 J4
Hyde Heath....22 E2
Hydestile....14 C1
Hynish....84 A5
Hyssington....40 E7
Hythe, Hants....13 G5
Hythe, Kent....17 J2
Hythe End....22 F5
Hythie....105 K3

I

Ibberton....11 J5
Ible....42 E1
Ibsley....12 D5
Ibstock....43 G5
Ibstone....22 C3
Ibthorpe....21 H7
Ibworth....21 K7
Ickburgh....46 D7
Ickenham....22 F4
Ickford....22 B2
Ickham....25 J7
Ickleford....34 E6
Icklesham....16 F4
Ickleton....35 H5
Icklingham....36 C2
Ickwell Green....34 E5
Icomb....32 E7
Idbury....32 E7
Iddesleigh....9 F5
Ide....9 J6
Ideford....5 J2
Ide Hill....23 K7
Iden....17 G3
Iden Green....16 F2
Idlicote....32 E5
Idmiston....12 E2
Idridgehay....42 E2
Idrigill....99 J6
Idstone....21 G4
Ifield....15 F2
Ifold....14 D2
Iford....15 H5
Ifton Heath....40 E3
Ightfield....41 G3
Ightham....24 B7
Iken....37 K4
Ilam....42 D1
Ilchester....11 G3
Ilderton....75 G2
Ilford....23 K4
Ilfracombe....8 F1
Ilkeston....43 G2
Ilketshall St Andrew....37 J1
Ilketshall St Lawrence....37 J1
Ilketshall St Margaret....37 J1
Ilkley....59 G6
Illey....32 B1
Illingworth....59 F8
Illogan....2 E5
Illston on the Hill....43 K7
Ilmer....22 C2
Ilmington....32 E5
Ilminster....10 E4
Ilsington....5 H2
Ilston....27 K7
Ilton, Somer....10 E4
Ilton, N. Yks....59 G3
Immingham....55 F2
Impington....35 H3
Ince....50 D6
Ince Blundell....50 C3
Ince-in-Makerfield....50 C4
Inchbare....89 J2
Inchberry....104 C3
Incheril....101 G6
Inchina....101 F3
Inchinnan....79 G5
Inchlaggan....93 H5
Inchmore....94 B1
Inchnadamph....108 D6
Inchture....88 E6
Indian Queens....3 H4
Ingatestone....24 C3
Ingbirchworth....52 E3
Ingestre....42 B4
Ingham, Suff....36 D2
Ingham, Lincs....54 D5
Ingham, Norf....47 J4
Ingleby Arncliffe....66 E7
Ingleby Greenhow....67 F7
Inglesbatch....20 B6
Inglesham....21 G3
Inglewhite....57 J6
Ingliston....81 G4
Ingoe....75 G7
Ingoldisthorpe....46 B3
Ingoldmells....55 K7
Ingoldsby....44 D3
Ingram....75 G3
Ingrave....24 C3
Ings....64 B8
Ingst....19 K4
Ingworth....47 G4
Inkberrow....32 C4
Inkhorn....97 J2
Inkpen....21 H6
Inkstack....111 J1
Innellan....78 D4
Innerleithen....81 J8
Innerleven....81 J1
Innermessan....68 B4
Innerwick, Lothn....82 F4
Innerwick, Tays....87 H4
Innsworth....32 A7
Insch....97 F3
Insh....95 G5
Inskip....57 H7
Instow....8 E2

Inver, Grampn....96 B6
Inver, Highld....103 G4
Inverailort....92 D7
Inveralligin....100 E7
Inverallochy....105 K2
Inveramsay....97 G3
Inveran....102 D3
Inveraray....86 C8
Inverarish....92 B2
Inverarity....89 G4
Inverarnan....86 F7
Inverasdale....100 E4
Inverbervie....89 L1
Inverbrough....95 G2
Invercharon....101 J7
Invercreran....86 C4
Inverdruie....95 H4
Inverebrie....97 J2
Inveresk....81 J4
Inverey....95 J7
Inverfarigaig....94 D3
Invergarry....93 K5
Invergordon....102 F6
Invergowrie....89 F5
Inverguseran....92 D5
Inverharroch....96 C2
Inverie....92 D6
Inverinate....93 F3
Inverkeilor....89 J4
Inverkeithing....81 G3
Inverkeithny....104 F4
Inverkip....78 E4
Inverkirkaig....108 B7
Invermoidart....92 C8
Invermoriston....94 C4
Invernaver....110 D2
Inverness....102 E8
Inverquhomery....105 K4
Inverroy....93 J7
Invershin....102 D3
Inverugie....105 L4
Inveruglas....86 F8
Inverurie....97 G3
Invervar....87 J4
Inwardleigh....9 F6
Inworth....24 E1
Iping....14 B3
Ipplepen....5 J3
Ipsden....22 B4
Ipstones....42 C1
Ipswich....37 G5
Irby....50 B5
Irby in the Marsh....55 J7
Irby upon Humber....55 F3
Irchester....34 C3
Ireby, Lancs....58 B3
Ireby, Cumbr....63 H4
Ireland, Orkney....112 D6
Ireland, Shetld....115 F6
Ireleth....57 F3
Ireshopeburn....65 F4
Irlam....51 G4
Irnham....44 D4
Iron Acton....20 A4
Iron Cross....32 C4
Ironbridge....41 H6
Ironmacannie....72 B7
Ironside....105 H3
Ironville....43 G1
Irstead....47 J4
Irthington....64 B1
Irthlingborough....34 C2
Irton....61 H2
Irvine....78 F8
Isauld....110 F2
Isbister, Orkney....112 C4
Isbister, Orkney....112 D5
Isbister, Shetld....115 H2
Isfield....15 H4
Isham....34 B2
Isle Abbotts....10 E3
Isle Brewers....10 E3
Isleham....36 B2
Isle of Whithorn....69 F7
Isleornsay or Eilean Iarmain....92 C4
Islesburgh....115 F2
Isleworth....23 G5
Isley Watton....43 G4
Islington....23 J4
Islip, Northnts....34 C2
Islip, Oxon....21 K1
Islivig....106 D6
Istead Rise....24 C6
Isycoed....40 F1
Itchen Abbas....13 H2
Itchen Stoke....13 H2
Itchingfield....14 E3
Itchington....20 A4
Itteringham....47 G3
Itton....9 G6
Itton Common....19 J3
Ivegill....63 K3
Ivelet....65 G8
Iver....22 F4
Iver Heath....22 F4
Iveston....65 J2
Ivinghoe....22 E1
Ivinghoe Aston....22 E1
Ivington....31 F4
Ivington Green....31 F4
Ivybridge....5 G4
Ivychurch....17 H3
Ivy Hatch....24 B7
Iwade....24 E6
Iwerne Courtney or Shroton....11 K4
Iwerne Minster....12 A4
Ixworth....36 E2
Ixworth Thorpe....36 E2

J

Jack Hill....59 H5

Jackstown....97 G2
Jackton....79 H6
Jacobstow....8 B6
Jacobstowe....9 F5
Jameston....26 E7
Jamestown, Highld....102 C7
Jamestown, Strath....79 F3
Jamestown, D. & G....73 H5
Jarrow....66 D1
Jawcraig....80 D4
Jayes Park....14 E1
Jaywick....25 H1
Jedburgh....74 C2
Jeffreyston....26 E6
Jemimaville....102 F6
Jevington....16 C5
Johnby....64 B4
John o' Groats....111 K1
Johnshaven....89 K2
Johnston....26 D5
Johnstone....79 G5
Johnstonebridge....73 G5
Jordans....22 E3
Jordanston....26 D3
Jump....53 F3
Juniper Green....81 G5
Jurby East....56 C2
Jurby West....56 Q2

K

Kaber....64 E6
Kaimes....81 H5
Kalnakill....100 C7
Kames, Strath....72 B2
Kames, Strath....78 B4
Kea....3 G5
Keadby....54 C2
Keal Cotes....55 H7
Kearsley....51 G3
Kearstwick....57 K2
Kearton....65 G8
Keasden....58 C4
Keddington....55 H5
Kedington....36 C5
Kedleston....43 F2
Keelby....55 F3
Keele....41 K2
Keeley Green....34 D5
Keeston....26 D5
Keevil....20 D7
Kegworth....43 G4
Kehelland....2 E5
Keig....96 F4
Keighley....59 F6
Keilarsbrae....80 D2
Keilhill....105 G3
Keillmore....77 F3
Keills....76 D5
Keils....76 E5
Keinton Mandeville....11 G2
Keir Mill....72 D5
Keisby....44 D4
Keiss....111 K2
Keith....104 D3
Keithock....89 J2
Kelbrook....58 E6
Kelby....44 D2
Keld, Cumbr....64 C6
Keld, N. Yks....65 F7
Keldholme....60 E2
Kelfield....60 C7
Kelham....44 A1
Kellan....85 G4
Kellas, Tays....89 G5
Kellas, Grampn....103 K7
Kellaton....5 J6
Kelleth....64 D7
Kelleythorpe....61 H5
Kelling....47 F2
Kellington....53 H1
Kelloe....66 D4
Kelly....4 D1
Kelly Bray....4 D2
Kelmarsh....33 K2
Kelmscott....21 G3
Kelsale....37 J3
Kelsall....50 F7
Kelshall....35 G6
Kelso....74 D1
Kelston....20 B6
Keltneyburn....87 K4
Kelton....65 G5
Kelton Hill or Rhonehouse....69 J5
Kelty....81 G2
Kelvedon....24 E1
Kelvedon Hatch....24 B3
Kelynack....2 B7
Kemacott....9 G1
Kemback....89 G7
Kemberton....41 J6
Kemble....66 J2
Kemerton....32 B6
Kemeys Commander....19 H2
Kemnay....97 G4
Kempley....31 H7
Kempsey....32 A5
Kempsford....21 F3
Kempston....34 D5
Kempston Hardwick....34 D5
Kempton....30 E1
Kemp Town....15 G5
Kemsing....23 L7
Kenardington....17 G2
Kenchester....31 F5
Kencott....21 G2
Kendal....57 J1
Kenfig....18 C4
Kenfig Hill....18 C4
Kenilworth....32 E2
Kenley, Shrops....41 G6

Kenley, G. Lon....23 J7
Kenmore, Highld....100 D7
Kenmore, Tays....87 K4
Kenn, Avon....19 J6
Kenn, Devon....9 K7
Kennacraig....77 H5
Kennerleigh....9 J5
Kennet....80 E2
Kennethmont....96 E3
Kennett....36 C3
Kennford....9 K7
Kenninghall....36 F1
Kennington, Kent....17 H1
Kennington, Oxon....21 K2
Kennoway....81 J1
Kenny Hill....36 B2
Kennythorpe....60 E4
Kenovdy....84 A4
Kensaleyre....99 K7
Kensington....23 H5
Kensworth....22 F1
Kentchurch....31 F7
Kentford....36 C3
Kentisbeare....10 B5
Kentisbury....9 G1
Kentmere....64 B7
Kenton, Suff....37 G3
Kenton, G. Lon....23 G4
Kenton, Devon....9 K7
Kentra....85 H2
Kents Bank....57 G3
Kent's Green....31 J7
Kent's Oak....13 F3
Kenwick....41 F3
Kenwyn....3 G5
Kenyon....51 F4
Keoldale....108 E2
Keose....107 H6
Keppoch....93 E3
Kepwick....60 B1
Keresley....33 F1
Kerne Bridge....19 K1
Kerridge....51 J6
Kerris....2 C7
Kerry....40 C7
Kerrycroy....78 D5
Kerrysdale....100 E5
Kerry's Gate....30 E6
Kersall....54 B7
Kersey....36 F5
Kershader....107 H6
Kershopefoot....74 A6
Kersoe....32 B5
Kerswell....10 B5
Kerswell Green....32 A5
Kesgrave....37 H5
Kessingland....37 L1
Kestle Mill....3 G4
Keston....23 K6
Keswick, Cumbr....63 H5
Keswick, Norf....47 H6
Keswick, Norf....47 J3
Kettering....34 B2
Ketteringham....47 G6
Kettins....88 E5
Kettlebaston....36 E4
Kettlebrook....42 E6
Kettleburgh....37 H3
Kettleness....67 G6
Kettleshulme....51 J6
Kettling Bottom....59 H5
Kettlestone....46 E3
Kettlethorpe....54 C6
Kettletoft....113 G3
Kettlewell....58 E3
Ketton....44 C6
Kew....23 G5
Kewstoke....19 H6
Kexbrough....53 F3
Kexby, Lincs....54 C5
Kexby, N. Yks....60 E5
Key Green....51 H7
Keyham....43 J6
Keyhaven....13 F6
Keyingham....55 G1
Keymer....15 G4
Keynsham....20 A6
Keysoe....34 D3
Keysoe Row....34 D3
Keyston....34 D2
Keyworth....43 J3
Kibblesworth....66 C2
Kibworth Beauchamp....43 J7
Kibworth Harcourt....43 J7
Kidbrooke....23 K5
Kiddemore Green....42 A6
Kidderminster....31 K2
Kiddington....33 G7
Kidlington....21 J1
Kidmore End....22 B5
Kidsgrove....41 K1
Kidstones....58 E2
Kidwelly....27 J6
Kielder....74 C5
Kiells....76 D5
Kilbarchan....79 Q5
Kilbeg....92 C5
Kilberry....77 G5
Kilbirnie....78 F6
Kilbride, Highld....92 B3
Kilbride, W. Isles....90 C4
Kilbride, Strath....85 K6
Kilburn, N. Yks....60 C3
Kilburn, Derby....43 F2
Kilby....43 J7
Kilchattan....76 C2
Kilchattan Bay....78 D6
Kilchenzie....76 B2
Kilchiaran....76 B5
Kilchoan....85 F2
Kilchoman....76 B5
Kilchrenan....86 C6
Kilconquhar....82 C1
Kilcot....31 H7
Kilcoy....102 D7

Kilcreggan....78 E3
Kildale....67 G7
Kildalloig....70 C3
Kildary....103 F5
Kildonan....70 F2
Kildonan....92 A7
Kildrummy....96 D4
Kidwick....58 F6
Kilfinan....77 J4
Kilfinnan....93 J6
Kilgetty....26 F6
Kilgwrrwg Common....19 J3
Kilham, Northum....74 E1
Kilham, Humbs....61 H4
Kilkenneth....84 A4
Kilkhampton....8 C4
Killamarsh....53 G5
Killay....27 L7
Killean....77 F7
Killearn....88 F8
Killen....102 E7
Killerby....66 B6
Killichonate....93 J7
Killiechonan....87 H3
Killiechronan....85 G4
Killiecrankie....88 B2
Killilan....93 F2
Killimster....111 K3
Killin....87 H5
Killinghall....59 H5
Killingholme....55 F2
Killington....57 K2
Killinochyett....82 C7
Killundine....85 G4
Kilmacolm....79 F5
Kilmahumaig....77 G2
Kilmaluag....99 K5
Kilmany....89 F6
Kilmarie....92 B4
Kilmarnock....79 G8
Kilmartin....77 H2
Kilmaurs....79 G7
Kilmelford....85 K7
Kilmeny....76 C5
Kilmersdon....20 A7
Kilmeston....13 H3
Kilmichael Glassary....77 H2
Kilmichael of Inverlussa....77 G3
Kilmington, Devon....10 D6
Kilmington, Wilts....11 J2
Kilmonivaig....93 H7
Kilmorack....102 C8
Kilmore....92 C5
Kilmory, Strath....70 E2
Kilmory, Highld....85 G1
Kilmory, Strath....77 G4
Kilmuir, Highld....102 E8
Kilmuir, Highld....103 F5
Kilmuir, Highld....99 H8
Kilmuir, Highld....99 J5
Kilnave....76 B4
Kilncadzow....80 D7
Kilndown....16 C2
Kilnhurst....53 G4
Kilninian....84 F4
Kilninver....85 K6
Kiln Pit Hill....65 H2
Kilnsea....55 J2
Kilnsey....58 E4
Kilnwick....61 G6
Kiloran....76 C2
Kilpatrick....70 C2
Kilpeck....31 F6
Kilpheder....90 C4
Kilphedir....111 F7
Kilpin....54 B1
Kilrenny....89 H8
Kilsby....33 H2
Kilspindie....88 E6
Kilsyth....80 C4
Kiltarlity....94 D1
Kilton....10 C1
Kilvaxter....99 J6
Kilve....10 C1
Kilvington....44 B2
Kilwinning....78 F7
Kimberley, Norf....46 F6
Kimberley, Notts....43 H2
Kimble....22 D2
Kimblesworth....66 C3
Kimble Wick....22 D2
Kimbolton, Cambs....34 D3
Kimbolton, H. & W....31 G3
Kimcote....33 H1
Kimmeridge....6 D7
Kimmerston....83 H8
Kimpton, Wilts....12 E1
Kimpton, Herts....23 G1
Kinbrace....110 E5
Kinbuck....87 K8
Kincaple....89 G7
Kincardine, Fife....80 E3
Kincardine, Highld....102 E4
Kincardine O'Neil....96 E6
Kincorth....97 J5
Kincraig....95 G5
Kineton, Glos....32 C7
Kineton, Warw....33 F4
Kinfauns....88 D6
Kingarth....78 C6
Kingcoed....19 J2
Kingerby....54 E2
Kingham....32 E7
Kingholm Quay....72 E7
Kinghorn....81 H3
Kinglassie....81 H2
Kingoodie....89 F6
King's Acre....31 F5
Kingsand....4 E4
Kingsbarns....89 H7
Kingsbridge, Somer....10 A2
Kingsbridge, Devon....5 H5
King's Bromley....42 D5
Kingsburgh....99 J7

Kingsbury, Warw....42 E7
Kingsbury, G. Lon....23 G4
Kingsbury Episcopi....11 F3
King's Caple....31 G7
Kingsclere....21 K7
King's Cliffe....44 D7
Kingscote....20 C3
Kingscott....9 F4
King's Coughton....32 C4
Kingscross....70 F2
Kingsdon....11 G3
Kingsdown....17 L1
Kingseat....81 G2
Kingsey....22 C2
Kingsfold....14 E2
Kingsford....31 K1
Kingshall Street....36 E3
King's Heath....32 C1
Kingskerswell....5 J3
Kingskettle....88 F8
Kingsland....31 F3
Kings Langley....22 F2
Kingsley, Hants....14 A2
Kingsley, Staffs....42 C2
Kingsley, Ches....50 E6
Kingsley Green....14 B2
King's Lynn....45 K5
King's Meaburn....64 D5
Kingsmuir, Tays....89 G4
Kings Muir, Border....81 H8
Kingsnorth, Kent....24 E5
Kingsnorth, Kent....17 H2
King's Norton, W. Mids....32 C2
King's Norton, Leic....43 J6
King's Nympton....9 G4
King's Pyon....31 F4
Kings Ripton....35 F2
King's Somborne....13 F2
King's Stag....11 J4
King's Stanley....20 C2
Kings Sutton....33 G6
Kingstanding....42 C7
Kingsteignton....5 J2
Kingston, Grampn....104 C2
Kingston, Lothn....82 D3
Kingston, Hants....12 D5
Kingston, Dorset....6 D7
Kingston, Cambs....35 G4
Kingston, Devon....5 G5
Kingston, Kent....25 H7
Kingston, Dorset....11 J5
Kingston, I. of W....7 J6
Kingston Bagpuize....21 J3
Kingston Blount....22 C3
Kingston by Sea....15 F5
Kingston Deverill....11 K2
Kingstone, Staffs....42 C4
Kingstone, Somer....10 E4
Kingstone, H. & W....31 F6
Kingston Lisle....21 H4
Kingston near Lewes....15 G5
Kingston on Soar....43 H4
Kingston Seymour....19 J6
Kingston St Mary....10 D3
Kingston upon Hull....61 H8
Kingston upon Thames....23 G6
Kingstown....63 J2
King's Walden....34 E7
Kingswear....5 J4
Kingswells....97 H5
Kingswinford....32 A1
Kingswood, Avon....20 A5
Kingswood, Bucks....22 B1
Kingswood, Glos....20 B3
Kingswood, Warw....32 D2
Kingswood, H. & W....30 D4
Kingswood, Powys....40 D6
Kingswood, Kent....24 E7
Kingswood, Surrey....23 H7
King's Worthy....13 G2
Kington, H. & W....30 D4
Kington, Powys....30 E4
Kington Langley....20 D5
Kington Magna....11 J3
Kington St Michael....20 D5
Kingussie....94 F5
Kingweston....11 G2
Kinharrachie....97 J2
Kinknockie....97 K1
Kinlet....31 J1
Kinloch, Highld....92 C4
Kinloch, Tays....88 D4
Kinloch, Highld....108 D3
Kinloch, Highld....91 K6
Kinlochard....79 G1
Kinlochbervie....108 D3
Kinlocheil....93 F8
Kinlochewe....101 G6
Kinloch Hourn....93 F5
Kinloch Laggan....94 D7
Kinlochleven....86 D2
Kinlochmore....86 D2
Kinloch Rannoch....87 J3
Kinlochspelve....85 H6
Kinloss....103 J6
Kinmel Bay....49 J2
Kinmuck....97 H4
Kinmundy....97 H4
Kinnadie....105 J4
Kinnaird....88 E6
Kinnell....89 J3
Kinnerley....40 E4
Kinnersley, H. & W....32 A5
Kinnersley, H. & W....30 E5
Kinnerton, Clwyd....50 C7
Kinnerton, Powys....30 D3
Kinnesswood....81 G1
Kinninvie....65 H5
Kinoulton....43 J3
Kinross....81 G1
Kinrossie....88 D5
Kinsham....30 E3

Kinsley....53 G2
Kintarvie....107 G7
Kintbury....21 H6
Kintessack....103 J6
Kintillo....88 D7
Kintocher....96 E5
Kintore....97 G4
Kintour....76 D6
Kinuachdrachd....77 G2
Kinveachy....95 H4
Kinver....31 K1
Kippax....59 K7
Kippen....79 J2
Kippford or Scaur....69 K5
Kirbister....112 D6
Kirbuster....112 C4
Kirby Bedon....47 H6
Kirby Bellars....43 K5
Kirby Cane....47 J7
Kirby Cross....37 H7
Kirby Grindalythe....61 G4
Kirby Hill, N. Yks....59 J4
Kirby Hill, N. Yks....65 J7
Kirby Knowle....60 B2
Kirby-le-Soken....37 H7
Kirby Mills....60 E2
Kirby Misperton....60 E3
Kirby Muxloe....43 H6
Kirby Row....47 J7
Kirby Sigston....59 K1
Kirby Underdale....60 F5
Kirby Wiske....59 J2
Kirdford....14 D3
Kirivick....107 F4
Kirk....111 J3
Kirkandrews-on-Eden....63 J2
Kirkbampton....63 J2
Kirkbean....62 E2
Kirk Bramwith....53 J2
Kirkbride....63 H2
Kirkbuddo....89 H4
Kirkburn....61 G5
Kirkburton....52 D2
Kirkby, Mers....50 D4
Kirkby, Lincs....54 E4
Kirkby, N. Yks....67 F7
Kirkby Fleetham....59 H1
Kirkby Green....44 D1
Kirkby in Ashfield....43 H1
Kirkby-in-Furness....57 F2
Kirkby la Thorpe....44 D2
Kirkby Lonsdale....57 K3
Kirkby Malham....58 D4
Kirkby Mallory....43 G6
Kirkby Malzeard....59 H3
Kirkby Mills....60 E2
Kirkbymoorside....60 D2
Kirkby on Bain....55 G7
Kirkby Overblow....59 J6
Kirkby Stephen....64 E7
Kirkby Thore....64 D5
Kirkby Underwood....44 D4
Kirkcaldy....81 H2
Kirkcambeck....74 B8
Kirkcarswell....69 J6
Kirkcolm....70 F8
Kirkconnel....72 C3
Kirkcowan....68 E4
Kirkcudbright....69 H5
Kirk Deighton....59 J5
Kirk Ella....61 H8
Kirkfieldbank....80 D7
Kirkgunzeon....72 D8
Kirkham, N. Yks....60 E4
Kirkham, Lancs....57 H7
Kirkhamgate....52 E1
Kirk Hammerton....60 B5
Kirkharle....75 G6
Kirkheaton, W. Yks....52 D2
Kirkheaton, Northum....75 G7
Kirkhill, Highld....102 D8
Kirkhill, Tays....89 J2
Kirkhope....73 J2
Kirkhouse....73 J1
Kirkibost, Highld....92 B4
Kirkibost, W. Isles....107 F5
Kirkinner....68 F5
Kirkintilloch....79 J4
Kirk Ireton....42 E1
Kirkland, D. & G....72 C3
Kirkland, Cumbr....64 D4
Kirkland, D. & G....72 D5
Kirkland, Cumbr....62 F6
Kirk Langley....42 E3
Kirkleatham....67 F5
Kirklevington....66 E7
Kirkley....47 L7
Kirklington, Notts....43 J1
Kirklington, N. Yks....59 J2
Kirklinton....73 K8
Kirkliston....81 G4
Kirkmaiden....68 C7
Kirk Merrington....66 C4
Kirkmichael, Tays....88 C2
Kirkmichael, Strath....71 J4
Kirk Michael, I. of M....56 Q2
Kirkmond le Mire....55 F4
Kirkmuirhill....80 C7
Kirknewton, Northum....74 F1
Kirknewton, Lothn....81 G5
Kirk of Shotts....80 D5
Kirkoswald, Cumbr....64 C3
Kirkoswald, Strath....71 H4
Kirkpatrick Durham....72 C7
Kirkpatrick-Fleming....73 H7
Kirk Sandall....53 J3
Kirksanton....56 E2
Kirk Smeaton....53 H2
Kirkstile....96 E2
Kirkton, Border....74 B3
Kirkton, Strath....77 E2
Kirkton, Highld....92 E3
Kirkton, D. & G....72 E6
Kirkton, Highld....93 F1
Kirkton, Highld....103 F3

Kirkton, Grampn....105 F3
Kirkton, Grampn....97 F3
Kirkton, Fife....89 F6
Kirkton, Tays....89 G4
Kirkton, Grampn....105 L3
Kirkton Manor....81 H8
Kirkton of Auchterhouse....89 F5
Kirkton of Auchterless....97 G1
Kirkton of Barevan....103 G8
Kirkton of Bourtie....97 H3
Kirkton of Collace....88 D5
Kirkton of Craig....89 K3
Kirkton of Culsalmond....97 F2
Kirkton of Durris....97 G6
Kirkton of Glenbuchat....96 C4
Kirkton of Glenisla....88 E2
Kirkton of Kingoldrum....89 F3
Kirkton of Largo....82 C1
Kirkton of Lethendy....88 D4
Kirkton of Logie Buchan....97 J3
Kirkton of Maryculter....97 H6
Kirkton of Menmuir....89 H2
Kirkton of Monikie....89 H5
Kirkton of Rayne....97 F2
Kirkton of Skene....97 H5
Kirkton of Tough....96 F4
Kirktown....105 K3
Kirktown of Alvah....104 F2
Kirktown of Bourtie....97 H3
Kirktown of Deskford....104 E2
Kirktown of Fetteresso....97 H7
Kirkwall....112 E5
Kirkwhelpington....75 F6
Kirk Yetholm....74 E2
Kirmington....54 F2
Kirmond le Mire....55 F4
Kirn....78 D4
Kirriemuir....89 F3
Kirstead Green....47 H7
Kirtlebridge....73 H7
Kirtling....36 B4
Kirtling Green....36 B4
Kirtlington....21 K1
Kirtomy....110 D2
Kirton, Lincs....45 G3
Kirton, Suff....37 H6
Kirton, Notts....53 J7
Kirton End....45 G2
Kirton Holme....45 F2
Kirton in Lindsey....54 D4
Kislingbury....33 J4
Kites Hardwick....33 G3
Kittybrewster....97 J5
Kitwood....13 J2
Kiveton Park....53 G5
Knaith....54 C5
Knaphill....22 E7
Knapp....10 E3
Knapton, N. Yks....60 C5
Knapton, N. Yks....61 F3
Knapton, Norf....47 J3
Knapwell....35 G3
Knaresborough....59 J5
Knarsdale....64 D2
Knaven....105 H4
Knayton....59 K2
Knebworth....35 F7
Kneep....106 E5
Kneesall....53 J7
Kneesworth....35 G5
Kneeton....43 K2
Knelston....27 J8
Knightacott....9 G2
Knightcote....33 F4
Knighton, Powys....30 D2
Knighton, Devon....4 F5
Knighton, Staffs....51 G7
Knighton, Staffs....41 J4
Knighton, Leic....43 J6
Knightwick....31 J4
Knill....30 D3
Knipton....44 B3
Knitsley....65 J3
Kniveton....42 E1
Knock, Cumbr....64 D5
Knock, Grampn....104 E3
Knock, Strath....85 G5
Knockally....111 H6
Knockan....101 J1
Knockandhu....96 B3
Knockando....95 K1
Knockbain....102 E7
Knockbrex....69 G6
Knock Castle....78 D5
Knockdee....111 H2
Knockenkelly....70 F2
Knockentiber....79 F8
Knockholt....23 K7
Knockholt Pound....23 K7
Knockin....40 E4
Knocknaha....70 B3
Knockrome....76 E4
Knocksharry....56 P3
Knodishall....37 K3
Knolls Green....51 H6
Knolton....40 E3
Knook....12 B1
Knossington....44 B6
Knott End-on-Sea....57 G6
Knotting....34 D3
Knottingley....53 G1
Knotty Green....22 E3
Knowbury....31 G2
Knowehead....72 B5
Knowesgate....75 F6
Knoweside....71 H3
Knowes of Elrick....104 F3
Knowetownhead....74 B3
Knowle, W. Mids....32 D2
Knowle, Devon....8 E2
Knowle, Shrops....31 G2
Knowle, Devon....9 H5
Knowle, Avon....19 L5
Knowle Green....58 B7

Knowl Hill....22 D5
Knowlton....25 J7
Knowsley....50 D4
Knowsley Hall....50 D4
Knowstone....9 J3
Knucklas....30 D2
Knutsford....51 G6
Knypersley....42 A1
Kuggar....2 F8
Kyleakin....92 D3
Kyle of Lochalsh....92 D3
Kylerhea....92 D3
Kylesmorar....92 E6
Kyles Scalpay....99 H3
Kyles Stockinish....99 G3
Kylestrome....108 D5
Kyloe....83 J7
Kynnersley....41 H5
Kyre Park....31 H3

L

Labost....107 G4
Laceby....55 G3
Lacey Green....22 D2
Lach Dennis....51 G6
Lache....50 C7
Lackalee....99 G3
Lackford....36 C2
Lacock....20 D6
Ladbroke....33 G4
Laddingford....16 D1
Lade Bank....45 G1
Ladock....3 G4
Ladybank....88 F8
Ladykirk....83 G7
Ladysford....105 J2
Lagavulin....76 D7
Lagg, Strath....70 E2
Lagg, Strath....76 E4
Laggan, Highld....94 E6
Laggan, Highld....93 J6
Lagganulva....85 F4
Laide....101 F3
Laindon....24 C4
Lair....101 G8
Lairg....102 D2
Lairgmore....94 D2
Lake....12 D2
Lakenham....47 H6
Lakenheath....36 C1
Lakesend....45 J7
Lakeside....57 G2
Laleham....22 F6
Laleston....18 C5
Lamarsh....36 D6
Lamas....47 H4
Lambden....82 F7
Lamberhurst....16 D2
Lamberton....83 H6
Lambeth....23 J5
Lambfell Moar....56 P3
Lambley, Northum....64 D2
Lambley, Notts....43 J2
Lambourn....21 H5
Lambourne End....23 K3
Lambs Green....15 F2
Lambston....26 D5
Lamerton....4 E2
Lamesley....66 C2
Lamington, Strath....72 E1
Lamington, Highld....103 F5
Lamlash....70 F1
Lamonby....63 K4
Lamorna....2 C7
Lamorran....3 G5
Lampeter....27 K2
Lampeter Velfry....26 E5
Lamphey....26 E6
Lamplugh....63 F5
Lamport....34 A2
Lamyatt....11 H2
Lana....8 D6
Lanark....80 D7
Lancaster....57 H4
Lanchester....66 B3
Landbeach....35 H3
Landcross....8 E3
Landerberry....97 G5
Landford....12 E4
Landimore....27 J7
Landkey....9 F2
Landore....27 L7
Landrake....4 D3
Landscove....5 H3
Landshipping....26 E5
Landulph....4 E3
Landwade....35 K3
Landywood....42 B6
Laneast....8 C7
Lane End....22 D3
Lane Green....42 B6
Laneham....54 C6
Laneshaw Bridge....58 B6
Langar....43 K3
Langbank....79 F4
Langbar....58 D4
Langcliffe....58 C3
Langdale End....61 G1
Langdon Beck....65 F3
Langdon Hills....24 C4
Langenhoe....25 G1
Langford, Devon....10 B5
Langford, Notts....54 C8
Langford, Essex....24 E2
Langford, Beds....34 E5
Langford, Oxon....21 G2
Langford Budville....10 C3
Langham, Leic....44 B5
Langham, Suff....36 E3
Langham, Norf....46 F2
Langham, Essex....36 F6

Langho....58 C7
Langholm....73 J6
Langleeford....75 F2
Langley, W. Susx....14 B3
Langley, Warw....32 D3
Langley, Kent....24 E7
Langley, Berks....22 F5
Langley, Herts....35 F7
Langley, Hants....13 G5
Langley, Essex....35 H6
Langley, Ches....51 J6
Langley Burrell....20 D5
Langley Marsh....10 B3
Langley Park....66 C3
Langley Street....47 J6
Langney....16 D5
Langold....53 H5
Langore....8 D7
Langport....11 F3
Langrick....45 F2
Langridge....20 B6
Langrigg....63 G3
Langrish....13 K3
Langsett....52 E3
Langshaw....82 D8
Langstone....13 K5
Langthorne....59 H1
Langthorpe....59 J4
Langthwaite....65 H5
Langtoft, Lincs....44 E5
Langtoft, Humbs....61 H4
Langton, Durham....66 B6
Langton, N. Yks....60 E4
Langton, Lincs....55 G7
Langton, Lincs....55 H6
Langton by Wragby....55 F6
Langton Green....16 C2
Langton Herring....11 H7
Langton Matravers....6 E7
Langtree....8 E4
Langwathby....64 C4
Langwith....53 H7
Langworth....54 E6
Lanivet....3 J3
Lanlivery....3 J4
Lanner....2 F6
Lanreath....4 B4
Lansallos....4 B4
Lanton, Border....74 C2
Lanton, Northum....74 F1
Lapford....9 H5
Laphroaig....76 C7
Lapley....42 A5
Lapworth....32 D2
Larbert....80 D3
Largie....96 F2
Largoward....89 G8
Largs....78 E6
Largybeg....70 F2
Largymore....70 F2
Larkfield....78 E4
Larkhall....80 C6
Larkhill....12 C1
Larling....46 E8
Larriston....74 B5
Lartington....65 H6
Lary....96 C5
Lasham....13 J1
Laskentyre....99 F3
Lassodie....81 G2
Lastingham....60 E1
Latchingdon....24 E2
Latchley....4 E2
Lately Common....51 F4
Lathbury....34 B5
Latheron....111 J5
Latheronwheel....111 H5
Lathones....89 G8
Latimer....22 F3
Latteridge....20 A4
Lattiford....11 H3
Latton....20 D3
Lauchintilly....97 G4
Lauder....82 D7
Laugharne....27 H5
Laughterton....54 C6
Laughton, Lincs....54 C4
Laughton, E. Susx....15 J4
Laughton, Leic....43 J8
Laughton-en-le-Morthen....53 H5
Launcells....8 C5
Launceston....8 D7
Launde Abbey....44 A6
Launton....33 J7
Laurencekirk....89 K1
Laurieston....69 H4
Lavant....14 B5
Lavendon....34 C4
Lavenham....36 E5
Laverhay....73 G5
Laverstock....12 D2
Laverstoke....13 G1
Laverton, Somer....20 B7
Laverton, Glos....32 C6
Laverton, N. Yks....59 H3
Law....80 D6
Lawers....87 J5
Lawford....37 F6
Lawhitton....8 D7
Lawkland....58 C4
Lawley....41 H6
Lawnhead....41 K4
Lawrenny....26 E6
Lawshall....36 D4
Lawton....31 F4
Laxay....107 H6
Laxdale....107 J5
Laxey....56 R3
Laxfield....37 H2
Laxfirth....115 G4
Laxo....115 G2
Laxobigging....117 F5
Laxton, Humbs....54 B1
Laxton, Notts....54 B7

Laxton, Northnts....44 C7
Laycock....58 F6
Layer Breton....25 F1
Layer de la Haye....36 E7
Layham....36 F5
Laytham....60 E7
Lazenby....67 F6
Lazonby....64 C4
Lea, Lincs....54 C5
Lea, Wilts....20 D4
Lea, Shrops....40 E8
Lea, Derby....43 F1
Lea, Shrops....41 F6
Lea, H. & W....31 H7
Leac Eskadale....99 H3
Leachkin....102 E8
Leadburn....81 H6
Leadenham....44 C1
Leaden Roding....24 B1
Leadgate, Cumbr....64 E3
Leadgate, Durham....65 J2
Leadhills....72 D3
Leafield....21 H1
Leagrave....34 D7
Leake Commonside....45 G1
Leake Hurn's End....45 H2
Lealholm....67 H7
Lealt, Highld....100 B6
Lealt, Strath....77 F2
Lea Marston....42 E7
Leamington Hastings....33 G3
Leamington Spa, Royal....33 F3
Leargybreck....76 E4
Learmouth....83 G8
Leasgill....57 H2
Leasingham....44 D2
Leask....97 K2
Leatherhead....23 G7
Leathley....59 H6
Leaton....41 F5
Lea Town....57 H7
Leaveland....25 G7
Leavenheath....36 E6
Leavening....60 E4
Leaves Green....23 K6
Lebberston....61 H2
Lechlade....21 G3
Leck....58 B3
Leckford....13 F2
Leckfurin....110 D3
Leckhampstead, Berks....21 J5
Leckhampstead, Bucks....33 K6
Leckhampton....20 D1
Leckmelm....101 H3
Leckwith....18 F5
Leconfield....61 H6
Ledaig....86 B5
Ledburn....34 C7
Ledbury....31 J6
Ledgemoor....31 F4
Ledicot....31 F3
Ledmore....108 D7
Lednagullin....110 E2
Ledsham, Ches....50 C6
Ledsham, W. Yks....59 K8
Ledston....59 K8
Ledwell....33 G7
Lee, Devon....8 E1
Lee, Shrops....40 F3
Lee, Hants....13 F4
Lee, Strath....84 F6
Lee, Lancs....57 J5
Leebotten....115 G6
Leebotwood....41 F7
Lee Brockhurst....41 G4
Leece....57 F4
Lee Clump....22 E2
Leeds, Kent....24 E7
Leeds, N. Yks....59 J7
Leedstown....2 E6
Leek....42 B1
Leekhampstead....21 J5
Leek Wootton....32 E3
Lee Mill....5 F4
Leeming....59 H2
Leeming Bar....59 H1
Lee Moor....4 F3
Lee-on-the-Solent....13 H5
Lees, Derby....42 E3
Lees, G. Man....51 J3
Leeswood....50 B7
Lee, The....22 E2
Legbourne....55 H5
Legburthwaite....63 J6
Legerwood....82 D7
Legsby....55 F5
Leicester....43 H6
Leicester Forest East....43 H6
Leigh, Kent....16 C1
Leigh, Wilts....20 E3
Leigh, Shrops....40 E6
Leigh, Surrey....15 F1
Leigh, G. Man....51 J3
Leigh, Dorset....11 H5
Leigh, H. & W....31 J4
Leigh Beck....24 E4
Leigh Delamere....20 C5
Leigh Green....17 F2
Leigh-on-Sea....24 E4
Leigh Sinton....31 J4
Leighterton....20 C3
Leigh, The....32 A7
Leighton, Powys....40 D6
Leighton, Shrops....41 H6
Leighton, Somer....11 J1
Leighton Bromswold....34 E2
Leighton Buzzard....34 C7
Leigh upon Mendip....11 H1
Leigh Woods....19 K5
Leinthall Earls....31 F3
Leinthall Starkes....31 F3
Leintwardine....30 F2
Leire....43 H7
Leirinmore....109 F2
Leiston....37 K3

Leith....81 H4
Leitholm....83 F7
Lelant....2 D6
Lelley....61 K7
Lem Hill....31 J2
Lemmington Hall....75 H3
Lempitlaw....74 D1
Lemreway....107 H7
Lendalfoot....71 G6
Lenham....24 E7
Lenham Heath....17 G1
Lenie....94 D3
Lennel....83 G7
Lennoxtown....79 J4
Lenton....44 D3
Lenwade....47 F5
Leoch....89 F4
Leochel Cushnie....96 E4
Leominster....31 F4
Leonard Stanley....20 C2
Lepe....13 G6
Lephin....99 G8
Lephinmore....78 B2
Leppington....60 E4
Lepton....52 E2
Lerryn....3 K4
Lerwick....115 G4
Lesbury....75 J3
Leslie, Grampn....96 E3
Leslie, Fife....81 H1
Lesmahagow....80 D8
Lesnewth....8 B6
Lessingham....47 J4
Lessonhall....63 H2
Leswalt....68 B4
Letchmore Heath....23 G3
Letchworth....35 F6
Letcombe Bassett....21 H4
Letcombe Regis....21 H4
Letham, Fife....88 F7
Letham, Tays....89 H4
Lethenty....97 H1
Letheringham....37 H4
Letheringsett....46 F3
Lettaford....9 G7
Letterewe....101 F5
Letterfearn....92 E3
Letterfinlay....93 J6
Letters....101 H4
Letterston....26 D4
Lettoch....95 K2
Letton, H. & W....30 E2
Letton, H. & W....30 E5
Letty Green....23 H1
Letwell....53 H5
Leuchars....89 G6
Leurbost....107 H6
Levedale....42 B3
Leven, Fife....81 J1
Leven, Humbs....61 J6
Levens....57 H2
Levenshulme....51 H4
Levenwick....115 G6
Leverburgh....98 F4
Leverington....45 H5
Leverton....45 G2
Levington....37 H6
Levisham....60 F1
Levishie....94 C4
Lew....21 H2
Lewannick....4 C1
Lewdown....8 E7
Lewes....15 H4
Leweston....26 D4
Lewisham....23 J5
Lewiston....94 D3
Lewknor....22 C3
Leworthy....9 G2
Lewtrenchard....8 E7
Ley....4 B3
Leybourne....24 C7
Leyburn....59 G1
Leycett....41 J2
Leyland....50 E1
Leylodge....97 G4
Leys....105 G3
Leysdown on Sea....25 G5
Leysmill....89 J4
Leys of Cossans....89 F4
Leysters....31 G3
Leyton....23 J4
Lezant....4 D2
Lhanbryde....104 B2
Lhen, The....56 Q1
Libanus....29 G7
Libberton....80 E7
Liberton....81 H4
Lichfield....42 D6
Lickey....32 B2
Lickey End....32 B2
Lickfold....14 C3
Liddington....21 G4
Lidgate....36 C4
Lidlington....34 C6
Lieurary....111 G2
Liff....89 F4
Lifton....8 D7
Lighthorne....33 F4
Lightwater....22 E6
Lightwood....42 B2
Lightwood Green....40 F2
Likisto....99 G3
Lilbourne....33 H2
Lilburn Tower....75 G2
Lilleshall....41 H4
Lilley....34 E7
Lilliesleaf....74 B2
Lillingstone Dayrell....33 K6
Lillingstone Lovell....33 K5
Lillington....11 H4
Lilstock....10 C1
Limbrick....50 F2
Limefield....51 H1
Limekilns....81 F3
Limerigg....80 D4

Limington	11	G3
Limmerhaugh	72	B2
Limpenhoe	47	J6
Limpley Stoke	20	B6
Limpsfield	23	J7
Linby	43	H1
Linchmere	14	B2
Lincoln	54	D6
Lincomb	31	K3
Lindale	57	H2
Lindal in Furness	57	F3
Linden	74	A1
Lindfield	15	G3
Lindford	14	B2
Lindores	88	E7
Lindridge	31	H3
Lindsell	36	B7
Lindsey	36	E5
Linford, Essex	24	C5
Linford, Hants	12	D5
Lingague	56	P4
Lingdale	67	G6
Lingen	30	E3
Lingfield	15	G1
Lingwood	47	J6
Liniclate	98	C8
Linicro	99	J6
Linkenholt	21	H7
Linkinhorne	4	D2
Linklater	112	E8
Linksness	113	F5
Linktown	81	H2
Linley	40	E7
Linley Green	31	H4
Linlithgow	80	F4
Linlithgow Bridge	80	E4
Linshader	107	G5
Linshiels	74	E4
Linsidemore	102	D3
Linslade	34	C7
Linstead Parva	37	J2
Linstock	63	K2
Linthwaite	52	D2
Lintlaw	83	G6
Lintmill	104	E2
Linton, Border	74	D2
Linton, Kent	16	E1
Linton, N. Yks	58	E4
Linton, Derby	42	E5
Linton, H. & W	31	H7
Linton, Cambs	35	J5
Linton-on-Ouse	60	B4
Linwood, Hants	12	D5
Linwood, Lincs	54	F5
Linwood, Strath	79	G5
Lional	107	K2
Liphook	14	B2
Liskeard	4	C3
Liss	14	A3
Lissett	61	J5
Liss Forest	14	A3
Lissington	54	F5
Lisvane	19	F4
Litcham	46	D5
Litchborough	33	J4
Litchfield	21	J7
Litherland	50	C4
Litlington, Cambs	35	G5
Litlington, E. Susx	15	J5
Little Abington	35	J5
Little Addington	34	C2
Little Alne	32	D3
Little Asby	64	D7
Little Aston	42	C6
Little Atherfield	7	J6
Little Ayre	112	D7
Little Ayton	67	F6
Little Baddow	24	D2
Little Badminton	20	C4
Little Bardfield	36	B6
Little Barford	34	E4
Little Barningham	47	G3
Little Barrington	21	G1
Little Barugh	60	E3
Little Bealings	37	H5
Little Bedwyn	21	G6
Little Bentley	37	G7
Little Berkhamsted	23	H2
Little Birch	31	G6
Little Blakenham	37	G5
Littleborough, Notts	54	C5
Littleborough, G. Man	51	J2
Littlebourne	25	J7
Little Bowden	34	A1
Little Bradley	36	B4
Little Brampton	30	E1
Little Brechin	89	H2
Littlebredy	11	G7
Little Brickhill	34	C6
Little Brington	33	J3
Little Bromley	37	F7
Little Budworth	50	E7
Little Burstead	24	C3
Littlebury	35	J6
Littlebury Green	35	H6
Little Bytham	44	D5
Little Carlton	55	J5
Little Casterton	44	D6
Little Cawthorpe	55	H5
Little Chalfont	22	E3
Little Chart	17	G1
Little Chesterford	35	J5
Little Cheverell	20	D7
Little Chishill	35	H6
Little Clacton	25	H1
Little Comberton	32	B5
Little Common	16	E5
Little Compton	32	E6
Little Cowarne	31	H4
Little Coxwell	21	G3
Little Cressingham	46	D6
Little Dalby	44	A5
Littledean	20	A1
Little Dens	105	K4
Little Dewchurch	31	G6
Little Downham	35	J1
Little Driffield	61	H5
Little Dunham	46	D5
Little Dunkeld	88	C4
Little Dunmow	36	B7
Little Easton	35	K7
Little Eaton	43	F2
Little Ellingham	46	F7
Little End	23	L2
Little Eversden	35	G4
Little Fakenham	36	E2
Little Faringdon	21	G2
Little Fenton	60	C7
Littleferry	103	G3
Little Fransham	46	E5
Little Gaddesden	22	E1
Little Gidding	34	E1
Little Glemham	37	J4
Little Gransden	35	F4
Little Gruinard	101	F4
Little Habton	60	E3
Little Hadham	35	H7
Little Hallingbury	23	L1
Littleham, Devon	8	E3
Littleham, Devon	5	L1
Little Hampden	22	D2
Littlehampton	14	D5
Little Harrowden	34	B2
Little Haseley	22	B2
Little Hautbois	47	H4
Little Haven	26	C5
Little Hay	42	D6
Little Haywood	42	C4
Littlehempston	5	J3
Little Hereford	31	G3
Little Horkesley	36	E6
Little Horsted	15	H4
Little Horwood	34	A6
Little Houghton, Northnts	34	B4
Littlehoughton, Northum	75	J3
Little Hucklow	52	D6
Little Hulton	51	G3
Little Kingshill	22	D3
Little Langdale	63	J7
Little Langford	12	C2
Little Laver	23	L2
Little Leigh	50	F6
Little Leighs	24	D1
Little Lever	51	G3
Little London, Hants	22	B7
Little London, E. Susx	16	C4
Little London, Hants	13	F1
Little London, Lincs	45	F4
Little Longstone	52	D6
Little Malvern	31	J5
Little Maplestead	36	D6
Little Marcle	31	H6
Little Marlow	22	D4
Little Massingham	46	C4
Little Melton	47	G6
Little Mill, Gwent	19	H2
Littlemill, Highld	103	H7
Littlemill, Strath	71	K3
Little Milton	22	B2
Little Missenden	22	E3
Littlemore	21	K2
Little Ness	41	F5
Little Newcastle	26	D4
Little Newsham	65	J6
Little Oakley, Northnts	34	B1
Little Oakley, Essex	37	H7
Little Orton	63	J2
Littleover	43	F3
Little Paxton	34	E3
Little Petherick	3	H2
Little Plumstead	47	J5
Littleport	35	J1
Little Raveley	35	F1
Little Ribston	59	J5
Little Rissington	21	F1
Little Ryburgh	46	E4
Little Ryle	75	G3
Little Salkeld	64	C4
Little Sampford	36	B6
Little Saxham	36	C3
Little Scatwell	102	B7
Little Shelford	35	H4
Little Smeaton	53	H2
Little Snoring	46	E3
Little Somerford	20	D4
Little Stainton	66	D5
Little Stanney	50	D6
Little Staughton	34	E3
Little Steeping	55	J7
Littlestone-on-Sea	17	H3
Little Stonham	37	G3
Little Stretton, Shrops	41	F7
Little Stretton, Leic	43	J6
Little Strickland	64	C6
Little Stukeley	35	F2
Little Tew	33	F7
Little Thetford	35	J2
Littlethorpe	59	J4
Little Thurlow	36	B4
Little Thurrock	24	C5
Littleton, Ches	50	D7
Littleton, Somer	11	F2
Littleton, Surrey	22	F6
Littleton, Hants	13	G2
Littleton Drew	20	C4
Littleton Panell	20	E7
Littleton-upon-Severn	19	K3
Little Torrington	8	E4
Little Totham	24	E1
Littletown, Durham	66	D3
Little Town, Cumbr	63	H6
Little Wakering	25	F4
Little Walden	35	J5
Little Waldingfield	36	E5
Little Walsingham	46	E3
Little Waltham	24	D1
Little Warley	24	C3
Little Weighton	61	G7
Little Welnetham	36	D3
Little Wenlock	41	H6
Little Whittingham Green	37	H2
Littlewick Green	22	D4
Little Wilbraham	35	J4
Little Witley	31	J3
Little Wittenham	21	K3
Little Wolford	32	E6
Littleworth, H. & W	32	A4
Littleworth, Staffs	42	C5
Littleworth, Oxon	21	H3
Little Wymondley	35	F7
Little Wyrley	42	C6
Little Yeldham	36	C6
Litton, Derby	52	D6
Litton, N. Yks	58	E3
Litton, Somer	19	K7
Litton Cheney	11	G6
Liverpool	50	C4
Liversedge	52	E1
Liverton	67	H6
Livingston	81	F5
Livingston Village	81	F5
Lixwm	50	A6
Lizard	2	F8
Llanaber	38	F5
Llanaelhaearn	38	C2
Llanafan	28	D2
Llanafan-fawr	29	G4
Llanallgo	48	E2
Llanarmon	38	D3
Llanarmon Dyffryn Ceiriog	40	C3
Llanarmon-yn-Ial	40	C1
Llanarth, Dyfed	28	B4
Llanarth, Gwent	19	H1
Llanarthney	27	K4
Llanasa	49	L2
Llanbabo	48	C2
Llanbadarn Fawr	28	D1
Llanbadarn Fynydd	30	C2
Llanbadarn-y-garreg	30	C5
Llanbadrig	48	C1
Llanbeder	30	H3
Llanbedr, Powys	30	C5
Llanbedr, Powys	30	D7
Llanbedr, Gwyn	38	E4
Llanbedr-Dyffryn-Clwyd	50	A8
Llanbedrgoch	48	E2
Llanbedrog	38	C3
Llanbedr-y-cennin	49	G4
Llanberis	48	E4
Llanbister	30	C2
Llanblethian	18	D5
Llanboidy	27	G4
Llanbradach	18	F3
Llanbrynmair	39	J6
Llancarfan	18	E5
Llancayo	19	H2
Llancynfelyn	39	F7
Llandaff	18	F4
Llandanwg	38	E4
Llandawke	27	G5
Llanddaniel Fab	48	D3
Llanddarog	27	K5
Llanddeiniol	28	C2
Llanddeiniolen	48	E4
Llandderfel	39	J3
Llanddeusant, Gwyn	48	C2
Llanddeusant, Dyfed	28	E7
Llanddew	29	H6
Llanddewi	27	J8
Llanddewi Brefi	28	D4
Llanddewi'r Cwm	29	H5
Llanddewi Rhydderch	19	H1
Llanddewi Velfrey	26	F5
Llanddewi Ystradenni	30	C3
Llanddoged	49	H4
Llanddona	48	E3
Llanddowror	27	G5
Llanddulas	49	J3
Llandefaelog, Powys	29	H6
Llandefaelog, Dyfed	27	J5
Llandefaelog tre'r-graig	30	C6
Llandefalle	30	C6
Llandegai	48	E3
Llandegfan	48	E3
Llandegla	40	C1
Llandegley	30	C3
Llandegveth	19	H3
Llandeilo	27	L4
Llandeilo Graban	29	H5
Llandeilo'r-Fan	29	F6
Llandeloy	26	C4
Llandenny	19	J2
Llandevenny	19	J4
Llandinabo	31	G7
Llandinam	29	H1
Llandissilio	26	F4
Llandogo	19	K2
Llandough, S. Glam	18	D5
Llandough, S. Glam	19	F5
Llandovery	28	E6
Llandow	18	D5
Llandre, Dyfed	28	D1
Llandre, Dyfed	27	L2
Llandrillo	40	B3
Llandrillo-yn-Rhos	49	H3
Llandrindod Wells	29	H3
Llandrinio	40	D5
Llandudno	49	G2
Llandudno Junction	49	H3
Llandudwen	38	B3
Llandwrog	48	D4
Llandybie	27	L5
Llandyfan	27	L5
Llandyfriog	27	H2
Llandyfrydog	48	D2
Llandygwydd	27	G2
Llandynrog	49	L4
Llandyssil	40	C7
Llandysul	27	J2
Llanegryn	38	F6
Llanegwad	27	K4
Llanelian-yn-Rhos	49	H3
Llanelidan	40	C1
Llanelieu	30	C6
Llanellen	19	H1
Llanelli	27	K6
Llanelltyd	39	G5
Llanelly	19	G1
Llanelly Hill	19	G1
Llanelwedd	29	H4
Llanelwy or St Asaph	49	K3
Llanenddwyn	38	E4
Llanengan	38	B4
Llanerchymedd	48	D2
Llanerfyl	40	B6
Llanethlu	48	C2
Llanfachraeth	48	C2
Llanfachreth	39	G4
Llanfaelog	48	C3
Llanfaes	48	F3
Llanfaethlu	48	C2
Llanfaglan	48	D4
Llanfair Caereinion	40	C6
Llanfair Clydogau	27	L1
Llanfair Dyffryn Clwyd	40	C1
Llanfairfechan	49	F3
Llanfair Kilgeddin	19	H2
Llanfair-Nant-Gwyn	26	F3
Llanfairpwllgwyngyll	48	E3
Llanfair Talhaiarn	49	J3
Llanfair Waterdine	30	D2
Llanfairyneubwll	48	C3
Llanfairynghornwy	48	C1
Llanfallteg	26	F5
Llanfaredd	29	H4
Llanfarian	28	C2
Llanfechain	40	C4
Llanfechan	29	G4
Llanfechell	48	C1
Llanfendigaid	38	E6
Llanferres	50	A7
Llanfflewyn	48	C2
Llanfihangel-ar-arth	27	J3
Llanfihangel Crucorney	30	E7
Llanfihangel Glyn Myfyr	39	J2
Llanfihangel Nant Bran	29	G6
Llanfihangel-nant-Melan	30	C3
Llanfihangel Rhydithon	30	C3
Llanfihangel Rogiet	19	J4
Llanfihangel Tal-y-llyn	30	C7
Llanfihangel-uwch-Gwili	27	J4
Llanfihangel-y-Creuddyn	28	D2
Llanfihangel-yng-Ngwynfa	40	B5
Llanfihangel yn Nhowyn	48	C3
Llanfihangel-y-pennant, Gwyn	38	E2
Llanfihangel-y-pennant, Gwyn	39	F6
Llanfihangel Ystum Llwern	19	J1
Llanfihangel-y-traethau	38	E3
Llanfilo	30	C6
Llanfoist	19	G1
Llanfor	39	J3
Llanfrechfa	19	H3
Llanfrothen	39	F2
Llanfrynach	29	H7
Llanfwrog, Clwyd	40	C1
Llanfwrog, Gwyn	48	C2
Llanfyllin	40	C5
Llanfynydd, Clwyd	40	D1
Llanfynydd, Dyfed	27	K4
Llanfyrnach	27	G3
Llangadfan	40	B5
Llangadog	28	E7
Llangadwaladr, Clwyd	40	C3
Llangadwaladr, Gwyn	48	C4
Llangain	27	H5
Llangammarch Wells	29	G5
Llangan	18	D5
Llangarron	31	G7
Llangasty-Talyllin	30	C7
Llangathen	27	K4
Llangattock	19	G1
Llangattock Lingoed	30	E7
Llangattock-Vibon-Avel	19	J1
Llangedwyn	40	C4
Llangefni	48	D3
Llangeinor	18	D4
Llangeitho	28	D4
Llangeler	27	H3
Llangelynnin	38	E6
Llangendeirne	27	J5
Llangennech	27	K6
Llangennith	27	J7
Llangenny	19	G1
Llangernyw	49	H4
Llangian	38	B4
Llangiwg	18	B2
Llangloffan	26	F4
Llanglydwen	26	F4
Llangoed	48	F3
Llangoedmor	27	G2
Llangollen	40	D2
Llangolman	26	F4
Llangorse	30	C7
Llangorwen	28	D1
Llangovan	19	J2
Llangower	39	J3
Llangranog	28	A4
Llangristiolus	48	D3
Llangrove	19	K1
Llangua	30	E7
Llangunllo	30	D2
Llangunnor	27	J4
Llangurig	29	G1
Llangwm, Dyfed	26	D6
Llangwm, Clwyd	39	J2
Llangwm, Gwent	19	J2
Llangwnnadl	38	B3
Llangwyfan	50	A7
Llangwyllog	48	D3
Llangwyryfon	28	C2
Llangybi, Gwyn	38	D2
Llangybi, Gwent	19	H3
Llangybi, Dyfed	27	L1
Llangyfelach	17	L7
Llangynhafal	50	A7
Llangynidr	18	F1
Llangynin	27	G5
Llangynog, Powys	40	B4
Llangynog, Dyfed	27	H5
Llangynwyd	18	C4
Llanhamlach	29	H7
Llanharan	18	E4
Llanharry	18	E4
Llanhennock	19	H3
Llanhilleth	19	G2
Llanidloes	29	G1
Llaniestyn	38	B3
Llanigon	30	D5
Llanilar	28	D2
Llanilid	18	D4
Llanishen, S. Glam	19	F4
Llanishen, Gwent	19	J2
Llanllechid	49	F4
Llanllowell	19	H3
Llanllugan	40	B6
Llanllwch	27	H5
Llanllwchaiarn	40	C7
Llanllwni	27	J2
Llanllyfni	38	D1
Llanmadoc	27	J7
Llanmaes	18	D6
Llanmartin	19	H4
Llanmerewig	40	C7
Llanmihangel	18	D5
Llanmiloe	27	G6
Llanmorlais	27	K7
Llannefydd	49	J3
Llannon	27	K6
Llannor	38	C3
Llanon	28	C3
Llanover	19	H2
Llanpumsaint	27	J4
Llanrhaeadr	49	K4
Llanrhaeadr-ym-Mochnant	40	C4
Llanrhian	26	C3
Llanrhidian	27	J7
Llanrhos	49	G2
Llanrhyddlad	48	C2
Llanrhystud	28	C3
Llanrothal	19	J1
Llanrug	48	E4
Llanrwst	49	H4
Llansadwrn, Dyfed	28	D6
Llansadwrn, Gwyn	48	E3
Llansaint	27	H6
Llansamlet	18	A3
Llansannan	49	J4
Llansannor	18	D5
Llansantffraed, Dyfed	28	C3
Llansantffraed, Powys	30	C7
Llansantffraed-Cwmdeuddwr	29	G3
Llansantffraed-in-Elvel	30	C6
Llansantffraid Glan Conwy	49	H3
Llansantffraid-ym-Mechain	40	D4
Llansawel	27	L3
Llansilin	40	D4
Llansoy	19	J2
Llanspyddid	29	H7
Llanstadwell	26	D6
Llansteffan, Dyfed	27	H5
Llanstephan, Powys	30	C5
Llanthony	30	D7
Llantilio Crossenny	19	H1
Llantilio Pertholey	19	H1
Llantrisant, Gwyn	48	C2
Llantrisant, M. Glam	18	E4
Llantrisant, Gwent	19	H3
Llantrithyd	18	E5
Llantwit Fardre	18	E4
Llantwit Major	18	D6
Llanuwchllyn	39	H3
Llanvaches	19	J3
Llanvair Discoed	19	J3
Llanvapley	19	H1
Llanvetherine	19	H1
Llanveynoe	30	E6
Llanvihangel Crucorney	30	E7
Llanvihangel Gobion	19	H2
Llanvihangel-Ystern-Llewern	19	J1
Llanwarne	31	G7
Llanwddyn	40	B5
Llanwenog	27	J2
Llanwern	19	H4
Llanwinio	27	G4
Llanwnda, Dyfed	26	D3
Llanwnda, Gwyn	48	D5
Llanwnnen	27	K2
Llanwnog	40	B7
Llanwrda	28	E6
Llanwrin	39	G6
Llanwrthwl	29	G3
Llanwrtyd	29	F5
Llanwrtyd-Wells	29	F5
Llanwyddelan	40	B6
Llanyblodwel	40	D4
Llanybri	27	H5
Llanybydder	27	K2
Llanycefn	26	E4
Llanychaer	26	D3
Llanycrwys	27	L2
Llanymawddwy	39	J5
Llanymynech, Shrops	40	D5
Llanymynch, Powys	40	D4
Llanynghenedl	48	C2
Llanynys	49	L4
Llan-y-pwll	40	E1
Llanyre	29	H3
Llanystumdwy	38	D3
Llanywern	30	C7
Llawhaden	26	E5
Llawnt	40	D3
Llawr Dref	38	B4
Llawryglyn	39	J7
Llay	40	E1
Llechcynfarwy	48	C2
Llechfaen	29	H7
Llechryd, M. Glam	18	F2
Llechryd, Dyfed	27	G2
Lledrod	28	D2
Llidiad-Nenog	27	K3
Llithfaen	38	C2
Llong	50	B7
Llowes	30	C5
Llwchmynydd	38	A4
Llwn-y-groes	28	C4
Llwydcoed	18	D2
Llwyn	30	D1
Llwyncelyn	28	B4
Llwyndafydd	28	A4
Llwynderw	40	D6
Llwyndyrys	38	C2
Llwyngwril	38	E6
Llwynhendy	27	K7
Llwynmawr	40	D3
Llwynypia	18	D3
Llynclys	40	D4
Llynfaes	48	D3
Llysfaen	49	H3
Llyswen	30	C6
Llysworney	18	D5
Llys-y-fran	26	E4
Llywel	29	F6
Loanend	83	H6
Loanhead	81	H5
Loans	71	J1
Lochaber	93	H6
Lochailort	92	D7
Lochaline	85	H4
Lochans	68	B5
Locharbriggs	72	E6
Lochawe	86	D6
Lochboisdale	90	C4
Lochbuie	85	H6
Lochcarnan	98	D8
Lochcarron	93	G2
Lochdon	85	J5
Lochearnhead	87	H6
Lochee	89	F5
Lochend, Highld	94	D2
Lochend, Highld	111	J2
Locheport	98	D6
Locherben	72	E5
Lochfoot	72	D7
Lochgair	77	J2
Lochganvich	107	G6
Lochgarthside	78	D1
Lochgelly	81	G2
Lochgilphead	77	H3
Lochgoilhead	78	D1
Lochhill	104	B2
Lochinver	108	B6
Lochlane	87	L6
Lochluichart	102	E3
Lochmaben	73	F6
Lochmaddy	98	E6
Lochore	81	G2
Lochranza	77	J6
Lochside	89	K2
Lochskipport	90	D2
Lochslin	103	G4
Lochton	97	G6
Lochwinnoch	79	F6
Lochwood	80	B5
Lockengate	3	J3
Lockerbie	73	G6
Lockeridge	21	F6
Lockerley	13	F3
Locking	19	H7
Lockinge	21	J4
Lockington, Leic	43	G4
Lockington, Humbs	61	G6
Lockleywood	41	H4
Locks Heath	13	H5
Lockton	60	F2
Loddington, Leic	44	A6
Loddington, Northnts	34	B2
Loddiswell	5	H5
Loddon	47	J7
Lode	35	J3
Loders	11	F6
Lodsworth	14	C3
Lofthouse	59	G3
Lofthouse Gate	53	F1
Loftus	67	H6
Logan	72	A2
Loggerheads	41	J3
Loggie	101	H3
Logie, Fife	89	G6
Logie, Tays	89	J2
Logie Coldstone	96	D5
Logie Hill	103	F5
Logie Newton	97	F2
Logie Pert	89	J2
Logierait	88	B3
Login	26	F4
Lolworth	35	G3
Lonbain	100	C7
Londesborough	60	F6
London	23	J5
London (Gatwick) Airport	15	F1
London (Heathrow) Airport	23	F5
London Colney	23	G2
Londonderry	59	J2
Londonthorpe	44	C2
Londubh	100	E4
Lonemore, Highld	100	D5
Lonemore, Highld	103	F5
Long Ashton	19	K5
Long Bennington	44	B2
Longbenton	75	J8
Longborough	32	D7
Long Bredy	11	G6
Longbridge, W. Mids	32	C2
Longbridge, Warw	32	E3
Longbridge Deverill	12	A1
Long Buckby	33	J3
Longburton	11	H4
Long Clawson	43	J4
Longcliffe	42	E1
Long Common	13	H4
Long Compton, Staffs	42	A4
Long Compton, Warw	32	E6
Longcot	21	G3
Long Crendon	22	B2
Long Crichel	12	B4
Longcroft	80	C4
Longden	41	F6

Long Ditton....23 G6
Longdon, Staffs....42 C5
Longdon, H. & W....31 K6
Longdon on Tern....41 H5
Longdown....9 J6
Longdowns....2 F6
Long Drax....60 D8
Long Duckmanton....53 G6
Long Eaton....43 G3
Longfield....24 C6
Longford, Derby....42 E3
Longford, W. Mids....33 F1
Longford, G. Lon....22 F5
Longford, Shrops....41 H3
Longford, Shrops....41 J5
Longford, Glos....31 K7
Longforgan....88 F5
Longformacus....82 E6
Longframlington....75 H4
Long Gill....58 C5
Longham, Dorset....12 C6
Longham, Norf....46 E5
Long Hanborough....21 J1
Longhirst....75 J6
Longhope, Glos....20 A1
Longhope, Orkney....112 D7
Longhorsley....75 H5
Longhoughton....75 J3
Long Itchington....33 G3
Long Lawford....33 G2
Longley Green....31 J4
Longload....11 F3
Longmanhill....105 G2
Long Marston, N. Yks....60 C5
Long Marston, Herts....22 D1
Long Marston, Warw....32 D5
Long Marton....64 D5
Long Melford....36 D5
Longmoor Camp....14 A2
Longmorn....104 B3
Long Newton....20 D3
Longnewton, Border....74 B2
Longnewton, Cleve....66 D6
Longney....20 B1
Longniddry....82 C4
Longnor, Staffs....52 C7
Longnor, Shrops....41 F6
Longparish....13 G1
Long Preston....58 D5
Longridge, Loth....80 E5
Longridge, Lancs....57 K7
Longriggend....80 D4
Long Riston....61 J6
Longsdon....42 B1
Longside....105 K4
Longslow....41 H3
Longstanton....35 G3
Longstock....13 F2
Longstowe....35 G4
Long Stratton....47 G7
Long Street....34 A5
Long Sutton, Somer....11 F3
Long Sutton, Lincs....45 H4
Long Sutton, Hants....13 K1
Longthorpe....44 E7
Long Thurlow....36 F3
Longton, Staffs....42 B2
Longton, Lancs....50 D1
Longtown, H. & W....30 E7
Longtown, Cumbr....73 J8
Longville in the Dale....41 G7
Long Whatton....43 G4
Longwick....22 C2
Long Wittenham....21 K3
Longwitton....75 G6
Longworth....21 H3
Longyester....82 D5
Lonmore....99 H8
Looe....4 C4
Loose....24 D7
Loosley Row....22 D2
Lopcombe Corner....12 E2
Lopen....11 F4
Loppington....41 F4
Lopwell....4 E3
Lorbottle....75 G4
Lorton....63 G5
Loscoe....43 G2
Lossiemouth....104 B1
Lostock Gralam....51 F6
Lostock Junction....51 F3
Lostwithiel....3 K4
Lothbeg....103 H1
Lothersdale....58 E6
Lothmore....110 F7
Loudwater....22 E3
Loughborough....43 H5
Loughor....27 K7
Loughton, Bucks....34 B6
Loughton, Shrops....31 H1
Loughton, Essex....23 K3
Lound, Lincs....44 D5
Lound, Notts....53 J5
Lound, Suff....47 L7
Lount....43 F5
Louth....55 H5
Love Clough....51 H1
Lover....12 E3
Loversall....53 H4
Loves Green....24 C2
Loveston....26 E6
Lovington....11 G2
Low Bentham....58 B4
Low Bradfield....52 E4
Low Bradley....58 F6
Low Braithwaite....63 K3
Low Brunton....74 F7
Low Burnham....54 B3
Lowca....62 E5
Low Catton....60 E5
Low Coniscliffe....66 C6
Lowdham....43 J2
Low Dinsdale....66 D6
Low Dovengill....64 E8
Low Ellington....59 H2

Lower Aisholt....10 D2
Lower Ashton....9 J7
Lower Assendon....22 C4
Lower Basildon....22 B5
Lower Beeding....15 F3
Lower Benefield....34 C1
Lower Boddington....33 G4
Lower Breinton....31 F6
Lower Bullingham....31 G6
Lower Cam....20 B2
Lower Chapel....29 H6
Lower Chedworth....20 E1
Lower Chute....21 H7
Lower Darwen....51 F1
Lower Diabaig....100 D6
Lower Down....30 E1
Lower Dunsforth....59 K4
Lower Farringdon....13 K2
Lower Frankton....40 E3
Lower Froyle....14 A1
Lower Gledfield....102 D3
Lower Green, Norf....46 E3
Lower Green, Berks....21 H6
Lower Halstow....24 E6
Lower Hardres....25 H7
Lower Heyford....33 G7
Lower Higham....24 D5
Lower Hordley....40 E4
Lower Killeyan....76 B7
Lower Langford....19 J6
Lower Largo....82 C1
Lower Lemington....32 E6
Lower Lye....30 F3
Lower Machen....19 G4
Lower Maes-coed....30 E6
Lower Moor....32 B5
Lower Nazeing....23 J2
Lower Penarth....19 F5
Lower Penn....42 A7
Lower Pennington....13 F6
Lower Peover....51 G6
Lower Quinton....32 D5
Lower Shelton....34 C5
Lower Shiplake....22 C5
Lower Shuckburgh....33 G3
Lower Slaughter....32 D7
Lower Stanton St Quintin....20 D4
Lower Stoke....24 E5
Lower Stondon....34 E6
Lower Sundon....34 D7
Lower Swanwick....13 H5
Lower Swell....32 D7
Lower Thurlton....47 K7
Lower Tysoe....33 F5
Lower Upham....13 H4
Lower Vexford....10 C2
Lower Weare....19 J7
Lower Welson....30 D5
Lower Wield....13 J1
Lower Winchendon or
  Nether Winchendon....22 C1
Lower Woodend....22 D4
Lower Woodford....12 D2
Lowesby....43 K6
Lowestoft....47 L7
Loweswater....63 G5
Lowe Withington....51 H1
Lowford....37 F6
Low Gate....65 G1
Lowgill, Lancs....58 B4
Lowgill, Cumbr....64 D8
Low Ham....11 F3
Low Hesket....64 B3
Low Hesleyhurst....75 G5
Lowick, Northnts....34 C1
Lowick, Cumbr....57 F2
Lowick, Northum....83 J8
Low Leighton....52 C5
Low Mill....60 D1
Low Moor....58 C6
Lownie Moor....89 G4
Lowood....82 D8
Low Row, Cumbr....64 C1
Low Row, N. Yks....65 G8
Lowsonford....32 D3
Lowther....64 C5
Lowthorpe....61 H4
Lowton....51 F4
Lowton Common....51 F4
Low Torry....80 F3
Low Worsall....66 D7
Loxbeare....9 K4
Loxhill....14 D2
Loxhore....9 G2
Loxley....32 E4
Loxton....19 H7
Loxwood....14 D2
Lubenham....33 K1
Luccombe....9 K1
Luccombe Village....7 K7
Lucker....75 H1
Luckett....4 D2
Luckington....20 C4
Lucklawhill....89 G6
Luckwell Bridge....9 K2
Lucton....31 F3
Ludag....90 C4
Ludborough....55 G4
Ludchurch....26 F5
Luddenden....52 C1
Luddesdown....24 C6
Luddington....54 C2
Luddington, Warw....32 D4
Ludford....55 F5
Ludgershall, Bucks....22 B1
Ludgershall, Wilts....21 G7
Ludgvan....2 D6
Ludham....47 J5
Ludlow....31 G2
Ludwell....12 B3
Ludworth....66 D3
Luffincott....8 D6
Lugar....72 A2
Luggate Burn....82 E4
Luggiebank....80 C4

Lugton....79 G6
Lugwardine....31 G5
Luib....92 B3
Lulham....30 F5
Lullington, Somer....20 B7
Lullington, Derby....42 E5
Lulsgate Bottom....19 K6
Lulsley....31 J4
Lulworth Camp....11 K7
Lumb....52 C1
Lumby....60 B7
Lumphanan....96 E5
Lumphinnans....81 G2
Lumsdaine....83 G5
Lumsden....96 D3
Lunan....89 J3
Lunanhead....89 G3
Luncarty....88 C6
Lund, N. Yks....60 D7
Lund, Humbs....61 G6
Lundie....88 E5
Lundin Links....82 C1
Lunna....115 G2
Lunning....115 H2
Lunsford's Cross....16 E4
Lunt....50 C3
Luntley....30 E4
Luppitt....10 C5
Lupton....57 J2
Lurgashall....14 C3
Lusby....55 H7
Luskentyre....98 F3
Luss....79 G2
Lussagiven....77 F3
Lusta....99 H7
Lustleigh....5 H1
Luston....31 F3
Luthermuir....89 J2
Luthrie....89 F7
Luton, Kent....24 D6
Luton, Beds....34 D7
Luton, Devon....5 F4
Lutterworth....33 H1
Lutton, Northnts....34 E1
Lutton, Devon....5 F4
Lutton, Lincs....45 H4
Lutworthy....9 H4
Luxborough....10 A2
Luxulyan....3 J4
Lybster....111 J5
Lydbury North....30 E1
Lydcott....9 G1
Lydd....17 H3
Lydden....17 K1
Lyddington....44 B7
Lydd-on-Sea....17 H3
Lydeard St Lawrence....10 C2
Lydford, Devon....8 F7
Lydford, Somer....11 G2
Lydgate....51 J1
Lydham....40 E7
Lydiard Millicent....20 E4
Lydiate....50 C3
Lydlinch....11 J4
Lydney....19 L2
Lydstep....26 E7
Lye....32 B1
Lye Green....22 E2
Lyford....21 H3
Lymbridge Green....17 J1
Lyme Regis....10 E6
Lyminge....17 J1
Lymington....13 F6
Lyminster....14 D5
Lymm....51 F5
Lymore....12 E6
Lympne....17 J2
Lympsham....19 H7
Lympstone....10 A7
Lynch....95 F5
Lynchat....95 G4
Lyndhurst....13 F5
Lyndon....44 C6
Lyne....22 F6
Lyneal....41 F3
Lyneham, Wilts....20 E5
Lyneham, Oxon....32 E7
Lynemouth....75 J5
Lyne of Gorthleck....94 D3
Lyne of Skene....97 G4
Lyness....112 D7
Lyng, Somer....10 E3
Lyng, Norf....46 F5
Lynmouth....9 H1
Lynsted....25 F6
Lynton....9 H1
Lyon's Gate....11 H5
Lyonshall....30 E4
Lytchett Matravers....12 B6
Lytchett Minster....12 B6
Lyth....111 J2
Lytham....50 C1
Lytham St Anne's....57 G8
Lythe....67 J6
Lythes....112 E8

M

Maaruig....99 H2
Mabe Burnthouse....2 F6
Mabie....72 E7
Mablethorpe....55 K5
Macclesfield....51 J6
Macclesfield Forest....51 J6
Macduff....105 G2
Macharioch....70 C4
Machen....19 G4
Machrihanish....70 B2
Machynlleth....39 G6
Mackworth....43 F3
Macmerry....82 C4
Madderty....88 B6
Maddiston....80 E4
Madehurst....14 C4

Madeley....41 J2
Madeley Heath....41 J2
Madingley....35 G3
Madley....31 F6
Madresfield....31 K5
Madron....2 C6
Maenaddwyn....48 D2
Maenclochog....26 E4
Maendy....18 E5
Maentwrog....39 F2
Maer....41 J3
Maerdy, Clwyd....40 B2
Maerdy, M. Glam....18 D3
Maesbrook....40 E4
Maesbury Marsh....40 E4
Maes-glas....19 H4
Maeshafn....50 B7
Maesllyn....27 H2
Maesmynis....29 H5
Maesteg....18 C3
Maesybont....27 K5
Maesycrugiau....27 J2
Maesycwmmer....18 F3
Magdalen Laver....23 L2
Maggieknockater....104 C4
Magham Down....16 D4
Maghull....50 C3
Magor....19 J4
Maiden Bradley....11 K2
Maidencombe....5 K3
Maidenhead....22 D4
Maiden Law....66 B3
Maiden Newton....11 G6
Maidens....71 H4
Maidenwell....3 K2
Maidford....33 J4
Maids Moreton....33 K6
Maidstone....24 D7
Maidwell....34 A2
Mail....115 G6
Main....94 C2
Mains of Clunas....103 G8
Mains of Drum....97 H6
Mains of Loch....104 C2
Mainstone....30 D1
Maisemore....31 K7
Makerstoun....74 C1
Malborough....5 H6
Malden....24 E2
Malham....58 E2
Mallaig....92 C6
Malltraeth....48 D4
Mallwyd....39 H5
Malmesbury....20 D4
Malmsmead....9 H1
Malpas, Ches....41 F2
Malpas, Corn....3 G5
Malpas, Gwent....19 H3
Maltby, Cleve....66 E6
Maltby, S. Yks....53 H4
Maltby le Marsh....55 J5
Maltman's Hill....17 G1
Malton....60 E3
Malvern Link....31 J5
Malvern Wells....31 J5
Mamble....31 H2
Manaccan....2 F7
Manafon....40 C6
Manaton....5 H1
Mancetter....43 F7
Manchester....51 H4
Mancot....50 C7
Mandally....93 J5
Manea....45 H8
Manfield....66 C5
Mangersta....106 E5
Mangotsfield....20 A5
Manish....99 G4
Mankinholes....51 J1
Manley....50 E6
Manmoel....19 F2
Mannal....84 A4
Manningford Bohune....21 F7
Manningford Bruce....21 F7
Mannings Heath....15 F3
Mannington....12 C5
Manningtree....37 G6
Mannofield....97 J5
Manorbier....26 E7
Manordeilo....27 L4
Manorowen....26 D3
Mansell Gamage....30 E5
Mansell Lacy....31 F5
Mansfield, Strath....72 B3
Mansfield, Notts....53 H7
Mansfield Woodhouse....53 H7
Manston....11 K4
Manswood....12 B5
Manthorpe....44 D5
Manton, Leic....44 B6
Manton, Humbs....54 D3
Manton, Wilts....21 F6
Manuden....35 H7
Maplebeck....54 B7
Maple Cross....22 F3
Mapledurham....22 B5
Mapledurwell....22 B7
Maplehurst....14 E3
Mapperley....43 G2
Mapperton....11 G6
Mappleborough Green....32 C3
Mappleton, Derby....42 D2
Mappleton....61 K6
Mappowder....11 J5
Marazion....2 D6
Marbury....41 G2
March....45 H7
Marcham....21 J3
Marchamley....41 G4
Marchington....42 D3
Marchington Woodlands....42 D4
Marchwiel....40 E2
Marchwood....13 F5
Marcross....18 D6

Marden, Kent....16 E1
Marden, Wilts....20 E7
Marden, H. & W....31 G5
Mardy....19 H1
Marefield....44 A6
Mareham le Fen....55 G7
Mareham on the Hill....55 G7
Maresfield....15 H3
Marfleet....61 J8
Margam....18 B4
Margaret Marsh....11 K4
Margaret Roding....24 B1
Margaretting....24 C2
Margate....25 K5
Margnaheglish....70 F1
Marham....46 C6
Marhamchurch....8 C5
Marholm....44 E6
Marian-glas....48 E2
Mariansleigh....9 H3
Marishader....100 A6
Mark....10 E1
Markbeech....15 H1
Markby....55 J6
Mark Causeway....10 E1
Mark Cross....16 C2
Market Bosworth....43 G6
Market Deeping....44 E5
Market Drayton....41 H3
Market Harborough....33 K1
Markethill....88 E5
Market Lavington....20 E7
Market Overton....44 B5
Market Rasen....54 F5
Market Stainton....55 G6
Market Warsop....53 H7
Market Weighton....61 F6
Market Weston....36 E2
Markfield....43 G5
Markham....19 F2
Markinch....81 H1
Markington....59 H4
Marksbury....20 A6
Marks Tey....36 E7
Markyate....22 F1
Marlborough....21 F6
Marlcliff....32 C4
Marldon....5 J3
Marlesford....37 J4
Marley Green....41 G2
Marlingford....47 G6
Marloes....26 B6
Marlow....22 D4
Marlow Bottom....22 D4
Marlpit Hill....15 H1
Marnhull....11 J4
Marnoch....104 E3
Marnock....80 C5
Marple....51 J5
Marr....53 H3
Marrick....65 H8
Marros....27 G6
Marsden....52 C2
Marsett....58 E2
Marsh....10 D4
Marshalls Heath....23 G1
Marsham....47 G4
Marshaw....57 J5
Marsh Baldon....21 K3
Marshborough....25 K7
Marshbrook....41 F8
Marshchapel....55 H4
Marshfield, Avon....20 B5
Marshfield, Gwent....19 G4
Marshgate....8 B6
Marsh Gibbon....33 J7
Marsh Green, Devon....10 B6
Marsh Green, Kent....15 H1
Marsh Green, Shrops....41 H5
Marshland St James....45 J6
Marshside, Mers....50 C2
Marshside, Kent....25 J6
Marsh, The....40 E7
Marshwood....10 E6
Marske....65 J7
Marske-by-the-Sea....67 G5
Marston, Lincs....44 B2
Marston, Staffs....42 B4
Marston, Wilts....20 D7
Marston, H. & W....30 E4
Marston, Warw....42 E7
Marston, Ches....51 F6
Marston, Oxon....21 K2
Marston, Staffs....41 K5
Marston Green....32 D1
Marston Magna....11 G3
Marston Meysey....20 E3
Marston Montgomery....42 D3
Marston Moretaine....34 C5
Marston on Dove....42 E4
Marston Stannett....31 G4
Marston St Lawrence....33 H5
Marston Trussell....33 J1
Marstow....19 K1
Marsworth....22 E1
Marten....21 G6
Marthall....51 H6
Martham....47 K5
Martin, Hants....12 C4
Martin, Lincs....54 F8
Martindale....64 B6
Martin Dales....55 F7
Martin Drove End....12 C3
Martinhoe....9 G1
Martin Hussingtree....32 A3
Martinscroft....51 F5
Martinstown....11 H7
Martlesham....37 H5
Martlesham Heath....37 H5
Martletwy....26 E5
Martley....31 J3
Martock....11 F4
Marton, Lincs....54 C5
Marton, Shrops....40 D6
Marton, N. Yks....60 E2

Marton, Cleve....66 F6
Marton, Warw....33 G3
Marton, Ches....51 H7
Marton, N. Yks....59 K4
Marvig....107 J7
Marwick....112 C4
Marwood....9 F2
Marybank....102 C7
Maryburgh....102 D7
Marygold....83 G5
Marykirk....89 J2
Marylebone, G. Man....50 E3
Marylebone, G. Lon....23 H4
Marypark....95 K2
Maryport, D. & G....68 C7
Maryport, Cumbr....62 F4
Marystow....8 E7
Mary Tavy....4 F2
Maryton....89 J3
Marywell, Grampn....96 E6
Marywell, Tays....89 J4
Masham....59 H2
Mashbury....24 C1
Masongill....58 B3
Mastrick....97 J5
Matching....23 L1
Matching Green....23 L1
Matching Tye....23 L1
Matfen....75 G7
Matfield....16 D1
Mathern....19 K3
Mathon....31 J5
Mathry....26 C3
Matlaske....47 G3
Matlock....53 F7
Matlock Bath....52 E8
Matson....20 C1
Matterdale End....64 B6
Mattersey....53 J5
Mattingley....22 C7
Mattishall....46 F5
Mattishall Burgh....46 F5
Mauchline....71 K2
Maud....105 J4
Maugersbury....32 E7
Maughold....56 R2
Maulden....34 D6
Maulds Meaburn....64 D6
Maunby....59 J2
Maund Bryan....31 G4
Mautby....47 K5
Mavesyn Ridware....42 C5
Mavis Enderby....55 H7
Mawbray....63 F3
Mawdesley....50 D2
Mawgan....2 F7
Mawla....2 F5
Mawnan....3 F7
Mawnan Smith....2 F7
Maxey....44 E6
Maxstoke....32 E1
Maxton....74 C1
Maxwellheugh....74 D1
Maybole....71 H4
Mayfield, E. Susx....16 C3
Mayfield, Staffs....42 D2
Mayfield, Surrey....22 F7
Mayfield, Loth....81 H3
Mayford....22 E7
Mayland....24 F2
Maypole....19 J1
Maypole Green....47 K5
Maywick....115 F6
Meadle....22 D2
Meadowtown....40 E6
Meal Bank....57 J1
Mealista....106 D6
Mealsgate....63 H3
Mearbeck....58 D4
Mearbrook....58 D4
Meare....11 F1
Meare Green....10 E3
Mears Ashby....34 B3
Measham....43 F5
Meathop....57 H2
Meaux....61 H7
Meavag....99 G3
Meavaig....99 F2
Meavy....4 F3
Medbourne....44 B7
Medburn....75 H7
Meddon....8 C4
Meden Vale....53 H7
Medmenham....22 D4
Medstead....13 J2
Meerbrook....51 J7
Meer End....32 E2
Meesden....35 H6
Meeth....9 F5
Meggethead....73 G2
Meidrim....27 G4
Meifod....40 C5
Meigle....88 D4
Meikle Earnock....80 C6
Meikleour....88 D5
Meikle Tarty....97 J3
Meikle Wartle....97 G2
Meinciau....27 J5
Meir....42 B2
Meir Heath....42 B2
Melbost....107 J3
Melbost Borve....107 J3
Melbourn....35 G5
Melbourne, Humbs....60 E6
Melbourne, Derby....43 F4
Melbury Abbas....12 A3
Melbury Bubb....11 G5
Melbury Osmond....11 G5
Melby....114 D3
Melchbourne....34 D3
Melcombe Bingham....11 J5
Meldon, Devon....9 F6
Meldon, Northum....75 H6
Meldreth....35 G5
Melfort....85 K7

Melgarve 94 C6
Meliden 49 K2
Melincourt 18 C2
Melin-y-coed 49 H4
Melin-y-ddol 40 B6
Melin-y-grug 40 B6
Melin-y-Wig 40 B2
Melkinthorpe 64 C5
Melkridge 64 E1
Melksham 20 D6
Melldalloch 77 J4
Melling, Mers. 50 C3
Melling, Lancs. 57 K3
Mellis 37 G2
Mellon Charles 100 E3
Mellon Udrigle 100 E3
Mellor, Lancs. 58 B7
Mellor, G. Man. 51 J5
Mellor Brook 58 B7
Mells, Somer. 11 J1
Mells, Suff. 37 K2
Melmerby, Cumbr. 64 D4
Melmerby, N. Yks. 59 F2
Melmerby, N. Yks. 59 J3
Melplash 11 F6
Melrose 74 B1
Melsonby 66 B7
Meltham 52 C2
Melton 37 H4
Meltonby 60 E5
Melton Constable 46 F3
Melton Mowbray 44 A5
Melton Ross 54 E2
Melvaig 100 D4
Melverley 40 E5
Melvich 110 E2
Membury 10 D5
Memsie 105 J2
Menai Bridge 48 E3
Mendham 37 H1
Mendlesham 37 G3
Mendlesham Green 37 F3
Menheniot 4 C3
Mennock 72 D4
Menston 59 G6
Menstrie 80 D2
Mentmore 22 E1
Meole Brace 41 F5
Meonstoke 13 J4
Meopham 24 C6
Meopham Station 24 C6
Mepal 35 H1
Meppershall 34 E6
Merbach 30 E5
Mere, Ches. 51 G5
Mere, Wilts. 11 K2
Mere Brow 50 D2
Mereclough 58 D7
Mere Green 42 D7
Mereworth 24 C7
Mergie 97 G7
Meriden 32 E1
Merkadale 91 J2
Merley 12 C6
Merlin's Bridge 26 D5
Merrington 41 F4
Merriott 11 F4
Merrivale 4 F2
Merrymeet 4 C3
Mersham 17 H2
Merstham 23 H7
Merston 14 B5
Merstone 13 H7
Merther 3 G5
Merthyr 27 H4
Merthyr Cynog 29 G6
Merthyr Dyfan 18 F5
Merthyr Mawr 18 C5
Merthyr Tydfil 18 E2
Merthyr Vale 18 E3
Merton, Norf. 46 E7
Merton, Devon 9 F4
Merton, G. Lon. 23 H6
Merton, Oxon. 21 K1
Mervinslaw 74 C3
Meshaw 9 H4
Messing 24 E1
Messingham 54 C3
Metfield 37 H1
Metheringham 54 E7
Methil 81 J2
Methley 53 F1
Methlick 97 H2
Methven 88 C6
Methwold 46 C7
Methwold Hythe 46 C7
Mettingham 47 J8
Mevagissey 3 J5
Mexborough 53 G3
Mey 111 J1
Meysey Hampton 20 F2
Miavaig 106 E5
Michael 56 D2
Michaelchurch 31 E7
Michaelchurch Escley 30 E6
Michaelchurch-on-Arrow 30 D4
Michaelstone-y-Fedw 19 G4
Michaelston-le-Pit 18 F5
Michaelstow 3 J2
Micheldever 13 F3
Michelmersh 13 F3
Mickfield 37 G3
Mickleby 67 J6
Micklefield 59 K7
Mickleham 23 G7
Mickleover 43 F3
Mickleton, Glos. 32 G5
Mickleton, Durham 65 H6
Mickley 59 H3
Mickley Square 65 H1
Mid Ardlaw 105 J2
Midbea 112 E4
Mid Beltie 96 F5
Mid Culbeuchly 104 F2

Middle Assendon 22 C4
Middle Aston 33 G7
Middle Barton 33 G7
Middlebie 73 H7
Middle Claydon 33 K7
Middleham 59 G2
Middlehope 31 F1
Middle Littleton 32 C5
Middle Maes-coed 30 E6
Middlemarsh 11 H5
Middle Mill 26 C4
Middle Rasen 54 E5
Middlesbrough 66 E5
Middlesmoor 59 F3
Middleston Moor 66 C4
Middlestown 52 E2
Middleton, Strath. 84 A4
Middleton, Norf. 46 B5
Middleton, Northnts. 44 B7
Middleton, Essex 36 D6
Middleton, Warw. 42 D7
Middleton, Shrops. 40 D7
Middleton, Derby 52 D7
Middleton, Derby 42 E1
Middleton, N. Yks. 60 E2
Middleton, Shrops. 40 E4
Middleton, Hants. 13 G1
Middleton, Northum. 75 G2
Middleton, Shrops. 31 G2
Middleton, H. & W. 31 G3
Middleton, Northum. 75 G6
Middleton, N. Yks. 59 G6
Middleton, G. Man. 51 H3
Middleton, Lancs. 57 H5
Middleton, Loth. 81 J6
Middleton, W. Yks. 59 J4
Middleton, Cumbr. 57 K2
Middleton, Suff. 37 K3
Middleton, Northum. 83 K8
Middleton Cheney 33 G5
Middleton Green 42 B3
Middleton Hall 75 F2
Middleton-in-Teesdale 65 G5
Middleton-on-Sea 14 C6
Middleton on the Hill 31 G3
Middleton-on-the-Wolds 61 G6
Middleton Priors 41 H7
Middleton Scriven 31 H1
Middleton St George 66 D6
Middleton Stoney 33 H7
Middleton Tyas 66 C7
Middletown 40 E5
Middle Tysoe 33 F5
Middle Wallop 12 E2
Middlewich 51 G7
Middle Winterslow 12 E2
Middle Woodford 12 D2
Middlewood Green 37 F3
Middlezoy 10 E2
Middridge 66 C5
Midfield 109 G2
Midge Hall 50 E1
Midgeholme 64 D2
Midgham 21 K6
Midgley 52 C1
Midhopestones 52 E4
Midhurst 14 B3
Midlem 74 B2
Midsomer Norton 20 A7
Midtown 100 E4
Midtown of Buchromb 104 C4
Midville 45 G1
Mid Walls 114 E3
Mid Yell 117 G3
Migvie 96 D5
Milborne Port 11 H4
Milborne St Andrew 11 K6
Milborne Wick 11 H3
Milbourne 75 H7
Milburn 64 D5
Milbury Heath 20 A3
Milcombe 33 G6
Milden 36 E5
Mildenhall, Suff. 36 C2
Mildenhall, Wilts. 21 G6
Milebrooke 30 E2
Milebush 16 E1
Mile Elm 20 D6
Mile End, Essex 36 E7
Mile End, Glos. 19 K1
Mileham 46 E5
Milesmark 81 F5
Milfield 75 F1
Milford, Staffs. 42 B4
Milford, Surrey 14 C1
Milford, Devon 8 C3
Milford, Derby 43 F2
Milford Haven 26 D6
Milford on Sea 12 E6
Milkwall 19 K2
Milland 14 B3
Mill Bank 52 C1
Millbounds 113 F3
Millbreck 105 K4
Millbrex 105 H4
Millbridge 14 B1
Millbrook, Beds. 34 D6
Millbrook, Corn. 4 E4
Millbrook, Hants. 13 F4
Millburn 71 K2
Mill Corner 16 F3
Mill End, Bucks. 22 C4
Mill End, Herts. 35 G6
Millerhill 81 J5
Miller's Dale 52 D6
Mill Green, Essex 24 C2
Mill Green, Shrops. 41 H4
Millheugh 80 C6
Mill Hill 23 H3
Millholme 57 J1
Millhouse, Strath. 77 J4
Millhouse, Cumbr. 63 J4
Millikenpark 79 G5
Millington 60 F5
Mill Lane 22 C7

Millmeece 41 K3
Millom 56 E2
Millport 78 D6
Mill Side 57 H2
Mill Street 46 F5
Milltrop 58 B1
Milltimber 97 H5
Milton of Corsindale 97 F5
Milton of Murtle 97 H5
Milltown, Devon 9 G4
Milltown, Derby 53 F7
Milltown, D. & G. 73 J7
Milltown of Aberdalgie 88 C6
Milltown of Auchindoun 96 C1
Milltown of Craigston 105 G3
Milltown of Edinvillie 96 B1
Milltown of Rothiemay 104 E4
Milltown of Towie 96 D4
Milnathort 88 D8
Milngavie 79 H4
Milnrow 51 J2
Milnthorpe 57 H2
Milovaig 99 G7
Milson 31 H2
Milstead 24 F7
Milston 12 D1
Milton, Staffs. 42 B1
Milton, Cumbr. 64 C1
Milton, Highld. 94 C2
Milton, D. & G. 68 D5
Milton, D. & G. 72 D7
Milton, Highld. 102 D8
Milton, Grampn. 104 E2
Milton, Dyfed 26 C6
Milton, Highld. 103 F5
Milton, Strath. 79 G4
Milton, Oxon. 33 G6
Milton, Central 79 H1
Milton, Cambs. 35 H3
Milton, Highld. 103 H7
Milton, Oxon. 21 J3
Milton, Highld. 111 K3
Milton, Highld. 101 K7
Milton Abbas 11 K5
Milton Abbot 4 E2
Milton Bridge 81 H5
Milton Bryan 34 C6
Milton Clevedon 11 H2
Milton Coldwells 97 J2
Milton Combe 4 E3
Milton Damerel 8 D4
Miltonduff 103 K6
Milton Ernest 34 D4
Milton Green 50 D8
Milton Hill 21 J3
Milton Keynes 34 B6
Milton Keynes Village 34 B6
Milton Libourne 21 F6
Milton Malsor 33 K4
Milton of Auchinhove 96 E5
Milton of Balgonie 81 J1
Milton of Buchanan 79 G2
Milton of Campfield 97 F5
Milton of Campsie 79 A4
Milton of Corsindae 97 F5
Milton of Cushnie 96 E4
Milton of Lesmore 96 D3
Milton of Murtle 97 H5
Milton of Tullich 96 C6
Milton on Stour 11 K3
Milton Regis 24 F6
Milton-under-Wychwood 21 G1
Milverton 10 C3
Milwich 42 B3
Milwr 50 A5
Minard 78 B2
Minchinhampton 20 C2
Mindrum 74 E1
Minehead 10 A1
Minera 40 D1
Minety 20 E3
Minffordd 38 E3
Mingary 90 C3
Miningsby 55 H7
Minions 4 C2
Minishant 71 J3
Minllyn 39 H5
Minnes 97 J3
Minnigaff 71 K8
Minskip 59 J4
Minstead 12 E4
Minster, Kent 25 F5
Minster, Kent 25 K6
Minsteracres 65 H2
Minsterley 40 E6
Minster Lovell 21 H1
Minsterworth 20 B1
Minterne Magna 11 H5
Minting 55 F6
Mintlaw 105 K4
Minto 74 B2
Minton 41 F7
Minwear 26 E5
Minworth 42 D7
Mirbister 112 D4
Mireland 111 K2
Mirfield 52 E2
Miserden 20 D2
Miskin 18 E4
Misson 53 J4
Misterton, Notts. 54 B4
Misterton, Somer. 11 F5
Misterton, Leic. 33 H1
Mistley 37 G6
Mitcham 23 H6
Mitcheldean 20 A1
Mitchel 3 G4
Mitchel Troy 19 J1
Mitford 75 H6
Mithian 2 F4
Mithian 42 A5
Mixbury 33 J6
Mixon 42 C1
Mobberley 51 G6
Moccas 30 E5

Mochdre, Powys 29 H1
Mochdre, Clwyd 49 H3
Mochrum 68 E6
Mockbeggar 12 D3
Mockerkin 63 F5
Modbury 5 G4
Moddershall 42 B3
Moelfre, Clwyd 40 C4
Moelfre, Gwyn. 48 E2
Moffat 73 F4
Mogerhanger 34 E5
Moira 43 F5
Molash 25 G7
Mol-chlach 91 K4
Mold 50 B7
Molehill Green 35 J7
Molescroft 61 H6
Molesworth 34 D2
Molland 9 J3
Mollington, Ches. 50 C6
Mollington, Oxon. 33 G5
Mollinsburn 80 C4
Mondynes 97 G8
Monewden 37 H4
Moniaive 72 C5
Monifieth 89 G5
Monikie 89 G5
Monimail 88 E7
Monington 26 F2
Monken Hadley 23 H3
Monk Fryston 60 D8
Monkhopton 41 H7
Monkland 31 E4
Monkleigh 8 E3
Monknash 18 D5
Monkokehampton 9 G5
Monks Eleigh 36 E5
Monk's Heath 51 H6
Monk Sherborne 21 L7
Monkshill 97 G1
Monksilver 10 B2
Monks Kirby 33 G1
Monk Soham 37 H3
Monks Risborough 22 D2
Monkswood 19 K1
Monkton, Devon 10 C5
Monkton, T. & W. 66 D1
Monkton, Strath. 71 J2
Monkton, Kent 25 J6
Monkton Combe 20 B6
Monkton Deverill 11 K2
Monkton Farleigh 20 B6
Monkton Heathfield 10 D3
Monkton Up Wimborne 12 C4
Monkwood 13 J2
Monmore 19 K1
Monmouth 19 K1
Monnington on Wye 30 E5
Monreith 68 E6
Monreith Mains 68 E6
Montacute 11 F3
Montford 41 F5
Montgarrie 96 E4
Montgomery 40 D7
Montgreenan 79 F7
Montrose 89 K3
Montsale 25 G3
Monxton 13 F1
Monyash 52 D7
Monymusk 97 F4
Monzie 88 A6
Moorby 55 G7
Moorcot 30 E4
Moordown 12 C6
Moore 50 E5
Moorends 53 J2
Moorhall 53 F6
Moorhampton 30 E5
Moorhouse, Notts. 54 B7
Moorhouse, Cumbr. 63 J7
Moorland or Northmoor Green 10 E2
Moorlinch 10 E2
Moor of Balvack 97 F4
Moorsholm 66 E5
Moorside 51 J3
Moor, The 16 E3
Moortown, Lincs. 54 E4
Moortown, I. of W. 13 G7
Morangie 103 F4
Morar 92 C6
Morborne 44 E7
Morchard Bishop 9 H5
Morcombelake 10 F6
Morcott 44 C6
Morda 40 D4
Morden, Dorset 12 B6
Morden, G. Lon. 23 H6
Mordiford 31 G6
Mordon 66 D5
More 40 E7
Morebath 9 K3
Morebattle 74 D2
Morecambe 57 H4
More Crichel 12 B5
Morefield 101 H3
Moreleigh 5 H4
Moresby 62 E5
Moresby Parks 62 E6
Morestead 13 H3
Moreton, Oxon. 22 B2
Moreton, Mers. 50 B4
Moreton, Staffs. 41 J5
Moreton, Dorset 11 K7
Moreton, Essex 23 L2
Moreton Corbet 41 G4
Moretonhampstead 9 H7
Moreton-in-Marsh 32 E6
Moreton Jeffries 31 H5
Moreton Morrell 33 F4
Moreton on Lugg 31 G5
Moreton Pinkney 33 H5
Moreton Say 41 H3
Moreton Valence 20 B2
Morfa Bychan 38 B2
Morfa Glas 18 C2
Morfa Nefyn 38 B2

Morgan's Vale 12 D3
Morland 64 C5
Morley, W. Yks. 52 E1
Morley, Derby 43 F2
Morley, Durham 65 J5
Morley Green 51 H5
Morley St Botolph 46 F7
Morningside 81 H4
Morningthorpe 47 H7
Morpeth 75 H6
Morrey 42 D5
Morriston 27 L7
Morston 46 F2
Morthoe 8 E1
Mortimer 22 B6
Mortimer's Cross 31 F3
Mortimer West End 22 B6
Mortlake 23 H5
Morton, Lincs. 54 C4
Morton, Lincs. 44 D4
Morton, Shrops. 40 D4
Morton, Norf. 47 G5
Morton, Derby 53 G7
Morton, Avon 19 L3
Morton Bagot 32 D3
Morton-on-Swale 59 J1
Morval 2 C4
Morvah 4 C4
Morvich, Highld. 103 F2
Morvich, Highld. 93 F3
Morville 41 H7
Morwenstow 8 C4
Mosborough 53 G5
Moscow 79 G7
Mosedale 63 J4
Moseley, W. Mids. 32 C1
Moseley, H. & W. 31 K4
Moss, Strath. 84 A4
Moss, Clwyd 40 E1
Moss, S. Yks. 53 H2
Mossat 96 D4
Mossbank, Shetld. 117 F5
Moss Bank, Mers. 50 E4
Mossblown 71 K2
Mossburnford 74 C3
Mossdale 72 B7
Mossend 80 C5
Mossgiel 71 K2
Mossley 51 J3
Moss of Barmuckity 104 B2
Moss Side 57 G7
Mosstodloch 104 C2
Mosterton 11 F5
Mostyn 50 A5
Motcombe 11 K3
Motherwell 80 C6
Mottingham 23 K5
Mottisfont 13 F2
Mottistone 13 G7
Mottram in Longdendale 51 J4
Mottram St Andrew 51 H6
Mouldsworth 50 E6
Moulin 88 B3
Moulsecoomb 15 G5
Moulsford 21 K4
Moulsoe 34 C5
Moulton, Northnts. 34 A3
Moulton, Suff. 36 B3
Moulton, N. Yks. 66 C7
Moulton, Ches. 51 F7
Moulton, Lincs. 45 G4
Moulton Chapel 45 F4
Moulton Seas End 45 G4
Mount, Corn. 3 F4
Mount, Corn. 3 K3
Mountain Ash 18 E3
Mountain Cross 81 G7
Mountbenger 73 J2
Mount Bures 36 E6
Mountfield 16 E3
Mountgerald 102 D6
Mount Hawke 2 F5
Mountjoy 3 G3
Mountnessing 24 C3
Mounton 19 K3
Mountsorrel 43 H5
Mousehole 2 C7
Mousen 75 H1
Mouswald 73 F7
Mow Cop, Staffs. 42 A1
Mow Cop, Ches. 42 A1
Mowhaugh 74 E2
Mowsley 43 J8
Moy 94 C7
Moyles Court 12 D5
Moylgrove 26 F2
Muasdale 77 F7
Muchalls 97 J6
Much Birch 31 G6
Much Cowarne 31 H5
Much Dewchurch 31 F6
Muchelney 11 F3
Much Hadham 35 H7
Much Hoole 50 D1
Muchlarnick 4 C4
Much Marcle 31 H6
Much Wenlock 41 H7
Mucking 24 C4
Mucklestone 41 J3
Muckleford 11 G6
Muckletown 96 E3
Muckton 55 H5
Mudale 109 G5
Muddiford 9 F2
Mudford 11 G1
Mudgley 11 F1
Mugdock 79 H4
Mugeary 91 K2
Muggington 42 E2
Muggleswick 65 H2
Muie 102 E2
Muir 95 J7
Muirden 105 G3
Muirdrum 89 H5

Muirhead, Strath. 80 B5
Muirhead, Tays. 89 F5
Muirhouses 80 F3
Muirkirk 72 B2
Muir of Fairburn 102 C7
Muir of Fowlis 96 E4
Muir of Lochs 104 C2
Muir of Ord 102 D7
Muirshearlich 93 H7
Muirtack, Grampn. 105 H4
Muirtack, Grampn. 97 J2
Muirton, Tays. 88 B7
Muirton, Tays. 88 F6
Muirton, Highld. 103 F6
Muirton of Ardblair 88 D4
Muirton of Ballochy 89 J2
Muker 65 G8
Mulbarton 47 G6
Mulben 104 C3
Mullion 2 E8
Mullion Cove 2 E8
Mumbles, The 27 L8
Mumby 55 K6
Munderfield Row 31 H4
Munderfield Stocks 31 H4
Mundesley 47 J3
Mundford 46 D7
Mundham, W. Susx 14 B5
Mundham, Norf. 47 J7
Mundon 24 E2
Munerigie 93 J5
Mungasdale 101 F3
Mungrisdale 63 J4
Munlochy 102 E7
Munsley 31 H5
Munslow 31 G1
Murch 18 F5
Murcott 21 K1
Murkle 111 H2
Murlaggan, Highld. 93 G6
Murlaggan, Highld. 93 K7
Murrow 45 G6
Mursley 34 B7
Murthly 88 C5
Murton, Durham 66 D3
Murton, N. Yks. 60 D5
Murton, Cumbr. 64 E5
Murton, Northum. 83 H7
Musbury 10 D6
Muscoates 60 D2
Musdale 86 B6
Musselburgh 81 J4
Muston, Leic. 44 B3
Muston, N. Yks. 61 H3
Mustow Green 32 A2
Mutford 37 K1
Muthill 88 A7
Muirton 10 B5
Mybster 111 H3
Myddfai 28 E6
Myddle 41 F4
Mydroilyn 28 B4
Mylor Bridge 3 G6
Mynachlog-ddu 26 F3
Myndtown 40 E8
Mynydd-bach 19 J3
Mynydd Isa 50 B7
Mynydd Llandegai 48 F4
Mynydd Mechell 48 C1
Mynytho 38 C3
Myrebird 97 G6
Mytchett 22 D7
Mytholm 51 J1
Mytholmroyd 52 C1
Myton-on-Swale 59 K4

N

Naast 100 E4
Naburn 60 D6
Nackington 25 H7
Nacton 37 H5
Nafferton 61 H5
Nailsea 19 J5
Nailstone 43 G6
Nailsworth 20 C3
Nairn 103 G7
Nancegollan 2 E6
Nancledra 2 C6
Nanhoron 38 B3
Nannerch 50 A7
Nanpantan 43 H5
Nanpean 3 H4
Nanstallon 3 J3
Nant-ddu 18 E1
Nanternis 28 A4
Nantgaredig 27 J4
Nantgarw 18 F4
Nant Glas 29 G3
Nantglyn 49 K4
Nantlle 38 E1
Nantmawr 40 D4
Nantmel 29 H3
Nantmor 38 F2
Nant Peris 48 F5
Nantwich 41 H1
Nant-y-derry 19 H2
Nantyffyllon 18 C3
Nantyglo 19 F1
Nant-y-moel 18 D3
Naphill 22 D3
Nappa 58 D5
Napton on the Hill 33 G3
Narberth 26 F5
Narborough, Norf. 46 C5
Narborough, Leic. 43 H7
Nasareth 38 D1
Naseby 33 J2
Nash, Bucks. 34 A6
Nash, H. & W. 30 E3
Nash, Shrops. 31 H4
Nash, Gwent 19 H4
Nash Lee 22 D2
Nassington 44 D7

Nasty....35 G7
Nateby, Cumbr....64 E7
Nateby, Lancs....57 H6
Natland....57 J2
Naughton....36 F5
Naunton, H. & W....32 A6
Naunton, Glos....32 D7
Naunton Beauchamp....32 B4
Navenby....44 C1
Navestock Heath....23 L3
Navestock Side....24 B3
Nawton....60 D2
Nayland....36 E6
Nazeing....23 K2
Neacroft....12 D6
Neal's Green....33 F1
Neasham....66 D4
Neath....18 B3
Neatishead....47 J4
Nebo, Dyfed....28 C3
Nebo, Gwyn....38 D1
Nebo, Gwyn....39 H1
Necton....46 D6
Nedd....108 C5
Nedging Tye....36 F5
Needham....37 H1
Needham Market....37 F4
Needingworth....35 G2
Neen Savage....31 H2
Neen Sollars....31 H2
Neenton....31 H1
Nefyn....38 C2
Neilston....79 G6
Nelson, Lancs....58 D7
Nelson, M. Glam....18 F3
Nelson Village....75 J7
Nemphlar....80 D7
Nempnett Thrubwell....19 K6
Nenthead....64 E3
Nenthorn....82 E8
Nerabus....76 B6
Nercwys....50 B7
Nerston....79 J6
Nesbit....75 F1
Ness, Ches....50 C6
Ness, N. Yks....60 D3
Nesscliffe....40 E5
Neston, Ches....50 B6
Neston, Wilts....20 C6
Nether Alderley....51 H6
Netheravon....12 D1
Nether Blainslie....82 D7
Netherbrae....105 G3
Nether Broughton....43 J4
Netherburn....80 D7
Nether Burrow....57 K3
Netherbury....11 F6
Nether Cerne....11 H6
Nether Compton....11 G4
Nether Dallachy....104 C2
Netherend....19 K2
Nether Exe....9 K5
Netherfield....16 E4
Netherhampton....12 D3
Nether Haugh....53 G4
Nether Heyford....33 J4
Nether Howcleuch....73 F3
Nether Kellet....57 J4
Nether Kinmundy....105 K4
Nether Kirkton....79 G6
Netherlaw....69 J6
Netherley....97 H6
Nethermill....73 F6
Nether Padley....52 E6
Netherplace....79 H6
Nether Poppleton....60 C5
Nether Ringorm....104 B4
Nether Row....63 J4
Netherseal....42 E5
Nether Silton....59 K1
Nether Stowey....10 C2
Netherthird....72 A3
Netherthong....52 D3
Netherton, H. & W....32 B5
Netherton, Mers....50 C3
Netherton, W. Yks....52 E2
Netherton, Northum....75 F4
Netherton, Tays....89 H3
Netherton, Central....79 H4
Netherton, Devon....5 J2
Nethertown, Cumbr....62 E7
Nethertown, Highld....111 K1
Nether Wallop....13 F2
Nether Wasdale....63 G7
Nether Whitacre....42 E7
Nether Winchendon or
  Lower Winchendon....22 C1
Netherwitton....75 G5
Nether Worton....33 G6
Nethy Bridge....95 J3
Netley....13 G5
Netley Marsh....13 F4
Nettlebed....22 C4
Nettlebridge....11 H1
Nettlecombe....11 G6
Nettleden....22 F1
Nettleham....54 E6
Nettlestead....24 C7
Nettlestead Green....24 C7
Nettlestone....13 J6
Nettleton, Wilts....20 C5
Nettleton, Lincs....54 F3
Neuk, The....97 G6
Nevendon....24 D3
Nevern....26 E2
New Abbey....72 E8
New Aberdour....105 H2
New Addington....23 J6
New Alresford....13 H2
New Alyth....88 E4
Newark, Orkney....113 H2
Newark, Cambs....45 F6
Newark-on-Trent....44 A1
Newarthill....80 C6
New Ash Green....24 C6

New Barn....24 C6
New Bewick....75 G2
Newbiggin, Cumbr....64 B5
Newbiggin, Cumbr....64 C3
Newbiggin, Cumbr....64 D5
Newbiggin, N. Yks....58 E1
Newbiggin, N. Yks....58 E2
Newbiggin, Cumbr....57 F4
Newbiggin, Durham....65 G5
Newbiggin-by-the-Sea....75 K6
Newbigging, Strath....88 E4
Newbigging, Tays....80 F7
Newbigging, Tays....89 G5
Newbigging, Tays....89 G5
Newbiggin-on-Lune....64 E7
Newbold, Derby....53 F6
Newbold, Leic....43 G5
Newbold on Avon....33 G2
Newbold-on-Stour....32 E5
Newbold Pacey....32 E4
Newbold Verdon....43 G6
New Bolingbroke....45 G1
Newborough, Staffs....42 D4
Newborough, Cambs....45 F6
Newbottle....33 H6
Newbourne....37 H5
New Brancepeth....66 C3
Newbridge, Corn....2 C6
Newbridge, Clwyd....40 D2
Newbridge, Hants....12 E4
Newbridge, Gwent....19 G3
Newbridge, Loth....81 G4
Newbridge, I. of W....13 G7
Newbridge-on-Usk....19 H3
Newbridge-on-Wye....29 H4
New Brighton....50 C4
New Brinsley....43 G1
Newbrough....74 E8
New Buckenham....47 F7
Newbuildings....9 H5
Newburgh, Lancs....50 D2
Newburgh, Fife....88 E7
Newburgh, Grampn....97 J3
Newburn....66 B1
Newbury....21 J6
Newby, N. Yks....58 C3
Newby, Cumbr....64 C5
Newby, N. Yks....58 F6
Newby Bridge....57 G2
Newby East....64 B2
New Byth....105 H3
Newby West....63 J2
Newby Wiske....59 J2
Newcastle, Shrops....30 D1
Newcastle, Gwent....19 J1
Newcastle Emlyn....27 F2
Newcastleton....74 A6
Newcastle-under-Lyme....42 A2
Newcastle upon Tyne....66 C1
Newchapel, Staffs....42 A1
Newchapel, Surrey....15 G1
Newchapel, Dyfed....27 G3
New Cheriton....13 H3
Newchurch, Powys....30 D4
Newchurch, Kent....17 H2
Newchurch, Dyfed....27 H4
Newchurch, I. of W....13 H7
Newchurch, Gwent....19 J3
Newchurch in Pendle....58 D7
New Clipstone....53 H7
New Costessey....47 G6
Newcott....10 D5
New Cross....28 D2
New Cumnock....72 B3
New Deer....105 H4
Newdigate....15 E1
New Duston....33 K3
New Earswick....60 D5
New Edlington....53 H4
New Ellerby....61 J7
Newell Green....22 D5
New Eltham....23 K5
New End....32 D3
Newenden....16 F3
Newent....31 J7
New Farnley....59 H7
New Ferry....50 C5
Newfield, Durham....66 C4
Newfield, Highld....103 F5
New Fryston....53 G1
Newgale....26 C4
New Galloway....72 B7
Newgate....46 F2
Newgate Street....23 J2
New Grimsby....2 N2
Newhall, Derby....42 E4
Newhall, Ches....41 H2
Newham....75 H2
Newham Hall....75 H2
New Hartley....75 K7
Newhaven....15 H5
New Hedges....26 F6
Newhey....51 J2
New Holland....54 E1
Newholm....67 J6
New Horndean....83 G7
New Houghton, Norf....46 C4
New Houghton, Derby....53 G7
Newhouse....80 C5
New Houses....58 D3
New Hutton....57 J1
New Hythe....24 D7
Newick....15 H3
Newington, Kent....24 E6
Newington, Kent....17 J2
Newington, Oxon....21 L3
New Inn, Gwent....19 H3
New Inn, Gwent....19 J2
New Inn, Dyfed....27 J3
New Invention....30 D2
New Kelso....101 F8
New Lanark....80 D7
Newland, N. Yks....53 J1
Newland, H. & W....31 J5
Newland, Glos....19 K2

Newlandrig....81 J5
Newlands, Grampn....104 C3
Newlands, Highld....103 F8
Newlands, Northum....65 H2
Newlands of Geise....111 G2
New Lane....50 D2
New Leake....45 H1
New Leeds....105 J3
New Longton....50 E1
New Luce....68 C2
Newlyn....2 C7
Newmachar....97 H4
New Malden....23 H6
Newmains....80 D6
New Marske....67 G5
New Marton....40 E3
Newmill, Border....74 B3
New Mill, Corn....2 C6
Newmill, Grampn....104 D3
New Mill, W. Yks....52 D3
New Mill, Herts....22 E1
Newmill of Inshewan....89 G2
New Mills, Powys....40 B6
New Mills, Ches....51 G5
New Mills, Corn....3 H4
New Mills, Derby....51 J5
New Mills, Gwent....19 K2
Newmiln....88 D5
Newmilns....79 H8
New Milton....12 E6
New Moat....26 E4
Newnham, Glos....20 A1
Newnham, Hants....22 C7
Newnham, Herts....35 F6
Newnham, Kent....25 F7
Newnham, H. & W....31 H3
Newnham, Northnts....33 H4
New Ollerton....53 J7
New Pitsligo....105 H3
New Polzeath....3 H2
Newport, Glos....20 B3
Newport, Dyfed....26 E3
Newport, Devon....9 F2
Newport, Humbs....60 F7
Newport, Gwent....19 H4
Newport, Highld....111 H4
Newport, I. of W....13 H7
Newport, Shrops....41 J5
Newport, Essex....35 J6
Newport, Norf....47 L5
Newport-on-Tay....89 G6
Newport Pagnell....34 B5
Newpound Common....14 D3
New Quay, Dyfed....28 A4
Newquay, Corn....3 G3
New Rackheath....47 H5
New Radnor....30 D3
New Romney....17 H3
New Rossington....53 J4
New Row....58 B7
New Sauchie....80 D2
New Scone....88 D6
Newseat....97 G2
Newsham, N. Yks....65 J6
Newsham, Northum....75 K7
Newsholme, Lancs....58 D5
Newsholme, Humbs....60 E8
New Silksworth....66 D2
Newstead, Border....74 B1
Newstead, Notts....43 H1
Newstead, Northum....75 H2
New Stevenston....80 C6
Newthorpe....60 B7
New Tolsta....107 K4
Newton, Northnts....34 B1
Newton, Border....74 B2
Newton, Lancs....58 B5
Newton, Strath....78 C2
Newton, Staffs....42 C4
Newton, M. Glam....18 C5
Newton, Lincs....44 D3
Newton, W. Isles....98 D5
Newton, Norf....46 D5
Newton, Strath....72 E1
Newton, Wilts....12 E3
Newton, Suff....36 E5
Newton, Ches....50 E6
Newton, H. & W....30 E6
Newton, Ches....50 E8
Newton, Cumbr....57 F3
Newton, Loth....81 F4
Newton, Highld....103 F6
Newton, Highld....103 F8
Newton, H. & W....31 G4
Newton, S. Glam....19 G5
Newton, D. & G....73 G5
Newton, Northum....65 H1
Newton, Warw....33 H2
Newton, Cambs....35 H5
Newton, Cambs....45 H5
Newton, Lancs....57 J3
Newton, Strath....79 J5
Newton, Highld....111 K4
Newton, Grampn....103 K6
Newton, W. Glam....27 L8
Newton Abbot....5 J2
Newton Arlosh....63 G2
Newton Aycliffe....66 C5
Newton Bewley....66 E5
Newton Blossomville....34 C4
Newton Bromswold....34 C3
Newton Burgoland....43 F6
Newton by Toft....54 E5

Newton Mearns....79 H6
Newtonmore....94 F6
Newton of Ardtoe....85 H1
Newton of Balcanquhal....88 D7
Newton-on-Ouse....60 C5
Newton-on-Rawcliffe....60 F1
Newton on the Moor....75 H4
Newton on Trent....54 C6
Newton Poppleford....10 B7
Newton Purcell....33 J6
Newton Regis....42 E6
Newton Reigny....64 B4
Newton Solney....42 E4
Newton Stacey....13 G1
Newton St Cyres....9 J6
Newton Stewart....68 F4
Newton St Faith....47 H5
Newton St Loe....20 B6
Newton St Petrock....8 E4
Newton Tony....12 E1
Newton Tracey....9 F3
Newton under Roseberry....67 F6
Newton upon Derwent....60 E6
Newton Valence....13 K2
Newton with Scales....57 H7
Newtown, Wilts....12 B3
Newtown, Highld....94 B5
Newtown, Cumbr....64 C1
New Town, Lothn....82 C4
Newtown, Dorset....12 C6
Newtown, Powys....40 C7
Newtown, Hants....12 E4
Newtown, Northum....75 F1
Newtown, Shrops....41 F3
Newtown, Hants....13 F3
Newtown, Northum....75 G2
Newtown, Northum....75 G4
Newtown, I. of W....13 G6
Newtown, Ches....41 H2
Newtown, H. & W....31 H5
Newtown, Hants....13 J4
Newtown, Ches....51 J5
Newtown, Derby....51 J5
Newtown, Hants....21 J6
Newtown, Staffs....51 J7
Newtown, I. of M....56 Q4
Newtown-in-St-Martin....2 F7
Newtown Linford....43 H5
Newtown St Boswells....74 B1
New Tredegar....18 F2
Newtyle....88 E4
New Waltham....55 G3
New Wimpole....35 G5
New Winton....82 C4
New Yatt....21 H1
New York, Lincs....45 F1
New York, T. & W....75 K7
Neyland....26 D6
Nibley....20 A4
Nicholashayne....10 C4
Nicholaston....27 K8
Nidd....59 J4
Nigg, Highld....103 G5
Nigg, Grampn....97 J5
Nine Ashes....24 B2
Ninebanks....64 E2
Ninemile Bar or Crocketford....72 D7
Ninfield....16 E4
Ningwood....13 G7
Nisbet....74 C2
Niton....7 K7
Nitshill....79 H5
Niwbwrch....48 D4
Noak Hill....23 L3
Nobottle....33 J3
Nocton....54 E7
Noke....21 K1
Nolton....26 C5
Nolton Haven....26 C5
No Man's Heath, Warw....42 E6
No Man's Heath, Ches....41 G2
Nomansland, Wilts....12 E4
Nomansland, Devon....9 J4
Noneley....41 F4
Noonsbrough....114 E3
Nor....83 H7
Noranside....89 G2
Norbury, Derby....42 D2
Norbury, Shrops....40 E7
Norbury, Ches....41 G2
Norbury, Staffs....41 J4
Nordelph....45 J6
Norden, Dorset....12 B7
Norden, G. Man....51 H2
Nordley....41 J2
Norham....83 H7
Norley....50 E6
Norleywood....13 F6
Normanby, Humbs....54 C2
Normanby, N. Yks....60 E2
Normanby-by-Spital....54 E5
Normanby le Wold....54 F4
Norman Cross....44 E7
Normandy....22 E7
Norman's Green....10 B5
Normanton, Lincs....44 C2
Normanton, Leic....44 C6
Normanton, W. Yks....53 F1
Normanton, Derby....43 F3
Normanton, Notts....43 K1
Normanton le Heath....43 F5
Normanton on Soar....43 H4
Normanton-on-the-Wolds....43 J3
Normanton on Trent....54 B7
Normoss....57 G7
Norrington Common....20 C6
Norris Hill....43 F5
Northallerton....59 J1
Northam, Devon....8 E3
Northam, Hants....13 G4
Northampton....34 A3
North Ascot....22 E6
North Aston....43 G7
Northaw....23 H2

North Roe....116 E4
North Runcton....46 B5
North Sandwick....117 G3
North Scale....56 E3
North Scarle....54 C7
North Seaton....75 K6
North Shields....75 K8
North Shoebury....25 F4
North Shore....57 G7
North Side....45 F7
North Somercotes....55 J4
North Stainley....59 H3
North Stainmore....65 F6
North Stifford....24 C4
North Stoke, Oxon....22 B4
North Stoke, Avon....20 B6
North Stoke, W. Susx....14 D4
North Street....13 J2
North Sunderland....75 J1
North Tamerton....8 D6
North Tawton....9 G5
North Thoresby....55 G4
North Tidworth....12 E1
North Tolsta....107 K4
Northton....98 B3
Northtown....113 E7
North Tuddenham....46 F5
Northwall....113 H2
North Walsham....47 H3
North Waltham....13 H1
North Warnborough....22 C7
North Water Bridge....89 J2
North Watten....111 J3
Northway....32 B6
North Weald Bassett....23 K2
North Wheatley....54 B5
North Whilborough....5 J3
Northwich....51 F6
Northwick, Avon....19 K4
North Wick, Avon....19 K6
North Widcombe....19 K7
North Willingham....55 F5
North Wingfield....53 G7
North Witham....44 C4
Northwold....46 C7
Northwood, Derby....52 E7
Northwood, G. Lon....23 F3
Northwood, Shrops....41 F3
Northwood, I. of W....13 G6
Northwood Green....20 B1
North Wootton, Norf....46 B4
North Wootton, Somer....11 G1
North Wootton, Dorset....11 H4
North Wraxall....20 C5
Norton, H. & W....32 A4
Norton, Glos....32 A7
Norton, Wilts....20 C4
Norton, W. Susx....14 C5
Norton, H. & W....32 C5
Norton, Suff....36 E3
Norton, Powys....30 E3
Norton, N. Yks....60 E3
Norton, Cleve....66 E5
Norton, Ches....50 E5
Norton, Shrops....31 F1
Norton, S. Yks....53 F5
Norton, Herts....35 F6
Norton, I. of W....13 F7
Norton, Shrops....41 G6
Norton, S. Yks....53 H6
Norton, Notts....53 H6
Norton, Northnts....33 J3
Norton, Shrops....41 J6
Norton Bavant....12 B1
Norton Bridge....42 A3
Norton Canes....42 C6
Norton Canon....30 E5
Norton Disney....54 C8
Norton East....42 C6
Norton Ferris....11 J2
Norton Fitzwarren....10 C3
Norton Green....13 F7
Norton Hawkfield....19 K6
Norton Heath....24 C2
Norton in Hales....41 J3
Norton-in-the-Moors....42 A1
Norton-Juxta-Twycross....43 F6
Norton-le-Clay....59 K3
Norton Lindsey....32 E3
Norton Malreward....19 L6
Norton Mandeville....24 B2
Norton St Philip....20 B7
Norton Subcourse....47 K7
Norton sub Hamdon....11 F4
Norwell....54 B7
Norwell Woodhouse....54 B7
Norwich....47 H6
Norwick....117 H1
Norwood Green....23 G5
Norwood Hill....15 F1
Noseley....43 K7
Noss Mayo....4 F5
Nosterfield....59 H2
Nostie....92 E3
Notgrove....32 D7
Notton, G. Man....18 C5
Nottingham....43 H2
Notington....11 H7
Notton, Wilts....20 D6
Notton, W. Yks....53 F2
Nounsley....24 D1
Noutard's Green....31 J3
Nox....41 F5
Nuffield....22 B4
Nunburnholme....60 F6
Nuncargate....43 F7
Nuneham Courtenay....21 K3
Nun Monkton....60 C5
Nunney....11 J1
Nunnington....60 D3
Nunnykirk....75 G5
Nunthorpe....67 F6
Nunton, W. Isles....98 C7
Nunton, Wilts....12 D3
Nursling....13 F4

Nursted...14 A3
Nutbourne...14 D4
Nutfield...15 G1
Nuthall...43 H2
Nuthampstead...35 H6
Nuthurst...15 E3
Nutley...15 H3
Nutwell...53 J3
Nybster...111 K2
Nyetimber...14 B6
Nyewood...14 B3
Nymet Rowland...9 H5
Nymet Tracey...9 H5
Nympsfield...20 C2
Nynehead...10 C3
Nyton...14 C5

O

Oadby...43 J6
Oad Street...24 E6
Oakamoor...42 C2
Oakbank...81 F5
Oakdale...19 F3
Oake...10 C3
Oaken...42 A6
Oakenclough...57 J6
Oakengates...41 J5
Oakenshaw, Durham...66 C4
Oakenshaw, W. Yks...52 D1
Oakford, Dyfed...28 B4
Oakford, Devon...9 K3
Oakgrove...51 J7
Oakham...44 B6
Oakhanger...14 A2
Oakhill...11 H1
Oakington...35 H3
Oaklands...23 H1
Oakle Street...20 B1
Oakley, Bucks...22 B1
Oakley, Beds...34 D4
Oakley, Fife...80 F3
Oakley, Suff...37 G2
Oakley, Hants...21 K7
Oakley Green...22 E5
Oakley Park...29 G1
Oakridge...20 D2
Oaks...41 F6
Oaksey...20 D3
Oakthorpe...43 F5
Oakwoodhill...14 E2
Oakworth...58 F7
Oare, Wilts...21 F6
Oare, Kent...25 G6
Oasby...44 D3
Oathlaw...89 G3
Oban...85 K5
Oborne...11 H4
Occlestone Green...51 F7
Occold...37 G2
Ochiltree...71 L2
Ockbrook...43 G3
Ockham...22 F7
Ockle...85 G1
Ockley...14 E1
Ocle Pychard...31 G5
Odcombe...11 G4
Odd Down...20 B6
Oddendale...64 C6
Oddingley...32 B4
Oddington, Glos...32 E7
Oddington, Oxon...21 K1
Odell...34 C4
Odiham...22 C7
Odstock...12 D3
Odstone...43 F6
Offchurch...33 F3
Offenham...32 C5
Offham, Kent...24 C7
Offham, E. Susx...15 H4
Offord Cluny...35 F3
Offord D'Arcy...35 F3
Offton...36 F5
Offwell...10 C6
Ogbourne Maizey...21 F5
Ogbourne St Andrew...21 F5
Ogbourne St George...21 G5
Ogle...75 H7
Ogmore...18 C5
Ogmore-by-Sea...18 C5
Ogmore Vale...18 D3
Okeford Fitzpaine...11 K4
Okehampton...9 F6
Okehampton Camp...9 F6
Old...34 A2
Old Aberdeen...97 J5
Old Alresford...13 H2
Old Basing...22 B7
Oldberrow...32 D3
Old Bewick...75 G2
Old Bolingbroke...55 H7
Oldborough...9 H5
Old Brampton...53 F6
Old Bridge of Urr...72 C8
Old Buckenham...46 F7
Old Burghclere...21 J7
Oldbury, W. Mids...43 B8
Oldbury, Warw...43 F7
Oldbury, Shrops...41 J7
Oldbury-on-Severn...19 L3
Oldbury on the Hill...20 C4
Old Byland...60 C2
Oldcastle...30 E7
Old Cleeve...10 B1
Old Clipstone...53 J7
Old Colwyn...49 H3
Oldcotes...53 H5
Old Daily...71 H5
Old Dalby...43 J4
Old Deer...105 J4
Old Denaby...53 G4
Old Ellerby...61 J7
Old Felixstowe...37 J6

Oldfield...31 K3
Oldford...20 B7
Old Hall, The...55 G2
Oldham...51 J3
Oldhamstocks...82 F4
Old Heath...36 F7
Oldhurst...35 G2
Old Hutton...57 J2
Old Kea...3 G5
Old Kilpatrick...79 G4
Old Kinnernie...97 G5
Old Knebworth...35 F7
Oldland...20 A5
Old Leake...45 H1
Old Malton...60 E3
Oldmeldrum...97 H3
Old Milverton...33 F3
Old Monkland...80 C5
Old Newton...36 F3
Old Park...41 H6
Old Philpstoun...81 F4
Old Radnor...30 D4
Old Rayne...97 F3
Old Romney...17 H3
Oldshore Beg...108 C3
Oldshoremore...108 D3
Old Sodbury...20 B4
Old Somerby...44 C3
Oldstead...60 C2
Old Swarland...75 H4
Old Town...57 J2
Old Town Farm...74 E5
Oldtown of Ord...104 F3
Old Warden...34 E5
Oldways End...9 J3
Old Weston...34 E2
Oldwhat...105 H3
Old Windsor...22 E5
Old Wives Lees...25 G7
Olgrinmore...111 G3
Oliver's Battery...13 G3
Ollaberry...116 E4
Ollach...92 B2
Ollerton, Ches...51 G6
Ollerton, Shrops...41 H4
Ollerton, Notts...53 J7
Olney...34 B4
Olton...32 D1
Olveston...19 L4
Ombersley...31 K3
Ompton...53 J7
Onchan...56 R4
Onecote...42 C1
Ongar Hill...45 J4
Ongar Street...30 E3
Onibury...31 F2
Onich...86 C2
Onllwyn...18 C1
Onneley...41 J2
Onslow Village...14 C1
Opinan, Highld...100 D5
Opinan, Highld...100 E3
Orby...55 J7
Orchard...11 K4
Orchard Portman...10 D3
Orcheston...12 C1
Orcop...31 F7
Orcop Hill...31 F7
Ord...92 C4
Ordhead...97 F4
Ordie...96 D5
Ordiquish...104 C3
Ore...16 F4
Oreton...31 H1
Orford, Ches...50 E4
Orford, Suff...37 K4
Orgreave...42 D5
Orinsay...107 H7
Orleton, H. & W...31 F3
Orleton, H. & W...31 H3
Orlingbury...34 B2
Ormesby...67 F6
Ormesby St Margaret...47 K5
Ormesby St Michael...47 K5
Ormiscaig...100 E3
Ormiston...82 C5
Ormsaigmore...85 F2
Ormskirk...50 D3
Orpington...23 K6
Orrell...50 E3
Orroland...69 J6
Orsett...24 C4
Orslow...41 K5
Orston...44 A2
Orton, Northnts...34 B2
Orton, Cumbr...64 D7
Orton Longueville...44 E7
Orton-on-the-Hill...43 F6
Orwell...35 G4
Osbaldeston...58 B7
Osbaston...43 G6
Osbournby...44 D3
Oscroft...50 E7
Ose...91 J1
Osgathorpe...43 G5
Osgodby, N. York...60 D7
Osgodby, Lincs...54 E4
Osgodby, N. Yks...61 H2
Oskaig...92 B2
Oskamull...85 F4
Osmaston...42 E2
Osmington...11 J7
Osmington Mills...11 J7
Osmotherley...66 E8
Osnaburgh or Dairsie...89 G7
Ospisdale...102 F4
Ospringe...25 G6
Ossett...52 E1
Ossington...54 B7
Ostend...25 F3
Oswaldkirk...60 D3
Oswaldtwistle...51 G1
Oswestry...40 D4
Otford...23 L7
Otham...24 D7

Othery...10 E2
Otley, Suff...37 H4
Otley, W. Yks...59 H6
Otterburn, N. Yks...58 D5
Otterburn, Northum...74 E5
Otterburn Camp...74 E5
Otterden Place...25 F7
Otter Ferry...77 J3
Otterham...8 B6
Ottershaw...22 F6
Otterswick...117 G4
Otterton...10 B7
Ottery St Mary...10 C6
Ottringham...55 G1
Oughtershaw...58 D2
Oughtibridge...53 F4
Oulston...60 C3
Oulton, Staffs...42 B3
Oulton, Norf...47 G4
Oulton, Cumbr...63 H2
Oulton, W. Yks...59 J8
Oulton, Suff...47 L7
Oulton Broad...47 L7
Oulton Street...47 G4
Oundle...34 D1
Ousby...64 D4
Ousden...36 C4
Ouseburn...59 K4
Ousefleet...54 C1
Ouston...66 C2
Outertown...112 C5
Outgate...63 J8
Outhgill...64 E7
Outlane...52 C2
Out Newton...55 H1
Out Rawcliffe...57 H6
Outwell, Cambs...45 J6
Outwell, Norf...45 J6
Outwood, W. Yks...53 F1
Outwood, Surrey...15 G1
Ovenden...52 C1
Over, Cambs...35 G2
Over, Avon...19 K4
Overbister...113 G2
Overbury...32 B6
Over Haddon...52 E7
Over Kellet...57 J4
Over Kiddington...33 G7
Over Norton...33 F7
Over Peover...51 G6
Overseal...42 E5
Over Silton...59 K1
Overstone...34 B3
Overstrand...47 H2
Overton, D. & G...62 E1
Overton, Clwyd...40 D2
Overton, Shrops...31 G2
Overton, Hants...13 H1
Overton, Grampn...97 H4
Overton, Lancs...57 H5
Overtown...80 D6
Over Wallop...12 E2
Over Whitacre...42 E7
Oving, W. Susx...14 C5
Oving, Bucks...33 J7
Ovingdean...15 G5
Ovingham...65 H1
Ovington, Essex...36 C5
Ovington, Norf...46 E6
Ovington, Northum...65 H1
Ovington, Hants...13 H2
Ovington, Durham...65 J6
Ower...13 F4
Owermoigne...11 J7
Owlswick...22 C2
Owmby-by-Spital...54 E5
Owslebury...13 H1
Owston...44 A6
Owston Ferry...54 C3
Owstwick...61 K7
Owthorne...43 J3
Oxborough...46 C6
Oxenholme...57 J2
Oxenhope...58 F7
Oxen Park...57 G2
Oxenton...32 B6
Oxenwood...21 H7
Oxford...21 K2
Oxhill...33 F5
Oxley...42 B6
Oxley's Green...16 D3
Oxnam...74 C3
Oxshott...23 G6
Oxspring...52 E3
Oxted...23 J7
Oxton, Border...82 C6
Oxton, Notts...43 J1
Oxwich...27 J8
Oxwick...46 E4
Oykel Bridge...102 B2
Oyne...97 F3

P

Pabail Iarach...107 K5
Pabail Varach...107 K5
Packington...43 F5
Padanaram...89 G3
Padbury...33 K6
Paddington...23 H4
Paddlesworth...17 J2
Paddockhaugh...104 B3
Paddock Wood...16 D1
Paddolgreen...41 G3
Padeswood...50 B7
Padiham...58 D7
Padstow...3 H2
Padworth...22 B6
Pagham...14 B6
Paglesham Churchend...24 F3

Paglesham Eastend...25 F3
Paible, W. Isles...98 C6
Paible, W. Isles...98 F3
Paignton...5 J3
Pailton...33 G1
Painscastle...30 C5
Painshawfield...65 H1
Painswick...20 C2
Paisley...79 G5
Pakefield...47 L7
Pakenham...36 E3
Pale...39 J3
Palestine...12 E1
Paley Street...22 D5
Palgrave...37 G2
Palmerstown...18 F6
Palnackie...69 K5
Palnure...68 F4
Palterton...53 G7
Pamber End...22 B7
Pamber Green...21 L7
Pamber Heath...22 B6
Pamphill...12 B5
Pampisford...35 H5
Panbride...89 H5
Pancrasweek...8 C5
Pandy, Clwyd...40 C3
Pandy, Gwent...30 E7
Pandy, Powys...39 J8
Pandy Tudur...49 H4
Panfield...36 C7
Pangbourne...22 B5
Panner...59 J5
Pannal...59 J5
Pant...40 D4
Panteg...26 D3
Pant Glas...38 D2
Pantgwyn...27 G2
Pant Mawr...29 F1
Panton...55 F6
Pant-pastynog...49 K4
Pantperthog...39 G6
Pant-y-dwr...29 G2
Pant-y-ffridd...40 C6
Pant-y-mwyn...27 L5
Pantyffynnon...27 L5
Panxworth...47 J5
Papcastle...63 G4
Papple...82 D4
Papplewick...43 H1
Papworth Everard...35 F3
Papworth St Agnes...35 F3
Par...3 J4
Parbold...50 D2
Parbrook...11 G2
Parcllyn...27 G1
Parc Seymour...19 J3
Pardshaw...63 F5
Parham...37 J3
Park Corner...22 B4
Park End, Northum...74 E7
Parkend, Glos...19 L2
Parkeston...37 H6
Parkgate, Ches...50 B6
Parkgate, Surrey...15 F1
Parkgate, D. & G...73 F6
Park Gate, Hants...13 H5
Parkham...8 D3
Parkham Ash...8 D3
Parkhouse...19 K2
Parkhurst...13 G6
Parkmill...27 K8
Parkstone...12 C6
Parley Cross...12 C6
Parracombe...9 G1
Parrog...26 E3
Parson Cross...53 F4
Parson Drove...45 G6
Partick...79 H5
Partington...51 G4
Partney...55 J7
Parton, D. & G...72 B7
Parton, Cumbr...62 E5
Partridge Green...15 E4
Parwich...42 D1
Passenham...34 A6
Paston...47 J3
Patcham...15 G5
Patchetts...14 D5
Patchole...9 G1
Patchway...19 L4
Pateley Bridge...59 G4
Pathfinder Village...9 J6
Pathhead, Strath...72 B3
Pathhead, Fife...81 H2
Pathhead, Lothn...81 J5
Patmore Heath...35 H7
Patna...71 K3
Patney...20 E7
Patrick...56 P3
Patrick Brompton...59 H1
Patrington...55 H1
Patrixbourne...25 J7
Patterdale...63 J6
Pattingham...41 K7
Pattishall...33 J4
Patton Bridge...64 C8
Paul...2 C7
Paulerspury...33 K5
Paull...55 F1
Paulton...20 A7
Pavenham...34 B4
Pawston...74 E1
Paxford...32 D6
Paxton...83 H6
Payhembury...10 B5
Paythorne...58 D5
Pcaston...82 C5
Peacehaven...15 H5
Peak Dale...52 C6
Peak Forest...52 D6
Peakirk...44 E6
Peanmeanach...92 D7
Peasedown St John...20 B7
Peasemore...21 J5
Peasenhall...37 J3
Pease Pottage...15 F2

Peaslake...14 D1
Peasmarsh...17 F3
Peaston Bank...82 C5
Peathill...105 J2
Peatling Magna...43 H7
Peatling Parva...43 H8
Peaton...31 G1
Pebmarsh...36 D6
Pebworth...32 D5
Pecket Well...58 E8
Peckforton...41 G1
Peckleton...43 G6
Pedmore...32 B1
Pedwell...11 F2
Peebles...81 H7
Peel...56 P3
Pegswood...75 J6
Peinchorran...92 B2
Peinlich...99 K7
Pelaw...66 C1
Pelcomb Cross...26 D5
Pelden...25 F1
Pelsall...42 C6
Pelton...66 C2
Peluth...63 G3
Pelynt...4 C4
Pembrey...27 J6
Pembridge...30 E4
Pembroke...26 D6
Pembroke Dock...26 D6
Pembury...16 D1
Penallt...19 K2
Penally...26 F7
Penare...3 J5
Penarth...19 F5
Pen-bont Rhydybeddau...28 D1
Pencader...27 G1
Pencaitland...82 C5
Pencarreg...27 K2
Pencelli...29 H7
Pen-Clawdd...27 K7
Pencoed...18 D4
Pencombe...31 H4
Pencoyd...31 G7
Pencraig, Powys...40 B4
Pencraig, H. & W...31 G7
Pendas Fields...59 J7
Pendeen...2 B6
Penderyn...18 D2
Pendine...27 G6
Pendlebury...51 G3
Pendleton...58 C7
Pendock...31 J6
Pendoggett...3 J2
Pendoylan...18 E5
Penegoes...39 G6
Penffordd...26 E4
Penffridd...38 E1
Penge...23 J5
Pengorffwysfa...48 D1
Penhalurick...2 F6
Penhow...19 J3
Penhurst...16 D4
Penicuik...81 H5
Peniel...49 K4
Penifiler...92 A1
Peninver...70 C2
Penisa'r Waun...48 E4
Penistone...52 E3
Penjerrick...2 F6
Penketh...50 E5
Penkridge...42 B5
Penley...41 F2
Penllergaer...27 L7
Pen-llyn, Gwyn...48 C2
Penllyn, S. Glam...18 D5
Penmachno...39 G1
Penmaen, Gwent...19 F3
Penmaen, W. Glam...27 K8
Penmaenmawr...49 G3
Penmaenpool...39 F5
Penmark...18 E6
Penmon...49 F2
Penmorfa...38 E2
Penmynydd...48 E3
Pennal...39 G6
Pennan...105 J2
Pennant, Dyfed...28 C3
Pennant, Powys...39 H7
Pennant, Clwyd...49 H5
Pennant-Melangell...40 B4
Pennard...27 K8
Pennerley...40 E2
Pennington...57 F3
Penn Street...22 E3
Penny Bridge...57 G2
Pennycross...85 G6
Pennymoor...9 J4
Penparc...27 G2
Penparcau...28 C1
Penperlleni...19 H2
Penpillick...3 J4
Penpol...3 G6
Penpont...72 D5
Penrherber...27 G3
Penrhiwceiber...18 E3
Penrhiw-llan...27 H2
Penrhiwpal...27 H2
Penrhos, Gwyn...48 B2
Penrhos, Powys...18 C1
Penrhos, Gwyn...38 C3
Penrhos, Gwent...19 J1
Penrhyn Bay...49 H2
Penrhyn-coch...28 D1
Penrhyndeudraeth...38 F3
Penrhyn-side...49 H2
Penrice...27 J8
Penrith...64 C4
Penrose...3 G2
Penruddock...63 K5
Penryn...3 F6
Pen-sarn, Gwyn...38 D2

Pen-sarn, Gwyn...38 E4
Pensarn, Clwyd...49 J3
Pensax...31 J3
Pensby...50 B5
Penselwood...11 J2
Pensford...19 L6
Penshaw...66 D2
Penshurst...15 J1
Pensilva...4 C3
Pentewan...3 J5
Pentir...48 E4
Pentire...3 F3
Pentney...46 C5
Penton Mewsey...13 F1
Pentraeth...48 E3
Pentre, Clwyd...40 C3
Pentre, Clwyd...40 D2
Pentre, Shrops...40 E5
Pentre, Powys...29 H1
Pentrebach, M. Glam...18 E2
Pentre-bach, Powys...29 G6
Pentre-bach, Dyfed...27 K2
Pentre Berw...48 D3
Pentre-bont...39 G1
Pentre-celyn...40 C1
Pentre-cwrt...27 H3
Pentre Dolau Honddu...29 G5
Pentre-dwr, W. Glam...18 A3
Pentredwr, Clwyd...40 C2
Pentrefelin, Gwyn...38 E3
Pentrefelin, Gwyn...49 H3
Pentrefoelas...39 H1
Pentregat...27 H1
Pentre-Gwenlais...27 L5
Pentre Halkyn...50 B6
Pentre-LLanrhaeadr...49 K4
Pentre-llyn-cymmer...39 J1
Pentre'r beirdd...40 C5
Pentre'r-felin...29 G6
Pentre-tafarn-y-fedw...49 H4
Pentre-ty-gwyn...28 F6
Pentrich...43 F1
Pentridge...12 C4
Pentwyn...19 G4
Pentyrch...18 E4
Penuwch...28 C3
Pen-y-banc...27 L4
Penybont, Powys...30 C3
Pen-y-bont, Clwyd...40 D4
Pen-y-bont, Dyfed...27 H4
Penybontfawr...40 B4
Penybryn, M. Glam...18 F3
Pen-y-bryn, Gwyn...39 F5
Pen-y-cae, Powys...18 C1
Penycae, Clwyd...40 D2
Pen-y-cae-mawr...19 J3
Pen-y-cefn...49 L3
Pen-y-clawdd...19 J2
Pen-y-coedcae...18 E4
Penycwm...26 C4
Penyffordd...50 C7
Pen-y-garn...27 K3
Penygarnedd, Powys...40 C4
Pen-y-garnedd, Gwyn...48 E3
Penygraig...18 D3
Penygroes, Gwyn...38 D1
Pen-y-groes, Dyfed...27 K5
Penysarn...48 D1
Pen-y-stryt...40 C1
Penywaun...18 D2
Penzance...2 C6
Peopleton...32 B4
Peover Heath...51 G6
Peper Harow...14 C1
Peplow...41 H4
Percie...96 E6
Percyhorner...105 J2
Perivale...23 G4
Perlethorpe...53 J6
Perranarworthal...2 F6
Perranporth...2 F4
Perranuthnoe...2 D7
Perranzabuloe...2 F4
Perry Barr...42 C7
Perry Green...23 K1
Pershore...32 B5
Pert...89 J2
Pertenhall...34 D3
Perth...88 D6
Perthy...40 E3
Perton...42 A7
Peterborough...45 E7
Peterburn...100 D4
Peterchurch...30 E6
Peterculter...97 H5
Peterhead...105 L4
Peterlee...66 E3
Petersfield...13 K3
Peter's Green...23 G1
Peters Marland...8 E4
Peterstone Wentlooge...19 G4
Peterston-super-Ely...18 E5
Peterstow...31 G7
Peter Tavy...4 F2
Petertown...112 D6
Petham...25 H7
Petrockstowe...8 F5
Pett...16 F4
Pettaugh...37 G4
Pettinain...80 E2
Pettistree...37 H4
Petton, Devon...10 B3
Petton, Shrops...41 F4
Petty...97 G2
Pettycur...81 H3
Pettymuick...97 J3
Petworth...14 C3
Pevensey Bay...16 D5
Pewsey...21 F6
Philham...8 C3
Philiphaugh...73 K2
Phillack...2 D6
Philleigh...3 G6
Philpstoun...81 F4

Phoenix Green	22	C7
Pica	62	F5
Piccotts End	22	F2
Pickering	60	E2
Picket Piece	13	F1
Pickhill	59	J2
Picklescott	41	F7
Pickmere	51	F6
Pickwell, Leic.	44	A5
Pickwell, Devon	8	E1
Pickworth, Leic.	44	C5
Pickworth, Lincs.	44	D3
Picton, Ches.	50	D6
Picton, N. Yks.	66	E7
Piddinghoe	15	H5
Piddington, Oxon	22	B1
Piddington, Northnts.	34	B4
Piddlehinton	11	J6
Piddletrenthide	11	J6
Pidley	35	G2
Piercebridge	66	C6
Pierowall	112	E2
Pigdon	75	H6
Pikehall	52	D8
Pilgrims Hatch	24	B3
Pilham	54	C4
Pill	19	K5
Pillaton	4	D3
Pillerton Hersey	33	F5
Pillerton Priors	32	E5
Pilleth	30	D3
Pilley	53	F3
Pilling	57	H6
Pilling Lane	57	G6
Pilning	19	K4
Pilsbury	52	D7
Pilsdon	11	F6
Pilsley, Derby	52	E6
Pilsley, Derby	53	G7
Pilton, Leic.	44	C6
Pilton, Northnts.	34	D1
Pilton, Somer.	11	G1
Pimperne	12	B5
Pinchbeck	45	F4
Pinchbeck West	45	F4
Pinfold	50	C2
Pinhoe	9	K6
Pinmore	71	H5
Pinner	23	G4
Pinvin	32	B5
Pinwherry	71	G6
Pinxton	43	G1
Pipe and Lyde	31	G5
Pipe Gate	51	G7
Piperhill	103	G2
Pipewell	34	B1
Pippacott	9	F2
Pirbright	22	E7
Pirnmill	77	H7
Pirton, H. & W.	32	A5
Pirton, Herts.	34	E6
Pishill	22	C4
Pistyll	38	C2
Pitblae	105	J2
Pitcairngreen	88	C6
Pitcalnie	103	G5
Pitcaple	97	G3
Pitchcombe	20	C2
Pitchcott	34	A7
Pitchford	41	G6
Pitch Green	22	C2
Pitch Place	22	E7
Pitcombe	11	H2
Pitcox	82	E4
Pitfichie	97	F4
Pitgrudy	103	F3
Pitlessie	89	F8
Pitlochry	88	B3
Pitmedden	97	H3
Pitminster	10	D4
Pitmunie	97	F4
Pitney	11	F3
Pitscottie	89	G7
Pitsea	24	D4
Pitsford	34	A3
Pitstone	22	E1
Pitstone Green	22	E1
Pittendreich	103	K6
Pittentrail	102	F2
Pittenweem	89	G2
Pittington	66	D3
Pitton	12	E2
Pixey Green	37	H2
Place Newton	61	F3
Plains	80	C5
Plaish	41	G7
Plaistow	14	D2
Plaitford	12	E4
Plas	27	J4
Plas Gogerddan	28	D1
Plas Isaf	40	B2
Plas Llwyngwern	39	G6
Plas Llysyn	39	J7
Plastow Green	21	K6
Platt	24	C7
Plawsworth	66	C3
Plaxtol	24	C7
Playden	17	G3
Playford	37	H5
Play Hatch	22	C5
Playing Place	3	G5
Pleasley	41	F6
Plean	80	D3
Pleasington	51	F1
Pleasley	53	H7
Plenmeller	64	E1
Pleshey	24	C1
Plockton	92	E2
Plocrapool	99	G3
Plocrapool Point	99	G3
Plowden	30	E1
Ploxgreen	40	E6
Pluckley	17	G1
Plumbland	63	G4
Plumley	51	G6
Plumpton, Cumbr.	64	B4
Plumpton, E. Susx.	15	G4
Plumpton, Lancs.	57	G7
Plumpton Green	15	G4
Plumpton Head	64	C4
Plumstead	47	G3
Plumtree	43	J3
Plungar	44	A3
Plush	11	J5
Plwmp	27	H1
Plymouth	4	E4
Plympton	4	F4
Plymstock	4	F4
Plymtree	10	B5
Pockley	60	D2
Pocklington	60	F6
Pode Hole	45	F4
Podimore	11	G3
Podington	34	C3
Podmore	41	J3
Point Clear	25	G1
Pointon	44	E3
Pokesdown	12	D6
Polapit Tamar	8	D7
Polbain	101	F1
Polbathic	4	D4
Polbeth	81	F5
Polebrook	34	D1
Polegate	16	C5
Pole of Itlaw, The	104	F3
Polesworth	42	E6
Polglass	101	G2
Polgooth	3	H4
Poling	14	D5
Polkerris	3	J4
Pollington	53	J2
Polloch	85	J2
Pollokshaws	79	H5
Pollokshields	79	H5
Polmassick	3	H5
Polnessan	71	K3
Polperro	4	C4
Polruan	3	K4
Polsham	11	G1
Polstead	36	E6
Poltalloch	77	H2
Poltimore	9	K6
Polwarth	82	F6
Polyphant	4	C1
Polzeath	3	H2
Ponde	30	C6
Pondersbridge	45	F7
Ponsanooth	2	F6
Ponsworthy	5	H2
Pontamman	27	L5
Pontantwn	27	J5
Pontardawe	18	B2
Pontardulais	27	K6
Pontarsais	27	J4
Pont Creuddyn	27	K1
Pontefract	53	G1
Ponteland	75	H7
Ponterwyd	28	E1
Pontesbury	40	F6
Pontfadog	40	D3
Pontfaen, Dyfed	26	E3
Pont-faen, Powys	29	G6
Pont Henri	27	J6
Ponthir	19	H3
Ponthirwaun	27	G2
Pontllanfraith	19	F3
Pontlliw	27	L6
Pont Llogel	40	B5
Pontllyfni	38	D1
Pontlottyn	18	F2
Pontneddfechan	18	D2
Pont Pen-y-benglog	49	F4
Pontrhydfendigaid	28	E3
Pont Rhyd-y-cyff	18	C4
Pontrhydyfen	18	B3
Pont-rhyd-y-groes	28	E2
Pontrilas	30	E7
Pontrobert	40	C5
Pont-rug	48	E4
Ponts Green	16	D4
Pontshill	31	H7
Pont-Sian	27	J2
Pontsticill	18	E1
Pontyates	27	J6
Pontyberem	27	K5
Pontybodkin	50	B8
Pontyclun	18	E4
Pontycymer	18	D3
Pontymister	19	G3
Pont-y-pant	39	G1
Pontypool	19	G2
Pontypridd	18	E3
Pontywaun	19	G3
Pooksgreen	13	F4
Pool	2	E5
Poole	12	C6
Poole Keynes	20	E3
Poolewe	100	E4
Pooley Bridge	64	B5
Poolhill	31	J7
Pool of Muckhart	80	F1
Pool Quay	40	D5
Poorton	11	G6
Popham	13	H1
Poplar	23	J4
Porchfield	13	G6
Poringland	47	H6
Porkellis	2	E6
Porlock	9	J1
Port-an-eorna	92	D2
Port Ann	77	J3
Port Appin	86	B4
Port Askaig	76	C5
Port Bannatyne	78	C5
Portbury	19	K5
Port Carlisle	63	H1
Port Charlotte	76	B6
Portchester	13	J5
Portclair	94	C4
Port Driseach	78	B4
Port Ellen	76	C7
Port Elphinstone	97	G3
Portencross	78	D7
Port Erin	56	N5
Portesham	11	H7
Port e Vullen	56	R2
Port-Eynon	27	J8
Portfield Gate	26	D5
Portgate	8	E7
Portgaverne	3	J1
Port Glasgow	78	F4
Portgordon	104	C2
Portgower	111	G7
Porth	18	E3
Porthallow	3	F7
Porthcawl	18	C5
Porthcurno	2	B7
Port Henderson	100	D5
Porthgain	26	C3
Porthkerry	18	E6
Porthleven	2	E7
Porthllechog	48	D1
Porthmadog	38	E3
Porthmeor	2	C6
Porth Navas	2	F7
Portholland	3	H5
Porthoustock	3	G7
Porthpean	3	J4
Porthtowan	2	E5
Portincaple	78	E2
Portington	60	E7
Portinscale	63	H5
Port Isaac	3	H1
Portishead	19	J5
Portknockie	104	D2
Portlethen	97	J6
Portlethen Village	97	J6
Portloe	3	H6
Port Logan	68	B6
Portmahomack	103	H4
Portmeirion	38	E3
Portmellon	3	J5
Port Mholair	107	K5
Port Mor	91	K8
Portmore	13	F6
Port Mulgrave	67	H6
Portnacroish	86	B4
Portnahaven	76	A6
Portnalong	91	J2
Portnaluchaig	92	C7
Portnancon	109	F2
Portobello	81	J4
Port of Menteith	79	H1
Porton	12	D2
Portpatrick	68	B5
Portquin	3	H1
Portreath	2	E5
Portree	99	K8
Portrye	78	D6
Portscatho	3	G6
Portsea	13	J5
Portskerra	110	E1
Portskewett	19	K4
Portslade	15	F5
Portslade-by-Sea	15	F5
Portsmouth	13	J5
Portsoy	104	E2
Port St Mary	56	P5
Port Sunlight	50	C5
Portswood	13	G4
Port Talbot	18	B3
Portway	32	C2
Port Wemyss	76	A6
Port William	68	E4
Portwrinkle	4	D4
Poslingford	36	C5
Postbridge	5	G2
Postcombe	22	C3
Postling	17	J2
Postwick	47	H6
Potarch	96	F6
Potsgrove	34	C7
Potten End	22	F2
Potterhanworth	54	E7
Potter Heigham	47	K5
Potteries, The	42	A2
Potterne	20	D7
Potterne Wick	20	E7
Potters Bar	23	H3
Potterspury	34	A5
Potter Street	23	K2
Potterton	97	J4
Potto	66	E7
Potton	35	F5
Pott Row	46	C4
Pott Shrigley	51	J6
Poughill, Corn.	8	C5
Poughill, Devon	9	J5
Poulshot	20	D7
Poulton	20	F2
Poulton-le-Fylde	57	G7
Pound Bank	31	J2
Pound Hill	15	F2
Poundon	33	J7
Poundsgate	5	H2
Poundstock	8	C6
Powburn	75	G3
Powderham	9	K7
Powerstock	11	G6
Powfoot	63	G1
Powick	31	K4
Powmill	80	F2
Poxwell	11	J7
Poyle	22	F5
Poynings	15	F4
Poyntington	11	H3
Poynton	51	J5
Poynton Green	41	G5
Poystreet Green	36	E4
Praa Sands	2	D7
Pratt's Bottom	23	K6
Praze-an-Beeble	2	E6
Predannack Wollas	2	E8
Prees	41	G3
Preesall	57	G6
Prees Green	41	G3
Preesgweene	40	D3
Prees Higher Heath	41	G3
Prendwick	75	G3
Pren-gwyn	27	J2
Prenteg	38	E2
Prenton	50	C5
Prescot	50	D4
Prescott	41	F4
Pressen	83	G8
Prestatyn	49	K2
Prestbury, Glos.	32	B7
Prestbury, Ches.	51	J6
Presteigne	30	E3
Presthope	41	G7
Prestleigh	11	H1
Preston, Leic.	44	B6
Preston, Lothn.	82	D4
Preston, Glos.	20	E2
Preston, Wilts.	20	E5
Preston, Herts.	34	E7
Preston, Border	83	F6
Preston, E. Susx.	15	G5
Preston, Northum.	75	H2
Preston, Glos.	31	H6
Preston, Devon	5	J2
Preston, Kent	25	J6
Preston, Humbs.	61	J7
Preston, Dorset	11	J7
Preston, Lancs.	57	J8
Preston Bagot	32	D3
Preston Bissett	33	J7
Preston Brockhurst	41	G4
Preston Brook	50	E5
Preston Candover	13	J1
Preston Capes	33	H4
Preston Gubbals	41	F5
Preston on Stour	32	E4
Preston on Wye	30	E5
Prestonpans	81	J4
Preston St Mary	36	E4
Preston-under-Scar	59	F1
Preston upon the Weald Moors	41	H5
Preston Wynne	31	G5
Prestwich	51	H3
Prestwick, Northum.	75	H7
Prestwick, Strath.	71	J2
Prestwood	22	D2
Price Town	18	D3
Prickwillow	35	J1
Priddy	19	K7
Priest Hutton	57	J3
Priest Weston	40	D7
Primrose Green	46	F5
Princes Risborough	22	D2
Princethorpe	33	G2
Princetown	5	F2
Priors Hardwick	33	G4
Priors Marston	33	G4
Priory, The	13	J6
Priory Wood	30	D5
Priston	20	A6
Prittlewell	24	E4
Privett	13	J3
Prixford	9	F2
Probus	3	G5
Proncy	103	F3
Prospect	63	G3
Prudhoe	65	H1
Puckeridge	35	G7
Puckington	10	E4
Pucklechurch	20	B5
Puddington, Ches.	50	C6
Puddington, Devon	9	J4
Puddledock	46	F7
Puddletown	11	J6
Pudleston	31	G4
Pudsey	59	H7
Pulborough	14	D4
Puleston	41	J4
Pulford	50	C8
Pulham	11	J5
Pulham Market	37	G1
Pulham St Mary	37	H1
Pulloxhill	34	D6
Pulverbatch	41	F6
Pumsaint	27	L2
Puncheston	26	E4
Puncknowle	11	G7
Punnett's Town	16	D3
Purbrook	13	J5
Purfleet	23	L5
Puriton	10	E1
Purleigh	24	E2
Purley	23	J6
Purley on Thames	22	B5
Purlogue	30	D2
Purls Bridge	35	H1
Purse Caundle	11	H4
Purslow	30	E1
Purston Jaglin	53	G2
Purton, Glos.	20	A2
Purton, Glos.	20	A2
Purton, Wilts.	20	E4
Purton Stoke	20	E3
Pury End	33	K5
Pusey	21	H3
Putley	31	H6
Putney	23	H5
Puttenham, Surrey	14	C1
Puttenham, Herts.	22	D1
Puxton	19	J6
Pwll	27	J6
Pwllcrochan	26	D6
Pwllgloyw	29	J6
Pwllheli	38	C3
Pwllmeyric	19	K3
Pwll-y-glaw	18	B3
Pyecombe	15	F4
Pye Corner	19	H4
Pyle, M. Glam.	18	C4
Pyle, I. of W.	7	J7
Pylle	11	H2
Pymore	35	H1
Pyrford	22	F7
Pyrton	22	B3
Pytchley	34	B2
Pyworthy	8	D5

Q

Quabbs	30	D1
Quadring	45	F3
Quainton	34	A7
Quarley	12	E1
Quarndon	43	F2
Quarrier's Homes	79	F5
Quarrington	44	D2
Quarrington Hill	66	D4
Quarry Bank	32	B1
Quarry, The	20	B3
Quarrywood	103	K6
Quarter	80	C6
Quatford	41	J7
Quatt	31	J1
Quebec	66	B3
Quedgeley	20	C1
Queen Adelaide	35	J1
Queenborough	24	F5
Queen Camel	11	G3
Queen Charlton	19	L6
Queensbury	59	G7
Queensferry, Clwyd.	50	C7
Queensferry, Lothn.	81	G4
Queenzieburn	80	B4
Quendale	115	F7
Quendon	35	J6
Queniborough	43	J5
Quenington	21	F2
Quernmore	57	J4
Quethiock	4	D3
Quholm	112	C5
Quidenham	36	F1
Quidhampton, Wilts.	12	D2
Quidhampton, Hants.	21	K7
Quidnish	99	F4
Quilquox	97	J2
Quindry	112	E7
Quine's Hill	56	Q4
Quinton	34	A4
Quoditch	8	E6
Quorndon or Quorn	43	H5
Quorn or Quorndon	43	H5
Quothquan	80	E8
Quoyloo	112	C4
Quoys	117	H1

R

Raby	50	C5
Rachub	49	F4
Rackenford	9	J4
Rackham	14	D4
Rackheath	47	H5
Racks	73	F7
Rackwick, Orkney	112	C7
Rackwick, Orkney	112	K1
Radcliffe, G. Man.	51	G3
Radcliffe, Northum.	75	J4
Radcliffe on Trent	43	J3
Radclive	33	J6
Radcot	21	G3
Raddery	102	F7
Radernie	89	G8
Radford Semele	33	F3
Radlett	23	G3
Radley	21	K3
Radnage	22	C3
Radstock	20	A7
Radstone	33	H5
Radway	33	F5
Radway Green	41	J1
Radwell	35	F6
Radwinter	35	K6
Radyr	18	F4
Rafford	103	J7
Ragdale	43	J5
Raglan	19	J2
Ragnall	54	C6
Rainford	50	D3
Rainham, Kent	24	E6
Rainham, G. Lon.	23	L4
Rainhill	50	D4
Rainow	51	J6
Rainton	59	J3
Rainworth	53	H8
Raisbeck	64	D7
Rait	88	E6
Raithby, Lincs.	55	H5
Raithby, Lincs.	55	H7
Rake	14	B3
Rame, Corn.	4	E5
Rame, Corn.	2	F6
Ram Lane	17	G1
Rampisham	11	G5
Rampside	57	F4
Rampton, Notts.	54	B6
Rampton, Cambs.	35	H3
Ramsbottom	51	G2
Ramsbury	21	G5
Ramscraigs	111	H6
Ramsdean	13	K3
Ramsdell	21	K7
Ramsden Bellhouse	24	D3
Ramsden Heath	24	D3
Ramsey, Cambs.	35	F1
Ramsey, Essex	37	H6
Ramsey, I. of M.	56	R2
Ramseycleuch	73	H3
Ramsey Forty Foot	35	G1
Ramsey Island	25	F2
Ramsey Mereside	45	F8
Ramsey St Mary's	35	F1
Ramsgate	25	K6
Ramsgill	59	G3
Ramshorn	42	C2
Ranby	53	J5
Rand	54	F6
Randwick	20	C2
Ranfurly	79	F5
Rangemore	42	D4
Rangeworthy	20	A4
Ranish	107	J6
Rankinston	71	K3
Ranskill	53	J5
Ranton	42	A4
Ranworth	47	J5
Rapness	113	F2
Rascarrel	69	J6
Raskelf	60	B3
Rassau	18	F1
Rastrick	52	D1
Ratagan	93	F4
Ratby	43	H6
Ratcliffe Culey	43	F7
Ratcliffe on the Wreake	43	J5
Rathen	105	K2
Rathillet	89	F6
Rathmell	58	D5
Ratho	81	G4
Ratho Station	81	G4
Rathven	104	D2
Ratley	33	F5
Ratlinghope	40	F7
Rattar	111	J1
Ratten Row	57	H6
Rattery	5	H3
Rattlesden	36	E4
Rattray	88	D4
Rauceby	44	D2
Raughton Head	63	J3
Raunds	34	C2
Ravenfield	53	G4
Ravenglass	56	D1
Raveningham	47	J7
Ravenscar	67	K7
Ravensdale	56	Q2
Ravensden	34	D4
Ravenseat	65	F7
Ravenshead	43	H1
Ravensmoor	41	H1
Ravensthorpe, W. Yks.	52	E1
Ravensthorpe, Northnts.	33	J2
Ravenstone, Bucks.	34	B4
Ravenstone, Leic.	43	G5
Ravenstonedale	64	E7
Ravenstown	57	G3
Ravenstruther	80	E7
Ravensworth	65	J7
Raw	67	K7
Rawcliffe, N. Yks.	60	C5
Rawcliffe, Humbs.	53	J1
Rawcliffe Bridge	53	K1
Rawdon	59	H7
Rawmarsh	53	G4
Rawreth	24	D3
Rawridge	10	D5
Rawtenstall	51	H1
Raydon	36	F6
Raylees	74	F5
Rayleigh	24	E3
Rayne	36	C7
Reach	35	J3
Read	58	C7
Reading	22	C5
Reading Street	17	G2
Reagill	64	D6
Rearquhar	103	F3
Rearsby	43	J5
Rease Heath	41	H1
Reaster	111	J2
Reawick	115	F4
Reay	110	F2
Rechullin	100	D4
Reculver	25	J6
Redberth	26	E6
Redbourn	23	G1
Redbourne	54	D3
Redbrook	19	K1
Redburn	103	H8
Redcar	67	G5
Redcastle	102	D8
Redcliff Bay	19	J5
Red Dial	63	H3
Redding	80	E4
Reddingmuirhead	80	E4
Reddish	51	H4
Redditch	32	C3
Rede	36	D4
Redenhall	37	H1
Redesdale Camp	74	E5
Redesmouth	74	E6
Redford, Tays.	89	H4
Redford, Durham	65	H4
Redfordgreen	73	J3
Redgrave	36	F2
Redhill, Grampn.	97	G3
Redhill, Grampn.	97	G5
Redhill, Surrey	23	H7
Redhill, Avon	19	J6
Redisham	37	K1
Redland, Orkney	112	D4
Redland, Avon	19	K5
Redlingfield	37	G3
Redlynch, Wilts.	12	E3
Redlynch, Somer.	11	J2
Redmarley D'Abitot	31	J6
Redmarshall	66	D5
Redmile	44	A3
Redmire	58	F1
Redmoor	3	J3
Rednal	40	E4
Redpath	82	D6
Redpoint	100	D6
Red Rock	50	E3

Red Roses....27 G5	Rhydycroesau....40 D3	Rochester, Kent....24 D6	Rothiesholm....113 G4	Rushlake Green....16 D4	St Eval....3 G3
Red Row....75 J5	Rhydyfelin, Dyfed....28 C2	Rochester, Northum....74 E5	Rothley....43 H5	Rushmere....37 K1	St Ewe....3 H5
Redruth....2 F5	Rhydyfelin, M. Glam....18 E4	Rochford, Essex....24 E3	Rothmaise....97 F2	Rushmere St Andrew....37 H5	St Fagans....18 F5
Red Street....41 K1	Rhyd-y-fro....18 B2	Rochford, H. & W....31 H3	Rothwell, Northnts....34 B1	Rushmoor....14 B1	St Fergus....105 K3
Red Wharf Bay....48 E2	Rhydymain....39 H4	Rock, Corn....3 H2	Rothwell, Lincs....55 F4	Rushock....32 A2	St Fillans....87 J6
Redwick, Gwent....19 J4	Rhydymwyn....50 B7	Rock, Northum....75 J2	Rothwell, W. Yks....59 J8	Rusholme....51 H4	St Florence....26 E6
Redwick, Avon....19 K4	Rhyd-yr-onen....38 F6	Rock, H. & W....31 J2	Rotsea....61 H5	Rushton, Northnts....34 B1	St Gennys....8 B6
Redworth....66 C5	Rhyl....49 K2	Rockbeare....10 B6	Rottal....89 F2	Rushton, Ches....50 E7	St George....49 J3
Reed....35 G6	Rhymney....18 F2	Rockbourne....12 D4	Rottingdean....15 G5	Rushton, Shrops....41 H6	St George's, S. Glam....18 F5
Reedham....47 K6	Rhynd....88 D6	Rockcliffe, Cumbr....63 J1	Rottington....62 E6	Rushton Spencer....51 J7	St Georges, Avon....19 H6
Reedness....54 B1	Rhynie....96 D3	Rockcliffe, D. & G....69 K5	Roud....7 K6	Rushwick....31 K4	St Germans....4 D4
Reef....106 F5	Ribbesford....31 J2	Rock Ferry....50 C5	Rougham....46 D4	Rushyford....66 C5	St Giles in the Wood....9 F4
Reepham, Lincs....54 E6	Ribble Head....58 C3	Rockfield, Highld....103 H4	Rougham Green....36 E3	Ruskie....79 J1	St Giles on the Heath....8 C6
Reepham, Norf....47 G4	Ribbleton....57 J7	Rockfield, Gwent....19 J1	Roughburn....94 B7	Ruskington....44 D1	St Harmon....29 G2
Reeth....65 H8	Ribchester....58 B7	Rockhampton....20 A3	Rough Close....42 B3	Rusland....57 G2	St Helen Auckland....66 B5
Regaby....56 R2	Riby....55 F3	Rockingham....44 B7	Rough Common....25 H7	Rusper....15 F2	St Helens, Mers....50 E4
Regil....19 K6	Riccall....60 D7	Rockland All Saints....46 E6	Roughlee....58 D6	Ruspidge....20 A1	St Helens, I. of W....13 J7
Regoul....103 G7	Riccarton....79 G8	Rockland St Mary....47 J6	Roughley....42 D6	Russell's Water....22 C4	St Hilary, Corn....2 D6
Reiff....108 A7	Richards Castle....31 F3	Rockland St Peter....46 E7	Roughsike....74 B7	Rustington....14 D5	St Hilary, S. Glam....18 E5
Reigate....23 H7	Richmond, N. Yks....66 B7	Rockley....21 F5	Roughton, Lincs....55 G7	Ruston Parva....61 H4	Saint Hill....15 G2
Reighton....61 J3	Richmond, G. Lon....23 G5	Rockwell End....22 C4	Roughton, Norf....47 H3	Ruswarp....67 J7	St Illtyd....19 G2
Reiss....111 K3	Rickarton....97 H1	Rodbourne....20 D4	Roughton, Shrops....41 J7	Rutherford....74 C1	St Ippollitts....35 E7
Rejerrah....3 G4	Rickinghall....36 F2	Rodd....30 E3	Roundhay....59 J7	Rutherglen....79 H5	St Ishmael's....26 C6
Relubbus....2 D6	Rickling....35 H6	Roddam....75 G2	Roundstreet Common....14 D3	Ruthernbridge....3 J3	St Issey....3 H2
Relugas....103 H8	Rickmansworth....22 F3	Rodden....11 H7	Roundway....20 E6	Ruthin....50 A8	St Ive....4 D3
Remenham....22 C4	Riddell....74 B2	Rode....20 C7	Rounton....66 E7	Ruthrieston....97 J5	St Ives, Corn....2 D5
Remenham Hill....22 C4	Riddlecombe....9 G4	Rode Heath, Ches....51 H7	Rousdon....10 D6	Ruthven, Grampn....104 E4	St Ives, Dorset....12 D5
Rempstone....43 H4	Riddlesden....59 F6	Rode Heath, Ches....41 K1	Rous Lench....32 C4	Ruthven, Tays....88 E4	St Ives, Cambs....35 G2
Rendcomb....20 E2	Ridge, Wilts....12 B2	Rodel....98 F4	Routh....61 H6	Ruthven, Highld....95 G2	St James South Elmham....37 J1
Rendham....37 J3	Ridge, Dorset....12 B7	Roden....41 G5	Row, Cumbr....57 H2	Ruthvoes....3 H3	St John....4 E4
Rendlesham....37 J4	Ridge, Herts....23 H2	Rodhuish....10 B2	Row, Corn....3 J2	Ruthwell....73 G8	St Johns, H. & W....31 K4
Renfrew....79 H5	Ridge Lane....42 E7	Rodington....41 G5	Rowanburn....73 K7	Ruyton-XI-Towns....40 E4	St John's, I. of M....56 P3
Renhold....34 D4	Ridgeway Cross....31 J5	Rodley....20 B1	Rowde....20 D6	Ryal....75 G7	St John's Chapel....65 F4
Renishaw....53 G6	Ridgewell....36 C5	Rodmarton....20 D3	Rowen....49 G3	Ryal Fold....51 F1	St John's Fen End....45 J5
Rennington....75 J3	Ridgewood....15 H4	Rodmell....15 H5	Rowfoot....64 D1	Ryall....10 F6	St John's Highway....45 J5
Renton....79 F4	Ridgmont....34 C6	Rodmersham....24 F6	Rowhedge....36 F7	Ryarsh....24 C7	St John's Town of Dalry....72 B6
Renwick....64 C3	Riding Mill....65 H1	Rodney Stoke....19 J7	Rowhook....14 C2	Rydal....63 J7	St Judes....56 Q2
Repps....47 K5	Ridlington, Leic....44 B6	Rodsley....42 E2	Rowington....32 E3	Ryde....13 H6	St Just....3 B6
Repton....43 F4	Ridlington, Norf....47 J3	Roecliffe....59 J4	Rowland....52 E6	Rye....17 G3	St Just in Roseland....3 G6
Resolis....102 E6	Ridsdale....74 F6	Roehampton....23 H5	Rowland's Castle....13 K4	Rye Foreign....17 G3	St Katherines....97 G2
Resolven....18 C2	Rienachait....108 B5	Roffey....15 F2	Rowlands Gill....66 B2	Rye Harbour....17 G4	St Keverne....3 F7
Reston....83 G5	Rievaulx....60 C2	Rogart....103 F2	Rowledge....14 B1	Ryhall....44 D5	St Kew....3 J2
Retew....3 H4	Rigg....73 H8	Rogate....14 B3	Rowlestone....30 E7	Ryhill....53 F2	St Kew Highway....3 J2
Retford....53 K5	Riggend....80 C4	Rogerstone....19 G4	Rowley, W. Mids....40 E6	Ryhope....66 E2	St Keyne....4 C3
Rettendon....24 D3	Rigside....80 D8	Rogerton....79 J6	Rowley Regis....32 B1	Rylstone....58 E5	St Lawrence, Essex....25 F2
Rettendon Place....24 D3	Rileyhill....42 D5	Rogiet....19 J4	Rowly....14 D1	Ryme Intrinseca....11 G4	St Lawrence, Corn....3 J3
Revesby....55 G7	Rilla Mill....4 C2	Roker....66 E2	Rowney Green....32 C2	Ryther....60 C7	St Lawrence, I. of W....7 K7
Rewe....9 K6	Rillington....60 F3	Rollesby....47 K5	Rownhams....13 H4	Ryton, N. Yks....60 E3	St Leonards, Dorset....12 D5
Reydon....37 K2	Rimington....58 D6	Rolleston, Notts....44 A1	Rowsham....22 D1	Ryton, T. & W....65 J1	St Leonards, Bucks....22 E2
Reymerston....46 F6	Rimpton....11 H3	Rolleston, Staffs....42 E4	Rowsley....52 F7	Ryton, Shrops....41 J6	St Leonards, E. Susx....16 E5
Reynalton....26 E6	Rimswell....61 L8	Rolleston, Leic....43 K6	Rowston....44 D1	Ryton, Glos....31 J6	St Levan....2 B7
Reynoldston....27 J7	Rinaston....26 D4	Rolston....61 K6	Rowton, Ches....50 D7	Ryton-on-Dunsmore....33 F2	St Lythans....18 F5
Rhadmad....28 C2	Ringasta....115 F7	Rolvenden....16 F2	Rowton, Shrops....41 H5		St Mabyn....3 J2
Rhandirmwyn....28 E5	Ringford....69 H5	Rolvenden Layne....16 F2	Roxburgh....74 C1		St Madoes....88 D6
Rhayader....29 G3	Ringland....47 G5	Romaldkirk....65 G5	Roxby, Humbs....54 D3		St Margarets....30 E6
Rhedyn....38 B3	Ringmer....15 H4	Romanby....59 J1	Roxby, N. Yks....67 H6	**S**	St Margaret's at Cliffe....17 L1
Rheindown....102 D8	Ringmore....5 G5	Romannobridge....81 G7	Roxton....34 E4		St Margaret's Hope....112 D7
Rhes-y-cae....50 A6	Ring's End....45 G6	Romansleigh....9 H3	Roxwell....24 C2	Saasaig....92 C5	St Margaret South Elmham....37 J1
Rhewl, Clwyd....40 C2	Ringsfield....37 K1	Romford....23 L4	Royal British Legion Village....24 D7	Sabden....58 C7	St Mark's....56 P4
Rhewl, Clwyd....49 L4	Ringshall, Herts....22 E1	Romiley....51 J4	Royal Leamington Spa....33 F3	Sacombe....23 J1	St Martin, Corn....4 C4
Rhiconich....108 D3	Ringshall, Suff....36 F4	Rochford, Essex....13 F3	Royal Tunbridge Wells....16 C2	Sacriston....66 C3	St Martin, Corn....2 F7
Rhicullen....102 E5	Ringshall Stocks....36 F4	Romsey....13 F3	Roybridge....93 J7	Sadberge....66 D6	St Martins, Tays....88 D5
Rhigos....18 D2	Ringstead, Norf....46 C2	Romsey, H. & W....32 B1	Roydon, Norf....46 C4	Saddell....70 C1	St Martin's, Shrops....40 E3
Rhilochan....103 F2	Ringstead, Northnts....34 C2	Romsley, Shrops....31 J1	Roydon, Norf....37 F1	Saddington....43 J7	St Mary Bourne....21 J7
Rhiroy....101 H4	Ringwood....12 D5	Ronague....56 P4	Roydon, Essex....23 K1	Saddle Bow....45 K5	St Mary Church....18 E5
Rhiw....38 B4	Ringwould....17 L1	Rookby....65 F6	Royston, S. Yks....53 F2	Saddlethorpe....60 F8	St Mary Cray....23 K6
Rhiwbryfdir....39 F2	Rinmore....96 D4	Rookhope....65 G3	Royston, Herts....35 G5	Sadgill....64 B7	St Mary Hill....18 D5
Rhiwderin....19 G4	Rinnigill....112 D7	Rookley....13 H7	Royton....51 J3	Saffron Walden....35 J6	St Mary Hoo....24 E5
Rhiwlas, Clwyd....40 C3	Rinsey....2 D7	Rooks Bridge....19 H7	Ruabon....40 E2	Saham Toney....46 D6	St Mary in the Marsh....17 H3
Rhiwlas, Gwyn....48 E4	Ripe....15 J4	Roos....61 K7	Ruaig....84 B4	Saighton....50 D7	St Mary's....112 E6
Rhiwlas, Gwyn....39 J3	Ripley, Hants....12 D6	Roosebeck....57 F4	Ruan Lanihorne....3 G5	St Abbs....83 H5	St Mary's Bay....17 H3
Rhodesia....53 H5	Ripley, Surrey....22 F7	Rootpark....80 E6	Ruan Minor....2 F8	St Agnes....2 F4	St Mawes....3 G6
Rhodes Minnis....17 J1	Ripley, Derby....43 G1	Ropley....13 J2	Ruardean....19 L1	St Albans....23 G2	St Mawgan....3 G3
Rhondda....18 D3	Ripley, N. Yks....59 H4	Ropley Dene....13 J2	Ruardean Woodside....19 L1	St Allen....3 G4	St Mellion....4 D3
Rhonehouse or Kelton Hill....69 J5	Riplingham....61 G7	Ropsley....44 C3	Rubery....32 B2	St Andrews....89 H7	St Mellons....19 G4
Rhoose....18 E6	Ripon....59 J3	Rora....105 K3	Rubha Bhocaig....99 G3	St Andrews Major....18 F5	St Merryn....3 G2
Rhos, W. Glam....18 B2	Rippingale....44 D4	Rorrington....40 E6	Rubha Cnan Gall....98 D8	St Annes....57 G8	St Mewan....3 H4
Rhos, Dyfed....27 H3	Ripple, H. & W....32 A6	Rose....2 F4	Rubha Crago....99 H3	St Ann's....73 F5	St Michael Caerhays....3 H5
Rhoscefnhir....48 E3	Ripple, Kent....25 K7	Roseacre....57 H7	Rubh' Aird-mhicheil....90 C2	St Ann's Chapel, Corn....4 C2	St Michael Penkevil....3 G5
Rhoscolyn....48 B3	Ripponden....52 C2	Rose Ash....9 H3	Ruckcroft....64 C3	St Ann's Chapel, Devon....5 G5	St Michaels, Kent....17 F2
Rhoscrowther....26 D6	Rireavach....101 G3	Rosebank....80 D7	Ruckinge....17 H2	St Anthony-in-Meneage....3 F7	St Michaels, H. & W....31 G3
Rhosesmor....50 B7	Risabus....76 C7	Rosebush....26 E4	Ruckland....55 H6	St Arvans....19 K3	St Michael's on Wyre....57 H6
Rhos-fawr....38 C3	Risbury....31 G4	Rosedale Abbey....60 E1	Ruckley....41 G6	St Asaph or Llanelwy....49 K3	St Michael South Elmham....37 J1
Rhosgadfan....38 E1	Risby, Humbs....54 D2	Roseden....75 G2	Ruddington....43 H3	St Athan....18 E6	St Minver....3 H2
Rhos-goch, Powys....30 C5	Risby, Suff....36 D3	Rosehall....102 C2	Rudge....20 C7	St Austell....3 J4	St Monance....82 D1
Rhosgoch, Gwyn....48 D2	Risca....19 G3	Rosehearty....105 J2	Rudgeway....19 L4	St Bees....62 E6	St Neot....4 B3
Rhoshirwaun....38 A4	Rise....61 J6	Rosehill....41 H3	Rudgwick....14 D2	St Blazey....3 J4	St Neots....34 E3
Rhoslan....38 D2	Risegate....45 F4	Roseisle....103 K6	Rudhall....31 H7	St Boswells....74 B1	St Newlyn East....3 G4
Rhoslefain....38 E6	Riseley, Berks....22 C6	Rosemarket....26 D6	Rudloe....20 C6	St Breock....3 H2	St Nicholas, Dyfed....26 D3
Rhosllanerchrugog....40 D2	Riseley, Beds....34 D3	Rosemarkie....103 F7	Rudry....19 F4	St Breward....3 H2	St Nicholas, S. Glam....18 E5
Rhosmeirch....48 D3	Rishangles....37 G3	Rosemary Lane....10 C4	Rudston....61 H4	St Briavels....19 K2	St Nicholas at Wade....25 J6
Rhosneigr....48 C3	Rishton....58 C7	Rosemount, Tays....88 D4	Rudyard....42 B1	St Brides....26 B5	St Ninians....80 C2
Rhosnesni....40 E1	Rishworth....52 C2	Rosemount, Strath....71 J2	Rufford....50 D2	St Bride's Major....18 C5	St Osyth....25 H1
Rhos-on-Sea....49 H2	Rising Bridge....51 G1	Rosenannon....3 H3	Rufforth....60 C5	St Bride's-super-Ely....18 E5	St Owen's Cross....31 G7
Rhossili....27 J8	Risley, Ches....51 F4	Rosewell....81 H5	Rugby....33 H2	St Brides Wentlooge....19 G4	St Paul's Cray....23 K6
Rhosson....26 B4	Risley, Derby....43 G3	Roseworthy....2 E6	Rugeley....42 C5	St Budeaux....4 E4	St Paul's Walden....35 E7
Rhostrehwfa....48 D3	Risplith....59 H4	Rosgill....64 C6	Ruilick....102 D8	Saintbury....32 D6	St Peter's....25 K6
Rhostryfan....38 D1	Rivar....21 H6	Roshven....92 D8	Ruishton....10 D3	St Buryan....2 C7	St Petrox....26 D7
Rhostyllen....40 E2	Rivenhall End....24 E1	Roskhill....99 H8	Ruisigarry....98 E4	St Catherine....20 B5	St Pinnock....4 C3
Rhosybol....48 D2	River Bank....35 J3	Rosley....63 J3	Ruislip....23 F4	St Catherines....86 D8	St Quivox....71 J2
Rhos-y-brithdir....40 C4	Riverhead....23 L7	Roslin....81 H5	Ruislip Common....23 F4	St Clears....27 G5	St Stephen....3 H4
Rhos-y-gwaliau....39 J3	Rivington....51 F2	Rosliston....42 E5	Rumbling Bridge....80 F2	St Cleer....4 C3	St Stephens, Corn....8 D7
Rhos-y-llan....38 B3	Roachill....9 J3	Rosneath....78 E3	Rumburgh....37 J1	St Clement....8 C7	St Stephens, Corn....4 E4
Rhu....78 E3	Roade....34 A4	Ross, D. & G....69 H6	Rumford....3 G2	St Colmac....78 C5	St Teath....3 J1
Rhuallt....49 K3	Roadmeetings....80 D7	Ross, Northum....83 K8	Rumney....19 G5	St Columb Major....3 H3	St Tudy....3 J2
Rhuddlan....49 K3	Roadside....111 H2	Rossett....40 E1	Runcorn....50 E5	St Columb Minor....3 G3	St Twynnells....26 D7
Rhue....101 G3	Roadside of Catterline....97 H8	Rossington....53 J4	Runcton....14 B5	St Columb Road....3 H4	St Vigeans....89 J4
Rhulen....30 C5	Roadside of Kinneff....97 H8	Rossland....79 G4	Runcton Holme....45 K6	St Combs....105 K2	St Wenn....3 H3
Rhunahaorine....77 G7	Roadwater....10 B2	Ross-on-Wye....31 H7	Runfold....14 B1	St Cross South Elmham....37 H1	St Weonards....31 F7
Rhyd, Gwyn....39 F2	Roag....99 H8	Roster....111 J5	Runhall....46 F6	St Cyrus....89 K2	St Winnow....3 K4
Rhyd, Powys....39 J6	Roath....19 F5	Rostherne....51 G5	Runham....47 K5	St David's, Dyfed....26 B4	Salcombe....5 H6
Rhydargaeau....27 J4	Robbingworth....23 L2	Rosthwaite....63 H6	Runnington....10 C3	St David's, Tays....88 B6	Salcombe Regis....10 C7
Rhydcymerau....27 K3	Roberton, Strath....72 E2	Roston....42 D2	Runsell Bay....67 J6	St Day....2 F5	Salcott....25 F1
Rhydd....31 K5	Roberton, Border....73 K3	Rosudgeon....2 D7	Runwell....24 D3	St Dennis....3 H4	Sale....51 G4
Rhyd-Ddu....38 E1	Robertsbridge....16 E3	Rosyth....81 G3	Ruscombe....22 C5	St Dogmaels....26 F2	Saleby....55 J6
Rhydding....18 B3	Roberttown....52 D1	Rothbury....75 G4	Rushall, W. Mids....42 C6	St Dominick....4 E3	Sale Green....32 B4
Rhyd-foel....49 J3	Robeston Cross....26 C6	Rotherfield....16 C3	Rushall, Wilts....20 F7	St Donats....18 D6	Salehurst....16 E3
Rhydlewis....27 H2	Robeston Wathen....26 E5	Rotherfield Greys....22 C4	Rushall, Norf....37 G1	St Endellion....3 G2	Salem, Dyfed....28 D1
Rhydlios....38 A3	Robin Hood's Bay....67 K7	Rotherfield Peppard....22 C4	Rushall, H. & W....31 H6	St Enoder....3 G4	Salem, Dyfed....27 L4
Rhydlydan....39 H1	Roborough....9 F4	Rotherham....53 G4	Rushbrooke....36 D3	St Erme....3 G4	Salen, Strath....85 G4
Rhydowen....27 J2	Roby Mill....50 E3	Rothersthorpe....33 K4	Rushbury....41 G7	St Erney....4 D4	Salen, Highld....85 H2
Rhyd-Rosser....28 C3	Rocester....42 D3	Rotherwick....22 C7	Rushden, Northnts....34 C3	St Erth....2 D6	Salesbury....58 B7
Rhydtalog....40 D1	Roch....26 C4	Rothes....104 B4	Rushden, Herts....35 G6	St Erth Praze....2 D6	Salford, Beds....34 C6
Rhydwyn....48 C2	Rochdale....51 H2	Rothesay....78 C5	Rushford....36 E1	St Ervan....3 G2	Salford, Oxon....32 E7
Rhyd-y-clafdy....38 C3	Roche....3 H3	Rothiebrisbane....97 G2	Rush Green....23 L4		Salford, G. Man....51 H4
			Rothienorman....97 G2		

Salford Priors............32 C4
Salfords...................15 F1
Salhouse.................47 H5
Saline.....................80 F2
Salisbury.................12 D3
Sallachy...................93 F2
Salle.......................47 G4
Salmonby.................55 H6
Salperton................32 C7
Salph End................34 D4
Salsburgh................80 D5
Salt.........................42 B4
Saltash.....................4 E4
Saltburn.................102 F6
Saltburn-by-the-Sea...67 G5
Saltby.....................44 B4
Saltcoats.................78 E7
Saltdean..................15 G5
Salter......................57 K4
Salterforth...............58 D6
Salterswall...............51 F7
Saltfleet..................55 J4
Saltfleetby All Saints...55 J4
Saltfleetby St Clement..55 J4
Saltfleetby St Peter.....55 J5
Saltford...................20 A6
Salthaugh Grange.......55 G1
Salthouse................46 F2
Saltmarshe..............54 B1
Salton.....................60 E2
Saltwood.................17 J2
Salum......................84 B4
Salwarpe.................32 A3
Salwayash................11 F6
Samala....................98 C6
Sambourne..............32 C3
Sambrook.................41 J4
Samlesbury.............57 J7
Samlesbury Bottoms..57 K8
Sampford Arundel.....10 C4
Sampford Brett.........10 B1
Sampford Courtenay....9 G5
Sampford Peverell.....10 B4
Sampford Spiney........4 F2
Samuelston.............82 C4
Sanachan.................92 E1
Sancreed....................2 C7
Sand, Shetld..........115 F4
Sand, Highld...........101 F3
Sandaig...................92 D5
Sandbach................51 G7
Sandbank.................78 D3
Sandbanks...............12 C7
Sandend.................104 E2
Sanderstead.............23 J6
Sandford, Dorset......12 B7
Sandford, Strath.......80 C7
Sandford, Cumbr.......64 E6
Sandford, Devon........9 J5
Sandford, Avon.........19 J7
Sandfordhill............105 L4
Sandford-on-Thames..21 K2
Sandford Orcas.........11 H3
Sandford St Martin....33 G7
Sandgate.................17 K2
Sandgreen................69 G5
Sandhaven..............105 J2
Sandhead.................68 B5
Sandhoe...................75 F8
Sandholme, Humbs...60 F7
Sandholme, Lincs.....45 G3
Sandhurst, Berks......22 D6
Sandhurst, Kent.......16 E3
Sandhurst, Glos.......31 K7
Sand Hutton, N. Yks...60 D5
Sandhutton, N. Yks...59 J2
Sandiacre................43 G3
Sandilands..............55 K5
Sandiway.................50 F6
Sandleheath.............12 D4
Sandleigh................21 J2
Sandling..................24 D7
Sandness................114 B2
Sandon, Staffs.........42 B4
Sandon, Essex..........24 D2
Sandon, Herts..........35 G6
Sandown...................13 H7
Sandplace..................4 C4
Sandridge................23 G1
Sandringham............46 B4
Sandsend................67 J6
Sandsound..............115 F4
Sandtoft..................54 B3
Sandwich.................25 K7
Sandwick, Orkney....112 E8
Sandwick, Shetld....115 G6
Sandwick, W. Isles...98 D8
Sandwick, W. Isles..107 J5
Sandwick, Cumbr......63 K6
Sandwith.................62 E6
Sandy......................34 E5
Sandycroft...............50 C7
Sandygate................56 Q2
Sandyhills...............69 K5
Sandy Lane.............20 D6
Sangobeg...............109 F2
Sannox...................78 C7
Sanquhar................72 C4
Santon.....................61 G7
Santon Bridge..........63 G7
Santon Downham.....36 D1
Sapcote..................43 G7
Sapey Common........31 J3
Sapiston..................36 E2
Sapperton, Glos......20 D2
Sapperton, Lincs......44 D3
Saracen's Head.......45 G4
Sarclet...................111 K4
Sarisbury.................13 H5
Sarn, M. Glam.........18 D4
Sarn, Powys............40 D5
Sarn, Powys............40 D7
Sarnau, Powys........40 D5
Sarnau, Dyfed.........27 H1
Sarnau, Dyfed.........27 H5
Sarnau, Gwyn.........39 J3

Sarn Bach...............38 C4
Sarnesfield.............30 E4
Sarn Meyllteyrn.......38 B3
Saron, Dyfed...........27 H3
Saron, Dyfed...........27 L5
Sarratt...................22 F3
Sarre......................25 J6
Sarsden..................32 E7
Satley.....................65 J3
Satterleigh................9 G3
Satterthwaite...........57 G1
Sauchen..................97 G4
Saucher...................88 D5
Sauchieburn............89 J2
Sauchrie..................71 J3
Saughall.................50 C6
Saughtree................74 B5
Saul........................20 B2
Saundby..................54 B5
Saundersfoot...........26 F6
Saunderton..............22 C2
Saunton....................8 E2
Sausthorpe...............55 H7
Saval....................102 D2
Savon Street............36 B4
Sawbridgeworth.......23 K1
Sawdon...................61 G2
Sawley, Lancs..........58 C6
Sawley, Derby..........43 G3
Sawley, N. Yks.........59 H4
Sawrey....................57 G1
Sawston..................35 H5
Sawtry....................34 E1
Saxby, Leic..............44 B4
Saxby, Lincs............54 E5
Saxby All Saints.......54 D2
Saxelbye.................43 K4
Saxilby...................54 C6
Saxlingham..............46 F3
Saxlingham Nethergate..47 H7
Saxmundham...........37 J3
Saxondale...............43 J3
Saxtead..................37 H3
Saxtead Green.........37 H3
Saxthorpe...............47 G3
Saxton....................60 B7
Sayers Common.......15 F4
Scackleton..............60 D3
Scadabay................99 G3
Scaftworth...............53 J4
Scagglethorpe..........60 F3
Scalasaig................76 C2
Scalby, N. Yks..........61 H1
Scalby Hill...............64 B1
Scaldwell.................34 A2
Scaleby...................64 B1
Scale Houses...........64 C3
Scales, Cumbr..........57 F3
Scales, Cumbr..........63 J5
Scalford..................44 A4
Scaling....................67 H6
Scalloway..............115 G5
Scamblesby.............55 H6
Scampston...............60 F3
Scampton.................54 C6
Scarastavore............98 F3
Scarborough............61 H2
Scarcliffe.................53 G7
Scarcroft.................59 J6
Scardroy................101 J7
Scarfskerry.............111 J1
Scargill...................65 H6
Scarinish................84 B4
Scarisbrick..............50 C2
Scarning.................46 E5
Scarrington..............43 K2
Scarth Hill...............50 D3
Scartho...................55 G3
Scaur or Kippford.....69 K5
Scawby...................54 D3
Scawton..................60 C2
Scayne's Hill...........15 G3
Scethrog.................30 C7
Scholar Green.........41 K1
Scholes, W. Yks.......52 D3
Scholes, W. Yks.......59 J7
Schoolhill................97 G5
Scleddau.................26 D3
Scole.....................37 G2
Scolpaig..................98 C5
Scolton...................26 D4
Sconser...................92 B2
Scoor.....................84 F7
Scopwick.................54 E8
Scoraig..................101 G3
Scorborough............61 H6
Scorrier....................2 F5
Scorton, N. Yks........66 C7
Scorton, Lancs.........57 J6
Sco Ruston..............47 H4
Scotasay.................99 G3
Scotby....................64 B2
Scotch Corner..........66 C7
Scotforth.................57 H5
Scothern..................54 E6
Scotland Gate..........75 J6
Scotlandwell............81 G1
Scotsburn..............102 F5
Scots' Gap..............75 G6
Scots Hole...............54 F7
Scotstown...............85 K2
Scottas...................92 D5
Scotter....................54 C3
Scotterthorpe...........54 C3
Scotton, Lincs..........54 C4
Scotton, N. Yks........59 G1
Scotton, N. Yks........59 J5
Scottow...................47 H4
Scoughall................82 E3
Scoulton.................46 E6
Scourie..................108 C4
Scousburgh............115 F7
Scrabster...............111 G1
Scrainwood.............75 F4
Scrane End..............45 G2

Scraptoft.................43 J6
Scratby....................47 L5
Scrayingham.............60 E4
Screapadal.............100 B8
Scredington..............44 D2
Scremby..................55 J7
Scremerston............83 J7
Screveton................43 K2
Scriven....................59 J5
Scrooby...................53 J4
Scropton..................42 D3
Scrub Hill................45 F1
Scruton....................59 J1
Sculcoates...............54 C2
Sculthorpe...............46 D3
Scunthorpe..............54 C2
Scurlage..................27 J8
Seaborough.............11 F5
Seacombe...............50 C4
Seacroft..................55 K7
Seaford...................15 H6
Seaforth..................50 C4
Seaforth Head........107 G7
Seagrave.................43 J5
Seaham...................66 E3
Seahouses...............75 J1
Sea Palling..............47 K4
Searby....................54 E3
Seasalter.................25 G6
Seascale..................62 F7
Seathorne...............55 K7
Seathwaite, Cumbr....57 F1
Seathwaite, Cumbr....63 H6
Seaton, Leic.............44 C7
Seaton, Durham.......66 D3
Seaton, Corn.............4 D4
Seaton, Devon.........10 D6
Seaton, Cumbr.........62 F4
Seaton, Humbs........61 J6
Seaton, Northum......75 K7
Seaton Burn.............75 J7
Seaton Carew..........66 F5
Seaton Delaval........75 K7
Seaton Ross............60 E6
Seaton Sluice..........75 K7
Seatown...................11 F6
Seave Green............67 F7
Seaview...................13 J6
Seavington St Mary...10 E4
Seavington St Michael..10 E4
Sebastopol..............19 G3
Sebergham..............63 J3
Seckington...............42 E6
Sedbergh.................58 B1
Sedbusk..................58 D1
Sedgeberrow............32 C6
Sedgebrook..............44 B3
Sedgefield...............66 D5
Sedgeford................46 C3
Sedgehill.................12 A3
Sedgley...................42 B7
Sedgwick.................57 J2
Sedlescombe............16 E4
Seend.....................20 D6
Seend Cleeve..........20 D6
Seer Green..............22 E3
Seething..................47 J7
Sefton.....................50 C3
Seghill....................75 J7
Seifton....................31 F1
Seighford.................42 A4
Seilebost..................98 F3
Seisdon....................41 K7
Seisiadar...............107 K5
Selattyn...................40 D3
Selborne..................13 K2
Selby......................60 D7
Selham...................14 C3
Selkirk....................74 A2
Sellack....................31 G7
Sellafirth...............117 G3
Sellindge.................17 J2
Selling.....................25 G7
Sells Green..............20 D6
Selly Oak................32 C1
Selmeston...............15 J5
Selsdon...................23 J6
Selsey.....................14 B6
Selsfield Common.....15 G2
Selside, N. Yks........58 C3
Selside, Cumbr........64 C8
Selston...................43 G1
Selworthy..................9 K1
Semer.....................36 F5
Semington...............20 C6
Semley....................12 A3
Send.......................22 F7
Senghenydd.............18 F3
Sennen.....................2 B7
Sennen Cove............2 B7
Sennybridge.............29 G7
Sereveton.................43 K2
Sessay.....................59 K3
Setchey...................46 B5
Setley.....................13 F5
Setter....................117 H4
Settiscarth.............112 D1
Settle......................58 D4
Settrington..............60 F3
Sevenhampton, Glos..32 C7
Sevenhampton, Wilts..21 G3
Seven Kings.............23 K4
Sevenoaks...............23 L7
Sevenoaks Weald......23 L7
Seven Sisters...........18 C2
Severn Beach...........19 K4
Severn Stoke............32 A5
Sevington................17 H1
Sewards End............35 J6
Sewerby..................61 J4

Seworgan...................2 F6
Sewstern.................44 B4
Sezincote.................32 D6
Sgiogarstaigh.........107 K2
Shabbington............22 B2
Shackerstone...........43 F6
Shackleford.............14 C1
Shader...................107 H3
Shadforth................66 D3
Shadingfield............37 K1
Shadoxhurst............17 G2
Shaftesbury.............12 A3
Shalbourne..............21 H6
Shalcombe...............13 F7
Shalden...................13 J1
Shaldon....................5 K2
Shalfleet..................13 G7
Shalford, Essex........36 C7
Shalford, Surrey.......14 D1
Shalford Green.........36 C7
Shalmsford Street.....25 H7
Shalstone................33 J6
Shamley Green.........14 D1
Shandon..................78 E3
Shandwick.............103 G5
Shangton.................43 K7
Shanklin...................7 K6
Shanquhar...............96 E2
Shap.......................64 C6
Shapwick, Dorset.....12 B5
Shapwick, Somer......11 F2
Shardlow................43 G3
Shareshill................42 B6
Sharlston.................53 F2
Sharnbrook..............34 C4
Sharnford................43 G7
Sharoe Green...........57 J7
Sharow....................59 J3
Sharpenhoe..............34 D6
Sharperton..............75 F4
Sharpness...............20 A2
Sharpthorne............15 G2
Sharrington.............46 F3
Shatterford...............31 J1
Shaugh Prior.............4 F3
Shavington..............41 H1
Shaw, Wilts.............20 C6
Shaw, G. Man.........51 J3
Shaw, Berks.............21 J3
Shawbost...............107 G4
Shawbury................41 G4
Shawell...................33 H1
Shawford.................13 G3
Shawforth................51 H1
Shawhead................72 D7
Shaw Mills..............59 H4
Shawhead................72 D7
Sheanwick...............59 J3
Shearsby.................43 J7
Shebbear...................8 E5
Shebdon...................41 J4
Shebster................111 G2
Shedfield..................13 H4
Sheen.....................52 D7
Sheepscombe..........20 C1
Sheepstor..................4 F3
Sheepwash................8 E5
Sheepy Magna.........43 F6
Sheepy Parva...........43 F6
Sheering..................23 L1
Sheerness................24 F5
Sheet......................14 A3
Sheffield.................53 F5
Sheffield Bottom......22 B6
Shefford..................34 E6
Sheinton..................41 H6
Shelderton...............30 F2
Sheldon, Devon.......10 C5
Sheldon, W. Mids....32 D1
Sheldon, Derby........52 D7
Sheldwich................25 G7
Shelf.......................59 G8
Shelfanger...............37 G1
Shelfield..................42 C6
Shelford..................43 J2
Shelley....................52 E2
Shellingford..............21 H3
Shellow Bowells.......24 C2
Shelsley Beauchamp..31 J3
Shelsley Walsh........31 J3
Shelton, Notts.........44 A2
Shelton, Northnts....34 D3
Shelton, Norf...........47 H7
Shelton Green..........47 H7
Shelve.....................40 E7
Shelwick..................31 G5
Shenfield.................24 C3
Shenington..............33 F5
Shenley...................23 G2
Shenley Brook End...34 B6
Shenleybury.............23 G2
Shenley Church End..34 B6
Shenmore................30 E6
Shenstone, H. & W...32 A2
Shenstone, Staffs....42 D6
Shenton...................43 F6
Shenval, Grampn......96 B3
Shenval, Highld........94 C3
Shepherd's Green.....22 C4
Shepherdswell or Sibertswold..17 K1
Shepley...................52 E2
Shepperdine.............19 L3
Shepperton..............23 F6
Shepreth..................35 G5
Shepshed.................43 G5
Shepton Beauchamp..10 F4
Shepton Mallet........11 H1
Shepton Montague....11 H2
Shepway..................24 D7
Sheraton..................66 E4
Sherborne, Glos.......21 F1
Sherborne, Dorset....11 H4
Sherborne St John....22 B7
Sherbourne..............32 E3
Sherburn, Durham....66 D3
Sherburn, N. Yks......61 G3

Sherburn in Elmet......60 B7
Shere......................14 D1
Shereford.................46 D4
Sherfield English.......12 E3
Sherfield on Loddon...22 B7
Sherford....................5 H5
Sheriffhales.............41 J5
Sheriff Hutton..........60 D4
Sheringham.............47 G2
Sherington...............34 B5
Shernborne..............46 C3
Sherrington..............12 B2
Sherston..................20 C4
Sherwood Green........9 F3
Shettleston..............79 J6
Shevington...............50 E3
Shevington Moor......50 E2
Sheviock...................4 D4
Shiel Bridge............93 F4
Shieldaig, Highld....100 E5
Shieldaig, Highld....100 E7
Shieldhill.................80 D4
Shielfoot..................85 H1
Shifnal....................41 J6
Shilbottle.................75 H4
Shildon...................66 C5
Shillingford, Devon...10 A3
Shillingford, Oxon....21 K3
Shillingford St George..9 K7
Shillingstone...........11 H4
Shillington................34 E6
Shillmoor.................74 E4
Shilton, Warw..........33 G5
Shilton, Oxon...........21 G2
Shimpling, Suff........36 D4
Shimpling, Norf........37 G1
Shimpling Street.......36 D4
Shiney Row..............66 D2
Shinfield..................22 C6
Shingay...................35 F5
Shinness................107 G7
Shipbourne..............24 C7
Shipdham................46 E6
Shipham...................19 J7
Shiphay....................5 J3
Shiplake..................22 C5
Shipley, W. Susx......14 E1
Shipley, W. Yks........59 G7
Shipley, Shrops........41 K7
Shipmeadow............47 J7
Shippon...................21 J3
Shipston-on-Stour....32 E5
Shipton, N. Yks........60 C5
Shipton, Glos...........20 D1
Shipton, Shrops........41 G7
Shipton Bellinger......12 E1
Shipton Gorge..........11 F6
Shipton Green..........14 B6
Shipton Moyne.........20 C3
Shipton-on-Cherwell..21 J1
Shiptonthorpe..........60 E6
Shipton-under-Wychwood..21 G1
Shirburn..................22 B3
Shirdley Hill.............50 C2
Shirebrook...............53 H7
Shirehampton...........19 K5
Shiremoor................75 K7
Shirenewton.............19 J3
Shire Oak.................42 C6
Shireoaks................53 H5
Shirkoak..................17 G2
Shirland..................53 F8
Shirley, W. Mids.......32 D2
Shirley, Derby..........42 E2
Shirley, Hants..........13 G4
Shirl Heath..............31 F4
Shirrell Heath...........13 H4
Shobdon..................30 F3
Shobrooke.................9 J5
Shocklach................41 F2
Shoeburyness...........25 F4
Sholden...................25 K7
Sholing....................13 G4
Sholver....................51 J3
Shop, Corn.................8 C4
Shop, Corn.................3 G2
Shoreditch...............23 J4
Shoreham................23 L6
Shoreham-by-Sea.....15 F5
Shoresdean..............83 H7
Shoreswood.............83 H7
Shoreton................102 E6
Shorncote................20 E3
Shorne....................24 C5
Shortgate.................15 H4
Short Heath, W. Mids..42 D7
Short Heath, Leic.....43 F5
Shortlanesend............3 G2
Shortlees.................79 G8
Shortley Bridge........65 H2
Shorwell..................13 G4
Shoscombe..............20 B7
Shotesham..............47 H7
Shotgate..................24 D3
Shotley....................37 H6
Shotley Gate...........37 H6
Shotleyfield.............25 H2
Shottenden..............25 H7
Shottermill..............14 B2
Shottery..................32 D4
Shotteswell.............33 G5
Shottisham.............37 J5
Shottle....................43 F2
Shotton, Clwyd........50 C7
Shotton, Northum.....74 E1
Shotton, Durham......66 E4
Shotts....................80 D5
Shotwick.................50 C6
Shoughlaige-e-Caine..56 Q3
Shouldham..............46 B6
Shouldham Thorpe....46 B6
Shoulton..................31 K4
Shrawardine............40 F1
Shrawley.................31 K3
Shrewley..................32 E3

Shrewsbury.............41 F5
Shrewton.................12 C1
Shripney..................14 C5
Shrivenham.............21 G4
Shropham................46 F7
Shroton or Iwerne Courtney..11 K4
Shrub End................36 E7
Shucknall................31 G5
Shudy Camps...........35 K5
Shulishader............107 K5
Shurdington.............20 D1
Shurlock Row...........22 D5
Shurrery.................111 G3
Shurton...................10 D1
Shustoke.................42 E7
Shute......................10 E4
Shutford..................33 F5
Shuthonger..............32 A6
Shutlanger...............33 K5
Shuttington..............42 E6
Shuttlewood............53 G6
Sibbertoft................33 J1
Sibdon Carwood.......31 F1
Sibertswold or Shepherdswell..17 K1
Sibford Ferris...........33 F6
Sibford Gower..........33 F6
Sible Hedingham......36 C6
Sibsey.....................45 G1
Sibson, Cambs.........44 D7
Sibson, Leic.............43 F6
Sibthorpe................44 A2
Sibton.....................37 J3
Sicklesmere............36 D3
Sicklinghall.............59 J6
Sidbury, Devon.........10 C6
Sidbury, Shrops........31 H1
Sidcup.....................23 K5
Siddington, Glos......20 E3
Siddington, Ches......51 H6
Sidestrand..............47 H3
Sidford....................10 C6
Sidinish...................98 D6
Sidlesham...............14 B6
Sidley.....................16 E5
Sidmouth.................10 C7
Sigford.....................5 H2
Sigglesthorne...........61 J6
Silchester................22 B6
Sileby......................43 J5
Silecroft..................56 E2
Silian......................27 K1
Silkstone.................52 E3
Silkstone Common....52 E3
Silk Willoughby........44 D2
Silloth.....................63 G2
Sillyearn................104 E3
Siloh.......................28 E6
Silpho......................61 G1
Silsden....................58 F6
Silsoe.....................34 D6
Silton.......................11 J3
Silverburn................81 H5
Silverdale, Cumbr......57 H3
Silverdale, Staffs......41 K2
Silver End................24 E1
Silvergate...............105 G2
Silverley's Green.......37 H2
Silverstone..............33 J5
Silverton...................9 K5
Silwick..................114 E4
Simonburn...............74 E7
Simonsbath................9 H2
Simonstone..............58 C7
Simprim..................83 G7
Sinclairston.............71 K3
Sinderby..................59 J2
Sinderhope..............65 F2
Sindlesham...............22 C6
Singleton, W. Susx...14 B4
Singleton, Lancs......57 G2
Singlewell...............24 C5
Sinnahard................96 D4
Sinnington..............60 D2
Sinton Green...........31 K3
Sipson.....................22 F5
Sirhowy....................18 F1
Sissinghurst.............16 E2
Siston.....................20 A5
Sithney.....................2 E7
Sittingbourne...........24 F6
Six Ashes................31 J1
Sixhills....................55 F5
Sixpenny Handley.....12 B4
Sizewell...................37 K3
Skares....................71 L3
Skateraw................82 F4
Skaw.....................115 H2
Skeabost..................99 K8
Skeabrae................112 C4
Skeeby.....................66 B7
Skeffington.............44 A6
Skeffling..................55 H4
Skegby....................53 G7
Skegness.................55 K7
Skelberry...............113 C6
Skelbo....................103 F3
Skeldyke..................45 G3
Skellingthorpe...........54 C6
Skellister................115 G3
Skellow....................53 H2
Skelmanthorpe.........52 E2
Skelmersdale............50 D3
Skelmorlie...............78 D5
Skelpick.................110 D3
Skelton, Cumbr........64 B4
Skelton, N. Yks........60 C5
Skelton, Cleve.........67 G6
Skelton, N. Yks........65 H7
Skelton on Ure.........59 J4
Skelwick................113 E2
Skelwith Bridge........63 J7
Skendleby................55 H7
Skenfrith.................31 F7

Skerne....61 H5
Skerray....109 H2
Sketty....27 L7
Skewen....18 B3
Skewsby....60 D3
Skeyton....47 H4
Skidbrooke....55 J4
Skidby....61 H7
Skilgate....10 A3
Skillington....44 B4
Skinburness....63 G2
Skinflats....80 E3
Skinidin....99 H8
Skinningrove....67 H6
Skipness....77 J6
Skipsea....61 J5
Skipton....58 E5
Skipton-on-Swale....59 J3
Skipwith....60 D7
Skirlaugh....61 J7
Skirling....81 F8
Skirmett....22 C3
Skirpenbeck....60 E5
Skirwith....64 D4
Skirza....111 K2
Skulamus....92 C3
Skullomie....109 H2
Skye of Curr....95 H3
Slack....58 E8
Slackhall....52 C5
Slackhead....104 D2
Slacks of Cairnbanno....105 H4
Slad....20 C2
Slade....8 F1
Slade Green....23 L5
Slaggyford....64 D2
Slaidburn....58 C5
Slaithwaite....52 C2
Slaley....65 G2
Slamannan....80 D4
Slapton, Bucks....34 C7
Slapton, Devon....5 J5
Slapton, Northnts....33 J5
Slaugham....15 F3
Slawston....44 A7
Sleaford, Hants....14 B2
Sleaford, Lincs....44 D2
Sleagill....64 C6
Sleapford....41 H5
Sledge Green....31 K6
Sledmere....61 G4
Sleightholme....65 G6
Sleights....67 J7
Slepe....12 B6
Slickly....111 K2
Sliddery....70 E2
Slimbridge....20 B2
Slindon, W. Susx....14 C5
Slindon, Staffs....41 K3
Slinfold....14 E2
Slingsby....60 D3
Slip End....23 F1
Slipton....34 C2
Slochd....95 G3
Slockavullin....77 H2
Sloley....47 H4
Sloothby....55 J6
Slough, Powys....30 E3
Slough, Berks....22 E4
Slyne....57 H4
Smailholm....82 E8
Smallbridge....51 J2
Smallburgh....47 J4
Smallburn, Strath....72 B2
Smallburn, Grampn....97 K1
Small Dole....15 F4
Smalley....43 G2
Smallfield....15 G1
Small Hythe....17 F2
Smallridge....10 E5
Smardale....64 E7
Smarden....17 F1
Smeatharpe....10 C4
Smeeth....17 H2
Smeeton Westerby....43 J7
Smerclate....90 C4
Smerral....111 H5
Smethwick....32 C1
Smirisary....92 C3
Smisby....43 F5
Smithfield....64 B1
Smithincott....10 B4
Smithton....102 F8
Snailbeach....40 E6
Snailwell....36 B3
Snainton....61 G2
Snaith....53 J1
Snape, N. Yks....59 H2
Snape, Suff....37 J4
Snarestone....43 F6
Snarford....54 E5
Snargate....17 G3
Snave....17 H3
Snead....40 E7
Sneaton....67 J7
Sneatonthorpe....67 K7
Snelland....54 E5
Snelston....42 D2
Snettisham....46 B3
Snishival....90 C2
Snitter....75 G4
Snitterby....54 D4
Snitterfield....32 E3
Snitton....31 G2
Snodhill....30 E5
Snodland....24 D6
Snowshill....32 C6
Soberton....13 J4
Soberton Heath....13 J4
Soham....35 J2
Soldon Cross....8 D3
Soldridge....13 J2
Sole Street, Kent....24 C6
Sole Street, Kent....17 H1
Solihull....32 D2

Sollas....98 D5
Sollers Dilwyn....31 F4
Sollers Hope....31 H6
Sollom....50 D2
Solva....26 C4
Somerby....44 A5
Somercotes....43 G1
Somerford Keynes....20 E3
Somerley....14 B6
Somerleyton....47 K7
Somersby....55 H6
Somersal Herbert....42 D3
Somersham, Suff....37 F5
Somersham, Cambs....35 G2
Somerton, Somer....11 F3
Somerton, Oxon....33 G7
Somerton, Norf....47 K5
Sompting....14 E5
Sonning....22 C5
Sonning Common....22 C4
Sopley....12 D6
Sopworth....20 C4
Sorbie....68 F6
Sordale....111 H2
Sorisdale....84 D2
Sorn....72 A2
Sortat....111 J2
Sotby....55 G6
Sots Hole....54 F7
Sotterley....37 K1
Soudley....41 J4
Soughton or Sychdyn....50 B7
Soulbury....34 B7
Soulby....64 E6
Souldern....33 H6
Souldrop....34 C3
Sound, Shetld....115 F3
Sound, Shetld....115 G4
Soundwell....20 A5
Sourhope....74 E2
Sourin....112 E3
Sourton....9 F6
Soutergate....57 F2
South Acre....46 D5
Southall....23 G4
South Allington....5 H6
South Alloa....80 D2
Southam, Glos....32 B7
Southam, Warw....33 G3
South Ambersham....14 C3
Southampton....13 G4
South Bank....67 F5
South Barrow....11 H3
South Benfleet....24 D4
Southborough....16 C1
Southbourne, W. Susx....14 A5
Southbourne, Dorset....12 D6
South Brent....5 G3
Southburgh....46 E6
South Burlingham....47 J6
South Cadbury....11 H3
South Carlton....54 D6
South Cave....61 G7
South Cerney....20 E3
South Chard....10 E5
South Charlton....75 H2
South Cheriton....11 H3
Southchurch....24 F4
South Cliffe....60 F7
South Clifton....54 C6
South Cove....37 K1
South Creake....46 D3
South Croxton....43 J5
South Dalton....61 G6
South Darenth....24 B6
South Duffield....60 D7
Southease....15 H5
South Elkington....55 G5
South Elmsall....53 G2
Southend, Strath....70 B4
South End, Cumbr....56 F4
Southend, Berks....21 K5
Southend-on-Sea....24 E4
Southerndown....18 C5
Southerness....62 E2
South Erradale....100 D5
Southery....45 K7
South Fambridge....24 E3
South Fawley....21 H4
South Ferriby....54 D1
Southfleet....24 C5
South Garvan....93 H3
Southgate, Norf....47 G4
Southgate, G. Lon....23 J3
Southgate, W. Glam....27 K8
South Godstone....15 G1
South Gorley....12 D4
South Green....24 C3
South Hanningfield....24 D3
South Harting....14 A4
South Hayling....13 K6
South Heath....22 E2
South Heighton....15 H5
South Hetton....66 D3
South Hiendley....53 F2
South Hill....4 D2
South Hole....8 C4
South Holmwood....14 E1
South Hornchurch....23 L4
South Hylton....66 D2
Southill....34 E5
South Kelsey....54 E4
South Kilvington....59 K2
South Kilworth....33 J1
South Kirkby....53 G2
South Kirkton....97 G5
South Kyme....44 E2
South Lancing....14 E5
Southleigh, Devon....10 D6
South Leigh, Oxon....21 H2
South Leverton....54 B5
South Littleton....32 C5
South Lochboisdale....90 C4
South Lopham....36 F1
South Luffenham....44 C6

South Malling....15 H4
South Marston....21 F4
South Milford....60 B7
South Milton....5 G5
South Mimms....23 H2
Southminster....25 F3
South Molton....9 H3
South Moor, Durham....66 B2
Southmoor, Oxon....21 J3
South Moreton....21 K4
South Mundam....14 B5
South Muskham....44 A1
South Newington....33 G6
South Newton....12 C2
South Normanton....43 G1
South Norwood....23 J6
South Nutfield....15 G1
South Ockendon....24 B4
Southoe....34 E3
Southolt....37 G3
South Ormsby....55 H6
Southorpe....44 D6
South Otterington....59 J2
Southowram....52 D1
South Oxhey....23 G3
South Perrott....11 F5
South Petherton....11 F4
South Petherwin....8 D7
South Pickenham....46 D6
South Pool....5 H5
Southport....50 C2
South Raynham....46 D4
Southrepps....47 H3
South Reston....55 J5
Southrey....55 F7
Southrop....21 G2
Southrope....13 J1
South Runcton....46 B6
South Scarle....54 C7
Southsea....13 J6
South Shields....75 K8
South Shore....57 G7
South Somercotes....55 J4
South Stainley....59 J4
South Stainmore....65 F6
Southstoke, Avon....20 B6
South Stoke, W. Susx....14 D4
South Stoke, Oxon....21 K4
South Street....15 G4
South Tawton....9 G6
South Thoresby....55 J6
South Tidworth....12 E1
Southtown, Orkney....113 D7
South Town, Hants....13 J2
Southwaite....64 B3
South Walsham....47 J5
South Warnborough....13 K1
Southwater....14 E3
Southway....11 G1
South Weald....24 B3
Southwell, Dorset....6 A7
Southwell, Notts....43 K1
South Weston....22 C3
South Wheatley....8 C6
Southwick, Wilts....20 C7
Southwick, T. & W....66 D2
Southwick, Northnts....44 D7
Southwick, W. Susx....15 F5
Southwick, Hants....13 J5
South Widcombe....19 K7
South Wigston....43 H7
South Willingham....55 F5
South Wingfield....43 F1
South Witham....44 C5
Southwold....37 L2
South Wonston....13 G2
Southwood....47 J6
South Woodham Ferrers....24 E3
South Wootton....46 B4
South Zeal....9 G6
Soutra Farm....82 C6
Sowerby, W. Yks....52 C1
Sowerby, N. Yks....59 K2
Sowerby Bridge....52 C1
Sowerby Row....63 J3
Sowton....10 A6
Spa Common....47 H3
Spalding....45 F4
Spaldington....60 E7
Spaldwick....34 E2
Spalford....54 C7
Sparham....46 F5
Spark Bridge....57 G2
Sparkford....11 H3
Sparkwell....5 F4
Sparrowpit....52 C5
Sparsholt, Hants....13 G2
Sparsholt, Oxon....21 H4
Spaunton....60 E2
Spaxton....10 D2
Spean Bridge....93 J7
Speen, Bucks....22 D3
Speen, Berks....21 J6
Speeton....61 J3
Speke....50 D5
Speldhurst....16 C1
Spellbrook....23 K1
Spelsbury....33 F7
Spencers Wood....22 C6
Spennithorne....59 G2
Spennymoor....66 C4
Spetchley....32 A4
Spetisbury....12 B5
Spexhall....37 J1
Spey Bay....104 C2
Speybridge....95 J3
Spilsby....55 J7
Spindlestone....75 H1
Spinningdale....102 E4
Spirthill....20 D5
Spithurst....15 H4
Spittal, Lothn....82 C4
Spittal, Dyfed....26 D4
Spittal, Highld....111 H3
Spittal, Northum....83 J6

Spittalfield....88 D4
Spittal of Glenmuick....96 C7
Spittal of Glenshee....88 D1
Spixworth....47 H5
Spofforth....59 J5
Spondon....43 G3
Spooner Row....47 F7
Sporle....46 D5
Spott....82 E4
Spratton....33 K2
Spreakley....14 B1
Spreyton....9 G6
Spridlington....54 E5
Springburn....79 J5
Springcorrie....107 G5
Springfield, W. Mids....32 C1
Springfield, Fife....89 F7
Springfield, Grampn....103 J6
Springholm....72 D8
Springside....79 F8
Springthorpe....54 C5
Sproatley....61 J7
Sproston Green....51 G7
Sprotbrough....53 H3
Sproughton....34 E5
Sprouston....82 F8
Sprowston....47 H5
Sproxton, Leic....44 B4
Sproxton, N. Yks....60 D2
Spurstow....41 G1
Square and Compass....26 C3
Stackhouse....58 D4
Stackpole....26 D7
Stacksteads....51 H1
Staddiscombe....4 F4
Staddlethorpe....60 F8
Stadhampton....21 L3
Staffield....64 C3
Staffin....99 K6
Stafford....42 B4
Stagsden....34 C5
Stainacre....67 K7
Stainburn....59 H6
Stainby....44 C4
Staincross....53 F2
Staindrop....65 J5
Staines....22 F5
Stainfield, Lincs....44 D4
Stainfield, Lincs....54 F6
Stainforth, N. Yks....58 D4
Stainforth, S. Yks....53 J2
Staining....57 G7
Stainland....52 C2
Stainsacre....67 K7
Stainton, Cumbr....64 B5
Stainton, Cleve....66 E6
Stainton, N. Yks....59 G1
Stainton, S. Yks....53 H4
Stainton, Durham....65 H6
Stainton, Cumbr....57 J2
Stainton by Langworth....54 E6
Staintondale....67 K8
Stainton le Vale....55 F4
Stainton with Adgarley....57 F3
Stair, Cumbr....63 H5
Stair, Strath....71 K2
Staithes....67 H6
Stakeford....75 J6
Stake Pool....57 H6
Stalbridge....11 J4
Stalbridge Weston....11 J4
Stalham....47 J4
Stalham Green....47 J4
Stalisfield Green....25 F7
Stallingborough....55 G2
Stalling Busk....58 E2
Stalmine....57 G6
Stalybridge....51 J4
Station Town....66 E4
Staughton Highway....34 E3
Staunton, Glos....31 J7
Staunton, Glos....19 K1
Staunton in the Vale....44 B2
Staunton on Arrow....30 E3
Staunton on Wye....30 E5
Staveley, Cumbr....64 B8
Staveley, Derby....53 G6
Staveley, N. Yks....59 J4
Staveley-in-Cartmel....57 G2
Staverton, Glos....32 A7
Staverton, Wilts....20 C6
Staverton, Northnts....33 H3
Staverton, Devon....5 H3
Stawell....10 E2
Staxigoe....111 K3
Staxton....61 H3
Staylittle....39 H7
Staythorpe....44 A1
Stean....59 F3
Stearsby....60 D3
Steart....10 D1
Stebbing....36 B7
Stedham....14 B3
Steele Road....74 B5
Steen's Bridge....31 G4
Steep....13 K3
Steeple, Dorset....6 D6
Steeple, Essex....25 F2
Steeple Ashton....20 D7
Steeple Aston....33 G7
Steeple Barton....33 G7
Steeple Bumpstead....36 B5
Steeple Claydon....33 J6
Steeple Gidding....34 E1
Steeple Langford....12 C2
Steeple Morden....35 F5
Steeton....58 F6
Steinmanhill....105 G4
Steisay....98 D8
Stelling Minnis....17 J1
Stemster....111 H2
Stenalees....3 J4
Stenhousemuir....80 D3
Stenton....82 E4
Stepney....23 J4
Steppingley....34 D6

Stepps....79 J5
Sternfield....37 J3
Stert....20 E7
Stetchworth....36 B4
Stevenage....35 F7
Stevenston....78 E7
Steventon, Hants....13 H1
Steventon, Oxon....21 J3
Stevington....34 C4
Stewartby....34 D5
Stewarton....79 G7
Stewkley....34 B7
Stewton....55 H5
Steyning....14 E4
Steynton....26 D6
Stibb....8 C4
Stibbard....46 E4
Stibb Cross....8 E4
Stibb Green....21 G6
Stibbington....44 D7
Stichill....82 F8
Sticker....3 H4
Stickford....55 H8
Sticklepath....9 G6
Stickney....45 G1
Stiffkey....46 E2
Stifford's Bridge....31 J5
Stillgarry....90 C2
Stillingfleet....60 C6
Stillington, N. Yks....60 C4
Stillington, Cleve....66 D5
Stilton....44 E8
Stinchcombe....20 B3
Stinsford....11 J6
Stirchley....41 J6
Stirling....80 C2
Stisted....36 D7
Stithians....7 F6
Stittenham....102 E5
Stivichall....33 F2
Stixwould....55 F7
Stoak....50 D6
Stobo....81 G8
Stoborough....12 B7
Stoborough Green....12 B7
Stock....24 C3
Stockbridge....13 F2
Stockbriggs....80 C8
Stockbury....24 E6
Stockcross....21 J6
Stockdalewath....63 J3
Stockerston....44 B7
Stock Green....32 B4
Stockingford....43 F7
Stocking Pelham....35 H7
Stockinish Island....99 G3
Stockland....10 D5
Stockland Bristol....10 D1
Stockleigh English....9 J5
Stockleigh Pomeroy....9 J5
Stockley....20 E6
Stockport....51 H4
Stocksbridge....52 E4
Stocksfield....65 H1
Stockton, Wilts....12 B2
Stockton, Warw....33 G3
Stockton, H. & W....31 G3
Stockton, Norf....47 J7
Stockton, Shrops....41 J7
Stockton Heath....50 F5
Stockton-on-Tees....66 E6
Stockton on Teme....31 J3
Stockton on the Forest....60 D5
Stock Wood....32 C4
Stodmarsh....25 J6
Stoer....108 B6
Stoford, Wilts....12 C2
Stoford, Somer....11 G4
Stogumber....10 B2
Stogursey....10 D1
Stoke, Devon....8 C3
Stoke, Kent....24 E5
Stoke, Hants....21 J7
Stoke, Hants....13 K5
Stoke Abbott....11 F5
Stoke Albany....34 B1
Stoke Ash....37 G2
Stoke Bardolph....43 J2
Stoke Bliss....31 H3
Stoke Bruerne....34 A5
Stoke by Clare....36 C5
Stoke-by-Nayland....36 E6
Stoke Canon....9 K6
Stoke Charity....13 G2
Stoke Climsland....4 D2
Stoke D'Abernon....23 G7
Stoke Doyle....34 D1
Stoke Dry....44 B7
Stoke Ferry....46 C6
Stoke Fleming....5 J5
Stokeford....12 A7
Stoke Gabriel....5 J4
Stoke Gifford....19 L4
Stoke Golding....43 F7
Stoke Goldington....34 B5
Stokeham....54 B6
Stoke Hammond....34 B7
Stoke Heath....41 H4
Stoke Holy Cross....47 H6
Stoke Lacy....31 H5
Stoke Lyne....33 H7
Stoke Mandeville....22 D1
Stokenchurch....22 C3
Stoke Newington....23 J4
Stokenham....5 J5
Stoke on Tern....41 H4
Stoke-on-Trent....42 A2
Stoke Orchard....32 B7
Stoke Poges....22 E4
Stoke Prior, H. & W....32 B3
Stoke Prior, H. & W....31 G4
Stoke Rivers....9 G2
Stoke Rochford....44 C4
Stoke Row....22 B4

Stokesay 31 F1
Stokesby 47 K5
Stokesley 66 F7
Stoke St Gregory 10 E3
Stoke St Mary 10 D3
Stoke St Michael 11 H1
Stoke St Milborough 31 G1
Stoke sub Hamdon 11 F4
Stoke Talmage 22 B3
Stoke Trister 11 J3
Stolford 10 D1
Stondon Massey 24 B2
Stone, H. & W. 32 A2
Stone, Glos. 20 A3
Stone, Staffs. 42 B3
Stone, Kent 24 B5
Stone, Bucks. 22 C1
Stone Allerton 19 J7
Ston Easton 19 L7
Stonebroom 53 G8
Stone Cross 16 D5
Stonegate 16 D3
Stonegrave 60 D3
Stonehaugh 74 D7
Stonehaven 97 H7
Stonehouse, Glos. 20 C2
Stone House, Cumbr. 58 C2
Stonehouse, Strath. 80 C7
Stonehouse, Northum. 64 D2
Stone in Oxney 17 G3
Stoneleigh 33 F2
Stonely 34 E3
Stonesby 44 B4
Stonesfield 21 H1
Stones Green 37 G7
Stoneybridge 90 C2
Stoneyburn 80 E5
Stoney Cross 12 E4
Stoneygate, Leic. 43 J6
Stoneygate, Grampn. 97 K2
Stoneyhills 25 F3
Stoneykirk 68 B5
Stoney Middleton 52 E6
Stoney Stanton 43 G7
Stoney Stratton 11 H2
Stoney Stretton 40 E6
Stoneywood 97 H4
Stonham Aspal 37 G4
Stonnall 42 C6
Stonor 22 C4
Stonton Wyville 43 K7
Stonybreck 112 N1
Stony Stratford 34 A5
Stoodleigh 9 K4
Stopham 14 D4
Stopsley 34 E7
Storeton 50 C5
Stornoway 107 J5
Storridge 31 J5
Storrington 14 D4
Storrs 57 H1
Storth 57 H3
Stotfold 35 F6
Stottesdon 31 H1
Stoughton, W. Susx 14 B4
Stoughton, Surrey 22 E7
Stoughton, Leic. 43 J6
Stoul 92 D6
Stoulton 32 B5
Stourbridge 32 B1
Stourpaine 12 A5
Stourport-on-Severn 31 K2
Stour Provost 11 J3
Stour Row 11 K3
Stourton, Staffs. 32 A1
Stourton, Warw. 32 E6
Stourton, Wilts. 11 J2
Stourton Caundle 11 J4
Stoven 37 K1
Stow 54 C5
Stow Bardolph 45 K6
Stow Bedon 46 E7
Stowbridge 45 K6
Stow cum Quy 35 J3
Stowe 30 E2
Stowe-by-Chartley 42 C4
Stowell 11 H3
Stowford 8 E7
Stowlangtoft 36 E3
Stow Longa 34 E2
Stow Maries 24 E3
Stowmarket 36 F4
Stow-on-the-Wold 32 D7
Stowting 17 J1
Stowupland 34 D3
Straad 78 C5
Strachan 97 G6
Strachur 78 C1
Stradbroke 37 H2
Stradishall 36 C4
Stradsett 46 B6
Stragglethorpe 44 C1
Straiton, Lothn. 81 H5
Straiton, Strath. 71 J4
Straloch 88 C2
Stramshall 42 C3
Stranraer 68 B4
Strata Florida 28 E3
Stratfield Mortimer 22 B6
Stratfield Saye 22 B6
Stratfield Turgis 22 B6
Stratford 23 J4
Stratford St Andrew 37 J3
Stratford St Mary 36 F6
Stratford Tony 12 C3
Stratford-upon-Avon 32 E4
Strath 100 D5
Strathan, Highld. 108 B6
Strathan, Highld. 93 F6
Strathaven 80 C7
Strathblane 79 H4
Strathdon 96 C4
Strath Kanaird 101 H2
Strathkinness 89 G7
Strathmiglo 88 E7

Strathpeffer 102 C7
Strathrannoch 102 B5
Strathtay 88 B3
Strathwhillan 78 C8
Strathy 110 E2
Strathyre 87 H7
Stratton, Corn. 8 C5
Stratton, Glos. 20 E2
Stratton, Dorset 11 H6
Stratton Audley 33 J7
Stratton-on-the-Fosse 20 A7
Stratton St Margaret 21 F4
Stratton St Michael 47 H7
Stratton Strawless 47 H4
Streat 15 G4
Streatham 23 H5
Streatley, Beds. 34 D7
Streatley, Berks. 21 K4
Street, Somer. 11 F2
Street, N. Yks. 67 H7
Street, Lancs. 57 J5
Street End 14 B6
Streethay 42 D5
Streetly 42 C7
Strefford 31 F1
Strensall 60 D4
Strensham 32 B5
Stretcholt 10 D1
Strete 5 J5
Stretford 51 G4
Stretford Court 31 F4
Strethall 35 H6
Stretham 35 J2
Strettington 14 B5
Stretton, Staffs. 42 A5
Stretton, Leic. 44 C5
Stretton, Staffs. 42 E4
Stretton, Ches. 41 F1
Stretton, Ches. 50 F5
Stretton, Derby 53 F7
Stretton en le Fields 43 F5
Stretton Grandison 31 H5
Stretton Heath 40 E5
Stretton-on-Dunsmore 33 G2
Stretton-on-Fosse 32 E6
Stretton Sugwas 31 F5
Stretton under Fosse 33 G1
Stretton Westwood 41 G7
Strichen 105 J3
Stringston 10 C1
Strixton 34 C3
Stroat 19 K3
Stromeferry 92 E2
Stromemore 92 E2
Stromness 112 C6
Stronachlachar 87 G7
Strond 98 F4
Strone, Strath. 78 D3
Strone, Highld. 94 D3
Strone, Highld. 93 H7
Stronenaba 93 J7
Stronmilchan 86 D6
Strontian 85 K2
Strood 24 D6
Stroud, Glos. 20 C2
Stroud, Hants 13 K3
Struan, Highld. 91 J2
Struan, Tays. 87 L2
Strubby 55 J5
Strumpshaw 47 J6
Strutherhill 80 C7
Struy 94 C2
Stuartfield 105 J4
Stubbington 13 H5
Stubbins 51 G2
Stubhampton 12 B4
Stubton 44 B2
Stuckton 12 D4
Studham 22 F1
Studland 12 C7
Studley, Warw. 32 C3
Studley, Wilts. 20 D5
Studley Roger 59 H3
Stuntney 35 J2
Sturbridge 41 K3
Sturmer 36 B5
Sturminster Marshall 12 B6
Sturminster Newton 11 J4
Sturry 25 H6
Sturton by Stow 54 C5
Sturton le Steeple 54 B5
Stuston 37 G2
Stutton, N. Yks. 60 B6
Stutton, Suff. 37 G6
Styal 51 H5
Suainebost 107 K2
Suckley 31 J4
Sudborough 34 C1
Sudbourne 37 K4
Sudbrook, Lincs. 54 E6
Sudbrook, Gwent 19 K4
Sudbury, Derby 42 D3
Sudbury, Suff. 36 D5
Sudgrove 20 D2
Suffield 47 H3
Sugnall 41 K3
Sulby 56 Q2
Sulgrave 33 H5
Sulham 22 B5
Sulhamstead 22 B6
Sullington 14 D4
Sullom 116 E5
Sully 18 F6
Sumburgh 115 F8
Summerbridge 59 H4
Summercourt 3 G4
Summerleaze 19 J4
Summerseat 51 G2
Summit 51 J2
Sunbiggin 64 D7
Sunbury 22 F6
Sunderland, T. & W. 66 D2
Sunderland, Cumbr. 63 G4
Sunderland Bridge 66 C4
Sundhope 73 J2

Sundon Park 34 D7
Sundridge 23 K7
Sunk Island 55 G2
Sunningdale 22 E6
Sunninghill 22 E6
Sunningwell 21 J2
Sunniside, T. & W. 66 C2
Sunniside, Durham 65 J4
Sunnylaw 80 C2
Sunnyside 15 G2
Surbiton 23 G6
Surfleet 45 F4
Surfleet Seas End 45 F4
Surlingham 47 J6
Sustead 47 G3
Susworth 54 C3
Sutcombe 8 D4
Suton 47 F7
Sutors of Cromarty 103 G6
Sutterton 45 F3
Sutton, Notts. 44 A3
Sutton, W. Susx 14 C4
Sutton, Cambs. 44 D7
Sutton, Beds. 35 F5
Sutton, Shrops. 31 G1
Sutton, Cambs. 35 H2
Sutton, Shrops. 41 H3
Sutton, G. Lon. 23 H6
Sutton, Oxon. 21 J2
Sutton, Staffs. 41 J4
Sutton, Norf. 47 J4
Sutton, Suff. 37 J5
Sutton, Notts. 53 J5
Sutton, Kent 17 L1
Sutton Abinger 14 E1
Sutton at Hone 23 L5
Sutton Bassett 44 A7
Sutton Benger 20 D5
Sutton Bonington 43 H4
Sutton Bridge 45 H4
Sutton Cheney 43 G6
Sutton Coldfield 42 D7
Sutton Courtenay 21 K3
Sutton Crosses 45 H4
Sutton Grange 59 H3
Sutton Hill 41 J6
Sutton Howgrave 59 J3
Sutton in Ashfield 53 G8
Sutton-in-Craven 58 F6
Sutton Lane Ends 51 J6
Sutton Leach 50 E4
Sutton Maddock 41 J6
Sutton Mallet 10 E2
Sutton Mandeville 12 B3
Sutton Montis 11 H3
Sutton-on-Hull 61 J7
Sutton on Sea 55 K5
Sutton-on-the-Forest 60 C4
Sutton on the Hill 42 E3
Sutton on Trent 54 B7
Sutton Scotney 13 G2
Sutton St Edmund 45 G5
Sutton St James 45 G5
Sutton St Nicholas 31 G5
Sutton-under-Brailes 32 E6
Sutton-under-Whitestonecliffe 60 B2
Sutton upon Derwent 60 E6
Sutton Valence 16 F1
Sutton Veny 12 A1
Sutton Waldron 12 A4
Sutton Weaver 50 E6
Swaby 55 H6
Swadlincote 43 F4
Swaffham 46 D6
Swaffham Bulbeck 35 J3
Swaffham Prior 35 J3
Swafield 47 H3
Swainby 66 E7
Swainshill 31 F5
Swainsthorpe 47 H6
Swalcliffe 33 F6
Swalecliffe 25 H6
Swallow 55 F3
Swallowcliffe 12 B3
Swallowfield 22 C6
Swanage 6 E7
Swanbister 112 D6
Swanbourne 34 B7
Swan Green 51 G6
Swanland 54 D1
Swanley 23 L6
Swanmore 13 H4
Swannington, Norf. 47 G5
Swannington, Leic. 43 G5
Swanscombe 24 C5
Swansea 27 L7
Swanton Abbot 47 H4
Swanton Morley 46 F5
Swanton Novers 46 F3
Swanwick, Derby 43 G1
Swanwick, Hants 13 H5
Swarby 44 D2
Swardeston 47 H6
Swarister 117 G4
Swarkestone 43 F4
Swarland 75 H4
Swarthmoor 57 F3
Swaton 44 E3
Swavesey 35 G3
Sway 12 E6
Swayfield 44 C4
Swaythling 13 G4
Swefling 37 J3
Swepstone 43 F5
Swerford 33 F6
Swettenham 51 H7
Swffryd 19 G3
Swilland 37 G4
Swillington 59 J7
Swimbridge 9 G3
Swinbrook 21 G1
Swinderby 54 C7
Swindon, Staffs. 42 A7
Swindon, Glos. 32 B7

Swindon, Wilts. 21 F4
Swine 61 J7
Swinefleet 54 B1
Swineshead, Northnts. 34 D3
Swineshead, Lincs. 45 F2
Swineshead Bridge 45 F2
Swiney 111 J5
Swinford, Leic. 33 H2
Swinford, Oxon. 21 J2
Swingfield Minnis 17 K1
Swinhoe 75 J2
Swinhope 55 G4
Swinithwaite 58 F2
Swinscoe 42 D2
Swinside Hall 74 D3
Swinstead 44 D4
Swinton, N. Yks. 60 E3
Swinton, G. Man. 51 G3
Swinton, S. Yks. 53 G4
Swinton, Border 83 G7
Swinton, N. Yks. 59 H3
Swintonmill 83 G7
Swithland 43 H5
Swordale 102 D6
Swordland 92 D6
Swordly 110 D2
Sworton Heath 51 F5
Swydd-ffynnon 28 D3
Swynnerton 42 A3
Swyre 11 G7
Sychdyn or Soughton 50 B7
Syde 20 D1
Sydenham, Oxon. 22 C2
Sydenham, G. Lon. 23 J5
Sydenham Damerel 4 E2
Syderstone 46 D3
Sydling St Nicholas 11 H6
Sydmonton 21 J7
Syerston 44 A2
Syke 51 J1
Sykehouse 53 J2
Sykes 58 B5
Syleham 37 H2
Sylen 27 K6
Symbister 115 H2
Symington, Strath. 80 E8
Symington, Strath. 71 J1
Symondsbury 11 F6
Symonds Yat 19 K1
Syre 109 H4
Syreford 32 C7
Syresham 33 J5
Syston, Lincs. 44 C2
Syston, Leic. 43 J5
Sytchampton 31 K3
Sywell 34 B3

T

Tabost 107 K2
Tackley 33 G7
Tacolneston 47 G7
Tadcaster 60 B6
Tadden 12 B5
Taddington 52 D6
Tadley 21 L6
Tadlow 35 H4
Tadmarton 33 F6
Tadworth 23 H7
Tafarnaubach 18 F1
Tafarn-y-Gelyn 50 A7
Taff's Well 18 F4
Tafolwern 39 H6
Taibach, W. Glam. 18 B4
Tai-bach, Clwyd 40 C4
Tain, Highld. 103 F4
Tain, Highld. 111 J2
Tai'n Lon 38 D1
Takeley 35 J7
Talachddu 29 H6
Talacre 50 A5
Talaton 10 B6
Talbenny 26 C5
Talerddig 39 J6
Talgarreg 27 J1
Talgarth 30 C6
Talisker 91 J2
Talke 41 K1
Talkin 64 C2
Talladale 101 F5
Tallarn Green 41 F2
Tallentire 63 G4
Talley 27 L3
Tallington 44 D6
Talmine 109 G2
Talog 27 H4
Tal-sarn 28 C4
Talsarnau 38 F3
Talskiddy 3 H3
Talwrn 48 D3
Tal-y-bont, Gwyn. 38 E4
Tal-y-bont, Dyfed 39 F8
Tal-y-Bont, Gwyn. 49 G4
Talybont-on-Usk 30 C7
Tal-y-cafn 49 G3
Talyllyn, Powys 30 C7
Tal-y-llyn, Gwyn. 39 G6
Talysarn 38 D1
Tal-y-Wern 39 H6
Tamerton Foliot 4 E3
Tamworth 42 E6
Tandridge 23 J7
Tanfield 66 B2
Tangasdale 90 B5
Tangley 21 H7
Tangmere 14 C6
Tangwick 116 D5
Tankerness 113 F6
Tankersley 53 F4
Tannach 111 K4
Tannadice 89 G3

Tannington 37 H3
Tansley 53 F8
Tansor 44 D7
Tantobie 66 B2
Tanton 66 F6
Tanworth-in-Arden 32 D2
Tan-y-fron 49 J4
Tangrisiau 39 F2
Tan-y-groes 27 G2
Taplow 22 E4
Tarbert, Strath. 76 F3
Tarbert, W. Isles 99 G2
Tarbert, Strath. 77 H5
Tarbet, Highld. 108 C4
Tarbet, Highld. 92 D6
Tarbet, Strath. 86 F8
Tarbock Green 50 D5
Tarbolton 71 K2
Tarbrax 80 F6
Tarfside 96 D8
Tarland 96 D5
Tarleton 50 D1
Tarlogie 103 F4
Tarlscough 50 D2
Tarlton 20 D3
Tarnbrook 57 J5
Tarporley 50 E7
Tarr 10 C2
Tarrant Crawford 12 B5
Tarrant Gunville 12 B4
Tarrant Hinton 12 B4
Tarrant Keyneston 12 B5
Tarrant Launceston 12 B5
Tarrant Monkton 12 B5
Tarrant Rawston 12 B5
Tarrant Rushton 12 B5
Tarrel 103 G4
Tarring Neville 15 H5
Tarrington 31 H5
Tarskavaig 92 B5
Tarves 97 H2
Tarvie 102 C7
Tarvin 50 D7
Tasburgh 47 H7
Tasley 41 H7
Taston 33 F7
Tatenhill 42 E4
Tatham 57 K4
Tathwell 55 H5
Tatsfield 23 K7
Tattenhall 50 D8
Tatterford 46 D4
Tattersett 46 D4
Tattershall 45 F1
Tattershall Bridge 45 E1
Tattershall Thorpe 55 G8
Tattingstone 37 G6
Tatworth 10 E5
Taunton 10 D3
Taverham 47 G5
Tavernspite 26 F5
Tavistock 4 E2
Taw Green 9 G6
Tawstock 9 F3
Taxal 52 C6
Tayinloan 77 F7
Taynish 77 G3
Taynton, Oxon. 21 G1
Taynton, Glos. 31 J7
Taynuilt 86 C5
Tayport 89 G6
Tay Road Bridge, Fife. 89 G6
Tay Road Bridge, Tays. 89 G6
Tayvallich 77 G3
Tealby 55 F4
Tealing 89 G5
Teanamachar 98 C6
Teangue 92 C5
Tebay 64 D7
Tebworth 34 C7
Tedburn St Mary 9 J6
Teddington, Glos. 32 B6
Teddington, G. Lon. 23 G5
Tedstone Delamere 31 H4
Tedstone Wafre 31 H4
Teeton 33 J2
Teffont Evias 12 B2
Teffont Magna 12 B2
Tegryn 27 G3
Teigh 44 B5
Teigngrace 5 J2
Teignmouth 5 K2
Telford 41 H5
Tellisford 20 C7
Telscombe 15 H5
Templand 73 F6
Temple, Strath. 79 H5
Temple, Lothn. 81 J6
Temple, Corn. 3 K2
Temple Bar 28 C4
Temple Cloud 19 L7
Temple Grafton 32 D4
Temple Guiting 32 C7
Temple Hirst 53 J1
Temple Normanton 53 G7
Temple Sowerby 64 D5
Templeton, Dyfed 26 F5
Templeton, Devon. 9 J4
Tempsford 34 E4
Tenbury Wells 31 G3
Tenby 26 F6
Tendring 37 G7
Ten Mile Bank 45 K7
Tenston 112 C5
Tenterden 17 F2
Terling 24 D1
Ternhill 41 H3
Terregles 72 E7
Terrington 60 D3
Terrington St Clement 45 J4
Terrington St John 45 J5
Teston 24 D7
Testwood 13 F4

Tetbury 20 C3
Tetbury Upton 20 C3
Tetchill 40 E3
Tetcott 8 D6
Tetford 55 H6
Tetney 55 H3
Tetney Lock 55 H3
Tettenhall 42 A6
Teversal 53 G7
Teversham 35 H4
Teviothead 73 K4
Tewin 23 H1
Tewkesbury 32 A6
Teynham 25 F6
Thainston 97 F3
Thakeham 14 E4
Thame 22 C2
Thames Ditton 23 G6
Thamesmead 23 K4
Thaneston 97 F8
Thanington 25 H7
Thankerton 80 E8
Tharston 47 G7
Thatcham 21 K6
Thatto Heath 50 E4
Thaxted 35 K6
Theakston 59 J2
Thealby 54 C2
Theale, Berks. 22 B5
Theale, Somer. 11 F1
Thearne 61 H7
Theberton 37 K3
Thedden Grange 13 J2
Theddingworth 33 J1
Theddlethorpe All Saints 55 J5
Theddlethorpe St Helen 55 J5
Thelbridge Barton 9 H4
Thelnetham 36 F2
Thelwall 51 F5
Themelthorpe 46 F4
Thenford 33 H5
Therfield 35 G2
Thetford 36 D1
Theydon Bois 23 K3
Thickwood 20 C5
Thimbleby, Lincs. 55 G7
Thimbleby, N. Yks. 59 K1
Thirkleby 60 B3
Thirlby 60 B2
Thirlestane 82 D7
Thirn 59 H2
Thirsk 59 K2
Thistleton 44 C5
Thistley Green 36 B2
Thixendale 60 F4
Tholomas Drove 45 H6
Tholthorpe 60 B4
Thomas Chapel 26 F6
Thomastown 96 E2
Thompson 46 F7
Thomshill 104 B3
Thong 24 C5
Thoralby 58 F2
Thoresway 55 F4
Thorganby, N. Yks. 60 D6
Thorganby, Lincs. 55 G4
Thorington 37 K2
Thorington Street 36 F6
Thorlby 58 E5
Thorley 23 K1
Thormanby 60 B3
Thornaby-on-Tees 66 E6
Thornage 46 F3
Thornborough, Bucks. 34 A6
Thornborough, N. Yks. 59 H3
Thornbury, Devon. 8 D5
Thornbury, H. & W. 31 H4
Thornbury, Avon. 19 L3
Thornby 33 J2
Thorncliffe 52 C8
Thorncombe 10 E5
Thorncombe Street 14 D1
Thorndon 37 G3
Thorndon Cross 9 F6
Thorne 53 J2
Thorner 59 J6
Thorne St Margaret 10 B3
Thorney, Notts. 54 C6
Thorney, Cambs. 45 F6
Thorney Hill 12 E6
Thornfalcon 10 D3
Thornford 11 H4
Thorngumbald 55 G1
Thornham 46 C2
Thornham Magna 37 G2
Thornham Parva 37 G2
Thornhaugh 44 D6
Thornhill, D. & G. 72 D5
Thornhill, Derby 52 D5
Thornhill, M. Glam. 18 F4
Thornhill, Hants. 13 G4
Thornhill, Central 79 J2
Thornhill Edge 52 E2
Thornicombe 12 A5
Thornley, Durham 66 D4
Thornley, Durham 65 J4
Thornliebank 79 H6
Thorns 36 C4
Thornthwaite, N. Yks. 59 G5
Thornthwaite, Cumbr. 63 H5
Thornton, Bucks. 34 A6
Thornton, Mers. 50 C3
Thornton, Humbs. 54 E2
Thornton, Humbs. 60 E6
Thornton, Lancs. 57 G6
Thornton, Lincs. 55 G7
Thornton, Fife 81 H2
Thornton, W. Yks. 59 G7
Thornton, Northum. 83 H7
Thorntonhall 79 H6
Thornton Hough 50 C5
Thornton-in-Craven 58 E6
Thornton-le-Beans 59 J1
Thornton-le-Clay 60 D4

Thornton-le-Dale....60 F2
Thornton le Moor, Lincs....54 E4
Thornton-le-Moor, N. Yks....59 J2
Thornton-le-Moors....50 D6
Thornton-le-Street....59 K2
Thorntonloch....82 F4
Thornton Rust....58 E2
Thornton Steward....59 G2
Thornton Watlass....59 H2
Thornwood Common....23 K2
Thoroton....44 A2
Thorp Arch....59 K6
Thorpe, Notts....44 A2
Thorpe, Cumbr....64 B5
Thorpe, Derby....42 D1
Thorpe, N. Yks....58 F4
Thorpe, Surrey....22 F6
Thorpe, Lincs....55 J5
Thorpe, Norf....47 K7
Thorpe Abbotts....37 G2
Thorpe Acre....43 H4
Thorpe Arnold....44 A4
Thorpe Audlin....53 G2
Thorpe Bassett....60 F3
Thorpe Bay....24 F4
Thorpe by Water....44 B7
Thorpe Constantine....42 E6
Thorpe End....47 H5
Thorpe Fendykes....55 J7
Thorpe Green....36 E4
Thorpe Hesley....53 F4
Thorpe in Balne....53 H2
Thorpe Langton....44 A7
Thorpe Larches....66 D5
Thorpe le Fallows....54 D5
Thorpe-le-Soken....37 G7
Thorpe Malsor....34 B2
Thorpe Mandeville....33 H5
Thorpe Market....47 H3
Thorpe Morieux....36 E4
Thorpeness....37 K4
Thorpe on the Hill....54 D7
Thorpe Salvin....53 H5
Thorpe Satchville....43 K5
Thorpe St Andrew....47 H6
Thorpe Thewles....66 E5
Thorpe Underwood....60 B5
Thorpe Waterville....34 D1
Thorpe Willoughby....60 C7
Thorp St Peter....55 J7
Thorrington....37 F7
Thorverton....9 K5
Thrandeston....37 G2
Thrapston....34 C2
Threapwood....41 F2
Three Bridges....15 F2
Three Cocks....30 C6
Three Crosses....27 K7
Three Holes....45 J6
Threekingham....44 D3
Three Leg Cross....16 D2
Three Legged Cross....12 C5
Three Mile Cross....22 G6
Threemilestone....3 F5
Threlkeld....63 J5
Threshfield....58 E4
Thrigby....47 K5
Thringarth....65 G5
Thringstone....43 G5
Thrintoft....59 J1
Thriplow....35 H5
Throcking....35 G6
Throckley....75 H8
Throckmorton....32 B5
Throphill....75 H6
Thropton....75 G4
Throwleigh....9 G6
Throwley....25 F7
Throwley Forestal....25 F7
Thrumpton....43 H3
Thrumster....111 K4
Thrunton....75 G3
Thrupp, Glos....20 C2
Thrupp, Oxon....21 J1
Thrushelton....8 E7
Thrushgill....58 B4
Thrussington....43 J5
Thruxton, Hants....12 E1
Thruxton, H. & W....31 F6
Thrybergh....53 G4
Thundersley....24 D4
Thundridge....23 J1
Thurcaston....43 H5
Thurcroft....53 G5
Thurgarton, Norf....47 G3
Thurgarton, Notts....43 J2
Thurgoland....52 E3
Thurlaston, Warw....33 G2
Thurlaston, Leic....43 H7
Thurlby, Lincs....44 D5
Thurlby, Lincs....54 D7
Thurleigh....34 D4
Thurlestone....5 G5
Thurloxton....10 D2
Thurlstone....52 E3
Thurlton....47 K7
Thurmaston....43 J6
Thurnby....43 J6
Thurnham, Kent....24 E7
Thurnham, Lancs....57 H5
Thurning, Northnts....34 D1
Thurning, Norf....47 F4
Thurnscoe....53 G3
Thursby....63 J2
Thursford....46 E3
Thursley....14 C2
Thurso....111 H2
Thurstaston....50 B5
Thurston....36 E3
Thurstonfield....63 J2
Thurstonland....52 D2
Thurton....47 J6
Thurvaston....42 E3
Thuxton....46 F6
Thwaite, N. Yks....65 F8

Thwaite, Suff....37 G3
Thwaite St Mary....47 J7
Thwing....61 H3
Tibbermore....88 C6
Tibberton, H. & W....32 B4
Tibberton, Shrops....41 H4
Tibberton, Glos....31 J7
Tibenham....47 G8
Tibshelf....53 G7
Tibthorpe....61 G5
Ticehurst....16 D2
Tichborne....13 H2
Tickencote....44 C6
Tickenham....19 J5
Tickhill....53 H4
Ticklerton....41 F7
Ticknall....43 F4
Tickton....61 H6
Tidcombe....21 G7
Tiddington, Oxon....22 B2
Tiddington, Warw....32 E4
Tidebrook....16 D3
Tideford....4 D4
Tidenham....19 K3
Tideswell....52 D6
Tidmarsh....22 B5
Tidmington....32 E6
Tidpit....12 C4
Tiers Cross....26 D5
Tiffield....33 J4
Tifty....97 G1
Tigerton....89 H2
Tigharry....98 C5
Tighnabruaich....78 B4
Tighnafiline....100 E4
Tigley....5 H3
Tilbrook....34 D3
Tilbury....24 C5
Tilbury Juxta Clare....36 C5
Tile Cross....32 D1
Tile Hill....32 E2
Tilehurst....22 B5
Tilford....14 B1
Tillathrowie....96 D2
Tillicoultry....80 E2
Tillingham....25 F2
Tillington, W. Susx....14 C3
Tillington, H. & W....31 F5
Tillington Common....31 F5
Tillycorthie....97 J3
Tillydrine....96 F6
Tillyfourie....97 F4
Tillygreig....97 H3
Tilmanstone....25 K7
Tilney All Saints....45 J5
Tilney High End....45 J5
Tilney St Lawrence....45 J5
Tilshead....12 C1
Tilstock....41 G3
Tilston....41 F1
Tilstone Fearnall....50 E7
Tilsworth....34 C7
Tilton on the Hill....44 A6
Timberland....54 F8
Timbersbrook....51 H7
Timberscombe....9 K1
Timble....59 G5
Timperley....51 G5
Timsbury, Avon....20 A7
Timsbury, Hants....13 F3
Timsgarry....106 E5
Timworth Green....36 D3
Tincleton....11 J6
Tindale....64 D2
Tingewick....33 J6
Tingley....52 E1
Tingrith....34 D6
Tinhay....8 D7
Tinshill....59 H7
Tinsley....53 G4
Tintagel....8 A7
Tintern Parva....19 K2
Tintinhull....11 F4
Tintwistle....52 C4
Tinwald....73 F6
Tinwell....44 D6
Tipperty....97 J3
Tipton....42 B7
Tipton St John....10 B6
Tiptree....24 E1
Tirabad....29 F5
Tirley....31 K7
Tirphil....18 F2
Tirril....64 C5
Tisbury....12 B3
Tissington....42 D1
Titchberry....8 C3
Titchfield....13 H5
Titchmarsh....34 D2
Titchwell....46 C2
Titley....30 D3
Titlington....75 G3
Tittensor....42 A3
Tittleshall....46 D4
Tiverton, Ches....50 E7
Tiverton, Devon....9 K4
Tivetshall St Margaret....37 G1
Tivetshall St Mary....37 G1
Tixall....42 B4
Tixover....44 C6
Toab, Orkney....113 F6
Toab, Shetld....115 F7
Tobermory....85 G3
Toberonochy....85 J8
Tobson....107 F5
Tocher....97 F2
Tockenham....20 E5
Tockenham Wick....20 E4
Tockholes....51 F1
Tockington....19 L4
Tockwith....60 B5
Todber....11 J3
Toddington, Glos....32 C6
Toddington, Beds....34 D7
Todenham....32 E6

Todhills, Tays....89 G5
Todhills, Cumbr....63 J3
Todmorden....51 J1
Todwick....53 G5
Toft, Lincs....44 D5
Toft, Cambs....35 G4
Toft Hill....65 J5
Toft Monks....47 K7
Toft next Newton....54 E5
Toftrees....46 D4
Toftwood....46 E5
Togston....75 J4
Tokavaig....92 C4
Tokers Green....22 B5
Tolland....10 C2
Tollard Royal....12 B4
Toll Bar....53 H3
Toller Fratrum....11 G6
Toller Porcorum....11 G6
Tollerton, N. Yks....60 C4
Tollerton, Notts....43 J3
Tollesbury....25 F1
Tolleshunt D'Arcy....24 F1
Tolleshunt Major....24 F1
Tolpuddle....11 J6
Tolsta Chaolais....107 F5
Tolworth....23 G6
Tomatin....95 G3
Tombreck....94 E2
Tomchrasky....93 J4
Tomdoun....93 H5
Tomich, Highld....102 F5
Tomich, Highld....93 K3
Tomintoul, Gramp....95 K4
Tomintoul, Gramp....95 K6
Tomnavoulin....96 B3
Tombridge....16 C1
Tondu....18 C4
Tong....41 J6
Tonge....43 G4
Tongham....14 B1
Tongland....69 H5
Tongue....109 G3
Tongwynlais....18 F4
Tonmawr....18 C3
Tonna....18 B3
Ton-teg....18 E4
Tonwell....23 J1
Tonypandy....18 D3
Tonyrefail....18 E4
Toot Baldon....21 K2
Toothill, Hants....13 F4
Toot Hill, Essex....23 L2
Topcroft....47 H7
Topcroft Street....47 H7
Toppesfield....36 C6
Toppings....51 G2
Topsham....9 K7
Torbay....5 J3
Torbeg....70 E2
Torbryan....5 J3
Torcross....5 J5
Tore....102 E7
Torksey....54 C6
Torlum....98 C7
Torlundy....93 H8
Tormarton....20 B5
Tormitchell....71 H5
Tormore....70 D1
Tornagrain....103 F8
Tornahaish....96 B5
Tornaveen....96 F5
Torness....94 D3
Torpenhow....63 H4
Torphichen....80 E4
Torphins....96 F5
Torpoint....4 E4
Torquay....5 K3
Torquhan....82 C7
Torran....100 B8
Torrance....79 J4
Torridon....100 E7
Torrin....92 B3
Torrisdale....109 H2
Torrisholme....57 H4
Torroble....102 D2
Torry, Grampn....96 D1
Torry, Grampn....97 J5
Torrylinn....70 E2
Torterston....105 K4
Torthorwald....73 F7
Tortington....14 D5
Tortworth....20 B3
Torvaig....100 A8
Torver....57 F1
Torwood....80 D3
Torworth....53 J5
Toscaig....92 D2
Toseland....35 F3
Tosside....58 C5
Tostock....36 E3
Totaig....99 H7
Totamore....107 F5
Totland....13 F7
Totley....53 F6
Totnes....5 J3
Totscore....99 J6
Tottenham....23 J3
Tottenhill....46 B5
Totteridge, Bucks....22 D3
Totteridge, G. Lon....23 H3
Totternhoe....34 C7
Tottington....51 G2
Totton....13 F4
Touknag....100 E4
Toux, Grampn....104 E3
Toux, Grampn....105 J3
Tovil....24 D7
Toward....72 B3
Towcester....33 J5
Towednack....2 C6
Towersey....22 C2

Towie....96 D4
Towiemore....104 C4
Tow Law....65 J4
Town End....45 H7
Townhead, Cumbr....64 D4
Townhead, D. & G....69 H6
Townhead of Greenlaw....69 J4
Townhill....81 G3
Townshend....2 D6
Town Yetholm....74 E2
Towthorpe....60 D5
Towton....60 B7
Towyn....49 J3
Toynton All Saints....55 H7
Toynton Fen Side....55 H7
Toynton St Peter....55 J7
Toy's Hill....23 K7
Trabboch....71 K2
Trabbochburn....71 K2
Traboe....2 F7
Tradespark, Orkney....112 G6
Tradespark, Highld....103 G7
Trafford Park....51 G4
Trallong....29 G7
Trallwng or Welshpool....40 D6
Tranent....82 C4
Trantlemore....110 E3
Tranwell....75 H6
Trapp....27 L5
Traprain....82 D4
Traquair....73 J1
Trawden....58 E7
Trawsfynydd....39 G3
Trealaw....18 E3
Treales....57 H7
Trearddur....48 B3
Treaslane....99 J7
Trebartha....4 C2
Trebetherick....3 H2
Treborough....10 B2
Trebudannon....3 G3
Treburley....4 D2
Trecastle....29 F7
Trecwn....26 D3
Trecynon....18 D2
Tredavoe....2 C7
Tredegar....18 F2
Tredington....32 E5
Tredinnick....3 H2
Tredomen....30 C6
Tredrizzick....3 H2
Tredunnock....19 H3
Treen....2 B7
Treeton....53 G5
Trefdraeth....48 D3
Trefecca....30 C6
Trefeglwys....39 J7
Trefenter....28 D3
Treffgarne....26 D4
Treffynnon....26 C4
Trefil....18 F1
Trefilan....28 C4
Trefnanney....40 D5
Trefnant....49 K3
Trefonen....40 D4
Trefor, Gwyn....48 C2
Trefor, Gwyn....38 C2
Treforest....18 E4
Trefriw....49 G4
Tregadillett....8 C7
Tregaian....48 D3
Tregare....19 J1
Tregaron....28 D3
Tregarth....48 F4
Tregeare....8 C7
Tregeiriog....40 C3
Tregele....48 C1
Tregidden....2 F7
Treglemais....26 C4
Tregole....8 B6
Tregonetha....3 H3
Tregony....3 H5
Tregoyd....30 C6
Tre-groes....27 J2
Tregurrian....3 G3
Tregynon....40 B7
Trehafod....18 E3
Treharris....18 E3
Treherbert....18 D3
Treknow....8 A7
Trelan....2 F8
Trelawnyd....49 K3
Trelech....27 G3
Treleddyd-fawr....26 B4
Trelewis....18 F3
Treligga....8 A7
Trelights....3 H2
Trelill....3 J2
Trelissick....3 G6
Trelleck....19 K2
Trelleck Grange....19 J2
Trelogan....49 L2
Tremadog....38 E2
Tremail....8 B7
Tremain....27 G2
Tremaine....8 C7
Tremar....4 C3
Trematon....4 D4
Tremeirchion....49 K3
Trenance....3 G3
Trenarren....3 J5
Trench....41 H5
Treneglos....8 C7
Trenewan....4 B4
Trent....11 G4
Trentham....42 A2
Trentishoe....9 G1
Treoes....18 D5
Treorchy....18 D3
Tre'r-ddol....39 F7
Tresaith....27 G1
Trescott....41 K7
Trescowe....2 D6
Tresham....20 B3
Tresillian....3 G5

Tresinwen....26 D2
Tresmeer....8 C7
Tressait....87 L2
Tresta....115 F3
Trethewey....2 B7
Trethomas....19 F4
Trethurgy....3 J4
Tretio....26 B4
Tretire....31 G7
Tretower....30 C7
Treuddyn....50 B8
Trevalga....8 A6
Trevanson....3 H2
Trevarrick....3 H5
Trevellas....2 F4
Treverva....2 F6
Trevethin....19 G2
Trevigro....4 D3
Trevine....26 C3
Treviscoe....3 H4
Trevone....3 G2
Trewarmett....8 A7
Trewarthenick....3 H5
Trewassa....8 B7
Trewellard....2 B6
Trewen....8 C7
Trewidland....4 C4
Trewint....8 B6
Trewithian....3 G6
Trewoon....3 H4
Treyarnon....3 G2
Treyford....14 B4
Trickett's Cross....12 C5
Trimdon....66 D4
Trimdon Grange....66 D4
Trimingham....47 H3
Trimley St Martin....37 H5
Trimley St Mary....37 H6
Trimpley....31 J2
Trimsaran....27 J6
Trimstone....9 F1
Trinafour....19 G2
Tring....22 E1
Trinity....89 J2
Trislaig....93 G8
Trispen....3 G4
Tritlington....75 J5
Trochry....88 B4
Troedyraur....27 H2
Troedyrhiw....18 E2
Trofarth....49 H3
Trondavoe....116 E5
Troon, Corn....2 E6
Troon, Strath....71 J1
Troston....36 D2
Trottiscliffe....24 C6
Trotton....14 B3
Troutbeck....63 K7
Troutbeck Bridge....63 K7
Trowbridge....20 C7
Trow Green....19 K2
Trowle Common....20 C7
Trows....74 C1
Trowse Newton....47 H6
Trudoxhill....11 J1
Trull....10 D3
Trumisgarry....98 D5
Trumpan....99 J5
Trumpet....31 H6
Trumpington....35 H4
Trunch....47 H3
Truro....3 G5
Trusham....9 J7
Trusley....42 E3
Trusthorpe....55 K5
Trysull....42 A7
Tubney....21 J3
Tuckenhay....5 J4
Tuckhill....31 J1
Tuddenham, Suff....36 C2
Tuddenham, Suff....37 G5
Tudeley....16 C2
Tudhoe....66 C4
Tudweiliog....38 B3
Tuffley....20 C1
Tufton....26 E4
Tugby....44 A6
Tugford....31 G1
Tullibody....80 D2
Tullich....86 C7
Tullich Muir....103 F5
Tulloch....89 K1
Tullynessle....96 E4
Tumble....27 K5
Tumby Woodside....45 F1
Tummel Bridge....87 K3
Tunbridge Wells, Royal....16 C2
Tunga....107 J5
Tunstall, Staffs....42 A1
Tunstall, Kent....24 E6
Tunstall, N. Yks....59 H1
Tunstall, Suff....37 J4
Tunstall, Lancs....57 K3
Tunstall, Norf....47 K6
Tunstall, Humbs....61 J7
Tunstead....47 H4
Tunworth....13 J1
Tupsley....31 G5
Tupton....53 F7
Turgis Green....22 B7
Turkdean....20 F1
Tur Langton....43 K7
Turnastone....30 E6
Turnberry....71 H4
Turnditch....42 E2
Turners Hill....15 G2
Turners Puddle....11 K6
Turnworth....11 K5
Turriff....105 G3
Turton Bottoms....51 G2
Turves....45 G7
Turvey....34 C4

Turville....22 C3
Turville Heath....22 C3
Turweston....33 J6
Tutbury....42 E4
Tutnall....32 B2
Tutshill....19 K3
Tuttington....47 H4
Tuxford....54 B6
Twatt, Orkney....112 C4
Twatt, Shetld....115 F3
Twechar....80 C4
Tweedmouth....83 H6
Tweedsmuir....73 G2
Twelveheads....2 F5
Twemloe Green....51 G7
Twenty....44 E4
Twerton....20 B6
Twickenham....23 G5
Twigworth....32 A7
Twineham....15 F4
Twinhoe....20 B7
Twinstead....36 D6
Twitchen, Shrops....30 E2
Twitchen, Devon....9 H2
Two Bridges....5 G2
Two Dales....52 F7
Two Gates....42 E6
Twycross....43 F6
Twyford, Berks....22 C5
Twyford, Norf....46 F4
Twyford, Hants....13 G3
Twyford, Bucks....33 J7
Twyford, Leic....43 K5
Twyford Common....31 G6
Twynholm....69 H5
Twyning....32 B6
Twyning Green....32 B6
Twynllanan....28 E7
Twyn-y-Sheriff....19 J2
Twywell....34 C2
Tyberton....30 E6
Tyburn....42 D7
Tycroes....27 L5
Tycrwyn....40 C5
Tydd Gote....45 H5
Tydd St Giles....45 H5
Tydd St Mary....45 H5
Ty-hen....38 A3
Tyldesley....51 G3
Tyler Hill....25 H6
Tylers Green....22 E3
Tylorstown....18 E3
Tylwch....29 G1
Ty-nant, Clwyd....39 J2
Ty-nant, Gwyn....39 J4
Tyndrum....86 F5
Tyneham....6 C6
Tynehead....81 J6
Tynemouth....75 K8
Tynewydd....18 D3
Tyninghame....82 E4
Tynron....72 D5
Tyn-y-ffridd....40 C3
Tynygraig, Dyfed....28 D3
Tyn-y-graig, Powys....29 H4
Ty'n-y-groes....49 G3
Ty Rhiw....18 F4
Tyringham....34 B5
Tythby....43 J3
Tythegston....18 C5
Tytherington, Avon....20 A4
Tytherington, Wilts....12 B1
Tytherington, Somer....11 J1
Tytherington, Ches....51 J6
Tytherleigh....10 E5
Tytherton Lucas....20 D5
Tywardreath....3 J4
Tywyn, Gwyn....38 E6
Tywyn, Gwyn....49 G3

U

Uachdar....98 D7
Uags....92 D2
Ubbeston Green....37 J2
Ubley....19 K7
Uckerby....66 C7
Uckfield....15 H3
Uckington....32 B7
Uddingston....80 B5
Uddington....72 D1
Udimore....16 F4
Udny Green....97 H3
Udny Station....97 J3
Uffcott....20 F5
Uffculme....10 B4
Uffington, Lincs....44 D6
Uffington, Shrops....41 G5
Uffington, Oxon....21 H4
Ufford, Cambs....44 D6
Ufford, Suff....37 H4
Ufton....33 F3
Ufton Nervet....22 B6
Ugadale....70 C2
Ugborough....5 G4
Uggeshall....37 K1
Ugglebarnby....67 J7
Ugley....35 J7
Ugley Green....35 J7
Ugthorpe....67 H6
Uig, Highld....99 G3
Uig, Highld....99 J6
Uigshader....99 K8
Uisken....84 E7
Ulbster....111 K4
Ulceby, Humbs....54 F2
Ulceby, Lincs....55 J6
Ulcombe....16 F1
Uldale....63 H4
Uley....20 B3
Ulgham....75 J5
Ullapool....101 H3

Ullenhall................32 D3
Ullenwood................20 D1
Ulleskelf................60 C6
Ullesthorpe................33 H1
Ulley................53 G5
Ullingswick................31 G4
Ullinish................91 J2
Ullock................62 F5
Ulpha................56 E1
Ulrome................61 J5
Ulsta................117 F4
Ulverston................57 F3
Ulzieside................72 C4
Umberleigh................9 G3
Unapool................108 D5
Underbarrow................57 H1
Underriver................23 L7
Underwood, Notts................43 G1
Underwood, Gwent................19 H4
Undy................19 J4
Unifirth................114 E3
Union Mills................56 Q4
Unstone................53 F6
Unthank................64 B4
Upavon................21 F7
Up Cerne................11 H5
Upchurch................24 E6
Upcott................30 E4
Upend................36 C4
Up Exe................9 K5
Uphall................81 F4
Uphall Station................81 F4
Upham, Hants................13 H3
Upham, Devon................9 J5
Up Hatherley................32 B7
Uphill................19 H7
Up Holland................50 E3
Uplawmoor................79 G6
Upleadon................31 J7
Upleatham................67 G6
Uploders................11 G6
Uplowman................10 B4
Uplyme................10 E6
Upminster................24 B4
Up Nately................22 B7
Upnor................24 D5
Uppottery................10 D5
Upper Affcot................31 F1
Upper Ardchronie................102 E4
Upper Arley................31 J1
Upper Astrop................33 H6
Upper Basildon................21 K5
Upper Beeding................15 F4
Upper Benefield................44 C8
Upper Boddington................33 G4
Upper Borth................28 D1
Upper Breinton................31 F5
Upper Broughton................43 J4
Upper Bucklebury................21 K6
Upper Caldecote................34 E5
Upper Chapel................29 H5
Upper Chute................21 G7
Upper Clatford................13 F1
Upper Dallachy................104 C2
Upper Dean................34 D3
Upper Denby................52 E3
Upper Derraid................95 J2
Upper Dicker................16 C4
Upper Dunsforth................59 K4
Upper Eathie................103 F6
Upper Elkstone................52 C8
Upper End................52 C6
Upper Farringdon................13 K2
Upper Framilode................20 B1
Upper Froyle................14 A1
Upper Gravenhurst................34 E6
Upper Green................21 H6
Upper Hackney................52 E7
Upper Hale................14 B1
Upper Hambleton................44 C6
Upper Hardres Court................25 H7
Upper Hartfield................15 H2
Upper Heath................31 G1
Upper Helmsley................60 D7
Upper Heyford, Oxon................33 G7
Upper Heyford, Northnts................33 J4
Upper Hill................31 F4
Upper Hopton................52 D2
Upper Hulme................52 C7
Upper Inglesham................21 G3
Upper Killay................27 K7
Upper Knockando................103 K8
Upper Lambourne................21 H4
Upper Lochton................97 F6
Upper Longdon................42 C5
Upper Longwood................41 H6
Upper Lydbrook................19 L1
Upper Maes-coed................30 E6
Uppermill................51 J3
Upper Minety................20 E3
Upper North Dean................22 D3
Upper Poppleton................60 C5
Upper Quinton................32 D5
Upper Sanday................113 F6
Upper Sapey................31 H3
Upper Seagry................20 D4
Upper Shelton................34 C5
Upper Sheringham................47 G2
Upper Skelmorlie................78 D5
Upper Slaughter................32 D7
Upper Soudley................20 A1
Upper Stondon................34 E6
Upper Stowe................33 J4
Upper Street, Hants................12 D4
Upper Street, Norf................47 J5
Upper Sundon................34 D7
Upper Swainswick................20 B6
Upper Swell................32 D7
Upper Tean................42 C3
Upperthong................52 D3
Upper Tillyrie................88 D8
Upperton................14 C3
Upper Tooting................23 H5
Uppertown................111 K1
Upper Tysoe................33 F5

Upper Upham................21 G5
Upper Wardington................33 G5
Upper Weald................34 B6
Upper Weedon................33 J4
Upper Wield................13 J2
Upper Winchendon................22 C1
Upper Woodford................12 D2
Uppingham................44 B7
Uppington................41 G6
Upsall................59 K2
Upshire................23 K2
Up Somborne................13 F2
Upstreet................25 J6
Up Sydling................11 H5
Upton, Somer................10 A3
Upton, Mers................50 B5
Upton, Dorset................12 B6
Upton, Notts................54 B6
Upton, Bucks................22 C1
Upton, Lincs................54 C5
Upton, Ches................50 D7
Upton, Cambs................34 E2
Upton, Berks................22 E5
Upton, Cambs................44 E6
Upton, Hants................13 F4
Upton, Leic................43 F7
Upton, W. Yks................53 G2
Upton, Hants................21 H7
Upton, Norf................47 J5
Upton, Notts................43 K1
Upton, Northnts................33 K3
Upton, Oxon................21 K4
Upton Bishop................31 H7
Upton Cheyney................20 A6
Upton Cressett................41 H7
Upton Cross................4 C2
Upton Grey................13 J1
Upton Hellions................9 J5
Upton Lovell................12 B1
Upton Magna................41 G5
Upton Noble................11 J2
Upton Pyne................9 K6
Upton Scudamore................12 A1
Upton Snodsbury................32 B4
Upton St Leonards................20 C1
Upton upon Severn................32 A5
Upton Warren................32 B3
Upwaltham................14 C4
Upware................35 J2
Upwell, Cambs................45 J6
Upwell, Norf................45 J6
Upwey................11 H7
Upwood................35 F1
Urafirth................116 E5
Urchfont................20 E7
Urdimarsh................31 G5
Urgha................99 G3
Urlay Nook................66 E6
Urmston................51 G4
Urquhart................104 B2
Urra................67 F7
Urray................102 D7
Urswick................57 F3
Usan................89 K3
Ushaw Moor................66 C3
Usk................19 H2
Usselby................54 E4
Utkinton................50 E7
Utley................59 F6
Uton................9 J6
Utterby................55 H4
Uttoxeter................42 C3
Uwchmynydd................38 A4
Uxbridge................22 F4
Uyeasound................117 G2
Uzmaston................26 D5

V

Valleyfield................80 F3
Valsgarth................117 H1
Valtos, Highld................100 B6
Valtos, W. Isles................106 E5
Vange................24 D4
Varteg................19 G2
Vatersay................90 B6
Vatten................99 H8
Vauld, The................31 G5
Vaynor................18 E1
Vaynor Park................40 C6
Veensgarth................115 G4
Velindre................30 C6
Veness................113 F4
Vennington................40 E6
Venn Ottery................10 B6
Ventnor................7 K7
Vernham Dean................21 H7
Vernham Street................21 H7
Vernolds Common................31 F1
Verran Island................90 C2
Verwood................12 C5
Veryan................3 H6
Vicarage................10 D7
Vickerstown................56 E4
Victoria................3 H3
Vidlin................115 G2
Viewpark................80 C5
Village Abberley, The................31 J3
Village, The................42 A8
Vinehall Street................16 E3
Vines Cross................16 C4
Virginia Water................22 E6
Virginstow................8 D6
Vobster................11 J1
Voe................115 G2
Vowchurch................30 E6

W

Waberthwaite................56 E1
Wackerfield................65 J5
Wacton................47 G7
Wadborough................32 B5
Waddesdon................22 C1
Waddingham................54 D4
Waddington, Lancs................58 C6
Waddington, Lincs................54 D7
Wadebridge................3 H2
Wadeford................10 E4
Wadenhoe................34 D1
Wadesmill................23 J1
Wadhurst................16 D2
Wadshelf................53 F6
Wadworth................53 H4
Waen-fach................40 D5
Wainfleet All Saints................55 J8
Wainfleet Bank................55 J8
Wainhouse Corner................8 B6
Wainscott................24 D5
Wainstalls................58 F8
Waitby................64 E7
Wakefield................53 F1
Wakerley................44 C7
Wakes Colne................36 D7
Walberswick................37 K2
Walberton................14 C5
Walcot, Lincs................44 D3
Walcot, Warw................32 D4
Walcot, Shrops................30 E1
Walcot, Shrops................41 G5
Walcote................33 H1
Walcott, Lincs................44 E1
Walcott, Norf................47 J3
Walden................58 F2
Walden Head................58 E2
Walden Stubbs................53 H2
Walderslade................24 D6
Walderton................14 A4
Walditch................11 F6
Waldridge................66 C2
Waldringfield................37 H5
Waldron................16 C4
Wales................53 G5
Walesby, Lincs................55 F4
Walesby, Notts................53 J6
Walford, H. & W................30 E2
Walford, Shrops................41 F4
Walford, H. & W................31 G7
Walgherton................41 H2
Walgrave................34 B2
Walkden................51 G3
Walker................66 C1
Walkerburn................81 J8
Walker Fold................58 B6
Walkeringham................54 B4
Walkerith................54 B4
Walkern................35 F7
Walker's Green................31 G5
Walkhampton................4 F3
Walkington................61 G7
Walk Mill................58 D7
Wall, Staffs................42 B6
Wall, Northum................74 F8
Wallacetown................71 J2
Wallasey................50 B4
Wallingford................21 L4
Wallington, Herts................35 F6
Wallington, Hants................13 H5
Wallington, G. Lon................23 H6
Wallis................26 E4
Walliswood................14 E2
Walls................114 E4
Wallsend................75 J8
Wall under Heywood................41 G7
Wallyford................81 J4
Walmer................25 K7
Walmer Bridge................50 D1
Walmersley................51 H2
Walmley................42 D7
Walpole................37 J2
Walpole Highway................45 J5
Walpole St Andrew................45 J5
Walpole St Peter................45 J5
Walsall................42 C7
Walsall Wood................42 C6
Walsden................51 J1
Walsgrave on Sowe................33 F1
Walsham le Willows................36 F2
Walsoken................45 H5
Walston................81 F7
Walterstone................30 E7
Waltham, Humbs................55 G3
Waltham, Kent................17 J1
Waltham Abbey................23 J2
Waltham Chase................13 H4
Waltham Cross................23 J2
Waltham on the Wolds................44 B4
Waltham St Lawrence................22 D5
Walthamstow................23 J4
Walton, Bucks................34 B6
Walton, Cumbr................64 C1
Walton, Powys................30 D4
Walton, Warw................32 E4
Walton, Somer................11 F2
Walton, W. Yks................53 F2
Walton, Derby................53 F7
Walton, Shrops................41 G5
Walton, Leic................33 H1
Walton, Suff................37 H6
Walton, W. Yks................59 K6
Walton Cardiff................32 B6
Walton East................26 E4
Walton Highway................45 H5
Walton-in-Gordano................19 J5
Walton-le-Dale................50 E1
Walton-on-Thames................23 G6
Walton-on-the-Hill, Staffs................42 B4
Walton on the Hill, Surrey................23 H7
Walton-on-the-Naze................37 H7

Walton on the Wolds................43 H5
Walton-on-Trent................42 E5
Walton West................26 C5
Walworth................66 C6
Walwyn's Castle................26 C5
Wambrook................10 D5
Wanborough................21 G4
Wandsworth................23 H5
Wangford................37 K2
Wanlip................43 H5
Wanlockhead................72 D3
Wansford, Cambs................44 D7
Wansford, Humbs................61 H5
Wanstead................23 K4
Wanstrow................11 J1
Wanswell................20 A2
Wantage................21 J4
Wapley................20 B5
Wappenbury................33 F3
Wappenham................33 J5
Warbleton................16 D4
Warborough................21 K3
Warboys................35 G1
Warbstow................8 C6
Warburton................51 G5
Warcop................64 E6
Warden................25 G5
Ward Green................36 F3
Wardington................33 G5
Wardle, Ches................41 H1
Wardle, G. Man................51 J2
Wardley................44 B6
Wardlow................52 D6
Wardy Hill................35 H1
Ware................23 J1
Wareham................12 B7
Warehorne................17 G2
Warenford................75 H2
Waren Mill................75 H1
Warenton................75 H1
Wareside................23 J1
Waresley................35 F4
Warfield................22 D5
Wargrave................22 C5
Warham................46 E2
Wark, Northum................74 E7
Wark, Northum................83 G8
Warkleigh................9 G3
Warkton................34 B2
Warkworth................75 J4
Warlaby................59 J1
Warland................51 J1
Warleggan................3 K3
Warlingham................23 J7
Warmfield................53 F1
Warmingham................51 G7
Warmington, Northnts................44 D7
Warmington, Warw................33 G5
Warminster................12 A1
Warmsworth................53 H3
Warmwell................11 J7
Warndon................32 A4
Warnford................13 J3
Warnham................14 E2
Warninglid................15 F3
Warren, Dyfed................26 D7
Warren, Ches................51 H6
Warren Row................22 D4
Warren Street................24 F7
Warrington, Bucks................34 B4
Warrington, Ches................50 F5
Warsash................13 G5
Warslow................52 C8
Warter................60 F5
Warthill................60 D5
Wartling................16 D5
Wartnaby................43 K4
Warton, Warw................42 E6
Warton, Northum................75 G4
Warton, Lancs................57 H8
Warton, Lancs................57 J3
Warwick, Warw................32 E3
Warwick Bridge................64 B2
Warwick-on-Eden................64 B2
Wasbister................112 D3
Wasdale Head................63 G7
Washaway................3 J3
Washbourne................5 H4
Washfield................9 K4
Washford................10 B1
Washford Pyne................9 J4
Washingborough................54 E6
Washington, T. & W................66 D2
Washington, W. Susx................14 E4
Wasing................21 K6
Waskerley................65 H3
Wasperton................32 E4
Wass................60 C3
Watchet................10 B1
Watchfield, Somer................10 E1
Watchfield, Oxon................21 G3
Watchgate................64 C8
Watendlath................63 H6
Water................51 H1
Waterbeach................73 H7
Waterbeck................64 B3
Waterden................46 D3
Water End, Herts................22 F1
Water End, Herts................23 H1
Waterfall................42 C1
Waterfoot, Lancs................51 H1
Waterfoot, Strath................79 H6
Waterford................23 J1
Waterhead, Strath................72 A3
Waterhead, Cumbr................63 J7
Waterhouses, Durham................66 B3
Waterhouses, Staffs................42 C1
Wateringbury................24 C7
Waterlip................11 H1
Waterloo, Mers................50 C4
Waterloo, Tays................88 C5
Waterloo, Dorset................12 C6
Waterloo, Strath................80 D6
Waterloo, Norf................47 H5
Waterlooville................13 J5

Watermeetings................72 E3
Watermillock................64 B5
Water Newton................44 E7
Water Orton................42 D7
Waterperry................22 B2
Waterrow................10 B3
Watersfield................14 D4
Waterside, Strath................79 G7
Waterside, Strath................79 H5
Waterside, Strath................79 J3
Waterside, Strath................71 K4
Waterstock................22 B2
Waterston................26 D6
Water Stratford................33 J6
Waters Upton................41 H5
Waterthorpe................53 G5
Water Yeat................57 F2
Watford, Herts................23 G3
Watford, Northnts................33 J3
Wath, N. Yks................59 G4
Wath, N. Yks................59 J3
Wath upon Dearne................53 G3
Watlington, Oxon................22 B3
Watlington, Norf................45 K5
Watnall................43 H2
Watten................111 J3
Watterow................10 B3
Wattisfield................36 F2
Wattisham................36 F4
Watton, Norf................46 E6
Watton, Humbs................61 H5
Watton at Stone................23 J1
Wattston................80 C5
Wattstown................18 E3
Wattsville................19 G3
Waunarlwydd................27 L7
Waunfawr................48 E5
Wavendon................34 C6
Waverton, Ches................50 D7
Waverton, Cumbr................63 H3
Wawne................61 H7
Waxham................47 K4
Waxholme................61 L8
Wayford................11 F5
Way Village................9 J4
Weachyburn................104 F2
Wealdstone................23 G4
Weare................19 J7
Weare Giffard................8 E3
Wearhead................65 F4
Weasdale................64 D7
Weasenham All Saints................46 D4
Weasenham St Peter................46 D4
Weaverham................50 F6
Weaverthorpe................61 G3
Webheath................32 C3
Wedderlairs................97 H2
Weddington................43 F7
Wedhampton................20 E7
Wedmore................11 F1
Wednesbury................42 B7
Wednesfield................42 B6
Weedon................22 D1
Weedon Bec................33 J4
Weedon Lois................33 J5
Weeford................42 D6
Week................9 H4
Weekley................34 B1
Week St Mary................8 C6
Weeley................37 G7
Weeley Heath................37 G7
Weem................87 L4
Weeping Cross................42 B4
Weeting................36 C1
Weeton, Lancs................57 F7
Weeton, N. Yks................59 H6
Weir................51 H1
Welborne................46 F6
Welborn................44 C1
Welbourn................44 C1
Welburn................60 E4
Welbury................66 D7
Welby................44 C3
Welches Dam................35 H1
Welcombe................8 C4
Weldon................44 C8
Welford, Northnts................33 J1
Welford, Berks................21 J5
Welford-on-Avon................32 D4
Welham................44 A7
Welham Green................23 H2
Welling................23 K5
Wellingborough................34 B3
Wellingham................46 D4
Wellingore................44 C1
Wellington, Somer................10 C3
Wellington, H. & W................31 F5
Wellington, Shrops................41 H5
Wellington Heath................31 J5
Wellow, Avon................20 B7
Wellow, I. of W................13 F7
Wellow, Notts................53 J7
Wells................11 G1
Wellsborough................43 F6
Wells-next-the-Sea................46 E2
Wellwood................81 F3
Welney................45 J7
Welshampton................41 F3
Welsh Bicknor................19 K1
Welsh End................41 G3
Welsh Frankton................40 E3
Welsh Hook................26 D4
Welsh Newton................19 K1
Welshpool or Trallwng................40 D6
Welsh St Donats................18 E5
Welton, Humbs................54 D2
Welton, Lincs................54 E6
Welton, Northnts................33 H3

Welton, Cumbr................63 J3
Welton le Marsh................55 J7
Welton le Wold................55 G5
Welwick................55 H1
Welwyn................23 H1
Welwyn Garden City................23 H1
Wem................41 G4
Wembdon................10 D2
Wembley................23 G4
Wembury................4 F5
Wembworthy................9 G5
Wemyss Bay................78 D5
Wendens Ambo................35 J6
Wendlebury................21 K1
Wendling................46 E5
Wendover................22 D2
Wendron................2 E5
Wendy................35 G5
Wenhaston................37 K2
Wennington, Cambs................35 F2
Wennington, Lancs................57 K3
Wennington, G. Lon................23 L4
Wensley, Derby................52 E7
Wensley, N. Yks................59 F2
Wentbridge................53 G2
Wentnor................40 E7
Wentworth, S. Yks................53 F4
Wentworth, Cambs................35 H2
Wenvoe................18 F5
Weobley................30 F4
Weobley Marsh................31 F4
Wereham................46 B6
Wergs................42 A6
Wernheolydd................19 H1
Werrington, Staffs................42 B2
Werrington, Corn................8 D7
Werrington, Cambs................44 E6
Wervin................50 D6
Wesham................57 H7
Wessington................43 F1
West Acre................46 C5
West Allerdean................83 H7
West Alvington................5 H5
West Anstey................9 J3
West Ashby................55 G6
West Ashling................14 B5
West Ashton................20 C7
West Auckland................66 B5
West Bagborough................10 C2
West Barns................82 E4
West Barsham................46 E3
West Bay................11 F6
West Beckham................47 G3
Westbere................25 H6
West Bergholt................36 E7
West Bexington................11 G7
West Bilney................46 C5
West Blatchington................15 F5
Westborough................44 B2
Westbourne, W. Susx................14 A5
Westbourne, Dorset................12 C6
West Bradford................58 C6
West Bradley................11 G2
West Bretton................52 E2
West Bridgford................43 H3
West Bromwich................42 C7
West Buckland, Somer................10 C3
West Buckland, Devon................9 G2
West Burrafirth................114 E3
West Burton, W. Susx................14 C4
West Burton, Lancs................58 E4
West Burton, N. Yks................58 F2
Westbury, Wilts................20 C7
Westbury, Shrops................40 E6
Westbury, Bucks................33 J6
Westbury Leigh................20 C7
Westbury-on-Severn................20 B1
Westbury-sub-Mendip................11 G1
Westby................57 G7
West Caister................47 L5
West Calder................80 F5
West Camel................11 G3
West Challow................21 H4
West Charleton................5 H5
West Chelborough................11 G5
West Chevington................75 J5
West Chiltington................14 D4
West Chinnock................11 F4
West Clandon................22 F7
West Cliffe................17 L1
Westcliff-on-Sea................24 E4
West Clyne................103 G2
West Coker................11 G4
Westcombe................11 H2
West Compton, Somer................11 G1
West Compton, Dorset................11 G6
Westcote................32 E7
Westcott, Devon................10 B5
Westcott, Bucks................22 C1
Westcott, Surrey................14 E1
Westcott Barton................33 G7
West Cross................27 L8
West Curthwaite................63 J3
West Dean, W. Susx................14 B4
West Dean, Hants................12 E4
Westdean, E. Susx................15 J4
West Deeping................44 E6
West Derby................50 C4
West Dereham................75 H2
West Ditchburn................75 H2
West Down................8 F1
West Drayton, G. Lon................22 F5
West Drayton, Notts................53 K6
West End, Beds................34 C4
West End, Surrey................22 E6
West End, Hants................13 G4
West End, N. Yks................59 G4
West End, Humbs................61 G7
West End, Oxon................21 J2
West End, Avon................19 J6
West End, Norf................47 K5
West End Green................22 B6
Westerdale, N. Yks................67 G2
Westerdale, Highld................111 H3
Westerfield, Shetld................115 G2

Westerfield, Suff Witton Gilbert 183

Westerfield, Suff 37 G5
Wester Fintray 97 H4
Westergate 14 C5
Wester Gruinards 102 D3
Westerham 23 K7
Westerleigh 20 B5
Wester Quarff 115 G5
Wester Skeld 114 E4
Westerton 89 J3
Westerwick 114 E4
West Farleigh 24 D7
West Felton 40 E4
Westfield, Lothn 80 E4
Westfield, Norf 46 E6
Westfield, E. Susx 16 F4
Westfield, Highld 111 G2
West Firle 15 H5
West Fleetham 75 H2
Westgate, Humbs 54 B3
Westgate, Norf 46 E2
Westgate, Durham 65 G4
Westgate on Sea 25 K5
West Gerinish 90 C1
West Ginge 21 J4
West Grafton 21 G6
West Green 22 C7
West Grimstead 12 E3
West Grinstead 14 E3
West Haddlesey 53 H1
West Haddon 33 J2
West Hagbourne 21 K4
West Hall, Cumbr 74 B8
Westhall, Suff 37 K1
West Hallam 43 G2
West Halton 54 D1
Westham, E. Susx 16 D5
Westham, Somer 10 F1
West Ham, G. Lon 23 K4
Westhampnett 14 B5
West Handley 53 F6
West Hanney 21 J3
West Hanningfield 24 D3
West Hardwick 53 G2
West Harptree 19 K7
West Hatch 10 D3
Westhay 11 F1
Westhead 50 D3
West Heath 22 D7
West Helmsdale 111 G7
West Hendred 21 J4
West Heslerton 61 G3
Westhide 31 G5
West Hill, Devon 10 B6
Westhill, Highld 102 F8
Westhill, Grampn 97 H5
West Hoathly 15 G2
West Holme 12 A7
Westhope, Shrops 31 F1
Westhope, H. & W 31 F4
West Horndon 24 C4
Westhorpe, Suff 36 F3
Westhorpe, Lincs 45 F3
West Horrington 11 G1
West Horsley 22 F7
West Hougham 17 K1
Westhoughton 51 F3
Westhouse 58 B3
Westhouses 53 G8
Westhumble 23 G7
West Hyde 22 F3
West Ilsley 21 J4
Westing 117 G2
West Itchenor 14 A5
West Kennett 20 F6
West Kilbride 78 E7
West Kingsdown 24 B6
West Kington 20 C5
West Kirby 50 B5
West Knighton 11 J7
West Knoyle 11 K2
Westlake 5 G4
West Langdon 17 L1
West Langwell 102 E2
West Lavington, W. Susx 14 B3
West Lavington, Wilts 20 E7
West Layton 65 J7
West Leake 43 H4
Westleigh, Devon 10 B4
Westleigh, Devon 8 E3
Westleton 37 K3
West Lexham 46 D5
Westley, Suff 36 D3
Westley, Shrops 40 E6
Westley Waterless 35 K4
West Lilling 60 D4
Westlington 22 C1
West Linton, Border 81 G6
Westlinton, Cumbr 63 J1
West Littleton 20 B5
West Lulworth 11 K7
West Lutton 61 G4
West Malling 24 C7
West Malvern 31 J5
West Marden 14 A4
West Markham 61 B6
Westmarsh 25 J6
West Marton 58 D5
West Meon 13 J3
West Mersea 25 G1
Westmeston 15 G4
Westmill 35 G7
West Milton 11 G6
Westminster 23 H5
West Monkton 10 D3
West Moors 12 C5
Westmuir, Tays 89 F3
West Muir, Tays 89 H2
West Newton, Norf 46 B4
Westnewton, Cumbr 63 G3
West Newton, Humbs 61 J7
West Norwood 23 J5
West Ogwell 5 J2
Weston, Dorset 6 A7
Weston, Staffs 42 B4
Weston, Avon 20 B6
Weston, Notts 54 B7
Weston, N. Yks 60 E4
Weston, Ches 50 E5
Weston, Lincs 45 F4
Weston, Herts 35 F6
Weston, Shrops 41 G4
Weston, N. Yks 59 G6
Weston, Shrops 41 G7
Weston, Northnts 33 H5
Weston, Ches 41 J1
Weston, Berks 21 J5
Weston, Hants 13 K3
Weston Bampfylde 11 H3
Weston Beggard 31 G5
Westonbirt 20 C4
Weston by Welland 44 A7
Weston Colville 35 K4
Weston Green 35 K4
Weston Heath 41 J5
Weston Hills 45 F4
Westoning 34 D6
Weston in Gordano 19 J5
Weston Jones 41 J4
Weston Longville 47 G5
Weston Lullingfields 41 F4
Weston-on-the-Green 21 K1
Weston-on-Trent 43 G4
Weston Patrick 13 J1
Weston Rhyn 40 D3
Weston-sub-Edge 32 D5
Weston-super-Mare 19 H6
Weston Turville 22 D1
Weston-under-Lizard 41 K5
Weston under Penyard 31 H7
Weston under Wetherley 33 F3
Weston Underwood, Bucks 34 B4
Weston Underwood, Derby 42 E2
Westonzoyland 10 E2
West Overton 21 F6
West Parley 12 C6
West Peckham 24 C7
West Pennard 11 G2
West Pentire 2 F3
West Perry 34 E3
Westport 10 E3
West Putford 8 D4
West Quantoxhead 10 C1
West Rainton 66 D3
West Rasen 54 E5
West Raynham 46 D4
Westrigg 80 E5
West Row 36 B2
West Rudham 46 D4
West Runton 47 G2
Westruther 82 E6
Westry 45 G7
West Saltoun 82 C5
West Sandwick 117 F4
West Scrafton 59 F2
West Stafford 11 J7
West Stockwith 54 B4
West Stoke 14 B5
West Stonesdale 65 F7
West Stoughton 11 F1
West Stour 11 J3
West Stourmouth 25 J6
West Stow 36 D2
West Stowell 21 F6
West Street 24 F7
West Tanfield 59 H3
West Tarbert 77 H5
West Thorney 14 A5
West Thurrock 24 B5
West Tilbury 24 C5
West Tisted 13 J3
West Tofts 88 D5
West Torrington 55 F5
West Town 19 J6
West Tytherley 12 E3
West Walton 45 H5
Westward 63 H3
Westward Ho! 8 E3
Westwell, Oxon 21 G1
Westwell, Kent 17 G1
Westwell Leacon 17 G1
West Wellow 12 E4
West Wemyss 81 J2
Westwick, Cambs 35 H3
Westwick, Norf 47 H4
West Wick, Avon 19 H6
West Wickham, G. Lon 23 J6
West Wickham, Cambs 35 K5
West Winch 46 B5
West Winterslow 12 E2
West Wittering 14 A6
West Witton 59 F2
Westwood, Devon 10 B6
Westwood, Wilts 20 C7
West Woodburn 74 E6
West Woodhay 21 H6
West Woodlands 11 J1
Westwoodside 54 B4
West Worldham 13 K2
West Wratting 35 K4
West Wycombe 22 D3
West Yell 117 F4
Wetheral 64 B2
Wetherby 59 K6
Wetherden 36 F3
Wetheringsett 37 G3
Wethersfield 36 C6
Wethersta 115 F2
Wetherup Street 37 G3
Wetley Rocks 42 B2
Wettenhall 51 F7
Wetton 42 D1
Wetwang 61 G5
Wetwood 41 J3
Wexcombe 21 G7
Weybourne 47 G2
Weybread 37 H1
Weybridge 22 F6
Weydale 111 H2
Weyhill 13 F1
Weymouth 11 H8
Whaddon, Bucks 34 B6
Whaddon, Glos 20 C1
Whaddon, Wilts 12 D3
Whaddon, Cambs 35 G5
Whale 64 C5
Whaley 53 H6
Whaley Bridge 52 C5
Whaley Thorns 53 H6
Whalley 58 C7
Whalton 75 H6
Wham 58 C4
Whaplode 45 G4
Whaplode Drove 45 G5
Wharfe 58 C4
Wharles 57 H7
Wharncliffe Side 52 E4
Wharram le Street 60 F4
Wharton, Ches 51 F7
Wharton, H. & W 31 G4
Whashton 65 J7
Whatcombe 11 K5
Whatcote 33 F5
Whatfield 36 F5
Whatley 11 J1
Whatlington 16 E4
Whatstandwell 43 F1
Whatton 44 A3
Whauphill 68 F6
Wheatacre 47 K7
Wheathampstead 23 G1
Wheathill 31 H1
Wheatley, Hants 14 A1
Wheatley, Oxon 21 K2
Wheatley Hill 66 D4
Wheatley Lane 58 D7
Wheaton Aston 42 A5
Wheddon Cross 9 K2
Wheedlemont 96 D3
Wheelerstreet 14 C1
Wheelock 51 G8
Wheelton 50 F1
Wheldrake 60 D6
Whelford 21 F3
Whelpley Hill 22 E2
Whenby 60 D4
Whepstead 36 D4
Wherstead 37 G5
Wherwell 13 F1
Wheston 52 D6
Whetsted 16 D1
Whetstone 43 H7
Whicham 56 E2
Whichford 33 F6
Whickham 66 C1
Whiddon Down 9 G6
Whigstreet 89 G4
Whilton 33 J3
Whimple 10 B6
Whimpwell Green 47 J4
Whinburgh 46 F6
Whinnyfold 97 K2
Whippingham 13 H6
Whipsnade 22 F1
Whipton 9 K6
Whissendine 44 B5
Whissonsett 46 E4
Whistley Green 22 C5
Whiston, Staffs 42 A5
Whiston, Northnts 34 B3
Whiston, Staffs 42 C2
Whiston, Mers 50 D4
Whiston, S. Yks 53 G4
Whitbeck 56 E2
Whitbourne 31 J4
Whitburn, T. & W 66 E1
Whitburn, Lothn 80 E5
Whitby, Ches 50 C6
Whitby, N. Yks 67 J6
Whitchurch, Bucks 34 B7
Whitchurch, Dyfed 26 C4
Whitchurch, Devon 4 E2
Whitchurch, S. Glam 18 F4
Whitchurch, Hants 13 G1
Whitchurch, Shrops 41 G2
Whitchurch, H. & W 19 K1
Whitchurch, Avon 19 L6
Whitchurch Canonicorum 10 E6
Whitchurch Hill 22 B5
Whitchurch-on-Thames 22 B5
Whitcott Keysett 30 D1
Whitebridge 94 C4
Whitebrook 19 K2
Whitecairns 97 J4
Whitechapel 57 J6
White Coppice 50 F2
Whitecraig 81 J4
Whitecroft 19 L2
Whiteface 102 F4
Whitefield 51 H3
Whiteford 97 G3
Whitegate 51 F7
Whitehall 113 G4
Whitehaven 62 E6
Whitehill 14 A2
Whitehills 104 F2
Whitehouse, Grampn 96 F4
Whitehouse, Strath 77 H5
Whitekirk 82 D3
White Kirkley 65 H4
White Lackington 11 J6
White Ladies Aston 32 B4
Whiteley Village 23 F6
Whitemans Green 15 G3
Whitemire 103 H7
Whitemoor 3 H4
White Notley 24 D1
Whiteparish 12 E3
Whiterashes 97 H3
White Rocks 31 F7
White Roding or
White Roothing 24 B1
White Roothing or
White Roding 24 B1
Whiterow 111 K4
Whiteshill 20 C2
Whiteside 80 E5
Whitesmith 15 J4
Whitestaunton 10 D4
Whitestone 9 J6
White Waltham 22 D5
Whiteway 20 D1
Whitewell 58 B6
Whitewreath 104 B3
Whitfield, Avon 20 A3
Whitfield, Northum 64 E2
Whitfield, Bucks 33 J6
Whitfield, Northnts 33 J6
Whitfield, Kent 17 L1
Whitford, Clwyd 50 A6
Whitford, Devon 10 D6
Whitgift 54 C1
Whitgreave 42 A4
Whithorn 68 F6
Whiting Bay 70 F2
Whitland 27 G5
Whitletts 71 J2
Whitley, Berks 22 C5
Whitley, Wilts 20 C6
Whitley, Ches 50 F6
Whitley, N. Yks 53 H1
Whitley Bay 75 K7
Whitley Chapel 65 G2
Whitley Row 23 K7
Whitlock's End 32 D2
Whitminster 20 B2
Whitmore 41 K2
Whitnage 10 B4
Whitnash 33 F3
Whitney-on-Wye, H. & W 30 D5
Whitney-on-Wye, H. & W 30 D5
Whitrigg 63 H4
Whitsbury 12 D4
Whitsome 83 G6
Whitson 19 H4
Whitstable 25 H6
Whitstone 8 C6
Whittingham 75 G3
Whittingslow 41 F8
Whittington, Staffs 32 A1
Whittington, H. & W 32 A4
Whittington, Norf 46 C7
Whittington, Glos 32 C7
Whittington, Staffs 42 D6
Whittington, Shrops 40 E3
Whittington, Derby 53 F6
Whittington, Lancs 57 K3
Whittlebury 33 J5
Whittle-le-Woods 50 E1
Whittlesey 45 F7
Whittlesford 35 H5
Whitton, Humbs 54 D1
Whitton, Border 74 D2
Whitton, Powys 30 D3
Whitton, Cleve 66 D5
Whitton, Shrops 31 G2
Whitton, Northum 75 G4
Whitton, Suff 37 G5
Whittonditch 21 G5
Whittonstall 65 H2
Whitwell, Leic 44 C6
Whitwell, N. Yks 66 C8
Whitwell, Herts 34 E7
Whitwell, Derby 53 H6
Whitwell, I. of W 7 K7
Whitwell-on-the-Hill 60 E4
Whitwick 43 G5
Whitwood 53 G1
Whitworth 51 H2
Whixall 41 G3
Whixley 59 K5
Whorlton, N. Yks 66 E7
Whorlton, Durham 65 J6
Whyle 31 G3
Whyteleafe 23 J7
Wibdon 19 K3
Wibtoft 33 G1
Wichenford 31 J3
Wichling 24 F7
Wick, Avon 20 B5
Wick, H. & W 32 B5
Wick, Wilts 12 D3
Wick, M. Glam 18 D5
Wick, W. Susx 14 D5
Wick, Dorset 12 D6
Wick, Highld 111 K3
Wickam Street 36 C4
Wicken, Northnts 34 A6
Wicken, Cambs 35 J2
Wicken Bonhunt 35 J6
Wickenby 54 E5
Wickersley 53 G4
Wickford 24 D3
Wickham, Hants 13 H4
Wickham, Berks 21 H5
Wickham Bishops 24 E1
Wickhambreaux 25 J7
Wickhambrook 36 C4
Wickhamford 32 C5
Wickham Market 37 J4
Wickhampton 47 K6
Wickham Skeith 37 F3
Wickham St Paul 36 D6
Wickham Street 37 F3
Wicklewood 46 F6
Wickmere 47 G3
Wick St Lawrence 19 H6
Wickwar 20 B4
Widdington 35 J6
Widdrington 75 J5
Widecombe in the Moor 5 H2
Widegates 4 C4
Widemouth Bay 8 C5
Wide Open 75 J7
Widewall 112 E7
Widford, Essex 24 C2
Widford, Herts 23 K1
Widmerpool 43 J4
Widnes 50 E5
Wigan 50 E3
Wiggaton 10 C6
Wiggenhall St Germans 45 J5
Wiggenhall St Mary
Magdalen 45 J5
Wiggenhall St Mary
the Virgin 45 J5
Wiggington 60 C5
Wigginton, Herts 22 E1
Wigginton, Staffs 42 E6
Wigginton, Oxon 33 F6
Wigglesworth 58 D5
Wiggonby 63 J2
Wighill 60 B6
Wighton 46 E3
Wigmore, Kent 24 E6
Wigmore, H. & W 31 F3
Wigsley 54 C6
Wigsthorpe 34 D1
Wigston 43 J7
Wigtoft 45 F3
Wigton 63 H3
Wigtown 68 F5
Wilbarston 34 B1
Wilberfoss 60 E5
Wilburton 35 H2
Wilby, Northnts 34 B3
Wilby, Norf 46 F8
Wilby, Suff 37 H2
Wilcot 21 F6
Wildboarclough 51 J7
Wilden, Beds 34 D4
Wilden, H. & W 31 K2
Wildhern 21 H7
Wildsworth 54 C4
Wilford 43 H3
Wilkesley 41 H2
Wilkhaven 103 H4
Wilkieston 81 G5
Willand 10 B4
Willaston, Ches 50 C6
Willaston, Ches 41 H1
Willen 34 B5
Willenhall, W. Mids 42 B7
Willenhall, W. Mids 33 F2
Willerby, N. Yks 61 H3
Willerby, Humbs 61 H7
Willersey 32 D6
Willersley 30 E5
Willesborough Lees 17 H1
Willesden 23 H4
Willett 10 C2
Willey, Warw 33 G1
Willey, Shrops 41 H7
Williamscot 33 G5
Willian 35 F6
Willingale 24 B2
Willingdon 16 C5
Willingham 35 H2
Willingham by Stow 54 C5
Willington, Durham 66 B4
Willington, Derby 42 E4
Willington, Beds 34 E5
Willington, Warw 32 E6
Willington, T. & W 75 K8
Willington Corner 50 E7
Willitoft 60 E7
Williton 10 B1
Willoughby, Warw 33 H3
Willoughby, Lincs 55 J6
Willoughby-on-the-Wolds 43 J4
Willoughby Waterleys 43 H7
Willoughton 54 D4
Wilmcote 32 D4
Wilmington, E. Susx 16 C5
Wilmington, Devon 10 D6
Wilmington, Kent 23 L5
Wilmslow 51 H5
Wilnecote 42 E6
Wilpshire 58 B7
Wilsden 59 F7
Wilsford, Lincs 44 D2
Wilsford, Wilts 12 D2
Wilsford, Wilts 20 F7
Wilsill 59 G4
Wilson 43 G4
Wilstead 34 D5
Wilsthorpe 44 D5
Wilstone 22 E1
Wilton, Wilts 12 C2
Wilton, N. Yks 60 F2
Wilton, Cleve 67 F6
Wilton, Wilts 21 G6
Wilton Dean 74 A3
Wimbish 35 J6
Wimbish Green 35 K6
Wimbledon 23 H5
Wimblington 45 H7
Wimborne Minster 12 C5
Wimbotsham 45 K6
Wimpstone 32 E5
Wincanton 11 J3
Wincham 51 F6
Winchburgh 81 F4
Winchcombe 32 C7
Winchelsea 17 G4
Winchelsea Beach 17 G4
Winchester 13 G3
Winchfield 22 C7
Winchmore Hill, Bucks 22 E3
Winchmore Hill, G. Lon 23 J3
Wincle 51 J7
Windermere 63 K8
Winderton 33 F5
Windlesham 22 E6
Windley 43 F2
Windmill Hill, E. Susx 16 D4
Windmill Hill, Somer 10 E4
Windrush 21 F1
Windsor 22 E5
Windygates 81 J1
Wineham 15 F3
Winestead 55 H1
Winfarthing 37 G1
Winford 19 K6
Winforton 30 D5
Winfrith Newburgh 11 K7
Wing, Leic 44 B6
Wing, Bucks 34 B7
Wingate 66 E4
Wingates, G. Man 51 F3
Wingates, Northum 75 G5
Wingerworth 53 F7
Wingfield, Wilts 20 C7
Wingfield, Beds 34 D7
Wingfield, Suff 37 H2
Wingham 25 J7
Wingrave 22 D1
Winkburn 54 B8
Winkfield 22 E5
Winkfield Row 22 D5
Winkhill 42 C1
Winkleigh 9 G5
Winksley 59 H3
Winless 111 K3
Winmarleigh 57 H6
Winnersh 22 C5
Winscales 62 F5
Winscombe 19 J7
Winsford, Ches 51 F7
Winsford, Somer 9 K2
Winsham 10 E5
Winshill 42 E4
Winskill 64 C4
Winslade 13 J1
Winsley 20 C6
Winslow 34 A7
Winson 20 E2
Winster, Derby 52 E7
Winster, Cumbr 57 H1
Winston, Suff 37 G3
Winston, Durham 65 J6
Winstone 20 D2
Winswell 8 E4
Winterborne Clenston 11 K5
Winterborne Herringston 11 H7
Winterborne Houghton 11 K5
Winterborne Kingston 12 A6
Winterborne Monkton 11 H7
Winterborne Stickland 11 K5
Winterborne Whitechurch 11 K5
Winterborne Zelston 12 A6
Winterbourne, Avon 20 A4
Winterbourne, Berks 21 J5
Winterbourne Abbas 11 H6
Winterbourne Bassett 20 F5
Winterbourne Dauntsey 12 D2
Winterbourne Earls 12 D2
Winterbourne Gunner 12 D2
Winterbourne Monkton 20 F5
Winterbourne Steepleton 11 H7
Winterbourne Stoke 12 C1
Winterburn 58 E5
Winteringham 54 D1
Winterley 41 J1
Wintersett 53 F2
Wintershill 13 H4
Winterton 54 D2
Winterton-on-Sea 47 K5
Winthorpe, Notts 44 B1
Winthorpe, Lincs 55 K7
Winton, Dorset 12 C6
Winton, Cumbr 64 E6
Wintringham 61 F3
Winwick, Cambs 34 E1
Winwick, Northnts 33 J2
Winyates 32 C3
Wirksworth 42 E1
Wirswall 41 G2
Wisbech 45 H6
Wisbech St Mary 45 H6
Wisborough Green 14 D3
Wiseton 54 B5
Wishaw, Strath 80 C6
Wishaw, Warw 42 D7
Wisley 22 F7
Wispington 55 G6
Wissett 37 J2
Wistanstow 31 F1
Wistanswick 41 H4
Wistaston 41 H1
Wiston, Strath 72 E1
Wiston, W. Susx 14 E4
Wiston, Dyfed 26 E5
Wistow, N. Yks 60 C7
Wistow, Cambs 35 F1
Wiswell 58 C7
Witcham 35 H2
Witchampton 12 B5
Witchford 35 J2
Witham 24 E1
Witham Friary 11 J1
Witham on the Hill 44 D5
Witherenden Hill 16 D3
Witheridge 9 J4
Witherley 43 F7
Withern 55 J5
Withernsea 55 H1
Withernwick 61 J6
Withersdale Street 37 H1
Withersfield 36 B5
Witherslack 57 H2
Withiel 3 H3
Withiel Florey 10 A2
Withington, Glos 20 E1
Withington, Shrops 41 G5
Withington, H. & W 31 G5
Withington, G. Man 51 H4
Withington Green 51 H6
Withleigh 9 K4
Withnell 51 F1
Withybrook 33 G1
Withycombe 10 B1
Withyham 15 H2
Withypool 9 J2
Witley 14 C1
Witnesham 37 G4
Witney 21 H2
Wittering 44 D6
Wittersham 17 F3
Witton Bridge 47 J3
Witton Gilbert 66 C3

Witton-le-Wear 65 J4
Witton Park 66 B4
Wiveliscombe 10 B3
Wivelsfield 15 G3
Wivelsfield Green 15 G4
Wivenhoe 36 F7
Wiveton 46 F2
Wix 37 G7
Wixford 32 C4
Wixoe 36 C5
Woburn 34 C6
Woburn Sands 34 C6
Wokefield Park 22 B6
Woking 22 F7
Wokingham 22 D6
Woldingham 23 J7
Wold Newton, Humbs 55 G4
Wold Newton, Humbs 61 H3
Wolferlow 31 H3
Wolferton 46 B4
Wolfhill 88 D5
Wolf's Castle 26 D4
Wolfsdale 26 D4
Woll 73 K2
Wollaston, Northnts 34 C3
Wollaston, Shrops 40 E5
Wollerton 41 H3
Wolsingham 65 H4
Wolston 33 G2
Wolvercote 21 J2
Wolverhampton 42 B7
Wolverley, Shrops 41 F3
Wolverley, H. & W. 31 K2
Wolverton, Bucks 34 B5
Wolverton, Warw 32 E3
Wolvesnewton 19 J3
Wolverton 21 K7
Wolvey 33 G1
Wolviston 66 E5
Wombleton 60 D2
Wombourne 42 A7
Wombwell 53 F3
Womenswold 25 J7
Wonastow 19 J1
Wonersh 14 D1
Wonson 9 G7
Wonston, Hants 13 G2
Wonston, Dorset 11 J5
Wooburn 22 E4
Wooburn Green 22 E4
Woodale 58 F3
Woodbastwick 47 J5
Woodbeck 54 B6
Woodborough, Wilts 20 F7
Woodborough, Notts 43 J2
Woodbridge 37 H5
Woodbury 10 B7
Woodbury Salterton 10 B7
Woodchester 20 C2
Woodchurch 17 G2
Woodcote 22 B4
Woodcroft 19 K3
Wood Dalling 47 F4
Woodditton 36 B4
Woodeaton 21 K1
Wood End, Warw 32 D2
Woodend, Cumbr 56 E1
Wood End, Warw 42 E7
Wood End, Herts 35 G7
Woodend, Northnts 33 J5
Wood Enderby 55 G7
Woodfalls 12 D3
Woodford, Northnts 34 C2
Woodford, Corn 8 C4
Woodford, Devon 5 H4
Woodford, G. Man 51 H5

Woodford, G. Lon 23 K3
Woodford Bridge 23 K3
Woodford Green 23 K3
Woodford Halse 33 H4
Woodgate, W. Mids 32 B1
Woodgate, H. & W. 32 B3
Woodgate, W. Susx 14 C5
Woodgate, Norf 46 F5
Woodgreen, Hants 12 D4
Wood Green, G. Lon 23 J3
Woodhall 58 E1
Woodhall Spa 55 F7
Woodham 22 F6
Woodham Ferrers 24 D3
Woodham Mortimer 24 E2
Woodham Walter 24 E2
Woodhaven 89 G6
Woodhead 97 G2
Woodhill 31 J1
Woodhorn 75 J6
Woodhouse, S. Yks 53 G5
Woodhouse, Leic 43 H5
Woodhouse Eaves 43 H5
Woodhouselee 81 H5
Woodhurst 35 G2
Woodingdean 15 G5
Woodland, Devon 5 H3
Woodland, Durham 65 H5
Woodlands, Dorset 12 C5
Woodlands, Hants 13 F4
Woodlands, Grampn 97 G6
Woodlands Park 22 D5
Woodlands St Mary 21 H5
Wood Lanes 51 J5
Woodleigh 5 H5
Woodlesford 59 J8
Woodley 22 C5
Woodmancote, W. Susx 14 A5
Woodmancote, Glos 32 B7
Woodmancote, Glos 20 E2
Woodmancote, W. Susx 15 F4
Woodmancott 13 H1
Woodmansey 61 H7
Woodmansterne 23 H6
Woodminton 12 C3
Woodnesborough 25 K7
Woodnewton 44 D7
Wood Norton 46 F4
Woodplumpton 57 J7
Woodrising 46 E6
Woodseaves, Shrops 41 H3
Woodseaves, Staffs 41 K4
Woodsend 21 G5
Woodsetts 53 H5
Woodsford 11 J6
Woodside, Berks 22 E5
Woodside, Tays 88 E5
Woodside, Herts 23 H2
Woodstock 21 J1
Wood Street 22 E7
Woodthorpe, Derby 53 G6
Woodthorpe, Leic 43 H5
Woodton 47 H7
Woodtown 8 E3
Woodville 43 F5
Woodwalton 35 F1
Woodyates 12 C4
Woofferton 31 G3
Wookey 11 G1
Wookey Hole 11 G1
Wool 11 K7
Woolacombe 8 E1
Woolage Green 17 K1
Woolaston 19 K3
Woolavington 10 E1
Woolbeding 14 B3

Wooler 75 F2
Woolfardisworthy, Devon 8 D3
Woolfardisworthy, Devon 9 J5
Woolfords Cottages 80 F6
Woolhampton 21 K6
Woolhope 31 H6
Woolland 11 J5
Woolley, Cambs 34 E2
Woolley, W. Yks 53 F7
Woolmer Green 23 H1
Woolpit 36 E3
Woolscott 33 G3
Woolsington 75 H7
Woolstaston 41 F7
Woolsthorpe Belvoir 44 B3
Woolston, Shrops 40 E4
Woolston, Shrops 31 F1
Woolston, Ches 51 F5
Woolston, Bucks 34 B6
Woolston, Devon 5 H5
Woolston, Hants 13 G4
Woolstone, Bucks 34 B6
Woolstone, Oxon 21 G4
Woolstone Green 5 H3
Woolton 50 D5
Woolton Hill 21 J6
Woolverstone 37 G6
Woolverton 20 B7
Woolwich 23 K5
Woore 41 J2
Wootton, Staffs 42 D2
Wootton, Northnts 34 A4
Wootton, Beds 34 D5
Wootton, Humbs 54 E2
Wootton, Hants 12 E6
Wootton, Oxon 21 J1
Wootton, Oxon 21 J2
Wootton, Kent 17 K1
Wootton, Staffs 41 K4
Wootton Bassett 20 E4
Wootton Bridge 13 H6
Wootton Common 13 H6
Wootton Courtenay 9 K1
Wootton Fitzpaine 10 E6
Wootton Rivers 21 F6
Wootton St Lawrence 21 K7
Wootton Wawen 32 D3
Worcester 32 A4
Worcester Park 23 H6
Wordsley 32 A1
Worfield 41 J7
Workington 62 E5
Worksop 53 H6
Worlaby 54 E2
World's End 21 J5
Worle 19 H6
Worleston 41 H1
Worlingham 47 K8
Worlington, Cambs 36 B2
Worlington, Devon 9 H4
Worlingworth 37 H3
Wormbridge 31 F6
Wormegay 46 B5
Wormelow Tump 31 F6
Wormersley 53 H2
Wormhill 52 D6
Wormhills 89 J5
Wormingford 36 E6
Worminghall 22 B2
Wormington 32 C6
Worminster 11 G1
Wormit 89 F6
Wormleighton 33 G4
Wormley 23 J2
Wormley West End 23 J2
Wormshill 24 E7
Wormsley 31 F5

Worplesdon 22 E7
Worrall 53 F4
Worsbrough 53 F3
Worsley 51 G3
Worstead 47 J4
Worsthorne 58 D7
Worston 58 C6
Worth, W. Susx 15 F2
Worth, Kent 25 K7
Wortham 37 F2
Worthen 40 E6
Worthenbury 41 F2
Worthing, Norf 46 E5
Worthing, W. Susx 14 E5
Worthington 43 G4
Worth Matravers 6 D7
Wortley 53 F4
Worton 20 D7
Wortwell 37 H1
Wotherton 40 D6
Wotter 4 F3
Wotton 14 E1
Wotton-under-Edge 20 B3
Wotton Underwood 22 B1
Woughton on the Green 34 B6
Wouldham 24 D6
Wrabness 37 G6
Wrafton 8 E2
Wragby 55 F6
Wramplingham 47 G6
Wrangham 97 F2
Wrangle 45 H1
Wrangway 10 C4
Wrantage 10 E3
Wrawby 54 E3
Wraxall, Wilts 20 C6
Wraxall, Somer 11 H2
Wraxall, Avon 19 J5
Wray 57 K4
Wraysbury 22 F5
Wrea Green 57 G7
Wreay, Cumbr 64 B3
Wreay, Cumbr 64 B5
Wrekenton 66 C2
Wrelton 60 E2
Wrenbury 41 G2
Wreningham 47 G7
Wrentham 37 K1
Wressle 60 E7
Wrestlingworth 35 F5
Wretham 46 E7
Wretton 46 B7
Wrexham 40 E1
Wribbenhall 31 J2
Wrightington Bar 50 E2
Wrinehill 41 J2
Wrington 19 J6
Writtle 24 C2
Wrockwardine 41 H5
Wroot 54 B3
Wrotham 24 C7
Wrotham Heath 24 C7
Wroughton 21 F4
Wroxall, Warw 32 E2
Wroxall, I. of W 7 K7
Wroxeter 41 G6
Wroxham 47 J5
Wroxton 33 G5
Wyaston 42 D2
Wyberton 45 G2
Wyboston 34 E4
Wybunbury 41 H2
Wychbold 32 B3
Wych Cross 15 H2
Wyche 31 J5
Wyck 14 A2

Wyck Rissington 32 D7
Wycombe Marsh 22 D3
Wyddial 35 G6
Wye 17 H1
Wyke, W. Yks 52 D1
Wyke, Shrops 41 H6
Wyke, Dorset 11 J3
Wykeham, N. Yks 60 F3
Wykeham, N. Yks 61 G2
Wyke Regis 6 A7
Wyke, The 41 J6
Wykey 40 E4
Wylam 65 J1
Wylde Green 42 D7
Wylye 12 C2
Wymering 13 J5
Wymeswold 43 J4
Wymington 34 C3
Wymondham, Leic 44 B5
Wymondham, Norf 47 G6
Wyndham 18 D3
Wynford Eagle 11 G6
Wyre Piddle 32 B5
Wysall 43 J4
Wythall 32 C2
Wytham 21 J2
Wyverstone 36 F3
Wyverstone Street 36 F3

Y

Yaddlethorpe 54 C3
Yafford 7 J6
Yafforth 59 J1
Yalding 24 D7
Yanworth 20 E1
Yapham 60 E5
Yapton 14 C5
Yarburgh 55 H4
Yarcombe 10 D5
Yardley 32 D1
Yardley Gobion 34 A5
Yardley Hastings 34 B4
Yardro 30 D4
Yarkhill 31 H5
Yarlet 42 B4
Yarlington 11 H3
Yarm 66 E6
Yarmouth 13 F7
Yarnfield 42 A3
Yarnscombe 9 F3
Yarnton 21 J1
Yarpole 31 F3
Yarrow 73 J2
Yarrow Feus 73 J2
Yarsop 31 F5
Yarwell 44 D7
Yate 20 B4
Yateley 22 D6
Yatesbury 20 E5
Yattendon 21 K5
Yatton, H. & W 31 F3
Yatton, Avon 19 J6
Yatton Keynell 20 C5
Yaverland 13 J7
Yaxham 46 F5
Yaxley, Cambs 44 E7
Yaxley, Suff 37 G2
Yazor 30 F5
Yeading 23 G4
Yeadon 59 H6
Yealand Conyers 57 J3
Yealand Redmayne 57 J3

Yealmpton 4 F4
Yearsley 60 C3
Yeaton 41 F5
Yeaveley 42 D2
Yedingham 61 F3
Yelden 34 D3
Yelford 21 H2
Yelling 35 F3
Yelvertoft 33 H2
Yelverton, Devon 4 F3
Yelverton, Norf 47 H6
Yenston 11 J3
Yeoford 9 H6
Yeolmbridge 8 D7
Yeo Mill 9 J3
Yeovil 11 G4
Yeovil Marsh 11 G4
Yeovilton 11 G3
Yerbeston 26 E6
Yesnaby 112 C5
Yetlington 75 G4
Yetminster 11 G4
Yettington 10 B7
Yetts o' Muckhart 80 F1
Y Fan 29 G1
Y Felinheli 48 E4
Y Ffor 38 C3
Yieldshields 80 D6
Yiewsley 22 F4
Ynysboeth 18 E3
Ynysddu 19 F3
Ynyshir 18 E3
Ynyslas 38 F7
Ynysybwl 18 E3
Yockenthwaite 58 E3
Yockleton 40 F5
Yokefleet 54 C1
Yoker 79 H5
Yonder Bognie 104 F4
York 60 D5
Yorkletts 25 G6
Yorkley 19 L2
Yorton 41 G4
Youlgreave 52 E7
Youlstone 8 C4
Youlthorpe 60 E5
Youlton 60 B4
Young's End 24 D1
Yoxall 42 D5
Yoxford 37 J3
Ysbyty Ifan 39 H2
Ysbyty Ystwyth 28 E2
Ysceifiog 50 A6
Ystalyfera 18 B2
Ystrad 18 D3
Ystrad Aeron 28 C4
Ystradfellte 18 D1
Ystradffin 28 E5
Ystradgynlais 18 B2
Ystradmeurig 28 E3
Ystrad Mynach 18 F3
Ystradowen, Dyfed 18 B1
Ystradowen, S. Glam 18 E5
Ythanbank 97 J2
Ythanwells 97 F2
Ythsie 97 H2

Z

Zeal Monachorum 9 H5
Zeals 11 J2
Zelah 3 G4
Zennor, Corn 2 C6

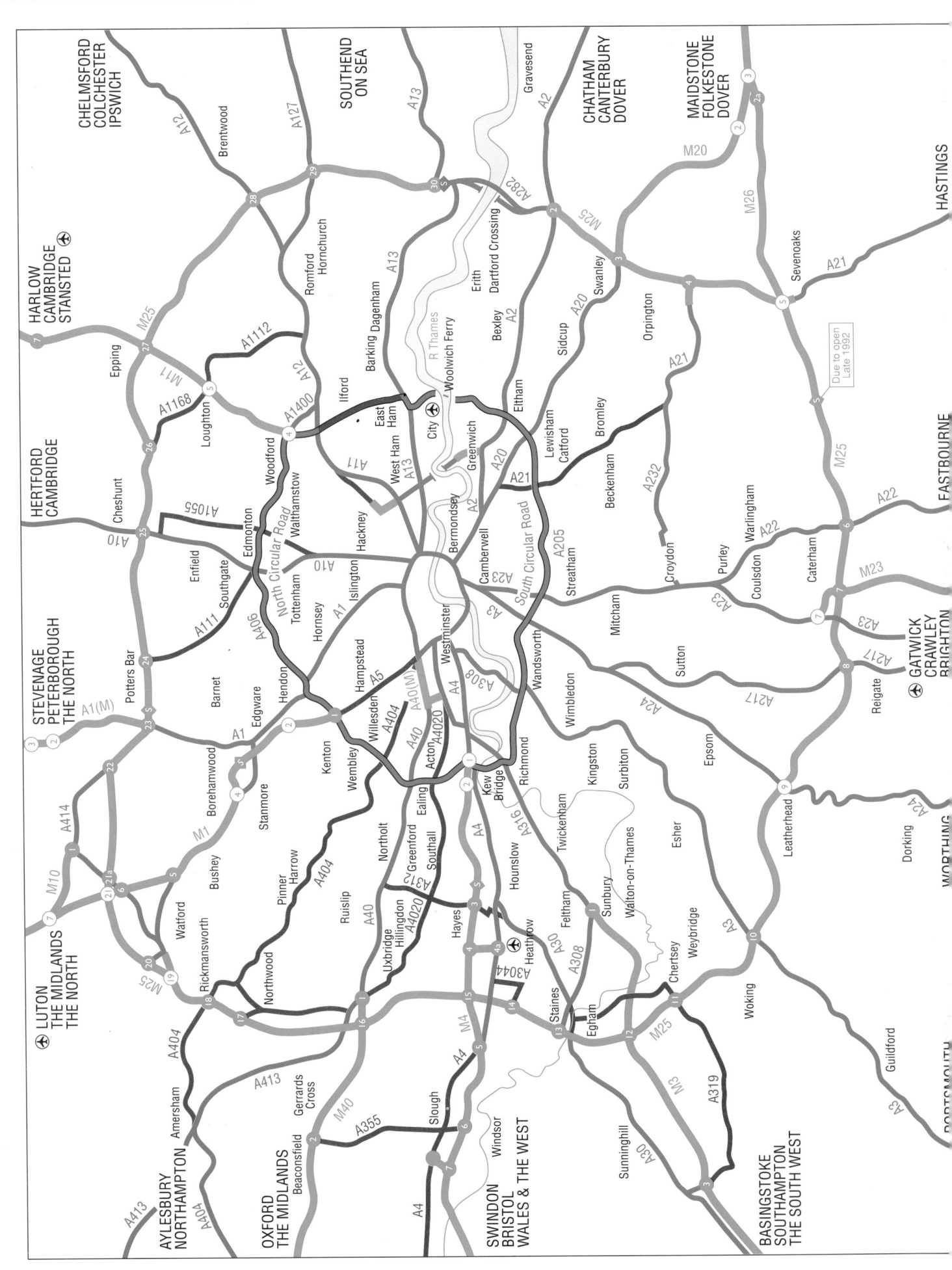